Literacy Assessment
and Instructional Strategies

Literacy Assessment and Instructional Strategies

Connecting to the Common Core

Kathy B. Grant
State University of New York at Plattsburgh

Sandra E. Golden
Sisters of Charity Foundation of Cleveland

Nance S. Wilson
State University of New York at Cortland

$SAGE

Los Angeles | London | New Delhi
Singapore | Washington DC

Los Angeles | London | New Delhi
Singapore | Washington DC

FOR INFORMATION:

SAGE Publications, Inc.
2455 Teller Road
Thousand Oaks, California 91320
E-mail: order@sagepub.com

SAGE Publications Ltd.
1 Oliver's Yard
55 City Road
London, EC1Y 1SP
United Kingdom

SAGE Publications India Pvt. Ltd.
B 1/I 1 Mohan Cooperative Industrial Area
Mathura Road, New Delhi 110 044
India

SAGE Publications Asia-Pacific Pte. Ltd.
3 Church Street
#10-04 Samsung Hub
Singapore 048763

Printed in the United States of America

A catalog record of this book is available from the Library of Congress.

ISBN: 978-1-4129-9658-7

This book is printed on acid-free paper.

Certified Chain of Custody
Promoting Sustainable Forestry
www.sfiprogram.org
SFI-01268
SFI label applies to text stock

Acquisitions Editor: Theresa Accomazzo
Editorial Assistant: Georgia McLaughlin
Production Editor: Melanie Birdsall
Copy Editor: Megan Granger
Typesetter: C&M Digitals (P) Ltd.
Proofreader: Wendy Jo Dymond
Indexer: Judy Hunt
Cover Designer: Anupama Krishnan
Marketing Manager: Terra Schultz

14 15 16 17 18 10 9 8 7 6 5 4 3 2 1

Brief Contents

Detailed Contents

Visit **www.sagepub.com/grantlit** to access additional appendices:

Appendix C. Phonological Awareness Sheets

Appendix D. Concepts of Print Assessment Booklet

Appendix E. Supplemental Forms for Literature Circles

Appendix F. Assessments for Literature Circles

Preface

This comprehensive textbook for literacy assessment and foundations of reading courses uses the Common Core State Standards for English Language Arts and Literacy as the backbone of the text. This textbook prepares early childhood and elementary teachers to effectively develop literacy assessments for classroom data collection. In addition, the volume includes literacy strategies that match objectives of each assessment. With 12 contributing authors who are experts in various areas of literacy assessment, the text features information to help teachers understand the dynamics of assessment through data analysis and instructional decision making.

Literacy Assessment and Instructional Strategies: Connecting to the Common Core can be adopted by college and university education departments in their undergraduate course work in literacy and reading assessment. The textbook is particularly powerful in nurturing teachers' understanding of elementary assessments, both informal and formal in nature. School districts could benefit from acquiring the text, as it provides a compendium of early and intermediate-level assessments and corresponding literacy strategies.

The philosophical underpinning of the text comes from our belief that authentic assessment drives instruction in childhood education. The heart of the text remains our commitment to prepare teachers to think critically about their assessment choices. We have an extensive literacy assessment background, including our work teaching reading foundations and assessment courses at colleges throughout the country. Combined, we have more than 35 years of college teaching experience. Moreover, we taught for many years in elementary schools, assessing and teaching literacy skills and strategies. These experiences formed the basis for realistic scenarios as well as practical activities and strategies found in the text and ancillary materials.

With the introduction of Common Core State Standards for English Language Arts and Literacy for preschool through sixth grade replacing or supplementing state curricula, teachers are accountable for assessing student literacy progress in their classrooms. The Common Core State Standards are integrated in each chapter to engage educators and reading specialists in developing strategies and assessments that align with the Common Core. Moreover, the textbook recognizes and is designed around the National Reading Panel's five components of reading instruction: phonemic awareness, phonics, vocabulary development, text comprehension, and fluency. National standards such as the International Reading Association Standards for Reading Teacher Preparation Programs in the area of assessment diagnosis, and evaluation promote principles and values intrinsic to student-centered assessment. Teachers need to adhere to these standards to strengthen their current evaluation practices.

A strong research base is embedded throughout the text chapters. Current research from peer-reviewed journals, such as *Elementary School Journal, Exceptional Children, Journal of Exceptional Children, Journal of Learning Disabilities, Journal of Literacy Research, Journal of Reading Education, Journal of Research in Technology in Education, New England Reading Association Journal, Reading Horizons, Reading Research Quarterly, The Reading Teacher, Review of Educational Research,* and *Teacher Librarian,* supports a growing literacy assessment knowledge base for new and practicing teachers. In addition, organizations promoting elementary literacy and assessment, such as Reading Rockets and the National Association for the Education of Young Children; regional educational laboratories, such as SEDL and Northwest Regional Educational Laboratory; and university centers, such as the University of Oregon Center for Teaching and Learning, the Curry School of Education, and the Harvard Graduate School of Education, provide best-practice ideas for literacy assessment and support. Moreover, research from leading authors in the field of literacy strategies and reading/writing assessment, such as Allington, Armbruster, Au, Clay, Clymer, Dechant, Diller, Fox, Gallagher, Gunning, Hempenstall, Johnston, Luke, Padak, Popham, Rasinski, Roskos, Samuels, Schnorr, Snow, and Strickland, adds richness to the text. To support our commitment to culturally responsive literacy and brain-based learning, groundbreaking work by Gay, Gonzalez, Moll, Sousa, Wolf, and others has been included.

Literacy Assessment and Instructional Strategies: Connecting to the Common Core is a theory-based, yet practical textbook for use by teacher educators. The textbook promotes collaborative interaction, a very important aspect of teaching, with opportunities for deliberative and engaging conversations on the realities of assessment, evaluation, and teaching literacy skills and strategies. This text provides many of the literacy tools teachers will need to plan instruction with appropriate strategies and assessments. Many new strategies were developed to connect with the Common Core State Standards. The strategies and activities have been field-tested across elementary classrooms and can be modified to meet the needs of instruction.

Assessment that is integrated with instruction forms the framework for this book. Our beliefs embrace this model for authentic assessment that builds teachers' knowledge of students' literacy understanding while supporting the differentiation of instruction.

- The goals of assessment and the reasons for progress monitoring are presented in Chapter 1.
- Literacy background knowledge is discussed in Chapter 2.
- Understanding the student factors that impact assessment and learning of literacy are delineated in Chapters 3, 4, and 5.
- Chapters 6 and 7 are devoted to early childhood assessments.
- Intermediate grade-level assessments are detailed in Chapter 8.
- Chapter 9 focuses on administering and analyzing informal reading inventories.
- The vocabulary and language of commercial assessments is defined in Chapter 10.
- Moving beyond assessment to plan for intervention is the focus of Chapter 11.
- Strategies for teaching literacy in the classroom, combined with assessment, are addressed in Chapters 12, 13, and 14.
- Chapter 15 describes various activities that connect students and texts.
- Assessing new literacies and media literacies is described in Chapter 16.

Last, this book is designed to engage our readers in gaining knowledge, skills, and competencies to reach and teach all children how to read for learning and enjoyment. Readers of this text will practice becoming self-reflective and collaborative educators.

Features of the Text

Focus Questions

The focus questions at the start of each chapter are designed to engage the readers in thinking critically about the reading and reflecting on their learning. These questions should guide readers in discovery, discussions, and ways to think about how to use the information to better understand the topics. Furthermore, these questions promote classroom collaboration.

Words in Action

Realistic scenarios involving literacy assessment and instruction open each chapter. The scenarios situate chapter topics through the real world of assessment, including the instructional decisions teachers engage in. Moreover, the Words in Action scenarios present a challenge for the reader: How can I best serve the assessment needs of my students?

Making Connections

In each chapter, readers will also have many opportunities to connect learning in authentic and collaborative ways with classmates. The Making Connections feature enables readers to engage with the reading by reflecting on their learning, assessing their own learning and that of peers, and gaining understanding through problem-based activities.

Literacy Assessment Terminology

Key terms are defined in the chapters and listed in a comprehensive glossary. We selected key literacy assessment vocabulary from each chapter to add to the readers' schema.

Website Resources

A list of research-based websites is provided at the end of each chapter. These websites provide readers with additional resources to explore, literacy strategies and activities to include in their toolboxes, and formative and summative assessments to consider when varying their assessment strategies.

Organization of the Text

The text is divided into four sections.

Section I. Foundations of Literacy Assessment and Instruction

What Is the Role of Literacy Assessment and Evaluation in Today's Schools?

Literacy assessment is at the heart of strong instructional practice. Assessment is how we obtain information about what students know and are able to do. Teachers assess students throughout the teaching and learning process. This continuous assessment of reading, writing, decoding, and comprehension skills remains a daily event for elementary teachers. Through formative checks for understanding as well as summative end-of-unit tests, teachers act as continuous decision makers. This ongoing instructional decision making is based on assessment results, knowledge of students' strengths and weaknesses, and conferring with colleagues and resource personnel.

With that in mind, Chapter 1 focuses on building or expanding a teacher's knowledge base for connecting the academic language of literacy assessment to realistic learning targets. Armed with the new terminology of testing—data-driven instructional decision making, benchmarking, high-stakes testing, and formative assessment—teachers will be prepared to collaborate with colleagues to process change. At the close of Chapter 1, readers are challenged to review literacy assessment roles they will assume when teaching and to rate their understanding of those roles.

Next, Chapter 2 takes the reader back, as a review, into the realm of literacy background information that may or may not have been taught during a Foundations of Reading course. The four cueing systems, developmental reading processes, and the brain and reading are covered in detail, with diagrams and explanations. Without a thorough understanding of the reading process, worthwhile assessment is limited.

Chapters 3, 4, and 5 delve into the factors that affect students' literacy achievement. Chapter 3 examines students who struggle to meet the developmental milestones of typical literacy development. It addresses the provisions of Response to Intervention (RtI) as well as developmental suggestions for teacher work with struggling readers in the classroom. With the advent of RtI, regular education teachers now act as first responders to institute literacy interventions. Clearly, the immediacy of well-planned intervention is critical. Chapter 4 addresses the developmental, physical, environmental, and cognitive factors that can affect students' literacy development. Throughout this chapter, readers will connect their understanding of educational psychology to literacy assessment and instruction. Chapter 5 sets the stage for assessment by addressing the affective issues that can influence students' literacy achievement. Like the previous chapters, this one describes the effects on literacy development while providing tools to build students' self-efficacy in literacy.

Section I is planned to start readers on a thoughtful journey into assessment that has changed the landscape of education. These initial chapters expose teachers to assessment terminology through practical application. Teachers will consider and explore the developmental and intervention models for literacy growth that will be a part of their teaching. Moreover, this section sets the stage to ensure that teachers are cognizant of the basis for authentic assessment: that the reading process drives all individuals' efforts in learning to read. Section I reminds us, most importantly, that assessment considers the strengths and challenges of individual readers, since all children learn to read in very different ways.

Section II. Grade-Level Literacy Assessments

What Characterizes Authentic Grade-Level Literacy Assessments?

As teachers integrate assessment throughout the teaching and learning process, they need a large toolbox of assessments that can support them. Authentic grade-level literacy assessment is integrated with classroom instruction. These assessments are given before instruction to determine what students need to meet the standards. They are given during instruction to gauge students' progress on the standards. After instruction, these assessments serve to measure the effectiveness of the teacher and to see if students need additional intervention to achieve the standards.

Section II focuses on providing teachers with the assessments that can equip their toolboxes. Chapters 6, 7, and 8 examine authentic formative assessment tools that can be used before, during, and after enacting instruction. Depending on the grade level and developmental reading level of the students, these chapters provide teachers with a series of assessments that can inform and guide the instructional process. Chapter 9 focuses on informal reading inventories (IRIs). These individually administered reading assessments provide teachers with a lens to zoom in on individual students' literacy strengths and weaknesses. In this chapter, readers will learn how to administer and interpret IRIs to inform their instruction. Chapter 10 moves away from teacher-administered assessments to commercial assessments. It focuses on both the formative and the summative commercial assessments that are part of the schoolwide data-collection initiatives. This chapter highlights the key vocabulary needed to interpret these assessments, as well as how the teacher can administer and use these assessments in the classroom.

Next, Chapter 11 describes how teachers can prepare their classroom as the center of literacy assessment through organized efforts to streamline the process. This chapter focuses on practical ideas for using the instruments of data collection, such as checklists, spreadsheets, and anecdotal records, among many suggestions.

Section III. Designing Instructional Strategies Based on Students' Needs

Many would argue that the primary responsibility of teachers is to guide students to become skilled, independent readers. The complex nature of reading has been studied by linguists, cognitive psychologists, and educators for nearly a century, and their discoveries and insights have provided valuable understandings of reading processes, the acquisition of reading, the difficulties some students face in learning how to read, and the complex skill set that helps readers develop proficient reading. Their contributions continue to assist us in equipping teachers to provide effective literacy instruction (Adams, 1990; Chall, 1996; National Reading Panel, 2000; Neuman & Dickinson, 2002; Rieben & Perfetti, 1991; Ruddell & Unrau, 2004; Snow, Burns, & Griffin, 1998; Stanovich, 2000). The complex processes of literacy continue to be studied, challenged, and modified as research unveils deeper understandings of the human brain, cognition, learning, and language.

While Section I of the text provides a foundational understanding of literacy and Section II dissects several components of literacy after providing a working definition and understanding of authentic literacy assessment, Section III examines the strategies that teachers can use to build students who are skilled readers and writers. Chapter 12 focuses on phonemic awareness and phonics instruction. Chapter 13 analyzes comprehension and writing strategies. Chapter 14 emphasizes building students' fluency and discusses comprehension and writing strategies that build fluency. In each of these chapters, readers will learn a wealth of information that will build their knowledge and repertoire for teaching literacy. The instructional strategies in this section will support teachers as they enact instruction based on what they have learned from administering previously discussed assessments.

Section IV. Connecting Readers to Texts

How Can Teachers Decide When Students Are
"Connected" to a Text That Meets Their Reading Needs?

Throughout this text, we have highlighted that assessment and instruction are not separate parts of teaching but, rather, crucial aspects of an integrated teaching and learning process. This final section continues the holistic view of literacy assessment and teaching. Chapter 15 discusses matching texts to readers. It highlights how teachers can use what they know about their students to find books and to implement classroom procedures that build students who are readers and writers. Chapter 16 takes reading and writing into the realm of new literacies. This chapter focuses on the skills and strategies students need to become successful readers and writers using Internet communication technologies, in addition to discussing assessment and classroom techniques that can develop student competencies.

Appendices

The collection of appendices at the end of this book and online at **www.sagepub.com/ grantlit** provides readers with supplemental resources that address standards reading practitioners should be aware of. These include the International Reading Association Standards for Reading Professionals and individual state websites that list the Common Core State Standards. Moreover, additional assessment forms for phonological awareness and literature circles are included. Another resource offers additional strategies for rhyming practice. We have provided these supplementary forms to further confirm our commitment to individualizing classroom assessment.

Six appendices are included to support the chapter content (access Appendices C through F at **www.sagepub.com/grantlit**):

- *Appendix A: International Reading Association Standards for Reading Professionals.* The Assessment and Evaluation Standard recognizes the need to prepare teachers for using a variety of assessment tools and practices to plan and evaluate effective reading and writing instruction.
- *Appendix B: Common Core State Standards, State Assessments.* Web addresses are provided for all states adopting the national Common Core State Standards, with their particular modifications.

- *Appendix C: Phonological Awareness Sheets.* Phonological awareness and phoneme identification skills assessment provides a method to assess young students' readiness to manipulate phonemes, thereby determining whether readers have mastered these important skills or need more time to mature in their understanding of phonemes.
- *Appendix D: Concepts of Print Assessment Booklet.* The concepts of print assessment in Chapter 6 was developed by a practicing teacher as an authentic preschool assessment. The instrument should be used in conjunction with the booklet included in this appendix.
- *Appendix E: Supplemental Forms for Literature Circles.* The discussion roles performed in literature circles are clarified, and focus questions are listed to aid the teacher in supporting students when enacting this strategy.
- *Appendix F: Assessments for Literature Circles.* Valuable group work rubrics, a note page form, and an analytic rubric are provided to support teachers in assessing student groups while engaged in literature circles.

Ancillary Materials

Instructor Teaching Site

A password-protected site, available at **www.sagepub.com/grantlit,** features resources that have been designed to help instructors plan and teach their courses. These resources include an extensive test bank, chapter-specific PowerPoint presentations, lecture notes, course projects and web resources.

Student Study Site

A web-based study site is available at **www.sagepub.com/grantlit.** This site provides access to several study tools including eFlashcards, web resources, as well as online-only appendices:

Appendix C. Phonological Awareness Sheets

Appendix D. Concepts of Print Assessment Booklet

Appendix E. Supplemental Forms for Literature Circles

Appendix F. Assessments for Literature Circles

Acknowledgments

We wish to sincerely thank our numerous reviewers for their helpful suggestions for revising and editing our early drafts, as well as those who reviewed this book. Our reviewers included the following individuals:

Jacqueline Collier, *Wright State University*

Mary Jo Finney, *University of Michigan–Flint*

Sue F. Foo, *Worcester State College*

Karen L. Ford, *Ball State University*

Kathleen A. Froriep, *Georgian Court University*

Sandra E. Gandy, *Governors State University*

Carolyn Ann Walker Hitchens, *Ball State University*

Patricia A. Jenkins, *Albany State University*

Belinda Laumbach, *New Mexico Highlands University*

Barbara Loebach, *Wilmington College*

Irene Nares-Guzicki, *California State University, Monterey Bay*

Timothy Rasinski, *Kent State University*

Pamela J. Riggs, *Missouri Valley College*

Jiening Ruan, *The University of Oklahoma*

Marva J. Solomon, *Angelo State University*

Carol Strax, *Dominican College*

Ana Taboada, *George Mason University*

Carol B. Tanksley, *University of West Florida*

We would like to acknowledge the powerful writing of our 12 contributing authors. Experts from the fields of literacy assessment and evaluation, reading foundations, library science, early childhood literacy, elementary literacy education, special education, secondary science content literacy, elementary administration, literacy research, and technological literacy all left their mark on our textbook. With their knowledge and experiences relating to the wide range of topics presented, their contributions have greatly enhanced our efforts, and we are extremely grateful for their scholarly contributions. We appreciate the work of the contributors to the text: Robert T. Ackland, Stephanie Affinito, Laura Baker, Colleen Carroll, Kimberly Davidson, Michael P. French, Justin Gray, Jolene Malavasic, Sheila Morris, Melanie O'Leary, Gwyn W. Senokossoff, and Penny Soboleski.

This text would not have been possible without the efficiency and dedication of assistant Melanie O'Leary. Many thanks to Justin Gray for his graphics work and to Kelly Lymberger for her editorial support at the start of the project. A note of deep appreciation goes out to the staff in the Fort Ann Central School District for opening their doors to us for our project. Finally, we wish to thank the staff at SAGE, especially Terri Accomazzo and Reid Hester, for providing support and encouragement through the publication process. As always, Diane McDaniel is inspirational on all levels.

SECTION I

Foundations of Literacy Assessment and Instruction

What Is the Role of Literacy Assessment and Evaluation in Today's Schools?

Literacy assessment is at the heart of strong instructional practice. The continuous assessment of reading, writing, decoding, and comprehension skills remains a daily event for elementary teachers. Through formative checks for understanding as well as summative end-of-unit tests, teachers act as continuous decision makers. This ongoing instructional decision making is based on assessment results, knowledge of students' strengths and weaknesses, and conferring with colleagues and resource personnel.

Literacy assessment and evaluation has never held a greater importance in schools than at the current time. The Common Core State Standards and national assessments are intended to boost literacy learning while assessing the growth of reading skills nationwide. Literacy assessment is at a critical juncture for school progress; therefore, the main goal of this text is to build a teacher knowledge base for literacy assessment and evaluation, with accompanying strategies and activities to support student literacy growth.

However, early in your reading of the text, you will note that the authors purposefully endorse authentic assessment. We have "experienced" scripted, canned, and stagnant assessment instruments that are counterintuitive; they pit teachers against students. The student is simply an object to be tested. Interestingly, the word *assessment* in French means "to sit next to." Authentic teacher-developed assessment is that in which the teacher and student sit next to each other to set goals and discuss results. One major aim of this text is to help new teachers make sound assessment decisions.

Let's focus on the format of the text, which includes resources to check your understanding of the literacy assessment process. Each chapter starts with a contemporary scenario or short vignette that functions as a hook to examine and begin thinking deeply about the challenges of administering appropriate assessments. Selected chapters also contain keys to indicate the specific Common Core State Standards that apply to information contained in the chapter. Interspersed within the chapters is a textbox labeled "Connections." This feature's purpose is to directly connect given assessments with appropriate strategies to support developmental reading growth or even Response to Intervention (RtI) Tier 1 and 2 activities. Moreover, each chapter after Chapter 1 contains suggestions for teacher literacy assessment and instruction with children who have special needs and with English language learners.

With that in mind, Chapter 1 focuses on building or expanding a teacher's knowledge base for connecting the academic language of literacy assessment to realistic learning targets. Armed with the new terminology of testing—data-driven instructional decision making, benchmarking, high-stakes testing, and formative assessment—teachers will be prepared to collaborate with colleagues to process change. At the close of Chapter 1, readers are challenged to review literacy assessment roles they will assume when teaching and to rate their understanding of those roles.

Next, Chapter 2 takes the reader back, as a review, into the realm of literacy background information that may or may not have been taught during a Foundations of Reading course. The four cueing systems, developmental reading processes, and the brain and reading are covered in detail, with diagrams and explanations. Without a thorough understanding of the reading process, worthwhile assessment is limited.

Chapter 3 addresses the provisions of RtI as well as developmental suggestions for teacher work with struggling readers in the classroom. With the advent of RtI, regular education teachers now act as first responders to institute literacy interventions. Clearly, the immediacy of well-planned intervention is critical.

Chapter 4 focuses on reading-related factors that impact reading assessment, such as home environment, the impact of poverty, psychological factors, health problems, and many other critical considerations. Last, Chapter 5 provides the reader with assessments that measure student motivation, interest, and self-efficacy while reading.

Section I is planned to start readers on a thoughtful journey into assessment that has changed the landscape of education. These initial chapters expose teachers to a whole set of new assessment terminology that must be brought into practical application. Teachers will consider and explore the developmental and intervention models for literacy growth that will be a part of their teaching. Moreover, teachers should be cognizant of the basis for authentic assessment: that the reading process drives all individuals' efforts in learning to read. Section I reminds us, most importantly, that assessment considers the strengths and challenges of individual readers, since all children learn to read in very different ways.

CHAPTER 1

Building Teacher Knowledge for Literacy Assessment, Evaluation, and Measurement

Kathy B. Grant, Jolene Malavasic, and Nance S. Wilson

Common Core State Standards

Key Ideas and Details	*CCRA.R.3* Analyze how and why individuals, events, or ideas develop and interact over the course of a text.
Craft and Structure	*CCRA.R.4* Interpret words and phrases as they are used in a text, including determining technical, connotative, and figurative meanings, and analyze how specific word choices shape meaning or tone.
Integration of Knowledge and Ideas	*CCRA.R.9* Analyze how two or more texts address similar themes or topics in order to build knowledge or to compare the approaches the authors take.
Range of Reading and Level of Text Complexity	*CCRA.R.10* Read and comprehend complex literary and informational texts independently and proficiently.

FOCUS QUESTIONS

1. How will your emerging goals of literacy assessment impact your future assessment undertakings? How do your goals compare or contrast with those held by the experts in the field of literacy? Also, how do your goals compare or contrast with those of the U.S. Department of Education or other educational policymakers or groups?

2. Formative literacy assessments can be used for ongoing checks of student understanding. What techniques to check for understanding would you like to try? Of what terms involving formative assessment should parents be aware?

3. Data-driven instruction and progress monitoring are complex concepts. How can you describe their purpose in your own words?

4. Teachers should be prepared and proactive concerning high-stakes testing. How can you prepare the parents of the students in your classroom for the reality of high-stakes testing?

5. What do reading specialists need to know about the special needs of English language learners, and how should those needs be addressed?

Words in Action

Ongoing Assessment and Checks for Understanding

As a veteran fifth-grade teacher, my commitment to teaching includes supporting new teachers in their understanding of classroom assessment and data-driven instruction. This year, I started to work with a new fourth-grade teacher who appeared to be struggling with the notion of data-driven instruction based on ongoing assessment. Her questions uncovered a deep skepticism about ongoing assessments and checks for understanding. She felt that these methods took too much time out of the instructional day. Our conversation started informally in the teachers' lounge, but we moved to her classroom to continue our debate of ongoing assessment.

Ms. Jones had trouble seeing the place in her lessons for ongoing assessment. She asked, "Won't students just raise their hands to ask questions when they don't understand the material?" and "How can I take time to check every 10 minutes or so whether students are getting the concepts?" I smiled and replied, thinking back to the day when I was a new teacher and overwhelmed, "Fifth-grade students may be hesitant to raise their hands for fear of standing out from the class, so you need a solid technique to get a reading on individuals and the whole class to gauge if the teaching is working. Ask yourself if you need to reengage or reteach based on the checks you enact." Next, I mentioned how ongoing assessment and continuous checks for understanding during a lesson can be fun, can be engaging for students, and can build a community of learners where everyone has the right to be wrong and correct his or her answers without fear.

I invited her into my class during her break to watch a lesson I was giving, where I used ongoing assessment such as exit/entrance slips and checks for understanding such as thumbs up/down. She noted, "Your checks for understanding flowed with the lesson, and you were able to pick out students who still struggled with the concept through stop-and-writes and turn-and-talks. I need to try these strategies."

I smiled and remembered when I was a new teacher and a veteran took me under her wing. Ms. Jones is a willing learner.

Before we proceed further into the chapters, as educators we must have clear goals for our classroom literacy assessment that feed into our school and district assessment goals.

Literacy Learning and Assessment

Before teachers can consider our goals for establishing a powerful literacy assessment classroom, they must understand and embrace the principles behind literacy learning as the heart of the developmental reading process. Literacy learning is a "complex process that requires the analysis, coordination and interpretation of a variety of sources of information" (Scanlon, Anderson, & Sweeney, 2010, p. 9). Multiple skills and strategies are involved in successfully decoding and understanding a given text. Furthermore, students have to orchestrate multiple strategic actions (Pinnell & Fountas, 2008) before, during, and after reading. Children must read the printed words, retrieve the word meanings, combine words to form ideas, and assemble a larger model of the text (Scanlon et al., 2010) for overall comprehension. Literacy learning is at the core of the developmental reading process.

One of the leaders in the field of literacy learning, Brian Cambourne (2001), poses the following questions hoping to elicit a deeper level of debate among teacher practitioners:

- What is good reading?
- How is it best learned?
- After it has been learned, what is it used for? (p. 416)

Effective teachers constantly wrestle with these questions (how could they not?): What characteristics do strong readers exhibit in their particular grade level? How should teachers be able to determine that proficiency through assessment? What instructional methods or activities promote good reading, and how can teachers self-assess their literacy teaching? And, last, how can teachers gauge student use of superior reading strategies through informed judgment?

As an educator, your emerging goals of literacy assessment clearly impact your future assessment undertakings. However, the choices you make concerning your assessment aims should target improved literacy instruction for readers. It is natural for readers to hit developmental stages in their reading levels at different times. Consequently, knowledge of various assessment options within a continuum, such as authentic teacher-developed assessments, observational surveys, and standardized tests, is mandatory. For example, at several key times during the year, kindergarten teachers administer a Concepts About Print (CAP) assessment, a beginning observational survey on students' knowledge of book handling and how to approach using a text. A CAP is a wonderful assessment that allows teachers to authentically connect with students one-on-one.

Goals of Literacy Assessment

The goal of a school assessment program should be to improve instruction for children. With anything less, we run the danger of assessment becoming an end unto itself rather than a means to an end. (Teale, 2008, p. 359)

As teacher candidates entering the complex world of literacy assessment and **evaluation**, the task may seem daunting and overwhelming! However, it is reassuring to know that even veteran teacher practitioners are struggling with new federal and state testing mandates, accountability issues, and the realities of student testing. It seems, then, that everyone is in the same boat, so to speak.

Having identified several priorities we feel are absolutely essential to the development of literacy assessment goals, the authors of this chapter—both former literacy specialists—are strong proponents of a mind-set of student-centeredness. As we discuss the culture of **"high-stakes testing,"** currently in vogue in American schools, we also remain aware of the importance of organizing assessment interactions (Johnston, 2005) based on the reading curriculum priorities—in other words, employing formative and summative assessment through "real-world" content during classroom instruction. This supplements and often supersedes the results disseminated through end-of-year testing.

Furthermore, we endorse assessment that promotes independent and collaborative learning in literacy through guided reading interactions, literature circles, and independent reading. When a classroom culture promotes student **metacognition** and self-evaluation of reading skills and abilities, the negative effects of high-stakes testing can be circumvented. When students articulate and support logical answers, their confidence is nurtured and grows.

A compilation of suggestions from experts in the field of literacy assessment outlines some characteristics they find valuable in creating a humane culture of assessment and evaluation:

- *Assessment should be grounded in the context of learning.* Assessment judges the quality of students' learning opportunities (context of learning) through teacher quality instruction (Darling-Hammond, 2006).
- *Assessment should be research based.* Assessment fosters a literate disposition toward joint learning tasks (Johnston & Costello, 2005).
- *Assessment opportunities should be multifaceted.* Testing can include a variety of assessments useful for multiple literacy evidences—for example, performance assessments (e.g., CAP), product assessments (e.g., analytical rubric for reader's theatre script), and writing assessments based on reading selections (e.g., response journals).
- *Assessment is ongoing.* It can include formative and summative assessments, as well as state-mandated assessment measures.
- *Assessment is useful and functional.* It is an integral part of the instructional process (Guskey, 2003).
- *Assessment is socially connected.* It "involves noticing, representing, and responding to children's literate behaviors" (Johnston & Costello, 2005, p. 258).

- *Assessment is fair and equitable.* Validity and reliability must be factored in and culturally biased items curtailed.
- *Assessment remains representational or interpretative.* Assessments are viewed through differing perspectives (teacher, parent, or administrator) as a part of differing goals (for school psychologist, teacher, or student), or used to categorize students for reading disabilities (Johnston & Costello, 2005).

Making Connections

A humane culture of testing in schools and classrooms is critical for students, teachers, and parents. After reviewing and discussing the goals of humane testing, develop a dialogue that you might use to explain to a parent, your principal, or a colleague how you intend to make this model of assessment a part of your classroom.

Formative Assessments

Formative assessment in literacy instruction is a "hot topic" as defined by the International Reading Association—and well it should be! Literacy teachers enact formative assessment of students' reading development by checking for understanding and modifying their instruction based on the results. By rejecting "trial-and-error" learning as random, inefficient, and harmful to student instructional growth (Sadler, 1989, p. 120), the teacher is alert to gaps in student learning as well as to the quality of responses. In addition, students assume responsibility for self-regulating their progress through peer collaboration and self-reflection.

Think of formative assessment as a two-step process: frequent interactive checks of student understanding and skills to pinpoint individual learning needs, followed by adjustment of instruction by the teacher. Roskos and Neuman (2012) state that formative assessment involves making judgments about the quality of students' responses, such as performances and classroom work, and then using those informed judgments on the spot to scaffold and improve student learning.

The Seven Dimensions of Formative Assessment as Applied to Teacher Expectations

1. Purpose of the assessment: Teachers ask where learners' gaps exist and whether their assessment validates the needs of learners.

2. On the run/in the moment: Teachers use spontaneous assessments within a planned activity.

3. Continuum-based: Teachers judge student progress with a continuum of learning.

4. Feedback and scaffolding: Teachers are provided with information, which is shared with readers. With that information, they are guided into the next steps of the process.

5. Peer and self-involvement: Teachers expect students to employ peer and self-assessments to react to their progress.

6. Time interval: Teachers facilitate short time spans between formative input and restructuring learning.

7. Teacher control: Teachers decide when and how to employ formative assessment strategies. (Bailey & Heritage, 2008, p. 45)

Table 1.1 delineates different types of formative literacy assessments.

Table 1.1 Types of Formative Literacy Assessments

- *Active response:* Hold-up cards, lineups, and thumbs-up/-down/-sideways
- *Written tasks:* Quick-writes, short creative pieces, minute persuasive essays, and gist papers
- *Personal communication:* 3-minute instructional conferences, paired conversations, turn-and-talks, graphic organizer notes, and sticky-note questions
- *Tests:* Exit quizzes, on-the-spot quiz, and informal text with matching terms, true/false, or fill-ins
- *Curriculum-embedded assessments:* Formative assessments that provide information on student achievement and learning embedded throughout the curriculum

---

Making Connections

Formative assessments should be used as vital checks for understanding throughout delivery of a literacy lesson. The teacher should frequently check key informational knowledge, vocabulary understanding, and concept attainment as the lesson progresses. As you learn more about formative assessments, develop a plan for infusing checks for understanding into your daily teaching.

Data-Driven Instruction

Exemplary teachers rely on ongoing data collection as a means to gauge and measure student literacy growth; this is called **data-driven instruction**. Collection, selection, interpretation, and use of data to inform practice are acts of "negotiating" with the results (M. Reilly, 2007, p. 770). Reilly notes that "being data rich does not necessarily translate into being data smart. Teachers form and reform themselves by the decisions they make" (p. 770). Clearly, the uncertainty and confusion of new practitioners can lead to a feeling of being overwhelmed by data at first. Yet data collection and interpretation is a critical skill to master under the tutelage of a veteran teacher.

The ultimate goal of using data to guide instructional decisions should be to prevent reading difficulties at the early grades as **emergent reading** occurs (M. Reilly, 2007). Some early reading skills that may be assessed include the following:

- Phonemic awareness
- Letter naming
- Sounds in words
- Initial sound fluency

- Concepts of print directionality, sequencing letters, letter formation, placement of words, spacing between words, visual discrimination of print, and visual memory
- Vocabulary identification and writing (p. 771)

Driven by Data, Bambrick-Santoyo's (2010) practical guide to improve instruction, is an invaluable tool for literacy assessors, even though the text focuses on the assessment needs of all practitioners. He mentions the following characteristics as crucial in the cycle of assessment in reading:

1. An assessment calendar makes time for data; otherwise, the school calendar drives everything. Teachers should block off time for interim assessments to be administered, scored, and interpreted.

2. The starting point for the assessment cycle must be transparent. Teachers should regard assessments as the beginning of each cycle and use them to define the road map for teaching.

3. The teacher should set the goals for reading-level attainment higher than grade-level expectations. In this way, above-grade-level progress continues to serve as a way to push for greater rigor in teaching and learning.

Data-Driven Dialogue Sample

Using Clay's CAP assessment with kindergartners yields varying results. Because this assessment involves a situated assessment for individual students reading a real book, the results are immediate and pertinent. Print awareness is a critical skill for emerging readers. Using the Concepts About Print Score Sheet, I individually test each student until they reach 24 items correct. Students reaching proficiency in Items 12 through 14 (order of words; letters at the beginning, end, or middle) indicate a control of these skills. Information from score sheets can then be placed into tables indicating student growth. (Taken in part from Clay, 2000)

Progress Monitoring

Progress monitoring is individual, ongoing assessment of how a child is responding to instruction; progress monitoring is conducted at least monthly, but more typically weekly or biweekly, by the child's teacher. (Teale, 2008, p. 358)

As part of data-driven instruction, **progress monitoring** is a term used to decide if instructional measures and intervention strategies are working. Decision making is based on whether students adequately progress through regular instruction and extra assistance or whether intervention should be discontinued. Progress-monitoring tests are given to decide if the level of instruction and intervention are actually producing academic growth in literacy (McKenna & Walpole, 2005). These tests are administered frequently to provide feedback concerning the effectiveness of intervention measures. When students do not respond as hoped, they can be given further diagnostic assessments to pinpoint weak areas according to the RtI model (Alber-Morgan, 2010).

Progress Monitoring Dialogue Sample

I just completed the final progress monitoring before the January assessments. I created a new, much smaller group of students who are still not performing as well as I would like to see and need intensive instruction. I will concentrate on teaching them how to isolate initial sounds using consonant sorting activities while building their oral language skills. Using data to inform my instruction has helped my children to achieve higher levels of success in literacy. I think years ago students at risk of reading difficulties made progress at a much slower pace because the instruction wasn't geared toward their needs. Using data to drive my instruction, certainly to intensify it, seems to assist the children in meeting benchmarks sooner. (Taken from Reilly, 2007, p. 772)

Accountability

Accountability often exists under the guise of "yearly progress goals" established by both the teacher and the school district. Under the outdated No Child Left Behind Act, schools that did not meet accountability goals were chastised or sanctioned by state or federal departments of education. This created tension and angst among teachers that has yet to dissipate. We support accountability as an individual teacher's goal; in reality, who has better knowledge of individual students than their teacher does? Articulating, recording, and measuring learning goals remain crucial daily tasks for every teacher.

Interim or Benchmark Assessments

Benchmark assessments are short tests administered throughout the school year that give teachers immediate feedback on how students are meeting academic standards. Regular use of benchmark assessments is seen by many as a tool to measure student growth and design curriculum to meet individual learning needs. (Coffey, 2012, para. 1)

Characteristics of Standardized Benchmark Assessments

Standardized benchmark assessments typically

- are given periodically, from three times a year to as often as once a month;
- focus on reading and mathematics skills, taking about an hour per subject;
- reflect state or district academic-content standards; and
- measure students' progress through the curriculum and/or on material in state exams. (Coffey, 2012, para. 4)

Making Connections

Turn to and discuss with your partner the concepts and realities of data-driven instruction, progress monitoring, accountability, and interim/benchmark assessments. These terms can be intimidating to new teachers at all grade levels. How can one lessen the level of uncertainty? What school resources or personnel would be useful to bridge the knowledge or experience gap for the new teacher?

High-Stakes Testing: Formal Measures

Current legislation has even gone so far as to specify which types of assessment will be approved for providing accountability evidence; to insist that yearly progress goals be set and reached; and to impose consequences on the educational system itself for failure to collect, analyze, and respond to data about student learning. (Reutzel & Mitchell, 2005, p. 606)

The purpose of high-stakes testing is to uphold school accountability and monitor student achievement. "Highly consequential" outcomes of high-stakes testing include teacher promotion or retention, student placement in remedial reading, school funding changes, labeling of schools as successes or failures, and lessening of community support for a school (Afflerbach, 2005, p. 151). Additionally, the testing of reading is now federally mandated for Grades 3–8.

Unfortunately, high-stakes-testing terminology has become a part of the terrain of teaching, and much misinformation and confusion abound. Some of the most commonly heard terms are shown in Figure 1.1.

There is a difference between teaching to the test and teaching what is going to be on the test. Popham (2005) wrote that if a teacher is "teaching to the content represented by the test" it is good teaching. (Hollingsworth, 2007, p. 340)

There is a disconnect between the requirements to meet the demands of high-stakes testing and the type of assessment information classroom teachers can profit from (Invernizzi, Landrum, Howell, & Warley, 2005). With that in mind, many teachers of reading feel that standardized testing yields little in the way of useful instructional information for present-year students. However, teachers should prepare themselves for the inevitable; the American public supports and accepts the premise of high-stakes testing (Afflerbach, 2005). Most important, *don't compromise what you know to be best practices in literacy instruction.* Calm student anxiety by holding informal conversations to build up confidence. Make sure students understand the nature of the tests and their purpose. Other suggestions to prepare for high-stakes testing include the following:

- Conduct your own alignment study between your state's curriculum standards and the Common Core State Standards, and lesson plans/units to ensure you are teaching what is expected for your grade level.

Federal and state initiatives and mandates
Reading First (now defunct)
Percentile Rankings and raw scores
Norm referenced tests: normative scores based on above or below average
National Assessment of Educational Progress (NAEP)   Fairness in testing
Criterion referenced test linked to state standards
Snapshot of student performance
Standardized administration

High Stakes Testing Terminology

Figure 1.1
Wordle List of High-Stakes-Testing Vocabulary Terms

Source: © Wordle.com.

- Routinely engage in formative assessment practices to provide feedback to students on their reading performance.
- Connect your literacy units to real-world reading contexts (Hollingsworth, 2007, pp. 339–341).

Concerns With High-Stakes Testing

A National Reading Conference policy brief (Afflerbach, 2005) on high-stakes testing and reading assessments articulates many concerns that are deserving of consideration. The brief's "talking points" address the following issues:

1. No existing research studies link increased testing with increased reading achievement.

2. Scores from high-stakes testing are not at all representative of the full range of the complexity of reading skills and performances.

3. Reading curriculum priorities are shrinking based on "fit" with high-stakes testing.

4. Testing concerns override teacher professional judgments about reading instruction and practice.

5. Significant blocks of time are dedicated to test-preparation exercises in the name of accountability.

6. High-stakes tests are expensive, taking funds from more worthy academic needs.

7. Young learners can be inadvertently labeled even though they are in the early developmental reading stages.

8. The practice of relying on one single test score for use in making educational decisions affecting children's academic futures remains a dangerous one.

How to Survive in a High-Stakes Testing Culture

Teachers need to be prepared to reflect critically on the culture of testing that currently exists in schools. They need to join district committees that support the discussion and revision of testing practices. Furthermore, they need to become members of professional organizations, such as the International Reading Association or National Council of Teachers of English, where blogs provide opportunities for rational discussion and organized planning. Don't be afraid to become more politically visible and to speak to stakeholders and parent organizations about the effects of testing on children.

When assessment and instruction work together seamlessly and each informs the other, instructional time is maximized and assessment time minimized. (Teale, 2008, p. 359)

Recommendations for Improving Reading Assessment

According to the National Reading Conference policy brief on high-stakes testing and reading assessment (Afflerbach, 2005), it is imperative that high-stakes testing be augmented with results from more effective reading assessments. The following traits are shared by these more student-friendly assessments:

1. Teachers must provide students with *multiple opportunities* daily in their lives as readers.

2. Teachers should assess students on a *wide range of skills* using a variety of formats and responses.

3. Teachers should become knowledgeable about the established guidelines concerning *ethics, fairness, and effectiveness* in testing.

4. Teachers should recognize that reading is *developmental in nature* and thus testing should reflect that differentiation between early and more skilled readers.

5. Teachers should allow students to *access information* that is formative to help shape their reading progress.

6. Teachers should be provided with useful *diagnostic* information to add classroom practice.

7. Teachers must provide *parents* with the results of assessment in comprehensible terms.

8. Teachers should recognize that assessments provide useful information to *administrators* in order to assess yearly progress.

9. Teachers pick assessments that align with *classroom curriculum.* (pp. 159–160)

Making Connections

Referencing the nine recommendations for improving reading assessment, hold a mock discussion with a colleague concerning the values you hold regarding classroom reading assessment. Reflect on why you hold these values. What might change your values related to literacy assessment? How can you counteract values that are opposite to your assessment methodology?

Value of Measurement

Common Core State Standards for Literacy

To build a foundation for college and career readiness, students must read widely and deeply from among a broad range of high-quality, increasingly challenging literary and informational texts. (Common Core State Standards Initiative, 2014a, "Note on Range and Content of Student Reading")

The above statement certainly sounds odd as a broad standard for K–5, with its reference to college and career readiness; however, **Common Core State Standards** delineate both broad (global) and reading foundational skills for K–5. Referencing the dialogue on the print concepts (Clay, 2000), the following standards for kindergarten should be assessed:

1. Demonstrate understanding of the organization and basic features of print.

   a. Follow words from left to right, top to bottom, and page by page.
   b. Recognize that spoken words are represented in written language by specific sequences of letters.
   c. Understand that words are separated by spaces in print.
   d. Recognize and name all upper- and lowercase letters of the alphabet. (Common Core State Standards Initiative, 2014b, "Print Concepts")

In many school districts, as of 2012, progress-monitoring literacy benchmarks are currently being redesigned based on the influence of the federal and state Common Core standards. At the time of this writing, the Partnership for Assessment of Readiness for College and Careers consortium is still at work developing specific assessments based on Common Core State Standards.

Measurement Frame of RtI

RtI is a "new approach to identifying students with specific learning disabilities and represents a major change in special education law, the Individuals with Disabilities Act (IDEA)" (Mesmer & Mesmer, 2008, p. 280). Previously, schools used a discrepancy model to identify students with learning disabilities; yet there are many problems with using the discrepancy model (Francis et al., 2005; O'Malley, Francis, Foorman, Fletcher, & Swank, 2002; Stanovich, 2005; Vellutino, Scanlon, & Lyon, 2000; Walmsley & Allington, 2007). Students are often caught in the middle until the gap between their IQ and achievement becomes large enough to warrant additional support. Within an RtI model, a learning disability may be present when a student's performance is not adequate to meet grade-level standards when provided with appropriate instruction and research-based interventions (Mesmer & Mesmer, 2008, p. 283).

RtI is a "comprehensive, systemic approach to teaching and learning designed to address learning problems for all students through increasingly differentiated and intensified assessment and instruction" (Wixson, 2011, p. 503). Through regular assessment, schools identify students who are at risk for learning difficulties early on in their schooling and provide support and responsive instruction tailored to their needs through a multitiered system of support. Often, instructional interventions are provided in a three-tier system. Interventions aim to prevent learning difficulties and reduce the number of children inaccurately identified as learning disabled (Scanlon et al., 2010).

When a child demonstrates difficulty learning literacy, we must not assume that the reasons for those difficulties reside in the child (Pinnell & Fountas, 2008); rather, we should assume they result from a mismatch between the instruction and the student's individual learning experiences and instructional needs. This belief demands meaningful and relevant assessment reflecting the multidimensional nature of literacy and diversity in students (International Reading Association, 2010a). Rather than using assessments to classify students, teachers must use data to make changes in their own instruction. Multiple measures must be used and looked at as a whole—not in isolation. Combined screening, diagnostic, and progress-monitoring tools, as well as informal observation and performance in the classroom, must be considered (International Reading Association, 2010a). Table 1.2 outlines the various types of assessment data. Assessment that informs instruction is critical; teachers must notice and respond to what children can and cannot do to influence the instruction they provide (Johnston, 2011).

Schools "are using RTI as a vehicle for school improvement, providing a high-quality core program that addresses the needs of all students, and then developing or selecting robust, research-based approaches that meet the needs of students needing more targeted or intensive instruction" (Bean & Lillenstein, 2012, p. 492).

Table 1.2 RtI Instructional Model in Literacy

Tier	Components
Tier 1	• Comprehensive, core literacy instruction in a classroom setting for all students. • Instruction is differentiated to meet all students' needs and experiences. • Includes responsive whole-group instruction, small-group teaching, and independent practice to prevent literacy difficulties.
Tier 2	• Supplemental intervention for students who need additional intervention beyond Tier 1 instruction. • Small-group instruction provided by expert teachers and specialists, tailored to students' individual needs, experiences, and rates of progress.
Tier 3	• Intensive intervention for students who need additional support beyond Tiers 1 and 2. • Very small group or one-to-one instruction provided by expert teachers and specialists, tailored to students' individual instructional needs, experiences, and rates of progress.

Beliefs Supporting Assessment

The premise supporting the current trend in administrating select assessments is strongly reflective of popular instructional models in teaching. Moreover, stakeholders in evaluation—administrators, teachers, and parents—are often excluded from national and state decision making when selecting a research-based assessment instrument.

Trends in Reading Assessments

As the nation's early teachers in one-room schoolhouses began to understand the importance of reading as connected to meaning (see 1914 on the timeline that follows), a revolution was happening in the arena of reading assessment. With the advent of reading research (see 1910), standardized testing was implemented in schools. Alternate reading programs throughout the decades drove the different choices for assessment and evaluation.

As you investigate the timeline below, notice the cyclical nature of assessment; for example, from 1900 to 1920, an emphasis on phonics skills was the mode of assessment. During the 1990s, phonics assessments came back in vogue. Researcher Edward Thorndike supported comprehension assessments, as did the whole language movement in the 1970s.

What assessment types do you recognize from this timeline? As you read through the chapters, note the specific assessments that were developed through the decades.

- 1879–1900: The McGuffey reader appears, along with oral recitation of stories by students as a measure of reading competence. *Measurement: Oral recitation*

- 1900–1920: Phonics-based readers are used in one-room schoolhouses throughout the nation. *Measurement: Phonics decoding skills*

- 1910–1924: Intense research interest is devoted to standardizing reading tests and how to administer such tests. *Measurement: Implementation of standardized testing*

- 1914: Thorndike proposes that meaning should be connected to the printed page while reading, a revolutionary concept at that time. *Measurement: Comprehension assessments*

- 1920s: Basal readers and their accompanying exercises come on the reading scene. *Measurements: Basal reading worksheets*

- 1921: Focus shifts to silent reading methods, and the variety of reading materials increases. *Measurement: Tests on meaning making*

- 1922–1937: Attention is given to reading disabilities and subsequent interventions. *Measurement: Diagnostic tests*

- 1930s: Gates's and Dolch's lists of sight words gain popularity, skill drills become common, and oral reading becomes a measure of comprehension. *Measurement: Sight-word lists*

- 1940s: Assessment grows more multifaceted, with readability of text as a goal. *Measurement: Remedial reading tests*

- 1950s: Programmed reading methods appear to answer the question. *Measurement: Programmed reading tests*

- 1960s: National Assessment of Educational Progress (1969); first national assessments of math and reading skills are brought into districts. *Measurement: National Assessments of Educational Progress*

- 1970s: Whole language movement; emphasis is placed on comprehension and valuing student input on their own learning. *Measurement: Comprehension assessments*

- 1980s: A return to testing basic reading skills and stressing student academic achievement occurs. *Measurement: Basic reading inventories*

- 1990s: Goals 2000; Educate America Act (1998); high-stakes-testing era dawns, with emphasis on phonics-only decoding and assessing. *Measurement: Phonics instruments*

- 2001: No Child Left Behind accountability standards for testing and sanctions for failing schools, based on test scores, are implemented. *Measurement: Standardized tests*

- 2010: Common Core State Standards are adopted; literacy modules are developed countrywide, with formative and summative assessments attached. *Measurement: Criterion-referenced state-developed tests* (Sears, n.d.)

> ### Making Connections
>
> *Assess yourself:* This helpful chart for students to realistically gauge their level of knowledge on a given topic was found in a teacher's classroom:
>
> **I am a novice:** I am just starting to learn this, and I don't really understand it yet.
>
> **I am an apprentice:** I am starting to get it, but I still need someone to coach me through it.
>
> **I am a practitioner:** I can mostly do it by myself, but I sometimes mess up or get stuck.
>
> **I am an expert:** I understand it well and could thoroughly teach it to someone else.
>
> Turn to a partner and explain how this gauge of self-assessment focuses on student strengths and realities. In labeling themselves as novices or apprentices, what risks might students be taking?

Making Choices: Teachers Assume Literacy Assessment Roles

No instrument or assessment practice can overcome the fact that the teacher is the primary agent of assessment. (International Reading Association and National Council of Teachers of English Joint Task Force on Assessment, 1994)

Exemplary teachers envision and critically connect student acts of literacy through classroom facilitation activities. These activities include reciprocal partnerships among learners, ongoing independent work with checks for understanding, kidwatching observational opportunities, selected conferencing, and on-the-spot assessment.

The role of teacher as literacy facilitator critically connects the "Daily Five" literacy tasks or other literacy structures to the ongoing literacy learning in the classroom. The Daily Five literacy structure includes reading to yourself, reading to someone, working on writing, listening to reading, and spelling/word work (Boushey & Moser, 2006; see Chapter 8 for more on this).

Teacher as Literacy Facilitator

- Teachers administer and score assessments based on instructional goals and flexible management (Risko & Walker-Dalhouse, 2010).
- Teachers promote the development of agency for learners—a sense that if they act strategically, they can accomplish their goals (J. Johnston, 2005).
- Teachers should act as collaborators in partnership with students to support their acclimation to the assessment process, stressing self-evaluation of learning goals.

Teacher as Literacy Assessor

- Teachers must be willing to develop authentic assessments based on the wide range of literacy skills and strategies that are a part of their literacy framework or structures within the class (Risko & Walker-Dalhouse, 2010).
- Teachers must plan for and manage a systematized practice of frequently collecting literacy assessment data, displaying it, and making on-the-spot decisions.

- Teachers must ensure their classroom assessments are trustworthy and valid or relevant to what is being taught (Risko & Walker-Dalhouse, 2010).

Teacher as Literacy Evaluator

- Teachers directly apply assessments to instructional adjustments when necessary (Risko & Walker-Dalhouse, 2010).
- Teachers help students understand that the learning process is paramount and that assessment and evaluation are not connected to their worth as human beings (Johnston, 2005).
- Teachers see and envision a transparent starting point at the beginning of their assessment cycle; they use their selection of assessments to define the road map for evaluation (Bambrick-Santoyo, 2010, p. 28)

Sound overwhelming? Relax! To facilitate the ease of development of classroom-based roles, the teacher should work with an expert literacy practitioner to gain the background knowledge to step into these complex roles. The job of a literacy coach, the district literacy curriculum coordinator, or the school reading specialist often involves supporting new reading teachers, modeling assessment practice and analysis. So seek out an expert, take copious notes, and reflect, reflect, reflect.

Let's close this chapter by reflecting in writing on the assessment, diagnosis, and evaluation standard for reading teacher preparation programs (International Reading Association, 2003, p. 2; see Table 1.3). How would you gauge your mastery of this critical standard? Are you a novice, apprentice, practitioner, or expert? Please cite specific activities that support your self-evaluation.

Table 1.3 Standards for Reading Teacher Preparation Programs

Category	Criteria
Assessment, diagnosis, and evaluation	- Know how to assess the progress of every child and change instruction when it is not working - Know how to communicate the results of assessments to various stakeholders, including parents

Source: International Reading Association (2003). Used with permission of the International Reading Association.

Key Terms

accountability

Common Core State Standards

data-driven instruction

emergent reading

evaluation

formative assessment

high-stakes testing

metacognition

progress monitoring

Website Resources

- **International Reading Association and National Council of Teachers of English Joint Task Force on Assessment** *Standards for Assessment of Reading and Writing* **(Rev. ed., 2010)**

The International Reading Association and the National Council of Teachers of English appointed a Joint Task Force on Assessment to establish *Standards for the Assessment of Reading and Writing* for both the teaching and learning of literacy in the 21st century. This joint task force determined that the primary purpose of assessment is for the improvement of both teaching and learning, the teacher is the most important agent in the assessment process, and assessment must be ever fair and equitable, as the students' interests are the foremost concern. The joint task force outlines its 11 standards at **www.reading.org/ General/CurrentResearch/Standards/AssessmentStandards.aspx.**

- **SEDL's Reading Assessment Database**

SEDL (formerly called the Southwest Education Development Laboratory) is a private, not-for-profit organization that provides educators, among other resources, the Reading Assessment Database, which describes early literacy assessment tools and tests, the skills and abilities the tools and tests measure, the reliability and validity of the tools or tests, as well as any restrictions of the assessment measures and the age range for which the assessments apply. SEDL's purpose is to inform the public of the diverse assessment measures available to educators in a time when state and federal mandates require comprehensive, summative assessment. The Reading Assessment Database can be accessed at **www.sedl.org/reading/rad.**

- **The Teachers College Reading and Writing Project's Assessment Materials**

The Teachers College Reading and Writing Project provides professional development services for teachers and schools, field-tested methodologies, curriculum development assistance, and guidance on differentiating instruction. The project offers free informal research-based reading inventories, writing continua, benchmarks for student progress, and assessment materials for Grades K–8. The project works closely with teachers and schools, with the goal of enabling students to become avid readers and writers. The project's assessment materials are available at **readingandwritingproject.com/ resources/assessments.**

Student Study Site: Visit the Student Study Site at **www.sagepub.com/grantlit** to access additional study tools including eFlashcards, web resources, and online-only appendices.

CHAPTER 2

Literacy Background Knowledge and Assessment

Kathy B. Grant

Common Core State Standards

Key Ideas and Details	*RF.K.1* Demonstrate understanding of the organization and basic features of print.
Craft and Structure	*RF.K.2* Demonstrate understanding of spoken words, syllables, and sounds.
Integration of Knowledge and Ideas	*RF.K.3* Know and apply grade-level phonics and word analysis skills in decoding words.
Range of Reading and Level of Text Complexity	*RF.K.4* Read emergent-reader texts with purpose and understanding.

Source: © Copyright 2010. National Governors Association Center for Best Practices and Council of Chief State School Officers. All rights reserved.

Author's Note: To my heroes in helping teachers understand all the intricacies involved in the act of reading: Maryanne Wolf and Constance Weaver.

FOCUS QUESTIONS

1. What does the reading process mean to you?

2. How do you assess the graphophonic or phonological development of your students? What assessments have you used in the past? Did they provide you with the information you needed?

3. Do you analyze your students' spelling errors? Have you taught them to analyze their errors? How can it help?

4. What are the background experiences of your students? How does this affect their reading?

5. Have you ever considered the effects of reading on your brain? If not, what have you learned to support your inquiry into brain-based learning?

Words in Action

Are You Will or Are You Well?

My best friend and I were in the same reading group in second grade, the Red Group. This made us very happy. Well, it certainly made me happy. I always wanted my friends to be in my classes and work groups. You know, social opportunities!

But along came some sort of a cueing breakdown in my friend's reading skills. I could not understand it. She would look at the word *will* and say *well*. What?! "No, no, Suzanne, it says WILL!" This was a disaster for me!

I would ask her what *will* means, and she would say, "I will go to school." "Yup, that's right, good! How about *well*? What does *well* mean?" I would ask. She would tell me it was a place to get water. "Yeah! That's right." I was delighted. She got it.

I would ask her, "How do you spell *will*?" She would spell W-I-L-L. "Yup! That's good. How do you spell *well*?" She would spell W-E-L-L. "Niiiice! Exactly! So, let's read this passage together: 'Where there is a will, there is a way!'" But, invariably, Suzanne would say *well* instead of *will*. Despite my best efforts and to my chagrin, she was promptly moved to the Green Group . . . perhaps to protect her from my incessant attempts to help her learn the difference between *will* and *well*.

Teachers and Assessment

Without a clear understanding of the process of reading and what occurs during the act of reading, assessing reading performance will be haphazard at best. Teaching reading is "rocket science." I put that metaphor on my Reading Foundations syllabus every spring semester, and by the end of the semester my undergraduate students agree with and fully comprehend that reading is indeed a complex and sometimes confusing process. In fact, some of the key areas assessed in reading—phonics, comprehension, and vocabulary—correlate directly to the cueing systems and assessment methods you will learn about in this chapter.

Teachers of reading need to reflect on the connections among the Common Core State Standards for English Language Arts and Literacy, the reading process, and brain-based considerations. That will be a daunting task! We start with excerpts from "Questions for Professional Reflections on Reader and Task Considerations" (see Table 2.1) and revisit this document at the end of the chapter. McLaughlin and Overturf (2012) state, "This document is one of very few associated with the Common Core that addresses the reading process as we know it" (p. 8). As you work through this document with a partner, decide which sections/questions correspond to the developmental reading process as outlined in Table 2.1.

Table 2.1 Questions for Professional Reflection on Reader and Task Considerations

Cognitive Capabilities

- Does the reader possess the necessary attention to read and comprehend the specific text?
- Will the reader be able to remember and make connections among the various details presented in this specific text?

Reading Skills

- Does the reader possess the necessary comprehension strategies to manage the material in this specific text?

Motivation and Engagement With Text and Task

- Will the reader be interested in the content of this specific text?
- Will the text maintain the reader's motivation and engagement throughout the reading experience?

Prior Knowledge and Experience

- Does the reader possess adequate prior knowledge and/or experience regarding the topic of this specific text to manage the material that is presented?

Content and/or Theme Concerns

- Does the reader possess the maturity to respond appropriately to any potentially concerning elements of content or theme?

Complexity of Associated Tasks

- Will the complexity of any before-, during-, or after-reading tasks associated with this specific text interfere with the reading experience?

As teachers think about assessments, they need to know the two key points of assessment: assessment for teaching and assessment for learning. Thus, the assessment system needs to provide behavioral evidence that is consistent with a shared understanding of the reading process. It should link directly to our teaching and recognize that good assessment is the foundation for effective teaching. Assessment in its simplest form means gaining information about the learners you will teach. A "noticing" teacher tunes in to the individual reader and observes how the reader works through a text and thinks about how the reading sounds (Fountas & Pinnell, 2012). As we delve into the reading process, simple and quick formative (checks for understanding) and on-the-spot diagnostic assessments are included. We encourage new teachers to try these measures out with students during their reading case study or literacy field experience and to reflect on the results and implications for reading practice.

Developmental Reading Process: Cueing Systems

Cueing systems help teachers understand the differing types of language cues or signals that readers consciously and unconsciously use to read a written text. When teachers note cues that students use efficiently or inefficiently (miscues), they can then "draw informed inferences" about strategies helpful to the struggling reader (Weaver, 2000).

Graphophonics

Graphophonic cueing system/phonological development involves a child's gradually learning to hear, segment (break apart and put together), and understand the small units of sound that compose words. This development is critical in decoding, which involves understanding and learning letter sounds (and various exceptions). Cues from letters and letter patterns (phonics) help students identify words automatically or try to sound words out letter by letter, which is inefficient (Weaver, 2000; Wolf, 2007).

Our alphabet of 26 letters contains 40 distinctive sounds. There is not one letter in our alphabet that is not represented by more than one sound (e.g., *k* in *knot* and *key*). In addition, letter combinations, such as *th*, variously represent different sounds when combined with other letters. Smith (1985) considers phonics the least efficient cueing system and states that phonics truly works only if you know the word in the first place. Also, he feels that knowing phonics rules and generalizations is "cumbersome and unreliable" (p. 71). For Smith, meaning rules. We witness new readers' struggle with traditional phonics every day. Table 2.2 offers an activity used to assess graphophonic skills.

The example above is just one of many common assessment methods used to assess students' skill levels. Multiple assessments are used to test for early childhood graphophonic or phonological development. We believe the most effective and student-friendly assessments rely on manipulating letters through the active use of magnetic letters, sentence strips, **Elkonin or sound boxes** (shown in Figure 2.1), and other phonics manipulatives. Elkonin or sound boxes work on the principle of letter–sound association. They are effective as formative assessment in supporting student growth in high-frequency words and Tier 1 words.

According to McCarthy (2008),

for some students, though, learning to differentiate sounds in words, especially on the phoneme level, is confusing. For these children, using sound boxes to add a kinesthetic aspect to this auditory process scaffolds their learning so that they may become more adept at manipulating the phonemes in words. (p. 346)

Table 2.2 Graphophonic Skill Assessment

Directions: Engage your students in sight-reading words from the table provided. Instruct your students to provide the sound of the grapheme for each phoneme and then write it in the third column. You will be able to formatively assess your students' skills based on whether their answers match the first-column phonemes.

Phoneme	Word Examples	Student's Grapheme Spelling Response
/t/	right, mutt, picked	
/ng/	bring, tank	
/s/	sat, task, scissor, psyche, suede, site	
/b/	bug, bubble, bright, bite, rub, beside, blue	

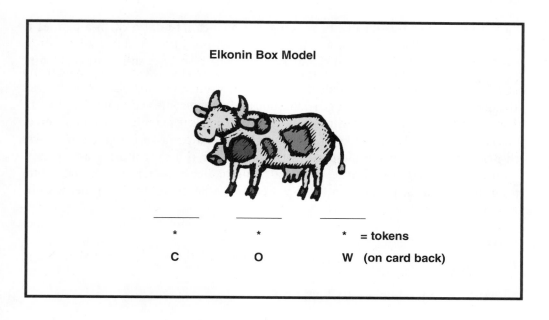

Elkonin Box Model

*   *   * = tokens

C   O   W (on card back)

Figure 2.1
Elkonin or Sound Box

Suggestions for Using Elkonin or Sound Boxes

1. The goal is to teach the process of hearing sounds in words, and so exposure to a collection of words is valuable.

2. Pick one-syllable words that are conceptually familiar to children, and select words that are phonemically regular so that stretching sounds can be heard distinctively.

3. Words with r-controlled vowels should be avoided; however, words with silent vowels can be included as long as the number of spaces represents sounds, not letters—for example, in the word *feet*.

4. McCarthy recommends:

Model how to stretch the word out into its phonemes. Then have the student repeat the slow, phoneme-by-phoneme articulation. By practicing a smooth pronunciation of the word, the student will learn how to hear each phoneme within a natural speech flow. Make sure that the student can stretch the word back, articulating each phoneme, before moving on to the next step. Occasionally, there will be a student for whom the slow articulation of words is very difficult. One way to help him or her is to use a large mirror showing both the instructor's and the student's mouths so that they can observe each other and match mouth positions as the word is segmented. (p. 348)

The three levels of difficulty that follow list words that work well for phoneme segmentation. Try the mirror activity for students who are beginning readers at the primary levels for Levels 1 and 2. Intermediate students may strive to pronounce Level 3 words. Maintain a checklist form that annotates student growth in word pronunciation and word automaticity.

Level 1

f-a-n, f-i-sh, f-ee-d, f-ee-t, f-i-le, f-i-ve, j-o-g, l-a-mb, l-ea-f, l-i-d, l-o-ck, m-a-p, m-ea-t, m-e-ss, m-i-ce, m-oo-n, m-o-p, n-ai-l, n-e-t, n-o-se, n-u-t, r-a-t, r-ai-n, r-a-ke, r-ea-d, r-i-de, r-oa-d, r-o-ck, r-o-pe, r-u-g, s-a-ck, s-ea-l, s-ea-t, sh-ee-p, sh-i-p, s-i-ck, s-oa-p, s-u-n, wr-i-te

Level 2

b-a-ke, b-a-g, b-a-t, b-e-d, b-i-ke, b-oo-k, b-u-g, b-u-s, c-a-p, c-a-ke, c-a-ge, c-a-n, c-a-ve, ch-i-ck, c-oa-t, c-o-mb, c-o-t, c-u-p, c-u-t, d-o-g, d-ee-r, d-u-ck, g-a-me, g-a-te, g-oa-t, g-u-m, h-a-m, h-a-t, h-i-t, h-o-se, h-o-t, j-a-ck, j-a-m, j-ee-p, j-e-t, j-ui-ce, k-i-ck, k-i-te, p-i-g, p-a-n, p-a-th, p-ea-k, p-o-t, t-o-p, t-ea-m, t-a-pe, t-i-re, t-u-b, t-u-be, w-a-sh, w-a-ve, w-e-b, w-i-g, w-i-pe

Level 3

Three Phonemes

b-l-ow, c-r-y, f-l-y, g-l-ue, s-k-i, s-t-ew, t-r-ee

Four Phonemes

b-l-a-ck, b-l-o-ck, b-r-i-de, b-r-oo-m, b-r-u-sh, b-r-i-ck, c-r-a-ck, d-r-o-p, d-r-e-ss, d-r-i-ve, f-l-a-g, f-r-o-g, f-l-oa-t, f-l-u-te, f-r-ui-t, g-l-a-ss, g-r-a-ss, g-r-i-ll, g-r-oo-m, h-a-n-d, p-l-u-g, p-l-u-m, p-r-e-ss, p-l-a-ne, p-r-i-ze, s-k-a-te, s-k-i-p, s-l-ee-ve, s-l-i-ce, s-l-e-d, s-l-i-p, s-m-i-le, s-n-i-p, s-p-i-ll, s-p-oo-n, s-p-o-t, s-t-o-p, s-t-ea-m, s-w-ee-p, s-w-i-m, t-r-ai-n, t-r-u-ck (McCarthy, 2008, p. 348)

Semantics

Semantics/meaning making involves meaning cues from sentences, paragraphs, and the whole selection as a student reads the text. Children progressively learn more about the words that are found in their world. This takes us to **schemas,** or organized chunks of knowledge or experience tied to feelings, memories, and actions that are a part of our daily lives. We can liken schemas to the "hanging files" of the mind (Weaver, 2000; Wolf, 2007). In addition, visuals—pictures, diagrams, maps, and other graphic features—in text can function as semantic cues. Newfound attention has been place on these critical features, especially for understanding informational selections.

Making Connections

The practice of assessing meaning making or the act of comprehension through multiple-choice questions should be thoroughly reconsidered. At best, multiple-choice answers are one-shot, reformulated responses not considerate of student cognitive and affective interpretations. Instead, comprehension monitoring should be a co-constructed activity at the formative level, with the teacher conferring with the child about the influences of schema/prior knowledge, context within a selection, cultural setting of reader and reading material, and supportive organizational features in informational text. Employ the graphic organizer in Figure 2.2 to enact this discussion.

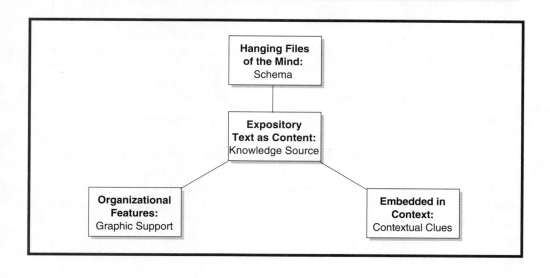

Figure 2.2
Semantic Knowledge Components

Syntactics

Syntactics/development involves how students learn and practice the grammatical forms and structures of sentences. They have a growing intuitive sense of how sentences are formed (subject/predicate); the rules for parts of speech (noun, verb, adjective, adverb, preposition, etc.), and how paragraphs are developed (Weaver, 2000). The assessment in Table 2.3 is designed to measure students' syntax skills.

Table 2.3 Syntactic Assessment

Directions: This assessment will measure students' syntax or grammar skills through identifying parts of speech and creating sentences using the provided parts of speech. The first part will be to ask students to define the parts of speech. Teachers may provide a definition of one part of speech (i.e., define *linking verb*, but have the student define *noun*). Teachers will direct students to create a sentence based on the parts of speech upon completion of definitions.

Parts of Speech	Define Parts of Speech	Create a Sentence
Noun/verb		
Noun/verb/noun		
Noun/verb/adverb		
Noun/linking verb/noun		
Noun/verb/noun/noun		

Making Connections

Different languages depend on various syntactic or sentence structures in their words. Second language learners who have started to understand their first language may be confused by the switch to English syntax. Investigate strategies to support these learners, using website resources listed at the end of the chapter. For example, bilingual learners benefit from measured teaching, reinforcement, and fun, engaging activities that stimulate their schema in their first language with scaffolds and supports to English. What are some other teacher strategies or activities that help support bilingual learners?

Common Assessments: For early readers, using sentence strips, generate several simple sentences—subject and predicate (noun, "who" or "what," and verb, "what happened")—based on student input, as in the **language experience approach.** Children can read what they generate into writing, even if the teacher acts as scribe. After the sentence is written on the strip, engage in a discussion about the "who" or "what" of the sentence at the start and "what happened," or the action taken. Cut the sentence strip at midpoint between subject and predicate. Rehearse this several times with three sentences.

Pragmatics

Pragmatics or situational contexts in reading are highly influenced by the culture, social connections, and worldview of the reader. These interpretations develop as students connect with the external world. Note that the meaning of a sentence develops only by means of transactions among words whose meanings are not identifiable except in context; the readers' schemas enable them to make use of grammatical, semantic, and situational contexts to comprehend language (Weaver, 2000).

> ### Making Connections
>
> I lived in Montana for several years, and my husband worked for the forest service there, fighting forest fires. Based on the schematic knowledge I held through living there, although originally from suburban upstate New York, my experiential base expanded and changed. In my undergraduate and graduate literacy courses, I cover cueing systems, and I invariably place the following sentence on the board and challenge my students (from upstate New York) to explain it: *The Phos-Chek fell to the right of the CAT.* They can decode it without problem, but what does it mean? In more than 10 years demonstrating this exercise, I have yet to see a student be able to explain the meaning of the sentence. It is grounded in western firefighting practices, Phos-Chek being a brand of long-term flame retardant and CAT standing for Caterpillar earth-moving equipment. The verb *fell* here means to land next to after being dropped from an airplane onto the forest floor.

Common Assessments: Pragmatics or situational context settings are best taught and assessed through focused discussions using pictures, visuals, **rebuses** (a form of word-play, such as H + a picture of an ear = HEAR), or oral traditions—poems, songs, or storytelling. Students can write or draw their understanding, perspectives, or interpretation of phrases or terms that are couched in the pragmatics of a culture or situational context. In addition, they can do a turn-to and explain to their partner the thinking that leads them to understanding. Assessment should remain as a check for understanding of word/phrase usage, not necessarily on the summative level.

The Venn diagram representing reading cueing systems (Figure 2.3) demonstrates the interwoven relationships among cueing system supports, inherent in the act of reading. Focal point questions are affixed to each cueing system for teachers to consider when administering running records (see Chapter 9).

Developmental Reading Processes: Language Conventions

In addition to the cueing systems we mentioned, morphological and orthographic development play critical roles in reading systems. Morphological development, or **morphology**, deals with how words are formed or put together from smaller, meaning-based affixes (roots, prefixes, and suffixes) and units of meaning (morphemes). Students need to learn the conventions of morphology through direct instruction and discovery learning. For example, using cut-up sentence strips supports recognition of prefixes, root words, and suffixes.

Figure 2.3
Venn
Diagram of
Cueing
Systems

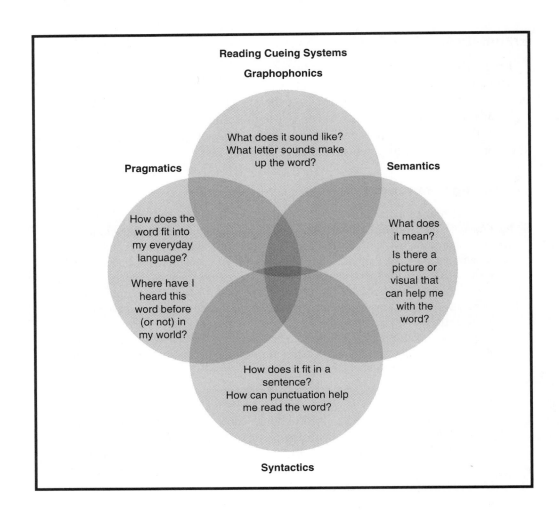

Orthographic development depends on a child learning that his or her writing system represents language and presents the conditions that follow through in oral expression. Knowledge of visual aspects of print, including letters, common letter patterns, and sight words, leads to adeptness in spelling new words (Weaver, 2000). The act of spelling is a developmental and conceptual process and can influence how young children feel about their writing (Newlands, 2011). The first guideline for the selection of spelling words is to include words that students can read and understand. If the student cannot read the word, he or she will likely be challenged to remember its spelling pattern (p. 532). Spelling words should remain at the instructional level for optimum growth and confidence building. For example, the difficulty level for a 10-word spelling list is shown in Table 2.4.

The analysis of spelling errors is critical. When spelling errors occur, students should analyze them through the process of self-evaluation. Through self-evaluation, students examine the types of errors they made and classify them. Table 2.5 shows an error analysis chart in which the student will record both the correct spelling of the list word and the spelling mistake. With the teacher's support, the student classifies the error with a check mark in the appropriate column. "In this activity, students engage episodic memory through a metacognitive analysis of their spelling behavior and gain an understanding of the types of errors they make and how to correct them" (Newlands, 2011, p. 533).

Table 2.4 Difficulty Level of a 10-Word Spelling List

Correct Spelling	Learning Opportunity Index
8–10 out of 10 words (80–100%)	Independent Level
5–7 out of 10 words (50–70%)	Instructional Level
0–4 out of 10 words (0–40%)	Frustration Level

Source: Newlands (2011, p. 532).

Table 2.5 Error Analysis Chart

Word:	Misspelling _____	What did I do?				
		Phonemic	Orthographic error	Missed letter(s)	Insertions	Letter reversals

Source: Newlands (1993). Adapted from Primary Junior Department, Hamilton Board of Education.

The Act of Reading

The act of reading engages students in an amazing experience through text. Good, quality literature books take the readers on a journey of co-creating with the words from the text. Through well-developed skills, the readers connect the words for meaning and, depending on the narrative, may also form images of what is being read as they construct meaning. The readers' experiences with the text will consist of their own personal experiences, cultural backgrounds, values, traditions, and, of course, interest and motivation.

Furthermore, Clay (1991) described the process of the act of reading as a generative one, with interlocking routes to get to meaning:

> This reading work clocks up more experience for the network with each of the features of print attended to. *It allows the partially familiar to become familiar and the new to become familiar in an ever-changing sequence.* Meaning is checked against letter sequence or vice versa, phonological recoding is checked against speech vocabulary, new meanings are checked against the grammatical and semantic contexts of the sentence and the story, and so on. Because one route to a response confirms an approach from another direction this may allow the network to become a more effective network. However the generative process only operates when the reading is "good," that is, successful enough to free attention to pick up new information at the point of problem-solving. An interlocking network of appropriate strategies which include monitoring and evaluation of consonance or dissonance among messages that ought to agree is central to this model of a system which extends itself. (pp. 328–329)

Skills View of Reading: Part-to-Whole or Bottom-Up Approach

When teachers and school districts fully endorse a **skills view of reading,** thus limiting the type of reading materials to easily "decoded" texts, children are denied the appreciation of quality books. This part-to-whole or bottom-up model, as it may be called, assumes incorrectly that once word decoding occurs, word meaning will naturally follow. This outside-in process belittles the role of context in getting meaning, as well as reading as a transaction between reader and text (Weaver, 2000). The skills model shown in Figure 2.4 ignores the interrelationships between the various cueing systems and the act of making meaning from text.

Figure 2.4
Skills Model
of Reading

Source: Weaver (2000, p. 34). From *Reading Process and Practice, 3rd Edition,* by Constance Weaver. Copyright © 2002 by Constance Weaver. Published by Heinemann, Portsmouth, NH. Reprinted with permission of the publisher.

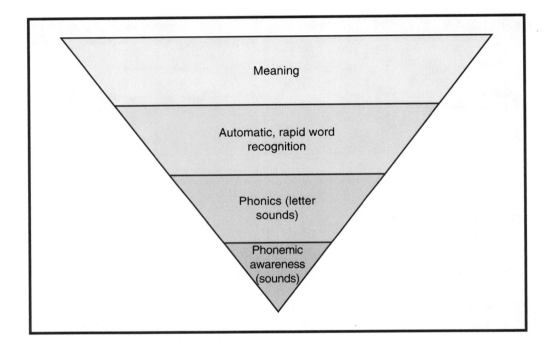

Sociopsycholinguistic (Dynamics) View of Reading: Top-Down, Whole-to-Part Approach

A transitional sociopsycholinguistic view of reading contrasts sharply with the skills approach discussed above. It assumes a whole-to-part model, with the reader constructing meaning from text rather than absorbing and regurgitating whatever is on the page. Making meaning reigns! Making sense of text emerges as meaning is negotiated within a specific situational context:

1. Words in isolation have a range of possible meanings—denotations, connotations, shadings, and nuances.

2. Words and phrases take on meaning as they transact with one another in sentences, paragraphs, and situations.

3. Meaning does not emanate from the text but is constructed by the reader.

4. Readers make meaning from text based on their schemas, or the hanging files of the mind that store knowledge, feelings, beliefs, and experiences (Weaver, 2000).

Complete the self-evaluation in Table 2.6 to gauge your current understanding of the different reading approaches.

Table 2.6 Self-Evaluation of Knowledge Base on Reading Approaches

Directions: With a partner, reflect on the statements on reading that follow. Do you agree or disagree, or are you unsure at this point? If you can support or refute a belief, provide an explanation of your reasoning or evidence of a reader's responses.

Belief	Agree/Disagree/Unsure	Evidence/Explanation
Once word decoding occurs, meaning will naturally follow.		
Various cueing systems all play a part in understanding text.		
Words and phrases take on meaning as they connect with other words and phrases.		
Readers create new meanings every time they encounter text.		

Let's continue our discussion of schemas. Remember that schemas are what students hold in their heads—the "hanging files of the mind"—each schema individual and unique to the student. As a teacher, do not allow your "expert blind spot" to supersede your respect for student perspective and experience.

The Role of Schemas

A schema is simply an organized chunk of knowledge or experience, often accompanied by feelings. (Weaver, 2000, p. 17)

Knowing that children's schemas develop as they interact with their external environment, they often lack requisite schemas to be able to attach meaning to what they read. One of the biggest errors made in reading instruction concerns decoding a word: If a reader can decode a word, he or she must understand its meaning. This is not true. Think about words you can pronounce or read correctly, yet you have no idea of their meaning. We can think of some that have recently confounded us: *glyph, hydrolysis,* and *logosyllabary* (Wolf, 2007). As a mature reader, you can most likely pronounce these words through graphophonics/syllabication but have probably (or maybe) not previously encountered them through schematic exchanges.

Consider: Look at these five sentences that use the word *drop* in different ways:

1. Drop everything and pay attention!
2. Do not drop that expensive clock.
3. The criminal was searching for the drop for the money.
4. The model was drop-dead gorgeous.
5. Do you drop the final *e* when adding "ment" to the word *judge*?

Deep and Surface Meanings

The nuances of language can be confounding for early readers. Our life experiences as adults have exposed us to various forms of **emotive language** to which we react in ways based on the "deeper" word connections. Each response is uniquely individual, yet powerful for the reader. Here are some words or pairs of words that can evoke strong reactions, either positive or negative or both. Obviously, they hold surface meanings based on their dictionary definitions; however, deeper meanings exist. Describe your reaction and try to trace the basis for that response:

1. Love/hate
2. Tornado/hurricane
3. Ice cream/Weight Watchers diet dinner
4. McDonald's fast food/homemade salad
5. Politicians/teachers

Making Connections

This quick formative exercise is a good warm-up for students. Generate five emotive terms about which students can express their feelings. Discuss the idea of deep versus surface meanings of words or phrases. Enact a think-aloud, where you make your thinking processes evident through dialogue, using three different terms as models. Use chart paper to annotate student responses or recollections. Talk about those connections to reading. Evaluate on the following points:

1. Do students understand what is meant by surface or outward meaning or definition/denotation (by dictionary)? This will vary by grade level and exposure to dictionary skills.
2. Are students able to express their interpretation of the "deeper" meaning of a word/phrase? If not, why not?
3. Are students able to describe why they connote the word/phrase as they do, to provide essential evidence or background reflection? Are some students unable to articulate this process?

The background of experience that a reader brings to the reading setting is crucial to generating meaning. Knowledge of the topic enhances the reader's ability to make predictions about the textual information, uncover the meaning of vocabulary words, and generate feelings about the text. We as adults are able to read what interests us, and students should also have this right. Would we care to read a topic about which we have no intrinsic knowledge? When students have little background in a topic, vocabulary becomes a challenge and they struggle with predictions about the text (R. Moore & Gilles, 2005).

Formative Assessment

Challenge students to express what they know about a text after previewing or engaging in a quick book walk, or develop four or five questions from the text to gauge understanding. Focusing on the title, author, pictures, selected sentences, or headings, ask students to predict (you can expand their vocabulary by asking them to *forecast, foretell, guess,* or *calculate*) what might happen in the text. Push them further by requesting evidence or proof of their predictions and then having them compare their answers to those of other students.

Context of Situation

Watson (1988) refers to the expectations of readers and the intentions of authors. Readers form literary anticipation based on prior reading experiences. Looking at certain genres of text, such as informational text, readers may come to expect factual information, diagrams, tables, and little if any character dialogue. Conversely, reading a fairy tale, students would expect fantasy, larger-than-life characters, and usually happy endings. Reflect on the activity in Table 2.7.

Table 2.7 Context of Situation Genre Expectations

Directions: Consider the expectations readers may hold when preparing to read the following genres in children's literature. The table below provides an opportunity for students to use their experiential knowledge in reading literature selections to generalize about author's style, content, vocabulary, and the inclusion of visuals (or not). Moreover, this table could be used as a formative assessment tool for classroom genre prediction activities.

Genre Type	Author's Style of Writing	Content	Vocabulary Use	Visuals/ Pictures
Fairy tale				
Rhyming book				
Informational text				
Autobiography				
Biography				
Humorous/riddle book				

Readers' cultures act as a filter in that everything they listen to or read silently, as well as whatever they hear instructionally or in the medium of conversation, is culturally bound. When text does not reflect passages from a reader's culture or background, **cultural discontinuity** can set in. This means a student is disconnected from the context of reading based on the lack of representation of his or her culture in the text.

A personal story will help explain cultural disconnects. As a white professor, I relocated to work at a historically black college in North Carolina, Winston-Salem State University. I recognized that my in-service education majors, mainly African Americans, would be prepared to work with their students who were mainly African American. Therefore, I knew I must develop a library of children's books that reflected the lives and stories of those children. I now have a wonderful collection of African American children's books, both narrative and nonfiction, that I am very proud of.

The Matthew Effect

The very children who are reading well and who have good vocabularies will read more, learn more word meanings, and hence read even better. Children with inadequate vocabularies—who read slowly and without enjoyment—read less, and as a result have slower development of vocabulary knowledge, which inhibits further growth in reading ability. (Stanovich, 2000, p. 184)

The concept of the **Matthew effect** emanates from research findings that students who have supportive early educational experiences are able to use new educational experiences more efficiently (Wahlberg & Tsai, 1983). Conversely, students who are labeled as less skilled and may not receive optimal reading instruction will continue to become weaker in reading as they progress through the grades. This idea of the "rich getting richer," with strong readers continuing to get more proficient, while the "poor get poorer" heightens chances of reading failure for weak readers. The students' out-of-school literacy environment—lacking reading materials, not visiting libraries, not being read to, engaging in intensive television viewing, and other factors—may limit the effects of well-intentioned interventions. Awareness of the research on the Matthew effect, coupled with gaps in the home literacy environment, has policymakers endorsing the implementation of universal preschool and quality early learning opportunities.

Wolf (2007) neatly explains the downward-spiral effect for reading and cognitive skills when children come from "impoverished language environments":

> Unbeknownst to them or their families, children who grow up in environments with few or no literacy experiences are already playing catch-up when they enter kindergarten and the primary grades. It is not simply a matter of the number of words unheard and unlearned. When words are not heard, concepts are not learned. When syntactic forms are never encountered, there is less knowledge about the events in a story. When story forms are never known, there is less ability to infer and predict. When cultural traditions and the feelings of others are never experienced, there is less understanding of what other people feel. (p. 102)

A critical longitudinal study by Hart and Risley (1995) cites the meaningful differences between the word usage of middle-class children and the "word poverty" of children from impoverished language environments. By age 5, children growing up in environments lacking rich language opportunities had heard 32 million fewer words spoken than had the average middle-class child (as cited in Wolf, 2007).

How does this pertain to assessment opportunities? Early childhood educators usually administer a questionnaire to the head of the family asking for details about at-home reading practices (see Table 2.8 for an example). Questions modeled after those used at Head Start centers can be used for intake forms (Green & Halsall, 2004).

Table 2.8 Alternative Questions for Families About At-Home Reading Activities

Alternative Questions for Families About At-Home Literacy	Possible Responses to Survey Questions
What family reading routines do you follow with your children?	Time, location, and reader
Please describe the daily learning activities you engage in with your children.	Counting, list making, discussions at home/in car, singing, reading stories, discussing TV shows, listening to educational tapes, focused discussions, discovery activities, library visits, nature walks, and so on
What books related to experiences does your family engage in?	Arts, crafts, cooking, outings
Specific Questions for Families	
Who reads to the children?	Mother, father, siblings, grandparents, others
What time(s) of day does reading occur?	Bedtime, early evening, afternoon, noon, morning
Where does the reading activity happen?	Living room, child's bedroom, kitchen table, outside, parents' bedroom, floor
What type of books does your child like to listen to?	Fairy tales, informational, reality, picture books, poetry, sports heroes, and so on

As a former family involvement coordinator, I urge teachers to be educators of parents also. Basic information about the benefits of continuous reading and exposure to literacy may be something unfamiliar to parents if they were not exposed to a rich home literacy environment themselves. Keeping in mind the learning standards in the Common Core, teachers should make parents aware that they can help by reading informational children's books, magazines, or pamphlets.

Making Connections

Carefully read over and complete Table 2.9. Share your ideas with a partner, and discuss the similarities and differences in answers you may receive from parents. Discuss why some parents might have a different view or perspective on the benefits of home literacy.

Table 2.9 Parental Perceptions of Benefits for Reading at Home

Directions: Read each statement and mark an X next to the level of measurement that best indicates your feelings.

1. I recognize the benefits that reading at home has for my family.

    _____ Strongly agree

    _____ Agree

    _____ Somewhat agree

    _____ Neutral

    _____ Somewhat disagree

    _____ Disagree

    _____ Strongly disagree

2. Reading at home has helped my child/children improve in their classes at school.

    _____ Strongly agree

    _____ Agree

    _____ Somewhat agree

    _____ Neutral

    _____ Somewhat disagree

    _____ Disagree

    _____ Strongly disagree

3. I recognize that it is important for my child/children to see me reading at home.

    _____ Strongly agree

    _____ Agree

_____ Somewhat agree

_____ Neutral

_____ Somewhat disagree

_____ Disagree

_____ Strongly disagree

4. I recognize the benefits of reading expository (informational) texts with my child/children at home.

_____ Strongly agree

_____ Agree

_____ Somewhat agree

_____ Neutral

_____ Somewhat disagree

_____ Disagree

_____ Strongly disagree

5. I recognize that reading with my child/children at home will reinforce a positive attitude toward learning English.

_____ Strongly agree

_____ Agree

_____ Somewhat agree

_____ Neutral

_____ Somewhat disagree

_____ Disagree

_____ Strongly disagree

Reading and the Brain

Neuroscientists at research universities continue to make exciting discoveries about the role of the brain in the reading process. It is clearly beyond the scope of this textbook to attempt to discuss even a minuscule portion of the recent research. We suggest you refer to Maryanne Wolf's fascinating 2007 book *Proust and the Squid: The Story and Science of the Reading Brain* for further enlightenment.

The diagram of the brain shown in Figure 2.5 indicates the areas responsible for word analysis, word formation, and phoneme processing. Broca's area is responsible for phoneme processing, a most important skill for beginning readers. The parieto-temporal area is where words are pulled apart and put back together as readers strive for word analysis. The occipito-temporal area promotes automaticity, meaning words and word chunks can be recognized automatically.

Nonetheless, there are brain facts we should be aware of as educators, taking in the health and nurturance of the brain. Frequent intake of water and lessening sugar intake help support the brain. Exercise for the brain in the form of whole-body physical exercise and mental exercise is critical; take interval breaks during class to let students engage in movements that are fun and invigorating. Let's turn to a brief explanation of reading and the brain for beginning and more fluent readers.

The Beginning Reader. This process, as articulated by Wolf (2007), outlines the attention networks on which the beginning reader is dependent. In the brain of a beginning reader, learning a skill expends a lot of cognitive and motor processing through expanding neural connections. As the skill becomes highly practiced, less brain effort is expended and the neural pathways become more streamlined and effective in meeting the learning task. The major job for a beginning reader is to strive to connect the parts of the brain through frequent reading and skills performance. "Learning to read changes the visual cortex of the brain" (p. 147).

The Fluent Reader. Because the visual cueing system of the expert reader is capable of instantaneous object recognition and specialization, the fluent reader's visual areas of the brain now have cell networks accountable for visual images of letters, letter patterns, and sounds. These areas of the brain function at lightning speeds, between 50 and 150

Figure 2.5

Brain Diagram for Reading

Source: From *Breakthrough in Beginning Reading and Writing* by Richard Gentry. Copyright © 2007 by Richard Gentry. Reprinted with permission of Scholastic, Inc.

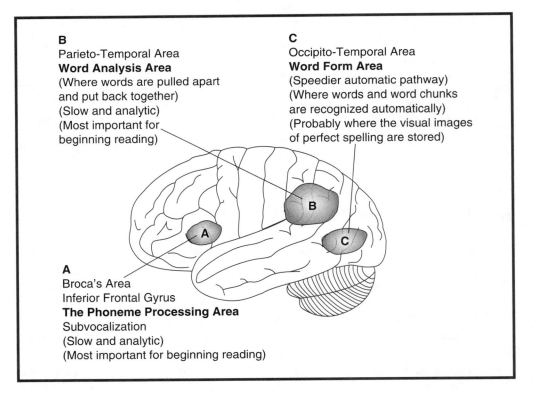

B
Parieto-Temporal Area
Word Analysis Area
(Where words are pulled apart and put back together)
(Slow and analytic)
(Most important for beginning reading)

C
Occipito-Temporal Area
Word Form Area
(Speedier automatic pathway)
(Where words and word chunks are recognized automatically)
(Probably where the visual images of perfect spelling are stored)

A
Broca's Area
Inferior Frontal Gyrus
The Phoneme Processing Area
Subvocalization
(Slow and analytic)
(Most important for beginning reading)

milliseconds. Eye movements, or the ways our eyes move across text, contribute to **automaticity**, which appears horizontal and flowing but is nonetheless made up of small, continuous movements, called saccades. Fixations, or when our eyes stop moving so we can gather information for the brain, have several critical characteristics:

- At least 10% of the time, eyes dash back (we don't realize this is happening) to pick up past information read.
- For children, the typical saccade is fewer than eight letters.
- Eyes allow children to "see ahead" to preview information that lies ahead.

The executive system tells the brain whether there is enough information about letters and word forms to move forward to a new saccade at 250 milliseconds or whether a regression backward to obtain more information is warranted.

This complex cognitive activity is accomplished simultaneously and at lightning speed; strong readers are largely unconscious of it. It is an efficient, effective, fluent process that allows readers to keep the greater part of their attention on the meaning of the text (Clay, 1991). However, the process can break down for readers who struggle in one or more cueing systems, as we discuss in Chapter 4.

Students With Special Needs, Reading, and the Brain

For students with special needs, learning to read may be a huge challenge. Factors impacting reading may include hearing, speech, vision, or other developmental disabilities such as dyslexia. Reading successfully involves two basic processes—decoding and comprehension—and the coordination of three neural systems—auditory, visual, and executive (Sousa, 2007). In some, problems may occur during early brain development and affect the ability to process the sounds of language and, eventually, to decode written text. According to Sousa, this developmental deficit appears to be the most common cause of reading difficulties and usually results in a lifelong struggle with reading.

It is not easy to pinpoint the causes of reading disabilities. An extensive number of cognitive, motor, and sensory systems are involved in reading. Striving readers may have impairments in any one or more of these systems. A word of caution: If a child shows signs of any of these indicators, experts in the area of reading difficulties should be notified. Carefully annotated observational notes from the teacher should be supplied to reading experts. Some indicators of reading disabilities that may act as "red flags" include

- phonological deficits (the inability to sound out words in one's head),
- differences in auditory and visual processing speeds,
- working memory (phonological memory) deficits,
- word blindness,
- inability to detect and discriminate among sounds presented in rapid succession,
- impairment in sound-frequency discrimination,
- inability to detect tones within noise,
- visual magnocellular deficits (deficits in the visual processing system, motor coordination, and the cerebellum),
- delays in speaking,

- difficulties with pronunciation,
- difficulty learning letters of the alphabet,
- recalling incorrect phonemes, and
- insensitivity to rhyme (Sousa, 2007).

Thus, building on phonemic awareness is key for children with reading disabilities. Also, the process of identifying a child with a disability, implementing appropriate screening, and accurately diagnosing the disability, or disabilities, is critical in developing essential instructional methods and strategies to address the child's needs.

Bilingual Language Development and the Brain

Learning two or more languages is an extraordinary, complicated cognitive investment for children, that represents a growing reality for a huge number of children. (Wolf, 2007, p. 105)

The plasticity of a young child's brain brings many advantages to second language learning if first language acquisition is well under way. A younger child's brain beats out the brain of an adolescent in the ability to learn a new language, based on ease of neural connections. Wolf (2007) suggests three principles that educators should keep in mind when working with bilingual learners:

1. English language learners who know concepts attached to words in their first language fare better in attaining a second language. Children from language-impoverished home environments have no cognitive or linguistic foundation for a second language.

2. Children who come to school as new English learners are unfamiliar with the phonemes they are expected to induce while reading. They need careful exposure to the new phonemes of the English language, along with its conventions.

3. Early bilingual exposure, before age 3, has a positive effect on language growth and reading development.

Translanguaging, or learning multiple languages at an early age, is a process that expands and enriches the brain. Educators, concerned with the learning standards in the Common Core, are seeking activities and strategies to support the English language learners in their classrooms. The following websites supply resources helpful for teachers, students, and parents:

- ¡Colorín Colorado! (www.colorincolorado.org)—This is a bilingual site for educators and families. The "ELL Research and Reports" section features a number of articles and resources about implementing the new Common Core State Standards with English language learners, including articles, presentations, video interviews, and information for bilingual parents.
- EngageNY: New York State Bilingual Common Core Initiative (www.engageny.org/resource/new-york-state-bilingual-common-core-initiative)—The New York State

Education Department launched the Bilingual Common Core Initiative to develop new English as a second language and native language arts standards aligned to the Common Core. As a result of this process, the department has developed New Language Arts Progressions and Home Language Arts Progressions for every New York State Common Core Learning Standard in every grade.

Literacy and the very act of reading, including what occurs in the brain of a reader, are fascinating and exceedingly complex. We suggest you take time to further explore the topics presented in this chapter, using the references and web resources provided. Happy exploring!

Key Terms

automaticity	morphology
cueing systems	orthographic development
cultural discontinuity	pragmatics
Elkonin or sound boxes	rebuses
emotive language	schemas
graphophonics	semantics
language experience approach	skills view of reading
Matthew effect	syntactics

Website Resources

- **"Ready to Read? Neuroscience Research Sheds Light on Brain Correlates of Reading,"** The Dana Foundation

The Dana Foundation is a private philanthropic organization that supports brain research through education, grants, and publications. This particular article focuses on the brain's "wiring" for reading and the subtle differences found in people with reading learning disabilities. To read this article in its entirety, visit **www.dana.org/media/detail.aspx?id=13124**.

- **"Science Bulletins: How Does Reading Change the Brain?" American Museum of Natural History**

This is a 2-minute YouTube video that you have to see. It shows images of the brain and how reading changes the brain, and compares literate brains with newly literate and illiterate brains. To view this video, go to **www.youtube.com/watch?v=AZ6HKCAhcAc**.

(Continued)

(Continued)

- **National Council of Teachers of English: A Professional Association of Educators in English Studies, Literacy, and Language Arts**

The National Council of Teachers of English is devoted to improving the teaching and learning of English and the language arts at all levels of education. The council's site offers a wide variety of resources, including lesson plans, journals, newsletters, magazines, and grants. It also offers professional development services and membership opportunities. For more information, go to **www.ncte.org.**

- **Scholastic**

This site includes resources for teachers, parents, children, and librarians. The teacher pages provide a wide variety of reading strategies and resources, professional support, and student activities, all designed to promote student development and growth in the language arts. See **www.scholastic.com/home**.

- **"Response to Intervention in Reading for English Language Learners," RTI Action Network**

This article highlights the knowledge base on reading and Response to Intervention for English language learners, and provides preliminary support for the use of practices related to Response to Intervention with this population. This site also provides links to other articles and resources supporting English language learners. In addition, the site offers articles and resources for students with special needs. To read the full article, visit **www.rtinetwork .org/learn/diversity/englishlanguagelearners.**

Student Study Site: Visit the Student Study Site at **www.sagepub.com/grantlit** to access additional study tools including eFlashcards, web resources, and online-only appendices.

CHAPTER 3

Students Who Struggle With Literacy Learning

Stephanie Affinito and Melanie O'Leary

Common Core State Standards

Key Ideas and Details	*CCRA.R.1* Read closely to determine what the text says explicitly and to make logical inferences from it; cite specific textual evidence when writing or speaking to support conclusions drawn from the text.
	CCRA.R.2 Determine central ideas or themes of a text and analyze their development; summarize the key supporting details and ideas.
	CCRA.R.3 Analyze how and why individuals, events, or ideas develop and interact over the course of a text.
Craft and Structure	*CCRA.R.4* Interpret words and phrases as they are used in a text, including determining technical, connotative, and figurative meanings, and analyze how specific word choices shape meaning or tone.
	CCRA.R.5 Analyze the structure of texts, including how specific sentences, paragraphs, and larger portions of the text (e.g., a section, chapter, scene, or stanza) relate to each other and the whole.
	CCRA.R.6 Assess how point of view or purpose shapes the content and style of a text.
Integration of Knowledge and Ideas	*CCRA.R.7* Integrate and evaluate content presented in diverse media and formats, including visually and quantitatively, as well as in words.

(Continued)

(Continued)

Integration of Knowledge and Ideas (continued)	*CCRA.R.8* Delineate and evaluate the argument and specific claims in a text, including the validity of the reasoning as well as the relevance and sufficiency of the evidence.
	CCRA.R.9 Analyze how two or more texts address similar themes or topics in order to build knowledge or to compare the approaches the authors take.
Range of Reading and Level of Text Complexity	*CCRA.R.10* Read and comprehend complex literary and informational texts independently and proficiently.

FOCUS QUESTIONS

1. What is literacy learning, and what components of a successful literacy learning program do you find most important?

2. With the advent of Response to Intervention, what three levels correspond with primary, secondary, and tertiary prevention?

3. What are some strategies that help circumvent difficulties in literacy learning? Explain why they may help support students?

4. What are some challenges in phonics, decoding, or word recognition that may impact developmental reading?

5. What are some challenges in vocabulary, comprehension, or fluency that may impact developmental reading?

6. How can teachers support English language learners who enter classrooms with minimal language skills?

Words in Action

Jake and Tyler

We want students to be able to glean meaningful information from expository text; however, learning this technique via imposed reading is counterproductive. By allowing students to pick the expository text and the answers they are looking for, we give purpose to their learning and maintain their natural curiosity.

Tyler and Jake epitomize the reasons for self-selected reading material. Tyler hates home-work and sees it as busywork with no inherent purpose. This is not for lack of fortitude, for the same fourth grader will spend 8 to 12 hours in a corn chopper making sure the harvest gets in on time.

Each afternoon, the struggle to get Tyler to do his assigned reading begins. "I hate read-ing" is not what a parent wants to hear. Alternatively, Tyler will spend hours reading and interpreting the complex directions for a LEGO Star Destroyer with articulating gun turrets and a full chassis antilock braking system.

Jake, while enjoying the playtime with LEGOs, has no interest in reading and interpreting the technical directions required to get the turrets working and the braking system function-ing correctly. But ask him what he likes to read and he will refer to a cadre of animal books about such creatures as his favorite pet, Spike the bearded dragon, and his next conquest, Mocha the ball python. Jake has been to classrooms from elementary to master's level to present all he knows about his pets and where they come from. He is a model of the insa-tiable interest to learn more about the natural world around him—why ice melts, wind blows, and spiders weave.

Jake and Tyler are brothers, yet each has a different interest and motivation for reading. To force either into the other's reading realm would be to instantly turn off the innate curi-osity they were born with. Each brother is seeking a different set of answers, and together they represent the differences among all students of reading and writing.

Developmental Reading Process

Multiple researchers have provided developmental descriptions of the reading process (Adams, 1990; Chall, 1983; Ehri, 1991; Ehri & McCormick, 2004; Stahl, 2006) suggesting that children move through particular stages as they learn to recognize words and construct meaning from the text. The double conceptualization of fluency and comprehension is central to understanding the stages of reading development (Institute of Reading Development, 2014). *Developmental reading* is a term used to describe classroom-based literacy taught by a teacher at the **instructional level** of individual students; however, this developmental approach does not imply that children proceed through rigid stages at a prescribed or predetermined rate. Table 3.1 outlines the general time frame, sequence, and fundamental ideas behind the developmental reading process.

Children bring their own **background information**, experiences, and instruction to the reading experience. Given the diversity of student experience and ability, children vary in their ease of learning to read (Scanlon, Anderson, & Sweeney, 2010). For most students, learning to read follows a predictable sequence (Strickland,

Table 3.1 Stages of Reading Development	
Stage 1: **Learning to Read**	This stage begins with letter recognition, when children are aged 4 or 5. At this time, the central focus is learning to decode: learning the alphabet, learning letter sounds, distinguishing sounds in speech, and learning to sound out words. This stage is complete when children achieve fluency in easy-to-read books with controlled vocabulary and simple sentences, as early as mid-first grade to mid-third grade.
Stage 2: **Developing** **Independent** **Reading Skills**	Reading practice and skill development at this stage are both primarily focused on fluency development. The central focus is lots of reading at the just-right level, progressing into chapter books. Students learn how to decode long words (three or more syllables). As fluency continues to develop, comprehension becomes an instructional and developmental focus. This stage is complete when children achieve fluency in children's novels, as early as Grade 2 to Grade 5.
Stage 3: **Reading With** **Absorption**	When students read with identification and absorption, the process is both transparent for the author's vision and intrinsically pleasurable. The central focus of this stage is to do a great deal of reading in children's novels at gradually increasing levels of difficulty, a process that enables a child to develop the levels of fluency and comprehension required to support identification and absorption. This achievement is also the basis for all subsequent reading development, including reading for concepts and information.
Stage 4: **Critical Reading**	The capability to read critically allows students to enter a new stage of reading development in which a critical dimension of experience is added to the basic substrata of experiences that are already present as a result of previous developments in reading ability. A student with a strong reading background who reads with solid levels of fluency and comprehension will experience a relatively automatic and accurate flow of understanding while reading, whether reading a novel or textbook. Training in critical reading is based on metacognitive techniques in which the readers learn to exercise conscious control of the reading process based on their purpose as readers and the demands of the text. Students develop the ability to recognize how material is organized, determine and synthesize main ideas, relate to main ideas, monitor comprehension and adjust reading rate or reread when necessary, and take notes and study them for a test.

Source: Institute of Reading Development (2014).

Ganske, & Monroe, 2002) over time and experience. Yet for others, literacy learning proves more difficult. For students with special needs and English language learners, this is especially true; the reading process and reading comprehension may present a multitude of challenges for these populations. Various aspects of print, **orthographic features,** and knowledge sources may cause difficulty based on the child's stage or level of reading (Leslie & Caldwell, 2011). Other challenges may occur, as listed in Table 3.2 and outlined in the following.

The literacy teacher uses assessment to observe these developmental differences in learning to read (Leslie & Caldwell, 2011). Furthermore, the Response to Intervention approach offers a different way of thinking about students who struggle with literacy learning and places particular importance on the match of instruction between a child and the instructional program in place.

Table 3.2 Signs of Reading Problems	
Grades	**Red Flags**
Preschool	• Doesn't know how to hold a book • Can't tell the difference between letters and squiggles • Can't recognize own name • Only says a small number of words • Doesn't like rhyming games and can't fill in the rhyming word in familiar nursery rhymes
Kindergarten	• Can't tell the difference between the sounds that make up a word (phonics) • Slow to name familiar objects and colors • Can't remember the names and sounds of the letters • By the end of kindergarten, can't write most of the consonant sounds in a word (it's normal for vowels to be missing until later)
Grades 1 and 2	• Has trouble pronouncing new words and remembering them • Has trouble blending sounds together to say words • Says reading is easier for their classmates • Falls way behind their classmates • Can't figure out unknown words • Avoids reading • Resists reading aloud
Grades 2 and 3	• Starts to withdraw • Has some troubling behavior • Seems to guess at unknown words • Does not get meaning from reading

Source: University of Michigan Health System (2013). Kyla Boyse, MS, RN, CPNP University of Michigan Health System, http://www.med.umich.edu/yourchild/topics/dyslexia.htm.

Making Connections

Red flags that alert teachers to students' reading problems are critical for early diagnosis of reading challenges. Pick one red flag listed in Table 3.2 that can form the focus of a virtual conversation with a veteran teacher on the topic of early identification. What additional questions might be posed to help you understand the importance of that particular red flag? For example, one possible red flag is that the student seems to guess at unknown words. With that in mind, the new practitioner may pose the following questions: (1) Is the word guessing consistent or intermittent? (2) Is the word guessing mainly in Tier 1, 2, or 3 words, or a mixture? (3) Is the word guessing supported by orthographic (similar spelling) or semantic (meaning) cues? These questions will be posed after reflection with your partner. Use pertinent information from Chapter 2 to help support your inquiries.

Response to Intervention and Literacy Learning

As discussed in Chapter 1, **Response to Intervention (RtI)** is a "comprehensive, systemic approach to teaching and learning designed to address learning problems for all students through increasingly differentiated and intensified assessment and instruction" (Wixson, 2011, p. 503). Lose's (2007) research study suggests that signs of struggling students usually surface after 1 year of school—hence, the immediacy of early intervention. The struggling student must receive intensive individually delivered instruction tailored to his or her needs.

According to RtI experts Fuchs and Fuchs (2009, pp. 250–251), the RtI framework was initiated with the following levels:

Primary prevention or Tier 1: Instructional practices general educators conduct with all students; the core instructional program, along with classroom routines for differentiating instruction; accommodations that permit access for all students, including those with disabilities; and problem-solving strategies to address motivational problems that interfere with student performance.

Secondary prevention or Tier 2: Involves the standard form of small-group tutoring, with instructional procedures that are typically 0 to 15 weeks of 20- to 40-minute sessions, occurring three to four times a week.

Tertiary prevention or Tier 3: Teachers establish individual year-end goals in instructional materials that match student needs; materials may come from below-grade-level sources. Tertiary prevention is individualized based on student failure to thrive academically at the primary or secondary level.

RtI demands meaningful and relevant assessment reflecting the multidimensional nature of literacy and diversity in students (International Reading Association [IRA], 2010a). Rather than using assessments to classify students, teachers must use data to make changes in their own instruction. Multiple measures must be used and looked at as a whole, not in isolation. Combined **screening**, diagnostic, and progress monitoring tools, as well as informal observation and performance in the classroom, must be considered (IRA, 2010a). Student progress should be monitored by the teacher as a skilled problem solver, diagnostician, and lesson designer versus "teacher-as-technician" (Lose, 2007, p. 277). Assessment that informs instruction is critical; teachers must notice and respond to what children can and cannot do so they can adapt the instruction they provide (Johnston, 2011).

When a child demonstrates difficulty in learning literacy, we must first assume not that the reasons for those difficulties reside in the child (Pinnell & Fountas, 2008) but, rather, that they result from a mismatch of instruction with students' individual learning experiences and instructional needs; "most learning problems exist not within the child, but in the inadequacy of the system to find a way to teach him" (p. 30). However, if a student with special needs has a reading disability, it is essential to pinpoint exactly where the difficulties lie so instruction can be focused and explicit.

Making Connections

RtI and the tiers will be a critical part of your screening, diagnosis, benchmarking, and intervention plans as a teacher. RtI is a substantive change for schools in the way they provide interventions for striving students. You will need to seek out professional opportunities to interact with teachers who have instituted RtI in their classrooms. Some topics to inquire about are understanding benchmarking, cut points, and state-allowed assessments. Think about developing some interview questions for teacher experts or special education teachers in the area of RtI. What might you ask?

Difficulties With Literacy Learning

Learning to read involves the orchestration of several systems (Pinnell & Fountas, 2008). These systems include language processing, phonological processing, visual processing, use of background knowledge to construct meaning, connecting reading and writing, reading fluency, attention, memory, processing/cognitive actions, emotion, and motivation (Pinnell & Fountas, 2011). Table 3.3 provides a description for each of these elements as well as their application to literacy learning through specific instructional strategies.

Table 3.3 Elements of Learning to Read With Specific Instructional Strategies

Elements of Learning to Read	Description	Specific Instructional Strategies
Language processing	Children live in a world that is rich with print and start to develop an awareness of language redundancy and predictability.	Primary: Exposure to environmental print, parent read-alouds, library visits, books on tape, encouraging word play, and labeling classroom features
Phonological processing	Children begin processing the sounds of language and how they work together in meaningful ways.	Primary: Employing words, rhyming words, onsets and rhymes, syllables, and individual sounds through active strategies
Visual processing	Children learn ways of word solving that include knowing how a word looks and using patterns and clusters of letters in a word.	Primary: Word shape activities, sight word practice, letter patterns and cluster activities, and word identification on word walls
Use of background knowledge to construct meaning	Through schemas or organized files of memory, students are supported in gaining meaning.	Primary and intermediate: Thinking beyond the text, bringing knowledge from personal experiences to make predictions
Connecting reading and writing	Children extend their understanding of a selection through a variety of writing genres and strategies, including functional, narrative, poetic, and informational writing.	Primary: Sketches, lists, short writes, heading labels, graphics, and supporting illustrations Intermediate: Longer written responses, journal entries, T-charts, and reader's theatre

(Continued)

Table 3.3 (Continued)

Elements of Learning to Read	Description	Specific Instructional Strategies
Reading fluency	Students are reading text continuously, with good momentum and phrasing, and appropriate pausing, stress, and intonation. Comprehension of text is the critical element in fluency.	Primary: Reading and echo reading nursery rhymes, and choral reading poems Intermediate: Poetry reading, echo reading, radio reading, and guided reading
Attention	Children are conscious of and attend to strategies in reading; they exhibit metacognitive recognition of the task of reading.	Primary: Teacher modeling, drawing attention to skilled reading, and modeling strong reading Intermediate: Self-reflection coaching activities and metacognitive teaching strategies
Memory	Students can achieve automatic recall of words through long-term memory.	Primary and intermediate: Cloze activities, prediction of story endings, and memory games
Processing actions	Children automatically process or make mindful daily choices about a large amount of written language.	Primary and intermediate: Opportunities to read choice books, guided reading, and partner reading
Cognitive actions	Students have the ability to comprehend ideas and use their language facility to share their thinking.	Primary and intermediate: Use of anchor charts, partner turn-and-talks, and think-alouds
Emotions	Students achieve emotional engagement with text, regardless of success in the reading task.	Primary and intermediate: Response journals, reader response activities, reader's theatre, and partner reading
Motivation	Students are interested and engaged in the act of reading.	Primary and intermediate: Student choice of books and individualizing books for students through literature circles

According to one teacher's recollections,

> It has always struck me that students who struggle with reading do so in such diverse ways. It is these reluctant and struggling readers who still haunt their teachers at night, long after they have left the classroom doors, and whose voices echo in their minds when they read about an approach that may have made sense to one of them. (Sableski, 2009, p. 30)

With proficient readers, the systems illustrated in Table 3.3 work together smoothly; yet some readers may experience and demonstrate difficulty decoding words, monitoring and correcting, and/or comprehending. Difficulty in learning to read should not be thought of as an overall cognitive deficit (Fink, 2006). In fact, "many intelligent children have difficulty learning to read" (Pinnell & Fountas, 2008, p. 30).

The term **struggling reader** has "become a label that places everything—all the challenges, difficulties, responsibilities, and possibilities related to reading—on students, which can result in self-fulfilling prophecies, leading to withdrawn behavior and negative feelings about reading, education, and themselves" (Enriquez, Jones, & Clarke, 2010, p. 74). Struggling readers are often defined as those readers who do not qualify for special services outside of the regular classroom but who struggle with grade-level reading assignments, often reading as many as two grade levels below their peers (Sableski, 2009). Fink (2006) proposes using the term **striving readers** instead, as it denotes the more positive qualities of motivation and effort, which are often overlooked in students who struggle.

Making Connections

Struggling Versus Striving Readers

Consider the differences in connotation between the terms *struggling reader* and *striving reader*. Discuss the positive versus negative messages sent through these labels attached to developmental readers. Is there another term that would be more comfortable for you as a teacher of developmental reading? If so, what is it?

Literacy experts Harste, Allington, and Enriquez, Jones, and Clarke weigh in with their opinions on struggling readers in Figure 3.1.

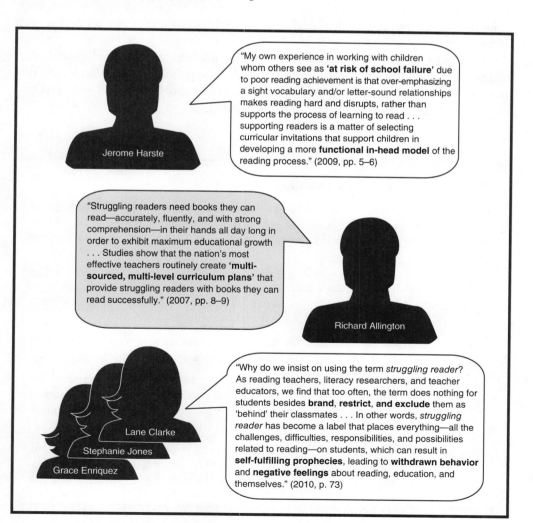

Figure 3.1
Literacy Experts and Struggling Readers

"My own experience in working with children whom others see as **'at risk of school failure'** due to poor reading achievement is that over-emphasizing a sight vocabulary and/or letter-sound relationships makes reading hard and disrupts, rather than supports the process of learning to read . . . supporting readers is a matter of selecting curricular invitations that support children in developing a more **functional in-head model** of the reading process." (2009, pp. 5–6)

Jerome Harste

"Struggling readers need books they can read—accurately, fluently, and with strong comprehension—in their hands all day long in order to exhibit maximum educational growth . . . Studies show that the nation's most effective teachers routinely create **'multi-sourced, multi-level curriculum plans'** that provide struggling readers with books they can read successfully." (2007, pp. 8–9)

Richard Allington

"Why do we insist on using the term *struggling reader*? As reading teachers, literacy researchers, and teacher educators, we find that too often, the term does nothing for students besides **brand, restrict, and exclude** them as 'behind' their classmates . . . In other words, *struggling reader* has become a label that places everything—all the challenges, difficulties, responsibilities, and possibilities related to reading—on students, which can result in **self-fulfilling prophecies**, leading to **withdrawn behavior** and **negative feelings** about reading, education, and themselves." (2010, p. 73)

Lane Clarke
Stephanie Jones
Grace Enriquez

Thus, accurate and authentic assessment is needed to document students' strengths and instructional needs. Given the range of difficulties a student may encounter throughout the reading process, assessment should focus on multiple aspects of reading. These areas of assessment include accuracy and automaticity in identifying words, word identification strategies used, ability to **decode** words in isolation versus connected text, differences in text types, modes of reading (silent vs. oral), familiar and unfamiliar text, using look-backs to facilitate comprehension, and comprehension strategies used to gain meaning from a text (Leslie & Caldwell, 2011). By reflecting on the assessment data gathered, teachers identify students' strengths, as well as the problematic actions (Clay, 2005b) they exhibit, to best design instructional interventions.

Furthermore, there is no one, typical profile of a student who struggles in literacy (Flanigan et al., 2011). Literacy learning is fluid and multidimensional, and students do not fit neatly into boxed categories and labels, nor should they. Students may struggle with different literacy skills for different reasons. Some students might struggle with decoding unfamiliar words. Others may easily decode unknown words but lack fluency and intonation while reading. Still others may have difficulty comprehending a text due to a lack of prior knowledge and reading experiences. Others may struggle with specific comprehension strategies, such as finding the main idea of a text or making higher-level connections.

Reflecting on the typical challenges some students face in their development helps teachers become more reflective about their students' needs and better plan for instruction. In the next section, we explore challenges in phonics, decoding, and word recognition, along with vocabulary, fluency, and comprehension.

Making Connections

Difficulties in Literacy Learning

Think of the last time you learned something new. How did you learn it? What contributed to your success? Cambourne (2001) proposed certain conditions that need to be in place to ensure students' success in learning oral language and literacy, as well as classroom strategies:

1. *Immersion:* Students need to be surrounded by an environment that is rich with learning and language. Classroom strategies include print walks, read-alouds, student work on walls, sustained silent reading, and choral reading.

2. *Demonstration:* Students need opportunities to observe learning occurring. Classroom strategies include modeling, think-alouds, and process demonstrations.

3. *Expectations:* Students learn in an environment where the teacher communicates high expectations, believing that the student can—and will—learn. Classroom strategies include student goal setting, mixed-ability groups, and avoiding negative comparisons.

4. *Responsibility:* Students are encouraged to assume responsibility for their learning. Classroom strategies include scaffolding structures for learning, using open-ended language that supports choices, and insisting that comments and judgments be justified.

5. *Approximation:* Students should feel free to take risks with their learning. For this to occur, students must experience success in a safe, supportive environment where a mistake is seen (and treated!) merely as a learning point. Classroom strategies include modeling good/bad miscues, spelling approximations, and community-based stories of how things are accomplished.

6. *Use and practice:* Students use their knowledge through their everyday lives (e.g., writing, presenting, exploring, experimenting, etc.). Classroom strategies include sustained silent reading and DEAR (drop everything and read), reading for a range of purposes, reading and retelling, and meaningful writing for authentic purposes.

7. *Engagement:* For learning to be effective, students must actively engage with learning and the process of learning. Classroom strategies include propagandizing: reading and its value to students, personal stories, and demonstrations of powerful reading.

8. *Response:* Students need to receive feedback from the teacher and classroom peers (e.g., critique, self-evaluations, peer evaluations, talk, etc.). Classroom strategies include receiving multiple-course feedback and modeling how readers use various cues to create meaning (Cambourne, 2001; Lilly & Green, 2004).

How did these conditions influence your own learning? How can you help ensure that they are met in your classroom?

Challenges in Phonics, Decoding, and Word Recognition

Phonics, decoding, and word recognition are skills needed to accurately read printed words. Phonics is the understanding that there is a predictable relationship between **phonemes**, which are the sounds of spoken language, and **graphemes**, the letters and spelling that represent those sounds in written language (National Reading Panel, 2000). It involves learning letter–sound correspondences (**phonological awareness**) and applying those skills while reading connected text. These skills sustain students' reading (Pinnell & Fountas, 2008) so they can read accurately to gain meaning from the text.

Some readers, however, have difficulty with word knowledge, which interferes with this process. Word knowledge includes three related areas: spelling, reading, and decoding and vocabulary knowledge (Flanigan et al., 2011). Students may have difficulty fluently decoding words or accessing the meaning of words (Biemiller, 2003; Chall & Jacobs, 2003; Leach, Scarborough, & Rescorla, 2003). Several observable behaviors accompany difficult reading: slower reading rate, finger-pointing and broken phrasing and intonation, word-by-word reading, and lack of self-monitoring (Allington, 2012). Word-level skills are foundational to other skills, including comprehension of text. Thus, students who struggle with reading words accurately and at a sufficient pace are more likely to struggle in other aspects of literacy as well (Deshler, Palincsar, Biancarosa, & Nair, 2007).

Challenges in Vocabulary, Comprehension, or Fluency

To adequately understand the text read, students not only have to read words accurately but also must read fluently and know the meanings of those words. The entire act of reading involves sustaining reading strategies, including phonics and word recognition, as well as expanding the meaning of the text (Pinnell & Fountas, 2008).

Vocabulary is stored information about the meanings and pronunciations of words necessary for communication (National Reading Panel, 2000). As students move into the upper elementary grades and beyond, this vocabulary knowledge becomes critical. Knowing words and their meanings is critical to comprehension (Allington, 2012) because vocabulary knowledge influences comprehension of texts (Anderson & Freebody, 1981). Some students might read words accurately but not be able to articulate the meanings of those words. Others may have difficulty decoding complex words as a result of limited vocabulary knowledge. Teachers can build vocabulary by focusing on a wide range of reading and explicit vocabulary teaching.

Strategies. **Reading comprehension** is the construction of the meaning of a written text through a reciprocal interchange of ideas between the reader and the message in a particular text (National Reading Panel, 2000). Comprehension involves thoughtful consideration and discussion of texts, focusing on understanding rather than on remembering. "Thoughtful literacy goes beyond the ability to read, remember and recite on demand" (Allington, 2012, p. 129). If students have difficulty with foundational reading skills such as decoding and word recognition, then comprehension may be compromised; however, some students read accurately and fluently but still struggle with reading comprehension.

Fluency is reading with speed and accurate and proper expression, without conscious attention (National Reading Panel, 2000). It has been referred to as the neglected reading skill (Allington, 1983), because many teachers and researchers assume that fluency will naturally follow word recognition skills. But one cannot assume that if a child can decode printed words fluency will automatically follow. Fluency involves reading accuracy, as well as **reading rate** and inflection. Students who have difficulty reading fluently may show it in different ways. Some students may read too slowly, with choppy expression, while others might read much too quickly and ignore critical punctuation of the text. This may be a result of limited experience reading texts, a learned response to reading aloud, or limited practice with appropriate materials (Allington, 2012). Fluency can be developed with proper instruction and has a positive impact on comprehension (Allington, 2012).

Let's take a look at some profiles of student performance. These profiles are helpful as typographies of struggling readers. To read the full article from which the profiles come, see Valencia and Buly (2004).

Student Profiles

Research conducted by Valencia and Buly (2004) describes the patterns of performance of students who failed to pass a fourth-grade reading test. This important study yields insight into the test failures of classroom students who are experiencing reading struggles but are not receiving remediation or intervention. Six profiles emerged, as described by prototypical characteristics (see Table 3.4).

Table 3.4 Student Profiles

Profile	Word Identification	Meaning Comprehension	Fluency	Strategy Suggestion
Automatic word callers	Can decode quickly and accurately	Fail to read for meaning	Strong fluency skills	Sticky note—stop and think—for each page read
Struggling word callers	Struggle with word identification	Lack of word identification creates comprehension problems	Read quickly, whether correct or incorrect	Slow it down with expressive reader's theatre
Word stumblers	Substantial difficulty in word recognition	Focused on reading for meaning; overreliance on context clues	Fluency rate slow, choppy, and lacking flow	Echo reading, partner reading
Slow comprehenders	Lack of automaticity hampered by multisyllabic words	Attends to meaning; comprehension is strong	Extremely slow reading rate	Introducing multisyllabic words prior to reading—word parts review
Slow word callers	Well-developed decoding skills	Difficulty with comprehension and text-based understandings	Slow reading rate; lack of expression or meaningful phrases	Fluency through radio reading
Students with special needs	Severe difficulties in all areas; limited word identification skills	Cannot read enough words to obtain meaning	Complete lack of fluency	Explicit systematic word identification instruction

Conclusions and implications from this research indicate that one-size classroom instruction will not meet the needs of struggling learners. Furthermore, additional diagnostic tests are indicated to "go beneath the scores on state tests" (Valencia & Buly, 2004, p. 78). The authors suggest that informal reading inventories, oral reading records, and other tailored, individualized assessments will provide useful information. Matching assessments to student needs is predicated on the flexibility to assess and teach students according to daily analysis.

What Students Know and Can Do

Virtually all children can learn to read (Scanlon et al., 2010; Vellutino & Fletcher, 2005). Before engaging with students, it is imperative that the teacher believes every child can learn and contribute to the learning community (Allington, 2006; Clay, 1998; P. Johnston, 2004; Lyons, 2003; Pinnell & Fountas, 2008). Each and every student possesses unique strengths that must be built on to continue their literate development, and this must be in the forefront of teacher thinking.

Making Connections

What Students Know and Can Do

Instruction needs to begin with students' strengths. Teachers need to engage in a variety of activities with students to learn about those strengths and decide where to begin instruction. Make a quick list of all the methods you can use to learn about your students' instructional needs. Then read on to learn additional ways you might learn about your students.

Teachers must observe and collect information about students' current levels of development—their strengths and instructional needs. Multiple observational, informal, and formal assessment measures are available to support this process. Table 3.5 provides a list of the more formal assessments explored in Chapters 6, 7, and 8. Also included are teacher-developed informal assessments that make up the "heart" of authentic assessment of individual student literacy. All the informal and formal assessment instruments are covered in detail in the chapters that follow. Standardized tests are listed in the third row; a thorough review of current standardized tests can be found in Chapter 10.

Teachers must pay close attention to students who experience difficulty acquiring literacy and carefully choose places to support them, while keeping them in control of processing. Instructional assessment does not make a difference for students' learning if it does not lead to action. Matching students' needs with instruction by using "if/then" thinking (Strickland, 2005) is at the heart of effective and efficient assessment instruction (Lipson, Chomsky-Higgins, & Kanfer, 2011).

This requires teachers to become "keen observers of how learners construct knowledge and then use that information to build on learners' strengths" (Dozier, Garnett, & Tabatabai, 2011, p. 11). As students read, teachers notice and name the literate behaviors and strategies they experiment with and those they use successfully (Johnston, 2004). Teachers "use this information to help learners build self-extending systems (Clay, 2001) whereby they use a range of strategies flexibly and competently in new situations" (Dozier et al., 2011, p. 637). These targeted and responsive literacy instructions and interventions are essential to change the growth trajectories of students who experience difficulty learning to read.

Table 3.5 Formal and Standardized Data

Informal	
• Target vocabulary assessment • Running records (teacher developed) • Elkonin boxes	• Field notes: Kidwatching • Names test • Response protocol

Formal	
• Observation Survey of Early Literacy Achievement • Prereading skills assessment • TROLL oral language assessment • Yopp–Singer Test of Phoneme Segmentation • Sight word inventories • Developmental spelling inventories • Peabody Picture Vocabulary Test	• Informal reading inventories • Qualitative Reading Inventory • Dynamic Indicators of Basic Early Literacy Skills • Texas Primary Reading Inventory • Fountas and Pinnell Benchmark Assessment • Rasinski's Multidimensional Fluency Scale

Standardized Assessment	
• Iowa Test of Basic Skills • Woodcock-Johnson III Normative Update • Texas Primary Reading Inventory	• State English language arts assessments • National Assessment of Educational Progress

Literacy Instruction and Exemplary Reading Teachers

In one of its position statements, *Making a Difference Means Making It Different: Honoring Children's Rights to Excellent Reading Instruction,* the IRA (2000b) states:

> Most children can, and do, learn to read and write. But too many children read and write poorly. When schools fail to teach any child to read and write, they fail all of us. We must ensure that all children receive the excellent instruction and support they need to learn to read and write. (p. 1)

While it is important to consider the origin of reading difficulties, "it is more productive to think about instruction that will help children overcome them" (Pinnell & Fountas, 2008, p. 31).

The quality of literacy instruction is the single greatest determinant of students' later literacy achievement (Sanders & Rivers, 1996). All students must have access to highly qualified teachers and instructional programs that are suited to their needs. The IRA (2000a) describes characteristics of effective reading teachers in another position statement, *Excellent Reading Teachers*. Effective teachers "have strong content and pedagogical knowledge, manage classrooms so that there is a high rate of engagement, use strong motivation strategies that encourage independent learning, have high expectations for children's achievement, and help children who are having difficulty" (p. 1).

Comber and Kamler (2005) advocate that teachers engage in what they call turn-around pedagogies. Here, teachers first work to understand who students are and what they are already capable of doing with texts. The underlying assumption is that

> real, meaningful, and effective instruction unfolds by capitalizing on students' strengths and interests as readers, rather than focusing on what they might lack or how far behind they might be. To turn students around as readers, teachers must first turn themselves around to see students differently and then to respond differently. (Enriquez et al., 2010, p. 73)

Students who experience difficulty in learning literacy and need more than effective classroom instruction must have access to additional, intensive, expert instruction (Allington, 2012). According to the IRA (2000a), effective reading teachers exhibit critical qualities of knowledge and practice. Table 3.6 outlines these critical qualities.

Table 3.6 Characteristics of Effective Reading Teachers

1. They understand reading and writing development and believe all children can learn to read and write.

2. They continually assess children's individual progress and relate reading instruction to children's previous experiences.

3. They know a variety of ways to teach reading, when to use each method, and how to combine the methods into an effective instructional program.

4. They offer a variety of materials and texts for children to read.

5. They use flexible grouping strategies to tailor instruction to individual students.

6. They are good reading "coaches" (that is, they provide help strategically).

Source: IRA (2000a, p. 1).

Furthermore, Blair, Rupley, and Nichols (2007) identified a set of common instructional features associated with effective teachers of reading. They label these the "what" and "how" of effective instruction. These features include

1. assessing students' reading strengths and weaknesses,

2. structuring reading activities around an explicit instructional format,

3. providing students with opportunities to learn and apply skills and strategies in authentic reading tasks,

4. ensuring that students attend to the learning tasks, and

5. believing in one's teaching abilities and expecting students to be successful. (p. 433)

Knowledgeable and effective reading specialists tailor literacy intervention programs to meet students' varied, individual needs and accelerate students' achievements. It is not enough for students who are not meeting grade-level expectations to progress alongside their peers. We must accelerate their literacy development so they can meet grade-level expectations by the end of the year, rather than continuing to progress behind other students. To do so, Allington (2012) proposes the 100/100 rule: 100% of students are engaged in instruction appropriate to their needs 100% of the time. This will change students' achievement patterns and learning trajectories (Vlach & Burcie, 2010).

Making Connections

Focusing on the characteristics of effective reading teachers (see Table 3.6), one characteristic that is reinforced by the information in this text is the ability to continually assess children's individual progress and relate reading instruction to children's previous experiences. Using information you have gathered in the chapters presented so far, design a T-chart. Label the columns of this chart *KNOW* and *NEED TO LEARN*. List three to five ideas that you understand or know about continual assessment and then three to five things you still need to learn.

Intervention Opportunities

Research has provided key elements of research-based interventions for students experiencing literacy difficulties. According to Allington (2012), key elements of research-based interventions include improving classroom instruction; enhancing access to intensive, expert instruction; and expanding available instructional time and support for older struggling readers.

In an RtI model, instructional interventions based on multiple assessment measures are provided in increasing intensity, depending on students' instructional needs. Based on student responses to interventions, more or less support can be provided. Teachers can alter the teacher–pupil ratio, the frequency of scheduling, and the pacing of the intervention (Allington, 2012).

Possible literacy interventions include one-to-one tutorial programs as well as small-group and even whole-group explicit instruction. Within the intervention, students might reread to meet a standard; participate in small-group reading, including choral reading and echo reading; engage in shared book experiences; and participate in reader's theatre (Allington, 2012). All students benefit when teachers construct lessons that make the invisible process of reading visible (Allington, 2012; Barnhouse & Vinton, 2012), not just those students who find literacy difficult. We must move beyond the traditional "assign and assess" method of reading to answer comprehension questions and, instead, demonstrate effective strategy use and provide multiple opportunities for reading and application (Allington, 2012).

Literacy interventions must be specific and tailored to students' strengths and instructional needs. They must be responsive to students and to how they change as readers over time. Schools and teachers must "develop the flexibility they need to adjust their programs to achieve a solid match with all students" (Applegate, Applegate, & Turner, 2010, p. 212).

English Language Learners as Literacy Learners

English language learners (ELLs) may be students whose first language is not English, students from communities that have maintained a distinct cultural and linguistic tradition, or children who have immigrated to the United States from countries whose primary language is not English. All ELLs vary in their understanding and experience with the English language. In addition to limited English language knowledge, ELLs may also have little or no former schooling and may not have learned to read in their native language.

ELLs have a wide variety of knowledge and experience, making it essential to know a student's ability before tailoring instruction to his or her specific needs. If it is necessary to start from the beginning, explicit instruction in phonological awareness is key and should include extensive experience (e.g., songs, poems, chants, etc.). This should be followed by systematic phonics instruction with a varied print-rich environment and with vocabulary building. Effective instruction eventually includes an integration of decoding skills, fluency building, and reading comprehension (Irujo, 2007).

Irujo (2007) offers seven key suggestions for working with ELLs, based on her summary of the U.S. Department of Education's 2002 findings from the National Literacy Panel on Language-Minority Children and Youth. These recommendations include additional work on English phonemes that are not present in the student's native language; focusing on differences between the student's native language and English; providing extra practice in reading words, sentences, and stories; using cognate words in the native language as synonyms when teaching vocabulary; identifying and clarifying difficult words and passages; consolidating knowledge of text through the use of summaries; and finding appropriate ways to use the student's native language. Irujo (2007) warns that these recommendations on their own do not necessarily constitute a reading program for ELLs, but they are a place to start.

Strategies for ELLs to retain word knowledge include the following:

1. *Hint cards:* Challenging concepts or vocabulary words are placed on separate index cards. Next, a mnemonic, synonym, or application to the student's life is written on the front of the card in abbreviated form. Hint cards can be posted on a unit/thematic wall or a word wall, or be kept on a ring for individual student access.

2. *Anchor charts:* Anchor charts are codeveloped by teacher and students to highlight important literacy processes or academic vocabulary used in lessons. They are displayed continuously, and teachers should frequently draw attention to anchor charts to scaffold understanding.

3. *Picture clues:* Early learners of English need support through diagrams, pictures, graphics, and language-equivalent words. Furthermore, ELLs need multiple reinforcements of words through direct instruction, reintroduction, and review.

Making Connections

Develop a picture clues strategy for an ELL in first grade who is being introduced to the word *car*. Locate the Spanish word, apply a letter box for letter learning, show a picture or graphic, use it in a short sentence, and have the student draw a picture (virtually). Provide direct instruction, reintroduce the concept on the second day, and then review. Provide the input or specific dialogue you will use to support the first grader. Keep the lesson direct, and check for understanding. How can you assess whether the student truly understood the concept of a car and can apply the English word correctly?

The striving readers in your future classroom deserve all the benefits of an exemplary reading teacher armed with the latest knowledge of literacy learning, classroom intervention, and models for successful reading. They deserve no less.

Key Terms

background information	reading comprehension
decode	reading rate
fluency	Response to Intervention (RtI)
graphemes	screening
instructional level	secondary prevention or Tier 2
orthographic features	striving reader
phonemes	struggling reader
phonological awareness	tertiary prevention or Tier 3
primary prevention or Tier 1	vocabulary

Website Resources

- **International Reading Association's Response to Intervention Resources**

The IRA's RTI Task Force developed *Response to Intervention: Guiding Principles for Educators*, a free RtI resource for its members, also available for purchase by nonmembers. The IRA, a joint partner with RTI Action Network, also offers many resources for educators, administrators, parents, and the community, including the most up-to-date research; free webinars on planning and implementing RtI for communities, schools, and individuals; and networks for literacy professionals. The IRA's RtI resources can be found at **www.reading.org/Resources/ ResourcesbyTopic/ResponseToIntervention/Resources.aspx**.

(Continued)

(Continued)

- **National Center on Response to Intervention**

The National Center on Response to Intervention emphasizes the importance of data-based decision making in formative assessment and instruction. Interventions need to be based on evidence from student performance and should be individualized for the students who require them. The center offers explicit information on implementing RtI in the classroom, provides research-based progress-monitoring tools for teachers, updates contemporary research in its database, and offers additional resources. The center's website can be accessed at **www.rti4success.org.**

- **RTI Action Network**

The RTI Action Network delineates tiered instruction for intervention, stresses the importance of ongoing student assessment, and offers highly effective suggestions for family involvement in intervention. The RTI Action Network helps develop and implement intervention plans that are not only designed for individual students but also tailored to specific communities and responsive to those communities' needs. The RTI Action Network offers resources for professional development so that intervention may always be implemented with fidelity. The network's website can be accessed at **www.rtinetwork.org.**

Student Study Site: Visit the Student Study Site at **www.sagepub.com/grantlit** to access additional study tools including eFlashcards, web resources, and online-only appendices.

CHAPTER 4

Student Factors Impacting Assessment

*Michael P. French
and Melanie O'Leary*

Common Core State Standards

Print Concepts	*RF.K.1* Demonstrate understanding of the organization and basic features of print.
Phonological Awareness	*RF.K.2* Demonstrate understanding of spoken words, syllables, and sounds (phonemes).
Phonics and Word Recognition	*RF.K.3* Know and apply grade-level phonics and word analysis skills in decoding words.
Fluency	*RF.K.4* Read emergent-reader texts with purpose and understanding.

FOCUS QUESTIONS

1. How will your assessment style impact the way you assess your students?

2. What are you doing to reach your students? Are your lesson plans varied and diverse enough to meet all students' needs? What about your English language learners and students with special needs?

3. The majority of standardized assessments require students to be able to read. Are you prepared to support students in your classroom with vision and hearing disabilities? What about your English language learners and students with special needs—will they be able to participate?

4. Health issues may impact a student's time spent in school, and you may be unable to assess him or her in a standard way. How are you going to adjust your assessments to meet such a student's needs?

5. Are you prepared to consider students' cognitive, physical, and sensory disabilities when designing your nonstandardized classroom assessments?

Words in Action

Allya

Take for instance Allya, in the third grade. Allya comes from a sociocultural background in which no parent or older sibling is proficient at reading and writing, and none have completed school. For her, just getting to school on a daily basis is a chore. The realities she faces at home are nearly insurmountable, such that on some days her only coping mechanism is to hole up and hide.

On the days she does make it to school, 1 day a week on average, she finds herself behind on material and connections the other students have made through discovery and discussion. Allya has honed her ability to learn verbally and has developed the ability to garner help from her peers. While not a behavioral problem in class, Allya derives her entertainment from drama among her schoolmates rather than from any scholar/performer/athlete scenario. Her teachers have noted her innate intelligence but are concerned about her motivation and connection with school tasks; for Allya, school represents a place she must visit occasionally to keep case workers from dropping by her home.

Allya's accommodations include "tests read." For a student who is present only 20% of the time, she understands about 40% of the material. She appears to be strong in understanding what is read to her but has missed so much school that her comprehension has suffered, as well as her ability to build schema for text connections.

How might you scaffold Allya's learning?

How might you assess Allya's learning?

In *Becoming a Nation of Readers* (Anderson, Hiebert, Scott, & Wilkinson, 1985), this definition of reading is presented:

> *Reading* is a process in which information from the text and the knowledge possessed by the reader act together to produce meaning. (p. 8)

Although indirectly, this definition does acknowledge the importance of various reader factors in the reading process. Since 1985, there have been a great deal more research studies with regard to student factors related to learning and the impact of these factors in the assessment of literacy abilities and differences.

Before examining these various factors that impact a student's assessment, it is important to revisit the purpose of assessment. Literacy instruction in the classroom primarily comprises reading, writing, and critical thinking, each of which is complex in its own right and requires multiple ways of assessing. Ultimately, through literacy, teachers work to instill a desire for lifelong learning within their students, to enable their students to achieve goals, develop their knowledge and potential, and participate fully in life.

Teaching and assessment are intertwined in the learning process. Assessments generally are either standardized or nonstandardized. "A standardized test is any test that's administered, scored, and interpreted in a standard, predetermined manner" (Popham, 2005b, "Instructionally Insensitive"). The same test is given to all test takers in the same manner. Questions and testing conditions are standard for everyone. Ideally, standardized tests are designed to assess everyone on an equal and level playing field. Historically, these tests were used to compare students in the same classroom from year to year, students in different schools across cities and states, and eventually students across the country. Now they are most often used to judge teaching ability and school accreditation.

Standardized tests are not designed to take into account the varying backgrounds and prior knowledge students bring with them to school. Nor do they take into account the different ways individual students learn, show creativity, use imagination, think, or explore with their curiosity. Standardized tests are designed to isolate specific skills and test them in a controlled manner, ideally with the testing situation the same for all students. "Standardized tests are designed to enable us to compare the performance of students in a relatively efficient way" (Fusaro, 2008, para. 3). These tests measure specific skills, specific facts, and content knowledge. The results of these assessments can be useful to inform teaching practice.

A nonstandardized assessment may also be called informal testing. These tests are usually teacher generated and look at an individual student's performance. They allow teachers to gain specific information about that student. Nonstandardized assessments include exhibitions of work, group discussions, informal questioning, interviews, oral tests, performance exams, pop quizzes, and portfolios. These nonstandardized assessments can be used before, during, and after academic units to measure growth, can be tailored to better match individual students' needs, and are more meaningful and authentic to students.

Whether an assessment is standardized or nonstandardized, informative judgments will be made from their results; therefore, it is essential to examine student factors that may impact these assessments to maximize assessment efficiency and student success. This chapter discusses readers' cognitive, social, physical, and health factors, and their impact on literacy abilities and differences.

Cognitive Factors

Cognitive development is the building of thought processes that include remembering, problem solving, and decision making. This begins in infancy and continues through adulthood. It refers to how people perceive, think, and gain understanding of their world through the interaction of genetic and learned factors. Some of the areas of cognitive development include information processing, reasoning, and language development.

Learning theories are the foundations that help educators understand diverse factors of individual student differentiation in perceiving information, encoding information, transferring information, scanning the representation of information, and working memory capacity (Danili & Reid, 2006). There are also unique differences in styles of thinking, remembering, and evaluating, and these individual variations are part of one's personality. Taken together, these differences suggest that individuals have different cognitive styles that influence intellectual abilities, personalities, skills, and teaching and learning performance (Danili & Reid, 2006).

Piaget

Traditional discussion of cognitive development and learning typically begins with the work of Jean Piaget (McLeod, 2009). His work provides a foundation for the understanding of differences in how cognitive development affects learning. McLeod summarizes Piaget's theory as containing three key elements: schemas, adaptation, and stages of development. These elements are outlined in Table 4.1.

Observe this classroom discussion in which a student shares her first experience eating at a sushi restaurant:

Student 1:   Can you believe all the fish was raw?

Student 2:   So, you like shrimp cocktail right?

Student 1:   Yeah, but that's not like eating raw fish . . .

Student 2:   Why not?

Student 1:   Well, I guess so . . .

Student 2:   So, did you try any?

Student 1:   Yeah, it wasn't so bad.

Table 4.1 Piaget's Three Key Elements	
Schemas	Schemas have been compared to building blocks of knowledge. Another way to visualize the concept of schemas is to think of elaborate file cabinets in the head in which all personal information and memories are filed. There is a clear relationship between a student's collective set of schemas and his or her ability to comprehend. As such, it is important to probe student's prior knowledge and prior learning in assessing literacy processes.
Adaptation	Piaget describes the process by which children transition from one stage of development to another, which consists of three key elements: • Assimilation: Using an existing schema to deal with a new situation (inner reality) • Accommodation: When an existing schema does not fully work and must be adjusted to understand the new situation (external reality) • Equilibration: When there is a state of cognitive balance between the child's schema and new information learned
Stages of Development	Piaget identified four stages of cognitive development: 1. Sensorimotor: This first stage in marked by children's awareness of their physical selves. 2. Preoperational: This stage is marked by egocentric behavior. Children at this stage will be able to express personal interests related to reading. 3. Concrete operational: This stage is marked by the beginning of formal reasoning about concrete objects. As children develop in this stage, they will be able to process inferences in reading. 4. Formal operational stage: This stage is marked by the ability to think abstractly, visualize, and apply previous learning to current learning.

In this example, the second student is helping the first use her shrimp cocktail schema to appreciate sushi. Over time, as the first student accommodates this type of thinking, she may come to further appreciate the range of sushi cuisine. As this happens, she will approach cognitive equilibration, which drives her learning process and allows for balancing the two complementary processes: assimilation and accommodation of the new information.

Piaget (1973) saw play as an imbalance between assimilation and accommodation. He theorized that play provides an opportunity to reinterpret experience and practice emerging skills. During the preoperational stage, pretend play allows children to use a variety of make-believe transformations of actions, objects, and words to stand for other actions, objects, and words. These transformations enable children to practice using and interpreting symbols, developing mental resources that will deal with the second-order symbolism of written language. Likewise, planning and acting out during dramatic play provide an opportunity to strengthen children's growing knowledge about narrative story structure—the foundation for understanding and writing stories (Roskos & Christie, 2011). The later preoperational stage of development is also when children are learning to become independent readers and conventional writers. By the concrete operational stage of development, students are reading for meaning and experimenting with various types of writing.

The Role of Misconceptions

Although not specifically included in Piaget's processes, teachers must be aware of misconceptions when assessing children's cognitive processes. For example,

> A young child goes to an ethnic restaurant where patrons eat with their fingers rather than utensils. Looking around at others eating and remembering being told at home that it is bad manners to eat with her fingers, she says, "Mom, all these people have terrible table manners."

If this logic persists, the child may come to believe that everyone from this ethnic background is ill mannered. Prior knowledge and misconceptions in knowledge influence the understanding and organization of new information. Misconceptions may impede learning for several reasons: Students may be unaware that the knowledge they have is wrong; misconceptions can be very entrenched in student thinking; new experiences, such as the one in the example above, are interpreted through erroneous understandings; and misconceptions tend to be very resistant to instruction because learning entails replacing or radically reorganizing student knowledge (Lucariello, 2012). For teachers to undo misconceptions, conceptual change must take place. Conceptual change requires uncovering a misconception and using various teaching techniques to help change student thinking.

Making Connections

Think of a time when you went through these processes. How did you come to achieve equilibration? Share the information with a classmate.

Examples:

Learning to appreciate a new kind of music

Learning to appreciate a new kind of food

Resolving a misconception

Most recognize that Piaget's theory does not take into account the social context of cognitive development. Two key theorists provide insight into the social context: Lev S. Vygotsky and Albert Bandura.

Vygotsky

Two key elements of Vygotsky's theory are the role of a More Knowledgeable Other (MKO) and the zone of proximal development (ZPD; McLeod, 2007). Vygotsky's MKO relates to the role of others in learning—teachers, tutors, and other students who have more information and experience (McLeod, 2007). This assistance from others is also known as scaffolding. The ZPD relates to the difference between what the child can learn alone and what the child can learn in cooperation with others (scaffolding).

Vygotsky viewed play as a "self-help" tool (McLeod, 2007). While engaging in play, children can create their own scaffolding or self-assistance. For example, pretend play activates change in representational abilities by dividing thought from action via gesture and language. It does this by challenging a new mental structure where thought takes precedence over action. This creates a ZPD where the child learns that a word can represent a thing, building a basic understanding of word meaning, and precipitates the use of words to stand for and express experience (Roskos & Christie, 2011).

Bandura

Bandura's (1977) social learning theory posits that children learn effectively when they are able to observe others performing the tasks to be learned. Through the process of modeling and reinforcement, children are able to assimilate these new behaviors (McLeod, 2011).

Bandura's work on self-efficacy also plays a role in learning. It is important for students to believe that they can accomplish goals they set for themselves, expend effort to achieve those goals, persevere during difficulties, and develop a strong resilience to failure. These four characteristics together determine the amount of success students will experience in their academic work (Scott, 1996). The components of Bandura's self-efficacy model are outlined in Table 4.2.

Table 4.2 Bandura's Self-Efficacy Model	
Performance	Past successes and failures, amount of effort and assistance necessary, task difficulty, persistence needed, and belief of effectiveness of the instruction
Observational Comparison	Comparison between self and classmates
Social Feedback	Direct and indirect input from teachers, classmates, and family
Physiological States	Acknowledged internal feelings during the task process, which may be demonstrated by physical manifestations—for example, sweaty palms

Source: Bandura (1977).

Students who view themselves as highly efficacious act, feel, and think differently than those who do not see themselves that way. Students who have high self-efficacy attribute their failure to lack of effort and will try harder the next time. Students with low self-efficacy attribute failure to insufficient ability and feel a loss of control over the situation. Motivation suffers when self-efficacy is low (Scott, 1996). This will negatively impact assessment results.

Contemporary Aspects

Although these classic views of cognitive development provide insight into the literacy and assessment processes, other contemporary aspects provide additional insight into a student's cognitive set. "A person's cognitive skill set is made up of several cognitive skills including auditory processing, visual processing, short and long term memory, comprehension, logic and reasoning, and attention skills" (LearningRx, 2012, para. 5). The first of these is a student's learning style. According to Keefe (1979), **learning styles** are "composites of characteristic cognitive, affective, and physiological factors that serve as relatively stable indicators of how a learner perceives, interacts with, and responds to the learning environment" (p. 1).

Generally, learning styles are presented in terms of three modalities: visual, auditory, and kinesthetic (Clark, 2000). It is commonly accepted that learners use all three modalities in learning but may display marked preferences for certain styles. Others posit that learners use all three modalities but that one may be more dominant than the others.

Applied to reading and reading processes, the visual, auditory, and kinesthetic modalities are described in Table 4.3.

Table 4.3 Modalities

Modality	Description of Learning Style	Relation to Literacy Processes
Visual	Learners who rely on written language and visual information such as diagrams and charts	These students may be more proficient in visual tasks such as sight-word reading than in decoding phonic-regular words. They may not be as proficient in assessment of phonics through pseudowords.
Auditory	Learners who rely on verbal language—listening to stories read or to information presented orally	These students may be more proficient in tasks such as retelling. They may be less proficient in tasks such as note taking or summary writing.
Kinesthetic	Learners who rely on movement and touch to learn better; often doodle during class as a brain-balancing mechanism	These students may be more proficient in tasks for which responses are written or provided through pointing.

Source: Adapted from Clark (2000).

Traditionally, learning style is forced on students according to a set pattern: From kindergarten until Grade 3, new information is given kinesthetically; from Grades 4 through 8, it is presented visually; and from Grade 9 forward, it is delivered auditorily. Visual, auditory, and kinesthetic theorists believe that new information should be presented from the beginning using all three styles. This provides all students the opportunity to become involved regardless of their preferred style (Clark, 2000).

Cognitive Factors and Intelligence

Traditional views of intelligence, such as learning style, have focused on verbal and nonverbal cognitive capacity. Recent advances in neuropsychology and child psychology have added additional domains (categories) to intelligence or cognition (Sparrow & Davis, 2000). These categories of cognition are shown in Table 4.4.

Table 4.4 Categories of Cognition		
Domain	**Description of Cognitive Domain**	**Relation to Literacy Processes**
Attention Auditory, visual, and tactile perceptual functions	Ability to focus on relevant information	Evaluation of attention in reading is essential for assessment of deep reading ability and potential for successful sustained silent reading.
Verbal and language functions	Ability in expressive and receptive language	Students with ability in expressive language are more able to perform retelling tasks. They are able to describe in their own words what they do and do not understand. Students with ability in receptive language are better able to listen to stories or instruction.
Spatial/constructional processing abilities	Ability to visualize newly learned information	Students with this information will be able to illustrate their understanding in diagrams and pictures. They will be able to create graphic organizers and charts.
Memory and learning	Ability to use information both short-term and long-term	Short-term memory is related to retelling of previously read text, whereas long-term memory is more related to recalling previously learned information for reading, lecture, homework, and other school-related experiences.

(Continued)

Table 4.4 (Continued)		
Domain	**Description of Cognitive Domain**	**Relation to Literacy Processes**
Executive functions (conceptual reasoning, problem solving, planning, flexibility in cognitive strategy, and implementing cognitive plans)	Ability to integrate new information and compare new information to known information Ability to be strategically planful and metacognitive	As in Piaget, this domain is related to the assimilation of new information. It is also the foundation for metacognitive thinking.

Source: Sparrow and Davis (2000, pp. 118–119).

Gardner's Multiple Intelligences

In 1983, Howard Gardner began his work on the formulation of multiple intelligences. As cited by Smith (2002, 2008), Gardner initially proposed seven intelligences. Later, in 1999, an eighth (naturalist) was added. Gardner's eight intelligences are listed in Table 4.5.

Table 4.5 Howard Gardner's Multiple Intelligences		
Gardner's Intelligence	**Description of Intelligence Domain Paraphrased**	**Relation to Literacy Processes**
Linguistic intelligence	Sensitivity to spoken and written language	Will have ability to learn languages and new vocabulary; generally will write at higher levels
Logical-mathematical intelligence	Ability to analyze problems, carry out mathematical processes, and think scientifically	Will be more visual than verbal; will be more systematic in problem solving
Musical intelligence	Skill in performance and appreciation of music	Will learn better when there is music in the environment
Bodily-kinesthetic intelligence	Ability to use one's whole body in learning	Will learn better through exercise and movement
Spatial intelligence	Ability to recognize and use patterns	Will be more proficient in the use of a graphic organizer in content reading
Interpersonal intelligence	Ability to tune in to others in learning situations	Will be especially fluent in group discussions, literature circles, and tuning in to others' thoughts
Intrapersonal intelligence	Ability to be personally reflective	Will be more likely to keep feelings about reading to oneself; may not be as willing to share writing products
Naturalist	Ability to relate to the environment and its impact on one's learning	Will tune in to texts dealing with environment; will be more likely to gravitate to nonfiction texts

Source: Smith (2002, 2008).

Students are unique in their thinking and learning; therefore, it is essential for educators to develop new and multiple approaches to meet the wide range of students in their classrooms. Students need to be given multiple ways to explore and show creativity. This also means that alternative assessments should be developed to allow all students to show what they know and can do.

Those students who display linguistic or logical-mathematical intelligences have been successful on traditional standardized assessments. However, according to Gardner (1991), a significant population lacks facility with formal examinations but can display relevant understanding when problems arise in natural contexts. Sometimes students who are unsuccessful with the usual measures of competence reveal significant mastery and understanding when these measures are elicited in a different, more appropriate way. Therefore, teaching and assessment methods can be adjusted to match learners' strengths.

Making Connections

When was the last time you planned your assessments based on Gardner's theory of multiple intelligences? Do you include activities such as debating, data collection, sketching, creative movement, rapping, peer editing, journal keeping, and gardening? How do you keep all your students involved, engaged, and successful?

Social Factors

When thinking about the social factors and reading, one generally considers aspects of the society in which the students live, where they attend school, the personal backgrounds of teachers (e.g., gender, race/ethnicity, socioeconomic status, religion), and expectations of the community. All these factors impact how ready to learn children are when they come to school, along with how well they are likely to learn there. A great deal of study has been conducted in this area—especially under the umbrella label of "funds of knowledge" (Gay, 2010; Moll, Amanti, Neff, & Gonzalez, 1992; Moll & Cammarota, 2010).

Funds of Knowledge

Understanding of funds of knowledge has evolved from the study of families and their impact on student learning. According to Moll and his colleagues (1992), funds of knowledge can be defined as "the historically accumulated and culturally developed bodies of knowledge and skills essential for household or individual functioning and well-being" (p. 133). Many educators have come to understand this definition in the context of the accumulation of students' prior knowledge and schemas that have been learned in their homes and neighborhoods. Whereas some might negatively view these funds of knowledge as baggage students bring with them, it is more correct to view them as opportunities for students to use their unique understandings and experiences in perceiving new content and as a springboard to comprehension.

Teachers of reading need to be keenly aware of the prevalence of different funds of knowledge within their classrooms. According to Au (2002),

> In the 1990s, students of diverse backgrounds constituted 35% of the enrollment in public schools in grades 1 through 12 (National Center for Education Statistics, 1997a), and approximately 13% of all students spoke a language other than English at home. In 2025, the population of students of diverse backgrounds will be even larger, and an equal or even greater proportion of children will be growing up in poverty. (p. 393)

The educational process is greatly enhanced when teachers learn about the everyday contexts of their students' lives. Table 4.6 is an example of an invaluable questionnaire that should be sent home with students very early in the school year. These questions are a great way to draw students into their learning by building on knowledge that is already familiar to them and also a good way to create partnerships with students' families. Culturally diverse families are a wealth of knowledge that can advance students' growth and development. The National Center for Research on Cultural Diversity and Second Language Learning has shown that numerous "funds of knowledge" found

Table 4.6 Funds of Knowledge		
Consider This	**You**	**Your Students**
What customs are important to your family?		
Does your family eat any special foods?		
Do you wear any special or traditional clothing?		
Which language(s) are spoken in your home?		
Which holidays specific to your culture does your family celebrate? What are they called, and when do they occur?		

Source: Adapted from Cohen (2009).

within students' households could form the foundation for curriculum units in language arts, math, science, and other subjects (Gonzalez et al., 1993).

Conversely, diversity, language abilities, and socioeconomic status may have a huge influence on students' lives, which will impact outcomes of assessment in many ways. For example, children who come from lower-income families may not have access to literacy materials in their homes. They may not have had opportunities to travel, which provides valuable experience, and they may have inconsistent access to contemporary technology such as the Internet or a wide variety of television programs. Finally, from Bandura's social learning theory, when students come to school from diverse neighborhoods they may have inconsistent models for appropriate academic literacy behavior. The impact of poverty and family literacy opportunities is more fully discussed later in this chapter.

In assessing literacy abilities of students, having an awareness of the students' home and neighborhood cultures is an important component of the assessment process. According to Sousa (2007),

> For these children, we should not be looking at what is wrong with them but how we can alter instruction to make them more successful in learning to read. Such alterations can be made when teachers of reading are properly trained to recognize when a child's reading problems are the result of linguistic clashes and not pathology. . . . That training should also help teachers understand how they can use some of the linguistic attributes . . . to help children pronounce, decode, and understand standard English. (p. 89)

Making Connections

With a classmate, discuss how you will use the "funds of knowledge" in your classroom. Will you develop a unit around foods from different countries and invite parents in to cook and share their cultural knowledge with your students? Or will you use traditional stories? Discuss and list ways you could use your students' experiences and cultures to promote learning in the classroom.

Physical Factors

When considering physical factors that impact reading and reading performance, the most obvious are vision and hearing. In the 2006–2007 school year, the National Center for Education Statistics estimated that 29,000 exceptional student education (ESE) learners had visual impairments, including blindness. Additionally, about 2.6 million ESE students had a specific learning disability, which likely includes some students with a "print" disability (U.S. Department of Education, 2010).

Vision Issues

Reading is a seeing act; students need to be able to see the print they are reading. In relation to schools, children not only need to be able to see print in front of them as they hold a book or e-reader, but they also need to be able to read text written on whiteboards or projected on interactive boards. As such, in literacy assessment, one needs to make sure students can see what they are reading.

Vision is also a critical element of written language. In learning to write, children must take in linguistic information and, through knowledge of letter formation, transform the linguistic information in their heads to written language on the page. While some aspects of visual perception relate to both reading and writing, others (as noted in the following) relate primarily to written language.

According to the Children's Vision Information Network (n.d.),

> Vision plays a vital role in the reading process. First of all, children must have crisp, sharp eyesight in order to see the print clearly. School vision screenings routinely check children's sharpness of vision at distance—measured by the 20/20 line on the eye chart—and refer children for glasses if they have blurry far-away vision and can't see the board from the back of the room. Unfortunately, this is all school vision screenings are designed to check, and children's vision involves so much more. (para. 3)

In addition to acuity, other aspects of vision related to reading are discussed next.

Eye Teaming (Binocular Reading). Since each eye functions independently, both must come together to allow the student to see a clear image of the text to be read. As seen in the following example, when eyes do not work together, the image can become most difficult to read (top line). However, when the eyes work together, the image can be read quite easily (Children's Vision Information Network, n.d.).

I can read this to myself.
I can read this to myself.

Tracking. Simply stated, **tracking** while reading is the ability to follow the words across the line and then jump back to the beginning of the next line below. Problems with tracking can cause children to lose their place while reading—especially when reading aloud. Children who struggle with tracking while reading will often point to words as they read; this becomes a coping strategy for them (Children's Vision Information Network, n.d.).

However, children who lose their place while reading may not be having tracking problems. In *Reading Without Nonsense*, Frank Smith (2006) presents a concept called **tunnel vision.** Tunnel vision is not a visual problem as such; rather, it is a condition in which the brain becomes overloaded by visual information and hyperfocuses on individual words. As Smith describes it, "we see a line of print as if we were looking at it through a narrow tube" (p. 60). When students have tunnel vision, they may have difficulty predicting the next word to be read. In addition to this, should that next word be at the beginning of the next line, they may have difficulty finding it. This condition would be further exacerbated by a reader's lack of metacognition. Not only might students fail to read the correct word at the beginning of the next line, but they might also fail to realize they read the wrong word.

Focusing. Very much related to acuity, in schools children need to read text near to them and farther away. Their eyes need to be able to focus and adjust as necessary (Children's Vision Information Network, n.d.).

Visual Perception. Visual perception is the act of giving meaning to what is seen. It requires the ability to analyze and interpret visual images. In reading and writing, this analysis and interpretation must happen with a high degree of automaticity.

Visual perception is not a single task but a set of interrelated cognitive functions. These areas of perception are usually included in comprehensive assessments of visual perception, such as Martin's (2006) *Test of Visual-Perceptual Skills* (non-motor). This test includes the subtests shown in Table 4.7.

Table 4.7 Visual-Perceptual Skills		
Domain	**Description**	**Relation to Literacy Processes**
Visual discrimination	The ability to perceive likeness and difference in visual information	Children must see differences in visual information.
Visual memory	The ability to retain visual information and use it at a later time (even if the later time is in milliseconds)	Ability to maintain visual information in tracking, turning the page, and copying information from whiteboards to paper.
Visual-spatial relationships	The ability to perceive visual information in relation to space	Relates to reading text in various shapes. May have difficulty writing without lines.
Form constancy	Ability to perceive relationship of shape to visual elements	Deals with letter formation and word formation cues.
Visual sequential memory	Ability to remember visual aspects in order	This skill is seen in written language—especially when copying information from a far point.
Visual figure-ground	Ability to perceive visual information both in foreground and background	This is seen in reading text superimposed on objects or as presented in picture books where the text is superimposed on an illustration.
Visual closure	Ability to perceive a whole entity from parts	Often in reading, word recognition is based on selected letters in a word. Efficient readers have strong visual closure skills.

Source: Martin (2006).

With regard to children's vision, it is important that teachers be able to recognize when their students might be having trouble in the classroom. If teachers or families identify children with vision problems, proper referrals should be made.

Hearing Issues

Phonological awareness is one of the essential components of reading. Children need to hear the differences in sounds and use their auditory processing abilities to learn decoding and phonics. As such, hearing is also essential to learning to read. Some children are not able to discriminate among these sounds even though their physical hearing abilities are within the normal range. Often, these children are evaluated for auditory processing deficits.

In the United States, about 1,000,000 people (0.38% of the population) over 5 years of age are "functionally deaf"; more than half of these are over 65 years of age. About 8,000,000 people (3.7%) over 5 years of age are hard of hearing (i.e., have some difficulty hearing normal conversation even with the use of a hearing aid; Reilly & Qi, 2011). As many as 1 in 10 students can have significant hearing loss. There are three main types of hearing loss: conductive, which affects the outer or middle ear; sensorineural, which is nerve-related; or a mixture of both types (Australian Disability Clearinghouse on Education and Training [ADCET], n.d.-b).

How hearing loss impacts a student depends on the type of disorder and the extent and timing of the loss. Sound frequencies or background noise may cause difficulty for students with a hearing impairment. Some students may have been born deaf, while other students may have hearing loss due to childhood illness. Students with hearing impairments may need accommodations and/or assistive devices to support their learning in the classroom. Having a hearing impairment affects students' learning in a variety of ways: Low self-esteem from past learning failure negatively impacts their approach to learning; quality of interaction with other students or participation in group activities impacts learning; these students tend to be visual learners, but most necessary information is spoken; and students with hearing impairment have a limited range of vocabulary, which affects reading and assessment-taking ability (ADCET, n.d.-b).

Making Connections

As an inner-city public school teacher, you have students regularly coming and going from your classroom. Midyear, you get a new student with a hearing impairment; this is a new experience for you. Where do you go for information to best support this student? With a partner, visit moleary31.blogspot.com, read through the posts and the blog list, and then make an instructional plan for this student.

Neurological and Psychological Considerations

In recent decades, a great deal of scientific and medical research on the brain has advanced our knowledge of neurology and reading. Without question, it is known that reading and the brain are related, but now, through imaging studies, we not only know that the brain is related to learning, but we can also see how and where the brain works in reading.

Neurological Considerations

Reading—successful decoding and comprehension—requires the synchronization of three neural networks: auditory processing (phonology), understanding meaning (semantics), and visual processing (orthography; see Figure 4.1). According to Sousa (2007),

> the optic nerves send signals to the visual cortex, and the visual processing system puts the alphabetic symbols of the word together. The decoding process alerts the auditory processing system that recognizes the alphabetic symbols representing the sound [of that word]. Other brain regions, such as Broca's and Wernicke's areas, are coordinated by the frontal lobe for comprehension. (p. 87)

Problems may occur anywhere within the network synchronization, causing reading disorders.

Students with learning disabilities often receive and/or process some information inaccurately. Learning disabilities can cause errors in discerning and processing information, unusual and inconsistent spelling, omission of parts of words or sentences, transposition of letters and numbers, and lack of proper order or demonstrated sequence in writing and mathematical calculations. Any one of these inaccurately processed pieces of information can have a negative impact on a student's success in assessments.

Through imaging studies, great advances have been made in the diagnosis and treatment of specific learning disabilities, such as dyslexia—the most common learning disability. For example, Shaywitz (1996) was able to demonstrate the relationship between

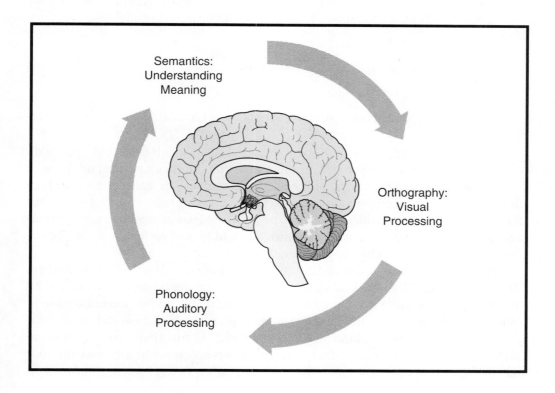

Figure 4.1

Neural Systems Involved in the Reading Process

neuroprocessing and learning phonologic skills. This line of inquiry leads to what is now referred to as the double-deficit hypothesis (Wolf & Bowers, 1999). Essentially, a double deficit is found when a child lacks both phonological skill and rapid naming skill (neuro-processing speed), leading to significant reading impairment.

As a result of this neuroscience research, teachers, doctors, and families can and should work together as a team to facilitate the diagnosis and remediation of reading problems. In summary, Shaywitz (1996), in discussing the historic difficulty of diagnosing reading problems, states,

> Heretofore, reading difficulties could be explained away in any number of ways. Now, however, men and women with dyslexia can point to an image of the brain's internal workings, made possible by new brain imaging technology and say, "Here. Look at this. This is the root cause of my problem." We now know exactly where and how dyslexia manifests itself in the brain. (p. 98)

Psychological Considerations

The toll of assessment can weigh heavily on the student's mind. For many, assessment can cause a great deal of distress, especially when the student may be suffering from anxiety, depression, or stress. For instance, children may suffer from the same six classes of anxiety disorders that adults experience:

1. Separation anxiety (fear of leaving or being left by primary caregiver)

2. Social anxiety (an intense fear of scrutiny and evaluation of peers or authority figures and/or performance situations)

3. Obsessive-compulsive disorder

4. Generalized anxiety disorder (excessive worry)

5. Posttraumatic stress disorder

6. Panic disorders (Anxiety Disorders Association of Canada, 2007)

Anxiety may create significant distress or partial functional impairment in a child's daily life, and those with an anxiety disorder may find it difficult to function in social interactions, family relationships, or school. These students are easily frustrated, have difficulty completing work, or worry about getting everything right, such that they either take too long to finish activities or refuse to begin. These fears can result in school avoidance and increased periods of absence, which also lead to poor performance (Minnesota Association for Children's Mental Health, n.d.).

Depression, generally classified as an adult disorder, is also found in children. About 5% of children and adolescents suffer from depression (Cohen, 2012). Symptoms of depression in children may vary but primarily revolve around persistent sadness and hopelessness for extended periods and may include withdrawal, difficulty concentrating or thinking, and reduced ability to function during events and activities at home and in school. Children with depression are at high risk for poor school performance.

A certain amount of stress is a regular part of everyday life; this is normal and can even be healthy. Some level of stress may be experienced when stuck in traffic, due to missing a deadline, when preparing for a test, or during an unexpected event such as a pop quiz. When situations are out of control, extremely intense, or out of control for a long time, it may result in the inability to cope. A change in behavior or regression of behavior could indicate that a student is abnormally stressed, and this will negatively impact school performance.

General Health Issues

A multitude of general health issues may impact students' performance on assessments. According to the UN Educational Scientific and Cultural Organization (2001), hunger, malnutrition, anxiety, alcohol and drug abuse, and violence and injury are just some of the health problems students may face. Sleep deprivation is another health issue that impacts students; lack of sleep makes it difficult to complete cognitive tasks. As a result of these issues, teachers must work toward promoting healthy activities to achieve student success. It is essential that students be healthy and well nourished to fully participate and gain maximum benefits from their education.

Hunger and malnutrition are widespread among school-aged children. In 2012, the National School Lunch Program provided nutritionally balanced, low-cost or free lunches to more than 31 million children each school day (U.S. Department of Agriculture Food and Nutrition Service, 2013). Hunger affects more than just the stomach: Without a proper supply of essential nutrients to fuel the brain, children may become apathetic, confused, distracted, and/or irritable. Hunger also reduces ability to concentrate on a task and interferes with a student's ability to perform to his or her highest potential. Even more than that, lack of proper nutrition inhibits the body's ability to fight illness and infection, which often means excessive absences from school. Many malnourished students have vision and hearing impairments and other forms of disabilities requiring special education in school. At least 20% of the children in each U.S. state are insecure about their food situation (Feeding America, 2014). According to the Children's Defense Fund (2012b),

- food-insecure preschool and school-aged children are more likely to suffer from problems such as anxiety,
- food-insecure elementary school children are 4 times more likely to require mental health counseling and 7 times more likely to be classified as clinically dysfunctional,
- children who had been food insecure in kindergarten saw a 13% drop in their reading and math test scores,
- food-insecure teens are more likely to have repeated a grade and missed more school days, and
- food-insufficient teenagers were more than twice as likely to have been suspended.

The 2007 National Survey on Drug Use and Health reports that 8.3 million children live with at least one parent who abused or was dependent on alcohol or an illicit drug during the past year (Office on Child Abuse and Neglect, Children's Bureau, ICF

International, 2009). These students are at an increased risk for abuse or neglect, in addition to emotional, social, physical, and academic problems. Students' emotional needs usually take a backseat to a parent's substance abuse and dependence, and these children have chaotic and unpredictable home lives. Furthermore, students who were exposed to alcohol prenatally may have functional and physiological problems as well as functional or mental impairments, such as attention-deficit disorder, inability to focus, and poor memory. Students who were exposed to prenatal or postnatal drugs are at risk for a range of academic, developmental, or emotional problems, including symptoms of anxiety and depression, psychiatric disorders, and behavior problems. As a result of exposure to alcohol or drugs, these students are likely to experience difficulties in school and achieve lower scores on assessments.

The Centers for Disease Control and Prevention (2014) reports that each year more than 740,000 children and youth are treated in hospital emergency departments as a result of violence, and more than 3 million reports of child maltreatment are received by state and local agencies. In addition, students who live in homes where violence takes place, either against them or a parent, may show emotional problems, cry excessively, or be withdrawn and shy. These students have trouble making friends, fear adults, suffer from depression, and are excessively absent from school (Centers for Disease Control and Prevention, 2014).

A recent study by Stickgold (2007) on positive sleep habits has shown the relationship between adequate, healthy sleep and learning. According to Stickgold,

> When we are sleep deprived, our focus, attention, and vigilance drift, making it more difficult to receive information. Without adequate sleep and rest, over-worked neurons can no longer function to coordinate information properly, and we lose our ability to access previously learned information. ("The Impact of Sleep Deprivation")

Children who come to school tired do not learn as well as those who are well rested. Teachers need to be aware that when children nod off in class, this may be an indicator of disrupted sleep or inappropriate sleep patterns. Furthermore, according to Börsch-Haubold (2006), sleep is especially important for consolidating long-term memory. As such, knowledge of children's sleep habits is important in assessment of long-term learning.

Chronic Health Issues

Teachers intuitively know that students who have poor health or chronic health problems generally do not do well in school. Some of this poor performance may be related to school absence or inability to focus while in school. According to Walsh and Murphy (2003), contemporary research has identified two specific trends: (1) Poor health leads to negative academic outcomes, and (2) school programs that intervene to improve children's health lead to improved academic learning. Furthermore, Walsh and Murphy list the following as potential causes of poor health in students:

- Health conditions such as epilepsy, asthma, and diabetes
- Dysfunctional family life
- School neighborhood environment

- Unsupervised after-school time
- Inadequate nutrition and learning

Walsh and Murphy (2003) also cite many types of programs that have a positive impact on health outcomes:

- Providing in-school health care and screenings by a school nurse or health clinic
- Involving the family in school programs and providing programs for parents and other caregivers
- Working with civic organizations to maintain a safe school-neighborhood environment
- Offering after-school programs for students
- Participating in free-food programs when applicable

When assessing children, teachers need to be aware of students' health and take this into account. A chronic health condition can be described as one that lasts longer than 3 to 6 months, is biologically based, has a significant impact on the person's life, and requires more than usual access to health care services for support (CLAN, 2012). About 15% to 18% of American children are affected by chronic illness (University of Michigan Health System, 2012). A wide range of chronic health conditions may impact students' success with assessments. Some of these conditions are allergies, epilepsy, arthritis, asthma, diabetes, kidney disorders, cystic fibrosis, cancer, hepatitis, lupus, sickle cell anemia, chronic fatigue syndrome, and HIV/AIDS. Many of these conditions may have associated mobility and/or vision impairments, damage parts of the brain affecting speech (e.g., epilepsy), or involve long and debilitating periods of nausea and fatigue, such as when undergoing cancer treatment. In addition, cardiac and respiratory diseases can affect mobility and impair coordination and dexterity, endurance, speed, and strength needed for moving, manipulating equipment, or writing (ADCET, n.d.-a).

Symptoms of chronic health issues are highly unpredictable. They can fluctuate in severity over relatively short or long periods; some may be progressively degenerative. Whatever the chronic health condition, students can be away from school for extended periods, and they may be unable to complete assignments within a specific time frame or to be assessed in a standard way. Medications may cause lethargy and concentration difficulties, while some conditions bring mood swings, depression, or anxiety (ADCET, n.d.-a).

Emotional and Behavioral Disability

Emotional and behavioral disability (EBD) is

a condition exhibiting one or more of the following characteristics over a long period and to a marked degree that adversely affects a child's educational performance:

- An inability to learn that cannot be explained by intellectual, sensory, or health factors.
- An inability to build or maintain satisfactory interpersonal relationships with peers and teachers.
- Inappropriate types of behavior or feelings under normal circumstances.

- A general pervasive mood of unhappiness or depression.
- A tendency to develop physical symptoms or fears associated with personal or school problems. (King, n.d., para. 1)

The U.S. Department of Education (2002) indicated that from 2000 to 2001, nearly 474,000 or about 18% of students served under the Individuals with Disabilities Education Act (IDEA) were identified as students with EBD. This condition can coexist with other disabilities. EBD includes children or youth with schizophrenia, affective disorders, and anxiety disorders but does not apply to students who are socially maladjusted (Lehr & McComas, 2005).

A student may or may not be placed in an Individualized Education Program, depending on the results of the school psychologist cognitive test and social/emotional measures (rating scales, interviews, and observations). In addition to this testing, the teacher provides results of educational testing, and a social worker conducts a sociocultural evaluation (King, n.d.).

Student achievement is linked to the state of the child's emotional and mental health. When students lack social and emotional connections to learning, educators, schools, and their peers, it often leads to behavior issues or disengagement. This inevitably leads to declining achievement and, in the worst cases, students' dropping out of high school (Finn, 1993).

Emotional Factors

Because social and emotional connections support engagement, they are critical prerequisites for student success. However, engagement is complex and may be defined in three ways: behavioral motivation, emotional engagement (comprising reactions to teachers and peers, activities in the learning task and school, as well as student attitudes, interests, and values), and cognitive engagement (Fredricks, Blumenfeld, & Paris, 2004).

Schools have many roles to play in building these connections, often beginning with establishing a learning environment that promotes healthy social and emotional interactions. Examples of these interactions are learning circles and cooperative and collaborative learning opportunities. Healthy social and emotional engagement can also be promoted through offering teacher support (both interpersonally and academically); facilitating connections with peers; providing a respectful, supportive, and academically challenging classroom structure; and presenting authentic and engaging tasks (including the level of interest and/or ownership it generates in the students plus opportunities for collaboration, task complexity, and links to the real world; Apple Classrooms of Tomorrow–Today, n.d.).

Many schools offer mentorship programs to promote positive emotional and mental health. This involves making a connection by assigning a staff member to each student. The mentor not only monitors the student's academic and personal development but is also there daily to celebrate successes and serve as an advocate.

Behavioral Factors

For a student to be identified with a behavioral disorder, certain characteristics must be demonstrated in a variety of settings, with little consideration or understanding of social or cultural rules. The academic characteristics are as follows:

- Disrupts classroom activities
- Impulsive

- Inattentive, distractible
- Preoccupied
- Does not follow or appear to care about classroom rules
- Poor concentration
- Resistance to change and transitions in routines
- Often speaks out with irrelevant information or without regard to turn taking rules
- Demonstrates aggressive behavior
- Intimidates and bullies other students
- Regularly absent from school
- Consistently blames others for their dishonesty
- Low self-esteem
- Difficulty working in groups
- Demonstrates self-injurious behavior
- Cannot apply social rules related to others' personal space and belongings
- Often manipulative of situations (Gallaudet University, n.d., "Academic Characteristics")

Students with EBD have many strengths, but effective, cohesive programming is necessary to reach them. Sugai and Horner (2002) recommend a three-tiered model of support:

- Tier 1—Includes strategies and programs that are designed to prevent the development of problems, target all students, and provide students and school staff with a strong foundation for teaching appropriate behaviors. Some examples are positive behavioral supports and school climate improvement projects.
- Tier 2—Includes programs that decrease the intensity of problems, designed to address alterable factors that place students at risk. Some examples are conflict-resolution lessons, peer-tutoring programs, and social skills instruction.
- Tier 3—Includes programs designed to remediate established problems, reduce duration, and preclude negative outcomes. Highly individualized, student-centered programs provide effective and efficient response to students most in need. An example is wrap-around services.

To support students with EBD, a sustained and cohesive program is essential, and this program must include collaborative efforts with others throughout the school, parents, and community members. In addition to the tiered approach, interventions must address relevant domains of competence for students with EBD. These interventions may include explicit and systematic instruction in reading, schoolwide social development programs, counseling, relevant opportunities to learn outside of school, and mentoring supports (Gaylord, Quinn, McComas, & Lehr, 2005).

Students With Special Needs and Assessment

In IDEIA 2004, the language about who will participate in assessments was changed to specify, "All children with disabilities are included in all general State and districtwide assessment programs . . . with appropriate accommodations and alternate assessments, where necessary and as indicated in their respective individualized educations programs. (Section 1412(c) (16)(A))" (Wright & Wright, 2005, "Participation in State and District Assessments").

There are more than 6.7 million children and youth with disabilities in the United States (U.S. Department of Education, 2006). These students have historically been excluded from assessment and accountability testing. Since IDEA and No Child Left Behind (NCLB), students with disabilities have been included in statewide accountability to promote their higher achievement. This is a positive step forward; however, it is a challenge to develop quality assessments for these students. Standardized assessments are meant to place all students on a level playing field, and so allowing for accommodations can compromise test validity. To increase the participation of students with special needs in testing, accommodations are often required (Abedi et al., 2009).

There are many ways accommodations can be used to support students with disabilities during assessment. They may take the form of adjustment to presentation of testing information, how students respond to assessment questions, the setting of the assessment environment, and the timing or scheduling of an assessment (Luke & Schwartz, 2007). When making these accommodations for an assessment, it is essential to ensure that they do not give one student an unfair advantage over another, or alter or compromise the test's ability to assess particular knowledge or skills.

Alternate assessments are designed to evaluate the progress of students who are unable to participate in regular assessments, even with accommodations (Luke & Schwartz, 2007). There are many students with special needs for whom an alternate assessment is the only way to appropriately evaluate what they know, have learned, or can do. For a student with special needs to receive an alternative assessment, IDEA requires that the student's Individualized Education Program team provide an explanation of why the statewide or districtwide assessment is not appropriate and a description of how the student will be assessed (Luke & Schwartz, 2007).

Making Connections

You are a second-grade teacher and about to assess your students on describing how characters in a story respond to major events and challenges. How are you going to alter your assessment to accommodate your nonverbal student with Down syndrome? Have you followed the proper procedures as laid out by the Individualized Education Program team (see Figure 4.2)?

English Language Learners, Culture, and Assessment

NCLB legislation has placed education accountability squarely in the public eye. As a result, overuse of standardized assessments has become the barometer to measure student achievement and success.

Although no one would disagree with the need for accountability in all facets of education, the extended use of standardized tests to make high stakes decision with regard to student placement, graduation, and promotion raises some fundamental issues relative to students, in general, and English language learners (ELLs) in particular. (Solórzano, 2008)

Figure 4.2
Individualized
Education Plan
Partial Sample

Individualized Education Plan: John Doe

Date: 2014/09/16 (yr/mo/day)
Student Name: John Doe
Student No.: 11187
Birth Date: 2007/06/21 (yr/mo/day)
Grade: 2
School: Best Choice Elementary
School Division: Anywhere
Referral Date: (yr/mo/day)
Case Manager: Mrs. M. Mann
Program Planning Team:

Name	Position	Signature
John Doe	Student	
	Parents	
	Principal	
	Classroom Teacher	
	Learning Center	
	Occupational Therapist	
	Physiotherapist	

(Signature indicates you understand the IEP)

Background Information

Relevant Medical/Diagnostic Information:

John is nonverbal and has Down syndrome, which impacts on his ability to perform grade level activities. He has poor muscle tone resulting in poor balance and an unsteady gait. John is right hand dominant. Although he can write, he is not able to keep up with his peers and his work can be illegible.

John has moderate intellectual disability (IQ level: 35–40) as demonstrated through formal assessments. He has a teaching assistant for all activities of daily living required in the school environment.

(Continued)

Figure 4.2
(Continued)

John has been identified as needing adaptive supports to compensate for his disability since entering school.

Other Information:

Language Spoken at Home: English

Agencies Involved: National Association for Down Syndrome

School Lego club, Swimming lessons, Boy Scouts, and Special Olympics

School History (*From Pertinent Cumulative File Information***):**

John has been integrated into the regular classroom for his entire school career; daily 80% time in classroom and 20% time learning center.

The school has had ongoing consultation from clinicians (PT, OT, SLP) who have assisted in developing strategies and adaptations which allow John be successful.

Student Specific Outcome: John will achieve the outcomes of the Grade 2 Language Arts curriculum using a variety of adaptations.

Strengths	Challenges
Works well in small groups; enjoys his classmates	Non-verbal
Visual learner	Difficulty following and remembering multiple step directions
Enjoys technology, i.e., computer and iPad, is able to stay on task 5 to 10 minutes when doing a high interest activity	Extremely easily distracted and requires verbal redirection and prompting to attend to task
Is able to follow simple one-step directions	Extreme difficulty completing tasks independently
Can recognized numbers up to 10	Limited bank of sight words
Successful with Picture Exchange Communication system (PECs) and continues to add new "words"	

There has been extraordinary growth in the number of ELLs in U.S. classrooms. From the 1997–1998 school year to the 2008–2009 school year, the number of ELLs enrolled in public schools increased from 3.5 million to 5.3 million (51%; National Clearinghouse for English Language Acquisition, 2011). The overwhelming numbers of ELLs bring unique challenges to teachers striving to ensure that these students get access to the core curriculum in schools and gain academic knowledge as well as English-language skills.

Most research contends that ELLs need 3 to 5 years to acquire English at reasonable levels and 4 to 7 years to acquire academic English proficiency (Solórzano, 2008). Now, assessments are most often used to judge teaching ability and school accreditation. These tests do not take into account the varying backgrounds and prior knowledge that students bring with them to school.

Some of the factors that influence the assessment of ELLs and their test accommodations are language, educational background, and culture. Language factors for ELLs may be broken down further into the range of linguistic backgrounds. There are about 400 different native languages among ELLs in the United States (Educational Testing Service, 2009). In addition, ELLs are at varying levels of proficiency not only in English but also in their respective native languages. When making accommodations to an assessment, it is essential to consider the literacy skills of the student both in English and in his or her native language.

An ELL's educational background also plays an important role in determining the necessary accommodations for an assessment. ELLs differ greatly in their level of schooling both in their native language and in the English language. In some cases, ELLs are learning English and academic content simultaneously. In addition to this, some ELLs may never have been exposed to standardized testing, even if they have a strong educational background and/or are proficient in English (Educational Testing Service, 2009).

ELLs' cultural factors also play a role in assessment. ELLs have varying degrees of acculturation to the mainstream U.S. culture. Cultural backgrounds and differences may place ELLs at a disadvantage in a standardized testing situation. If students lack familiarity with mainstream American culture, this can impact their test scores due to differences in prior knowledge and testing experience, or values and beliefs that can affect their responses to questions. In addition, some cultures value cooperation over competition, and students from these cultures may not be accustomed to performing at their personal best (Educational Testing Service, 2009). Standardized assessment makers tend to come from a middle-class, white background; therefore, test questions are based on this discourse—its values, habits, and background. They do not take into account those from other cultures and their knowledge and values. Is it reasonable to expect success for these students?

Making Connections

You are a new teacher in a Grade 5 class that comprises more than 80% ELLs. You know that there will be two rounds of standardized assessments for your students this year. What are you going to do to ensure their success on the standardized test?

Environmental Factors: Poverty and Assessment

One of the most striking correlations between poor health and learning is poverty. Walsh and Murphy (2003) state that

> It has long been known that children who live in poverty are more likely to experience educational difficulties that place them at risk for school failure. Research demonstrates that poor children, as well as children living near the poverty level, perform less well than non-poor or middle class children on many academic indicators. (p. 18)

"Children represent 24 percent of the population. Yet, they comprise 34 percent of all people in poverty" (Addy & Wight, 2012, p. 1). In the United States, there are more than 72 million children under age 18: 44% (31.9 million) live in low-income families and 21% (15.5 million) live in poor families (Addy & Wight, 2012).

Child poverty is defined as children who live in families below the federal poverty level. In 2011, the federal poverty level for a family of four was $22,350 (Addy & Wight, 2012). Poverty dictates the extent to which an individual goes without resources. These may include emotional, financial, mental, physical, and spiritual resources. In addition, they may also include support systems, relationships, and role models. According to Lacour and Tissington (2011), "poverty directly affects academic achievement due to lack of resources available for student success. Low achievement is closely correlated with lack of resources, and numerous studies have documented the correlation between low socioeconomic status and low achievement" (p. 522).

Poverty's effect seems to be the most detrimental when it occurs early in the child's life, when it is persistent, and when the child lives well below the poverty threshold. In 2011, "more than one in four children under 6 years old were poor in 21 states and the District of Columbia during their years of greatest brain development" (Children's Defense Fund, 2012a, para. 3). Poverty can impact a child's development in many ways, the most common including health and nutrition, parent mental health and affective interactions, a stimulating home environment, school and child-care quality, and neighborhood conditions (Fauth, Brady-Smith, & Brooks-Gunn, 2012).

Parents in poverty are more likely to have worse emotional and physical health than those who are not. Poor parental mental health is coupled with more conflict with children and less stimulating home environments. This results in less-than-optimal emotional, social, and cognitive outcomes (Fauth et al., 2012).

Income is directly related to the amount of material resources available to children. Typically, the higher the income, the higher the levels of cognitively stimulating materials; this leads to more cognitively developed preschool and elementary school children. This is one of the most detrimental effects of poverty. Income is also directly related to housing choice, and in poverty situations choice is limited. Families in poverty may typically live in neighborhoods with high crime and unemployment rates, neighborhoods that lack resources and efficacy among their residents.

Child-care subsidies assist low-income parents for child-care arrangements chosen by the family. However, as Phillips, Voran, Kisker, Howes, and Whitebook (1994) point out, up to 60% of subsidized and low-income child-care centers failed to conform to legal child-to-staff ratios in toddler classrooms, and most (70%) received low ratings on scales of appropriate caregiving and provision of appropriate activities. This reduced-quality child care results in lower cognitive development.

Making Connections

You are a fourth-grade teacher; every day, one particular student cries and is disruptive all morning. It takes some time, but you eventually find out that this student has no breakfast or snack for recess. Where can you go for help? What resources are available to you? How can you talk to the parent about this without crossing a line or creating distrust? Discuss this situation with a partner and share with the class.

Key Terms

cognitive development

learning styles

tracking

tunnel vision

Website Resources

• **Partnership for Accessible Reading Assessments**

The Partnership for Accessible Reading Assessments is a research and development project funded by the National Center for Special Education Research to make reading assessments more accessible for students with disabilities that affect reading. Presentations and publications regarding information relevant to the partnership's work can be found at **www.reading assessment.info/resources/index.htm.**

• **National Accessible Reading Assessment Projects**

The National Accessible Reading Assessment Projects is a collaboration of projects funded by the U.S. Department of Education Office of Special Education Programs to conduct research to make large-scale assessments of reading proficiency more accessible to students who have disabilities that affect reading. *Implications of NARAP Accessibility Principles for School and Classroom Practices* can be found at **www.narap .info/publications/PracticesForm.pdf.**

(Continued)

(Continued)

- **Technology Assisted Reading Assessment**

The Technology Assisted Reading Assessment project focuses on a program of research and development to improve reading assessments for students with visual impairments or blindness. The report *Field-Based Perspectives on Technology Assisted Reading Assessments: Results of an Interview Study With Teachers of Students With Visual Impairments (TVIs)* can be found at **www.naraptara.info/reports/TARAteacherInterviewStudy.pdf.**

- **Children's Vision Information Network**

This site is designed to provide parents and teachers information about frequently overlooked vision problems. It includes resources on the development of vision, a vision checklist, visual skills needed for reading, vision therapy, links to specialists in specific areas, instructional videos, and eye activities to try. The website is located at **www.childrensvision.com/index.htm.**

- **"Assessment and Accommodations," National Dissemination Center for Children with Disabilities**

This is a comprehensive site focusing on accommodations for assessments and alternative assessments for students with special needs. It includes procedures for teachers and parents as mandated by IDEA and NCLB. The site also provides links to a range of possible accommodations, an accommodations manual, and informative fact sheets and practical teaching tools for parents and schools. For more information, visit **nichcy.org/research/ee/assessment-accommodations.**

- **Guidelines for the Assessment of English Language Learners, Educational Testing Services (2009)**

This document is a comprehensive booklet that breaks down the recommendations and guidelines for assessing ELLs. It guides the user through planning, developing, and scoring assessments; development of assessment specifications and items; reviewing and field testing items; and using statistics to evaluate the assessment and scoring. It essentially provides a framework to assist with decision making regarding ELLs and assessments in the academic content areas. The document can be found at **www.ets.org/s/about/pdf/ell_guidelines.pdf.**

Student Study Site: Visit the Student Study Site at **www.sagepub.com/grantlit** to access additional study tools including eFlashcards, web resources, and online-only appendices.

CHAPTER 5

Setting the Stage for Literacy Assessment Through Affective Measures

*Kathy B. Grant
and Sandra E. Golden*

Common Core State Standards	
Comprehension and Collaboration	*SL.1.1* Participate in collaborative conversations with diverse partners about *grade 1 topics and texts* with peers and adults in small and larger groups.
	SL.2.1 Participate in collaborative conversations with diverse partners about *grade 2 topics and texts* with peers and adults in small and larger groups.
	SL.3.1 Engage effectively in a range of collaborative discussions (one-on-one, in groups, and teacher-led) with diverse partners on *grade 3 topics and texts*, building on others' ideas and expressing their own clearly.
	SL.4.1 Engage effectively in a range of collaborative discussions (one-on-one, in groups, and teacher-led) with diverse partners on *grade 4 topics and texts*, building on others' ideas and expressing their own clearly.
	SL.5.1 Engage effectively in a range of collaborative discussions (one-on-one, in groups, and teacher-led) with diverse partners on *grade 5 topics and texts*, building on others' ideas and expressing their own clearly.

Source: © Copyright 2010. National Governors Association Center for Best Practices and Council of Chief State School Officers. All rights reserved.

Words in Action

Affective Measures

As a new teacher in a fifth-grade classroom, Sheila's struggles include getting students into a reading regiment whereby they self-select books from the classroom library during their independent or free reading time at the end of the day. She notices smirks, frowns, and opposition when she announces free reading, especially from a small group of boys. Their resistance is palatable and makes for a difficult closing to the school day. Under-the-breath mutterings such as "Not again" and "Do we have to?" and other not-so-civilized terms are used. Sheila is in a quandary about how to make free reading enjoyable, yet instructional for students.

Thinking back to early in the school year, she had set up her classroom library with required fifth-grade text selections, as well as some fictional favorites of intermediate students. Where had she gone wrong? She steered away from informational texts because they were used for instructional resources. Sheila remembered students had asked if they could bring their own reading materials, but as a new teacher she was wary of the principal stopping by and seeing students reading *Car and Driver* magazine or some teenage fluff.

During the end-of-the-day reading, clock watching had become a favorite pastime of the students. *Gosh*, she thought, *when I was a student I looked forward all day to free reading. But is this really "free" for them? What steps can I take to reach a happy medium where students look forward to connecting with a good book? Or does that connection always need to be with a book? What will the administration or parents think if I allow other literacy resources such as comics, newspapers, magazines, graphic novels, or e-books on tablets?*

Sheila decided to reflect deeply on her quandary, ask other teachers what they did, and also approach her principal about the situation. Oh, yes, and she decided to ask the most important stakeholders—the students themselves.

Setting the Stage for Literacy Assessment Through Affective Measures

Research has confirmed that students who enjoy reading perform significantly better than those who do not. Unfortunately, 37% of the students in the study reported they do not read recreationally at all (Gambrell, 2011). This could be attributed to lack of reading in the home; absence of books, magazines, or newspapers in the home; and low awareness of the genres of literature that students may find engaging. In Ontario, Canada, People for Education noted that in the group of third and sixth graders surveyed (240,000) only about half liked to read (Pattenaude, 2012).

However, reasons for the lack of student enthusiasm concerning reading can be varied and complex, as we shall see. Moreover, with the advent of Literacy 2014, educators need to embrace alternative methods of connecting students to reading through Internet resources, multimedia, as well as graphic novels, comic books, and magazines. Engaging students in various forms of literature is essential, especially when teachers can guide them in **purposeful reading**. For instance, introducing students to autobiographies, biographies, or memoirs is an opportunity for them to connect with subjects who may share similar traits, values, or cultural backgrounds. Literature and informational texts can also be purposeful for learning about other countries, states, or cities, and comparing and contrasting them with their own lives. Teaching students to read for purpose could increase their interest and motivation to read.

Reading motivation, or the likelihood of **engagement** in reading or choosing to read, is critical for students to develop their full literacy potential. Engaging in reading is even more important than a student's family background of strong literacy promotion. Thus, stressing the importance of reading and promoting many opportunities for reading is critical to students' academic success and, ultimately, to their success and contribution as citizens in their community. Student motivation to read at home and in school decreases as children get older. Regrettably, decline in reading motivation appears to be the greatest from first through fourth grade (Guthrie & Wigfield, 2000). Therefore, as teachers, we need to ensure that students find enjoyment, value, and authenticity in reading.

It is important that we ask students the following: What makes a good reader? What strategies are crucial in proficient reading? What are weak readers lacking (Johnson, 2005)? By allowing students to understand what strong readers do to process text—through **strategies** such as inferencing, making connections, visualizing, determining importance, synthesizing, questioning, and using effective text structures—weaker readers can be taught to approach text more like strong readers (p. 766).

Edmunds and Bauserman (2006) found that teachers voice definitive concerns about students' motivation, and it can be concluded that teachers must become active literacy educators in the classroom and promote the importance of literacy. In surveying teachers, they noted the need to

- foster a genuine love of literacy in the classroom;
- boost the confidence of reluctant readers;
- promote at-home recreational reading;
- stress intrinsic, instead of extrinsic, motivation to read;

- address peer reading opportunities; and
- turn negative comments about reading into positive ones.

As found in Edmunds and Bauserman's (2006) study, motivating students as readers is complex and requires a high level of literacy engagement that students will find interesting, relevant, and meaningful. Throughout this chapter, issues of reading engagement, motivation, and identity will be addressed.

> Adolescent students who participate in programs that connect literacy with real-life out-of-school issues and personal interests indicate more positive feelings about reading and writing in school. (Ivey & Broaddus, 2001, p. 354)

Establishing Purposes for Reading and Writing

As you have learned in earlier chapters of this book, no two students are alike; thus, how teachers facilitate reading instruction in the classroom is critical to how students will approach reading and writing, specifically younger students. As teachers of reading, we have to guide students to become self-engaged readers. To engage students in becoming successful readers and writers, it is important to set the stage for reading and writing by providing them with skills and strategies for purposeful reading and writing. As children explore the academic content areas, they need to know and understand purposeful strategies for reading and writing that are based on context. These contexts should be authentic so that students can connect what they are learning and reading to their lives. These meaningful experiences can include learning about their community, learning about the socio-cultural aspects of their lives, reading for entertainment, and reading for real-life experiences, such as desired careers.

Furthermore, teachers need to provide students with opportunities to explore various genres of reading and writing to pique their interest (Ivey & Broaddus, 2001). When students have a choice in reading and writing, engagement and motivation are dynamic. Ivey and Broaddus contend that teaching strategies for reading and writing are critical and "should be embedded in the context of diverse genres and multiethnic children's and adolescent literature that inspires students and evokes personal responses" (2001, p. 356). A growing body of research on motivation, choice, and interest is showing that young adolescents engage in purposeful and strategic reading outside of the classroom, further suggesting that when given a choice students possess the necessary skills to have good literacy experiences. For instance, young adolescent girls are more likely to choose books that relate to them socially, personally, or in their future career goals.

Therefore, children need to have a purpose for reading and writing to engage them in ways that motivate and interest them to read and write in the classroom. A study conducted by Fisher and Frey (2012) found that when students are given essential questions that evoke critical thinking, they are more likely to read for inquiry, which leads to reading with a purpose.

Allington and Gabriel (2012, p. 10) noted that the two most powerful design factors for improving reading motivation and comprehension were student access to many books and personal choice of what to read.

Reading is a multifaceted process involving word recognition, comprehension, fluency, and motivation. Learn how readers integrate these facets to make meaning from print. (Leipzig, 2001, para. 1)

As readers ourselves, we come to the act of reading with certain preconceptions and beliefs. It is critical to note that our students, likewise, enter into reading with various preconceptions (e.g., trepidation or enjoyment), specific interests (e.g., wolves or princesses), and motivations (e.g., "How fast can I get through this task?" or "How long will the teacher let us read?") that impact a classroom literacy community. The questions in Table 5.1 are designed to help you get a handle on your own preconceptions regarding reader preference.

Table 5.1 Prereading and Postreading Preference Guide

Directions: As you read Chapter 5, think about your preconceptions in the areas of student literacy interests, motivations, and sustaining a classroom literacy community.

After a collaborative discussion, label A for general agreement with the statement or D for general disagreement with the statement. The lines following the statements are provided for any "well . . . buts." After completing Chapter 5, go back to review your preferences and indicate an A or D on the second line. Be prepared to support you decision and/or revision in thinking.

_____ _____ 1. Engaged readers will always remain that way, while disengaged readers will remain unmotivated to read.

_____ _____ 2. Teachers should always choose books students should read during their sustained reading time; choices should be limited.

_____ _____ 3. Reading incentives such as small gifts to get students to read should be used to provide extrinsic motivation.

_____ _____ 4. A student's reading identity can be positive or negative; teachers should gather this information through individual conferences and surveys.

_____ _____ 5. Buddy reading activities can serve to benefit student efficacy in literacy.

Making Connections

Take a moment and work in small groups to discuss how content-specific reading and writing can be developed to engage students in purposeful activities that promote strong academic and literacy experiences. Think of essential questions that address students' social and personal lives and evoke purposeful reading and writing activities. Explain why and how those questions will arouse interest and motivation.

> ### Making Connections
>
> Now, reflect on your own unconscious process for purposeful reading and writing. What do you do that is automatic when you read? What is your conscious approach for purposeful reading and writing? Do you develop questions in your mind that keep your reading and writing focused on the overall purpose for reading? Write on your process for purposeful reading and writing, and then share with your colleagues.

Student Definitions of Reading and Writing

Definitions of reading and writing vary widely. Walcutt (1967) defined reading as the ability to decode symbols to develop mastery skills for comprehending printed materials. The development and teaching of reading is a complex process that involves skills and strategies to help students read fluently with comprehension. But it is not just the ability to decode symbols, read fluently, and comprehend what is read; it also involves sustaining engagement and motivation to read (Leipzig, 2001). As teachers, providing students with reading skills and reading strategies is essential to how they experience reading and reading success. Afflerbach, Pearson, and Paris (2008) offer two unique interpretations of reading skills and reading strategies:

- Reading skills are automatic actions that result in decoding and comprehension with speed, efficiency, and fluency and usually occur without awareness of the components or control involved.
- Reading strategies are deliberate, goal-directed attempts to control and modify the reader's efforts to decode text, understand words and construct meanings of test. (p. 368)

Effective reading instruction should engage students in authentic and meaningful skills and strategies that foster cognitive responses to reading, responses such as motivation, self-regulation, and self-assessment. Effective reading instruction should also influence students to automatically use good strategies for comprehension and reading for purpose (Cziko, Greenleaf, Hurwitz, & Schoenbach, 2000). When students are equipped with various strategies and the skills needed to decode text, engagement and interest are strengthened and students are able to experience various reading tools. They will have greater opportunity to try different skills when text meaning requires more complex thinking.

We now know with greater certainty that children who have made positive associations with reading tend to read more often, for longer periods of time, and with greater intensity. (Henk & Melnick, 1995, p. 470)

> ### Making Connections
>
> With a partner, identify effective skills and strategies that promote children's reading for purpose, develop comprehension, and encourage motivation. How do you know that these serve those purposes?

Literacy Agency Self-Assessment: Self-Efficacy

Students' self-perceptions of their ability to read influence their reading experiences. Henk and Melnick (1995) suggest that students who perceive high self-efficacy in their reading abilities are more engaged than those students with low self-efficacy in their reading abilities. Consequently, self-efficacy will have a huge impact on how students experience the text and their motivation to read. Thus, providing students with ways to affirm their beliefs about their reading abilities could be beneficial not only for the students but also for the teacher. The Reader Self-Perception Scale (RSPS; Henk & Melnick, 1995) measures how students perceive themselves as readers. Reading success or lack thereof could be attributed to the students' perception of their reading. The RSPS is based on four sources:

1. Progress: A child's perception of present reading performance compared with past performance.

2. Observational comparison: How a child perceives his or her reading performance as compared with those of classmates.

3. Social feedback: Direct and indirect input about reading from teachers, classmates, and people in the child's family.

4. Physiological states: Internal feelings the child experiences during reading (p. 472).

The RSPS can be a valuable tool in the classroom to inform and perhaps affirm students' perceptions of themselves as readers (see Table 5.2). Teachers can then use the information to develop instruction and strategies to help engage struggling readers with more positive reading experiences.

Literacy Self-Regulation

Starting young readers on the path to **self-regulated learning** is a critical component of literacy instruction that begins in preschool (McTigue, Washburn, & Liew, 2011). This means a student should strive to maintain a positive attitude when encountering reading difficulties, remaining flexible and seeking support when needed. Furthermore, **eco-resiliency** is the ability to exert control over the reading task when called for (Block & Block, 1980). Coupled with academic resiliency (defined in the next paragraph), students intuitively recognize the difference between conscious behaviors in a reading setting and those on the playground. Underlying all is the socioemotional skill of self-esteem, which gives students confidence that they can reach their reading goals through self-monitoring and checking.

In a responsive classroom, students are engaged in literacy tasks, yet do not hesitate to seek help from knowledgeable others. This may be the teacher, aide, another student, or a classroom volunteer. In this manner, students develop **academic resiliency**—that is, the ability to persevere through challenging academic tasks. Table 5.3 contains a checklist of academic resilient behaviors observed during literacy activities.

Table 5.2 Reader Self-Perception Scale

Student: _____ Grade: _____

Date: _____ Teacher: _____

Answer each question.

1. How often do you read per week?

2. What do *you* like to read (text genres: fiction, fantasy, biography/autobiography, informational; other media: comic books, magazine articles, blogs, e-books, etc.)?

3. What was most memorable for you in your recent reading? *Why* was that?

4. Who are *two* of your favorite writers?

5. Where do you find your favorite reading material (e.g., online, magazines, books, library)?

6. What do you do well as a reader? What would you like to improve?

7. What have you *learned* as a reader that makes you proud (e.g., better comprehension, fluency, inference)?

8. What literacy skills have helped you with your fictional reading?

9. What literacy skills have helped you with your informational reading?

Teacher's comments:

Source: Adapted from the *Fountas and Pinnell Benchmark Assessment System.*

Table 5.3 Teacher Checklist of Academic Resilient Behaviors in Literacy

Engagement

❏ Eager for reading time (teacher read-alouds, partner reading, books on tape, literature circles, guided reading, or other literacy tasks)
❏ Needs only occasional teacher redirection to stay on task
❏ Enjoys teacher or student read-alouds, reader's theatre, or poetry, and reacts appropriately to the text (nonverbally or verbally)
❏ Other evidence:

Self-Monitoring

❏ Recognizes meaning-changing errors and tries to self-correct during oral reading
❏ Strives for correct syntax through paragraphs and sentences
❏ Rereads own writing in response to reading and can identify parts that may confuse another reader
❏ Other evidence:

Help-Seeking

❑ Uses class resources (e.g., dictionary, Internet) for academic growth
❑ Asks other students or adults for explanations when confused
❑ Other evidence:

Source: Adapted from McTigue et al. (2011).

Making Connections

Reflect on your own experience as a reader and/or writer, and write about that experience. Think about a time when you were successful, and then think about a time when you were not as successful. Describe specific literacy incidents demonstrating self-regulated learning, eco-resiliency, self-efficacy, and academic resiliency. How have these incidents changed your notions of reading and seeking support when confused?

Enjoyment of Reading: Interest and Attitudes

Greenwood (2007) and his in-service teachers had pupils in Grades 1 through 8 complete the sentence stem, "Reading is . . . " (p. 37). This research acknowledged how critical it is to converse with students about their definitions of reading and to take the time to listen to their responses, noting the variety of definitions and complexities of literacy. Some powerful definitions of reading begin this section. Interesting to note is the **transformational literacy** perspective these students choose to include.

- "Reading is a separate definition for everyone because when people read they see different things than those around them."
- "Reading is powerful words on a page to transform a reader."
- "Reading is staying up all night to find out what happens next."
- "Reading is comprehension and understanding of text. Though to many reading a book can mean simply saying aloud the words, truly understand[ing] the words is a bigger part of reading. In addition, thinking afterwards about what you read is a big part of the reading process." (p. 37)

In this chapter's introduction, we provided quotes citing the declining lack of interest in text-based reading, as well as ongoing teacher concerns about reader motivation, negativism, goal setting, confidence, and **extrinsic rewards** for reading, especially for reluctant and/or struggling readers. We should note, students who are strong readers but choose not to pick up a book for leisure reading were previously labeled **alliterate**, able to read but choosing not to. We prefer to call them **reluctant readers**.

We highly recommend, as the school year starts, that teachers take the time to understand their students' interest or lack of interest in reading, as well as their attitudes when approaching reading tasks. There are various ways to uncover interest in and attitudes about reading for diverse learning styles: drawing pictures, performing oral reading, employing symbols, and observing body response, as well as using traditional question-naires or surveys. The data from these interest and attitude questionnaires and surveys will determine how instruction is designed. Additionally, the information gathered will provide teachers with information as to who is struggling, who is a reluctant reader, and who lacks motivation. Our advice is to make use of ongoing observations of readers through on-the-spot analysis of responses and to make the inventory sessions engaging for students.

What Makes a Good Reader?

Little information is available on how to assess student understanding of what makes a proficient reader. Johnson (2005) developed a "good reader" open-ended series ques-tionnaire (see Table 5.4) to name some things students have observed strong and poor readers do.

Table 5.4 What Makes a Good Reader?

1. Do you know any good readers? Who?

2. How do you know he or she is a good reader?

3. Name some things good readers do when they read.

4. Name some things poor readers do when they read.

5. What kind of reader are you? Tell why.

Source: Johnson (2005).

Johnson administered the questionnaire at the beginning of school in August, then readministered it in January to note changes in responses. Overall "good readers" were found to have the following characteristics:

- Read with expression
- Make no mistakes/read fast
- Read a lot
- Memorize
- Correct/reread
- Sound out
- Don't skip pages
- Monitor/don't give up
- Ask questions/make connections
- Take their time/understand
- Use strategies/infer
- Overview/preview
- Retell

On the other hand, "poor" readers exhibited the following characteristics:

- Read with little expression/read too fast
- Don't read a lot/pretend to be done
- Don't correct
- Become bored with reading
- Don't select "just right" books
- Don't enjoy reading
- Don't finish books

- Don't make connections/use strategies
- Don't ask questions
- Only look at pictures
- Sound out/skip parts

- Don't understand what they read
- Don't monitor or go back
- Can't finish/get stuck
- Read slowly

The changing definitions of students as strong or weak readers evolved as students observed peer literacy behaviors. By watching peers and conversing about the current reading selection, a powerful connection with literacy was established. Moreover, students developed **stamina** as they followed a classroom schedule assigning reading times. They became more aware that they have control over their reading behaviors and gained resiliency and became mature readers.

Reader's Interest Inventory Analysis

We developed a Reader's Interest Inventory to learn more about students and also to help discern their affective responses to questions. This inventory elicits verbal responses, but as an observant teacher, you can also learn about students through their affective reactions. Oftentimes, students will give answers they believe the teacher wants to hear; however, nonverbal cues may yield more authentic reactions. Using verbal and nonverbal cues may yield more accurate information needed to develop instruction for students. This is especially important in working with English language learners (ELLs).

The Reader's Interest Inventory Analysis in Table 5.5 is meant to be administered orally prior to an individual reading case study and contains 16 broad-based questions (that can be shortened) to prompt student responses. Observational opportunities exist for teachers to note an **affective** responses based on each question, along with a 4-point

Table 5.5 Reader's Interest Inventory Analysis

Teacher: _____ Grade: _____
Study Pseudonym: _____ Date: _____

1. Do you like reading?
Response:

4-Scale Rating	Affective Response
3—High Reading Interest 2—Moderate Reading Interest 1—Low Reading Interest 0—No Reading Interest	☺ 😐 ☹

(Continued)

Table 5.5 (Continued)

2. What is your favorite thing about reading?

Response:

4-Scale Rating	Affective Response
3—High Reading Interest 2—Moderate Reading Interest 1—Low Reading Interest 0—No Reading Interest	☺ ☺ ☹

3. What is your least favorite thing about reading?

Response:

4-Scale Rating	Affective Response
3—High Reading Interest 2—Moderate Reading Interest 1—Low Reading Interest 0—No Reading Interest	☺ ☺ ☹

4. What is your favorite book you have ever read?

Response:

4-Scale Rating	Affective Response
3—High Reading Interest 2—Moderate Reading Interest 1—Low Reading Interest 0—No Reading Interest	☺ ☺ ☹

5. Do you have books of your own? What types?

Response:

4-Scale Rating	Affective Response
3—High Reading Interest 2—Moderate Reading Interest 1—Low Reading Interest 0—No Reading Interest	☺ ☺ ☹

6. What do you like to do in your free time?

Response:

4-Scale Rating	Affective Response
3—High Reading Interest 2—Moderate Reading Interest 1—Low Reading Interest 0—No Reading Interest	☺ ☻ ☹

7. Do you like to go to the library? Why? Why not?

Response:

4-Scale Rating	Affective Response
3—High Reading Interest 2—Moderate Reading Interest 1—Low Reading Interest 0—No Reading Interest	☺ ☻ ☹

8. Do you read at home or read with your family? How so?

Response:

4-Scale Rating	Affective Response
3—High Reading Interest 2—Moderate Reading Interest 1—Low Reading Interest 0—No Reading Interest	☺ ☻ ☹

9. Do you like to read at school? Why? Why not?

Response:

4-Scale Rating	Affective Response
3—High Reading Interest 2—Moderate Reading Interest 1—Low Reading Interest 0—No Reading Interest	☺ ☻ ☹

(Continued)

Table 5.5 (Continued)

10. What school subject(s) do you like the most?

Response:

4-Scale Rating	Affective Response		
3—High Reading Interest 2—Moderate Reading Interest 1—Low Reading Interest 0—No Reading Interest	☺	😐	☹

11. What do you do well when you are reading?

Response:

4-Scale Rating	Affective Response		
3—High Reading Interest 2—Moderate Reading Interest 1—Low Reading Interest 0—No Reading Interest	☺	😐	☹

12. What's your favorite thing to do during reading instruction? Why?

Response:

4-Scale Rating	Affective Response		
3—High Reading Interest 2—Moderate Reading Interest 1—Low Reading Interest 0—No Reading Interest	☺	😐	☹

13. How do you feel when you are reading?

Response:

4-Scale Rating	Affective Response		
3—High Reading Interest 2—Moderate Reading Interest 1—Low Reading Interest 0—No Reading Interest	☺	😐	☹

14. If you could change one thing about your reading class, what would you change? Why?	

Response:

4-Scale Rating	Affective Response
3—High Reading Interest 2—Moderate Reading Interest 1—Low Reading Interest 0—No Reading Interest	☺ ☺ ☹

15. What do you feel about reading different kinds of books?	

Response:

4-Scale Rating	Affective Response
3—High Reading Interest 2—Moderate Reading Interest 1—Low Reading Interest 0—No Reading Interest	☺ ☺ ☹

16. What goals would you like to set with me to accomplish by the end of the year?	

Response:

4-Scale Rating	Affective Response
3—High Reading Interest 2—Moderate Reading Interest 1—Low Reading Interest 0—No Reading Interest	☺ ☺ ☹

rating scale to quickly check as each question is addressed. We recognize the importance of analyzing student responses for facial and body responses—hence the inclusion of the scale and affective check-offs.

Using Visuals to Gauge Reading Engagement

When teachers match learning styles with interest inventory preferences, there is greater opportunity to determine how best to encourage reading engagement and results in gaining feedback that acknowledges and respects students' diversity. For younger students, familiar pictures and bright colors can bring into play a level of comfort in making choices about early reading endeavors. The Butterfly Visual Learning Styles Inventory queries use learning style choices: tactile (teddy bear), visual (lots of pictures), listening (reading aloud), or musical (songs and music). This inventory could elicit a discussion about various ways young children connect to reading, why differing approaches all contribute to a life of literacy, and how they can value them. Teachers can find various templates that relate to the pictures or themes in a **picture book** and develop their own visual learning styles interest inventory. The sample provided in Figure 5.1 was developed by graduate student Alicia Sherman, MST program, SUNY Plattsburgh (2011).

Figure 5.1
Butterfly Visual

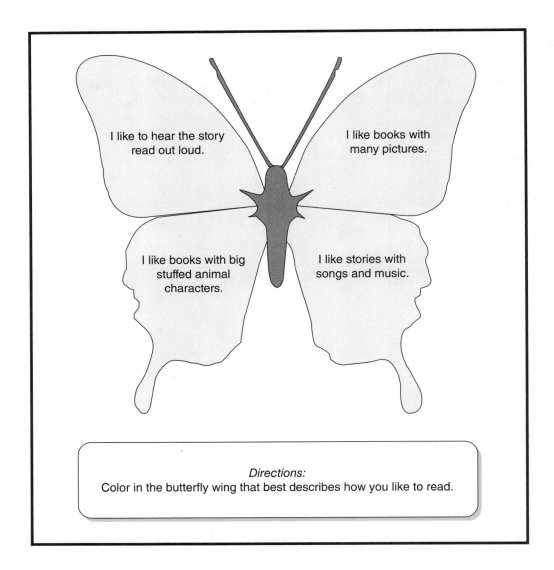

I like to hear the story read out loud.

I like books with many pictures.

I like books with big stuffed animal characters.

I like stories with songs and music.

Directions:
Color in the butterfly wing that best describes how you like to read.

Thought-Bubble Picture Self-Assessment

Many readers have positive literacy identities; however, many reluctant readers do not. As struggling students progress through the grades, they become adept at hiding their true feelings about the act of reading. "As teachers, we need to recognize the importance of how students perceive reading and the emotions they feel" (Zambo, 2006, p. 802). The following scenario describes the feelings and actions of a struggling student:

> A fifth grade student, Lee, feels no joy in reading. He has struggled as a reader since first grade and feels overwhelmed by the demands of science and social studies texts. Consequently, he avoids reading for pleasure, even though he loves to know about NASCAR. He is convinced he will never be a good reader and when he is in guided reading, he often stares around the room, asks to go to the bathroom, or puts his head down on the table. He becomes anxious when he hears the teacher call for guided reading groups to form. In his mind, reading is linked to failure and negative experiences. (p. 798)

Zambo (2006) suggests that teachers gauge their students' perceptions about reading through thought-bubble pictures. Samples of blank thought bubbles are provided in Figures 5.2 and 5.3. Thought bubbles can contain negative or positive perceptions

Figure 5.2

Sample Thought-Bubble: Boy

Directions:
Pretend this boy is you reading a book. Draw his expression, including his eyes and mouth. Then write or draw what he is thinking about while reading.

Figure 5.3
Sample
Thought-
Bubble: Girl

Directions:
Pretend this girl is you reading a book. Draw her expression,
including her eyes and mouth. Then write or draw
what she is thinking about while reading.

and emotions concerning reading. Through drawings and captions, readers are encouraged to express what a character (they as readers) is thinking or feeling during the act of reading.

Zambo (2006) cautions teachers to ensure the reliability and validity of their interpretations by asking another observer to score the bubbles. Positive, neutral, and negative ratings based on physical features of characters, as well as symbols, signs, and emotive words, aid teachers in interpreting student self-assessment of their reading. Thought bubbles serve as a valuable check for positive reading attitudes and negative reactions. Teachers can offer varied reading choices, including graphic novels, comics, and e-texts, to stimulate reading interest.

Motivation: Reading Resiliency and Maturity

Reading resiliency is a critical habit that supports a love of reading. However, reluctant readers do not habituate resiliency since their negative attitudes about reading prevail. As noted, there are many reasons for student pessimism, but as facilitators of literacy, we hold the key to turning that attitude around. One fun and easy way to change student attitudes is through buddy reading.

Buddy Reading

Along with book choice and allocating chunks of time for pleasure reading during the school day, setting up a **buddy reading** program can foster positive attitudes toward reading, improve confidence, develop a love of books, and perk up self-esteem (Friedland & Truesdell, 2004). There are many configurations of cross-age reading— older students with primary students or high school students with intermediate or middle school students—however, the point of the program is promoting an experience of mentorship or **reading resiliency**. Some caveats for a successful student program include these basic elements:

- Primary students should have the ability to read independently.
- Grade levels should be spaced out enough to provide a mentoring experience—for example, second grade and sixth grade.
- Partners should remain together throughout the program and be same-gender pairs.
- The program should span several months and consistently occur at a designated time and day (for about 30 minutes).
- Buddies should have a quiet, comfortable place to read.
- A significant number of books should be available for self-selection, with a variety of reading levels and genres represented.
- Materials should be stored together, including a large plastic bag to tote books, reading logs, and writing materials (Friedland & Truesdell, 2004).

Cross-age tutoring can be beneficial for both students involved, with the positive elements of reading aloud to and with younger students, appropriate book choices, reading with fluency and expression, and follow-up questions. A reading log that lists the books read and how well the students liked each book is recommended. Teacher modeling of the procedure as well as monitoring of the relationships in student pairs is essential. Obtaining feedback midway through the program will gauge students' interest and engagement in the process (Friedland & Truesdell, 2004). A Buddy Reading Survey can provide a clue to the reluctant reader's resiliency and maturity in taking on the mentorship of a younger student (see Table 5.6).

Buddy reading is a powerful motivator for students disinclined to read. When such a reader engages in reading aloud to a younger student a text he or she has practiced reading and feels a level of comfort with, that reader will experience a measure of success. As Vacca, Vacca, and Mraz (2010) contend, "Reading aloud can spur student interest in a topic. After hearing a book read aloud, students are much more likely to pick up books on this topic, and related ones, on their own" (p. 383). **Maturity** in making informed book choices is the sign of an advancing reader. With maturity, students are aware of their reading abilities, including likes and dislikes, strengths and limitations. For example, students might recognize that informational books on choice topics are more engaging to them than fairy tales or tall tales. Moreover, they discover that informational books contain glossaries of challenging terms to support fluency.

Table 5.6 Buddy Reading Survey

Student:_____ Date:_____

Reading Buddy: _____

Please answer the following questions about your buddy reading experience.

1. Do you look forward to your buddy reading? Why or why not?

2. What do you think you do well in your buddy reading program? How is working with a reading buddy helping you improve?

3. Is your reading buddy a good reader?

4. What does your reading buddy do well? What are you helping him or her improve?

5. Do you ever come to something you don't know? What do you do about it?

6. Does your reading buddy ever come to something he or she doesn't know? What does he or she do about it?

7. Do you practice reading your material aloud before your buddy session? _____ Yes _____ No

8. What kinds of questions do you ask your reading buddy during or after your reading?

9. Do you think you are a good reading buddy?

10. On a scale of 1 to 10, with 10 being the highest, how would you rate your buddy reading experience?

    1   2   3   4   5   6   7   8   9   10

11. What do you like and/or dislike about buddy reading?

Reading Choice

Reluctant oral readers should be supported by the teacher in their choice of what to read aloud to the class, an activity suggested by Hurst, Scales, Frecks, and Lewis (2011). By signing up beforehand for a designated day and time to read aloud to the class, students have the opportunity to prepare for their performance. **Reading choice** can be a powerful motivating factor; however, students must explain their rationale for choosing that particular text, song lyrics, script, letter, book series, children's book, joke, quote, excerpt from a novel, piece from a magazine or the Internet, or poem (Hurst et al., 2011). "The reading aloud activity cultivates civility toward classmates through audience participation, fosters reading confidence, and provides a platform for social learning" (p. 442).

Reading Incentives

Teachers struggle with decisions about the use of reading incentives. Various groups offer reading incentives, some dubious or even detrimental to true literacy motivation. Other incentives support reading recognition, expertise, and celebration. Typical incentives include the following:

- Classroom incentives: "Place a check on our classroom reading chart for completing the book. Good work!" (Recognition)
- Reader's chair: Like writer's chair, the student highlights the book read. (Expertise)
- Home-based incentives: "If you finish reading your chapter, we will go get ice cream." (Food) "You cannot go out to play with Sam until the book is read." (Leisure time)
- District incentives: "Let's turn in our parent-signed reading sheets toward our Pizza Hut reading points." (Group pressure)
- Community incentives: "Join us Tuesday, November 12 for our Celebration of Literacy at the Rotterdam Library." (Celebration of literacy)
- Commercial incentives: "Let's get on the computers to use Accelerated Reader." (Commercial reading incentive program software; not recommended)

Our advice is to carefully consider the use of reading incentives and check with parents/guardians about their allocation of incentives. Also, remember that the previous grades' teachers may have used incentives that benefited students. Find out what incentives were used and why. Reading motivation can be broken down into two main components: intrinsic and extrinsic (Hilden & Jones, 2011). As teachers, our primary aim is to nurture the intrinsic love of reading and book choice over other activities.

Teachers' Questions About Reading Motivation

1. *Should I provide rewards for student reading?* Books as prizes are the best! Offer students rewards that are directly related to the act of reading, such as a bookmark or book cover. Check out the Scholastic Reading Club, which offers teachers inexpensive book sets.

2. *What intrinsic rewards can teachers employ to engage reluctant readers?* Social motivation to read can act as an intrinsic reward. To boost intrinsic motivation, allow students to share with others through book chats, while eating lunch with the principal, or by turning a book into a reader's theatre enactment.

3. *What can I do to help a young reader who has consistently received extrinsic rewards from parents for at-home reading?* What well-meaning parents do to provide incentives is a family matter; however, if students react when no extrinsic reward is given for reading in the class, the teacher may discuss with parents his or her viewpoint as far as reward giving in school.

4. *What is the reward proximity hypothesis (Gambrell, 1996)?* This hypothesis suggests that the type of reward for reading can influence the type of motivation engendered. According to this hypothesis, if a book is given as a reward, students will be more likely to read than if given a token such as candy or a pencil.

English Language Learners and Motivation to Read

ELLs' motivation to read may rely on dynamic variables different from those for a first-language learner. A study by Protacio (2012) found variables that focused on ELLs' acclimatization to American schooling and social networks as a rationale for reading motivation. She identified instrumental motivation—meaning that reading is taken on for the value of the task tied to academics, such as passing a test. Another motivation for ELLs concerns integrative motivation, or using reading to acclimate and learn about a new culture. Another factor to consider is the second-language student's perceived competence in the reading task. Sometimes levels of higher English proficiency account for higher reading motivation but not always. Coupled with this factor is the use of engaging and exciting reading materials for ELLs.

Here are some factors Protacio (2012) identified through her research study of six male ELLs. After each factor, some activities to support reading motivation are also listed.

- Sociocultural environment—ELLs are motivated to read because of family members and friends in their immediate environment.
  - Families are encouraged to share in at-home reading with students, check homework, and read aloud in their native language and English at home.

- Integrative orientation—ELLs use reading as a way to form bonds with their American peers and learn more about their new culture.
  - Buddy reading is the perfect reading venue to connect with peers. Consider reader's theatre and dramatic readings.

- Instrumental motivation—ELLs are motivated to read because they realize the value of reading in further developing their competence in English.
  - Celebrate small steps in the acquisition of English for students, label classroom objects in other languages, and support cultural exchange opportunities.

- Perceived competence—ELLs' perception of their English abilities is related to their motivation to read in English.
  - Discuss student's perceptions of their reading abilities to form a plan for progress, highlight student readers as experts in student read-alouds, and have students journal about their reading successes.

In sum, this chapter provides usable ideas, assessments, and strategies to support reading motivation, as research clearly validates the affective nature of reading. Getting students to a level of self-regulated learning and academic resiliency is crucial to developing goal-oriented readers as well as circumventing resistance to reading. Work hard to develop drive to read as a top priority in your daily literacy dialogue with students.

Key Terms

academic resiliency	purposeful reading
affective	reading choice
alliterate	reading motivation
buddy reading	reading resiliency
eco-resiliency	reluctant readers
engagement	self-regulated learning
extrinsic rewards	stamina
maturity	strategies
picture book	transformational literacy

Website Resources

- **International Children's Digital Library**

More than 4,000 children's books from 64 countries in 54 languages are available at this site, located at **en.childrenslibrary.org.**

- **Google Books**

Children can read sample chapters or even full texts of a number of books. Search for a specific topic or browse the list of available titles at **books.google.com.**

- **Project Gutenberg**

Project Gutenberg is a collection of more than 36,000 free e-books in the public domain. Access the collection at **www.gutenberg.org.**

- **Wonderopolis**

This is a website created by the National Center for Family Literacy that can help parents and teachers draw elementary-age children into literacy-strengthening conversations and activities too fun to resist. Find a wealth of resources at **wonderopolis.org.**

Student Study Site: Visit the Student Study Site at **www.sagepub.com/grantlit** to access additional study tools including eFlashcards, web resources, and online-only appendices.

SECTION II

Grade-Level Literacy Assessments

What Characterizes Authentic Grade-Level Literacy Assessments?

As teachers integrate assessment throughout the teaching and learning process, they need a large toolbox of assessments that can support them. Authentic grade-level literacy assessment is integrated with classroom instruction. These assessments are given before instruction to determine what students need to meet the standards. They are also given during instruction to gauge students' progress on the standards. After instruction, these assessments serve to measure the teacher's effectiveness and to determine if students need additional intervention to achieve the standards.

Section II focuses on providing teachers with the assessments that can make up their toolbox of assessments. Chapters 6, 7, and 8 examine authentic formative assessment tools that can be used before, during, and after enacting instruction. Depending on the grade level and developmental reading levels of your students, these chapters will provide you with a series of assessments that can inform and guide the instructional process. Chapter 9 focuses on informal reading inventories (IRIs). These individually administered reading assessments provide teachers with a lens to zoom in on an individual student's literacy strengths and weaknesses. In Chapter 9, readers will learn how to administer and interpret IRIs to inform their instruction. Chapter 10 moves away from teacher-administered assessments to look at commercial assessments. It focuses on both the formative and summative commercial assessments that are part of the schoolwide data collection initiatives. This chapter highlights the key vocabulary needed to interpret these assessments, along with how the classroom teacher can administer and use them in the classroom. Last, Chapter 11 describes how teachers can prepare their classroom as the center of literacy assessment through organized efforts to streamline the process.

This chapter focuses on practical ideas for using the instruments of data collection, such as checklists, spreadsheets, and anecdotal records, among many suggestions. The primary purpose of this section is to provide teachers with the vocabulary and applications of authentic, commercial, formative, and summative assessments.

CHAPTER 6

Early Childhood–Level Assessments

Breaking the Code

*Sandra E. Golden
and Gwyn W. Senokossoff*

Common Core State Standards	
Print Concepts	*RF.K.1.A* Follow words from left to right, top to bottom, and page by page.
Phonological Awareness	*RF.K.2.E* Add or substitute individual sounds (phonemes) in simple, one-syllable words to make new words.
Phonics and Word Recognition	*RF.K.3.C* Read common high-frequency words by sight (e.g., *the, of, to, you, she, my, is, are, do, does*).
Fluency	*RF.K.4* Read emergent-reader texts with purpose and understanding.

FOCUS QUESTIONS

1. What are some complexities to be aware of when assessing kindergartners?
2. How does authentic instruction increase higher-order thinking?

(Continued)

(Continued)

3. Analysis of assessment data is instrumental in making decisions for instruction. In what ways can these data influence literacy development instruction?

4. How can you develop instruction in phonics, phonemic awareness, and fluency that promotes growth, fosters opportunities for practice and application, and engages students in authentic, relevant, and meaningful ways?

Words in Action

Maddie Tells the Story

"Maddie, ya wanna read a book with me?" Maddie is a 5-year-old and about to start school, but due to her birth order—the youngest of three children—she is driven to keep up and perform as well as her older brother and sister do. Since they are already reading, she is confident that she can read, too. I have been using a ploy with her. First, I ask if she'll read a book with me, but she always insists on reading it to me now. She can't really read yet, but she knows just what the story is about and/or can make up anything to fit the pictures.

The ploy I use is to tell her what a great job she did reading the story to me, and then I ask if she'll read it to me again. This is plausible because all my nieces and nephews made me read the same story over and over to them. She is delighted and reads the story to me again. This time, I am listening for the details, mentally comparing them to the first version. I am visualizing the story, and so is Maddie! I comment on the differences that I notice, never pointing out that they were not in the first version. She often embellishes Version 2, wanting to make it as good as or better than the first time. More important, Maddie is visualizing. This is one of the best foundations for good readers. Learning to visualize gives students a point of reference. Does the story make sense? Is the story consistent? Is it believable to the listener/reader?

Try this technique with your students. Get them "reading" early and often, and ensure that they visualize by listening for and commenting on the new details.

The Complexities of Preschool and Kindergarten Assessments

There is a need for informative preschool and kindergarten data. These data identify gaps in students' early experiences before they come to school. Accurate information about students' strengths and weaknesses is used to plan activities that will best support learning. Schools look for an accurate picture of skills and abilities as a baseline for understanding results from standardized tests in later grades.

However, assessment of preschool and kindergarten students may be difficult for many reasons. These young students could be harmed by misguided assessment systems and poor use of the data. Some schools have implemented a "readiness" assessment system and, depending on the results, can suggest that some children are "not ready" for school (National Research Council, 2000). Table 6.1 outlines a number of reasons why assessment of young students is complex.

As Table 6.1 indicates, assessing preschool and kindergarten students is a balancing act. The need for information on skills and abilities must be balanced with the difficulties innate to early childhood assessments. Assessment of kindergarten students should be appropriate, beneficial, and useful; these assessments should not be used to make "high-stakes" decisions and should not be paper-and-pencil tests. Table 6.2 contains a list of recommendations by Scott-Little and Niemeyer (2001) for kindergarten assessments.

Table 6.1 Complexities of Preschool and Kindergarten Assessments

Child Development	This includes cognitive, emotional, language, physical, and social development. They are interrelated, and each impacts a student's success in school.
Unpredictable Development	Development is rapid and uneven in young children. Young students can change dramatically in a short period and may be highly developed in one area while behind in another area.
Standardized Assessments	Young students have not experienced standardized assessments, are still learning how to use pencils, have limited reading abilities, and have short attention spans.
Appropriate Assessments	Young students are better able to show what they know. Therefore, they need the right kind of assessment to share what they know and can do.
Previous Experiences	Preschool children have widely diverse experiences that will be reflected in their performance on assessments, instead of their potential for success in school.

Source: Adapted from Shepard, Kagan, and Wurtz (1998).

Table 6.2 Kindergarten Assessments

Kindergarten assessments must

- be consistent with purpose,
- be age appropriate,
- collect information on a range of child development indicators,
- be authentic,
- be culturally and linguistically aware,
- accommodate students with disabilities,
- collect information from multiple sources, and
- have reliability and validity.

Source: Adapted from Scott-Little and Niemeyer (2001, p. 11).

Designing a Kindergarten Assessment

So far in this chapter, the shoulds and should-nots of kindergarten assessments have been discussed. Also mentioned were the literacy assessments typically used with kindergarten students. It is necessary to assess kindergarten students, because the information that results is essential for planning lessons and monitoring progress. Good assessments benefit students, families, teachers, and the educational systems that support student learning. At this age, kindergarten students are developing rapidly. Table 6.3 outlines the steps involved in the process of designing a kindergarten assessment.

Table 6.3 Steps in Designing a Kindergarten Assessment

1. Form a team with people from many different perspectives. This team agrees to design the assessment, oversee its implementation, and interpret the results.

2. Determine the purpose of the assessment.

3. Specify what skills, abilities, or characteristics will be assessed. What types of information or data will you need to gather?

4. Select the appropriate assessment approach.

5. Identify specific assessment measures appropriate for collecting the necessary information.

6. Obtain as much information on each instrument as possible.

7. Evaluate instruments based on age-appropriate design and school population, application to development domain, authenticity, and logistical school requirements.

8. Evaluate the most promising instruments carefully.

9. Develop consensus from the team on which assessment instruments are best suited for your school.

10. Develop a plan for implementing the assessment system, including training, communication with all involved, obtaining the assessment instruments, logistical details for implementing, consent (if needed), collecting supplemental information, sharing assessment results, using the results, and evaluating the assessment process.

11. Conduct a trial run with a diverse, age-appropriate group of students.

12. Make revisions where necessary.

13. Implement the assessment system.

14. Evaluate the system's effectiveness.

15. Develop recommendations for revisions. These will be implemented in the next round of information collection.

Source: Adapted from Scott-Little and Niemeyer (2001, pp. 30–33).

Keep in mind that the cycle of review assessments should occur yearly. Considerations of validity, or whether the assessment tests what is being taught, as well as reliability, or whether the assessment shows consistent scores over multiple test administrations, are overriding. Work with your team to modify the early assessment and then field-test for these factors.

Making Connections

As you prepare for a brand-new year of kindergarten, make a list of what you want to know your students can do at the beginning of the year. How will you assess this? What types of assessments will you use? Will you use assessments already available in the school, or will you create your own? Will they be authentic assessments?

What Characterizes Authentic Grade-Level Literacy Assessments?

Authentic assessment and instruction, according to Newmann, King, and Carmichael (2007), comprises three criteria "as *construction of knowledge*, through the use of *disciplined inquiry* to produce discourse, products or performances that have *value beyond school*" (p. 3). **Construction of knowledge** is defined as the learners' ability to analyze and interpret new information or situations by applying basic and prior knowledge at higher levels of thinking. The discipline inquiry of authentic assessment and instruction refers to the learners' ability to apply prior knowledge to construct deep structures and convey these ideas through effective communication skills. The last criterion suggests that the learners are developing skills, knowledge, and competency beyond the classroom. That is, the learners should be acquiring knowledge that is transferable from grade to grade and beyond the school environment.

Research indicates that when learners are exposed to high levels of authentic assessment and instruction, they are more likely to experience greater academic achievement (Newmann et al., 2007). Thus, authentic assessment engages learners in authentic ways of learning, such as inquiry and problem-based learning. Inquiry and problem-based instruction engage students in critical and creative thinking and require teachers to instruct students how to think at higher levels and for deep understanding (Newmann et al., 2007). Student-generated portfolios and teacher observations are types of authentic assessment that are engaging, relevant, and meaningful. Assessment data from these types of measurements can drive how literacy instruction is developed and ensure that the students are gaining the skills and knowledge needed to be academically successful. Furthermore, student-generated portfolios encourage students to think critically about themselves as learners.

The use of authentic instruction and assessment go hand in hand. They are dependent on each other to ensure that learners are achieving high academic performance and teachers are providing the highest level of effective instruction. Assessment is a critical component in becoming an effective teacher, ensures that instruction is appropriate based on assessment data, promotes differentiation of instruction, and improves instruction.

Authentic Measures

> Reading assessment allows us to assess and understand the strengths and needs of each of our students. (Afflerbach, 2007, p. 4)

Authentic measures are instruments that inform us what learners have learned and are capable of doing. Employing authentic measures is a valuable way to assess learners' deep knowledge throughout the curriculum.

Through the use of authentic measures, students are engaged in critical thinking and developing their own learning goals based on instructional standards. For example, the use of student-generated portfolios is beneficial for promoting critical thinking, motivating learners, increasing self-esteem, and encouraging self-regulation, especially when assessment is used to focus on what learners are learning to improve academic achievement.

Hart (1994) suggests that authentic assessments have three components: design, structure, and grading. A few examples of Hart's concept on authentic assessments suggest that the design component of instruction should focus on learning relevant to the students' lives and encourage learning that engages a depth of knowledge. The structure component of instruction should promote ways of learning based on the needs of the students, and the grading component of instruction should be focused less on punitive errors but more on the students' strengths. The characteristics of these components demonstrate that instruction is constructed to engage learners in engaging, meaningful, and relevant learning activities. It is also evident that, with such assessments, learners will have more opportunities for higher-order thinking and greater depth of understanding. Furthermore, authentic assessments promote meaningful and real-life learning opportunities to engage and motivate learners as participants in their learning.

Making Connections

Reflect on a time when an assessment of your learning was based on an authentic assessment. Describe the assessment and use the components from Table 6.3 to describe the design, structure, and grading. How did the design support ease of administration? Did you generate a product or performance? How was the authentic assessment graded? What criterion was employed? Explain the implications for learning.

Authentic assessments ask students to perform engaging, real-world tasks that demonstrate meaningful application of essential knowledge and skills. Authentic assessments are also known as performance, alternative, or direct assessments. Authentic assessment allows for the integration of teaching, learning, and assessing. Students are learning in the process of developing a solution to a problem, teachers are facilitating the process, and the students' solutions to the problem become an assessment of how well they can meaningfully apply concepts (Mueller, 2014). Table 6.4 lists the basic steps in creating an authentic assessment.

Table 6.4 Creating an Authentic Assessment	
1. Questions to Ask	What should the students know and be able to do? List knowledge and skills they do have.
2. Standards	What indicates students have met these standards? Design or select a relevant authentic task to determine if standards have been met.
3. Authentic Tasks	What does good performance on the task look like? Identify and look for characteristics of good performance.
4. Criteria	How well did the students perform? Develop a rubric to discriminate among students' performances.
5. Rubric	How well should most students perform? List the minimum level at which most students should perform—the benchmark. What do students need to improve on? Information from the rubric will give students feedback and allow for adjustment of instruction.

Source: Adapted from Mueller (2012).

Early Childhood Literacy Assessments

Children start school with a diverse range of early literacy knowledge, skills, and understanding. Educators of young learners will want to employ student-centered assessments with care and consideration. Heed students' signals of boredom, tiredness, or anxiety, and halt testing if necessary. Fortunately, many early childhood assessments request oral responses from students, are brief, and are easily scored.

Kindergarten literacy assessments allow teachers to find out about each student's abilities. The assessments outlined below will help teachers develop effective lesson plans that build on what kindergarten students know and can do. By the end of kindergarten, most students should be able to

- read all or most of a simple book;
- give a short summary of a story that includes beginning, middle, and end;
- write a recognizable sentence;
- point to the first word to read when beginning a story and know about periods and capital letters;
- provide the first sound of words (New South Wales Department of Education and Training, n.d.).

Developmental differences should be kept in the forefront. We know young students learn to read at varying rates, and that is perfectly fine. Kindergartners who can barely write their names at the beginning of the school year may forge ahead and, by the end of the school year, write complete sentences.

Alphabetic Awareness

Teachers should also be aware that, in addition to reading alphabet books, they should provide children with further opportunities to learn about the alphabet and to use it in meaningful contexts. (Bradley & Jones, 2007, p. 459)

Alphabetic awareness refers to the ability to recognize the shapes, names, and sounds each letter represents, as well as the ability to write the letters (Bradley & Jones, 2007). Many researchers suggest that knowledge is critical to achieve academic success in alphabetic literacy. According to Hammill (2004), children's knowledge of letter names and sounds is the best predictor of their later reading and spelling abilities. These are the basic skills required to enhance the building blocks of reading and writing. In addition, a study conducted by Piasta, Purpura, and Wagner (2010) suggests that it is more advantageous to teach letter name and letter sound together than to teach them as isolated skill sets. Planning instruction that combines both skill sets fosters authentic instruction to engage learners in developing the skills needed to recognize letter name and make a connection to letter sound.

Furthermore, Rosenberg (2006) contends that learners must have the skills and abilities in phonemic awareness and alphabetic knowledge to be proficient in understanding the alphabet principle (awareness). Rosenberg further defines phonemic awareness "as the understanding that a word is made up of a series of discrete sounds (phonemes) and the ability to identify and manipulate those sounds in spoken words" (2006, p. 3), both of which are necessary to read fluently. Thus, for learners to be academically successful, they need frequent opportunities to become skillful and knowledgeable in alphabetic awareness. Instructional and remediation plans must integrate rich activities that engage learners in practical, relevant experiences that have meaningful applications not only for academic growth but also in real-life situations. Bradley and Jones (2007) recommend that, in addition to reading alphabet books, teachers should

1. encourage children to recognize their names and the names of their peers to help them think critically about the letters in the names,

2. promote dramatic play,

3. create a writing center,

4. engage children in writing class books to help learn the alphabet,

5. develop activities that allow children to create alphabet books, and

6. construct opportunities with alphabet books to maximize children's interaction with text.

Recommended Alphabet Books

Reading a variety of alphabet books holds students' interest with engaging stories and new concepts developed through pictures or photographs. As teachers read the book aloud, they should focus on two or three aspects, such as the storyline, illustrations, and alphabetic recognition. For kindergartners, books should be read multiple times; that way, you can engage students by attending to different features of the book as well as asking them to articulate letter names (Bennett-Armistead, Duke, & Moses, 2005).

Alphabet Under Construction by Denise Fleming (2002, Holt)

Baseball ABCs by Dorling Kindersley (2001, Dorling Kindersley)

The Butterfly Alphabet Book by Kjell Bloch Sandved (1996, Scholastic)

Chicka Chicka Boom Boom by Bill Martin Jr. and John Archambault (1989, Simon & Schuster)

Firefighters From A to Z by Chris L. Demarest (2000, Scholastic)

Girls A to Z by Eve Bunting (2002, Boyd Mills Press)

Q Is for Duck: An Alphabet Guessing Game by Mary Elting and Michael Folsom (1985, Clarion Books)

The Underwater Alphabet Book by Jerry Pallotta (1991, Charlesbridge) (Bradley & Jones, 2007, pp. 458–459)

Opportunities for Authentic Assessment of Alphabetic Knowledge

Classroom Alphabet Books. Along with commercial alphabet books, handmade alphabet books compiled as a classroom generate authentic opportunities for students to alphabetize and label classroom items. Use a disposable camera to allow students to take pictures of classroom items, and then place each picture on the correct alphabetical title page. Furthermore, use this collection as an ongoing assessment of alphabetic knowledge or interval progress monitoring.

Children's Alphabet Books. Have students select personal pictures, drawings of family members, or pictures of other things important to them that can be displayed on the correct pages, labeled with both lower- and uppercase letters. Assemble the book by singing the alphabet song slowly, and then laminate and bind it with string. Children can add to it throughout the year. What a morale booster!

Family Alphabet Books. When families compile alphabet books together, it offers a wonderful chance for parents and children to collaborate on choosing and labeling important "family treasures." Pets, relatives, vacation spots, neighbors, and other things surrounding the child's life can be placed in the alphabet book. A midyear "Family Night" could celebrate different family books.

Making Connections

Research and identify learners' literature books to focus on letter shape, name, sounds, and writing. Use these books to develop instructional strategies to teach letter shape, letter name, and letter sounds. Then think of and develop strategies to personalize these concepts. For example, engage learners in creating picture books with alliterations based on the letter(s) learned.

Print Awareness

To become skilled readers and writers, young children need to develop a conceptual grasp of the functions and conventions of printed language as well as an understanding of the instructional language used by teachers to talk about printed language. (Reutzel, Oda, & Moore, 1989, p. 197)

Print awareness refers to **print concepts** and print language. Research shows that when learners have early experiences in print awareness and print concepts, they will attain greater reading achievement. Concepts of print and its relationship to oral language are best understood when the teacher provides learners with "demonstrations, modeling and explanation" (Reutzel et al., 1989, p. 200). The authors also recommend instruction that is explicit and implicit. That is, learners should be engaged in instruction that clearly connects the new concepts to prior knowledge. Eliciting learners' prior knowledge is one way of ensuring depth of understanding and higher-order thinking.

Checklist of Skills for Concepts of Print

The child should know the following:

1. Functions of print

   - Print contains a message, makes sense, tells a story.
   - Print corresponds to speech—word for word.

2. Conventions of print

   - Print is print, no matter where it appears.
   - Printed words are made up of individual letters/sounds.
   - There is a difference between a letter and a word.
   - There is a difference between the first and the last letters of a word.
   - Words are separated by spaces.
   - Sentences are made up of words.
   - Sentences begin with a capital letter and end with a punctuation mark.
   - There is a particular starting point when reading.
   - Text is read from left to right with a return sweep to the next line.
   - Lines of text go from the top to the bottom of the page.
   - Text goes from the left page to the right page, and then the page is turned.

3. Book conventions

- The book has front and back covers.
- The book has a spine.
- The book is held right-side up.
- The book has a title page.
- The book has an author and sometimes an illustrator.
- The book has pages, and the left page is read before the right page.
- Pages are turned one at a time in order, from front to back (EducationFever.com).

The Concepts About Print (CAP) test developed by Clay (1979) assesses what children know about printed language. The CAP assessment evaluates learners' understanding of printed language, directional concepts (up/down, left/right, top/bottom, etc.), and text versus pictures when telling a story. The Observation Survey, another popular assessment developed by Clay (2002, 2005a), was approved as a tool to identify learners for Response to Intervention. This instrument is made up of six literacy tasks that measure the following:

- Letter identification—to determine which letters the child knows and the preferred mode of identification
- Word test—to determine if the child is building a personal resource of reading vocabulary
- Concepts about print—to determine what the child knows about the way spoken language is represented in print
- Writing vocabulary—to determine if the child is building a personal resource of known words that can be written in every detail
- Hearing and recording sounds in words—to assess phonemic awareness by determining how the child represents sounds in graphic form
- Text reading—to determine an appropriate level of text difficulty and to record what the child does when reading continuous text (using a running record; Clay, n.d.)

Developing an assessment for literacy development that is based on the concept of print awareness should be an integral part of every teacher's pedagogical repertoire. To support this proposal, a CAP instrument was codeveloped by one of our authors and a preschool teacher in the Fort Ann School District in New York. The CAP instrument was fine-tuned to meet the learning needs of kindergartners in rural northern New York State. The CAP test meets the assessment needs of prekindergarten students in this particular locale. It mirrors objectives the teacher evaluates and also reflects the New York State Common Core preschool literacy standards and Fountas and Pinnell's (2010) prekindergarten literacy skills.

The dialogue that ensued when developing Fort Ann's CAP instrument (reproduced in Table 6.5) was based on the following factors:

1. Instructional priorities: Will this objective be covered in the classroom? At what point in the year will the objective be covered? How critical is coverage of this objective, or would it be considered tertiary? Are all children able to fulfill this objective?

2. Aligning the CAP test with New York Common Core literacy objectives and the work of researchers in the field—in this case, that of Fountas and Pinnell.

3. CAP format: The traditional CAP test as developed by Clay uses premade books that align with the tasks required. We decided to do something similar, using both a children's book that students could hold (to check if they are read to) and cards to simplify the tasks for early learners.

4. Time allocated for the test: Our preschool teacher wrestled with time considerations (having students for only a little longer than 2 hours daily) for administering this instrument. We both agreed that quality student responses overrode time considerations. Also, we decided that three administrations of the instrument during the school year would provide an authentic snapshot of student literacy growth.

5. Reporting results to parents: Relaying student literacy progress to parents using the tasks found in the CAP instrument can appear simplistic and may be confusing; therefore, we did not feel that the report card was the best format for providing this information. We decided to attach a printout of the results alongside the instrument for discussion at a parent–teacher literacy conference.

The preschool teacher and another teacher constructed a little book similar to Clay's (2000) CAP test books *Sand, Stones,* and *Follow Me, Moon.* Because of size limitations, it is include in Appendix D (available at **www.sagepub.com/grantlit**). Please refer to it when you review the CAP test.

Reliability of the CAP test for each administration is considered; in other words, is the test consistent in measuring student print skills among test takers? Yearly, the preschool teacher will review the validity of the test to determine if it continues to measure what she plans to teach. We remain confident that the Fort Ann CAP test will assess the strengths and weaknesses of her preschool students in the areas of function of print, conventions of print, and book handling.

Letter–Sound Identification Assessment

Just as fluency is an important process in reading, so is phonemic awareness. Assessing learner ability in phonemic segmentation is not complicated and can yield important information about learners' reading skills. Rasinski, Padak, and Fawcett (2010) adapted the Yopp-Singer Test of Phonemic Segmentation to create a 22-item test (see Chapter 12), a short assessment that takes only a few minutes to administer.

Elkonin Boxes

Another tool that supports students as they learn to segment and blend is Elkonin boxes. Originally developed by the Russian psychologist David Elkonin, this strategy helps students identify the individual phonemes in a word and then blend them back together (Joseph, 1998). To begin, a rectangle divided into three or four boxes is placed in front of the child. The boxes correspond to the number of phonemes in the word. For instance, the word *fox* has three phonemes, /f/, /o/, and /x/. In addition to the boxes, the child is given a set of manipulatives such as bingo chips, beans, pennies, or tokens. Then, the teacher and the child pronounce the word slowly and count the number of phonemes

Table 6.5 Fort Ann Central School Pre-K Concepts of Print Assessment

Student Name:

- Circle Y for correct response; Circle N for incorrect
- Objectives in *italics*
- Teacher prompts in **bold**
- Use the *A Day on the Farm* book

	Beginning Test Date: _____	Mid-Year Test Date: _____	End-of-Year Test Date: _____
Beginning-of-Year Assessment* (two successful tests do not need to be administered a third time)			
1. *Identify parts of a book* Place book in front of child and prompt: **Point to the front of this book.**	Y N	Y N	Y N
2. *Purpose of print: Text vs. illustration* Show child the book open to pages 2 and 3, and prompt: **Point to the words on this page.**	Y N	Y N	Y N
3. *Identify point of origin* Show child the book open to pages 2 and 3, and prompt: **Point to the word I would read first.**	Y N	Y N	Y N
4. *Directionality: Left to right* Show child the book open to pages 2 and 3, and prompt: **Use your finger to show me which way I go when I read.**	Y N	Y N	Y N
5. *Letter in isolation* Show child the book open to pages 2 and 3, and prompt: **Point to one letter on this page.**	Y N	Y N	Y N
6. *Word in isolation* Show child page 4, and place word card "the" in front of him or her. Prompt: **The word on this card is *the*. Point to *the* word the on this page of the book.**	Y N	Y N	Y N
7. *Understands positional words* Show child page 5 and prompt: a. **Point to the first picture on this card.** b. **Point to the last picture on this card.**	a. Y N b. Y N	a. Y N b. Y N	a. Y N b. Y N

(Continued)

Table 6.5 (Continued)

	Beginning Test Date: _____	Mid-Year Test Date: _____	End-of-Year Test Date: _____

8. *Demonstrates prior experiences with literature*
Pretend you are reading this book to me.
Hand child the book, look for
   a. **Correct upright position**
   b. **Starts at beginning**
   c. **Turns each page until end**
	a. Y N
	b. Y N
	c. Y N
		a. Y N
		b. Y N
		c. Y N
			a. Y N
			b. Y N
			c. Y N

*Beginning-of-year assessment includes skills students are expected to master by the end of pre-K.

Mid-Year Assessment			

9. *Distinguish between upper-/lowercase letters*
Show child page 6, and prompt child to
   a. **Point to an uppercase letter.**
   b. **Point to a lowercase letter.**
	a. Y N
	b. Y N
		a. Y N
		b. Y N
			a. Y N
			b. Y N

10. *One-to-one letter/sound correspondence*
Show student page 9.
Point to the word *pig* and prompt:
   a. **Point to the letter that makes the sound /p/.**
Point to the word *cat* and prompt:
   b. **Point to the letter that makes the sound /t/.**
Point to the word *barn*, prompt:
   c. **Point to the letter that makes the sound /r/.**
	a. Y N
	
	b. Y N
	
	c. Y N
		a. Y N
		
		b. Y N
		
		c. Y N
			a. Y N
			
			b. Y N
			
			c. Y N

11. *Differentiates between letters/numerals* Show child page 7 and prompt: **Point to the two numbers in this sentence.**	Y N	Y N	Y N
12. *Recognizes words are a specific sequence* Show student page 7. Point to the word *live* in the text and prompt: **Tell me how many letters are in this word.**	Y N	Y N	Y N
13. *Recognizes common environmental print* Show child page 10 and prompt: **Point to the sign that says *Exit*.**	Y N	Y N	Y N

End-of-Year Assessment						
14. *Directionality: Top to bottom* Read first line of page 7 to child; point to each word as you read. Stop at end of first line and prompt: **Point to the line I read next.**	Y	N	Y	N	Y	N
15. *Conventions of writing: Punctuation* Show child page 7 and prompt: **A period tells me to stop at the end of a sentence. Can you point to a period on this page?**	Y	N	Y	N	Y	N
16. *One-to-one match of voice to print* Show child page 8 and prompt: **I am going to read this sentence to you. I want you to point to each word as I say it.**	Y	N	Y	N	Y	N

17. *Identifies role of author/illustrator*
Place book with title page facing child and prompt:
At least two people create a book. One is the author, and one is the illustrator.
   a. **Which one writes the words?**
   b. **Which one draws the pictures?**
   c. **Can you point to the title of this book?**
	a. Y
	b. Y
	c. Y
		N
		N
		N
			a. Y
			b. Y
			c. Y
				N
				N
				N
					a. Y
					b. Y
					c. Y
						N
						N
						N

they hear. As each phoneme is pronounced, the child pushes a chip into the corresponding box. After using the chips, the teacher and the student go back and write the letter that matches each phoneme in each the box. Then the child pronounces the phonemes again and pushes one chip into each box. Finally, the child removes all the chips from the boxes and then practices blending the phonemes back together several times as he or she drags one chip across the boxes (see Figure 6.1).

Figure 6.1
Elkonin Boxes

> **Making Connections**
>
> Develop several Elkonin boxes for practice. Remember, the number of phonemes heard is the basis for the use of Elkonin or sound boxes. Explain how this exercise is helpful for early word skills.

High-Frequency Word Lists

As we read words that flow across the pages of text, we are constructing meaning, creating visual images, and interpreting text in a dynamic process. Thus, to read for comprehension, readers must develop some basic skills such as phonics and phonemic awareness, and the ability to read fluently. The strength of skills and competency to read while automatically recognizing words plays an integral role in how we construct meaning of text. Engaging and instructing learners in developing and building vocabulary through lists of **high-frequency words** (see Table 6.6) is one way to improve fluency as well as construct meaning. Rasinski and colleagues (2010) assert that the weaker and less proficient reader will expend excessive time decoding and deciphering the words and commit less time to constructing meaning of the text. Thus, as teachers, you must be able to develop instruction to help learners automatically recognize and decode words.

To locate high-frequency lists for Grades 1 and 2, look toward online resources. Remember, identification of high-frequency words is developmental in nature. A degree of automaticity in identifying these common words should be the goal for the end of each primary grade.

> **Making Connections**
>
> Discuss the development of appropriate authentic assessments to evaluate learners' ability to recognize and use high-frequency word lists. How does instruction and assessment of high-frequency words prepare the learner beyond the classroom?

Phonics

Phonics can be defined as the study of the relationship between the phonological aspects and the written symbols or graphic elements of language (Clay, 1993; Fountas & Pinnell, 1996; Reutzel & Cooter, 2013). Phonics instruction should be systematic and predictable (National Reading Panel, 2000; Reutzel & Cooter, 2013). Children in the early grades need a variety of experiences with letters, digraphs, clusters, vowels, syllables, prefixes, suffixes, root words, and phrases (Clay, 1993). Systematic phonics instruction is an important part of any successful classroom reading program (National Reading Panel, 2000). Prior to beginning instruction, it is important to

Table 6.6 High-Frequency Word List Assessment

Directions: Check off as kindergarten students can say each word on the list. Administer three or four times in the course of the school year. Make sure to date when students achieve word pronunciation.

Word	Yes	Date
a		
am		
an		
and		
at		
can		
do		
go		
he		
I		
in		
is		
it		
like		
me		
my		
no		
on		
see		
so		
the		
to		
up		
we		
you		

Source: Pinnell, Fountas, and Giacobbe (1998). Taken from *Word Matters: Testing Phonics and Spelling in the Reading/Writing Classroom* by Gay Su Pinnell and Irene C. Fountas. Copyright © 1998 by by Gay Su Pinnell and Irene C. Fountas. Published by Heinemann, Portsmouth, NH. Reprinted by permission of the publisher.

determine students' strengths and needs. Three assessments that may be used to screen young students will be discussed in this chapter: the Letter Naming Test, the Phonics Inventory, and the Consortium on Reading Excellence (CORE) Phonics Survey.

Letter Identification Assessment

Of all the readiness skills that are traditionally evaluated, letter identification seems to be the strongest predictor on its own (Snow, Burns, & Griffin, 1998). Measuring a young child's ability to name the letters of the alphabet, when shown in random order, is nearly as successful as an entire battery of assessments in predicting that child's future reading accomplishments (Snow et al., 1998). Letter identification or alphabet knowledge is a very easy assessment to administer. The teacher provides the student with a copy of both the upper- and lowercase letters of the alphabet. The letters should be arranged randomly, with the uppercase letters grouped together on one sheet and the lowercase letters on another. The student is asked to say the name of the letter when the teacher points to it (University of Oregon Center on Teaching and Learning, 2014). Benchmarks or expectations are identified for each grade level, usually kindergarten and first grade. Most districts have developed their own version of this assessment. Clay (1979) has developed a version as well.

Making Connections

Set up a letter identification assessment that you could use with primary learners. The letters should be arranged randomly using a large font size. In addition, pick a font style that replicates a simple alphabetic form that young learners might see often. Avoid font styles that have elaborate swirls or sharp lines. Use two sheets, and place uppercase letters on one and lowercase letters on the other. Make up a scoring function on the sheets for data collection. If you laminate this assessment, it can be filed away for future use.

Note: Keep in mind that recognition of letters in isolation may prove difficult for primary learners. It is beneficial to place letters in the context of something children know or can relate to.

The Phonics Inventory

The Phonics Inventory was developed by Thomas Gunning (2013) and is fairly simple to administer. The inventory contains a list of 50 words that assess a student's knowledge of vowels and vowel patterns (Gunning, 2013). First, the teacher creates a series of word cards for each word on the list. Next, he or she presents one card at a time to the student and asks the student to read the word. When the student misses a word or does not respond within 5 seconds, the teacher reads the word to the student. Students continue to read the words until they miss five in a row. Once this happens, the teacher stops and calculates the student's score. There are five levels in the inventory: 1 to 10, short-vowel patterns; 11 to 20, short vowels with clusters; 21 to 30, long vowels; 31 to 40, r-vowels; 41 to 50, other vowels. The level at which the teacher should begin teaching is the highest level where the student identifies 8 out of 10 words correctly.

Consortium on Reading Excellence (CORE) Phonics Survey

Another phonics assessment that may be used as a screening tool or an outcome measure is the Consortium on Reading Excellence (CORE) Phonics Survey. This assessment contains 12 sections that test students' knowledge of letter names, consonants, vowels, blends, digraphs, single-syllable words, and multisyllabic words. The assessment spans Grades K–3, and the instructions include charts outlining a suggested timeline for administration. Students work toward mastery, and guidelines are identified so teachers can group their students based on their scores. Students may be grouped into three levels: benchmark, strategic, and intensive.

Phonological Awareness Literacy Screening (PALS)

Oral language is the foundation for literacy development, and children with impairments in speech and language often experience difficulty developing literacy skills (Justice, Invernizzi, & Meier, 2002). Therefore, it is very important that teachers screen their students early to identify any gaps in phonological awareness. PALS 1–3 consists of four parts: an entry-level screening that includes spelling and word recognition in isolation; Level A, which includes running records, timed passage readings, comprehension, and fluency assessments; Level B, which includes alphabet recognition, letter sounds, and concept of word assessments; and Level C, which includes blending and sound-to-letter assessments (Invernizzi, Meier, & Juel, 2010).

Level C: Phonemic Awareness

To assess blending, the teacher reads a word aloud, separating each phoneme, and asks the student to blend the phonemes back together and tell him or her the word. For example, the teacher might say, "/s/-/a/-/t/," and the student would respond with "sat." To assess segmenting, the teacher reads a word aloud and asks the student to identify the letter or sound at the beginning, middle, or end of the word. For instance, the teacher might say "mop" and ask the student to tell him or her which letter or sound the word begins with. The student would respond with either *m* or /m/.

Tile Test

Another assessment that is both practical and efficient is the Tile Test. The Tile Test is a diagnostic tool used to assess individual students' understanding of letters, sounds, words, and sentences (Norman & Calfee, 2004). It can be given in about 15 minutes and is very manageable for the classroom teacher. To administer the test, the teacher uses letter tiles similar to those used in the game Scrabble® by Hasbro. The test includes four sections. In the first section, the teacher places two vowel tiles (*a, i*) and six consonant tiles (*p, m, n, s, d, t*) in front of the student and asks the student to point to each letter as he or she names it. Next, the teacher points to a letter tile and asks the student to tell him or her the name of the letter and the sound the letter makes. In the second section of the test, the teacher uses the letter tiles to create several three-letter words for the student to read. Then, the teacher will read a word and ask the student to use the tiles to spell the word. Throughout this section, the teacher will also ask the student several metalinguistic questions to better understand the student's thinking and problem-solving abilities (Norman & Calfee, 2004). In the third section of the test, students are asked to read a series of 17 sight words. The last section of the test includes several sentences that the student is asked to read and several sentences that the student is asked to build. An example of two items on the Tile Test is shown in Figure 6.2.

Figure 6.2
Sample Items
From Tile Test

Letters and Sounds

Display letter tiles M, A, P, I.

M	A	P	I

"Here are some letters. I'll say the name of a letter and ask you to point to the letter. Point to the tile that has the letter *M*."

Record. Continue procedure with each letter.

"Now, I'll point to a tile and you'll tell me two things about the letter: first, the name of the letter and, second, the sound it makes."

Record.

Identification	Name	Sound
M		
A		
P		
I		

Words

Add letter tile T.

M	A	P	I	T

Decoding

"Now let's put some letters together to make words. I'll go first and make a word, and then I'll ask you to read it for me."

Manipulate only necessary letters. Stop after sat and ask the first metalinguistic question.

pat _____

P	A	T

sat* _____

S	A	T

Metalinguistic question:

"How did you know to say *sat* (or other pronunciation) that way?"

_____

_____

_____

Source: Adapted from Norman and Calfee (2004).

Letter Naming Test

The Letter Naming Test is an alphabet identification assessment designed to assess student knowledge of letters. For this assessment, primary students are shown a sheet with upper- and lowercase letters mixed together randomly and asked to name as many letters as they can within a time frame designated by the test administrator. If a student does not recognize a letter, he or she is told the letter. There are a total of 48 letters on the sheet. The student's score is based on the number of letters he or she named correctly in 1 minute. Students are considered at risk if they rank in the lowest 20% of all students tested in their district. (See Figure 6.3 for a sample test template.)

Test												
K	r	S	h	J	m	Q	g	s	l	o	d	U
P	f	n	a	e	G	b	x	A	y	B	s	
Q	D	F	H	j	k	M	b	V	C	i		
L	Z	X	c	v	N	l	p	O	z	f	u	

Number correct _____ /48

Figure 6.3
Sample Letter Naming Test Template

Assessing phonics knowledge using commercial inventories is one way teachers can save time in undertaking assessment tasks. However, if the test item does not make sense for the learner, little data of any significance will be yielded. We believe all forms of evaluation are meant to be modified with learners in mind. Many districts select certain test components to administer, while others generate their own district-based tests. Phonics assessments are easily modified based on learners' needs, especially those of English language learners.

Assessing Kindergarten Students Who Are English Language Learners

Any English-speaking student who is at the beginning of his or her literacy education goes through five stages related to learning parts of speech, patterns of words, vocabulary meanings, reading/writing, and spelling. By Grades 3–5, English language learners, or ELLs, have already developed an extensive vocabulary in their first language; their transition into using English parts of speech and literacy requires focusing on the study of sounds. Depending on their first language, these ELL students may be able to link words together to form *cognate understandings*; that is, because certain words sound similar in their first language and in English, they may assume that the meanings of the words are the same. With some words, this can be beneficial; however, there is a great possibility of forming *false cognates*. To prevent such misunderstandings, using a strategy involving words and visuals is crucial to help ELLs make the correct connections. In addition to using a visual tool, such as Elkonin boxes, to promote literacy links, using music, such as the alphabet song, promotes word and sound identification repetition. One strategy to support early second-language learners is the vocabulary visual strategy, shown in Figure 6.4.

Using a four-square template, choose a vocabulary word to work on with your ELL student. Fold the paper into four so you can isolate the information and present the strategy in steps. In the first square (top left), draw a detailed picture that represents the vocabulary word. In the second square (bottom left), write the word. Say the word to your student, and ask him or her to identify the letters in the word. In the third square (bottom right), spell the word phonetically. Encourage your student to identify the letters in this representation of the word and attempt to sound out the word. Finally, in the fourth square (top right), direct your student to draw his or her own version of the word and, if appropriate, to write the word. This strategy will assist with the student's vocabulary connections to real-world applications and can be easily varied to incorporate individual interests and abilities (you may choose to use two or three boxes instead of four, for example).

Stages of Literacy

ELLs as well as students with special needs must experience 10 stages of English literacy development, despite their preexisting literacy capabilities in their first language. At the core of the English language, there are three basic areas of growth: sound, pattern,

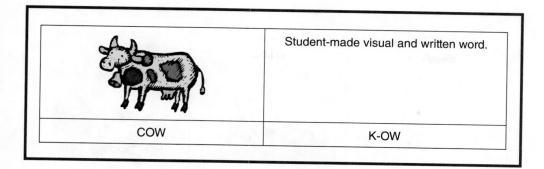

	Student-made visual and written word.
COW	K-OW

Figure 6.4
Elkonin Box
Sample

and meaning. These areas are applied within reading, writing, and spelling, which must be taught together. The stages for reading/writing are as follows:

1. *Emergent:* Pretending to read and write.

2. *Beginning:* Reading aloud, sentences not fluent; tracking words with finger while reading; writing letters, words, basic sentences, small paragraphs.

3. *Transitional:* Reading becomes more fluent—students recognize phrases and begin to read somewhat expressively; writing begins to have more organization and longer paragraphs.

4. *Intermediate/advanced:* Fluent, expressive reading; reading various genres; continued vocabulary growth with experience; fluent writing with expression and a personal voice; critical thinking, creativity, and reflection.

Spelling has different stages than does reading/writing. Spelling in the English language can be a difficult and frustrating transition for ELL students, and it is not uncommon to see students use words in their first language intermittently within their writing. In some cases, you will have students whose alphabets are radically different from the English alphabet, such as Cyrillic (Russian), Arabic, African indigenous languages, Asian languages, and Hebrew. With these students, they may have some understanding of the English alphabet and can write in their language using conventional English letters, or they may have no understanding and must be taught from the most emergent level of English literacy education.

In this situation, one of the best strategies is to find an example of a bilingual alphabet, or create one of your own, including how the letter sounds in both languages and a picture that starts with the letter that can become a word–visual connection. Teachers can make up their own bilingual alphabet charts (see the sample in Figure 6.5).

An underlying assessment principle in kindergarten is to encourage children to show what they know and can do. This is especially important when working with ELLs because we want them to take the risks involved in becoming functioning members of their English-language instructional setting (Ontario Ministry of Education, 2007). ELLs face many challenges, all of which must be considered during assessment. For example, their ability to acquire and demonstrate new knowledge may be influenced by an inability to understand or use the language of the classroom.

Figure 6.5
Spanish Translation of High-Frequency Words

Source: Adapted from SpanglishBaby (2011).

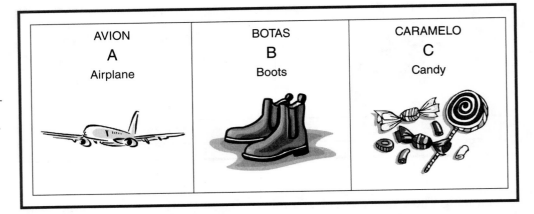

AVION	BOTAS	CARAMELO
A	B	C
Airplane	Boots	Candy

Asking probing questions of ELLs in the early stages of acquiring English may be unproductive. At this stage, observation would be more suited to collecting assessment information. There are a number of alternative strategies for assessing ELLs' learning if they can't tell you what they know:

- Observing ELLs in small and large groups, at centers, during routines, using familiar materials, trying new things, and when taking turns
- Observing book handling skills, modeling the rhythm of language after hearing read-alouds, pointing to familiar words, writing samples, vocabulary recognition, making names with classroom materials, and computer interaction
- Observing ELLs copying or demonstrating what they observe, beginning to use contextualized language, using classroom materials, and following actions (Ontario Ministry for Education, 2007)

Making Connections

Refer back to the kindergarten assessments listed earlier in this chapter, such as print awareness, sound–letter identification, and high-frequency words. How would you accommodate your kindergarten students who are ELLs?

Assessing Kindergarten Students With Special Needs

Kindergarten students with special needs may also require accommodations or alternative standardized and nonstandardized assessments. Often, the assessment instrument is not sensitive to their needs. The resulting test scores can actually be meaningless because they do not represent these students' abilities.

No Child Left Behind forbids schools from excluding students with special needs from the educational accountability system. Most students with special needs should attempt to take the same assessment as their peers; however, the Individuals with

Disabilities Act outlines accommodations/modifications for when the traditional assessment situations are not applicable. Accommodations provide different ways for students to receive information or communicate their knowledge back to the teacher; standards or expectations remain the same. Modifications refer to changes in the delivery, content, or instructional level of districtwide or statewide tests for students receiving special education services; expectations or standards are lowered (GreatSchools Staff, 2014).

Students with physical disabilities may not be physically able to perform the task requirements (Scott-Little & Niemeyer, 2001). Some students with special needs do not follow the typical developmental pattern and have not yet developed the skills of their peers. These students may have difficulty with sequence items on an assessment. Other students may have sensory impairments, such as hearing or vision impairments, and during assessments communication is often essential. For these students to be successful, gestures, sign language, or explicit and detailed verbal instructions will be necessary. In addition, kindergarten students with cognitive or emotional disabilities typically require a longer response time for particular items (Scott-Little & Niemeyer, 2001). These are just a few examples of factors requiring consideration when selecting reading or writing assessments for students with special needs.

In addition to the previously mentioned areas, parent participation should be considered as well. Parents are a wealth of knowledge where their children are concerned. They know their children's abilities and are excellent sources regarding adaptations. Also, take advantage of school specialists, such as the resource and learning center teacher; they are invaluable during the assessment planning process and will ensure that assessment strategies are fair and valid for students with special needs (Scott-Little & Niemeyer, 2001).

Sometimes, even with the appropriate accommodations, alternative assessments may be necessary. Alternate assessments are designed for the small number of students with special needs who are unable to participate in the regular assessments even with accommodations. An alternative assessment may include materials collected under several different circumstances, such as teacher observation, student work samples produced during regular classroom instruction that show mastery of a specific instructional strategy, or standardized performance tasks. Currently, an alternate assessment must be aligned with the state's content standards to serve the purposes of assessment under Title I and must be implemented in a manner that supports use of the results as an indicator of adequate yearly progress. An alternate assessment may be scored against grade-level standards or alternate achievement standards (American Speech-Language-Hearing Association, 2009).

Some additional alternative assessment solutions include the following:

- Using assistive technology, such as iPad, iPod, or iPhone apps
- Extending standard example—connecting text to own experience, exploring and responding to different forms of text, and following oral–graphic directions
- Using self-selected text rather than teacher-selected text
- Demonstrating response to voice and/or sounds within a literacy context or response to visual text
- Assessing a student with special needs only after repeated exposure to materials (Marentette, 2009)

Making Connections

Refer back to the kindergarten assessments listed earlier in the chapter, such as print awareness, sound–letter identification, and high-frequency words. How would you accommodate your kindergarten students who have special needs?

Key Terms

alphabetic awareness

authentic measures

construction of knowledge

high-frequency words

print awareness

print concepts

Website Resources

- **"Informal Reading Assessments: Examples," Reading Rockets**

This site provides informal reading assessments for one-on-one use. The site gives explicit instruction on how to assess kindergarten students on concepts of print, rhyming, identifying initial sounds, blending words, phoneme segmentation, phoneme manipulation, and phoneme deletion. The site also includes an easy to re-create sample of a recording chart for each assessment. For more information, go to **www.readingrockets.org/article/3411**.

- **PALS: Phonological Awareness Literacy Screening**

This site offers assessment tools for pre-K through Grade 3. The kindergarten assessments measure students' knowledge of several literacy fundamentals: phonological awareness, alphabet recognition, concept of words, knowledge of letter sounds, and spelling. Each assessment is accompanied by a video showing a teacher giving the assessment and scoring it. For more information, go to **http://pals.virginia.edu**.

Student Study Site: Visit the Student Study Site at **www.sagepub.com/grantlit** to access additional study tools including eFlashcards, web resources, and online-only appendices.

CHAPTER 7

Early Childhood Grade-Level Assessments

Spelling, Vocabulary, Fluency, Comprehension, and Writing

Gwyn W. Senokossoff

Common Core State Standards	
Conventions of Standard English	*L.2.2* Demonstrate command of the conventions of standard English capitalization, punctuation, and spelling when writing.
Vocabulary Acquisition and Use	*L.1.4* Determine or clarify the meaning of unknown and multiple-meaning words and phrases based on *grade 1 reading and content*, choosing flexibly from an array of strategies.
Writing Standards	*W.1.2* Write informative/explanatory texts in which they name a topic, supply some facts about the topic, and provide some sense of closure.
Fluency	*RF.1.4* Read with sufficient accuracy and fluency to support comprehension.

Source: © Copyright 2010. National Governors Association Center for Best Practices and Council of Chief State School Officers. All rights reserved.

FOCUS QUESTIONS

1. How are anecdotal records best used in observational kidwatching? What questions should a teacher reflect on before deciding his or her purpose for engaging in student observation?

2. Identify and characterize the spelling stages students advance through. How would you characterize the growth through each stage?

3. What different types of vocabulary do students hold? How do you believe you could effectively assess vocabulary growth authentically?

4. How can the reading teacher measure fluency in the primary reader? What considerations should be taken into account?

5. Describe the components of the six traits of writing. How could you authentically assess beginning writers based on emergent writing components?

Words in Action

Objective Evidence

One of your future frustrations may be taking the obvious student conversations and observations, and turning them into "objective evidence" that an administrator can use to defend your effectiveness in assessing. Here are some suggestions from an auditing expert that may prove helpful:

1. Have a basic checklist of behaviors you are assessing for. This helps demonstrate that you are looking for the behaviors equally from all students, not just assuming you see it in your most competent students (see Table 7.1).

2. Have a comments section where you can note exceptional behaviors, or ones you hadn't necessarily intended to assess for that day.

3. Carry sticky notes or index cards or whatever with you, but be sure to keep the sticky, card, or whatever. Scan them and save them for your records. Review them and look for trends.

4. Date your observations.

Table 7.1 Basic Observation Template

Name	Vocabulary	Spelling	Phonics	Teamwork
Morgan	X	X		X
Abby	X		X	X

Name	Vocabulary	Spelling	Phonics	Teamwork
AJ	X		X	X
Tony			X	X
Comments:				

Assessment for young children should be "developmentally appropriate, culturally and linguistically responsive, tied to children's daily activities, supported by professional development, inclusive of families," and used for instructional decision making, to identify individual needs, and to improve early interventions (National Association for the Education of Young Children and National Association of Early Childhood Specialists in State Departments of Education, 2003, p. 1).

What Is Assessment, and How Is It Employed in the Early Grades?

Assessment is collecting and analyzing data to make decisions about how children are performing and growing. (Cunningham & Allington, 2011, p. 205)

Rather than becoming one more item on a to-do list, assessment should be an extension of good teaching (Cunningham & Allington, 2011). Effective early childhood teachers learn to observe and document their students' attempts at reading and writing in a variety of informal and formal instructional situations (Rasinski, Padak, & Fawcett, 2010). Yetta Goodman (1985) coined the term **kidwatching** for this type of observation, and you will encounter this term throughout the text. Observation is a great first step in the assessment process. Teachers can develop a general idea of how their students are performing in the classroom, identify the students who may need more support, and monitor progress.

Observation or Kidwatching as Assessment

To begin using observation, teachers develop a plan (Billman & Sherman, 2003). They decide each of the following:

- Who will be observed
- In what setting (i.e., word work, reading group, learning centers)

- What behaviors will be noted
- When and how long the observation will be
- How the observation will be documented
- For what purpose the information will be used

Teachers use observation to screen and monitor students' progress in three main areas: physical development, cognitive development, and social/emotional development (Billman & Sherman, 2003). In relation to physical development, teachers need to note any problems with fine motor skills that may affect students' ability to write, type, or draw. They also monitor students' vision and note any potential problems that could affect a student's ability to read. In addition, they document any differences in students' speech and hearing that may prevent them from hearing or speaking the language correctly. Finally, nutrition and good sleep habits are important to ensure students' focus on learning. If teachers notice a student falling asleep repeatedly in class, this could indicate the need for a parent–teacher conference to determine better ways to support the student at home and at school.

With cognitive development, teachers monitor students' thinking, learning, and problem solving. They observe students' language and interactions with texts for authentic purposes to develop insights about the effect of literacy instruction on their growth (Rasinski et al., 2010). As effective kidwatchers, they notice delays in language, reading, and writing development. They also notice whether students have trouble paying attention. These teachers learn to recognize the difference between a recurring pattern of behaviors and an isolated behavior by observing students often and over time (Rasinski et al., 2010).

The third area of development that effective early childhood teachers monitor through observation is the social/emotional area (Billman & Sherman, 2003). A child's success in school affects his or her self-esteem. By first grade, children are moving out of Piaget's (1954) egocentric stage of development and becoming more social. Learning moves from a focus on self to recognizing oneself as part of a group, with family, friends, and culture. Effective teachers observe the ways their students interact with one another and in a variety of group settings. By noting any developmental delays, behavioral issues, or emotional needs, the teacher is able to seek and provide the support required for each child.

To make the best use of classroom observations, teachers must maintain good records (Rasinski et al., 2010). These records may take a variety of forms, including anecdotal records, checklists, charts, interviews, and inventories. One of the simplest forms to use, the anecdotal record, is a brief description of an activity or behavior that offers information about a student (Gunning, 2010). According to Gunning, an anecdotal record includes a brief summary of an event and the date and time the event occurred. When recording observations, teachers should describe the student's behaviors exactly as they see them and avoid making judgments about the student based solely on one observation. Repeated observations over time provide the evidence needed to evaluate a student accurately. To prevent failure in reading, teachers observe what children are able to do and use what they cannot do to plan for instruction (Clay, 2005a). By recording a student's strengths and areas where growth is needed, teachers will see patterns that help them plan instruction (Gunning, 2010).

Using Anecdotal Records

Anecdotal records may be recorded in several ways. Some teachers choose to carry around sticky notes on a clipboard because the notes can be easily transferred to a notebook later. Others may choose to use index cards that can later be dropped into the child's folder. Or, with the advent of smartphones and iPads, some teachers prefer to record their observations electronically. An example of an anecdotal record sheet that can be copied and later placed in a binder is provided in Figure 7.1.

Student(s): _____ Date: _____
Event: _____ Time: _____
Description:

Figure 7.1
Anecdotal
Record Sheet

While anecdotal records are probably the simplest way to record observations, some teachers prefer checklists that outline relevant behaviors to guide the observation. An example of a reading/writing behaviors checklist for early readers is shown in Table 7.2.

Table 7.2 Literate Behaviors Checklist

Name:

Behaviors to Observe	Date	Comments
Reading Behaviors		
Enjoys listening to stories		
Chooses to read independently		
Shows enjoyment of books through discussion or creative means		
Developing the ability to retell longer stories in sequence		
Developing the ability to recall facts from informational texts		
Uses illustrations as a clue to make meaning		

(Continued)

Table 7.2 (Continued)

Behaviors to Observe	Date	Comments
Beginning to use language structure to figure out new words		
Uses visual information (letters and words) to figure out new words		
Rereads to self-correct or confirm		
Makes several attempts to figure out new words		
Expects to get meaning from text		
Beginning to cross-check using a number of meaning-making strategies		
Self-corrects most of the time		
Recognizes high-frequency words		
Reads with phrasing and fluency		

Writing Behaviors		
Enjoys writing stories		
Uses invented spelling in writing		
Uses known sight words in writing		
Beginning to use punctuation in writing		
Uses capital letters correctly		
Adding more detail to stories		
Stories make sense		

Positive Literacy Behaviors		

Participates confidently in
  ❑ shared reading
  ❑ shared writing
  ❑ guided reading
  ❑ guided writing
  ❑ writer's workshop		

Source: Adapted from Fountas and Pinnell (1996) and Orange County Public Schools, Orlando, FL (1992).

Regardless of the format used, observation is an important and effective form of assessment for early childhood teachers.

Making Connections

The Literate Behaviors Checklist (Table 7.2) provides a format for teachers to comment on early literacy growth in a positive manner. How might you use this checklist effectively for ongoing student assessment? Talk with your text partner and decide on organizational considerations that will aid use of the checklist.

English Orthography

Understanding the layers inherent in English orthography is critical for teachers. Good readers consciously connect the dots to be effective spellers; however, they must be willing to apply their orthographic skills to their advantage.

Orthographic awareness is the knowledge of the symbols in a writing system (Fountas & Pinnell, 1998). When combined with phonological awareness, students have the key elements they need to study words. Children use phonological information such as words, letter clusters, syllables, and phrases to connect their oral language with written language while they read (Fountas & Pinnell, 1998).

English orthography comprises three layers: the alphabetic, pattern, and meaning layers (Bear, Invernizzi, Templeton, & Johnston, 2008; see Figure 7.2). Each layer provides information about different aspects of the English language. As students progress through the layers, they develop stronger reading and writing skills. In the alphabetic layer, students learn that sounds are represented by letters and that English is read from left to right (Bear et al., 2008). Next, in the pattern layer, children learn that letters combine to form patterns and that there are patterns within syllables and syllable patterns within words. Finally, in the meaning layer, readers learn that groups of letters can signify meaning directly.

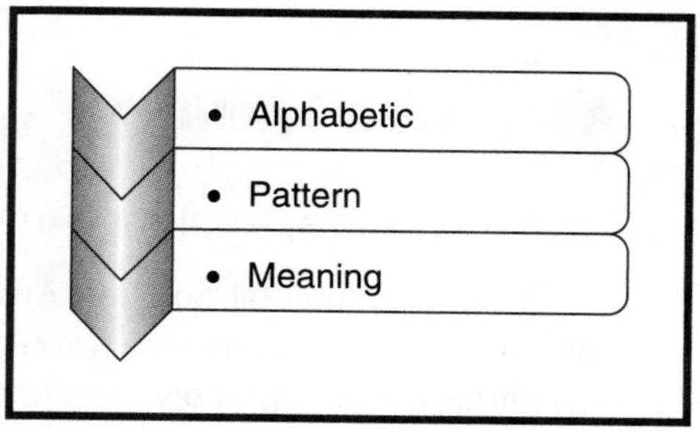

The acquisition of orthographic knowledge, like phonological knowledge, is developmental (Bear et al., 2008). The stages used most often are emergent, letter-name alphabetic, within-word pattern, syllables and affixes, and derivational relations (Bear et al., 2008). These are the stages teachers should consider when planning instruction in word work.

Figure 7.2

English Orthography

Source: Adapted from Bear et al. (2008).

- Alphabetic
- Pattern
- Meaning

Making Connections

Consider various types of spelling challenges students may face as emergent spellers. Plan your method for supporting young students as spellers through explaining emergent spelling and writing to parents. How would you explain to the parent of a first grader that attempts at spelling through trial and error are normal and encouraged?

Spelling Stages

The stages of spelling are characterized from early emergent spellers through conventional spellers. As students proceed through the stages, they grow in spelling proficiency and ease.

- *Emergent spelling:* Students in this stage of spelling have no sense of the alphabetic principle and have not yet developed the concept of words (Bear et al., 2008). They do create scribbles, mock letters, and symbols (Bear et al., 2008). They also engage in pretend reading and writing.
- *Letter-name alphabetic:* Students in this stage of development move from partial to full phoneme segmentation (Bear et al., 2008). They focus primarily on beginning and ending sounds. Toward the end of this stage, they begin to identify short vowel sounds as well as consonant blends and digraphs (Bear et al., 2008).
- *Within-word pattern:* Children in the within-word pattern stage have a good grasp of consonant blends and digraphs, short and long vowels in single-syllable words, r-controlled vowels, and some common suffixes (Bear et al., 2008).
- *Syllables and affixes*: In the syllables and affixes stage, students continue to build on their previous knowledge and are also beginning to understand consonant doubling (Bear et al., 2008). In addition, they understand long-vowel patterns in accented syllables (Bear et al., 2008).
- *Derivational relations*: Students in this stage spell most words conventionally (Bear et al., 2008). Instruction for students in this stage usually focuses on word histories and etymologies.

Assessing Spelling

Developmental Spelling Analysis

The Developmental Spelling Analysis (DSA) consists of two parts: the Screening Inventory and the two Feature Inventories (Ganske, 2014). The first part of the DSA, the Screening Inventory, allows teachers to determine their students' spelling stages. To begin, the teacher dictates a list of 20 words to students and asks them to do their best to spell each word. The teacher also lets the students know that this assessment will not be graded but will be used to provide information to help in teaching spelling. The list of 20 words is divided into sets of five, and each set is more difficult than the previous one. When a student is unable to spell fewer than two words out of five in a given set, the teacher may stop assessing that student.

After the Screening Inventory has been administered and the teacher is able to predict the students' spelling stages, he or she will select the Feature Inventory that matches each student's stage of spelling development. With the Feature Inventory, the teacher is able to determine a student's specific strengths and needs within his or her spelling stage. Like the Screening Inventory, students are asked to spell a series of words, and based on their spelling errors, the teacher is able to ascertain each student's specific needs.

Elementary Spelling Inventory

The Elementary Spelling Inventory is similar to the DSA. Like the DSA, the teacher explains to the students that they may be asked to spell some words they do not know and have not studied yet (Bear et al., 2008). The teacher reassures the students that they will not be graded. Students will be asked to number a sheet of paper from 1 to 25, and then the teacher will dictate the words. During the assessment, the teacher observes the students' progress and if a student appears frustrated or is not attempting to spell a word, the teacher may choose to stop testing that student. After the students complete as much of the assessment as they can, the teacher analyzes and interprets their spelling errors. Like the Feature Inventories of the DSA, the words included in the Elementary Spelling Inventory contain features from each of the five stages of spelling development, as described earlier. The teacher is able to analyze students' errors and determine their specific needs.

Vocabulary

Vocabulary can be defined as the collection of words and their meanings that a person uses. There are four types of vocabulary: receptive or listening, oral or speaking, print or reading, and productive or written (Kamil & Hiebert, 2005; Reutzel & Cooter, 2013). According to Reutzel and Cooter, the four vocabulary types are defined this way:

- Listening vocabulary includes the words students hear and understand.
- Speaking vocabulary is made up of the words we speak.
- Reading vocabulary includes the words we comprehend when we read.
- Written vocabulary is composed of the words we use in our writing.

Making Connections

In thinking about the types of vocabulary—listening, speaking, reading, and writing—judge their predominance through the different ages of students. In other words, for early learners, what type of vocabulary would contain the largest number of retrievable words? Why do you believe that to be true? For Grades 3–5, what vocabulary would contain the most words and which would contain the least? Provide evidence for your thinking. For middle school students, what vocabulary might be predominant? As an adult learner, which vocabulary is your strength? Explain your answer.

A student's vocabulary knowledge and skill directly influences his or her proficiency in reading comprehension (National Reading Panel, 2000). Therefore, vocabulary should be an important part of daily reading instruction. To develop students' vocabulary skills, teachers must encourage wide reading, individual word instruction, the use of vocabulary strategies, and an interest in words and their meanings (Graves, 2000, as cited in Lane & Allen, 2010).

The average high school student has a vocabulary of 50,000 words and learns about 3,500 new words each year (Graves & Watts-Taffe, 2002, as cited in Lane & Allen, 2010). To help students build a vocabulary of this size, teachers must provide multiple opportunities for "incidental learning" as well as direct instruction (National Reading Panel, 2000). It is unreasonable to think that direct instruction alone will suffice.

One method that many teachers use to help students become word conscious is modeling the use of sophisticated labels for everyday concepts (Lane & Allen, 2010). For example, teachers may ask students to "distribute" papers to each other rather than to "pass" them (Lane & Allen, 2010). Instead of simplifying their language, teachers model the familiar names for the concepts first and then demonstrate the use of more sophisticated synonyms.

Assessing Vocabulary

While formal, norm-referenced instruments such as the Peabody Picture Vocabulary Test can be used to assess vocabulary knowledge, this type of assessment is often time-consuming and not recommended for frequent use. Many school districts also include a formal vocabulary test in their battery of grade-level assessments. However, there are several simple methods that teachers can employ to assess their students' progress in vocabulary. These methods include teacher observation, Marie Clay's (1979) test of writing vocabulary, and the Consortium on Reading Excellence (CORE) Vocabulary Screening (Diamond & Thornes, 2008).

Teacher Observation of Vocabulary

In their book *Word Matters*, Fountas and Pinnell (1998) recommend that teachers develop a classroom assessment plan to systematically collect data on what their students know and are able to do. They recommend asking the following questions:

- Is there evidence of growth in the student's speaking vocabulary?
- Does the student show an interest in learning new words and searching for their meanings?
- Does the student use strategies to figure out the meaning of unknown words?
- Is there evidence that the student is learning words with a range of meanings?
- Does the student have a growing body of words he or she can write and/or read?
- Does the student try to use more interesting words in his or her writing?
- Does the student have a growing body of words he or she can use in context correctly?

Clay's Test of Writing Vocabulary

With the test of writing vocabulary, children are asked to write all the words they know how to write (Clay, 1979). Often, the teacher begins by asking the student to write his or her own name and then encourages the student to think of any other words he or she knows how to write. By observing the student as he or she writes, the teacher may learn how one word prompts the student to think of other words and how fluently the child writes these words (Fountas & Pinnell, 1998). The teacher may also learn more about the child's spelling development by looking at the spelling errors he or she makes.

Consortium on Reading Excellence (CORE) Vocabulary Screening

Another tool teachers may use to screen and monitor progress in vocabulary is the Consortium on Reading Excellence (CORE) Vocabulary Screening (Diamond & Thornes, 2008). In this assessment, students read a word and select a synonym for that word from one of three choices. This screening may be given to students in first through eighth grade and comes with two forms of each assessment. Scores for this assessment fall into one of three levels: benchmark (75% or more correct), strategic (between 50% and 74% correct), and intensive (49% or less correct).

Fluency

Oral reading fluency serves as a link between decoding and comprehension (Carnine, Silbert, Kame'enui, & Tarver, 2004, as cited in Therrien & Kubina, 2006). It is also a strong predictor of and support for reading comprehension (Samuels, 1997; Therrien & Kubina, 2006). Two strategies that serve to develop fluency and may be used to assess it are words correct per minute and repeated reading.

Fluency Assessments

The words correct per minute (WCPM) test is a simple 1-minute reading assessment. To administer it, a teacher needs a grade-level passage of 100 to 300 words, depending on the student's reading level, a timer or stopwatch, and a running record sheet. The teacher tells the student that he or she will be timed but to do his or her best. Then the teacher asks the student to begin and times him or her for 1 minute. While the student is reading, the teacher completes a running record. When the test is over, he or she subtracts the total number of errors from the total number of words read in 1 minute to determine the number of words read correctly. The target for words read correctly in 1 minute for students in the latter half of first grade is 60 and for second grade is 90 (Rasinski, 2003).

Repeated reading is a method that requires students to reread a "short, meaningful passage several times until a satisfactory level of fluency is reached" (Samuels, 1997, p. 377). This method has been implemented successfully with students reading at first-grade level and above. The purpose of repeated reading is for students to become fluent decoders and enhance their reading comprehension (Samuels, 1997). As reading speed increases with repetition, the number of errors a student makes decreases, and the student is better able to process the meaning of the text (Samuels, 1997).

To implement this method, teachers select an interesting passage of between 50 and 200 words on the child's instructional level. Then the student is paired with a tutor or the teacher and asked to read the passage aloud as quickly as possible. During the reading, the tutor notes the errors the student makes and corrects the student only if he or she hesitates on a word for more than 3 seconds (Therrien & Kubina, 2006). All other feedback is given after the student finishes. Next, the tutor spends a few minutes providing corrective feedback for any words that were mispronounced or omitted and lets the student know how he or she performed (Therrien & Kubina, 2006). Performance goals are set for each student based on his or her reading level. The criteria for a reader at the first-grade level would be between 60 and 70 WCPM; at the second-grade level, 90 to 100 WCPM; and at the third-grade level, 110 to 120 WCPM (Therrien & Kubina, 2006). See Table 7.3 for a sample repeated reading tracking sheet.

Table 7.3 Sample Repeated Reading Tracking Sheet

Student: _____ Tutor: _____

Date	WCPM Goal	Passage Title	Reading (1, 2, 3, etc.)	Errors	Words Read Correctly	Goal Met

Source: Adapted from Therrien and Kubina (2006).

Reading Comprehension

For a reader to comprehend a text, he or she must be able to decode the words and attach meaning to them. Keene (2008) likens reading comprehension to the development of intellect. As readers make meaning from a text, they are developing their "intellectual muscle" (p. 6). Recent research (Daniels, 2011) in reading comprehension has focused on developing students' thinking skills, but according to Cunningham and Allington (2011) most children already know how to think; they just don't know that they should think while reading. These children are able to predict that their soccer game will be canceled when the weather changes and dark clouds roll in or that their mother is angry about something when she greets them with a stern face. Children with limited literacy experiences, who are taught to read with a "phonics-first method" and decodable texts, do not learn that thinking is the goal of reading (p. 118). While early childhood teachers do have a responsibility to teach their students the alphabetic and pattern systems of English, it is doubly important that they also focus on the meaning system. Without meaning, students become "word callers," not readers.

Comprehension of Narrative Text

Effective comprehension instruction depends partly on identifying the text structures students are able to read effectively as well as those they have more difficulty understanding (Reutzel & Cooter, 2013). Many students come to school with some understanding of narrative text structure. They may have been read bedtime stories or listened to oral retellings of family members' exploits. In the early grades, teachers build on those experiences through read-alouds and journal writing. Children soon learn the features of narrative text structure. They learn that stories have a setting, a problem, a solution, and events. As they are learning the structure of narrative texts, they are also learning about sequencing and time; that stories have a beginning, middle, and end; and what happens first in a story and next and after that. When teachers assess a student's understanding of a narrative text, all these features are taken into account. One assessment that is fairly simple to use is a retelling.

Assessing Comprehension of Narrative Texts

Retelling. With a **retelling,** the student is asked to listen to or read a story and then retell as much of the text as he or she can remember. Unlike a summary, where students are including only two or three important ideas from the text, students must re-create all the major story elements, the details, and the sequence of the story. Brown and Cambourne (1990) developed a list of several types of retellings:

- Oral to oral
- Oral to written
- Oral to drawing
- Written to oral
- Written to written
- Written to drawing

In each case, the students are either listening to a story being read or reading a story themselves and then retelling the story orally, in writing, or by drawing. Teachers select the type that best fits the needs of their students.

As with any assessment, the teacher needs to instruct students how to complete a retelling prior to using it as an assessment. The teacher should begin by explaining and modeling retellings for the class. For young children, the retelling may be done as a whole-group shared writing activity before it is used as an individual assessment.

To teach the retelling procedure, the teacher would first share the title of the story he or she is going to read and ask students to make predictions about the story. Next, he or she would read the story and either confirm or disprove their predictions. Then the teacher would ask the students to tell him or her everything they remember. As they retell the story, the teacher would write it out on chart paper. Once the retelling is complete, he or she would review it with the students to see if they left out any important information. The teacher would use the retelling process several times during instruction before ever using it to assess.

Rubrics are often used to evaluate the retellings. Table 7.4 provides some categories for consideration based on Brown and Cambourne's (1990) work.

Table 7.4 Categories for Retelling Rubrics		
Meaning	**Structure**	**Conventions**
• Ideas • Clarity • Relevance	• Organization (characters, setting, problem resolution, events) • Unity between parts • Sequence	• Spelling • Usage • Punctuation

Comprehension Questions. One of the simplest ways to assess comprehension is by asking students questions (McKenna & Dougherty-Stahl, 2011). One approach is to think of questions in terms of levels of comprehension (McKenna & Dougherty-Stahl, 2011). The first level, *literal,* requires students to recall facts that have been stated explicitly in the text. The second level, *inferential,* requires students to make connections between different facts in a story. The answers to inferential questions are not stated explicitly but derived from the way a student interprets what he or she has read. The third level, *evaluative,* asks students to make value judgments about an issue in the story they are reading. Students must decide whether a character's actions are right or wrong. Many districts use prepackaged comprehension assessments that contain stories and a series of comprehension questions; however, teachers may easily create their own list of questions for any story their students are reading.

Maze. Another assessment that may be used to assess comprehension is the **maze** task (Diamond & Thornes, 2008; McKenna & Dougherty-Stahl, 2011). This assessment was introduced by Guthrie, Seifert, Burnham, and Caplan (1974). It is fairly easy to administer and may be used as a group or individual assessment. To create a maze task, the teacher uses a narrative passage at the appropriate reading level for the student and replaces certain words in the passage with a choice of three words (Diamond & Thornes, 2008; McKenna & Dougherty-Stahl, 2011). Students must select the word that makes sense based on the context of the story. According to Diamond and Thornes (2008), capable readers understand the syntax and meaning of what they are reading. The maze task will identify students who do not understand syntax and meaning so teachers can target those students for further instruction.

Sample Maze Passage

The cat ran up the tree.

It was chasing a (snake, squirrel, tire).

The squirrel (jumped, crawled, and) into another tree.

The cat gave up.

Comprehension of Informational Text

Students today are reading more informational text (Temple, Ogle, Crawford, & Freppon, 2011); so, in an effort to prepare students for the challenges they will face with content literacy in the older grades, more primary teachers are using informational text. Informational texts contain very different text features than do narrative texts. With informational texts, students learn about both the external and internal text features (Temple et al., 2011). The external text features include the table of contents, index, glossary, headings, sidebars, diagrams, charts, graphs, maps, and illustrations with captions. The internal text features encompass the type of writing found in the text. The text may be written as a description, a comparison and contrast, a problem and resolution, a cause and effect, or a sequence of events.

There are a variety of ways to assess students' comprehension of informational text. Two assessments that the early childhood classroom teacher may implement easily are summaries and think-alouds.

Assessing Comprehension of Informational Texts

Summarizing. Reading for important ideas is crucial when students are working with informational texts. To begin, the teacher must explain that a summary is a list of the most important ideas in a passage. Then he or she must model the strategy several times. This may be done through shared reading and writing using an informational big book and chart paper. Once students understand how to summarize a passage and have practiced, the teacher can ask them to try summarizing on their own.

Prior to giving the students their own text to summarize, the teacher would preread the text and create a list of the important ideas he or she expects the students to find. Later, once the students have read the text and created their own summaries, the teacher would use the symbols shown in Table 7.5 to score their summaries.

Think-Aloud. A think-aloud is a strategy a teacher uses to model his or her thinking by stating aloud what he or she is thinking. It allows a student to "see" the thought processes of

---

Table 7.5 Summary Scoring Guide

Scoring

1 point for each important idea

0 for an unimportant idea

X for an idea that does not come from the text

The student's score is calculated as a percentage.

[# of important ideas ÷ total # of important ideas in the passage]

Source: Adapted from Taylor, Harris, Pearson, and Garcia (1995).

an expert reader in action. Students may be taught to "think aloud" as they are reading. As they talk themselves through a text, the teacher understands the strategies they are using to comprehend. A checklist may be created to monitor students' use of comprehension strategies. A sample checklist can be found in Table 7.6.

Table 7.6 Think-Aloud Checklist

Student: _____ Date: _____

Text: _____ Evaluator: _____

Behaviors Evident in Think-Aloud	Frequency
Restates text ideas (i.e., paraphrase, summary)	
Recognizes when he or she does not understand • Words • Sentences • Larger ideas	
Rereads	
Recalls prior knowledge	
Predicts	
Forms an opinion about text	
Asks a question	
Makes a connection . . . to self, text, world	

Other Behaviors Observed by Teacher	
• Uses the glossary • Refers to a diagram • Studies an illustration • Uses the table of contents • Uses the index	

Writing Assessments

The best writing assessments support the efforts of students to improve their writing without penalizing them for what they have not yet learned (Strickland, Ganske, & Monroe, 2002). "Good assessment is never about [the] entrapment of students" (Spandel,

2009, p. 16). A good writing assessment should acknowledge what students are doing well while helping them understand what they need to work on (Strickland et al., 2002).

Writing Criteria Chart

Criteria charts or rubrics are fairly simple to create, and they provide a practical tool for teachers and students to assess writing (Strickland et al., 2002). Strickland and colleagues suggest that teachers invite students to participate in constructing the charts. The teacher would begin by asking students what they think good writers do and what makes writing good. Most student responses fall into three categories: the writing process, qualities of good writing, and conventions of good writing (Strickland et al., 2002). Once the teacher has listed all the students' suggestions, he or she would create charts that can be posted around the classroom. See Table 7.7 for an example of a writing criteria chart.

Table 7.7 Primary Writing Performance by Stages

Stage	Knowledge of Print	Expression of Ideas	Writing Process Behaviors
1	• Uses pictures to communicate • Scribbles • Writes mock letters • Writes random strings of letters	• Copies print	• Intends print to carry a message • Shares writing in a conference
2	• Uses left-to-right directional pattern • Uses correct return sweep • Writes phonetically related approximations • Writes correct first letter in approximations • Writes approximations using some phonemes • Places spaces between words	• Copies message • Uses single words or lists of words • Writes one complete phrase or sentence	• Can identify audience • Is able to identify a topic • Can verbalize the topic
3	• Correctly spells and uses sight words	• Writes a simple, logical sentence • Writes a sentence that makes sense • Writes specific details in a phrase or sentence • Writes a list of the same pattern sentences • Uses capital letters at the beginning of a sentence	• Seeks peer response for revision
4	• Writes approximations using all phonemes	• Writes three or more complete thoughts focused on one topic • Writes three or more thoughts telling how or why	• Rereads own written work to check for meaning (does it make sense?) and syntax (does it sound right?)

(Continued)

Table 7.7 (Continued)

Stage	Knowledge of Print	Expression of Ideas	Writing Process Behaviors
		• Is able to write a story that includes at least two story elements (character, setting, etc.) • Is able to write one sentence that elaborates another sentence • Uses figurative language • Writes a simple beginning • Can use pronouns • Can use periods and question marks	
5	• Uses more correct spelling than approximations	• Writes a logically ordered paragraph focused on one topic • Writes a story that includes three story elements • Writes a piece telling why or how • Uses specific, vivid language • Uses a variety of sentence types (questions, statements, exclamations) • Edits for at least one item	• Preplans and thinks about writing • Self-initiates revision • Self-initiates editing
6		• Writes more than one paragraph focused on a single topic • Writes a story that includes all the story elements • Writes a piece telling why or how • Uses transitional words • Writes more than one sentence that elaborates on another • Writes a simple ending • Uses generally correct grammar • Uses generally correct punctuation • Uses correct capitalization	• Writes for a variety of audiences and purposes • Demonstrates the ability to prewrite, compose, revise, edit, and publish

Source: Adapted from Primary Writing Continuum for Pinellas County Schools (1998).

Student Self-Evaluation Chart

Teachers may also encourage students to begin evaluating their own writing. One example that Strickland et al. (2002) recommend is a student self-evaluation T-chart. See Table 7.8 for a sample.

Table 7.8 Student Writing Self-Evaluation Chart	
Writing Self-Evaluation Chart	
Things I Am Doing Well	One Thing I Will Work On

Source: Adapted from Strickland et al. (2002).

Six Traits of Writing

According to Spandel (2009), the original six-trait rubric for assessing and teaching writing came from a group of 17 teachers who made up the Analytical Writing Assessment Committee in the Beaverton, Oregon, school district in 1984. The teachers met to develop a writing continuum and assessment system for their district. Their work was based on the work of Diederich (1974), Murray (1982), and Purves (1992; Spandel, 2009). Today, many school districts nationwide have adopted the six traits and developed their own versions of the rubrics. The six-trait program currently includes the following categories for teaching and assessing writing (Spandel, 2009):

- Ideas, or the writer's message
- Organization, or the structure of the piece of writing
- Voice, or the writer's voice that is unique to that student
- Word choice, or the ability to select the right words to make the piece clear for the reader
- Sentence fluency, or the rhythm and flow of the language
- Conventions, or the spelling, punctuation, and grammar

Six-Traits Rubrics

Detailed rubrics have been created for teachers using the six traits. The rubrics were constructed to be specific, positive, and to benefit the students. The following criteria describe how the rubrics were created (Spandel, 2009):

- Clarity
- Positive language
- Horizontal integrity
- Vertical integrity
- User-friendliness
- Absence of quantifiable criteria

Clarity and Positive Language. The language in a rubric should clearly describe the most important features of writing that the teacher is looking for. The words should be carefully chosen, because students will begin to think about themselves and their writing based on the language that is used. The language should remain positive. A score of 1 should show that a student is in the beginning stages of writing, not that he or she is a poor writer.

Horizontal and Vertical Integrity. A good rubric has horizontal integrity. The characteristics being scored are distinct so the teacher does not end up scoring the same characteristic twice. The rubric will also have vertical integrity, which means that there are very clear differences between a score of 2 and a score of 3.

User-Friendliness and Absence of Quantifiable Criteria. Rubrics should be constructed so that they are easy to use and understand. A teacher should be able to take a student's scored paper and use it to teach the student. The rubric should also be free of quantifiable criteria. Sometimes, writing rubrics measure things that are unimportant and do not help the student become a better writer. These rubrics may measure the length of the paper or the number of complex sentences in it. Writing assessment is not about counting words or complex phrases.

Six-Point Scale

Spandel (2009) recommends a six-point scoring scale in writing rubrics. First, the writer's performance can be clearly defined at all six levels. Second, a six-point scale is sensitive enough to document even modest growth in writing. See Table 7.9 for an example.

Observing and Conferring

Paying attention to children as they talk about their writing can provide insight into how they think about writing and where they are in their writing development. For example, a child in the beginning stages of writing may ask, "What will I write or draw today?" This question lets the teacher know that the child understands that messages may be created on and retrieved from a page (Education Department of South Australia, 1990). If the student asks, "What am I interested in writing today?" the teacher will know that the child understands that print can be manipulated according to a writer's intentions (Education Department of South Australia, 1990).

Table 7.9 Portion of Rubric for Ideas and Development Trait

Ideas and Development

The writing is clear, focused, and well developed, with many important, intriguing details.

- The writer is selective, avoiding trivia and choosing details that keep readers reading.
- The topic or story is narrow, focused, and manageable.

The writer has made a solid beginning. It is easy to see where the piece is headed, though more expansion would be helpful.

- Global information provides the big picture, making the reader long for more specifics.
- Greater focus might help narrow or shape the topic.

Sketchy, loosely focused information forces the reader to make inferences. Readers notice one or more of these problems.

- The topic or central idea is undefined or unclear.
- The topic is so big that it is hard for the writer to focus in and say anything meaningful.

Source: Based on Spandel (2009) and Pasco County Schools rubric.

Teachers may also write anecdotal notes as they observe their students during independent writing (Kendall & Khuon, 2006). They may watch to see if students begin to write immediately or if they reread their writer's notebook or journal first. They may notice whether they use a mentor text to get ideas or how they organize their work. They should also notice whether students have conversations with peers about their writing or if they revise or edit their work. Everything that students do during writing is a clue to their development and their needs.

In addition to listening to and observing their students, effective writing teachers meet with their students in one-on-one conferences. These student–teacher conferences provide the teacher with an opportunity to work with students in an apprenticeship model; the teacher is the expert, and the student is the novice writer. The conferences usually last about 5 to 10 minutes. The teacher begins the conference by listening to the student read his or her story, and then the teacher may ask the student questions to motivate him or her to add to or clarify the writing. Most teachers are able to conference with each student at least once a week, and they usually keep records of their conferences.

Making Connections

Kidwatching, mentioned earlier in this chapter, is an excellent way to come up with ideas for reluctant writers. In my anecdotal notes, I like to keep a list of interests, conversation notes, and repeat drawings—anything a student brings up multiple times. These become topics for those reluctant writers and can hook them into completing a writing piece.

Conference records can be kept in a variety of ways: sticky notes, index cards, class record sheets, or online via an iPad. The conference record usually includes the date the teacher met with the student and notes about their discussion. These records inform the teacher's writing instruction and provide an informal means of assessment.

Promoting Fluency in English Language Learners

Fluency in literacy when working with English language learners (ELLs) is intricately linked to their ability to use the vocabulary words developed in class within conversations. One strategy that will help in improving fluency is modeling fluent speech with your students. In a classroom activity, pair your ELL with a student who has good conversational skills. Assign a topic—discussing a book that was read to them, for example— and provide question queues that will prompt your English-speaking student to read the question out loud and give his or her answer. Then guide your ELL student to respond to his or her partner's answer.

Another powerful fluency lesson strategy is creating a student-directed book. This strategy requires one-on-one attention. When working with your ELL student, ask him or her to draw a picture. When your student is done drawing, ask him or her questions to tell you a story using the picture as a guide. As your student tells you the story, write every word down on a large piece of chart paper. This will show your student that he or she can create sentences in English, even if he or she is not comfortable with writing sentences yet. When your student is done telling you the story, read what you have written on the chart paper out loud to him or her and model the basic literacy skills (orientation of reading left to right, using your finger to point to each word, observing punctuation in the sentences, etc.). That will complete Part 1 of your activity. Part 2 requires you to create a "book" using your student's drawing and the story you wrote down. In the next one-on-one session, present the book to your student and model partner reading: You will read one page, your student will read the next, and so on. Learning objectives for this "experience approach" type of activity can be checked off as a form of assessment.

Early language users and ELLs share some of the same challenges while learning to embrace English as their primary school-based language. Teachers who thoughtfully prepare dialogues aimed at developing literacy learning and who pose critical questions to early learners can see powerful results:

> Culturally informed teaching supports the learning needs of all children, regardless of their cultural or linguistic background. The challenge is not to create the perfect "culturally matched" learning situation for each ethnic group, but to capitalize on diversity. (Ontario Ministry of Education, 2003, p. 49)

Students' culture and home language will greatly impact their performance on assessments, and this must be taken into account when choosing assessments and interpreting the results. Cultural experiences affect what students know, how they show/share knowledge and abilities, and how they might respond during assessment situations. Home language may also influence how assessment directions are understood and how responses are given (Scott-Little & Niemeyer, 2001).

As mentioned in Chapter 10, there are many concerns involved in the selecting of standardized and nonstandardized assessments. Both standardized and nonstandardized assessments should accommodate the home language of the student, the assessor should be fluent in the student's home language, and any translators should be well trained in using the assessment to maximize student success. See Table 7.10 for a list of considerations in choosing assessments for ELLs.

Table 7.10 Developmentally and Linguistically Appropriate Assessments for ELLs

- *Time:* ELLs need sufficient time to adjust to the cognitive, social, and physical demands of a new classroom and school environment.
- *Information:* The teacher should gather information about the student's literacy abilities in the student's first language.
- *Lack of response:* A variety of factors can impact an ELL's lack of response to an oral question or request. These factors could include the following:
  o Lack of English language proficiency to understand the question
  o Inability to access the knowledge or skill
  o Inability to formulate a response
  o Cultural influences, reluctance to speak in the presence of adults in positions of authority

- Assessments should allow ELLs to demonstrate what they can do with limited or no English.
- Assessments should address the "whole child" and not just the student's ability to acquire a language.

Source: Adapted from Ontario Ministry of Education (2007).

Cultural and linguistic differences can also impact the assessment data collection practice. Any measure is produced within a particular cultural and linguistic context. The type(s) of skill assessed, the importance placed on the skill(s) or particular item or developmental domain assessed, and the way the information is collected are all impacted by the cultural and linguistic background of the assessment development process. Bias may be found in the student, the observer collecting the information, or the "lens" of evaluating the results (Scott-Little & Niemeyer, 2001).

Promoting Fluency in Students With Special Needs

The importance of motivation for striving readers and writers cannot be ignored. Active learning employing movement to support fluency is a valuable strategy for disfluent readers. Always remember to select reading passages or poems that engage students at the independent level to promote the growth of "muscle" in reading—in other words, to strengthen their motivation to read with attention to fluency.

Moreover, requesting that disfluent students participate in traditional fluency activities such as popcorn or round-robin reading without prior practice is unfair and unethical;

once humiliated in front of a group of peers, disfluent readers may turn away from future directives on oral reading. Never put a child in this situation.

Special education teacher Peebles (2011) uses what she calls "Rhythm Walks" to draw attention to the natural breaks and phrasing of text through focused steps or movements. Repetition throughout the Rhythm Walk aids both fluency and comprehension. The planning steps behind a Rhythm Walk with the whole class might look like this:

1. Choose a short poem, story, or informational text for the Rhythm Walk.

2. Analyze the text, and decide where there are natural stops and appropriate chunks as indicated through punctuation, line breaks, or contextual cues.

3. Write each "chunk" of text on a rectangular strip of cardstock.

4. Place the strips, in order, in a curvy or straight pathway on the floor around the classroom, making sure that each strip is within one step of another as students line up in single file at the start of the Rhythm Walk.

Enactment of the Rhythm Walk might look like this:

1. Starting at the first strip, the first student reads it aloud and then takes a step to the next strip and reads that one. The student continues walking and reading as he or she makes his or her way through the Rhythm Walk and completes the poem or passage.

2. Each student begins when the student in front of him or her has completed the first three strips.

3. As each student gets to the end of the Rhythm Walk, he or she lines up at the beginning and repeats the process.

4. Allow each student to circulate through the Rhythm Walk 3 to 10 times, depending on the length of the passage, which has been anywhere from 4 to 25 strips.

At the end, the teacher requests that students return to the original passage to practice transferring their new reading skills to the text. An activity such as a response journal or discussion questions to monitor comprehension of the passage may follow.

Writing and Students With Special Needs

Students with special writing needs require an organized writing program with the opportunity to observe modeled writing on a small scale. The Write-Aloud, when modeled frequently, is a powerful strategy to support the special needs writer.

My version of this strategy employs a photograph of an event in my life: a vacation to a museum, my daughter fishing when she was very young, or my pets. Using a "think-aloud" strategy to frame my writing, I make on-the-spot decisions about word choice, conventions, sentence structure, and colorful words. I always use cover-up tape, flags, sticky notes, and colored markers as editing devices that students love to manipulate. One suggestion is to keep the Write-Aloud very short, around five sentences or a well-written paragraph to support striving writers. I make this modeled writing interactive at certain points, asking for student input based on a writing skill recently taught through a mini-lesson.

We coassess the writing by using a simple Write-Aloud checklist (see Table 7.11).

Table 7.11 Write-Aloud Checklist	
Write-Aloud	**Comments**
Picking "just-right" words	
Using engaging sentences we want to read	
Using right-on punctuation that lets us know where to pause or stop	
Including starting and ending sentences that tie up the writing	

Chapter 7, with its focus on assessing early learners in the areas of comprehension, spelling, and writing, offers the practitioner many assessment ideas useful for informal assessment. Keep in mind that developmental differences among students of this age group can account for differences that are perfectly acceptable and expected.

Key Terms

English orthography

kidwatching

maze

orthographic awareness

repeated reading

retelling

Website Resources

- "Teaching Metalinguistic Awareness and Reading Comprehension With Riddles," Reading Rockets

Reading Rockets is funded by a grant from the U.S. Department of Education and is a national multimedia project that offers research-based best-practice information. This particular article offers riddling as a way to expose students to metalinguistic awareness and positively influence reading comprehension. Sample riddles are given and steps provided to show students how to work with words that have multiple meanings and are considered ambiguous language, and to show how riddles can be incorporated into lessons. For more details, go to **www.readingrockets.org/article/28315**.

(Continued)

(Continued)

- **Words and Pictures**

This site from the BBC offers a variety of games and activities designed to help children develop their knowledge of phonics. The games and activities are a combination of online videos and worksheets based on the consonant-vowel-consonant words, consonant clusters, long-vowel sounds, and high-frequency words. For more information, go to **www.bbc.co.uk/ schools/wordsandpictures/teachers/intro.shtml.**

- **Big Ideas in Beginning Reading**

This website from the University of Oregon Center on Teaching and Learning provides information, technology, and resources for teachers, administrators, and parents. The main focus is the five components of early literacy: phonemic awareness, alphabetic principle, accuracy and fluency with text, vocabulary, and comprehension. Each of the five components also includes links that provide information on assessments, how to teach in the classroom, and the latest research and theories. For more information, go to **reading.uoregon.edu.**

- **"Strategies for the Reluctant Writer," LD Online**

LD Online offers information and resources on learning disabilities and attention-deficit hyperactivity disorder. The site features articles, multimedia, monthly columns by noted experts, and work samples and is a comprehensive resource guide. LD Online is a national educational service of WETA-TV, the PBS station in Washington, D.C. This particular article is loaded with useful, practical strategies for encouraging reluctant writers to become successful. For more information, go to **www.ldonline.org/article/6215.**

- **"Chart: Review of Progress Monitoring Tools," Reading Rockets**

This chart is an evaluation of scientifically based tools used to measure students' progress. The chart includes information on the major literacy and math assessments, such as AIMSwab, DIBELS, EdCheckup, iSTEEP, MBSP, PASeries, STAR, TOWRE, TOSWRF, VIP, and Yearly Progress Pro. The chart also provides a breakdown of the features of each assessment tool. These features include reliability, validity, and five progress monitoring standards. For more information, go to **www.readingrockets.org/article/30680.**

- **"Informal Reading Assessments: Examples," Reading Rockets**

This site provides informal reading assessments for one-on-one use. The site gives explicit instruction on how to assess kindergarten students on concepts of print, rhyming, identifying initial sounds, blending words, phoneme segmentation, phoneme manipulation and phoneme deletion. The site also includes an easy to re-create sample of a recording chart for each assessment. For more information, go to **www.readingrockets.org/article/3411.**

- PALS: Phonological Awareness Literacy Screening

This site offers assessment tools for pre-K through Grade 3. The kindergarten assessments measure students' knowledge of several literacy fundamentals: phonological awareness, alphabet recognition, concept of word, knowledge of letter sounds, and spelling. Each assessment is accompanied by a video showing a teacher giving the assessment and scoring it. For more information, go to **pals.virginia.edu.**

Student Study Site: Visit the Student Study Site at **www.sagepub.com/grantlit** to access additional study tools including eFlashcards, web resources, and online-only appendices.

CHAPTER 8

Intermediate Grade-Level (3–6) Assessments and Strategies

Kathy B. Grant, Nance S. Wilson, and Kimberly Davidson

Common Core State Standards

Key Ideas and Details	RI.K.1 With prompting and support, ask and answer questions about key details in a text.	RI.1.2 Identify the main topic and retell key details of a text.	RI.2.3 Describe the connection between a series of historical events, scientific ideas or concepts, or steps in technical procedures in a text.
Craft and Structure	RI.K.4 With prompting and support, ask and answer questions about unknown words in a text.	RI.1.5 Know and use various text features (e.g., headings, tables of contents, glossaries, electronic menus, icons) to locate key facts or information in a text.	RI.2.6 Identify the main purpose of a text, including what the author wants to answer, explain, or describe.

(Continued)

(Continued)

Integration of Knowledge and Ideas	*RI.K.7* With prompting and support, describe the relationship between illustrations and the text in which they appear (e.g., what person, place, thing, or idea in the text an illustration depicts).	*RI.1.8* Identify the reasons an author gives to support points in a text.	*RI.2.9* Compare and contrast the most important points presented by two texts on the same topic.
Range of Reading and Level of Text Complexity	*RI.K.10* Actively engage in group reading activities with purpose and understanding.	*RI.1.10* With prompting and support, read informational texts appropriately complex for grade 1.	*RI.2.10* By the end of year, read and comprehend informational texts, including history/ social studies, science, and technical texts, in the grades 2–3 text complexity band proficiently, with scaffolding as needed at the high end of the range.

Source: © Copyright 2010. National Governors Association Center for Best Practices and Council of Chief State School Officers. All rights reserved.

FOCUS QUESTIONS

1. How has the introduction of the Common Core standards changed the emphasis on reading narrative texts to an emphasis on reading more informational texts?

2. What are some problems with standardized tests that exist? How can employing authentic teacher-made assessments solve some of the issues with standardized tests?

3. Why is it critical that vocabulary learning be embedded into active teaching strategies?

4. What new challenges might be posed for readers as they encounter expository or informational texts? How can teachers support these encounters?

5. What special features found in biographies will students need to be aware of as tied to the Common Core standards? How will you support this learning as a reading teacher?

6. What assessments in the area of narrative text do you believe fit your style of teaching? Discuss why authentic, teacher-generated assessments work well with literacy instruction.

Words in Action

Boys and Informational Text Assessments

Boys in my fourth-grade classroom have special reading needs and wants. They look forward to self-selecting their reading materials for Reader's Workshop and are especially drawn to informational books about daredevils, the Loch Ness monster, outer space, and other exciting topics. With allowing students to self-select their reading materials, I wonder how I can assess or judge their understanding of the vocabulary contained in the trade book as well as their understanding of the technical and conceptual ideas found within the text. How can I seek evidence of their growing knowledge of the topic, say the Loch Ness monster, without appearing to control their reading selection? How deep an understanding of the selection is deep enough for an individual reader? Should I intervene and conduct informal reading conferences with students as a quick check for their understanding of vocabulary and context? Maybe I should stop students intermittently as a check for fluency and ask them to read a couple of paragraphs. Many critical decisions to make!!!

I decided to step back and consider what measure of reading proficiency I would accept as evidence for the class overall and for individual students who continue to strive to read better. I came to the conclusion that an exciting reading selection would propel students into the world of reading while they engaged in self-assessment by developing learning targets they articulated during informal conferences. I felt I was getting on track here—maybe if I layered my ongoing assessments, did occasional checks for understanding of vocabulary, and then monitored oral reading fluency, that would be a good start. I questioned how in the world I would be able to meet with each student each assigned reading period, or if I would need to. Being highly organized is the key to differentiating instruction for readers. I guess I now had some sort of plan.

PHEW! I definitely felt more at ease—at least I had some concrete "first steps" to form some judgments about reading progress and interventions. I scanned the classroom to see my fourth graders happily engaged in reading their choice books, and felt a sense of triumph.

Intermediate elementary–level assessments offer teachers of Grades 3–6 multiple opportunities to employ informational as well as narrative texts and trade books to assess students' ability to "read to learn." As students progress into higher elementary grades, they are challenged to use their expository reading materials to gain informational knowledge as well as to understand the intricacies of narrative text, such as literary terms, character motivation, story setting, and author's perspective. The educator's responsibility is to assess for understanding and evaluate for **mastery** through student data collection. Assessment and evaluation are related and complementary elements of the ongoing process of gathering and analyzing the evidence of student learning; the two processes are inseparable (Fountas & Pinnell, 2001, p. 483).

Fountas and Pinnell reiterate that quality teaching involves assessment, which involves collecting and categorizing evidence of student learning, as well as evaluation, or "taking stock" by gathering various data collected. They endorse the use of authentic assessment that involves students in "real-time" tasks of readers and writers (Fountas & Pinnell, 2001). Bridges (1995) notes that authentic assessment is

- continual and informs teaching;
- integral to the curriculum and invites collaboration; and
- developmentally appropriate, culturally responsive, and self-evaluative.

In our first section, we will address the literacy area of academic subjects or content, also known as disciplinary or content area literacy. Content literacy requires robust assessment (Kovalik & Olsen, 2010); as sampled by the *National Assessment of Educational Progress* (Institute of Education Sciences, 2008), 55% of eighth-grade passages and 70% of twelfth-grade passages are information based. Teachers must be able to gauge students' understanding of academic subjects through lessons employing differing sources, including subject textbooks at the intermediate level. Furthermore, the struggle with academic vocabulary and writing that is dense and structured differently than fiction (Ogle & Correa-Kovtun, 2010) has been brought into the forefront. Teachers must be able to gauge students' understanding of academic subjects with lessons that employ a range of text, including subject-area textbooks and trade books, to build students' strategies for informational text, vocabulary, and writing.

As you proceed through this chapter, it will highlight many authentic, easily constructed assessments based on selections students read and respond to. The goal of this chapter is to challenge teacher-practitioners to develop their own assessments based on ideas from the models and exemplars. By using genuinely engaging reading selections, undertaking the quest of appraising student mastery of information becomes straightforward.

Literacy in the Academic Subjects

Reading and writing in the academic subjects is central to students' building knowledge in the various academic disciplines. Assessment and instruction in strategies for reading and writing in the academic subjects are important because a troubling disparity exists among intermediate readers when encountering disciplinary-specific text sources: Nearly 70% of all students may be unable to accurately decode or comprehend their textbooks, according to McGrath (2005). Brozo and Simpson (2007) posit that striving readers are especially vulnerable to failure with content text. The preponderance of technical vocabulary, charts, tables and diagrams, and conceptually dense writing in informational text can defeat well-intentioned readers.

Focusing on a typical third-grade classroom, it is not uncommon to see student instructional levels ranging from pre-primer through sixth grade or higher. The differing levels of prior content knowledge students bring to the learning setting create instructional challenges. Furthermore, many phenomena and processes are invisible to the eyes of children; big ideas and concepts need to be made accessible through reading strategies (Gregg & Sekeres, 2006).

Subject-matter learning is currently in the spotlight with implementation of the Common Core State Standards. However, the "right to be able to read" content materials at independent (100% to 90% comprehension) or instructional (89% to 75% comprehension) levels in content textbooks, as well as to understand the academic or specialized vocabulary, often goes unmet for elementary students in social studies, math, science, health, and English language arts. Disciplinary language, or the "lingo" represented by a particular content area, should be taught through a repertoire of strategies. In particular, students with early literacy problems, students living in poverty, and students with limited English proficiency are challenged by the rigors of content literacy (Brozo & Flynt, 2007).

The two approaches for providing students with the strategies for academic subjects are content area literacy and disciplinary literacy. **Content area literacy** provides students with generic reading and writing strategies that can be applied across all content areas. One such strategy is summarizing. We can teach students to summarize ideas in all the content areas.

Disciplinary literacy provides students with the specific literacy skills and strategies used by experts in a specific discipline. For instance, when mathematicians read, they tend to focus on patterns and proofs, requiring them to ask questions such as, Can I generalize this pattern? Does this fit the pattern? How can I prove it? (Johnson, Watson, Delahunty, McSwiggen, & Smith, 2011).

Students in Grades 3–6 are learning both content and disciplinary literacy strategies (Fang & Coatoam, 2013). Students will need to learn how to summarize, but they will also need to understand that within different academic subjects, different questions will lead the summarization process. For instance, in history, students may summarize by looking for the major events that led to the Revolutionary War; in science, they may summarize by listing the characteristics of mammals. Both require students to give a brief overview of a topic, but with a different question in mind depending on the discipline.

As elementary teachers, you will need to orchestrate the reading and writing of informational texts throughout your instruction in the academic subjects. You will use your knowledge of the academic subjects, reading strategies, and your students' assessment results to explore "how to overlay adaptable generic content and discipline-dependent literacy practices to meet the learning needs of all students" (Brozo, Moorman, Meyer, & Stewart, 2013, p. 356). You must assess students in the academic subjects because research indicates the following:

1. The *National Assessment of Educational Progress* (Institute of Education Sciences, 2007) found that two thirds of children in the United States fail to read at or above proficiency levels by fourth grade; that rate is even higher for children living in poverty. As students progress into higher grade levels, the content challenges get more difficult.

2. Many reading experts once assumed that if a student can decode text fluently, understanding will follow; however, research shows that this "inoculation theory" does not work for most students (Shanahan & Shanahan, 2008). Fluency measures, although valuable, may be seen as stumbling blocks when asking students to apply these measures to content passages.

3. Misconceptions about content information abound; students need to read well-chosen resources to ensure they receive accurate information about concepts (Rice, 2002). Self-selection of topical texts should be monitored closely by the teacher.

4. Teaching students how to comprehend text readings while teaching content may aid in increasing reading proficiency (Duke & Pearson, 2002).

Assessment in the academic subjects should include both summative and authentic measures.

Content/Disciplinary Literacy

Let's compare summative assessments in the form of standardized tests with teacher-developed authentic literacy-based assessments. "A Declaration About Summative Assessments for Content/Disciplinary Literacy," developed by Kovalik and Olsen (2010), articulates the problems with standardized tests that serve as summative assessments. Summative assessments range from standardized tests to criterion-referenced instruments, either teacher-made or expensive commercial varieties. Standardized tests that employ true/false items, multiple choice, matching items, or even essay questions (lower level of Bloom's taxonomy) fail to measure authentic learning. Keep in mind the following:

> The idea of authentic achievement requires students to engage in disciplined inquiry to produce knowledge that has value in their lives beyond simply proving their competence in school. (Kovalik & Olsen, 2010, p. 8.1)

Although standardized tests are easy to score and quick to administer, and the majority of teachers appear to use them to check factual regurgitation of informational text knowledge, many complaints are leveled against them (see Table 8.1).

Table 8.1 Problems With Standardized Tests

- Standardized tests rely on reading ability, not the ability to apply content concepts and skills.
- Test items fail to connect to real-world scenarios and real-life dilemmas.
- These tests sample only the early stages of learning, not the higher levels of Bloom's taxonomy such as application, synthesis, and analysis.
- True/false items can be answered through the "sound of familiarity," that little bell that rings in one's head and afterward is quickly dumped from short-term memory.
- Multiple choice can be turned into "multiple guess" by eliminating distracters and employing test-taking savvy.
- Essay answers can often be "parroted back" through memorization studying with note cards and self-testing.

Source: Kovalik and Olsen (2010, pp. 8.2–8.3).

Making Connections

Explain why standardized testing is most likely the least effective way to judge student acquisition of knowledge from informational or content texts. Think about the levels of knowledge and concept development nurtured through encounters with well-written informational texts. As you read the chapter, focus on authentic assessments that tie to informational text knowledge retention and application. Turn and talk to your partner concerning your initial thoughts on developing such assessments.

Assessment experts and brain-based researchers suggest other ways to test the content thinking processes. These authentic (teacher-developed) assessment methods include analytical or holistic rubrics and individual conferences. These authentic (as well as valid and reliable) assessment instruments are discussed in this chapter.

Making Connections

Explain how characteristics of quality instruction in content or informational literacy translate into opportunities for authentic assessment based on the instructional needs of students. What are some of the tenets of quality instruction in the area of teaching and learning for informational texts? How does quality instruction open up opportunities for genuine assessment? Turn and talk to your partner about your initial thoughts in this area.

Authentic Assessments for Informational or Expository Texts

A narrative text includes such elements as a theme, plot, conflict(s), resolution, characters, and a setting. Expository texts, on the other hand, explain something by definition, sequence, categorization, comparison, contrast, enumeration, process, problem-solution, description, or cause-effect. Where the narrative text uses story to inform and persuade, the expository text uses facts and details, opinions and examples to do the same. (Burke, 2000, p. 142)

The first step in developing a classroom reading program using **informational or expository texts** is to gauge each student's interest and prior experience involving informational texts. The Reader Self-Awareness Survey for Informational Text allows classroom educators to gauge student interest in informational text topics, as well as helping students self-rate their skills in responding to this literacy genre.

Reader Self-Awareness

The Reader Self-Awareness Survey focusing on preparation for reading informational text in Grades 3–5 can be answered with teacher prompts or read and answered independently. Students will indicate their level of efficacy based on each statement by checking a Likert-scale rating that best expresses their feeling at the time (see Table 8.2). Further discussion concerning their knowledge of informational texts should follow.

Informational Retellings

Retellings are oral or written post-reading recalls during which children relate what they remember from reading or listening to a particular text. . . . Retellings provide insights about children's ways of constructing meaning from texts and their ability to organize information. (Moss, 2004, pp. 710, 712)

Table 8.2 Reader Self-Awareness Survey for Informational Text (Grades 3–5)

Directions: This Grades 3–5 self-awareness survey focusing on preparation for reading informational text can be answered through teacher prompting or read and answered independently. Students will indicate their level of efficacy (strong, good, or needs support) based on each statement by circling the Likert-scale rating that best expresses their feeling at the time. Further discussion concerning their knowledge of informational texts should follow.

What kinds of informational books do you like to read? Explain why?				
Earth	Space	Technology	Airplanes	Cars
Animals	Sports	Historical events	Motorcycles	Future travel
Oceans	Geology	Famous people	Boats	Ancient travel
Weather	Equipment	Physics	Trains	

Others: _____

_____

Response Key		
1	**2**	**3**
I would rate myself strong in this category.	I would rate myself good in this category.	I would rate myself needing support in this category.

Statement	Response
I am good at identifying the main topic in a paragraph as supported by details.	1–2–3
I am able to go over the main points of the text after I have read it.	1–2–3
I can draw inferences or read between the lines in a text.	1–2–3
I can explain how an author uses evidence or reasons to support particular points in the text.	1–2–3
I feel a sense of accomplishment when I find the information I am looking for through search activities.	1–2–3
I can tell about the connection between two people, events, ideas, or subjects of information in texts.	1–2–3

I feel good about being able to read and understand text features such as charts, tables, timelines, and graphs.	1–2–3
I can understand how specific images or diagrams help make clear the surrounding text.	1–2–3

Source: Adapted from New York State Education Department (2011, p. 21), the New York State Education Department. New York State Common Core Literacy Standards for Informational Text K–5. Available from http://www.p12.nysed.gov/ ciai/common_core_standards/pdfdocs/p12_common_core_learning_standards_ela.pdf

Informational trade book retellings, according to Moss (2004), can be used as assessment instruments to gauge student comprehension of expository text structures. Why use retellings with expository text when they have traditionally been used with the childhood fiction genre? Research and common sense support the following reasons:

- Comprehending nonnarrative text is an essential literacy skill for success in our fast-paced technological society.
- English language learners benefit from retellings, because the concrete nature of expository text can help scaffold understanding between their first and second languages.
- When students gain facility with retelling in early grades, their future retellings are increasingly complex and sophisticated. (Moss, 2004)

Multiple versions of commercially developed retelling rubrics are available; however, we suggest that teacher-made, simple, holistic rubrics best serve to match the text retelling with student understanding. A more general sample rubric is provided as an example in Table 8.3.

Preparation for individual student retellings should start with teacher modeling of an informational text retelling through a **think-aloud process**. The teacher should prompt students in elements of the retelling assessment identified in particular expository selections. Next, partner retelling enactments would be beneficial for students to gain confidence in practicing retelling elements. Last, scheduling individual informational retellings with all students, especially striving readers, bolsters student confidence.

Multiple retelling assessments can be given throughout the year as the child grows in technical vocabulary sophistication and understanding of the textual format and style of informational texts. Keep in mind that the informational retelling instrument is meant to be modified to meet content needs as well as student literacy ability levels.

Comprehension Conversations

Fountas and Pinnell (2008) have developed an assessment system aptly named Comprehension Conversation that can be applied to expository texts. Instead of a series of questions, this technique lets the teacher gather evidence of comprehension while engaging the student in a conversation about the nonfiction book. It develops student confidence as the student reads the text, discusses it with the teacher, and

Table 8.3 Retelling Assessment Rubric	
Retelling Score	
Exemplary (4) Comments:	**Exemplary Retelling** Retelling hits all the major points, including main idea, key facts; inferences applied to facts; summarizes; explains the importance of pictures/diagrams (captions); understands author's viewpoint, comparing/contrasting; sequences material accurately; and can point out examples of text aids such as diagrams, maps, timelines, glossary, table of contents, charts, tables, or graphs.
Proficient (3) Comments:	**Proficient Retelling** Retelling hits several of the major points, including main idea, key facts; inferences applied to facts; may forget summary; explains the importance of pictures/diagrams (captions); understands author's viewpoint, comparing/contrasting; sequences material accurately; and can point out examples of text aids such as diagrams, maps, timelines, glossary, table of contents, charts, tables, or graphs.
Emerging (2) Comments:	**Emerging Retelling** Retelling hits few major points, including or excluding main idea or key facts; lacks inferences applied to facts; leaves out summary; lacks explanations of important pictures/diagrams (captions); may be confused on author's viewpoint; struggles with text patterns, such as cause/effect and comparison/contrast; and may be unable to point out examples of text aids such as maps, charts, timelines, glossary, table of contents, tables, or graphics.
Beginning (1) Comments:	**Beginning Retelling** Retelling is weak overall. Prompting from teacher is essential to illicit minimal retelling. Lacks ability to understand inferences or patterns; may be able to name some key facts; explicit attention to textual aids is required, as well as understanding of author's viewpoint. Student may be stymied because of technical vocabulary or overwhelmed by content demands.

Source: Moss (2004).

then responds in writing. It may be completed employing expository trade books on the student's easy (independent), instructional, and hard (frustration) levels—although we feel the last level can be omitted. Fountas and Pinnell's recording form for the Comprehension Conversation probes for evidence that the reader is doing the following:

- *Thinking within the text* through word solving, literal meanings, monitoring understanding and accuracy, searching for information, summarizing, adjusting for purpose, and sustaining fluent reading.
- *Thinking beyond the text* by making predictions, connections with prior knowledge, using personal experience, connecting with other texts, inferring, and synthesizing information by adjusting ideas.
- *Thinking about the text* by focusing on text features, ways factual information is written, and thinking critically about the topic or subject. (2008, pp. 30–31)

Although the conversation assessment is located within the Fountas and Pinnell Benchmark Assessment System that your school may have purchased (it is expensive but worth every cent!), the idea behind this assessment mirrors the discussions you have every day in reading groups. The extensive kit contains recording forms as well as comprehension scoring keys that are copyrighted. A valuable point made by the authors of the Comprehension Conversation is that teachers should use **wait time**—we generally are rushed and don't allow students enough time to think and formulate their responses. As in a conversation with friends or acquaintances, we can pose questions, ask for details, prompt (probe gently) for further information, and then even summarize. If you think about it, we as conversationalists may use phrases (or prompts) such as these:

- So how did it start?
- What else happened?
- Tell me more about that . . .
- Did that affect your thinking or decision?
- Why do you believe that?
- How did things end?
- What would you do differently?
- What did you learn?

Like everyday conversations, teachers can conference with students in the same manner, with results that help inform their data collection on student progress with informational texts.

Let's now consider an instructional framework for reading that is commonly used in daily literacy practice. It has stood the test of time as a successful methodology to support comprehension and content understanding.

Content Material Assessments for Pre-, During, and Postreading

The instructional framework for reading for content understanding includes prereading activities to prepare the reader for engagement with the text, during reading activities to monitor and check textual understanding, and postreading follow-through strategies to take the reader beyond the text to find applications for real-world information. Authentic teacher-made assessments, such as **analytic** or **holistic rubrics**, inventories, lab rubrics, and individual conferences, form the checks and balances for knowledge building. In addition, student self-assessment is a powerful reality check for content reading ability.

Sample assessments for pre-, during, and postreading activities are supplied in the following sections; keep in mind that authentic assessment is based on requirements for student knowledge building.

Prereading Assessments

The self-appraisal in Table 8.4, focusing on supportive organizational aids and disciplinary language concerns, could be given to students prior to individual conferences or even peer conferences.

Table 8.4 Friendliness of Text Assessment

Directions: Rate your (social studies, science, math) textbook based on organizational aids or text features that help you with your assignment. What features could be helpful to you? Mark those features with a (+) and provide an explanation. Why are the other features not as helpful (−)? Please provide an explanation.

Purpose of Assignment: (Student provides target learning of reading assignment.)

Feature	Feature Friendliness (+/−)	Explanation
Table of contents		
Chapter introductions		
Chapter summaries		
Headings		
Key terms		
Signal words		
Pictures		
Graphs		
Index		
Glossary		

Source: Schumm and Mangrum (1991, pp. 120–124).

Next, let's focus on text organizational features that can scaffold student acquisition of disciplinary material. Conferencing with students while having them describe organizational features acts as an observational form of assessment that proves powerful for learning.

Prereading Conference Rubric

The rubric in Table 8.5 can be used as a grid to compile evaluations of student understanding of text organizational features such as the table of contents, glossary, index, graphics, maps, timelines, text boxes, sidebars, highlighted quotes, and other elements as tied to their assignment. What needs reteaching? Who can become a text features expert for readers who struggle? Who needs more support? Individual conferences with students will uncover difficulties with text that can be remediated.

Table 8.5 Textbook Organizational Aids Rubric (Teacher Rubric/Individual Conference)

Directions: Expand the rubric and take some annotated notes on individual or group results. Use results to formulate mini-lessons on text features for small groups of students or the whole class.

Criteria	Text Feature (Specific)	Explanations (Teacher Notes)	Students + (Mastery) or – (Nonmastery)
Expert status	Contrast	Well understood, with multiple evidences supplied	Mike, Sara, Jenny, and Tom
Strong work	Contrast	Only one evidence—look for more	Leigh, Sandy, and Manny
Proficient	Contrast	Appears to understand—check again	Sue, Kathy, and – or + Nancy
Needs support	Contrast	Needs reengagement—use everyday examples (check interests)	– Lisa and – Todd

Next, the content assessment template allows readers to compare and contrast several diverse text sources in similar content areas. It is best accomplished through partner or group work, and it is important that the activity is modeled first by the teacher and can be employed during reading as students analyze each text individually or after reading, with students comparing and contrasting the elements of the three texts.

During Reading Assessment

The following example of a science content assessment template (see Table 8.6) compares and contrasts three informational texts within the framework of focus questions. The three texts are *The Forest in the Clouds* (Collard, 2000), *Coral Reef: A City That Never Sleeps* (Cerullo, 1996), and *Meadowlands: A Wetland Survival Story* (Yezerski, 2011). Students are required to provide specific evidence from each of the selections to fill in the template and to discuss.

Moreover, informational texts offer opportunities to challenge students to apply what they are learning to the real world they live in.

Prereading prompts may include the following:

- Who can tell me a little about the environment?
- What kind of environment do we have here (in New York)?

Table 8.6 Science Content Assessment Template and Model

Questions	The Forest in the Clouds	Coral Reef	Meadowlands
What can you tell me about the environment in this book?	• Moist • Wet • Misty	• It is underwater • It is in salt water • It is in the ocean	• Wetlands • Marshes • Garbage dump
Was it warm? Cold? Wet? Dry?	• Warm • Wet	• Warm • Aquatic	• Temperate • Warm and cold
What creates this type of environment in this area?	• Clouds • Mountains • Warm, wet wind • Condensation	• Reef-building corals • Skeletons of sea animals • Build-up of calcium carbonate	• Estuary—Hackensack River empties into Newark Bay • Fresh and salty water soaking spongy, flat ground
Can you give me an example of where we might find this environment?	• Costa Rica • Caribbean Sea • Tropical places	• Around the equator • Australia, Indonesia • Caribbean Sea, Indian Ocean	• Meadowlands, New Jersey • Many other city wetlands
What are some of the plants and animals that thrive in this environment?	• Ferns, orchids, figs, avocados, epiphytes • Birds, bellbirds, quetzals, parrots • Frogs, salamanders, golden toads	• Snails, crabs, shrimp, clams • Clown fish, parrot fish, • Lion fish • Sea slugs, eels, octopus, sponges, zooplankton, algae, anemone	• Prepollution—oysters, ducks, rabbits, deer, bears, turkeys, fish • Postpollution—fiddler crabs, red foxes, pickerel frogs, box turtles, ospreys
How does the environment support these types of organisms?	• Trees to live in • Water puddles in leaves • Clouds contain water and nutrients • Plants support animals	• Provides shelter and protection • Provides food • Provides oxygen	• Volunteers clean garbage, build nest boxes • Marsh algae and plants clean water • People soak up floodwater and keep soil in place
Where do the plants or animals get their nourishment?	• Birds and bats eat fruit • Plants get moisture and nutrients from the clouds • Animals eat insects	• Algae • Parasites • Sunlight • Other animals	• Marsh algae • Grasses and reeds • Other animals—little • Fish
What are some of the threats to this type of environment?	• Global warming • Pesticides • Drying out • Pollution	• Global warming, fossil fuels • Pollution, poisonous chemicals • Dynamite and divers break up reef	• Pollution and chemicals • Overpopulation • Flooding • Lack of volunteers for cleanup
What evidence from the story supports your answer?	• Disappearance of the golden toad • Disappearance of frogs, toads, snakes	• Coral turns white (coral bleaching)	• Birds of prey disappeared with pesticides in the 1940s

Sources: Cerullo (1996), Collard (2000), Heisey and Kucan (2010), and Yezerski (2011).

- Can anyone tell me what a rainforest is?
- Where might we find one of those?
- What is one aspect of what makes a "rainforest"?
- Who can tell me some animals or plants that live in a rainforest?

Examples of during reading cues and text-supported evidence include the following:

1. Locate the picture that demonstrates the effect of chemicals on waterways. How does the image help you understand the author's message?

2. Find the map that will tell you in what country the "forest in the clouds" is located? What part of the world is it located in? Why might it be located there?

3. A glossary provides definitions of terms important for the book. Locate one that might be helpful to you and explain how so.

4. What additional resources (books and Internet sources) might be helpful if you were assigned a report on this topic? How so?

Example of postreading cues and text-supported evidence are as follows:

- Using the evidence (key facts) you located in the three texts and through peer discussion, tell us about three facts that are similar (compare) for the books and three that are different (contrast).
- What new information changed your ideas about the different environments described in the three texts?
- How do the key facts from the books tie to the environment you currently live in?

As we move on to postreading assessment, the text pattern of sequencing and providing specific evidence will be an instructional strategy that supports text visualization.

Postreading Assessment

The series of events or sequential inventory for *The Forest in the Clouds* uses a graphic chain to help students visualize or manipulate events as they unfold in the text. Readers can work as partners to check information. The teacher should ask students to locate the proof of sequential events and place them on chart paper (see Table 8.7).

The suggested assessments for pre-, during, and postreading of content materials displayed in this section are models that fit in the instructional framework for reading comprehension. As we move on, let's explore the critical role of vocabulary strategies and assessment for intermediate literacy.

Making Connections

Discuss the framework for informational reading that involves pre-, during, and postreading assessments and activities. Why does ongoing assessment go hand in hand with activities that support acquisition of key facts and application of knowledge? What instructional design ideas are you formulating to meet the criteria of pre-, during, and postreading activities? Turn to your partner and describe some of your inspirations.

Table 8.7 Series of Events Authentic Inventory

_____ As the winds climb the mountain, rising higher and higher, they cool and moisture is squeezed out of them.

_____ At the highest point in the cloud forest, damp clouds rush past, making everything wet even if it doesn't rain.

_____ In March and April the birds fly up to the cloud forest to mate and raise their young.

_____ In 1963, the golden toad was discovered when it gathered in shallow pools to mate and lay eggs.

_____ The clouds that surround the cloud forest drop 10 feet of rain per year.

_____ As the trade winds travel over the ocean, they suck up moisture.

_____ Bellbirds and quetzals spend part of the year in the lowlands looking for food.

_____ The disappearance of the golden toad indicates how everything on Earth is connected in some way.

A > B > C > D > E > F > G > H

Answer Key

A. As the trade winds travel over the ocean, they suck up moisture.
B. As the winds climb the mountain, rising higher and higher, they cool and moisture is squeezed out of them.
C. Bellbirds and quetzals spend part of the year in the lowlands looking for food.
D. In March and April the birds fly up to the cloud forest to mate and raise their young.
E. The clouds that surround the cloud forest drop 10 feet of rain per year.
F. At the highest point in the cloud forest, damp clouds rush past, making everything wet even if it doesn't rain.
G. In 1963, the golden toad was discovered when it gathered in shallow pools to mate and lay eggs.
H. The disappearance of the golden toad indicates how everything on Earth is connected in some way.

Vocabulary-Based Strategies and Assessments

Instead of using dictionaries as the sole source for word information, allow students to hear and practice using the target words in many contexts, in their speech *and* writing, so that they can grapple with shades of meaning and better understand all the ways that words can be used. (Kelley, Lesaux, Kieffer, & Faller, 2010, p. 9)

Outdated vocabulary-teaching techniques such as workbook fill-ins or dictionary exercises to look up word definitions must be supplanted with active, interest-based vocabulary exploration for children. The dos and don'ts of vocabulary instruction in Table 8.8 provide sound advice for the new practitioner.

Table 8.8 The Dos and Don'ts of Vocabulary Instruction and Assessment	
DON'T	• Use a dictionary as the main source for word information. • Give students lists of unknown words to look up in isolation. • Teach low-utility words highlighted in textbooks. • Test students with multiple-guess formats or matching. • Establish a vocabulary program of memorizing "superficial" word meanings. • Promote a vocabulary program where students become "word callers."
DO	• Focus on a *deep* understanding of a small number of high-utility words. • Balance direct word teaching with word-learning strategies. • Promote student "ownership" of content vocabulary. • Strive to incorporate "student-friendly" definitions or explanations. • Select words that students will use across contexts. • Employ active and partner learning to support acquisition of word meaning. • Evaluate vocabulary understanding through authentic, teacher-developed assessments.

The Role of Active Learning in Vocabulary Instruction

The role of active learning in vocabulary development has been well established. Students who engage with words by hearing them, using them, manipulating them semantically, and playing with them are more likely to learn and retain new vocabulary. (Blachowicz & Obrochta, 2005, p. 263)

Strive to increase the quality and duration of vocabulary work in your classroom! Nurturing **word consciousness** in students, or awareness of and interest in all sorts of words and their meanings, should be a part of your daily routine. Developing word consciousness involves both a cognitive and affective stance regarding words. Word consciousness promotes a motivation to learn new words and a deep and inquisitive interest in words (Graves & Watts-Taffe, 2008).

To promote word consciousness, set up a word wall and encourage students to "walk the wall" and hang their favorite words, new or known, on it. Classmates are allowed to add sticky notes with pictures or graphics, synonyms, antonyms, related words, or word etymologies, and then student partners walk along the wall to quiz each other on the words (Graves & Watts-Taffe, 2008). Teachers can use this opportunity to gently assess student word wall submissions, additions, and partner cross-preview (see Table 8.9). Since words are left up the whole year and students walk the wall one or more times a week, word consciousness is nurtured.

Table 8.9 Word Wall Checklist

Directions: The classroom word wall should function as an ongoing authentic, student-generated vocabulary activity and review. Keeping track of students who are posting words and responding to those words with synonyms (S), antonyms (A), pictures/graphics (P/G), sentences (SE), related words (RW), etymologies (E), and any other posting criteria is critical to vocabulary growth. Even more critical is noting students who are not adding words to the wall and exploring their hesitancy with an individual conference. Keep observational notes that will be moved to a checklist for each student (see the abbreviated sample below).

Word Wall Date Observed: _____

Word Wall Additions	S	A	P/G	RW	E	SE	? NOT ADDING	Partners	Notes
Justin							X		CONF.
Kelly	X		X		X			X	
Lindsay		X			X			X	

Observation Notes:

Vocabulary, conceptual, and technical terms should be generated through students' literacy endeavors. Reading selections, news articles, Internet information, and discussions should be the sources for authentic word exploration. When students have a stake in learning a word—that is, when it is important to them—the end goal of vocabulary acquisition is genuine. Active strategies make the process all the more fun and engaging.

Authentic Strategies and Assessments for Rich Vocabulary Development

Interrogate a Term

In this modification of Bromley's (2002) "Interview a Word" strategy, we have repurposed the interactive interview technique to focus on expository selections. Students pose questions to words or terms in their content unit that they are interested in knowing more about. Partners supply answers, on behalf of the terms, based on their content knowledge. Applying this to informational text provides powerful opportunities for growth in academic vocabulary. Here are some sample questions students might ask of the vocabulary terms:

- Are you useful? What is your purpose (inform, entertain)?
- What part of speech is your job (noun, verb, adjective, or adverb)?
- How do you fit in with the topic (weather) we are studying?
- Can you provide evidence of that connection?
- Who are your word relatives? (Word trees)
- Can I draw a picture of you or design a visual? If so, how? (Conceptual development)
- What other functions do you have outside of _____? (Multiple-meaning words)
- What do you like? What don't you like? (Synonyms, antonyms)
- What are favorite words or phrases that could partner with you? Why? (adapted from Bromley, 2002)

This fun activity can be vetted through a simple checklist with the questions addressed, student–teacher quick conferences, or partner-based assessments.

Vocabulary Notebooks

Maintaining vocabulary notebooks throughout the year allows students to get comfortable with new words and then present their vocabulary to the class, thereby practicing presentation skills in the process. One veteran teacher who is sold on vocabulary notebooks explains the process this way:

My students love sharing their vocabulary notebooks. I assign students a different word each week. Together we thoroughly research the word and its meaning. After this is done, I have students sketch a picture to illustrate the word. At the end of the week children present their drawings to the class. (Taylor, 2011, "Share Them")

Vocabulary notebooks should be assessed through informal conferences with the teacher, routinely established at certain points throughout the school year. We recommend encouraging students to sign up for and present a word from their vocabulary journal while the teacher applies a heuristic rubric, such as the one in Table 8.10. Ensure that students are aware of the criteria for their word presentations, and conference with students individually after their showcasing of the word.

Multimodal Vocabulary Strategies

Multimodal vocabulary strategies will appeal to students who learn and retain the meaning of a new word through multimodal exploration. Teachers must be willing to present new vocabulary through multimodal strategies such as the ones discussed in the following; otherwise, multimodal learners will miss the opportunity to connect with challenging terms. When the teacher stresses a variety of ways words can be retained, students benefit and their lexicons grow.

Table 8.10 Vocabulary Journal Rubric		
Vocabulary Notebook Presentation Criteria	Competent/Expert	Needs Support
Definition is student's own/ synonyms provided	New word is defined through student-generated sentence(s). Added points for synonyms provided.	Struggles with defining new word. Unable to provide synonym.
Visual representation of the word	Word visualization is accurate and reflects meaning.	Word visualization is not reflective of word; student may be thinking of another word.

As far as assessing these active vocabulary practices, simply employing sticky-note comments addressed to individual students would work well. Make sure you challenge them to improve their work in some way and check for that improvement.

> Timothy: I enjoyed the way you talked about your word in the fourth-grade class. Your stance demonstrated your knowledge of a difficult word and a synonym. I am proud of you.
> Just an idea for next time; I will look for a full sentence being used to define the new word.

Vocabulary Trails. The teacher attaches sequence vocabulary words to the floor, and students must follow the correct trail and describe the journey. For example, using connecting words such as *first, next,* and *finally,* students are encouraged to practice with transitional words.

Vocabulary Parade. Students attach a word to their person or to a hat and parade to other classrooms to explain the word to their parade audience. At each stop, selected students present their new word to the audience, defining it through their own meaning and/or presenting synonyms.

Human Make a Word. Students hold up placards with either single letters or word parts to make a complete word. They must pronounce and define the new term. This activity can potentially combine vocabulary comprehension with word work, spelling, practice with word parts (affixes), word families, and syllabication.

Word Why? Plus Pictures! The use of pictures or graphics is crucial to reinforce a vocabulary word that may be conceptually loaded or connected with time or space. The teacher employs oral questions as well as images to gauge student understanding of words in context.

Create the question cards with images that embed the target words. These can be laminated easily. Students will indicate "yes" or "no" to the teacher query. A quick assessment of overall class responses as well as individual responses will prove valuable (White, n.d.):

1. Pose the question to students: "Would you be *drowsy* if you were in an amusement park?"

2. Have them answer "yes" or "no" and explain why.

Word Boxes. This weekly vocabulary strategy relies on student word choice, partner work, and individual presentations. The process of integrating the vocabulary word into the student's schema is the key component to this method (Feezell, 2012).

Students select words to submit to the word box on Friday. These are words they find interesting or ones they want to understand better. They use the word in a sentence from the text where it was found or design a sentence themselves. The teacher selects five words to teach the following week.

Monday: "Here is an interesting word ___ found this week." Read the word in context, read the definition, and then talk about inferences based on the word's meaning. If appropriate, attach pictures. Tack to the word wall.

Tuesday: Sentences are written for the words, then a shared writing experience with chart paper follows. Start with a prompt and allow think-pair-shares. Combine responses and record them on chart paper.

Wednesday: Reinforce meaning and share understanding. Draw pictures or visuals.

Thursday: Play tic-tac-toe with words; then students move to one side of the room when a cloze sentence is read for word to be filled in orally.

Friday: One student is in the spotlight to answer fill-ins for five words and to review words. Students receive red, yellow, and green cards they can hold up to show that they agree, are unsure, or disagree. This provides a clear picture of whole-class understanding. For assessing, the teacher formats a checklist with the vocabulary running horizontally across the top margin and the class list running vertically down the side. An Excel spreadsheet could serve the same function. This checklist can easily be reused for weekly word box activities.

Lift-the-Flap Words. This strategy can aptly function as a review for content vocabulary—in addition, the images reinforce the meanings.

1. Fold an 8 1/2-by-10-inch piece of paper in half lengthwise and make four equal flaps by cutting the folds.

2. Students pick four words from the reading that they want to learn.

3. Under each flap, students define the word, add a synonym, add an antonym, and use the word in a sentence outside of the reading context.

4. When all information is filled in, students take turns reading the sentence, saying "blank" where the word should be inserted.

5. They call on a partner to guess the word and lift the flap to check (Bromley, 2002).

Mountain (Picture should be located below each flap word)			
A raised part of the earth's surface. SYNONYM = gigantic hill ANTONYM = valley The avalanche roared down the mountain and caught the skier.	Plateau	Valley	Stream

Engaging with vocabulary through fun activities as review and reinforcement merits no formal assessment, but a quick check with student partners as to how well they are doing will suffice.

Color My World. This is a great vocabulary technique to teach the nuances of words with differing shades of meaning by connecting them to colors.

1. Collect a variety of paint chips from home improvement stores (they are generally free).

2. From student reading selections or unit topics, select nouns, adjectives, or descriptive words that contain nuances of meaning that lend themselves to aligning with certain colors.

3. Hand out a variety of paint chips to groups, partners, or individuals. Ask them to match words with colors. For example, *furious* might align with bright red, *depressed* might be represented by a shade of blue, and *pristine* might be open to student interpretation (I would align it with a light purple). Ask students to explain and defend their choices.

4. Another technique involves using science or social studies terms, such as *camouflage*. Students might combine greens, browns, and oranges to show that *camouflage* means to use color to hide or deceive.

5. Ideally, a color word wall could be used for this technique, with students cutting the paint chips into separate shades, aligning them with new vocabulary terms, and then using sticky notes to comment on other students' choices.

6. Teacher assessment might involve positioning sticky-note comments on the color word wall after the activity, with students next being allowed to read and respond to the comments. Last, the teacher would collect and annotate these comments and student rebuttals.

Vocabulary Chains. Students love to make vocabulary chains and attach them to their desks as a reminder of the connections between words.

For this activity, challenge students to connect words through synonyms (similar words), antonyms (opposites), or word characteristics or descriptors to reinforce vocabulary. For younger students, use Tier 2 everyday terms; for older students, request academic vocabulary. Use arrows to show relationships between synonyms, antonyms (e.g., *spiral* and *straight* for math), and word characteristics (e.g., *mechanic*, *mechanical*, and *mechanism*).

Formative Vocabulary Assessments

Ongoing, formative vocabulary assessments offer opportunities for teachers to check students' vocabulary understanding. But keep in mind that this strategy can be inadequate with striving readers who have limited background knowledge, because they may not respond during group questioning. To remedy that, have all students use hold-up cards that are small placards with response prompts such as a letter, yes or no, or numbers to designate sequence.

- *Choice:* Students select the word that best fits the context.

  The wealthy man in the ___ vehicle zoomed past the other cars quickly.

  (a) automobile (b) luxurious (c) swiftly (d) blue

- *Cloze:* Students provide the missing word, choosing from a word bank.

  In science class, the students learned about cold-blooded and warm-blooded _____.

- *Retell:* Students place a word on a continuum of synonyms.

  Big > large > huge > gigantic

- *Analogies:* Features of a familiar word are tested.

  Gigantic is like _____. Which of these words means about the same thing as gigantic?

  Mammoth, enormous, tiny, huge, diminutive

- *Oddities:* Students hear or read attributes of a noun and determine which word does not belong.

  House > wood > concrete > car > shingles

Key Word Dance

The power of movement and dance in learning vocabulary should not be underestimated. Truly active and engaging for students, the Key Word Dance serves as a physical "mnemonic" for troublesome vocabulary.

1. Select vocabulary and create hand motions to go with the words. For example, *trestle*, a type of bridge, may be indicated with fingers intertwined to form a bridge-like arch.

2. Put words on flashcards, and have a student hold up one card at a time.

3. A group of six to eight students move in a conga line, or the latest dance craze, as they make the hand motion that goes with the word.

4. Next, students change the movement to match the card being held up.

Making Connections

Considering the active vocabulary strategies described previously, explain how a teacher could use one of them for authentic assessment of terms. Remember, literacy assessments mirror the goals of vocabulary growth. What format appeals to you and your teaching style? Can you explain why that particular vocabulary strategy appeals to your teaching style and also how it connects with the Common Core language requirements?

Let's transition our focus to comprehension of informational texts. Attention to new instructional shifts and methods of assessing student connections with informational text are vital to prepare students for attaining 21st century skills.

Comprehension of Informational Texts

The majority of elementary-aged students are excited to engage with informational trade books on topics of their choosing. With the advent of Common Core State Standards, the switch from narrative text to a renewed focus on informational text reigns. Instruction in informational text structure should be ongoing, explicit, and integrated throughout the curriculum. Children are generally less familiar with expository text, and for the striving reader it can present a specific set of challenges that focus on density of information, passage length, and lack of vocabulary knowledge.

Striving readers often attempt to decode accurately but exit the passage not understanding what they have read. They are unable to use fix-up strategies or to monitor comprehension (Hedin & Conderman, 2010). **Fix-up strategies** are on-the-spot strategies such as rereading, using context, partner reading, or reading-reflection pauses (among many others) to support students in monitoring their reading.

We present a variety of assessments—formative, informal (teacher made), and summative—to aid teachers in recognizing student strengths and weaknesses in understanding expository text. As teachers expose their students to expository or informational trade books, we recommend using a preassessment to gauge student self-awareness and prior knowledge in recognizing the features of and engaging with expository trade books. Both **text features**, or **organizational aids** (headings, subheadings, table of contents, glossary, maps, timelines, charts, and indexes), and expository text structures (Bluestein, 2010) need to be explicitly taught to students, along with fix-up strategies.

Why assess student comprehension of informational trade books? Research indicates the following reasons:

1. Struggling readers can have severe difficulty in selecting the main idea of an expository text selection (Rapp, van den Broek, McMaster, Kendeou, & Espin, 2007); consequently, a pre–post assessment should be administered.

2. Standardized reading test content is 70% to 80% expository (Daniels, 2002a); so students should practice test items similar to those found on these end-of-year tests.

3. Informational trade books are a powerful means to get across content knowledge in primary grades, instead of using a textbook (Reutzel, Read, & Fawson, 2009); thus, students should be made aware of external and internal features that are generally found in informational trade books, including picture books.

A high-quality informational book provides opportunities for students to experience visual imagery, figurative language, and powerful descriptions. Check out this passage from *Coral Reef: A City That Never Sleeps* (Cerullo, 1996):

Ghost Town

About ten minutes after sunset, an eerie quiet descends on the reef. Swaying sea fans provide the only visible movement, like tumble weeds blowing through a ghost town in a Western movie. The coral passages are silent, deserted, and vaguely menacing. The daytime fishes have retreated to their shelters. Many large predators have headed off with the setting sun into deeper waters beyond the reef. Others— some groupers, snappers, and reef sharks—remain hidden in the shadows where they can ambush any lone stragglers.

The quiet period lasts only about 15–20 minutes. Then, as abruptly as if a film director had shouted "Cut!" nocturnal creatures burst onto the set and the scene changes to night maneuvers. (pp. 34–35)

Gorgeous photographs mirror the textual descriptions, thereby aiding visual connections. Keep in mind that all students benefit from multimodal connections with text. As a reading teacher, strive to choose quality informational texts whose visuals leave lasting impressions for students.

Assessment of Prior Knowledge

Prior knowledge assessments for informational text can take many forms; however, we suggest trying the assessment of prior knowledge (for informational texts) developed by Langer (1982). Students are required to access and verbalize their familiarity with terminology or content language taken from an intermediate-level informational text, in response to verbal prompts from the teacher.

Student responses are evaluated as objectively as possible using a scoring rubric. Refer to Table 8.11 for the assessment tool, and give it a try!

Table 8.11 Assessment of Prior Knowledge

Directions: Teacher prompts students with the following after reading each term or phrase singly:

- What comes to mind when you hear _____?
- So what does _____ mean?
- Do you have any ideas about _____?

Note: Prompts can be modified to meet the needs of the students and/or text.

Employ the scoring rubric to your best judgment to rate students' knowledge of the terms.

Book Title: *The Forest in the Clouds*

Name of Student: _____ Teacher: _____

Term or Phrase	1 Much Knowledge	2 Some Knowledge	3 Minimal Knowledge
	Able to define Provides examples Labels Attributes Shows relationships Compares/contrasts	Provides examples or comparisons Attributes Defining characteristics	Personal associations Sounds like . . . Personal experiences
Camouflage			
Migrant			
Nocturnal			
Nutrient			
Tropical cloud forest			
Predator			
Trade wind			

Text Structures/Patterns

Many well-written informational children's texts clearly illustrate the text pattern being taught. Text structures can be found within sentences, throughout paragraphs, or throughout the book. Strong informational text often showcases a mixture of patterns as well as narrative (story) elements (Moss, 2004).

Furthermore, helping readers explicitly "dig out" transitional words and clue words that signal text patterns is critical. As texts gain complexity, readers are prepared to locate and connect transitional phrases with the main idea of the text.

Expository text structures should be taught early and individually as patterns, not conglomerated. Text structures or patterns include the following elements:

1. *Description:* Vivid writing used to present a visual image for the reader

2. *Sequence:* A series of events or processes that follow a certain order

3. *Comparison:* Demonstrates how events in the story or other topics are alike or similar

4. *Contrast:* Illustrates how events in the story or other topics are dissimilar or different

5. *Cause and effect:* Presents a cause followed by an effect, such that one thing leads to another

6. *Problem/solution:* Presents a problem situation and a solution, or how the problem is solved

Author David Macaulay (2003), in his highly acclaimed book *Mosque*, relates the mosque's role in the center of Muslim social and religious life. This sophisticated text is supported by multiple transitions that effectively guide the mature reader into the world of mosque building. The following paragraph highlights that process:

Admiral Suha Mehmet Pasa had done well by war. For *more than thirty years* his successful naval campaigns had made him a highly respected member of the Ottoman aristocracy, a favorite of two sultans, and a very rich man. *For most of his life* his eyes were firmly fixed on the borders of the empire he worked so valiantly to protect. *But as another decade* slipped away, he found himself confronting less familiar boundaries—those of his own mortality. (Macaulay, 2003, p. 9; emphasis added)

Remember, **graphic organizers** are very useful in helping students conceptualize a pattern as it applies to informational text. In addition, text-pattern graphic organizers can be provided to students to complete based on the structures in their reading selection.

Identifying key ideas as well as locating the main idea of a reading selection can be challenging for striving readers who are reading below grade level. As they strive to decode, comprehension suffers, particularly when they are asked to identify the main idea.

Location of Main Idea

Striving readers often struggle with locating the main idea of a paragraph, particularly when it is not in the first sentence or not highlighted. Once the student locates the main idea, rereading the paragraph is suggested. Main ideas are generally located in three ways: implicit or understood, embedded within the body of the paragraph, or occurring at the end. Readers should be able to identify the main idea through teacher modeling and practice—not by filling out worksheets. We recommend using authentic trade books and sentence strips, sticky notes, and text highlighting. When main ideas fall at the end of a paragraph, help students reconfigure the paragraph by (a) highlighting the main idea and reading it first and (b) reminding students that all other sentences should connect to the main idea in some way. We recommend using sentence strips to write out supporting detail sentences, noting the text structure, and having students verbalize how these details support the main idea. Graphic organizers can be useful to reinforce relationships among the various supporting sentences, as shown in Table 8.12.

Table 8.12 Location of Main Ideas in Childhood Informational Trade Books		
Location	How Found	Example
Early in the passage	Introduction, implicit, embedded, end of paragraph	"The forest here is called the elfin forest. Trees in the elfin forest grow only 10–20 feet high, but they aren't short by nature. They are stunted by the constant winds howling past" (Collard, 2000).
End of passage	Conclusion	"No one knows who invented the wheel. People may have invented wheels in different parts of the world at different times. Carts with wheels were made in Egypt more than 5,000 years ago" (Glover, 1997).

Source: Hedin and Conderman (2010).

Developing the expertise of summarizing is a higher-level skill necessary for filtering out the myriad details located in dense, technical informational text. It is a challenging reading skill to master and one that needs to be taught, modeled, and reinforced frequently as vocabulary demands increase in difficulty.

Generating Summaries

Magnet summaries can aid students in organizing important information into summaries. The approach is based on the use of key words or concepts (magnet words) as concrete structures for writing summarizations (Wood & Harmon, 2001). Use this strategy for a selection to help keep in mind key ideas, following these steps:

As you are reading, pick a section and locate four key words or concepts (magnet words). Find details to support each magnet word, and write these words and phrases around the term/concept. Next, take the terms/phrases from the cards and write brief summary statements (see Table 8.13 for a sample). Use the meat of those summary statements to write a summary paragraph. You may have to change words around and use transition words. Read your paragraph aloud to the group.

Original Passage. The majority of elementary-aged students are excited to engage with *informational trade books* on topics of their choosing. With the advent of Common Core State Standards, the switch from narrative text to *expository text structures*

Table 8.13 Sample Magnet Summary

This sample magnet summary demonstrates how the strategy can be applied to informational texts.

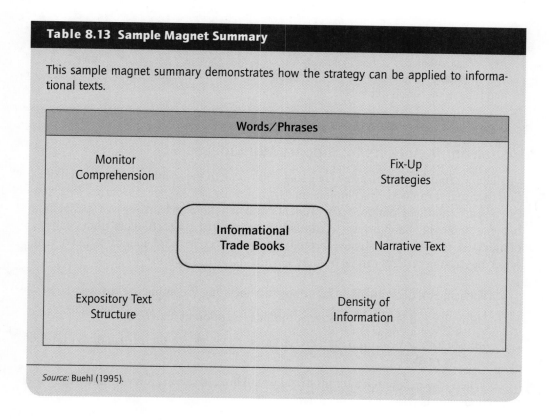

Source: Buehl (1995).

predominates. *Expository text structures* include question/answer, problem/solution, main idea, cause/effect, comparison/contrast, and order/sequence. Instruction in text structure should be ongoing, explicit, and scaffolded. Children are generally less familiar with expository text, and for the striving reader it can present a specific set of challenges that focus on *density of information, passage length,* and lack of vocabulary knowledge. Struggling readers often strive for decoding accuracy but exit the passage not understanding what they have read; they are unable to use *fix-up strategies* or to *monitor* comprehension (Hedin & Conderman, 2010). We present a variety of assessments—formative, informal (teacher made), authentic, and summative—to aid teachers in recognizing the strengths and weaknesses of students in understanding expository text.

Summary Paragraph. The Common Core State Standards have placed a greater emphasis on informational trade books, switching instruction from narrative text to expository text structures. These structures include question/answer, problem/ solution, main idea, cause/effect, comparison/contrast, and order/sequence. Since children are usually less familiar with expository text, it is important to address the challenges of density of information, passage length, and lack of vocabulary knowledge. Due to this, many students have difficulty comprehending the passages and are unable to use fix-up strategies or monitor comprehension. A variety of assessments is presented that can help teachers recognize student weaknesses and strengths in understanding expository text.

> ⌐ **Making Connections** ─────────────────────────────────
>
> As practice, develop a magnet summary for the sample summary paragraph in Table 8.13. With your partner, replicate the graphic for the magnet summary, designating the key idea and supporting details in the box.

Visualizing Key Facts to Support Main Ideas

Helping children organize key facts that contribute to the main idea or essential question in visual formats such as bubble maps, graphic organizers, or structured overviews can be particularly helpful for those students who benefit from learning in a spatial manner. Try employing bubble maps as formative measures to gauge students' understanding of the construction of a main idea through key facts. Keep in mind, identification of main ideas for striving readers can be hindered by the following factors:

1. Focusing on decoding is so laborious that meaning is completely lost.

2. Difficulty and length of passages prohibits retention of material.

3. Informational texts may be several grade levels above the instructional level of striving readers.

4. When readers attempt a fix-up strategy with limited success, they tend to extinguish their efforts (Hedin & Conderman, 2010).

Allington (2007) has consistently written that all readers need texts they are comfortable reading all the time. The tremendous effort readers expend identifying the main idea when they are reading text at a frustration or hard level is defeating to watch and must be avoided. Daniels and Steineke (2011) advise allowing students to self-select short, easier reading passages that spark their interests as they attempt to construct the main idea. Bubble maps for formative assessment can be useful instruments in a teacher's toolbox, because they help pinpoint challenges with main idea recognition.

Pronoun Referents and Appositives

Readers of informational texts, particularly novices or recipients of frequent read-alouds, may struggle with pronoun referents. A problem all too common in informational text is that of students not knowing what the *it*, *these*, or *them* in the selected text might refer to. Teachers should model explicit connections between pronoun referents and the proper or common nouns they represent. Likewise, appositives—or key terms and definitions occurring in the same sentence, with commas separating vocabulary words from descriptors—can be challenging. Make clear the representation of the appositive through sentence substitution and rereading. Table 8.14 provides some quick tips for identifying referents and appositives.

Special attention should be paid to the use of pronouns in sentences; casual readers can miss the connection or not understand what the pronoun represents. Clearly, the power of appositives should not be ignored.

Table 8.14 Pronoun Referents and Appositives

		Aids for Readers of Informational Texts		
Term	Definition	Use in Informational Text	Example/Clue	Challenges
Pronouns	Short, decodable words—*it, that, these, she, he*	Decrease redundancy in writing	"A lock is a canal with gates at each end. *It* is used to raise and lower boats from one level of water to another" (Glover, 1997).	A problem in informational text is students' not knowing what the *it, these,* or *them* might refer to.
Pronoun referents	What a pronoun refers to as connected to a noun	Remind yourself what the "referent" is to substitute the real thing for the pronoun	"*It* is a time of abundance. Fig trees and wild avocados burst with fruit that the birds and their babies eat" (Collard, 2000).	A large number of sentences in informational text begin with pronouns referring to key terms at the end of previous sentences.
Appositives	Key terms and definitions occurring in the same sentence; commas separate vocabulary words from descriptors	Comma acts as an equal sign. Explicitly connecting the key term to the synonym is a good strategy. Transform to cloze and maze sentences.	"The minaret, the tower from which Muslims are called to pray five times a day, was erected in just 30 days" (Macaulay, 2003).	Students may not fully understand target sentences if they miss the appositive connection.

Let's now focus on a genre of nonfiction that has been underused in classrooms. Under the category of nonfiction, students enjoy biographies they have chosen to read. Recently written biographies highlight heroes (Nelson Mandela), presidents (John F. Kennedy), and social activists (Woody Guthrie).

A Special Note on Biographies

Biographies are great beginning bridges from fiction to nonfiction because they are typically narrative and sequential. (Bluestein, 2010, p. 597)

Biographies offer a literacy opportunity unlike many other forms of informational text: They present real people from all walks of life with whom students can connect or empathize. Many exciting and engaging biographies are available for intermediate students. Recent trends in the writing of biographies focus on using more dynamic styles, including comic strips, graphic novels, and nonlinear formats. Author Vicki Cobb relates her approach:

I've recently had the fun of writing *Harry Houdini: A Photographic Story of a Life* for DK books. Telling the story of Harry's life chronologically like so many other people have done did not appeal to me. After absorbing their work by reading dozens of books, it occurred to me that there were recurring themes running through Houdini's life as a multifaceted person, and I used these themes to organize my book: Harry as a young man, a showman, a self-promoter, a scholar and author, a family man, and as a champion of science against spiritualists. (Kurkjian, Livingston, & Cobb, 2006, p. 92)

Biographies offer reading opportunities in the arena of civic ideas and actions and social justice, along with increasingly sophisticated illustrations. In fact, starting in 2001, the Robert F. Sibert Medal and Honors have been given annually for "informational books commended for their quality in writing, illustrations, documentation, and appropriateness of presentation of topic for the intended audience" (Kurkjian et al., 2006, p. 87); the award celebrates "nonfiction as works of art" (Kurkijian et al., 2006, p. 86). Biographies should be used frequently in the social studies, reading, science, and other content areas. Childhood lives of famous people, highlighting Hispanic American, African American, Asian America, and Native American heroes and heroines, offer students a connection to their own struggles.

Under the Common Core State Standards for students reading informational text (K–5), students are responsible for recognizing connections and relationships among individuals, events, ideas, concepts, and pieces of information, all of which would apply to reading a biography. In addition, they should be able to identify text features and structure, as well as quote accurately from the text and compare and contrast accounts of the same event or topic.

Many biographies contain organizational features and structures that aid new readers of biographies, including the following:

- A table of contents that highlights important periods, events, and places in a person's life
- Sidebars that highlight information, bulleted information, and fact files
- Nonlinear expository writing that may focus on themes, illustrations, or graphics
- An index that highlights certain concepts, vocabulary, or information pertinent to the text
- Timelines or graphics displaying life events, encapsulating the most important events in a person's life
- Photographs or drawings with captions, which provide important visual connections (Bluestein, 2010; Kurkjian et al., 2006)

Intermediate readers of quality biographies should be exposed to multiple organizational features and text structures through a text walk led by the teacher, who points out the "friendly text features" outlined in Table 8.15.

Often, famous individuals or heroes will stand out as characters or subjects of popular biographies. Facts and dates may overshadow the human element so critical in children's biographies; however, many fascinating **characterizations** of lesser-known figures, such as inventors or artists, can engage students. Suggestions from the *Salisbury Post* (Kosin, 2011) include the following biographies:

- *Mary Smith* by A. U'Ren—Ever wonder what people did before alarm clocks? How did they get to work or school on time? This story about Mary Smith tells of how the townspeople in one English village made sure they got up on time using a pea shooter.
- *The Magical Garden of Claude Monet, Picasso and the Girl With a Ponytail,* and *Camille and the Sunflowers: A Story About Vincent Van Gogh,* by Laurence Anholt—This series

Table 8.15 Biography Pathways: Friendly Text Features

A Biography Pathway:
Friendly Text Features

BIOGRAPHY TITLE	SIDEBARS OR SIDE NOTES	ILLUSTRATIONS
Is there a subtitle that helps explain the person? What does the illustration on the cover depict? How might the picture influence your reading? **1 MILE**	Does the author employ sidebars or embedded notes, quotes, or other devices to summarize key information? If so, how are they helpful to the reader? **4 MILES**	What is the power of the illustrations for the reader? How did the illustrations help you personally to understand the individuals? **7 MILES**
BIOGRAPHY AUTHOR	GLOSSARY OR KEY TERM BANK	APPENDIX
Have you read other books by this author? If so, what is their style of writing? Copyright—what year was the book written and would that affect the content? **2 MILES**	Does the book highlight key terms/phrases in the text or defined in the glossary? What would be the author's purpose in doing so? **5 MILES**	Did the biography contain an appendix that listed additional sources of material on the individual? If so, how would that be useful to the reader? **8 MILES**
TABLE OF CONTENTS	TIMELESS OR GRAPHIC ORGANIZERS	ADDITIONAL UNIQUE FEATURES
Is there a table of contents? How is this helpful? If not, how does the pattern of the text support your reading? **3 MILES**	Is there a chronological listing of life events such as a timeline or graphic organizer? Is it used effectively to support the story and how? **6 MILES**	Described additional unique text features that add to the richness of the text. Explain how they support the reader. **9 MILES**

of three books contains stories about young people and their encounters with famous artists. All inspired by real people, these are great story books for a child's first look at some famous artists.

- *The Day-Glo Brothers* by Chris Barton—Have you ever seen a traffic cone with that bright orange color? This fun biography tells the story of Bob and Joe Switzer, who invented fluorescent colors and how these colors changed the way we live today.
- *Stone Girl, Bone Girl: The Story of Mary Anning* by Laurence Anholt—Ever find a fossil hidden in the earth? Mary Anning discovered one of the most important fossils, the great ichthyosaur, when she was 12 years old in Lyme Regis in Dorset, England. Learn about her path to discovery, starting with her surviving a lightning strike at 15 months old. (Kosin, 2011, n.p.)

Kay Vandergrift (2014) of Rutgers University poses reflective questions teachers should consider when connecting intermediate-grade students with biographies:

Modern media bring real life characters into our homes and our lives "close-up" but very fragmented. Literary biographies may also present only a fragment of a life; but, even then, they often give a sense of wholeness or continuity within a context in their presentations of a life.

1. What degree of fictionalization, if any, is acceptable in biography for children and young people?

2. Do the kinds of fictionalization change with the age of the intended audience?

3. Is it necessary for the characters of children's biography to be inspiring to or role models for readers?

4. Is it true that children are not interested in most aspects of the adult lives of famous individuals?

5. Does biography for young people adequately represent the faces of our society: race, gender, class, religion, etc.?

6. Do young people read biography as an opportunity to "try on" various occupations or life styles?

7. Does biography introduce young people to those from other social or national groups? Do biographies of authors interest children?

8. Are author videos helpful to children trying to find out about an author?

9. How would you characterize youth biographies of "media stars"? What role do these biographies play in the lives of children?

10. How do contemporary societal concerns influence the selection of subjects for biographies?

Making Connections

Focus on the 10 questions Vandergrift poses to teachers when addressing the use of biographies with intermediate readers. With your partner, discuss selected questions, particularly numbers 3, 4, 9, and 10. The issues put forth by Vandergrift as potential considerations impact the connectedness of students when reading biographies.

Comprehension of Narrative Texts

Teachers often lament that their students can read but do not understand. The most important thing about reading is comprehension. It is the reason we read. (Scharlach, 2008, p. 20)

The rollout of the national Common Core standards, leading to state-generated Common Core standards, has definitively transformed the teaching of narrative or story texts for intermediate grades. The Common Core instructional shifts to prepare students for college readiness and career preparedness include the following:

- *They demonstrate independence* by comprehending and evaluating complex texts across genres without significant help.
- *They value evidence* as they are able to cite specific proof or key details when offering an oral or written interpretation of a text.
- *They comprehend as well as critique,* being engaged and open-minded, yet questioning the author's assumptions or opinions.
- *They respond to varying demands of audience, task, and purpose* as they set and adjust purposes for reading, recognize nuances of language, and relate tone to audience composition.
- *They come to understand other perspectives and cultures* through great classics and contemporary works of literature.

Materials and selections employed in teaching are evolving; in addition to high-quality children's literature, comparative presentations among genres such as mystery and adventure are encouraged through the instructional shifts in the Common Core standards, because they build strong content knowledge. In addition to the old favorites such as fables, folktales, and myths, the graphic novel is brought into the mix. Furthermore, expectations for multimedia presentations exist, whereby students use technology and digital media strategically and capably (New York State Education Department, 2011).

Making Connections

Locate and download your state's Common Core standards or the national Common Core State Standards for English Language Arts and Literacy. Locate and highlight the intermediate English language arts/literacy standards that apply to narrative or story text standards for one particular grade. Then pick one and turn to your partner to discuss a teacher instructional activity with an assessment from this chapter that fits your teaching style. Explain why you believe this is a potent and valuable activity/assessment for student learning of informational text content.

Eight Comprehension Strategies and Question–Answer Relationship

Teacher-constructed formative assessments that check for comprehension skills are vital in judging student mastery and metacognitive awareness of the eight comprehension strategies for narrative or fiction texts. Sentence starters for students are written in italics following the comprehension strategies below. Post this list in the form of an **anchor chart** on your classroom wall, where students can access the information daily.

1. Predicting/inferring: *"In this chapter, I think . . . "*

2. Visualizing: *"In my mind, I see . . . "*

3. Making connections: *"This reminds me of . . . "*

4. Questioning: *"I wonder . . . "*

5. Determining main idea: *"I think the most important thing . . . "*

6. Summarizing: *"In 10 words or fewer . . . "*

7. Checking predictions: *"My original prediction . . . "*

8. Making judgments: *"My favorite part . . . "* (Scharlach, 2008, p. 22)

We recognize that reading strategies can be effectively used before reading, during reading, and after reading, as we discussed previously in this chapter. Raphael and Au (2005) developed the question–answer relationship strategy. Students connect with the text ("Right There," "Think and Search"), their prior knowledge ("On My Own"), and personal experiences ("Author and You") to frame questioning within phases of reading (see Table 8.16).

Table 8.16 Types of Questions for Question–Answer Relationship Strategy	
In the Book	**In My Head**
Right There	Author and You
Think and Search	On My Own

Key Ideas and Details

The Reading Standards for Literature in Grades 3–5 (New York State Education Department, 2011) are highlighted in the sections that follow through assessment options and active strategies, beginning with the standards for key ideas and details (Table 8.17).

Table 8.17 Reading Standards for Literature: Key Ideas and Details (Grades 3–5)		
Grade 3	**Grade 4**	**Grade 5**
Describe characters in a story (e.g., their traits, motivations, and feelings) and explain how their actions contribute to the sequence of events.	Describe in depth a character, setting, or event in a story or drama, drawing on specific details in the text (e.g., a character's thoughts, words, or actions).	Compare and contrast two or more characters, settings, or events in a story or drama, drawing on specific details in the text (e.g., how characters interact).

Source: New York State Education Department (2011, p. 18).

Interactive Think-Aloud

Oczkus (2012) recommends an interactive think-aloud. A think-aloud modeled by the teacher, focusing on reading strategy identification and application in the text, allows students to visualize the teacher's thinking as applied to text-reading strategies.

The teacher says, "When good readers read, they (name the strategy—connect, predict, infer, monitor, clarify, summarize, synthesize, or evaluate), and it helps them . . . ." The teacher then carries out the following steps:

1. Ask students what they know about the strategy.

2. Explain the strategy by using sequential process cues—first, next, then, and finally.

3. Model the strategy through the think-aloud. Select a brief passage to read aloud, and apply the steps you would use in a specific strategy. Say, "I am stopping here to connect. . . . Watch me as I show you how it helps me understand what I am reading." You can add props or strategy starters to support the think-aloud.

4. Partner connections and then independent practice follow. See the rubric in Table 8.18 for "noticing" behaviors.

Table 8.18 Interactive Think-Aloud Rubric Process		
Strategy Identification	**Guided Practice: Evidence of Partner Discussion**	**Independent Practice: Evidence of Sticky-Note Locating Strategies**
Connect	"This reminds me of . . . because . . ."	Students use sticky notes to locate sections of the text where the modeled strategy might be used correctly.
Predict/infer	"I think . . . will happen because . . ."	
Question	"I wonder . . ."	
Monitor/clarify	"I didn't get the word . . . , so I (reread, read on, broke up the word, etc.)."	
Summarize/synthesize	"This is mainly about . . ."	
Evaluate	"I used to think . . . , but now I think . . ." "I rate . . . because . . ."	

An interactive think-aloud encourages students to reproduce "teacher-like" behaviors in noting evidence of the reading strategies aiding comprehension.

Now let's move in the direction of deep character analysis involving locating evidence of character traits, motivations, and feelings.

Character Chains

Provide students with three arrow-shaped strips of paper in three contrasting colors. On one arrow, students will write the character's name from a book being read. The next piece will be for character traits, motivations, or feelings. The final piece will be the "evidence" arrow, on which the student will write specific evidence or an exact quote from the selection to support the character traits, motivations, or feelings. Next, the three strips are stapled together to indicate the connections in this the process. Finally, this chain should be shared with a partner and then presented in class.

A modified character grid (Fountas & Pinnell, 2001) is appropriate to catalogue and discuss evidenced-based responses in presenting a fully developed character. A sample has been completed as a model for the reader (see Table 8.19).

Table 8.19 Character Chains				
Main Character *Lisa, 10-year-old neighbor*	**Appearance/ Looks Contribute to Character Traits**	**Dialogue/ Conversation Contribute to Actions of Character**	**Actions Contribute to Sequence of Events**	**Feelings and Motivation(s) Expressed by Character or Inferred by Actions**
What the text says specifically or infers	*Lisa was a pretty blond child who always had her wishes met. The persistent pout sketched on her face indicated dissatisfaction with her life.*	*Mrs. Smith said, "Mr. Smith, you have gone beyond spoiling that girl . . . she is downright entitled." Mr. Smith replied, "But she is only asking for a dog, every child should have a dog."*	*A small toy dog, Poe, goes missing in the neighborhood. Lisa climbs into her tree house.*	*Lisa demonstrates anger and is upset with her parents for not getting her a toy dog.*
What other characters say or infer	*Her next-door neighbor Sam says he heard barking at night from Lisa's yard. It crossed his mind that Lisa had Poe, the missing dog.*	*Sam says to his mother, "I woke up last night hearing a dog barking in the Smith's yard—they don't have a dog."*	*Sam asks Lisa what she thinks happened to Poe. Lisa shrugs her shoulders and hurries away.*	*Lisa ignores Sam's comments about the missing dog and hurries away.*
Your analysis of the character	Lisa is a person who puts her wants above others.	Lisa believes she deserves to own Poe even though he is a neighbor's dog.	The evidence points to Poe being in Lisa's tree house in her yard.	Lisa's reactions indicate she is trying to avoid telling the truth.

Character trait vocabulary (see Table 8.20) should be addressed in conjunction with character analysis. How do specific character traits contribute to actions and motivations of the main character and other characters?

Action–Character Trait Links

As students come to recognize a variety of character traits from the list in Table 8.20, the next step will be to interpret actions taken by a specific character and connect them to the corresponding character trait(s). Teachers should keep a list of character traits that

Table 8.20 Recommended Character Traits by Grade Level	
Grade 3	Admirable, appreciative, carefree, demanding, indecisive, egotistical, innocent, insensitive, irritable, modest, persistent, prudent, rambunctious, rash, sensitive, spiteful, sympathetic, tolerant, trustworthy, unsympathetic
Grade 4	Assertive, cordial, cunning, defiant, fickle, haughty, hesitant, indifferent, meek, menacing, noble, perceptive, pompous, reckless, ruthless, skeptical, submissive, surly, unassuming, uncompromising
Grade 5	Apprehensive, compliant, corrupt, cross, depraved, dignified, discreet, docile, ethical, frank, glum, ingenious, lackadaisical, malicious, plucky, prudent, rebellious, selfless, sheepish, sullen

Source: Manyak (2007).

were introduced (Richardson, 2012, p. 229). Deep, prolonged discussions about character traits will prove beneficial for students; oftentimes, character trait terms are not a part of learners' lexicons. As Tier 2 vocabulary, character traits can be difficult for striving readers with limited vocabulary to name. Autobiographies would serve well as text selections to practice character traits.

The simple rubric sampled below can be enlarged to list student names, dates, character traits discussed, and narrative texts used as exemplars.

Action	Character Traits
Her mother selected the clothes she was to wear that day in high school.	Mother: Assertive and controlling

Inferences

Teaching students to infer or develop inferences that go beyond the text can be a challenging process (Richardson, 2012). The writer provides hints or clues that lead the reader to make an inference about a character or event; however, those hints or clues can often be vague, and directing students to "read between the lines" can be puzzling for them. Richardson (2012) notes that

authors leave clues that help us discover implied meanings in the following ways:

1. Dialogue between characters
2. Actions a character decides to take
3. Physical descriptions of characters
4. Inner thoughts of characters not spoken as dialogue (p. 231)

Speaker tags, or words or phrases that explain how a character says something, provide additional clues. For example,

- The politician said *poignantly*
- The politician said *blandly*
- The politician said *sarcastically*

Without knowledge of speaker tags and nuances of expression, students can be at a loss as to how a character is saying something and the implied meaning behind the words. First, teacher modeling should occur, using highly expressive language to check for student understanding of the speaker tag (Richardson, 2012). For practice sessions, allow students to whisper-read the sentences and practice the intonation of dialogue with a partner. When assessing student mastery of speaker tags, set aside time for 1-minute discussions to check for understanding. These discussions should include specific dialogue with an individual student:

1. How does this particular speaker tag relate to how a character says something? How do you know?

2. Read the dialogue as the character might say it, based on what you infer from the speaker tag.

3. What did you learn about this character by understanding the speaker tag?

A quick check for understanding assesses whether students can name the function of the speaker tag and how it influences what a character says.

Character Interviews

Character interviews are an active way to engage groups of students in developing questions used for interviewing characters in a chapter book or picture book the class is currently reading. Once a list of main characters is generated, groups of students should develop thought-provoking questions that each character can address. Based on the Common Core reading standards, emphasis should remain on locating evidence to develop questions in the following areas:

- Exploring character traits, motivations, and feelings
- Explaining how character actions contribute to a series of events
- Describing a character in depth, drawing on specific details from the text through a character's thoughts, words, or actions
- Comparing and contrasting two or more characters, describing how the characters interact

Next, have groups distribute their questions and then assume the role of a character through designation of a prop—for example, eyeglasses, hats, or other symbols associated with the character. Make sure students who are being interviewed know to reflect on a character's actions, thoughts, and motivations (Johns & Lenski, 2001). A rating rubric similar to the one in Table 8.21 may be used to judge student interview responses as connected to textual references.

Table 8.21 Rating Rubric on Character Interviews

Ratings:

    1 = Strong evidence

    2 = Minimal evidence

    3 = No evidence provided

Level I: Explores character traits, motivations, and feelings.

                            1   2   3

Comments:

Level II: Explains how character actions contribute to a series of events.

                            1   2   3

Comments:

Level III: Describes a character in depth, drawing on specific details from the text through a character's thoughts, words, or actions.

                            1   2   3

Comments:

Level IV: Compares and contrasts two or more characters, describing how the characters interact

                            1   2   3

Comments:

Keep in mind, it is important to encourage students to pay attention to other characters' reactions to the character studied and to what others say about the character. Ask students to talk about the dynamics of this situation:

Jasmine asked Ashleigh and Haley if she could be their partner on the science lab.

Neither Ashleigh nor Haley even looked up when they answered sarcastically, "Sorry, we've already begun the experiment, and it's too late." Then Jasmine heard Ashleigh mumble to Haley, "Maybe now she knows how it feels to be left out." (Really Good Stuff, 2008, p. 2)

Making Connections

Checks for understanding and other formative assessments should be ongoing and continuously used throughout a literacy lesson. Although teachers are adept at asking questions, they may fail to annotate student responses as being on target or not.

Turn to a partner and explain how you could organize a system of checks for understanding, using some of the ideas mentioned in this section of the chapter.

Craft and Structure

Recognizing the point of view a text is written in is an essential skill for intermediate readers. Judging first-person or third-person point of view is a stepping-stone for higher-level literary knowledge. Furthermore, being able to compare and contrast varying points of view adds to student expertise (see Table 8.22).

Table 8.22 Reading Standards for Literature: Craft and Structure (Grades 3–5)		
Grade 3	Grade 4	Grade 5
Distinguish their own point of view from that of the narrator or those of the characters.	Compare and contrast the point of view from which different stories are narrated, including the difference between first- and third-person narrations.	Describe how a narrator's or speaker's point of view influences how events are described. Recognize and describe how an author's background and culture affect his or her perspective.

Source: New York State Education Department (2011, p. 18).

Point of View

An explanation of the literary element of point of view warrants discussion. It may be a challenging concept for students to grasp, particularly when comparing differing points of view across narrative excerpts.

First-Person Narration. The narrator is usually the central character in the story, but even if this character is not the protagonist, he or she is directly involved in the events of the story and is telling the tale "firsthand." Readers should watch for the narrator's use of first-person pronouns—*I, me, my, our, us, we, myself,* and *ourselves*—as these will usually indicate that the passage is narrated from the first-person perspective.

Third-Person Narration. With this mode of narration, the narrator tells the story of another person or group of people. The narrator may be a peripheral character or may not involved in the story, or he or she may be a supporting character supplying narration for a hero. The narrator's frequent use of *he, she, them, they, him, her, his, her,* and *their* may signal that a passage is narrated from the third-person perspective. In third-person omniscient, the narrator allows readers the most access to characters' thoughts and feelings. Third-person omniscient narration *reveals more than one character's inner thinking.* The base *omni-* means "all," and *-scient* means "knowing" (Ereading Worksheets, 2011).

The point-of-view appraisal strategy helps students actively "compare and contrast the point of view from which different stories are narrated, including the difference between first- and third-person narrations" (New York State Education Department, 2011, p. 18). There is safety in numbers for this activity, so form students into small groups. This activity is best suited for during and postreading, when students are working through or have completed two books—one using first-person narrative and the other using third-person narrative (see Table 8.23).

Table 8.23 Point-of-View Appraisal Strategy and Assessment

	Text	Steps	Teacher Appraisal of Student Understanding
First-Person Point of View *Reminder:* While first-person point of view can allow a reader to feel very close to a specific character's *point of view*, it also limits the reader to that one perspective. The reader can know only what this character knows. First-person narrators are not always trustworthy. It is up to you to determine what is the truth and what is not.	*Rotten Richie and the Ultimate Dare* (Polacco, 2006) This text works particularly well for the purpose of first-person point of view and changing values between competitive siblings. A brother who plays hockey and a sister who is into ballet dare each other to do the other's sport, with results that surprise each of them and change their opinions.	1. Read the picture book as partners, taking turns out loud. 2. Stop at three to five points where evidence of the main character's point of view is evidenced through narration. Place a sticky note on that page and line. 3. Determine if the narration is the truth or not, based on the events of the story. Label the sticky note as such and write evidence to back up your findings.	1. Collect the text read, *Rotten Richie and the Ultimate Dare,* with sticky notes left in pages. 2. Check student work for point-of-view narration and evidence as truth or not.

(Continued)

Table 8.23 (Continued)

	Text	Steps	Teacher Appraisal of Student Understanding
Third-Person Point of View *Reminder:* Here the narrator does not participate in the action of the story as one of the characters but lets us know exactly how the characters feel. We learn about the characters through this outside voice.	*January's Sparrow* (Polacco, 2009) This text works particularly well for indicating the deep feelings of characters through third-person narration. The book focuses on the Underground Railroad in Michigan and how townspeople saved a family of escaped slaves.	1. Read the picture book as partners, taking turns out loud. 2. Stop at three to five points where the author allows the reader to know how a character feels through narration. Place a sticky note on that page and line. 3. Label the sticky note as to how the reader learns about specific characters through the outside voice.	Check sticky note responses. Same as above.
Compare and Contrast Points of View	The two books by the same author work particularly well to contrast the differing points of view used in the books. Students should also understand the author's style in the way she creates feelings of care and sympathy through both books.	How does the point of view affect your responses to the characters in the two different stories by the same author? How is your response influenced by how much the third-person narrator knows and how objective she is?	Check discussion responses contrasting the two books even though they are by the same author. In addition, make sure students pick up on the stylistic similarities, such as feelings of care and sympathy or understanding.

Sources: Annenberg Foundation (2014) and Wiehardt (n.d.).

Table 8.24 Book Sources for Point of View at Fourth-Grade Level

Examples of first-person point of view:

Let's Be Enemies by Janice May Udry

Gila Monsters Meet You at the Airport by Marjorie Weinman Sharmat

Wagon Wheels by Barbara Brenner

The Wednesday Surprise by Eve Bunting

Bigmama's by Donald Crews

One of Three by Angela Johnson

How I Became a Pirate by Melinda Long

Math Curse by Jon Scieszka and Lane Smith

Dory Story by Jerry Pallota

My Rotten Redheaded Older Brother by Patricia Polacco

Don't Let the Pigeon Drive the Bus! by Mo Williams

Diary of a Worm by Doreen Cronin

Because of Winn Dixie by Kate DiCamillo

Examples of third-person point of view:

Slithery Jake by Rose Marie Provencher

The Sweetest Fig by Chris Van Allsburg

Chicken Sunday by Patricia Polacco

The Dot by Peter H. Reynolds

Bedhead by Margie Palatini

Dirty Bertie by David Roberts

Pigsty by Mark Teague

The Greedy Triangle by Marilyn Burns

Jubal's Wish by Audrey Wood

Many Moons by James Thurber

Ludlow Laughs by Jon Agee

Source: Ohio Department of Education (n.d., p. 4).

Allowing students to explore and discuss texts written in differing points of view enriches their reading. Specific narrative texts are written from the viewpoint of a first- or third-person narrator, and teachers should compile an extensive collection of texts exhibiting varied writing styles. Table 8.24 lists some children's books that meet the criteria for Grade 4.

The use of sticky notes was mentioned in the point-of-view appraisal strategy and assessment in Table 8.23. Let's explore how sticky notes can aid teachers in their daily assessment endeavors. Sticky notes are the teacher's best friend as far as on-the-spot assessment opportunities (see Table 8.25). They are useful for jotting observations of student work goals and progress, and several sizes are available for differing purposes. At some point, transfer the sticky notes into a literacy notebook under each student's name, making sure to date the observation. These carefully taken notes will come in handy for progress monitoring and parent conferences.

Table 8.25 Sticky Note Assessments

- Carry a clipboard for coaching conferences and on-the-spot reading conferences.
- Place four to six sticky notes on the clipboard with student's names and the date of the interaction.
- Keep the conversation directive, reinforcing, and quick (1–3 minutes).
- Use phrasing such as "I understand your goal was to ____. How have you progressed so far?"

Making Connections

Consider the many forms of assessment for narrative or fictional text. We discussed checklists, individual conferences, simple rubrics, and sticky-note responses. Assessments can be flexible for use as formative checks for understanding or summative measures in many cases. Discuss the forms of assessment that fit best for you in evaluating student learning for the Common Core reading skills we highlighted. Why do those work for you?

Integration of Knowledge and Ideas

Visual connections, illustrations, and graphics have a purpose in narrative text. Readers should explain, make connections, and analyze how these visual elements impact meaning in the story (see Table 8.26).

Table 8.26 Reading Standards for Literature: Integration of Knowledge and Ideas (Grades 3–5)

Grade 3	Grade 4	Grade 5
Explain how specific aspects of a text's illustrations contribute to what is conveyed by the words in a story (e.g., create mood, emphasize aspects of a character or setting).	Make connections between the text of a story or drama and a visual or oral presentation of the text, identifying where each version reflects specific descriptions and directions in the text.	Analyze how visual and multimedia elements contribute to the meaning, tone, or beauty of a text (e.g., graphic novel, multimedia presentation of fiction, folktale, myth, poem).

Source: New York State Education Department (2011, p. 18).

The visual aspects of a piece of fiction, including illustrations, drawings, photos, and book cover pictures reinforce what is conveyed in the story. Furthermore, dramatic presentations of stories, plays, radio readings, and monologues can serve to bring a piece of fiction to life for students. As children, when we watched a special play or theatre presentation, we were riveted—and we remain so after many years. Drama has the power to capture the imagination of students, as well as enhance understanding of story.

Multimedia Book Club

One strategy, called multimedia book club, allows students the opportunity to read and analyze a quality piece of fiction while comparing and contrasting the text and a multimedia presentation of the work. Resources for locating quality children's literature that have been made into movies or film trailers are listed at the end of the chapter. Included as well are author's and illustrator's websites, which are excellent resources for visuals such as drawings, illustrations, and graphics.

The book club can take the form of a voluntary activity for students who work well independently in a group setting, a small guided group with the teacher as facilitator, or a multimedia project enactment. In all cases, the teacher must model the manner of conducting the multimedia book club and the goals of the sessions:

1. Showing respect for book club members and shared discussion time

2. Locating and supporting evidence of multimedia contributions to the richness of the work of fiction, graphic novel, poem, folktale, or myth

3. Annotating student learning through journaling, anecdotal notes, or learning charts (chart paper hang-ups)

Try this engaging activity! Focus on illustrations and interpreting their impact on the setting, character actions, and story mood (e.g., sunny, dark, suspenseful, humorous, etc.). Break apart illustrations to highlight specific details and minute or subtle nuances of meaning. The four-quadrant strategy allows students to block off three quadrants or three fourths of the picture with a piece of paper, with one fourth showing. They can then note important details in the illustration that reinforce the author's use of story mood, setting details, or character expressions, motivations, or likes/dislikes. After engaging in discussion and taking notes for one quadrant, move to each of the other quadrants for discussion and connection to the text narrative. This activity allows teachers to assess student understanding in the following areas:

Able to explain how each quadrant of selected illustrations contributes to what is conveyed in the story line. *Yes/No*

Notes:

Provides specific descriptions of the impact of the illustration on the setting, character motivations, or story mood. *Yes/No*

Notes:

Responding to Literature

Responding to literature invites students to recognize, interpret, and make connections to a variety of narrative sources, not just traditional fiction but also poetry and drama. Personal perspectives as well as those of readers from other cultures become paramount in helping readers examine multiple ideas (see Table 8.27).

Table 8.27 Reading Standards for Literature: Responding to Literature (Grades 3–5)		
Grade 3	**Grade 4**	**Grade 5**
Recognize and make connections in narratives, poetry, and drama to other texts, ideas, cultural perspectives, personal events, and situations. Self-select text based upon personal preference.	Recognize, interpret, and make connections in narratives, poetry, and drama, to other texts, ideas, cultural perspectives, personal events and situations. Self-select text based upon personal preferences.	Recognize, interpret, and make connections in narratives, poetry, and drama, to other texts, ideas, cultural perspectives, eras, personal events, and situations. Self-select text to develop personal preferences regarding favorite authors.

Source: New York State Education Department (2011, p. 19).

Making connections to other texts, ideas, cultural perspectives, and personal events is part of the dual focus of this reading standard. In addition, self-selecting texts based on personal preferences is the primary learning goal, while developing preferences regarding favorite authors is the final learning goal. Responding to literature is a complex, multifaceted strand that asks assessors to judge if students "recognize," "make connections," "interpret," and, ultimately, "self-select text based on personal preferences" (New York State Education Department, 2011, p. 19). How can teachers accurately make these judgments? Our suggestion is to use assessment protocols that allow the freedom of discussion and interpretation by students, with the teacher as a facilitator of the conversations.

Using multicultural literature is a powerful way to fulfill the standard. The following publishers or resources for multicultural books are the very best sources of multicultural literature:

- Asia for Kids (www.asiaforkids.com)
- Lee & Low Books (www.leeandlow.com/books)
- The National Education Association's "50 Multicultural Books Every Child Should Read" (www.nea.org/grants/29510.htm)
- Oyate (www.oyate.org; check out *How to Tell the Difference: A Guide for Evaluating Children's Books for Anti-Indian Bias*, by Slapin, Seale, & Gonzales, 1996)

Making Connections

Group work employing a Venn diagram could stand as an assessment of this learning standard's application. With text in hand, students would strive to make connections through narratives, poetry, and drama, to various ideas, cultural perspectives, and personal events. Holding focused discussions on diverse cultural perspectives using multicultural books is essential for students. The Venn diagram could serve as a "placeholder" for notes, ideas, and evidence students provide to support connections. Encourage visualizations, drawings, use of quotes, and direct evidence from text (see Figure 8.1).

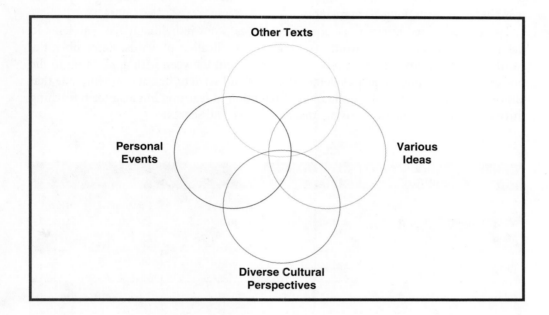

Figure 8.1
Venn Diagram

Vocabulary Assessment for English Language Learners

Developing a cache of English words held by English language learners (ELLs) is a worthwhile objective. However, vocabulary routines used for ELL students in many classrooms involve worksheets and boring, controlled-vocabulary texts. Clearly, vocabulary we choose to highlight should be embedded in interesting and engaging texts that students can connect to.

One technique—word experts—that works well for second-language students involves placing a target word from a read-aloud book on a sentence strip. Each word expert is responsible for defining and providing characteristics of the word for the school year. The teacher rotates through the class, making each student responsible for knowing and teaching several words. Finally, the teacher displays the sentence strips prominently in class.

The process for enacting word experts starts with presenting a small number of pages from a book you know students will connect with and using "word play" in multiple ways. For example, when teaching about reindeer using a nonfiction text with photos and colorful pictures, I used a stuffed animal I purchased while in Finland and paint chips to highlight nuances of the reindeer's color, with the aim of teaching the animal's physical traits. In addition, I asked for comparisons with other animals, such as deer, bulls, and elk, when we hit the word *antlers*, and asked them to close their eyes and visualize the softness of the velvet found on antlers. Prior to this, when recording the word *antlers* on the sentence strip, I wrote it on a large whiteboard and asked students to help me with spelling through initial sounds. Repetition and multiple opportunities to connect with words through multimodalities using touch, taste, hearing, and visualizing helped the word enter students' long-term memory.

Using determined intervals as assessment times, work individually with students to determine their retention of word meanings and application of words. Remember, the word experts present the words repeatedly throughout the year, with application to the book topic or real life. Table 8.28 demonstrates what I term a "flex assessment," one that allows not only for authentic evaluation of retention of learning but also for reteaching through multimodal methods using images, actions, and senses.

Table 8.28 Word Expert Flex Assessment			
Vocabulary Word	Fully Remembers: Can Define and Apply	Has Forgotten Definition and Cannot Apply	Incorrect Definition/ Incorrect Application of Word
Responsibility			
Reindeer			
Antlers			
Velvet			
Knobs			

Try word experts! We find that children retain and connect to the words selected much more strongly than they would through routines that use worksheets to practice by rote.

Furthermore, recognizing that ELLs need the opportunity to read and listen to culturally connected texts that celebrate their world, many books published recently meet that need. Publisher Lee & Low Books offers many award-winning children's books that use straightforward vocabulary and engaging images (see Table 8.29).

Table 8.29 Sample of Multicultural Children's Books

Cooper's Lesson, Sun Yung Shin, illustrated by Kim Coogan (Grade 3)

A Song for Cambodia, Michelle Lord, illustrated by Shino Arihara (Grade 5)

Honoring Our Ancestors, Harriet Rohmer (Grades 4–5)

Coming to America: A Muslim Family's Story, Bernard Wolf (Grade 3)

Around the World, John Coy, illustrated by Antonio Reonegro and Tom Lynch (Grades 3–4)

Say Hola to Spanish, Susan Middleton Elya, illustrated by Loretta Lopez (Grades 3–4)

Summer of Mariposas, Guadalupe Garcia McCall (Grades 5–6)

My Papa Diego and Me/Mi Papa Diego y Yo, Guadalupe Rivera Marín, illustrated by Diego Rivera (Grade 4)

Source: Lee & Low Books (2014).

Assessments for Students With Special Needs

Tiered Assessments Using Checklists

Tiering involves adjusting assignments to the learning needs and abilities of individual students (Robb, 2009). When we tier reading materials for struggling readers, we focus on meeting their instructional needs through choice materials at a comfortable instructional level. We also need to assess and evaluate their efforts. Through checklists, mini-checklists, observational notes, and scaffolding conferences, teachers can provide insight for further instruction and choice activities.

Choice activities are offered to meet the needs of diverse learners. Robb (2009) suggests projects to connect student work to issues and themes discussed through classroom or independent reading:

- Illustrated timeline of four to six events
- Cartoons that show problems/solutions
- Interview between two characters
- Letters between two characters
- Advice column responding to a character's letter
- Interview between two people from the same or different biographies
- Illustrations of key settings with title
- Radio play
- Diary entry
- Advertisement for a book
- Song lyrics about a character, a person, a conflict, or an event

This chapter has offered strategies and assessments to informally measure student learning of informational and narrative text selections. By offering authentic assessment options and activities for readers in Grades 3–6, teachers can meet the instructional demands put forth by the learning standards of their state's Common Core. Excellent teachers have always recognized the power of informal assessments at the intermediate grade levels. Assessments closely tied to the Common Core State Standards are a fresh addition to their teaching repertoire.

Key Terms

analytic rubric	informational or expository texts
anchor chart	mastery
characterizations	organizational aids
content area literacy	text features
disciplinary literacy	think-aloud process
fix-up strategies	tiering
graphic organizers	wait time
holistic rubric	word consciousness

Website Resources

- **"Critical Issue: Integrating Assessment and Instruction in Ways That Support Learning," North Central Regional Educational Laboratory**

This North Central Regional Educational Laboratory (NCREL) page briefly examines the aim of literacy assessment in determining how well students are meeting educators' goals, to determine what adjustments to instruction may benefit students according to assessment results. The NCREL stresses that unless the content and format of assessment complement what is taught and how, the results are meaningless. This page is a resource for teachers to determine reliability and validity, as well as fairness, of assessments. It includes links to case studies and additional material by topic. To access NCREL's page, visit **www.ncrel.org/ sdrs/areas/issues/methods/assment/as500.htm.**

- **"Reading Assessment Techniques," Southwest Educational Development Laboratory**

Southwest Educational Development Laboratory (SEDL), a private, not-for-profit organization, provides educators with detailed explications of the cognitive, phonological, and decoding reading skills students require; how these skills interrelate in the holistic reader; and multiple assessment techniques commonly used by educators to test these skills. This page explains how multiple measures may assess single skills and how single assessments may measure multiple skills to develop a comprehensive analysis of each reader. The page can be accessed at **www.sedl.org/reading/framework/assessment.html.**

- **"Assessment in Literacy," University of Connecticut**

The University of Connecticut provides an entire webpage of links to all issues relating to the assessment of literacy. The site provides links to diverse topics, from brief tables outlining classroom procedures for formative and summative assessment of literacy to full-length articles and essays delineating the importance of aligning assessment with instruction and maintaining authentic instruction in the classroom. To access the many links provided, visit **www.literacy.uconn.edu/evalit.htm.**

- **Movie Adaptations of Children's Books**

Abebooks' Reading Copy, **www.abebooks.com/blog/index.php/2009/08/12/childrens-books-becoming-movies/**

Goodreads, **www.goodreads.com/list/show/16227.Best_Children_s_Books_That_Are_Movies**

Waterford Township Public Library, **waterford.lib.mi.us/content/childrens-books-made-movies**

- **Authors and Illustrators on the Web**

Children's Literature Web Guide, **people.ucalgary.ca/~dkbrown/authors.html**

- **Multimedia Resources for Teachers and Students**

Pics4Learning.com: Royalty-free pictures for student use, **pics4learning.com/index.php**

Student Study Site: Visit the Student Study Site at **www.sagepub.com/grantlit** to access additional study tools including eFlashcards, web resources, and online-only appendices.

CHAPTER 9

Informal Reading Inventories

Robert T. Ackland

Common Core State Standards	
Key Ideas and Details	*RL.5.3* Compare and contrast two or more characters, settings, or events in a story or drama, drawing on specific details in the text (e.g., how characters interact).
Craft and Structure	*RL.5.6* Describe how a narrator's or speaker's point of view influences how events are described.
Integration of Knowledge and Ideas	*RL.5.9* Compare and contrast stories in the same genre (e.g., mysteries and adventure stories) on their approaches to similar themes and topics.
Range of Reading and Level of Text Complexity	*RL.5.10* By the end of the year, read and comprehend literature, including stories, dramas, and poetry, at the high end of the grades 4–5 text complexity band independently and proficiently.

Source: © Copyright 2010. National Governors Association Center for Best Practices and Council of Chief State School Officers. All rights reserved.

FOCUS QUESTIONS

1. How have you assessed student reading in the past? Have you tried administering an informal reading inventory (IRI)?

2. What can IRIs tell you about reading?

3. How do I administer an IRI? What do I do with the results?

4. How do I complete an IRI with my English language learners or students with special needs?

Words in Action

Looking Into the Administration of an IRI

Joyce, a fourth-grade teacher, is sitting at a table in the corner of her classroom next to Fred, an energetic 10-year-old who has low self-esteem in regard to academics and has joyfully proclaimed, "I hate reading!" more than once to his peers. Joyce is right-handed, so she has asked Fred to sit on her left—she doesn't want the materials she writes on to distract him from his reading. Joyce has decided to administer the informal reading inventory (IRI) herself because Fred is very leery of testing situations. He has never met the literacy coach recently hired by the school, and Joyce feels that sitting with an unfamiliar person or going out of the classroom to a new space may increase his anxiety and influence his performance. She has, however, consulted with the coach and taken her advice regarding the selection of an IRI that provides an assortment of narrative and expository materials with increasing complexity, and presents comprehension questions that go beyond recall of factual information. Joyce also likes that the IRI provides an easy way to record the order in which the reader retells parts of a passage (she has never been able to write fast enough when she tries to do this on her own).

Joyce has been using IRIs for 3 years. She usually has four or five students in her room who she feels will benefit from the information that surfaces from this kind of assessment. Joyce has decided to focus today on Fred's oral reading skills. She has chosen not to time his reading because she wants him to focus on trying to understand the text—not simply rush through it to beat the clock. She will start with a series of word lists and then move on to a graded set of expository passages with a few questions for each.

The other 23 students in Joyce's classroom are engaged in work at their table groups throughout the room. That activity is being facilitated by a college student who is assisting Joyce two mornings a week prior to his semester of student teaching. Her students have become accustomed to working in small groups while she meets with an individual learner. Joyce feels that the combination of independent and shared work in reading and writing that her students enjoy is a result of the study group that the primary and intermediate teachers at Joyce's school decided to do last year. The group, meeting once a week after school, focused on the Daily Five approach to balanced literacy instruction (Boushey & Moser, 2006).

This scenario is continued at the end of the chapter. After reading the chapter, you will understand how Joyce is able to best support Fred using the results of his IRI.

Reading Is the Active Construction of Meaning From Text

Reading is a dynamic process where familiarity with print, attention to graphics, activation of background knowledge, degree of interest, status of language development, and many other factors interact. Without making meaning, the process is incomplete.

Reading is the active construction of meaning from text. This statement has its roots in the work of Louise Rosenblatt, Ken Goodman, Yetta Goodman, Frank Smith, P. David Pearson, Stephen Krashen, Irene Fountas, Gay Su Pinnell, Richard Allington, and many others. The key here is that meaning is constructed by an active reader from "text." Text is more than print—think of the wordless picture book *Tuesday* by David Wiesner (1991) or the graphic novel *Maus* by Art Spiegelman (1986). In addition, reading is more than decoding letters into sound or "barking at print," as the title of an article by Jay Samuels (2007) reminds us. Reading goes beyond words correct per minute, and the depth of a reader's understanding is rarely explored by a multiple-choice test.

Here's the dilemma: We can never "see" anyone read. We can watch as eyes move across a page. We can listen when words on a list are voiced in isolation or when sentences from a magazine article are delivered in context. We can peer at a screen that displays a brain's electric activity or marvel as "nonsense words" are spoken aloud. We can ask what a reader remembers from a story, and we can grade the results of a test on Chapter 3 in a science book. But how do we know when someone is reading? How can we get a sense of the internal process of constructing meaning? We need concrete evidence. We need something that teachers, and readers themselves, can use to assist the development of reading abilities.

Informal Reading Inventories

Informal reading inventories (IRIs) provide tangible records of performance and action. A passage that is marked with symbols to identify particular miscues allows us to see how often a reader has gone back into the text to repeat a phrase or to correct a word that didn't fit during oral reading. The answers to a series of thoughtful questions asked one-on-one in a conversational setting can give us a sense of what is remembered after a passage is read silently. A written account of what a reader says when asked to retell a story or to reflect on the key points of a scientific theory can help us understand how a reader organizes new information.

IRIs can also help teachers move beyond a limited focus on the mechanical aspects of reading by providing time to have a one-on-one conversation about text. Especially when we revisit IRI data with readers, we can entertain the notion that the reader becomes part of the text through the action of reading. As German philosopher Hans-Georg Gadamer put it (1960/1989):

> Not just occasionally but always, the meaning of a text goes beyond its author. That is why understanding is not merely a reproductive but always a productive activity as well. . . . All reading involves application so that a person reading a text is himself [sic] part of the meaning he apprehends. He belongs to the text that he is reading. (pp. 296, 340)

Description of IRIs

As a teacher, I ask myself, "What is an effective way to determine how well my students read?" First, it's necessary to unpack the question. By "effective way," do I mean quick, accurate, or useful? By "read," do I mean make inferences, identify digraphs, or understand vocabulary? Then my practical concerns come to the surface: How many students can I assess at one time? What will I have them read (part of a fiction book, passages from a textbook, word lists)? Should I listen to them read aloud or watch them read silently? Is it important to record how fast they move through the text? How do I find out if their comprehension score is influenced by prior knowledge or distorted by the tension of testing?

Making Connections

New educators often wonder about the usefulness of IRIs. After reading the following section, compile a list of what the results of an IRI can tell you. Share this with a classmate and outline lessons to best support a student performing below grade level.

IRIs (pronounced eye-are-eyes) are designed to help educators address these questions. Whether they are commercially produced or teacher made, IRIs provide multiple ways to explore literacy development. Their "informal" nature allows educators to deviate from tightly structured testing protocols and enables them to select approaches that may uncover specific information. For example, a teacher may choose to ask a student to engage in silent reading of expository text followed by retelling activities. Or the teacher may ask for oral reading of a series of passages with greater and greater complexity to monitor automaticity (automatic word recognition) or to focus on **prosody** (reading with expression). The person administering the IRI uses a coding system such as the Oral Reading Key (see Table 9.1) to mark miscues (deviations from print) and observable reading behaviors so that colleagues—and readers—can examine evidence of performance and growth.

As you can see from Table 9.1, there are many codes to use when scoring an IRI. Be sure to become familiar with them and practice scoring a few IRIs before giving your first official one. Being able to score an IRI fluently can result in an accurate "snapshot" assessment of that student's abilities.

Table 9.1 Oral Reading Key

Oral Reading Key

During the administration of an informal reading inventory (IRI) or when listening to a learner who is reading other materials aloud, the following symbols can be used on your own copy of the text. Upon completion of the reading, mark "1" or "1/2" near the errors. The point value draws attention to significant miscues (deviations from print which alter meaning).

A. Count as 1 error if the miscue alters the meaning of the text; 1/2 error if not:

1. **Addition**	Write the word above a caret.	the brown dog walked.
2. **Omission**	Circle the word or word part.	the brown dog walked
3. **Substitution**	Write what the student says; draw a line through the text.	the brown dog walked.

When scoring substitutions, determine if the miscue was contextually appropriate or inappropriate, a nonsense word, a mispronunciation, or a reversal. Count proper nouns as 1/2 error. If the miscue is made with the same word over and over, count it only once.

B. Count as 1/2 error:

1. **Punctuation ignored or misinterpreted**	Circle the punctuation mark; write anything added above a caret.	the brown dog walked.
2. **Repetition**	Underline the word or word part.	the brown dog walked.

Only count if two or more words are repeated. Mark a single word, but don't count it as an error.

C. Count as 1 error:

1. **Omission of an entire line**	Circle the line.	the brown dog walked.
2. **Assistance, prompt**	Put parentheses around a word supplied.	the brown dog walked.

If the word supplied by the examiner after an uncomfortable pause is a proper noun, count as 1/2 error. If the miscue is made with the same word over and over, count it only once.

D. Do not count as errors:

1. **Self-correction**	Place a check near the correction.	the brown dog walked.
2. **Hesitation, pause**	Draw two vertical lines before the word.	the brown dog walked.
3. **Cultural, regional, or social dialect**	Write what the student says; add "Ⓓ."	the brown dog walked.
4. **Finger pointing**	Write "FP" in margin with "started" or "stopped."	
5. **Noteworthy behaviors**	Write marginal notes about fidgeting, possible vision problems, signs of tension, etc.	

Note: A version of this coding sheet first appeared in Ackland (1994).

IRIs are administered with one student at a time and, depending on the choice of content and procedures, may take from 10 to 45 minutes to complete. Key components can be selected to gather information about a student's vocabulary, decoding abilities, **oral reading fluency**, **self-monitoring strategies**, **silent reading proficiency**, and **comprehension**. The results are often used to identify reading levels, select instructional material, highlight progress, and pinpoint reading skills and strategies that need additional work. IRIs can be helpful in many grades. They are most commonly used with readers who have difficulty reading the material that is presented in their classrooms.

Nearly 20 IRIs produced by major publishers are available, some of which have had more than nine editions over the years (see Table 9.2). Generally, each published IRI includes a series of graded word lists, followed by passages of increasing difficulty, greater length, and smaller font size for oral and/or silent reading. The materials usually start at the preprimer (use a short *i* sound in *primer*) level and can go up into high school grades or beyond. Several different sets of passages (called "alternate forms") are often provided for each level, along with a variety of narrative and expository types of text. Some IRIs include simple graphic illustrations for passages below second grade. IRIs also present techniques for determining comprehension through questions or retelling activities. Reviews comparing format, approaches, and measures of reliability and validity of selected IRIs can be found in professional journals (e.g., Nilsson, 2008). Suggestions are also available if teachers want to create their own IRIs for particular instructional purposes (e.g., Provost, Lambert, & Babkie, 2010).

Table 9.2 IRIs From Major Publishers

Title	Author	Publishing Company
The Critical Reading Inventory: Assessing Students' Reading and Thinking (2nd ed., 2008)	M. D. Applegate, K. B. Quinn, and A. J. Applegate	Upper Saddle River, NJ: Pearson
Bader Reading and Language Inventory (7th ed., 2013)	L. A. Bader and D. L. Pearce	Upper Saddle River, NJ: Pearson
Adolescent Literacy Inventory, Grades 6–12 (2011)	W. G. Brozo and P. P. Afflerbach	Boston, MA: Pearson
Comprehensive Reading Inventory: Measuring Reading Development in Regular and Special Education Classrooms (2007)	R. B. Cooter, E. S. Flynt, and K. S. Cooter	Upper Saddle River, NJ: Pearson
English–Español Reading Inventory for the Classroom (1999)	E. S. Flynt and R. B. Cooter	Upper Saddle River, NJ: Prentice Hall
Reading Inventory for the Classroom (5th ed., 2004)	E. S. Flynt and R. B. Cooter	Upper Saddle River, NJ: Prentice Hall
Retrospective Miscue Analysis: Revaluing Readers and Reading (1996)	Y. M. Goodman and A. M. Marek	Katonah, NY: Richard C. Owen
Reading Miscue Inventory: From Evaluation to Instruction (2nd ed., 2005)	Y. M. Goodman, D. J. Watson, and C. L. Burke	Katonah, NY: Richard C. Owen

Title	Author	Publishing Company
Basic Reading Inventory (10th ed., 2012)	J. L. Johns	Dubuque, IA: Kendall/Hunt
Qualitative Reading Inventory (2011)	L. Leslie and J. S. Caldwell	Boston, MA: Allyn & Bacon
Informal Reading–Thinking Inventory (1995)	A. V. Manzo, U. C. Manzo, and M. C. McKenna	Belmont, CA: Wadsworth/ Thomson
Informal Reading Inventory: Preprimer to Twelfth Grade (7th ed., 2007)	B. D. Roe and P. C. Burns	Boston, MA: Houghton Mifflin
Ekwall/Shanker Reading Inventory (5th ed., 2009)	J. L. Shanker and W. A. Cockrum	Boston, MA: Allyn & Bacon
The Stieglitz Informal Reading Inventory: Assessing Reading Behaviors From Emergent to Advanced Levels (2nd ed.,1997)	E. L. Stieglitz	Needham Heights, MA: Allyn & Bacon
Classroom Assessment of Reading Processes (2nd ed., 2000)	R. Swearingen and D. Allen	Boston, MA: Houghton Mifflin
Classroom Reading Inventory (12th ed., 2012)	W. H. Wheelock and C. J. Campbell	New York: McGraw-Hill
Analytical Reading Inventory (9th ed.)	M. L. Woods and A. J. Moe	Boston, MA: Allyn Bacon

Some Purposes for Using IRIs

Teachers can use IRIs to gather data that will help them address a wide variety of questions, such as the following:

- "How do I get an idea of the student's ability to read different types of materials (such as expository or narrative)?"
- "What reading strategies are being used?"
- "How might this student perform in a one-on-one testing environment compared with a standardized test given to a group?"
- "How can I communicate with the student and the student's family regarding individual progress in reading?"
- "What books, magazines, and websites might challenge this student during assisted reading, and which ones might provide encouragement during independent reading?"

Scott Paris and Robert Carpenter (2003) draw attention to the fact that "teachers can use informal reading inventory data immediately to alter their teaching so that students are not drilled on skills already mastered or neglected on skills that are a struggle" (p. 580).

The discussion highlights outlined in Table 9.3 were generated by elementary teachers who participated in a series of workshops related to IRIs, facilitated by their school's reading specialist (Ackland, 1994, pp. 133–134).

Table 9.3 Discussion Highlights: IRI Workshops Conducted With Teachers

A. Reasons for Giving an IRI

1. Form of assessment to check for comprehension, vocabulary in isolation and context, oral miscues, reading rate, fluency

2. Useful in understanding an inconsistency between a standardized reading test result and the child's classroom performance

3. Better informs teacher about skills, approaches, and strategies child currently uses in the reading process; codifies specific strengths and weaknesses; specifics make the process more manageable for the teacher to understand and to identify appropriate strategies to teach or reinforce

4. Helps teacher determine reading level, assign appropriate materials, and design an individualized reading program

5. Allows screening to find out if a reading problem exists; can be used for program eligibility determinations and to write goals

6. Helps teacher find out about the child's attitude toward reading and own interpretation of what is read; may indicate how the reader thinks while reading

7. Gives a comparison between a child's oral response to questions and silent written answers

8. Gives time alone with a child (one-on-one)

9. Encourages a process approach rather than an end-product approach; more of a real reading situation than the contrived setting for paper-and-pencil tests; can be kept in context of classroom materials, subject matter, and approaches

10. Helps teacher see different levels in one class; indicates that children may be higher in one area but having difficulty in another

11. Gives something tangible to help communicate with parents regarding a child's reading ability

12. Can inform teacher about a child's background knowledge and interests

13. Can raise questions in the teacher's mind about types of text, reasons for reading, and strategies for both reading and teaching

B. Concerns About the Design of IRIs

1. Due to readability formulas, passage reading levels may be inaccurate.

2. Is there gender or culture bias in the passages? How is background knowledge accounted for?

3. Comprehension is difficult to assess using any procedure (including questions and oral retelling); what is "comprehension"?

4. How well does it tap word-attack, phonics, and decoding skills?

5. Parents or teachers may misinterpret the results (this is just one piece of assessment; the level of understanding may vary).

C. Concerns About the Administration of IRIs

1. How do we ensure interrater reliability? (One rater may say the child answered the question correctly; another wouldn't.)

2. Are instructions written clearly enough so that it can be given by anyone?

3. The task may cause mistakes (psychological response to the pressure of taking a test).

4. Time-consuming for either teacher or reading specialist (especially if tape-recorded).

5. Tester variability (knowledge/experience with procedures, whether or not prompting is used, etc.) needs to be accounted for.

6. How much does rapport between examiner and student influence results?

7. How do we account for time of day and whether it's a good day or a bad day to test?

8. Is this best used as one part of a battery of instruments? What is the goal, purpose for using this IRI with this student? If a commercial IRI is used, does it "carry more weight" than observations and portfolios?

9. Does readministration demonstrate progress or mastery over time? How often should it be given so that patterns can emerge? Are there enough forms available?

Guidelines for Giving an IRI to a Student

Each commercial IRI gives detailed directions for administration. Here are some general guidelines for teachers and other educators:

• *Determine what you intend to explore.* For example, you may want to know more about

1. strategies the student uses to read challenging material orally without practice,

2. recognition of high-frequency sight words,

3. familiarity with word beginnings and endings,

4. comprehension of key components of a brief narrative story, or

5. the ability to return to expository text after silent reading to find segments that supply answers to specific questions.

• *Gather the testing materials.* It is important to have the following items: a "student copy" of word lists and passages or portions of books the student will read; a "teacher copy" of the same materials (in an identical format but with larger spacing between lines) on which the teacher will make a record of what has been read; an audio-recording device, if necessary; and a stopwatch or other timing device, if desired. For each passage, the teacher needs a set of comprehension questions and/or a copy of a retelling framework listing key ideas. A summary chart is necessary for use after the IRI to assemble results.

- *Ensure your readiness to administer the IRI.* Some IRIs include disks or give access to websites where teachers can see educators administering the assessments to students. These also provide opportunities to practice coding oral reading by marking miscues on a teacher copy of the text being read aloud. Different commercial IRIs present particular ways to mark reading behaviors such as substitutions, omissions, repetitions, and self-corrections. Any system with which you are familiar can be used, as long as you can look at the markings on the text in the future and understand what the reader did. Until you are very experienced, it is vital to make an audio recording so the coding can be done later if necessary. Additional practice and training (especially with colleagues from your school) can be very helpful to determine how to interpret and communicate the information that comes to the surface during the use of a commercial or teacher-made IRI.

- *Find a comfortable setting and be ready to establish rapport with the reader.* Be alert to any interference that may skew the results. Find a place that will be free from distractions. Do what you can to put the student at ease.

- *Remember that this is an opportunity for assessment, not instruction.* Think of this as a snapshot of what the student does when reading. Resist the urge to respond to what might look like "teachable moments." You can revisit those moments if you choose to show the results to the reader at a future time.

- *Consider the implications of the data.* After giving an IRI, you can count **oral reading miscues** to get an accuracy score and look at responses to questions to estimate comprehension. Keep in mind that using these scores to identify a student's reading levels (independent, instructional, frustration) is based on many assumptions regarding, for instance, the connection between oral and silent reading behaviors (see Halladay, 2012). Ask yourself: What do the data imply about the way this particular student reads material similar to the passages in this IRI? Published IRIs provide recommendations for analyzing miscues to pinpoint challenges readers face. As Ken Goodman (1973) said many years ago, miscues are "windows on the reading process." Readers can look at their own miscues—as suggested in *Retrospective Miscue Analysis* by Yetta Goodman and Ann Marek (1996)—or can listen to themselves reading if you give them access to audio recordings. Data from IRIs can also be shared with a student's family to cast light on academic progress and with colleagues to provide evidence for the selection of instructional approaches.

Reading Levels: Independent, Instructional, and Frustration

Teachers use summary forms provided in published IRIs to tabulate percentage scores for the data to indicate how accurately the student read and comprehended the material presented in each of the graded passages. This provides a general idea of the grade level at which students can read text independently, a range of grade levels at which they can read with instructional assistance, and the grade level at which the material will probably frustrate the reader.

The concept of reading levels is generally attributed to Emmett A. Betts and his early role in the development of IRIs (Cramer, 1980; Johns & Lunn, 1994). In his textbook, published in 1946, Betts identified and described the characteristics of four different levels: basal (later renamed "independent"), instructional, frustration, and capacity (later renamed "listening capacity"). The listening capacity level was purported to be the highest level of material a student could comprehend while listening to it read aloud. Betts proposed that an appraisal of a reader's performance in terms of these levels could provide valuable information to both the teacher and the student (1946, p. 438).

Based on a reader's performance during an IRI, Betts proposed the following criteria:

Independent level: at least 99% oral accuracy with at least 90% comprehension

Instructional level: at least 95% oral accuracy with at least 75% comprehension

Frustration level: less than 90% oral accuracy with less than 50% comprehension

He supported the criteria for the instructional level with reference to an unpublished dissertation by his student Patsy A. Killgallon (1942/1983). Killgallon's study looked at the reading performance of 41 fourth-grade students.

Over the years, several studies have been undertaken to refine the criteria (see overviews in Ackland, 1994, and Halladay, 2012). As Johns and Magliari (1989) pointed out, the Betts criteria were developed on the basis of counting all miscues as errors. Their study indicated that these criteria may be too stringent for primary-grade students; however, "if teachers decide to count only miscues that affect the meaning of a passage, the word-recognition criterion should generally meet or exceed 95% for all students" (p. 131). Pikulski and Shanahan (1982, p. 102) caution against counting only the significant miscues, believing that this procedure could inflate scores and result in inaccurate placement of students for reading materials. In response to the debate, Johnston and Allington (1983) stated that there will never be a clear-cut percentage of accuracy, asking, to illustrate the problem, "How sharp is a unicorn's horn?"

Often overlooked is that the Betts criteria were based at least in part on oral rereading of material that had already been read silently (Betts, 1946, p. 456). Powell and Dunkeld (1971, pp. 638–639) draw attention to this procedure. Betts did recommend using oral reading at sight to get a quick appraisal of the independent level (p. 457), but when listing the principles of systematic observation through the administration of an IRI, he stated that "silent reading should *precede* oral reading" (p. 456). In contrast, published IRIs continue to use the process of oral reading at sight. This practice is supported by Johnson, Kress, and Pikulski (1987): "Oral reading at sight seems justifiable for diagnostic purposes since it reveals as fully as possible the difficulties a child encounters when reading" (p. 45).

During a conversation with Betts, Johns (1991) asked why, considering his emphasis on reading behaviors, he established the numerical criteria for reading levels. Betts replied: "I'm sorry I did!" (p. 493).

Halladay (2012) has suggested that we revisit the reading levels framework. For instance, she points out that "students can be emotionally frustrated by difficult texts. However, they can also be highly motivated by these texts, depending on factors such as interest, prior knowledge, and social considerations" (p. 60).

We may think it's desirable to proclaim that a student reads at the third-grade level and that more challenging material should not be provided. But Schön (1983) prompts us, as reflective practitioners, to move beyond the "comforting certainty of expertise" (p. 301). Fountas and Pinnell (2001, p. 228) clearly indicate that there is an overlap in the grades connected to the leveled texts they mark with the letters A to Z. Like the graded passages in published IRIs, these proponents of guided reading encourage teachers to view the gradient as "a continuum of progress" for readers (p. 228).

Interpreting IRIs

Vygotsky's Zone of Proximal Development: An Instructional Range for Reading

Pikulski's (1990) definition of instructional level—"the optimal level of text difficulty for stimulating student growth in reading when that student is working with the support, guidance, and instruction of a teacher" (p. 516)—is remarkably similar to Vygotsky's (1930–1935/1978) definition of the **zone of proximal development** (ZPD)—"the distance between the actual developmental level as determined by independent problem solving and the level of potential development as determined through problem solving under adult guidance or in collaboration with more capable peers" (p. 86).

Instead of attempting to specify an instructional "level," let's consider a zone or "range" similar to the ZPD. The instructional range can be envisioned as the space on a column above a mark for the level of independent performance and below a mark for the level of frustration. When instructional activities are directed toward the upper end of this range—the upper end of the ZPD—the learner is encouraged, with support, to move higher on the column. As this happens, the level of independent performance moves upward as well. There are probably several ranges for each student, especially when we consider the importance of a learner's interest and prior knowledge. A book about dinosaurs that is at the tenth-grade level may be within a fifth grader's instructional range if she is interested in dinosaurs. The same child may have difficulty reading an adventure story about talking mice that is classified as a fourth-grade text if she doesn't think mice should be personified.

IRI results that indicate an instructional range, together with the findings of other informal assessments such as running records (Clay, 1985), observations, and attitude surveys, can be vital components in a movement toward authentic assessment. One school district in Ohio moved away from a requirement that teachers give time-consuming IRIs to all their students when it was determined that a 3-minute Multidimensional Fluency Scale helped them identify proficiency in four areas—expression and volume, phrasing, smoothness, and pace (Rasinski, Ackland, Fawcett, & Lems, 2011, p. 23)—yet the teachers know they still have IRIs as an option to obtain more detailed information if needed.

James Wertz (1985) tells us that "Vygotsky (1930–35/1978, 1934/1986) introduced the notion of the zone of proximal development in an effort to deal with two practical problems in educational psychology: the assessment of children's intellectual abilities and the evaluation of instructional practices" (p. 67). It is curious that IRI literature rarely refers to Vygotsky. One exception is an article by Katherine Stahl (2012) in which she states, "Consistent with Vygotsky's concept of the zone of proximal development, children can work independently at low levels of difficulty but can still work productively with tasks at a higher level of difficulty by increasing the amount of support" (p. 48).

Oral Reading: Coding, Counting, and Analyzing Miscues

The determination of oral reading accuracy depends on what kinds of reading behaviors are counted as errors. There has been interest for many years in the distinctions among different kinds of miscues and their relation to three cueing systems: graphophonic, syntactic, and semantic (Goodman, 1969). Some miscues can be identified as significant because they alter the meaning of the text and may affect comprehension. But others, such as repetitions, self-corrections, slight omissions, or contextually appropriate substitutions, may actually indicate that a student is interacting with a text to make meaning. In addition, some miscues, such as dialect variations, may have no impact on the reader's understanding. The debate continues, because some authors feel that word recognition is the basis for building effective reading abilities (McKenna & Picard, 2006).

In an attempt to decrease the amount of examiner subjectivity in counting errors, the authors of two books (Harris & Sipay, 1990, pp. 227–228; Richek, List, & Lerner, 1989, p. 96) have proposed the following:

A serious or major miscue should be counted as one error.

A minor miscue should be counted as one-half error.

Self-corrections, hesitations, disregard for punctuation, and dialect variations should be marked but not counted.

However, this solution is not as straightforward as it may seem. There is no consensus concerning what constitutes major and minor miscues, and there is a plethora of ways to mark oral reading behaviors. This variety makes it difficult to compare performances on different commercial IRIs and to decipher what the reader actually did. For instance, if a *P* is marked near a word, it may indicate either a partial mispronunciation or a word prompted by the examiner. In addition, some marks are so cumbersome that they can't be made spontaneously while a student is reading, requiring the teacher to wait until the IRI is over and then listen to an audio recording of the passage. It is hoped that the Oral Reading Key (see Table 9.1) will serve as an effective way to code oral reading consistently and to give guidelines for distinguishing insignificant miscues from errors.

Making Connections

Whether you decide to use commercial IRIs or your own generated IRIs, consistency in scoring is important. This is especially true if you plan to give IRIs regularly to track student literacy growth. Any change in scoring can influence your findings and affect the support you provide your students.

One advantage of using a published IRI is that the directions and summary sheets assist teachers in the interpretation of the data from oral reading. How many miscues are substitutions? How often does the student need to repeat words to construct meaning? What is the frequency of difficulty with the initial portion of words compared with the final portions? As with other features of IRIs, once the data are collected, there are many ways teachers can put them to productive use for the learners.

Students Can Use IRIs to Inform Their Own Efforts to Grow as Readers

If there is to be a shift from what Frank Smith (1992) calls the "official view of learning," in which learning is difficult work, to an "informal view" (renamed by Smith in 1998 as the "classical view"), in which learning is envisioned as a continuous, social process, then

IRIs can play a part. Readers can be invited to explore the reading process by developing an explicit awareness of the challenges they face and the joys they will encounter.

IRIs and English Language Learners

Continuing assessments are extremely important for English language learners (ELLs). Standardized tests in English rarely reflect ELLs' abilities or content knowledge. Using informal assessments, teachers can target ELLs' specific problem areas, adapt instruction, and intervene earlier. IRIs can provide a more informed picture of ELLs' abilities, skills, and ongoing progress. The No Child Left Behind legislation requires detailed evidence of the progress of ELLs. Records from informal assessments make it easier when questions of grading, program placement, and special services arise (Colorín Colorado, 2007a).

As with all students, the instructional goal is for ELLs to meet or exceed grade-level expectations in curriculum goals and objectives. Table 9.4 provides effective tips for and benefits of using IRIs with ELLs.

Table 9.4 Using IRIs With ELLs

Here are a few things to keep in mind:

- A student's L1 (first language) abilities in reading can be explored by a teacher who is proficient in that language. Word lists, passages, and questions in the L1 can be used. Sharing data from a first-language IRI can draw a student's attention to what he or she does in the L1 to make sense of text. The student can then be encouraged to apply those strategies to reading in the target language—English.
- The one-on-one nature of the IRI procedures allows a monolingual English teacher to establish a comfortable and friendly setting for an assessment of English reading abilities.
- Thanks to the "informal" aspects of IRIs, it is possible to move freely between words in isolation (word lists) and various forms of connected text (passages). Word lists can be developed and passages found or composed that focus on particular onsets and rimes (word families), letter combinations, sight words (words that can't easily be decoded phonetically), high-frequency words, or specific vocabulary. The coding system for oral reading used during the IRI can then allow a teacher to test what has been taught in the classroom and can uncover particular L1 sounds and pronunciations that don't transfer into English.
- Some IRIs have illustrations that accompany the lower-level passages. These graphic representations may provide information that will assist students in their decoding of printed words. For older ELLs who may feel demeaned by the juvenile nature of the drawings and stories at these levels, consider finding high-interest picture books (including informational text with photographs) that can be used in a cycle of instruction and assessment.
- Audio recordings of comprehension activities can provide rich data about a student's ability to understand text and convey information in English. There is no dependence on writing skills when the questions, answers, and retellings are delivered orally.
- Some ELLs are adding English as a third or fourth language. Others may speak a language other than English at home or in the community but may have very limited literacy skills in that language. Gather information about the linguistic background of the unique individual who is expanding his or her literacy repertoire.

IRIs and Students With Special Needs

As stated earlier in the chapter, IRIs are designed to identify a student's reading needs. Performance on an IRI will help determine the instructional level and the amount and kind of support that may be beneficial for an individual. This is essential for students with special needs who may require directed emphasis in areas such as word recognition, vocabulary development, reading strategies, and comprehension techniques. The results of an IRI can highlight a student's strengths and weaknesses to inform instruction.

As with ELLs, IRIs are detailed records of student progress and can be used to assist with program placement and special services. Table 9.5 details how using IRIs with students with special needs is beneficial to instructional and program planning.

Table 9.5 Using IRIs With Students Identified With Special Needs (Special Education)

- Assessments using IRIs can be very valuable for children with special needs. Based on the data collected, targeted instructional strategies can be developed. These can be listed in a student's Individualized Education Program (IEP).
- Progress in areas such as oral reading accuracy and ability to comprehend narrative stories can be documented by examination of specific evidence from IRIs given at multiple times throughout the school year. However, educators need to be careful not to chart growth with numerical scores for accuracy and comprehension. The informal nature of the protocols for administering IRIs, coupled with the fact that there may be limited reliability in terms of content and level distinctions between the passages in different IRIs, makes comparisons problematic.
- Before administering an IRI with a child who is receiving special education services, it can be useful to know the particular characteristics and goals that have been identified within his or her IEP.
- Consultation with teachers and care providers who are familiar with a child's personality, emotional well-being, academic attitudes, and physical abilities can help a reading specialist or literacy coach determine effective ways to develop rapport that will improve the likelihood of a productive IRI experience.

Scenario Conclusion

Looking Into the Administration of an IRI

Preparation

On the table in front of her, Joyce has her teacher copies of the material she wants Fred to read. A week ago, she made a full set of photocopies of the word lists, reading passages, comprehension questions, and retelling frameworks ranging from first to sixth grade. She

(Continued)

(Continued)

will replenish the set for the student she works with next week by making new copies of what she uses today with Fred. She knows full well that the materials don't necessarily identify the expectations of each grade level, but she also knows that they are clearly more complex from one level to the next.

Joyce hands the IRI manual to Fred. "This is an IRI," she tells him. "You saw me do one of these with Lashon last week."

"Yeah, she said it was kind of fun. I figured I'd get a turn."

Joyce lets him know that he will be reading a few lists of words and some short passages that she has marked in the manual with sticky notes. She explains that the purpose of the IRI is to help her understand what he does when he is reading. She requests that he try to do his very best work.

Joyce places her cell phone on the table. "I'm going to use this to record your reading. Shall we see what you sound like?"

She asks him to say his name and give the date, and then she plays it back to make sure the device is working. She has a digital recorder nearby as a backup in case her preferred technology lets her down.

Word Lists

Joyce opens the manual to the first sticky note. It is a first-grade word list—a list she has selected as a starting point because she is sure that Fred will be able to read all the words correctly. She plans to use these word lists to help her decide where to start the oral reading of passages. After turning on the cell phone recorder, she picks up her pen with her right hand and gets ready to mark the teacher copy of the list in front of her. She points with her left hand to the first word on the list in front of Fred and says, "Please start here and continue reading down the column."

As Fred says each word aloud correctly, Joyce marks a plus sign next to the word on her teacher copy. When he reads the first five words without difficulty, she asks him to move on to the next column (the second-grade list). Fred pauses for a moment when he encounters the fourth word on the list. Joyce makes two vertical marks near that word (the symbol she uses for hesitation) and decides to have him continue reading the entire column of 20 words. When he completes the list, she sees that he read all the words without error. She asks Fred to move to the next column. He reads a few words on the third-grade list inaccurately, so she marks what he said next to those words and continues to put plus signs next to the others. She wants him to get used to the fact that she is always writing as he reads.

Passages

"OK, let's move on to reading some short passages," Joyce says when Fred is obviously stumped by the eighth word on the third-grade list. There is no need to have him struggle to read any more words in isolation at this time. She knows that a word recognition task (it would be word "identification" if she asked for meanings) is not the purpose of this assessment. She determines that Fred should start with the second-grade passage because that is the highest-level word list that he read with 100% accuracy. She wants him to have very little difficulty during his first encounter with connected text.

Joyce finds the second-grade passage in her photocopies and puts the word lists and lower-level passages at the bottom of her materials. The target passage is now on top. She turns her pile over so Fred doesn't see the passage before she is ready to record his reading performance.

Joyce reaches over and opens the IRI manual to the second-grade passage. She is happy that this published IRI uses a code to indicate the level of the passage (there is no need for Fred to know the grade level for the selection). Joyce puts a blank piece of paper over the passage but allows Fred to see the title. Joyce says, "The title of this passage is 'Rocks and Stones.' It's about the different kinds of rocks and stones that someone could find in the mountains. Tell me a few things you already know about rocks and stones."

Joyce has recently learned, thanks to the literacy coach, that some authors of IRIs suggest that the teacher engage the student in a brief discussion before oral reading. Joyce has decided to do this to set the scene for Fred, because she knows that during this assessment he will be compelled to read several passages in quick succession. Joyce also realizes that a student may know so much about the topic of the passage that he or she could answer the comprehension questions correctly even before reading the passage—ah, the joys of testing. In those cases, she has switched to one of the alternate passages that is at the same grade level as the one she had intended to use. If the passage she wanted Fred to read were about, for instance, automobile engines, she would move to an alternate; after having him in class for the past 2 months, she knows that he could write a passage on that topic.

Fred tells Joyce a few things about rocks and stones. Joyce thanks him, turns over her photocopies, picks up her pen, and looks to make sure her cell phone is still recording.

"I'd like you to read the passage out loud. When you've finished, I will ask you a few questions about what you've read. OK?" After a nod from Fred, Joyce uncovers the passage.

Coding Oral Reading

As Fred begins to read aloud, Joyce moves her pen beneath the words on her copy of the text. She's happy that she has practiced the technique for marking miscues with one of her fellow fourth-grade teachers, José. They've decided to use what they call the ORK (the Oral Reading Key in Table 9.1) whenever they code oral reading. It allows them to create a record that can be commonly understood among teachers who wish to share results of their students' efforts. When a student substitutes a different word for what is in print, a quick line can be drawn through the word in the text and the substituted word written in the space above. When a student omits a word, the teacher circles it. If the student then self-corrects by saying the right word, all the teacher needs to do is place a check mark above the word to indicate the correction. Some IRIs direct teachers to circle substitutions and draw a line through omissions, so Joyce is happy to use one coding system, regardless of which published IRI she selects for a student. There are also times when she uses the ORK to do a quick assessment of oral reading performance by simply marking on a photocopied page of a book that a student has selected from the library. Joyce has become proficient at marking miscues as they arise—rarely does she have to take the time to go back through audio recordings.

As expected, Fred is able to read the second-grade passage successfully. Joyce uses her pen only once—to draw a line under one word that Fred repeats. Joyce decides to ask him only 3 of the 10 questions about that passage. When he answers them all correctly, she moves to more complex text.

(Continued)

(Continued)

Joyce introduces the third-grade passage in the same way as the previous passage. She marks two substitutions that Fred makes and is happy to place a check mark over the second when Fred corrects what he said the first time he looked at the word. She makes a mental note to remember to show this to him after the IRI is over—his ability to self-correct means that he is monitoring his own reading. Perhaps Fred and the other students in the room have been influenced by the times during shared reading in small groups when Joyce has pointed to the small sign she made for the classroom wall that prompts a reader to ask, "Am I making sense?"

Comprehension

Joyce continues to mark a few other miscues as Fred reads. She then asks him all 10 questions provided by the IRI. It is such a time-saver to have these questions at her disposal.

The same process is repeated for the fourth-grade passage. As they move into the fifth-grade material, Fred is showing signs of his frustration. Joyce jots "started fidgeting" near a word on the third line—a word he may never have encountered before. After multiple miscues during his reading, Fred moves on to the comprehension questions. When Joyce asks Question 4, identified as "Inference" on her sheet, Fred says, "I have no idea what the answer is." Joyce decides that she doesn't need to continue. The "informal" aspect of IRIs indicates that she can determine it is in the best interest of this learner to stop here.

"Well, that's enough for today," Joyce says. "Oh, before you go, I'd like to show you something." Joyce flips through her papers and finds the passage where she made a check mark above a substituted word. "Look what you did here. This shows that you corrected what you said at first."

"Yeah, it didn't make sense when I read it."

Joyce smiles. "That's what readers do. They make sense."

Key Terms

comprehension (reading)

informal reading inventories

oral reading fluency

oral reading miscues

prosody

self-monitoring strategies

silent reading proficiency

zone of proximal development

Website Resources

- *Informal Reading Inventory*, Steve Rutledge (1998)

This website takes the reader step-by-step through an IRI assessment. It begins with tips and suggestions for preparing reading materials, determining books' levels, creating questions, giving the assessment, scoring, and interpreting the results. For more information, go to **lrs .ed.uiuc.edu/students/srutledg/iri.html**.

- **Informal Reading Inventory Video**

This YouTube video shows a literacy coach describing her analysis of an IRI given to a Grade 2 student. She reviews the results of the word list and passage reading, and she shares how the errors indicate where the student is lacking in knowledge and what activities she does to remediate. To see the video, go to **www.youtube.com/watch?v=dq6MdQO35-c.**

Student Study Site: Visit the Student Study Site at **www.sagepub.com/grantlit** to access additional study tools including eFlashcards, web resources, and online-only appendices.

CHAPTER 10

Reading Commercial Screening and Diagnostic Assessments

Nance S. Wilson

Common Core State Standards	
Anchor Standards for Reading	*CCRA.R.10* Read and comprehend complex literary and informational texts independently and proficiently.
Range of Reading and Text Complexity	*RL.3–5.10* By the end of the year, read and comprehend literature, including stories, dramas, and poetry, at the high end of the grades [K–5] text complexity band independently and proficiently.
Reading and Informational Text	*RI.K–5.10* By the end of the year, read and comprehend informational texts, including history/social studies, science, and technical texts, at the high end of the grades [K–5] text complexity band independently and proficiently.
Range of Writing	*W.3–5.10* Write routinely over extended time frames (time for research, reflection, and revision) and shorter time frames (a single sitting or a day or two) for a range of discipline-specific tasks, purposes, and audiences.

Source: © Copyright 2010. National Governors Association Center for Best Practices and Council of Chief State School Officers. All rights reserved.

Words in Action

Kevin and Quinton

Accountability and data analysis, as two of the most important aspects of student progress, should be student centered and student driven. We see how this can work in the following classroom.

Kevin and Quinton are starting third grade. They are nervous about this school year because they know at the end of the year they will have to take "The Test." Reading was difficult for both boys in second grade. They have heard from kids on the bus that "The Test" is very hard and that if they don't do well they may have to go to summer school. After a summer of baseball, swimming, and playing outside, neither boy is interested in summer school.

In the first week of school, Kevin and Quinton had to take a preliminary test to check their vocabulary and comprehension. This is supposed to help predict how they will do on "The Test." Their teacher planned lessons based on the results of the test they took during the first week of school. The boys had a lot of fun reading books together, creating graphic organizers around vocabulary words, and engaging in close readings.

After about 6 weeks of working together, the boys took another test to measure their progress on comprehension and vocabulary. After this test, the boys learned that they would be assigned new partners to work with in their reading and vocabulary activities. The boys were disappointed but not surprised. Quinton had been reading the books with ease and had no trouble identifying vocabulary terms, while Kevin was still struggling with some of the words in their readings. Kevin is determined to work hard so that by the time they take their next test in 6 weeks the boys will be in the same group again. Kevin plans to start reading outside of school so he can "catch up" to Quinton.

As the boys progress through the school year, their teacher continues to assess them every 6 weeks to see how they are doing. She uses the assessments to plan her instruction and knows that by the time the boys take "The Test" they will be prepared.

There are many different reasons for assessment in a comprehensive assessment program. We assess students to identify if they are at risk, we monitor students' progress to ensure that they are learning, we gather information to inform instruction, and we assess the effectiveness of the instruction. To accomplish all these tasks, teachers must use a variety of assessments, from the informal assessment tools we implement throughout our daily teaching to more standardized commercial tools. The assessments discussed in previous chapters are considered informal in nature; they are key to helping teachers monitor students' progress and supply information

that informs instruction. In this chapter, commercial assessments are introduced to provide a deeper understanding of the language of standardized assessments and the different purposes for assessment. The commercial assessments identify students who are struggling and determine whether instructional techniques are effective.

Commercial assessments are formal in nature in that they have undergone psychometric analysis to determine if they are reliable and valid. An assessment is **reliable** when it yields the same results when given to the student again under the same circumstances. An assessment is **valid** when it has demonstrated that it assesses what it claims to assess. Commercial screening, progress monitoring, diagnostic, and outcome measures are standardized tests because they are administered to a group of students under "standardized" conditions.

When considering standardized tests, three categories are used to describe them: diagnostic, criterion referenced, and norm referenced. **Diagnostic tests** are used to identify a student's strengths and weaknesses in a particular skill area. **Criterion-referenced tests** compare the performance of the test taker with a fixed criterion, the standard or specific learning task. **Norm-referenced tests** are standardized tests in which the student's results are compared with the norming population having taken the test. Due to the standardization of these tests, the ways the scores are reported are often confusing to parents and teachers.

Making Connections

Hark back to your early testing experiences. What memories remain concerning the tests you were given and your positive/negative experiences related to the testing events? How might these experiences influence your administration of tests with your future students?

Understanding Test Scores on Commercial Standardized Tests

The Score Report

Students' achievements on these assessments are communicated in the form of score reports. These score reports contain several measures that can sometimes cause confusion and misunderstanding. The trouble arises from the fact that score reports do not communicate achievement with a percentage-correct score. For instance, norm-referenced tests often report scores on a bell-shaped or normal curve. The curve represents the average or norm performance of a population and the scores that are above or below the average within that population. The **bell curve** compares a student's test performance to those of their same-age peers. The most commonly referenced scores on the bell curve are **percentile rank** and **stanine**. The percentile rank shows the student's position relative to the **norm group**. If a student receives an 85-percentile rank, that student is equal to or greater than 85% of his or her same-age peers; it does not mean that the student scored 85% of the items correctly. Stanines are another type of scale score; they range from 1 to 9, with 5 being average (Ford, 2009). Stanines group percentile ranks into relative areas of achievement (see Figure 10.1). They are considered poor measures of an individual's achievement because of their lack of specificity.

Figure 10.1
Commonly Reported Scores on the Bell Curve

Source: Huck (2012).

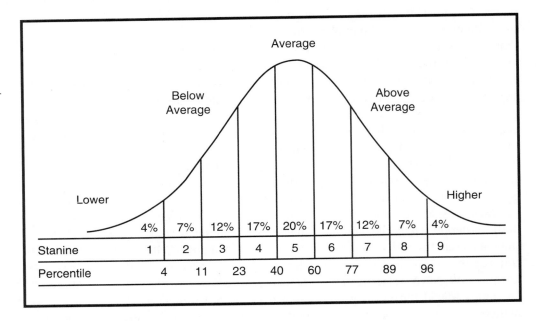

The **standard score** represents how well a student performed on an assessment compared with the mean, or average. This score can estimate if a student's performance is above average, average, or below average compared with the norm group. The standard score can be used across assessments to compare student achievement on different tests. One type of standard score that you will see on student score reports is the **normal curve equivalent** (NCE). The NCE shows where a student falls along the normal bell curve of achievement. The score is reported from 1 to 99 and is similar to the percentile scores discussed previously. The advantage of NCE scores over percentile scores is that they can be averaged when analyzing school and/or classroom performance.

Other commonly used scores that lead to confusion are the **grade- and age-equivalent scores**. Similar to other scores, these scores compare the student being tested with others in his or her same age or grade. A grade-equivalent score of 5.5 on a third-grade reading test means that the third grader who took the test read the material as a fifth grader with 5 months of fifth grade would have read that same test.

It does not mean the third grader can read fifth-grade material. Percentile ranks, stanines, and grade-equivalent scores are used on most standardized score reports for norm-referenced tests.

Criterion-referenced tests measure student achievement based on specific standards and/or a particular body of knowledge. State standardized assessments given at the end of each academic year and state-designed, end-of-course exams are criterion-referenced tests. These tests will report percentile ranks, stanines, and age or grade equivalences, but they will also include a **raw score**, **scaled score**, and **performance level**. The raw score is often tallied by total number of questions the student has answered correctly on an assessment. The scaled score converts a student's raw score to a common scale to adjust for differences in test items and/or form. The higher the scaled score, the higher the student's performance—like the score you received on your college entrance exam, the ACT (1–36) or SAT (200–800). The scaled score is similar to what happens when converting pounds to kilograms. That is, the student's performance does not change; only the units used to measure the performance change. Since scaled scores are representative of student performance, they allow for a direct comparison from year to year. Scaled scores are key in teacher evaluation systems.

Another score you will see on the end-of-year criterion-referenced tests is the performance level. The performance level refers to an assigned level of performance that correlates with a range of scaled scores. This score is often grouped by achievement categories such as basic, proficient, or advanced.

Some states also report a **Lexile** score with the results of their criterion-referenced test. The Lexile score represents a rough calculation of a student's reading level based on the student's achievement on the test given. Computing the student's Lexile requires an analysis of both the text difficulty of the assessment and the reader's achievement on the assessment. A student's Lexile score could be used in combination with the Lexile of a text as part of the formula to determine if the text is appropriate for students. You will know a score is a Lexile measure because it is shown as a number with an *L* after it. For example, 640L is a 640 Lexile (MetaMetrics, 2012).

Figure 10.2 shows a sample individual score report from the *Stanford Achievement Test Series* (2009). According to Pearson Education, publisher of the series, "*Stanford 10* provides reliable data to help measure student progress toward content standards and high expectations. This multiple-choice assessment helps to identify student strengths and needs, leading to effective placement and instructional planning" ("Product Details"). The report in Figure 10.2 represents a student's results on all the subtests, including but not limited to reading, mathematics, and science.

Beyond the Score Report: The Language of Assessment

Since standardized tests play such a large role in both teacher and student evaluation, it is important to understand the language of assessments. These terms describe the questions being asked and are helpful for students when answering these questions. Table 10.1 describes the terminology that will help you understand the language of assessment and be able to explain it to students and parents.

Understanding the language of the score reports and the language of assessments will help you prepare your students for assessments as well as explain and understand the score reports.

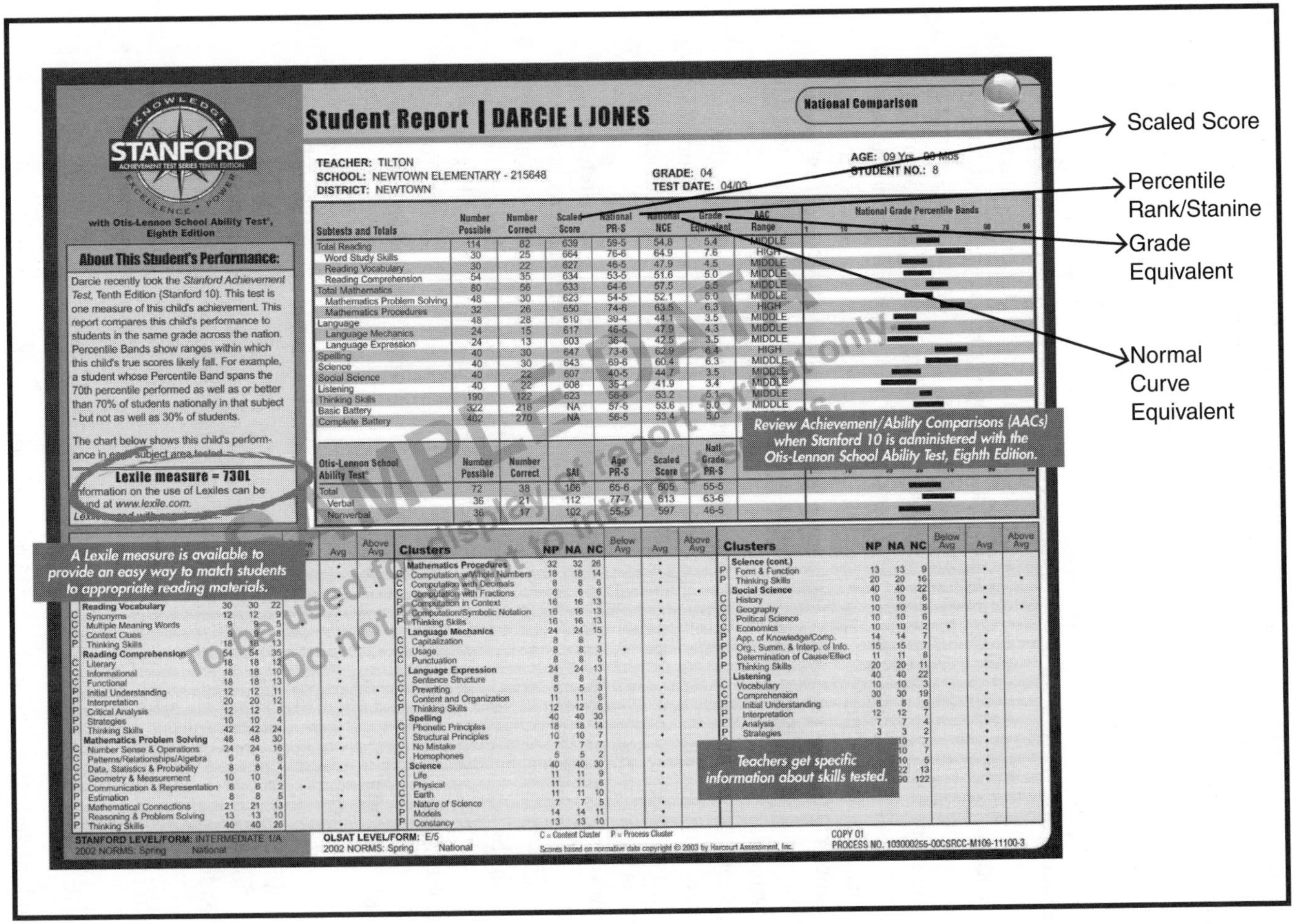

Figure 10.2
Sample Individual Score Report

Source: Pearson Education (http://images.pearsonassessments.com/images/dotCom/sat10/sat10_student_report.pdf).

Table 10.1 Testing Terminology	
Term	**Description**
Item	A test item refers to any question or exercise within a test. Test items include multiple choice and constructed response.
Multiple choice	Multiple-choice questions ask students to select a response that best answers the question. In reading assessments, they are used to assess a variety of reading skills, from vocabulary to comprehension. For example, questions may ask students to identify a small piece of text that best supports the central idea. To answer correctly, a student must first comprehend the central idea and then show understanding of how that idea is supported.
Distractors	A distractor is an incorrect choice in a multiple-choice test. Distractors are plausible responses. Students will need to truly comprehend the question to discern the correct response.
Constructed response	A constructed response item requires the student to create his or her own response through a written paragraph or essay, rather than simply choosing from a set of answers as in multiple choice. There are different types of constructed response questions (i.e., extended response and short-answer response), depending on the specific test. A short response will typically require students to write a single paragraph, whereas an extended response will require a complete writing sample or essay.
Prompt	A prompt activates a student's prior knowledge and requires a student to analyze it to answer the question. It can include a reading passage, graphic, or photograph.
Rubric	A rubric contains the criteria established for assessing a constructed response item. It includes what will be evaluated and what distinguishes an excellent to poor response.

Test Administration

Administration Practices for Standardized Assessments

The directions for administering for each assessment product provide specific instructions for procedures to follow before, during, and after test administration. They are each developed and evaluated prior to test standardization. During standardization, the materials are verified for accuracy and utility. Care should be taken in following a test's directions for administering. (Zucker, 2004, p. 4)

An important feature of commercial assessments is that they all have standard procedures for administration. Each test has specific instructions for materials, timing, and setting. Prior to giving a test, it is important to prepare for its administration, schedule testing periods as suggested by the testing company, and select an appropriate testing environment.

Administrators of a standardized assessment should familiarize themselves with the materials and procedures well before the testing periods. If permitted by the school district, they should carefully read and examine the directions for administering, student test booklets, answer documents, and any other materials provided for testing.

Testing periods should be scheduled for times that encourage maximum student performance. Scheduling testing before or after a vacation, on the days of school events, on Monday mornings, or on Friday afternoons is discouraged. It is suggested that no more than two subtests be administered in one sitting and a rest period be given between subtests.

The test setting for administering assessments should parallel the classroom environment as closely as possible. Standardized educational assessments should be administered to classroom-sized groups of about 25 students. In larger groups, the test administrator should have one assistant for every 25 students. Students perform better when they are familiar with the test administrator; therefore, the persons administering the tests should, if possible, be the students' own teachers. All the people who assist the test administrator should also be known to students (Zucker, 2004).

Although many of the administration practices for standardized tests are meant for school administrators, as a teacher, you will be asked to **proctor** these exams. The tips listed below will help you and your students throughout the test administration:

1. Be prepared.

    - Check that you have all the testing materials and extra sharpened pencils.
    - Read the testing script completely prior to the test administration.
    - Make sure your room is organized so distractions are limited.
    - Know the policy for emergencies and bathroom breaks.
    - Make sure you have a working clock to keep time during the test.

2. Help students relax before the test begins.

    - Convey a calm demeanor (this will be easier if you are prepared).
    - Tell some jokes.
    - Be ready to answer students' questions about testing procedures.

3. Stick to the script.

    - Read the script in a slow, clear voice.
    - If it is not permitted in the procedure manual, you cannot do it.

4. Stay alert.

    - Be available to assist with test procedures.
    - Monitor student testing behavior.
    - Do *not* engage in distracting behaviors such as side conversations, eating, texting, or grading papers.

5. Maintain test material security.

    - Before testing, learn the security measures prescribed by the test and your school.
    - During testing, make sure you follow these procedures.
    - After testing, make sure you have collected all the materials by counting everything at least three times.

When proctoring standardized tests, remember that what makes the test standardized is that students take the exam under the same conditions with the same directions, regardless of the school and/or teacher. Deviation from standardized procedures comes only when a student has a written plan for testing accommodations.

> **Making Connections**
>
> Standardized testing, usually held in the spring, can be very stressful for students. As a regular-education classroom teacher, what considerations for lessening students' anxiety would be suitable? Formulate a checklist of actions the school district, as well as you the classroom teacher, could take.

Assessment Modification and Accommodation

An **assessment modification** is a change in administration that alters the constructs or skills assessed or the comparability of scores (Phillips, 1993). When making changes to an assessment to meet a student's needs, policymakers (in state education agencies or large school districts) must conclude whether the change is an accommodation or a modification. If the change is an accommodation, then the scores can be compared to the scores of other students within the norm group. If the change is a modification, the student's results may need to be reported separately from those of the other students and can be compared only to the results of students who were administered the test with the same modification.

It is important to note that changes to the administration of a standardized assessment are occasionally necessary. No Child Left Behind (NCLB), as well as the 1997 reauthorization of the Individuals with Disabilities Education Act (IDEA), requires changes to an assessment to accommodate the needs of students with disabilities and English language learners.

An **assessment accommodation** can be a change in format, response, scheduling, setting, or timing that does not alter in any significant way what the test measures or the comparability of scores (Phillips, 1993). A change to an assessment counts as an accommodation when it has been shown as not invalidating a student's results.

Appropriate accommodations are often detailed in the Individualized Education Program (IEP) for a student with a disability and should already be present in the classroom environment (Nitko, 2004). For example, as written in a student's IEP, a student with a paraeducator may take the test alone in an alternate setting with headphones to support a distraction-free environment.

> **Making Connections**
>
> Assessment modifications are different from accommodations in that accommodations can occur within a regular classroom setting with minor changes. Brainstorm some possible modifications. Keep in mind that these are formulated by special educators in conjunction with the school psychologist and the regular-education teacher.

Commercial Assessments in the Classroom

Commercial assessments are not all standardized end-of-year tests; they are also used in the classroom throughout the teaching and learning process. We use these assessments to screen students' literacy abilities, to monitor progress throughout the school year, and to diagnose or identify students with learning disabilities.

> Screening measures are one "indicator" of children who may need additional support in literacy. . . . Progress monitoring in ALL settings holds the promise of growth for ALL students regardless of context. (Stahl, 2010, p. 6)

To identify students who are having difficulties acquiring literacy skills, teachers can use screening tests. Screening tests not only help teachers differentiate their instruction based on what students already know and can do, but they also provide teachers with the data to determine if the students need further assessment for special education. Screening tests tend to be brief. They are comparative to checking a car's oil level with a dipstick—a quick look to see how students are doing in a particular area of literacy.

Progress monitoring assessments are used to determine how students are doing on the path to achieving grade-level expectations. Commercial progress monitoring assessments have established targets for performance for various points in the school year. These targets can be used to predict student success in meeting grade-level standards at the end of the year. They can guide instruction to ensure that students will be able to meet the end-of-year goals. Progress monitoring assessments should be administered three times a year to ensure that students are making progress.

Both screening assessments and progress monitoring assessments are designed to provide quick measures of student achievement. Diagnostic tests are formal assessments that can help teachers develop information regarding a student's performance in an area of literacy. Diagnostic tests provide more detailed information than screening and progress monitoring, and they are often used when questions about individual students arise that cannot be answered using screening, progress monitoring, observation, and other forms of assessment.

Diagnostic, screening, and progress monitoring assessments are formative in nature and are used to determine how teachers can improve their instruction to help students meet the educational objectives. Outcome tests are administered toward the end of the year and are typically given to the whole class at once. These assessments are usually state exams.

Schools, districts, and states most often determine the commercial assessments administered in classrooms. These assessments generally follow some prescribed schedule for administration and data collection and discussion. Screening assessments are given at the beginning of the school year, progress monitoring assessments three times in the middle of the year, and outcome tests at the end of the year.

Using Assessment to Identify Students With Learning Disabilities in Reading

The process of identifying students with learning disabilities in reading is complex and requires a wide range of assessments and instructional interventions. Previously, students were identified with learning disabilities when there was a discrepancy between a student's IQ and his or her academic achievement. However, with the advent of Response to Intervention (RtI), students are identified with learning disabilities only after screening, progress monitoring, and diagnostic assessments demonstrate that regular classroom instruction has been ineffective.

RTI is a framework for providing comprehensive support to students and is not an instructional practice. RTI is a prevention oriented approach to linking assessment and instruction that can inform educators' decisions about how best to teach their students. A goal of RTI is to minimize the risk for long-term negative learning outcomes by responding quickly and efficiently to documented learning or behavioral problems and ensuring appropriate identification of students with disabilities. (National Center on Response to Intervention, 2010, p. 4)

A mixture of assessments is now used to identify and support readers who struggle daily at a sufficiently noticeable level in the regular education classroom. The screening assessments tell teachers which students are struggling with reading, and the progress monitoring assessments inform teachers how the classroom instructional techniques are working with individual students. If students are not demonstrating progress, it is up to the teacher to try alternative instructional techniques prior to suggesting that the student receive diagnostic testing for the identification of learning disabilities.

The following section includes information about assessments that are used in screening and progress monitoring students' literacy skills. The wide range of assessments below includes some you will encounter in your state or district. In addition, associated web addresses are included to provide avenues for further test exploration. Please remember that teachers should use the data gathered from all the assessments to plan classroom instruction.

Assessments for Screening and Progress Monitoring

- **AIMSweb:** AIMSweb is a complete web-based solution for progress monitoring and data management for Grades K–12. It provides assessments in early literacy and language arts. The assessments are computer based, aligned with the Common Core State Standards, and claim to be predictive of success on outcome assessments. Web address: www.aimsweb.com/products.

- **DIBELS:** The Dynamic Indicators of Basic Early Literacy Skills (DIBELS) are a set of assessments used for universal screening and progress monitoring in Grades K–6. These standardized, efficient, and extensively researched screening and progress monitoring assessments help educators identify students who may need additional literacy instruction to become proficient readers. DIBELS can be an integral part of most RtI programs. Web address: dibels.uoregon.edu.

- **Discovery Education Assessment:** This tool combines diagnostic assessment with Discovery Education's digital assets to provide an item library of more than 60,000 items where teachers can generate, assign, and share assessments. A variety of progress monitoring assessments that are reliable, state specific, and built on the most up-to-date research are available. This tool also falls under the RtI umbrella. Web address: www .discoveryeducation.com/administrators/assessment.

- **EasyCBM:** This free progress monitoring system provides a wide range of reading assessments based on the National Reading Panel's suggestions for literacy assessments. Literacy skills addressed include reading comprehension, passage reading fluency, word reading fluency, letter names, letter sounds, and phoneme segmenting. Web address: easycbm.com/info/reading_assessments.php.

- **Edcheckup Standard Reading Passages:** These consist of equivalent sets of 23 reading passages for each grade level. Three passages in each set are used for screening to establish students' current level of proficiency in reading aloud from text and to determine cut scores for identifying students who are academically at risk as readers. This is a progress monitoring assessment. Web address: www.edcheckup.com.

- **Maze Curriculum-Based Measurement:** This is one of the assessments on AIMSweb. It is a progress monitoring tool that assesses reading competence and is used with individuals or groups of students. Students are given grade-level passages with every seventh word missing and three word choices for each blank. Students are given 2.5 minutes to read and restore meaning to the passage. This assessment covers Grades 1–8 and progress monitors a student's overall reading competence at the relevant grade. Web address: www.aimsweb.com/products/features/assessments/maze.

- **Measures of Academic Progress (MAP) for Primary Grades:** These are diagnostic and computerized adaptive assessments in reading, specifically tailored to the needs of early learners. This progress monitoring assessment includes skills checklists that provide teachers with a way to continually monitor students' achievement relative to the skills of phonological awareness and phonics. Web address: www.nwea.org/products-services/assessments/help-all-kids-learn.

- **Phonological Awareness Literacy Screening (PALS):** This assessment identifies students at risk of reading difficulties in Grades 1–3. PALS is a screening tool intended to measure young children's knowledge of important literacy basics. It assesses students' oral reading in context, alphabetics, and phonemic awareness. Web address: pals.virginia.edu/tools-1-3.html.

- **Standardized Testing and Reporting (STAR):** Five domains of skill for individual students are tested by computer: word knowledge and skills, comprehensions and meaning, analyzing literacy text, understanding author's craft, and analyzing argument and evaluating text. This is a progress monitoring assessment. Web address: www.renlearn.com/se.

- **Test of Word Reading Efficiency:** This assessment tests word reading efficiency. It is individually administered and contains two subtests: The Sight Word Efficiency subtest assesses the number of real printed words that can be accurately identified within 45 seconds, and the Phonemic Decoding Efficiency subtest measures the number of pronounceable printed nonwords that can be accurately decoded within 45 seconds. This is a screening assessment. Web address: www.riverpub.com/products/Towre2/index.html.

Assessments for Diagnostics

- **Developmental Reading Assessment 2:** This assessment determines each student's reading level with an evaluation of reading engagement, oral reading fluency, and comprehension. It is administered individually and uses rubrics and running records to assess students' reading strengths and weaknesses. Web address: www.pearsonschool.com/index.cfm?locator=PSZw5u&PMDbSiteId=2781&PMDbSolutionId=6724&PMDbSubSolutionId=&PMDbCategoryId=3289&PMDbSubCategoryId=28139&PMDbSubjectAreaId=&PMDbProgramId=23661.

- **Dynamic Assessment of Test Accommodations (DATA):** DATA is used for individuals or groups of students with learning disabilities in Grades 2–7. It can assist multidisciplinary teams objectively to determine appropriate test adaptations to meet IDEA reauthorization and Americans with Disabilities Act requirements. Students are tested with and without accommodations, and results are compared with those of a nondisabled normative sample. When scores specify that a student would benefit from adaptations more than would be expected in the nondisabled normative sample, the accommodation is recommended. Web address: www.pearsonclinical.com/education/products/100000579/dynamic-assessment-of-test-accommodations-data.html.

- **Group Reading Assessment and Diagnostic Evaluation (GRADE):** GRADE is a diagnostic assessment that determines what developmental literacy skills Pre-K–12 students have mastered and areas of weakness where intervention is required. It is used to assess word identification, vocabulary, phonics/decoding, and comprehension skills such as compare and contrast, drawing conclusions, and making inferences. Web address: www.pearsonassessments.com/learningassessments/products/100000646/group-reading-assessment-and-diagnostic-evaluation-grade-grade.html.

- **Iowa Test of Basic Skills:** This test is administered to a group of students to supply a comprehensive assessment of each student's progress in the literacy content areas. It assesses vocabulary, word analysis, listening, and reading comprehension. Web address: www.riverpub.com/products/itbs/details.html.

- **Woodcock-Johnson Diagnostic Reading Battery:** This is a diagnostic test that assesses reading achievement and important related reading abilities. It is administered individually and measures phonemic awareness, phonics, fluency, vocabulary, and reading comprehension. Web address: riversidepublishing.com/products/wdrb/index.html.

Making Connections

Find out what tests (or others) are administered in your local school district or educational region. Investigate district websites by clicking on the testing toolbar to determine this information.

Using Assessment With English Language Learners to Assess Proficiency or Learning Disability in Reading

In 2010–2011, English language learners (ELLs) made up 10%, or nearly 5 million, of all school-age students in the U.S. educational system (National Center for Educational Statistics, 2013). ELLs are students who are developing proficiency in English but still must be assessed to progress through the educational system. Like their peers, it is critically important that the collection and content of assessments are fair and valid.

Regular and ongoing assessments are vital for ELLs, not only to monitor and advance progress but also for NCLB record keeping. However, depending on an ELL's level of

English language proficiency, standardized assessments do not truly reflect content knowledge or abilities. ELLs should be expected to take standardized assessments when possible. Table 10.2 lists a variety of commercial assessments that may be used to determine English language proficiency or if an ELL has a learning disability.

Table 10.2 Commercial Assessments for Use With ELLs

Aprenda	A native Spanish achievement test for K–9 students that assesses student achievement and critical thinking skills in language arts. Available through Harcourt Assessment Inc.
Batería Woodcock-Muñoz Revisada	A Spanish test through Riverside Publishing. Similar to the Woodcock-Johnson Diagnostic Reading Battery.
Bilingual Verbal Ability Test	Available in 15 languages, assesses a bilingual student's academic readiness, assisting with appropriate program placement and planning. Scores are based on knowledge and reasoning in English and the student's native language. Available through Riverside Publishing.
Brigance Diagnostic Assessment of Basic Skills (Spanish)	For K–6 native Spanish-speaking students, determines English proficiency and specific learning disability. Assessments include listening, oral reading, readiness, speech, word analysis, and writing and alphabetizing. Available through Curriculum Associates Inc.
Kaufman Test of Education Achievement (Second Ed.)	In English only, assesses academic skills in reading and oral and written language. The focus is pinpointing difficulties and assisting in appropriate program placement and planning. Available through the American Guidance Service Inc.
Language Assessment System Links in English or Spanish	Assesses English or Spanish language ability and proficiency for K–12 students. Assessing in one or both languages, it determines primary language proficiency.
Logramos	A Spanish achievement test for language, listening comprehension, reading, vocabulary, and word analysis for K–12 students. Determines native-language proficiency and appropriate instruction. Available through Riverside Publishing.
Test of Nonverbal Intelligence (Third Ed.)	A language-free assessment designed for those who may have communication or thinking disorders. Assesses abstract reasoning intelligence, aptitude, and problem solving. Available through Pearson.
Wechsler Individual Achievement Test (Second Ed.)	An English-only assessment for ages 4 through adult, assessing listening comprehension, oral language, spelling, and written expression. Assesses achievement skills and possible learning disabilities. Available through the Psychological Corporation and Pearson.
Woodcock-Johnson III Normative Update Test of Achievement	Assesses K–12 students, determining the need for special services. Tests basic reading skills, listening comprehension, oral expression, reading comprehension, reading fluency, and written expression. Available through Riverside Publishing.

Source: Adapted from Connecticut Administrators of Programs for English Language Learners (2011).

Common Core Assessment Shifts

The adoption of the Common Core State Standards (CCSS) has brought new assessments, and with these new assessments come new terminology and expectations for literacy. Although some states have revised their existing assessments to meet the criteria of the standards, others are planning to use the Smarter Balanced and Partnership for Assessment of Readiness for College and Careers (PARCC) assessments. Smarter Balanced and PARCC are not simply outcome measures; they also propose to provide schools with screening and progress monitoring assessments that could be used to evaluate students' achievement of the CCSS. (More information on each of the assessments can be found on their websites: www.parcconline.org and www.smarterbalanced.org.) These assessments would contain multiple-choice questions and a variety of constructed response sections and would strive to assess all literacy skills: reading, writing, speaking, and listening.

To begin preparing students for these assessments, it is important that educators clearly understand not just the basic testing terminology but also the terminology associated with the CCSS. Parents, administrators, and support staff should be aware of the "assessment shifts." Samples of terms with their definitions, along with "parent-friendly" language suggestions, are listed in Table 10.3.

Table 10.3 Common Core Assessment Terminology

Common Core Assessment Term	Testing Definition	Parent-Friendly Explanation
Computer adaptive tests	As a student progresses through a test, the level of difficulty will be adjusted based on his or her responses. For instance, if a student gets Question 3 wrong, the computer will follow it up with an easier question on the same skill. If the student gets it correct, the computer will provide a more difficult question. Since there is a lot of variability in student responses, these tests have a larger pool of questions for each assessment category and achievement level.	A computer adaptive test is not a "one-size-fits-all" assessment that requires that all students attempt to answer the same questions. This assessment will provide your child with questions based on how they do on previous questions.
Embedded support	Since these assessments are computer based, there are some tools embedded in the testing system to support students during testing. These tools are not required but can help students keep track of what they are reading. "For example, students who take the PARCC assessments will have access to a highlight tool, which will enable them to highlight text, as needed, to recall and emphasize certain material" (Partnership for Assessment of Readiness for College and Careers [PARCC], 2013, p. 2).	These are tools that students can use to assist them in being active during the test-taking process. They can access these tools through a menu or toolbar. The tools include but are not limited to highlighting and annotation.

(Continued)

Table 10.3 (Continued)

Common Core Assessment Term	Testing Definition	Parent-Friendly Explanation
Aligned CCSS	Acronym means "Common Core State Standards" and provides a basis for interpreting the way standards are conceptualized in each question.	The Common Core State Standards for Literacy cover reading, writing skills.
Level of text complexity	Quantitatively and qualitatively, the selection has been validated for use and deemed suitable at a certain grade level. Passages come from high-quality children's literature, including Newbery Medal winners, and informational text recommended by content organizations, such as the National Council of the Social Studies.	Grade-level expectations are rigorous and challenging but on grade level. Selections are taken from prize-winning children's literature and high-quality informational books; therefore, texts are worth reading and reflecting on.
Reading passages	Teachers are responsible for building a "staircase of text complexity" within their classroom curriculum. In addition, careful, close reading of quality, authentic text is valued. Texts worth reading include expository (70%) and high-quality narrative texts (30%).	Students are given high-quality and challenging texts to engage in close reading or reading that focuses on the key ideas and opposing viewpoints in a passage. Moreover, types of texts used in classroom literacy will be informational (70%) and story texts (30%).
Anchor text	Students will be asked to analyze topics that are presented with several reading passages. The first passage, which introduces the topic, is the anchor text.	This is the first text in a series of reading passages and is meant to introduce a topic to students.
Extended constructed response	When answering these questions, students will be asked to read passages to develop a coherent essay that cites textual evidence to support their ideas. Students will be assessed against the CCSS for writing.	Extended constructed response sample questions are designed to assess a student's ability to write from sources. Extended constructed response questions allow students to demonstrate the ability to write a strong essay using evidence from text to support their ideas.
Short constructed response	Short constructed response questions are questions in which students are asked to respond to a prompt or question by stating their answer and providing textual evidence to support it. Students will need to respond in complete sentences. Their responses should not be more than three complete sentences.	Short constructed response questions are single questions in which students are asked to respond to a prompt or question by stating their answer and providing evidence from the text to support it in no more than three complete sentences.
Evidence-based selected response	Combines a traditional selected response with a second selected response asking children to show evidence of their answer from the passage.	Combines the traditional multiple-choice response with a second multiple-choice response asking children to show evidence or proof of their answer from the reading.

Common Core Assessment Term	Testing Definition	Parent-Friendly Explanation
Technology-enhanced construction response	Uses technology, such as drop-down boxes, cut and paste, text move, to test student comprehension in authentic ways.	Uses technology to test student comprehension in different ways.
Range of prose constructed response	Students demonstrate their understanding through written response as well as knowing language and conventions.	Students demonstrate their understanding through writing as well as knowing language and conventions.

Sources: EngageNY (2013), PARCC (2013), and Smarter Balanced Assessment Consortium (2012).

In this chapter, you have read about different types of commercial assessments. We have reviewed the language of score reports so you can interpret the results of your students' tests. You have also learned the language of tests in general as well as that of the new CCSS assessments so you can prepare your students accordingly. As a classroom teacher, you should now understand some of what your administrators do to prepare for assessments and also what you will need to do as a test proctor. This knowledge will help you as you administer commercial screening and progress monitoring assessments. Remember, the assessments discussed in this chapter are standardized because they have been evaluated as reliable and valid by psychometricians and follow the same procedures for each administration.

Key Terms

assessment accommodation

assessment modification

bell curve

criterion-referenced tests

diagnostic tests

grade- and age-equivalent scores

Lexile

norm group

normal curve equivalent

norm-referenced tests

percentile rank

performance level

proctor

raw score

reliable

scaled score

standard score

stanine

valid

Website Resources

- **Smarter Balanced Assessment Consortium**

This website provides information about the Smarter Balanced assessment system. It contains information on test construction, sample questions, descriptions of score descriptors, and much more. If you are in a state using the Smarter Balanced assessment system, review this website to become familiar with it: **www.smarterbalanced.org/about.**

- **Partnership for Assessment of Readiness for College and Careers (PARCC)**

This website provides information about the PARCC assessment system. It contains information on test construction, sample questions, descriptions of score descriptors, and much more. If you are in a state using the PARCC assessment system, review this website to become familiar with it: www.parcconline.org.

The PARCC group has also included numerous sample items to help teachers understand how this test works. The sample items are organized by grade level, and you can view them at **practice.parcc.testnav.com/#.**

- *Elementary Assessments: Universal Screening, Diagnostic, and Progress Monitoring*, **State Education Resource Center of Connecticut**

This document is designed to break down the three types of assessments used in elementary schools. It explains each type of assessment in detail, including who would take it, why it's used, and the usefulness of the results. Assessments are organized in tables by subject, use, concepts and skills assessed, sample assessments, and resources. Assessments are also hyperlinked should you want more specific information. Find the document at **www.sde .ct.gov/sde/lib/sde/pdf/curriculum/cali/elementary_assessments_4-9-12.pdf.**

- **All About Adolescent Literacy: Resources for Parents and Educators of Kids in Grades 4–12**

This website is a national multimedia project offering information and resources to the parents and educators of struggling adolescent readers and writers. In addition, it explains why schools use assessments to evaluate students' reading performance and which assessments work well for evaluating fluency, comprehension, and vocabulary. It also includes an outline for teachers to set up a beginning-of-year general reading skills screening, plus links to classroom strategies, a glossary, webcasts, newsletters, and experts. For more information, visit **www.adlit.org.**

- **The Center on Standards and Assessment Implementation**

This website provides technical assistance and resources that support improved student learning and achievement. It features a "Data Use" site that provides tools for states using data to inform assessment and accountability decisions, and information about formative assessments. It also provides information regarding alternative assessments for students with special needs and ELLs. For more information, visit **www.aacompcenter.org.**

- *Linking Assessment and Instruction: Teacher Preparation and Professional Development*, National Comprehensive Center for Teacher Quality

This document, released by the National Comprehensive Center for Teacher Quality, links assessment results to instruction. This is a comprehensive document, broken into six components: fundamentals of assessments, standards for comparison of performance, considerations for making decisions, assessment procedures, identification of content to teach, and identification of student response. For more information, visit **nwcc.educationnorthwest.org/resource/928.**

- "Best Practice for ELLs: Screening," U.S. Department of Education

This article provides information on best practices for screening and monitoring ELLs. It recommends the use of three types of assessment—phonological processing, letter and alphabet knowledge, and reading word lists or connected text—as valid for identifying which ELLs will benefit from typical classroom instruction and which require extra support. It also provides steps on how to effectively monitor progress and track growth. For more information, go to **www.readingrockets.org/article/28879.**

Student Study Site: Visit the Student Study Site at **www.sagepub.com/grantlit** to access additional study tools including eFlashcards, web resources, and online-only appendices.

CHAPTER 11

Planning for Interventions

Kathy B. Grant

Common Core State Standards	
Anchor Standards for Reading	*CCRA.R.10* Read and comprehend complex literary and informational texts independently and proficiently.
Range of Reading and Text Complexity	*RL.2–5.10* By the end of the year, read and comprehend literature, including stories, dramas, and poetry, at the high end of the grades [K–5] text complexity band independently and proficiently.
Reading and Informational Text	*RI.2–5.10* By the end of the year, read and comprehend informational texts, including history/social studies, science, and technical texts, at the high end of the grades [K–5] text complexity band independently and proficiently.
Range of Writing	*W.3–5.10* Write routinely over extended time frames (time for research, reflection, and revision) and for shorter time frames (a single setting or a day or two) for a range of discipline-specific tasks, purposes, and audiences.

FOCUS QUESTIONS

1. What do you believe are your strongest skills in organizing a classroom for assessment? What weak areas of organization do you hope to improve?

2. Kidwatching is a skill you as a teacher will use daily. How can you effectively annotate literacy actions and affective behaviors? What format works best for your purposes of annotation, reflection, and analysis? Why?

3. Why is daily systematic assessment of student literacy, including formative assessment strategies, crucial to informed decision making for the teacher?

4. School-based peers can be especially helpful in supporting the novice assessment practitioner. List some school personnel you might feel comfortable approaching for mentorship.

5. Book lists, including independent- and guided-reading lists, can be used to promote choice in reading as well as instructional reading goals. They can be an impetus for further recreational reading. Devise a template that works as a reading or book list to record at-home and classroom choices.

Words in Action

Mrs. D.

As a novice teacher, Mrs. D struggled with what and how to assess. While graduate school had taught her numerous approaches, limited time led to a need to develop an efficient tool to report progress or regression on a weekly basis. For this, she turned to her peers for advice. "Keep it simple!" was their mantra.

Mrs. D found, after weeks of trying to keep up with the "weekly report" forms circulated by the establishment, that an altogether different tool worked for her. A journal, a blog, an e-mail thread with a parent—each had an essence of merit. Why report on nothing if nothing of note happened that week? Ultimately, Mrs. D had to adhere to prior training and her instincts to identify what worked for her.

For validation, she turned to peers such as Mike, a veteran teacher unfazed by rhetoric, who assured her that her instincts were right on and to stick with what she thought was appropriate. She turned to Phil, a resource room teacher, to celebrate the progress some of her at-risk students made at incremental rates. She turned to Russ, another resource teacher, who prompted her for scaffolds to her lessons, those that graduate school had taught her to provide but that a lack of time and an abundance of self-doubt had pushed from her mind.

Each of these mentors provided Mrs. D with a different piece of the puzzle, and all were invaluable in making her first assessment development experience meaningful, enjoyable, and survivable.

Organizing for Classroom Assessment

No instrument or assessment practice can overcome the fact that the teacher is the primary agent of assessment. (International Reading Association and National Council of Teachers, 1994)

Implementation of national and state-level Common Core State Standards changed the thrust of literacy assessment in major ways. The following paragraph sums up the expectations for assessment, analysis, and action as demonstrated through the assessment cycle. Moreover, the watch words of *accountability*, *professional development*, *action plans*, and *monitoring* are in the forefront of the discussion. With reenvisioned literacy assessments, it becomes imperative to prepare for classroom literacy evaluation through thoughtful and efficient organization.

Under the provisions of the Common Core State Standards all teacher teaching decisions should be **driven by data**, specifically the collection and analysis of literacy data. An **assessment calendar** will date the common interim assessments administered two to three times a year. Teachers will be held accountable for implementing action plans and will be monitored closely by administrators and others. Teachers will be provided with professional development to be able to apply the tenets of assessment, analysis, and action, thereby owning the analysis of results. Significant changes are outlined by the Common Core State Standards that play an important role in how educators envision literacy assessment (EngageNY, 2011).

Obviously, this is challenging to a new teacher practitioner who is striving to process the existing language of reading as well as get a jump start on the burgeoning list of assessment terms that prove confounding to even veteran teachers. This is most definitely the brave new world of teaching! Following the introduction in Chapters 1 and 10 to the components of high-stakes testing, this chapter focuses on organizational strategies for actual literacy classrooms, available resources, and ideas for collecting, documenting, and analyzing data.

Making Connections

Before moving forward with this chapter, realistically appraise your overall skills in classroom organization, but particularly for assessment. With your partner, make a T-chart of strengths and weaknesses. Discuss those areas that need work and the organization efforts you feel proud of.

The assessment cycle (see Figure 11.1) based on the Common Core State Standards requires organizational thinking to be used to best advantage. Each section—assessment, analysis, and action—requires that organizational components be firmly in place. Data collection, or the act of assessing and collecting evidence, necessitates essential materials such as teacher notebooks, portfolios, checklists, or other forms of systematized aids. Next, the analysis step requires making and storing informal and formal teacher notes and annotations through class profile summaries and scatter plots. Last, the action phase finalizes the cycle by enacting instructional interventions, as well as beginning the cycle anew.

Figure 11.1

Assessment Cycle Based on Common Core State Standards

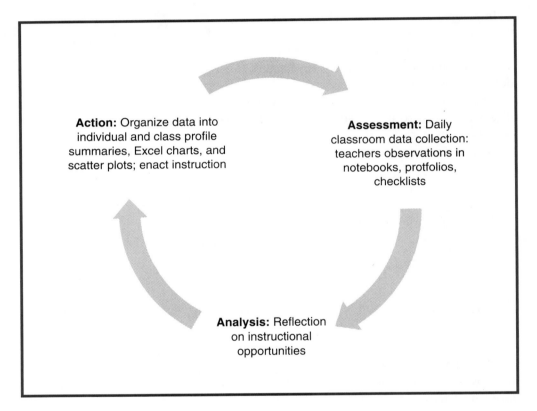

Action: Organize data into individual and class profile summaries, Excel charts, and scatter plots; enact instruction

Assessment: Daily classroom data collection: teachers observations in notebooks, protfolios, checklists

Analysis: Reflection on instructional opportunities

Making Connections

Review the assessment cycle in depth, discussing the components with your learning partner. It is critical that you have a practical understanding of the processes within the cycle and also that, at the end of this chapter, you can clearly articulate how each process works in conjunction with the previous and following steps to make the whole. Keep talking this through with your partner, and look for examples in classrooms you visit.

Let's start by focusing on observational assessment and the record-keeping organizational challenges that connect with this potent form of assessment.

Observations of Reading Behaviors

Excellent reading teachers are constantly observing children as they go about their daily work. (International Reading Association, 2000a, p. 2)

Even with the changes brought about by national and state implementation of the Common Core State Standards, teachers still ask themselves these two driving questions (Weaver, 2002):

- How and when will I get the data to be able to make critical literacy decisions?
- How can I record the data to make sure they are useful?

According to Weaver (2002) the "trickiest part is recording anecdotal observations made on the run—during read-aloud, shared reading experience time, guided reading and so forth" (p. 291). Nonetheless, daily assessment opportunities must be built into the teaching routine to ensure that continuous checks for progress are in place. Organized observations of students and reflection are the two key components of anecdotal records.

Anecdotal Records: Kidwatching

Keeping and organizing anecdotal records can be challenging for the best of teachers under optimum circumstances. Throw in a fast-paced classroom and attention seeking from individual students, and attempting to maintain anecdotal records sometimes seems like wishful thinking. However, scheduling when and how anecdotal records are gathered solves this quandary.

Record keeping reflecting the method developed by Yetta Goodman (1985), coined *kidwatching*, can be described as "direct, intentional, and systematic observations by teachers" (O'Keefe, 1997, p. 4). Characteristics of kidwatching are listed in Figure 11.2. With practice, novice teachers can become expert observers of students. Through trial and error, anecdotal notes can be developed.

- Observes authentic learning
- Values literacy contributions of each student
- Provides rich informal assessment aimed at acknowledging student strengths
- Gives voice to students who are otherwise silent
- Showcases students in different instructional settings
- Helps teacher get to know children deeply

Figure 11.2

Characteristics of Kidwatching

Source: O'Keefe (1997).

Becoming a skilled kidwatcher is a practiced art where teachers observe students, record impressions, and then analyze information collected. Notes are used to record both objective (factual) and subjective (impressions) information, as well as affective information such as motivation, interest for task, curiosity, and even unintended literacy outcomes (Boyd-Batstone, 2004). The teacher, as a "sensitive observer," remains in a "unique position to see and communicate a reliable and valid instructional perspective of the child" (Clay, 1993, p. 230).

Making Connections

"Daily systematic assessment of student literacy is essential to an informative practice." Write out a short response to this statement after taking time to reflect. Include in your response how you envision this connecting to kidwatching. Read your response to your partner.

Each teacher must invent his or her own way to maintain **anecdotal record keeping** by observing children and writing daily. Forms of anecdotal record keeping for silent reading may resemble the example below:

Juliet (1/13/2013)

Selection: *Out of the Dust*

Difficulty: Medium, poetic form

Notes: Quiet, intense reading, quick page turning, moves from group to beanbag chairs, finished early

Anecdotal recording keeping can work well for a literature response group. Codes indicate strong evidence of understanding (++), competent (+), or in need of work (–). For questions still remaining for the teacher, a question mark (?) reminds the teacher to connect with the student when an opportunity arises (see Table 11.1 for an example).

Table 11.1 Anecdotal Record Keeping Example			
	Karl	**Sandy**	**Lynn**
Connect/text	++ strong	+ scaffold (T)	– unsure (T support)
Connect/life	+	++ specific ex.	– no resp.
Connect/world	++ too easy text?	+ instructional (?)	– frustration (?)

Teachers employ kidwatching annotations to make authentic instructional decisions. Similar to a form of journaling, review and reflection of observation notes should be frequent and ongoing. Evidence of student progress can be shared with parents and school faculty in conferences and meetings.

A sample form for daily anecdotal records that can be modified for use is shown in Figure 11.3. In addition, Figure 11.4 provides a list of verbs with possible abbreviations to use as quick notations when conducting student observational assessment. As you become more proficient in noting students' affective reactions, you will want to explore their responses to judge motivation, interest, and engagement.

Using specific verbs in anecdotal records results in a discussion format for student progress. For example, a teacher tells her reader, "I really appreciated the way you planned for the activity beforehand—good organization!"

Student's Name: _____	Evaluator's Name: _____
Date: _____	Date: _____

Summary:

Recommendation:

Needs:

Strengths:

Figure 11.3
Form for Daily
Anecdotal Records

Source: Adapted from
Boyd-Batstone (2004).

Furthermore, employing an abbreviation key makes the teacher's job easier. Again, using words specific to student classroom actions, the teacher is able to choose precise terms in his or her conferencing.

Figure 11.4

Verbs for Notating Anecdotal Records and Abbreviation Key (Sample)

ACTIONS	
Demonstrates (D)	Pantomimes (P)
Describes (DS)	Presents (PR)
Acts Out (AO)	
READING	
Retells (RT)	Decodes (DC)
Summarizes (SU)	Comprehends (CM)
ACTIVITIES OR STRATEGIES	
Organizes (O)	Think-Aloud (TA)
Generalizes (G)	Question–Answer Relationship (QAR)
COLLABORATION	
Shares (S)	Plans (PL)
Partners (P)	Discusses (Dis)
AFFECT	
Disengaged (DIS)	Tired (T)
Motivated (M)	Leadership (L)

Making Connections

With your learning partner, brainstorm additional verbs you might add to the list, particularly in the areas of reading skills and comprehension. Apply learning styles or modalities to the mix: listening, hands-on, and written skills. How would a teacher notate student activities through these methods, besides using oral evidence through discussions? Would this be beneficial to observing student literacy progress? If so, how?

Kidwatching is a commonsense way to describe observational assessment: learning to see what is there and then using that information to make a better classroom as a goal for all teachers. Draw on your collection of anecdotal records to collaborate with peers, compare observations, and make generalizations about student progress noted or interventions needed.

Conferring With Peers

Collaboration with peers and specialists through discussions about student literacy progress varies among school districts. More formal meetings are scheduled through districtwide meetings, while less formal meetings may occur daily. The following are possible resources and personnel:

Schoolwide professional learning communities/inquiry teams can provide the organizational framework for continuous discussion, collaboration, and action focusing on supporting reading instruction, teacher knowledge, and school performance (Mokhtari, Thoma, & Edwards, 2009).

Credentialed reading specialists and literacy coaches have the knowledge and expertise to support the classroom reading teacher and recommend assessment options. They often function as experts in the area of data collection instruments, interpretation of data, and suggestions for instructional decision making (Mokhtari et al., 2009).

Teacher teams and literacy leaders may support the process of preventing reading failure by guiding teachers to list important literacy skills measured by screening, diagnostic, and outcome assessments used to monitor progress (Moore & Whitfield, 2009).

Data teams in some districts have traditionally been the group most involved in data interpretation, analysis, and action recommendations. However, under new provisions in the Common Core State Standards, "teacher-owned" analysis will drive the assessment analysis team meetings (EngageNY, 2011).

The differing groups of resource personnel within and outside school settings can support new teachers in their quest to organize for literacy assessment. Don't pass up professional development opportunities for systematizing and organizing assessment data.

Systematic Classroom Organization

Taken together, data from a variety of assessments (depending on grade level) can help advise a teacher about the text difficulty that students can handle, in addition to pinpointing their specific strengths and weaknesses. (Rubin, 2011, p. 606)

Data Management

Record-keeping protocols or formats for reporting, visualizing, and analyzing literacy data results can take the form of various models based on teachers' preferences. Many schools rely on data collection teams to develop protocols and maintain records; however, the teacher is the primary data collector, so comprehensive data "snapshots" should be housed in the classroom.

Both individual and classroom profiles emerge when comprehensive data collection is organized into tables or charts. A variety of assessments form an authentic snapshot for a whole class or individual student. These include

- literacy interest inventory;
- literacy attitude or self-efficacy survey;
- kidwatching of literacy behaviors;
- informal reading assessments: cloze, informal reading inventory, or running records; and
- composite scores on reading assessments: standardized tests.

Table 11.2 outlines the variety of assessments for a record-keeping form. It allows the teacher to sort out the data collected from individual as well as whole-class evaluations and acts as a valuable reference for daily instruction decisions and individual interventions.

Table 11.2 Record Keeping: Individual and Classroom Snapshots

Snapshots: Individual and Whole-Class Instruments	Protocols/Formats for Reporting, Visualizing, or Analyzing	Purpose/Planning
Literacy interest inventory	Narrative summary of interest inventory/student reaction protocol	Reflective interpretation of student reactions to interest inventory oral statements judging student affect
Literacy attitude or self-efficacy survey	Likert scale of emotional ratings/observational notes based on student reading affect	Nonjudgmental way to gauge student emotions about reading and then set realistic goals
Kidwatching of literacy behaviors	Observational field notes and analyses	Supports goal setting, literacy groupings, and individual reading goals
Informal reading assessments: cloze, informal reading inventory, or running records	Table: Mapping reading assessment scores to ability levels	Maps scores for range of three reading levels: frustration, instructional, and independent
Composite scores on reading assessments: standardized tests	Scatter plot or Excel spreadsheet and class profile table	Class profile to guide instructional decisions for whole-class activities; visual picture of how class as a whole relates to reading levels

Source: Based on Rubin (2011) and Vlach and Burcie (2010).

Management Plus

Many online assessment systems have been purchased by school districts. It is beyond the scope of this text to explore all the current offerings, but a few are listed in Table 11.3, along with their features. The authors highly recommend the Fountas and Pinnell Benchmark Online Data Management System, although all systems require training in the various management formats. Oftentimes, districts will offer new teachers in-house training on their online assessment systems.

The benefits of online management systems are numerous. They connect teacher formal assessment to district data banks to explicate data analysis. Furthermore, many of these expensive systems allow reporting to parents through a district portal or generated paper reports. Generally easy to interpret, some reports rely on the use of abbreviations that are foreign to parents and even some teachers. Many districts offer families workshops on reading generated reports, and teachers must become conversant in interpreting scores.

Organizing Literacy Data Collection

A loose-leaf notebook with dividers for each student, using mailing labels for each student's name, is one method elementary teachers use for literacy data collection. Space is left for comments regarding instruction, strengths, and needs, including student goal setting. Some teachers employ sticky notes on a clipboard that are then transferred to a sectioned sheet to generate student profiles. Other teachers use a checklist that may be used for writer's workshop, including who is publishing, dates, and process notes (O'Keefe, 1997).

Table 11.3 Online Data Management Systems		
Management System	**Features**	**Benefits (+) and Barriers to Use (−)**
Fountas and Pinnell Benchmark Online Data Management System	Universal screening Progress monitoring Integrated reporting tools Customizable reports Adequate yearly progress accountability	+ Collect, analyze, and report data + Individuals and classroom + Share data + Determine student growth and effectiveness in benchmark instruction and independent reading + Teacher subscription $30 − Training recommended
EDGE$_4$ (Education Data Gathering Engine)	Works with *all* student management systems Transparent data accessed at school and board levels Customizable reports Built-in workflow processes such as transportation, inventory, and Individualized Education Programs	+ 24-hour data updates + Enhances communication between school, board, and community + Increases accountability + Allows multiyear planning + Supports strategies to increase student achievement and reduce achievement gap − Costly
Schoology's K–12 LMS	Easy management/customizable Professional skill building Enhanced student learning Active/reactive education Money saving Guaranteed security	+ Individuals and classroom + Share data + Support via phone, e-mail, and ticketing system + One easy-to-use package − Training necessary

Sources: EDGE$_4$ (n.d.), Fountas and Pinnell (2009), and Schoology (2014).

Record sheets with a continuum or grid can be useful for check-off options. Other teachers use online resources to annotate observations of student reading progress. It is worthwhile to try a method to judge if it works for you as a busy teacher or to decide how the method may be revised to meet your assessment targets.

Making Connections

Try a method to judge if it works for you or to decide how it may be revised to meet your assessment targets. Weigh your options in revising a form to meet the needs of your assessment targets through ongoing observation and reflection. Are you the type of educator to use technology, such as a spreadsheet or word table? Do you prefer sticky notes on a clipboard that can then be placed on a grid and labeled? Have a discussion with your partner about the pros and cons of your chosen method.

Organizing Physical Space for Literacy Instruction

Effective data collection happens best in an organized classroom. An organized literacy classroom cannot be set up the week before class starts; planning needs to begin at the end of the previous year as teachers reflect on their successes in group work and share literacy accomplishments (Roskos & Neuman, 2012). A well-considered physical layout for a literacy classroom enhances productive routines, scheduling of learning, daily formative assessment, and modeling of procedures and rules. For new teachers preparing for their first literacy classrooms, Reutzel and Clark (2011) make the following excellent suggestions:

1. Gain access to your assigned classroom several months before the first day of school.

2. Take an inventory of the supplies, furnishings, instructional materials, trade books, and technology available.

3. Measure the size of your classroom and then draw a "scale" floor plan on graph paper or on the computer.

4. Take digital pictures of the walls to determine future placement of classroom displays, student work, daily schedules, and so on.

5. After completing this, arrange furniture and supplies available, and then make a list of other necessary furniture and supplies. Take this list to the principal, who will often want to accommodate new teachers.

A sample classroom schematic is provided in Figure 11.5. A variety of schematics will work; however, the key is to provide open areas, good flow of movement, and organized centers for literacy.

Envisioning your classroom in terms of "literacy areas" will serve to effectively and efficiently move students from activities designated by Four Blocks or The Daily Five.

Consider setting up your room to include a whole-class teaching area (read-alouds, skills and comprehension mini-lessons, shared reading, and reader's theatre), small-group instruction area (guided reading, literature reading), independent work area (sustained reading, work projects, inquiry reading, partner work, fluency practice, and computer stations), and classroom library.

Whole-Class Teaching Area

- Designated by a large piece of carpet or a rug, where students gather for instruction and read-alouds.
- Close to computer stations; contains whiteboards and teacher easels.

Small-Group Instruction

- Contains U-shaped table, student chairs (5–8), teacher chair, and rolling cart (Reutzel & Clark, 2011).
- Includes tabletop easel, magnetic boards or whiteboards, pocket chart (tabletop), and highlighter tape.

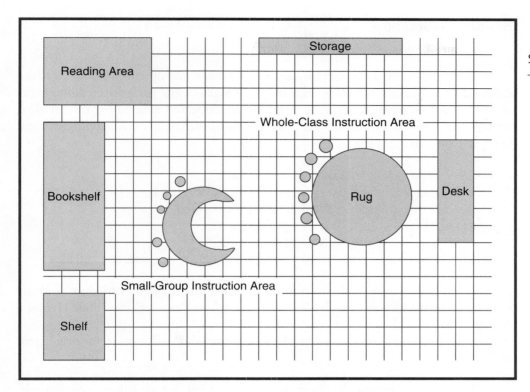

Figure 11.5
Classroom
Schematic Example

Source: Adapted from
Reutzel and Clark
(2011).

- Chart paper in long rolls can be taped on tables for student responses. In addition, individual mini-clipboards can be provided at seats for student responses, reflections, or comments.

Independent Work

- Use a management board or chart to organize independent work or literacy centers (Roskos & Neuman, 2012).
- Should include a rug or comfortable furniture for students to relax on while reading.

Classroom Library

- Organize in a quiet, peaceful area with comfortable seating (couches or beanbag chairs).
- Clearly mark library shelves by genre and reading level/Lexile, or color-code within genre tubs (Reutzel & Clark, 2011). Vinyl rain gutters can be mounted on book shelves to display selected book covers.
- On the average, 10 books per student is the recommended minimum number for a classroom library.

In addition, the leveled book room is a centrally located area (closet, room, part of the library) that contains the leveled book choices for guided reading and supplemental activities. Multiple copies of these small texts are housed in bins labeled by readability level.

Reading Workshop

Gathering and Recording Data

Weaver (2002) compiled a list of **authentic data collection** options for teachers to use during reading workshop, as "ongoing assessment is an integral part of the reading workshop" (p. 290). Students set reading goals and describe and assess their own reading strengths and weaknesses. Start with questions about each child's reading progress, and query to what extent the reader

- shows an interest in books in a range of genres,
- reads for meaning and makes meaning from suitable texts,
- uses effective strategies and various "fix-up" activities,
- uses word-level skills to deal with problem words,
- participates in conversations about books, and
- makes connections among books, authors and illustrators, text, and real life.

To record the data, teachers can create record sheets displaying a continuum or Likert scale with options such as "usually," "often," "seldom," and "not yet." (See Table 11.4 for a sample record sheet.)

In addition, the following aspects of reading workshop offer powerful assessment opportunities:

- *Read-alouds*: Interest, listening, meaning making, conversations, connections, genres, strengths, and problems
- *Shared reading*: Interest, meaning, strategies, word-level skills, connections, genres, strengths, and problems
- *Guided reading*: Interest, meaning, strategies, conversations, word-level skills, connections, genres, strengths, and problems
- *Sustained reading*: Interest, meaning, strategies, conversations, connections, choice, genres, strengths, and problems
- *Individual reading*: Interest, meaning, strategies, word-level skills, conversations, connections, choice, genres, strengths, problems, and goal setting
- *Literature reading*: Interest, meaning, strategies, conversations, connections, genres, strengths, and problems
- *Inquiry reading*: Interest, meaning, strategies, genres, strengths, and problems (Weaver, 2002, pp. 290–292)

Book Lists

Independent Reading and Guided Reading Lists

A clear and organized method for annotating books read throughout the year can take various forms. Students should maintain their own lists that can be shared during reading conferences. Table 11.5 provides a sample yearly record chart to help the student keep track of books read independently in class and at home. Table 11.6 shows an example of a critical guided reading book list maintained by both teacher and student.

Table 11.4 Reading Workshop Record Sheet				
	Usually	Often	Seldom	Not Yet
Read-Alouds				
Interest				
Listening				
Meaning making				
Conversations				
Connections				
Genres				
Strengths				
Problems				
Shared Reading				
Interest				
Meaning				
Strategies				
Word-level skills				
Connections				
Genres				
Strengths				
Problems				
Guided Reading				
Interest				
Meaning				
Strategies				
Conversations				
Word-level skills				
Connections				
Genres				
Strengths				
Problems				

(Continued)

Table 11.4 (Continued)	Usually	Often	Seldom	Not Yet
Sustained Reading				
Interest				
Meaning				
Strategies				
Conversations				
Connections				
Choice				
Genres				
Strengths				
Problems				
Individual Reading				
Interest				
Meaning				
Strategies				
Word-level skills				
Conversations				
Connections				
Choice				
Genres				
Strengths				
Problems				
Goal setting				
Literature Reading				
Interest				
Meaning				
Strategies				
Conversations				
Connections				
Genres				

	Usually	Often	Seldom	Not Yet
Strengths				
Problems				
Inquiry Reading				
Interest				
Meaning				
Strategies				
Genres				
Strengths				
Problems				

Source: Adapted from Weaver (2002).

Table 11.5 Independent Reading Book List

Student Name: _____

Date	Fiction	Nonfiction	Favorite Genres	Comments

Table 11.6 Guided Reading Book List

Student Name: _____

	Level: Initial	Level: Midyear	Level: Final
Text level: Lexiles			
Benchmarks			
Future goals			

Developing a Writing Notebook

Working writing portfolios can take various forms. One option is to keep two folders—one containing models, drafts, and notes, and the other containing a collection of finished work "to be used in parent conferences as a record of students' growth" (Whitney et al., 2008, p. 225).

Documenting Student Progress

Visual documentation of student literacy progress can take the form of graphs, scatter plots, charts, or spreadsheets. The advantage of a visual representation for the teacher is invaluable; a visual could be shown to the reader during an individual conference as a way to help him or her picture goal attainment, making it seem more realistic and doable.

Fountas and Pinnell Assessment Levels Graph

This graph shows the progress of one student over the course of the school year. In addition, independent- and instructional-level scores can be isolated by period.

Whole-Class Data Displays

Visual representations providing a class profile help the teacher understand how the whole class relates to each reading level: independent, instructional, and frustration. Taking the composite scores from standardized reading tests, informal reading inventories, cloze tests, running records, or other administered assessments, the teacher can use this information for differing activities. Such activities might include mixed-ability grouping, whole-class readings, and targeted instruction (Rubin, 2011). The scatter plot technique is a quick and useful method to visually share information with other resource personnel (see Figure 11.6).

Figure 11.6
Classroom
Literacy Profile
Using Scatter
Plot

Source: Adapted from
Rubin (2011).

Recording and Analyzing Individual Conferences

The individual conference provides authentic opportunities for the teacher to observe, record, and discuss reading behaviors with students. Data collection can involve a student reading a passage and the teacher keeping a running record for later analysis of miscue patterns. In addition, the teacher can interview or talk with the student about reading preferences—genres, formats, favorite authors or topics—conduct a book conversation, or establish reading goals or benchmarks (Weaver, 2002). Further examination of a student's reading journal or log kept on reader-generated record sheets can focus on extent of books read, levels of choices, and goals for the year.

Storing Student Records

Storing student records is based on teacher preference, along with space requirements. Common methods for storing records include the following:

- Student folders (plastic)
- Loose-leaf notebooks
- Plastic storage bins with sliding drawers
- Commercial moving boxes
- Index-card boxes
- Accordion folders
- Online storage options, such as memory sticks
- File cabinets with dividers

Student literacy records should be maintained as confidential, yet accessible to the teacher. They should be clearly labeled and dated. Records are normally passed to the next year's teacher.

Reporting to Families: Family Conferences

Research demonstrates that when parents and teachers partner together, at-risk student achievement increases. (Darling, 2005, p. 476)

Communicating with parents on a regular basis is essential, and involvement should be carefully planned and documented. Communicating with parents in a **family conference** about their child's mastery of literacy skills and objectives, especially for striving students, presents an opportunity for collaboration. Select opportunities to provide positive comments about a student's literacy work before noting any deficiencies. The following documents can be shared with parents:

- Progress-monitoring reports
- Report cards
- Student Education Plans (Reutzel & Clark, 2011).

Keep in mind that sitting with parents and explaining the contents of these documents, rather than just providing copies for independent reference, can circumvent problems of misinterpretation.

A literacy folder, maintained jointly by students and teacher, should be presented to families often throughout the school year. Independent reading lists should be kept at home as well as at school, along with leveled book lists maintained jointly by teacher and students. Writing portfolios can highlight student growth in writing by displaying graphic organizers of writing topics, rough drafts, final writing products, and displays. These student products can be highlighted and discussed during conferences.

Making Connections

List and describe the contents of a literacy folder that could be used for a parent conference. Why would you pick these components? Please explain their importance.

Presenting the literacy folder to parents/guardians should be a time for celebration of reading progress and attainment. The following dialogue starter can be used during a family literacy conference (with the student present). For Spanish speakers, translation should be provided during the conference.

Welcome to our family literacy conference. Your child _____ will talk about [his/her] progress in reading and writing this year. Also, [he/she] will be displaying the work [he/she] is most proud of and explaining why [he/she] feels that way. Together, we will discuss challenges in reading and writing and how your child used strategies to "fix up" those areas. Please feel free to ask questions and make comments.

Our overall purpose in Chapter 11 was to get educators thinking about systematic organization of records reflecting both informal and formal assessment results. Many of us are challenged to ensure that our records are comprehensive enough to present a full picture of individual student as well as whole-class progress. Seeking support from data-collection–savvy personnel is fine; don't be afraid to ask questions. When you streamline your assessment records, a comprehensive picture of student literacy achievement will emerge and strengthen your teaching expertise.

Key Terms

anecdotal record keeping

assessment calendar

authentic data collection

driven by data

family conference

Website Resources

- **"Data-Driven Decision Making and Electronic Learning Assessment Resources (ELAR)," California Learning Resource Network**

The California Learning Resource Network (CLRN) reviews materials for publishers and producers of Electronic Learning Assessment Resources (ELAR). Although the program began for the purpose of including such resources in the California Department of Education, current reviews include content-specific resources that address Common Core State Standards. CLRN answers emerging questions about the latest advances in data collection; storage and analysis; the use of assessment to plan for district, school, and individual instructional needs; and the professional development required for proper implementation of these resources. For information on ELAR, see **www.clrn.org/elar/dddm.cfm#A.** For information on literacy and language development, see **www.clrn.org/eld.**

- *Fountas and Pinnell Literacy*, **Heinemann**

Heinemann is a publisher of professional resources and a provider of educational services for teachers, kindergarten through college. The Fountas and Pinnell Online Data Management Systems, available through Heinemann, enable teachers to collect, analyze, and report data on individual and class progress; determine growth in benchmark instructional and independent reading levels; evaluate effectiveness of instruction; share data; and customize reports according to district requirements—among other essential educational and administrative processes. For information on assessment, data storage and analysis, leveled literacy intervention, and other Fountas and Pinnell classroom resources, see **www .heinemann.com/fountasandpinnell/default.aspx.**

- **American Institutes for Research**

The American Institutes for Research and Learning Point Associates have merged, forming an education research company that provides a continuum of education research, assessment, technical assistance, and policy analysis from the school level up to the national level. The company's newest multimedia resource, known as Stepping Stones, includes a scientifically based observation tool for data collection, a guide for analyzing the data, and a professional development workshop for teachers. For a list of literacy assessment techniques, visit **www.ncrel.org/sdrs/areas/issues/content/cntareas/reading/li7lk29.htm.**

Student Study Site: Visit the Student Study Site at **www.sagepub.com/grantlit** to access additional study tools including eFlashcards, web resources, and online-only appendices.

SECTION III

Designing Instructional Strategies Based on Students' Needs

Many would argue that the primary purpose of teachers is to help students become skilled, independent readers. The complex nature of reading has been studied by linguists, cognitive psychologists, and educators for nearly a century, and their discoveries and insights have provided valuable understanding about reading processes, the acquisition of reading, the difficulties some students face in learning how to read, and the complex skill set that helps readers develop reading proficiency. Their contributions continue to help us equip teachers to provide effective literacy instruction (Adams, 1990; Chall, 1996; National Reading Panel, 2000; Neuman & Dickinson, 2002; Rieben & Perfetti, 1991; Ruddell & Unrau, 2004; Snow, Burns, & Griffin, 1998; Stanovich, 2000). The complex processes of literacy continue to be studied, challenged, and modified as research unveils deeper understandings of the human brain, cognition, learning, and language. Section I of the text provided a foundational understanding of literacy, and Section II dissected several components of literacy after providing a working definition and understanding of authentic literacy assessment. Section III examines the strategies teachers can use to build students who are skilled readers and writers. The first chapter in this section, Chapter 12, focuses on phonemic awareness and phonics instruction. Chapter 13 addresses comprehension and writing strategies. Chapter 14 emphasizes how to build students' fluency, as well as comprehension and writing strategies that build fluency. In each of these chapters, you will learn a wealth of information that will build your knowledge and repertoire for teaching literacy.

Phonemic Awareness, Phonics, and Word Work Strategies and Assessments

Sandra E. Golden,
Penny Soboleski,
and Kathy B. Grant

Common Core State Standards

Phonological Awareness	*RF.K.2* Demonstrate understanding of spoken words, syllables, and sounds (phonemes).
	RF.K.2.A Recognize and produce rhyming words.
	RF.K.2.B Count, pronounce, blend, and segment syllables in spoken words.
	RF.K.2.C Blend and segment onsets and rimes of single-syllable spoken words.
	RF.K.2.D Isolate and pronounce the initial, medial vowel, and final sounds (phonemes) in three-phoneme (consonant-vowel-consonant, or CVC) words. (This does not include CVCs ending with /l/, /r/, or /x/.)
	RF.K.2.E Add or substitute individual sounds (phonemes) in simple, one-syllable words to make new words.

(Continued)

(Continued)

Phonics and Word Recognition	*RF.K.3* Know and apply grade-level phonics and word analysis skills in decoding words.
	RF.K.3.A Demonstrate basic knowledge of one-to-one letter-sound correspondences by producing the primary sound or many of the most frequent sounds for each consonant.
	RF.K.3.B Associate the long and short sounds with the common spellings (graphemes) for the five major vowels.
	RF.K.3.C Read common high-frequency words by sight (e.g., *the, of, to, you, she, my, is, are, do, does*).
	RF.K.3.D Distinguish between similarly spelled words by identifying the sounds of the letters that differ.
Vocabulary Acquisition and Use	*L.3.4.A* Use sentence-level context as a clue to the meaning of a word or phrase.
	L.3.4.B Determine the meaning of the new word formed when a known affix is added to a known word (e.g., *agreeable/disagreeable, comfortable/uncomfortable, care/careless, heat/preheat*).
	L.3.4.C Use a known root word as a clue to the meaning of an unknown word with the same root (e.g., *company, companion*).

FOCUS QUESTIONS

1. What is the difference between phonemic awareness and phonics instruction?
2. Describe how the ability to decode, blend, and segment impacts reading success.
3. What is explicit and systematic instruction?
4. How can you develop instruction in phonics and phonemic awareness that promotes literacy growth, fosters opportunities for practice and application, and engages students in authentic, relevant, and meaningful ways?

Words in Action

Growing Word Banks With Phonics

As a beginning teacher, Sage understood the notion of phonics instruction but was overwhelmed by the number of words that needed to be taught in first grade. How could she ensure that her first graders could grow through the word work they did in class? She struggled with how best to teach, reinforce, and assess phonics. She remained concerned about struggling readers who were challenged with first-grade sight words and identifying the sounds in those words. Many still could not spell high-frequency words correctly—should she worry?

Through her college classes, she found out that phonics generalizations did not stand up as reliable. Furthermore, asking students to memorize rules was deemed counterproductive to learning. She investigated literacy theories on early "code" reading, and now she must apply them to her classroom.

She needed a yearlong plan to implement phonics work daily. Her plan was to use read-alouds to create word connections. Sage was determined to set up learning centers that she would rotate by phonics skills throughout the year. Yes, word families offered solid connections, and she decided to display word family learning charts that were codeveloped by teacher and students.

But prior to implementing all this, she needed to have a discussion with her first graders about "growing" the word banks in their heads along the way by practicing reading new words with each other. Finally, Sage needed to connect with parents to encourage their help with her first graders in developing word consciousness through building community and family connections with words. The stakes were too high not to.

In 2000, the National Reading Panel (NRP) identified five components of skills and reading instruction strategies to improve or enhance children's reading levels: **phonics, phonemic awareness**, vocabulary, comprehension, and fluency. Members of the NRP believe that if children acquire solid phonemic awareness and phonics skills, with balanced instruction in vocabulary development, comprehension skills, and fluency, they will be more likely to achieve high levels of academic reading success. Furthermore, research indicates that children with strong skills in phonics and phonemic awareness achieve more success in reading. That is, when children have a deep understanding and recognition of phonemes and strong decoding abilities, reading will be enjoyable and effortless.

Phonemic awareness is the spoken word and the recognition that words consist of parts: words, syllables, and phonemes (Cheyney, n.d.). Phonemes are the "smallest part of a word" (Center for the Improvement of Early Reading Achievement, 2010, p. 5) and require children to demonstrate their ability to segment and blend the spoken word. Phonics refers to the sounds the letters of the alphabet represent, and for some children it is an effective approach to reading development. Furthermore, phonics strategies and instruction for young learners require direct guidance coupled with opportunities for practice and application. That is, children will connect better to the skills if they are engaged in meaningful, relevant, and engaging instruction (Rasinski & Padak, 2008). To ensure that instruction is explicit and systematic (NRP, 2000), it needs to include opportunities for practice and application. The instruction, practice, and application should apply to the learners' prior knowledge (meaningful) and their world (relevant) to make learning engaging.

When addressing the needs of beginner and English language learner (ELL) readers, one of many first steps is to determine the needs of the readers through an informal assessment. Moreover, as teachers, it is important to know what strategies to employ and how those strategies could enhance and improve reading. When referring to beginner or ELL readers, the skills that are most appropriate to strengthen are phonics, phonological awareness, and phonemic awareness. Thus, assessment should determine whether the child is capable of recognizing letters (alphabetic principle) and the sounds the letters represent (phonics), if the child is aware of the phonological aspect of the spoken word (Cheyney, n.d.; words, syllables, and phonemes), and if the child is capable of recognizing the smallest part of a spoken word (phonemic awareness). The latter of these skills is seen as the most complex (Cheyney, 2011), and it takes highly skilled and trained teachers to help children grasp this concept. These skills, along with oral language development, print knowledge, and writing, are recommended by the National Literacy Panel as those skills children should acquire from birth to age 5 for reading success.

Teachers must become conversant in the specialized vocabulary of phonemic awareness, phonics, and **word work**. National Common Core State Standards, as well as state-level standards, define critical terms for teacher implementation of phonics instruction. Check your state Common Core documents for specific code-based terms to become familiar with. Throughout this chapter, pay attention to highlighted terms and refer to the glossary for definitions. Work with your learning partners to connect terms to teaching strategies.

Test of Phonemic Segmentation

As mentioned in earlier chapters, the alphabetic principle and oral language development are key indicators of children's success toward achieving skills in phonological and phonemic awareness. Most children enter kindergarten classrooms with sufficient understanding of the **alphabetic principle** and oral language skills; however, those children still need formal learning and strategies to improve or enhance their reading ability. Identifying the specific needs of children struggling with reading is essential in determining their individual needs.

By the end of first grade, most students can manipulate phonemes in their speech; they can break spoken words into their constituent sounds. Phonemic awareness tasks are the best indicators of early reading acquisition. One popular instrument, the Yopp–Singer Test of Phoneme Segmentation (Yopp, 1988), is a research-based assessment used to gauge children's phonemic segmentation skills (see Table 12.1 for a sample). This teacher-administered assessment is highlighted early in the chapter as an archetype for phonics assessments. It is informally given by the teacher in a comfortable setting, is connected to breaking-the-code targets for early readers, and can be employed as an interim evaluation for segmentation.

Table 12.1 The Yopp–Singer Test of Phoneme Segmentation

Directions: Today we're going to play a word game. I'm going to say a word, and I want you to break the word apart. You are going to tell me each sound in the word in order. For example, if I say "old," you will say "o-l-d."

Let's try a few words together.

Practice Items

ride	go	man

Test Items

dog	lazy	keep	race
fine	zoo	no	three
she	job	wave	in
grew	ice	that	at
red	top	me	by
	sat	do	

Source: Yopp (1988).

We all know that no two children are alike, that developing instruction to meet individual needs is critical to their success, and that assessment is necessary. This chapter will focus on reviewing and providing resources and examples of various research-based strategies used to develop children's skill levels in phonemic awareness and phonics.

Making Connections

Reflect on and list the sequence of early reading skills involved in phonemic awareness and phonics knowledge. To do this, refer to your state's Common Core standards or the national version located at the beginning of the chapter. Try to "unpack" the standards; in other words, focus on the action the learner is supposed to master. For example, "demonstrate understanding of . . . ," "recognize and apply . . . ," "distinguish between . . . ," or other verbs indicating what students should be able to do. Connect those actions with "knowing"—for example, long and short vowel sounds, onsets and rimes, or specific high-frequency words.

Overall, what should students in Grades K–2 know and be able to do?

Phonemic Awareness Strategies

Phonemic awareness is the ability to conceptualize that the sounds of letters create the spoken word. Children need to recognize and segment the smallest part of a word and then blend the sounds of the letters to make the spoken word (Armbruster, 2010; Cheyney, 2011; Hempenstall, 2011) if they are to achieve success in reading. Phonemic awareness strategies provide teachers with opportunities to integrate in their instruction various ways to engage learners in developing phonemic awareness to ensure reading success.

Many of the strategies discussed in this section will focus on using activities that are enjoyable, engaging, meaningful, and relevant. Additionally, the strategies presented will demonstrate **explicit and systematic phonics** instruction. Activities such as the use of children's clapping songs are enjoyable and engaging while also promoting explicit and systematic instruction. *B-I-N-G-O* is an excellent clapping song that integrates sound–letter correspondence as well as blending of sounds for the spoken word. The *Miss Mary Mack* clapping song can be used to focus on rhyming, sound–letter correspondence, and ending words with similar sounds. These clapping songs and others are available at FunClapping.com (funclapping.com/list.php).

Furthermore, the overall purpose of engaging children in phonemic awareness strategies is to enhance or improve their abilities to automatically and seamlessly pronounce and recognize words while reading. When children demonstrate strong phonemic awareness skills, there is greater opportunity for them to read fluently and engage in reading for understanding—thus, the importance of promoting instruction that is explicit and systematic and not just drilling exercises. That is, children should be involved in authentic phonics instruction that is engaging and meaningful and that they can connect to. For example, if teaching the blending sounds of *bl* and *br*, authentic activities such as showing objects, reading books, playing games, or writing using those blending sounds allow for higher levels of engagement and provide greater opportunities for grasping the concepts. Additionally, instruction should include opportunities for practice and application.

Making Connections

When teaching *br*, bring in objects or visuals that start with *br* and that children can connect with. Also introduce students to *Brown Bear, Brown Bear, What Do You See?* by Bill Martin to encourage reading, and have them write a poem or grocery list (e.g., bread, bran, broccoli, Brussels sprouts, bratwurst, brown rice, brown sugar) or draw a picture using the letters *br*. ELL children could listen to the story read by Bill Martin, available on YouTube (www.youtube.com/watch?v=pdHCYgO9zh8).

Word Level

Phonemic awareness strategies are designed to improve or enhance the learner's ability to blend letters to form the spoken word. In this section, we will examine word, syllable, onset–rime, and phoneme levels for developing phonemic awareness. You will see how seamlessly these strategies can be aligned with the Common Core State Standards.

Many researchers (Cheyney, n.d.; Dechant, 1993; Hempenstall, 2011) posit that children must develop a deep phonological awareness to reach higher achievement in reading. Table 12.2 illustrates the various stages of phonological awareness. These stages suggest that phonemic awareness is contingent on sequencing instruction, strategies, and activities that are engaging and meaningful.

Table 12.2 Phonological Awareness Levels

Cheyney	Hempenstall	Dechant
Words—sentence segmenting	Recognition that sentences are made up of words	**Level 1** Awareness of gross differences
Rhyming words—ending word parts that sound the same	Recognition that words can rhyme	Awareness of rhyme
Compound words—segmenting and blending	Recognition that words can be broken down into syllables	Segmentation of words into syllables
Syllables—segmenting and blending	Recognition that words can be broken down into onsets and rimes	**Level 2** Awareness of initial consonant segment
Consonant sounds in the initial parts of words	Recognition that words can begin with the same sound	Alliterations—awareness that two words begin with the same sounds
Alliterations—words that begin with the same sounds	Recognition that words can end with the same sound	Awareness and segmentation of onset and rime
Onsets and rimes	Recognition that words can have the same medial sound(s)	**Level 3** Phonemic segmentation
Phoneme—segmenting, blending, and manipulating	Recognition that words can be broken down into individual phonemes	Phonemic synthesis (blending) of phonemes and syllables
	Recognition that sounds can be deleted from words to make new words	Phonemic manipulation (additions, deletions, substitutions, and reversals)
	Ability to make sounds to make words	
	Ability to segment words into constituent sounds	

Gross Difference

Awareness of gross differences refers to the child's ability to recognize individual words. For example, if a sentence reads, *I ran down the hill*, the child must demonstrate that there are five different words in the sentence. Cheyney (n.d.) describes Dechant's

Level 1 as first engaging students in gross differences, then rhyming and syllable awareness, and then segmenting and blending. Cheyney suggests that "as children progress through Level 1, they move from segmenting sentences into words to concentrating on word endings to determining the number of syllables in a word" (n.d., p. 2).

One strategy idea to practice gross differences involves using a popular children's literature book to create and cut out words that are in turn mounted on poster board or construction paper. Guide children, or have children use the words to make new sentences or write a poem.

Rhyming

As teachers, you can engage children in instruction that uses rhyming children's books or poetry to assist children in recognizing how ending sounds in some words sound similar. As described in Table 12.2, integrating rhyming and sentence segmentation is seen as the first stage of phonological instruction that moves children toward phonemic awareness and reading. Effective strategies and activities could include song, dance, drawing, writing, and visual opportunities. Table 12.3 provides a list of books characterized by Goodreads.com as popular rhyming and poetry books for children. See Table 12.4 for an activity to assess children's rhyming skills.

Table 12.3 Popular Rhyming and Poetry Books for Children

Book Title	Author
Noisy Nora	Rosemary Wells
A Giraffe and a Half	Shel Silverstein
Moose on the Loose	Kathy-Jo Wargin
Fox in Socks	Dr. Seuss
Barn Dance	Bill Martin Jr.

Poetry Collection Title	Author
Rainy Day Poems	James McDonald
Where the Sidewalk Ends	Shel Silverstein
When We Were Very Young	A. A. Milne
The New Kid on the Block	Jack Prelutsky
Poetry for Young People: Langston Hughes	David Roessel

Syllable Level

Hempenstall (2011) asserts that when children have a deep understanding of the phoneme, they will be better at grasping the concept of syllables. A syllable contains a vowel, several vowels, or a vowel and a consonant. The number of times you hear the vowel (*a*, *e*, *i*, *o*, *u*) is equal to the number of syllables in a word. The letter *Y* can be counted as a syllable only if it creates the sound of a vowel.

Table 12.4 Early Readers: Recognizing Rhyme Assessment

Directions:

    I am going to say two words: *cat–fat.*

    I want you to tell me if the two words sound alike. This is called a rhyme.

    Let me show you.

Model:

Cat and *fat* have the same sound at the end, so they rhyme. *Cat* and *mop* do not rhyme, because they do not have the same sound at the end.

Share:

    Listen to these two words: *pail–tail.*

    Now say the two words with me: *pail–tail.*

    Do these two words rhyme? *(Yes)*

    Put your thumbs up like this if they rhyme.

    Listen to these two words: *cow–pig.*

    Now say the two words with me: *cow–pig.*

    Do these two words rhyme? *(No)*

    Put your thumbs down like this if they do not rhyme.

Assess:

Listen to these sets of words. Thumbs up if they rhyme. Thumbs down if they do not rhyme. Here we go . . .

    1. *fin–win*

    2. *rug–mug*

    3. *hat–dress*

    4. *pan–man*

    5. *bird–book*

    6. *lock–rock*

    7. *bet–get*

    8. *cup–dog*

Source: Klein (n.d.).

Making Connections

Let's make sure you feel comfortable hearing the sounds in a word that make up a syllable. With your partner, decide on the number of syllables in the following words: *try*, *bee*, *cat*, *eating*, *skin*, *warns*, and *singing*. Practice voicing the sounds, and prepare a short teaching practice using recognition of syllables for primary students.

The simple instrument Assessing Syllable Recognition (Table 12.5) can easily be administered to individual students to evaluate their knowledge of sounds, specifically vowel sounds. A solid base for word learning will be developed when students can consistently break words into parts or syllables.

Table 12.5 Assessing Syllable Recognition

Directions: We are going to practice hearing the vowel sounds in our words. Pretend you are a robot in the future. Say the words as a robot would. Pay attention to the pauses in the word. How many parts did you break the word into? That is the number of syllables in the word.

Word list: For example, let's say the word *robot* together as a robot would. How many sounds do you hear?

    robot—ro-bot (two syllables) _____

    talking—talk-ing (two syllables) _____

    walk—walk (one syllable) _____

    dusted—dust-ed (two syllables) _____

    try—try (one syllable) _____

After several examples, use classroom words that students have heard through literacy connections, high-frequency words, or community-based words.

Source: How Many Syllables (2014).

A few notations on this assessment are in order. Words taken from current classroom read-alouds provide powerful connections for readers—so include those words in this assessment. Moreover, diphthongs—when two vowels make only one sound—should be taught explicitly and avoided for this assessment, because they may cause confusion for young readers. As students progress, engage them in practicing more complex syllable recognition. Some researchers suggest the use of compound words to assist in this practice.

Onset–Rime Level

Some researchers suggest that rhyming has strong value in reading development since students can easily recognize rhymes that are fun and engaging. These skills help the student recognize differences between the initial sound of the word—the **onset**—and other parts of the word—the **rime** (Cheyney, n.d.; Rasinski & Padak, 2008). Armbruster (2010) defines the onset as the "initial consonant(s) sound of a syllable." For example, the onset of *food* is *f* and of *bike* is *b*. Rimes consist of spelling patterns or "chunks," such as *-ate*, *-ile*, and *-ake* (see Table 12.6). One-syllable words can be divided into onsets and rimes; the onset is the letter or letters before a vowel, while the rime is the vowel(s) and letters following it. For example, in the word *late*, *l* is the onset and *-ate* is the rime (Gill, 2006).

Teaching onsets and rimes is a better approach to phonics than teaching individual letter sounds because onsets and rimes are much more consistent than single letters. . . . Clymer (1963) found that many of the phonics rules traditionally taught are not reliable; only half of the vowel generalizations he tested worked at least 60% of the time. Rimes, like *-all*, however, almost always make the same sound. Furthermore, Moustafa's (1997) research showed that children tend to figure out new words by analogy—that is, by thinking of other similar words they know. Students who learn a rime can apply this knowledge to help them figure out new words. (pp. 191–192)

Table 12.6 List of 37 Rimes

-ack, -ail, -ain, -ake, -ale, -ame, -an, -ank, -ap, -ash, -at, -ate, -aw, -ay

-eat, -ell, -est

-ice, -ick, -ide, -ight, -ill, -in, -ine, -ing, -ink, -ip, -it

-ock, -oke, -op, -ore, -ot

-uck, -ug, -ump, -unk

Source: Gill (2006).

Furthermore, **word families** are formed through the combination of onsets or initial consonants and rimes, such as using the *-ack* rime to form *sack*, *tack*, *jack*, *lack*, *track*, *knack*, *whack*, and so forth. Using word families in word work and play can be a powerful method to help grow vocabulary, especially at the Tier 1 level for early readers. Daily practice in manipulating and recognizing word families is recommended for primary grades. Guided practice involves substitution of onsets or consonants at the start of words. Also, students can make a word wheel using provided cut-out and sectioned wheels and a metal brad.

Start stockpiling classroom supplies that will form the basis for phonemic awareness, word families, vocabulary, or phonics practice centers. Centers can be rotated as primary classes advance in word work. Materials for phonics instruction may include the following:

- Magnetic letters
- Letter tiles
- Sentence strips
- Pocket charts
- Wiki sticks
- Dice
- Colored strips
- Chart paper
- Tic-tac-toe boards
- Small dry-erase boards
- Sound charts
- Bingo cards
- Newspapers and magazines to cut out words (Diller, 2007)

Teachers can easily set up a word learning center with practice materials, taped rhymes and other reading materials, and file folders of partner phonics matching activities (see Figure 12.1 for an example). Activities offer an opportunity for differing student learning configurations: self-monitoring individual practice and collaborative partner learning. Centers are a valuable part of word learning and practice.

Figure 12.1
Word Family
(-*ack*)

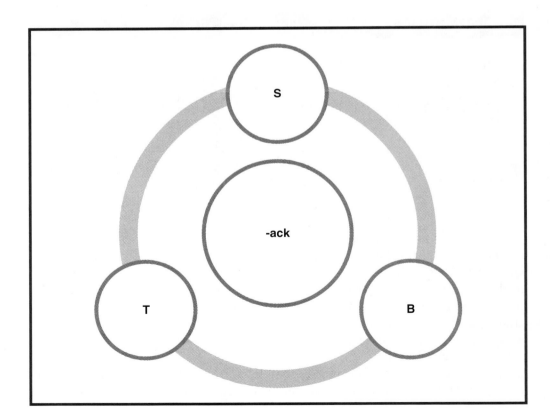

In addition, file-folder review games such as word ladders can be placed in centers to promote partner exploration of word families. Word ladders can be designed in many formats (a sample is shown in Figure 12.2; check the Internet or texts for others). Learning centers set up in elementary classrooms offer authentic assessment opportunities and student self-evaluation.

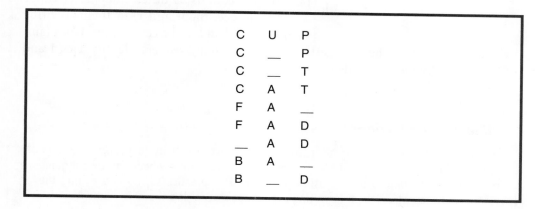

Figure 12.2
Word Ladders

Evaluating student learning through repetition and practice in learning centers should definitely be undertaken. Being flexible and allowing students to proceed through a learning center at their own pace is important. Through use of an exit slip (see Table 12.7), teachers can appraise student skills practice.

Table 12.7 Sample of an Exit Slip

Learning Center: Word Families Work
(Circle what you finished)

What word families file folders did you complete?   -at   -ade   -ack

How did you do with your partner?   Strong   Good   Still need practice

How do you know?

I was able to read all words in family. _____

I was able to read just some words in family. _____

I was not able to read any words in family. _____

What is your goal for the next time you work in this center? Talk to the teacher about this.

**When done with word family practice, fill this out and drop in box.*

Figure 12.3
Word Family
Book

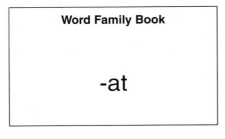

Word family books (see Figure 12.3) are a great way for primary readers to actively collect and get to know word families. Student arrangement of a personalized word family book can be a long-term project, with the end goal of celebrating completion of the books by having students display their creations as other students circulate around the classroom and read them. Inviting families would add to the celebration. Word family learning is one of the strongest ways to help young readers identify Tier 1 and selected high-frequency words.

Making Connections

In preparing for teaching, create a word family practice activity (e.g., *cap, flap, gap, lap, map, nap, rap, tap*). Create flashcards, word ladders, word wheels, or a word game to introduce children to the words; have the children practice saying and writing the words; and then guide them in writing a poem or story using the new words. You can also engage them in making nonsense words with the same ending, or extend their understanding by having them brainstorm and create a new list of words with similar ending sounds. Hint: If you laminate your flashcards, you can reuse them for multiple classroom phonics activities.

Phonics-Based Strategies

Phonics is the ability to recognize the sounds the letters represent (NRP, 2000; Rasinski & Padak, 2008; Reutzel & Cooter, 2013). In addition, children should have a good understanding of the alphabetic principle needed for decoding words. Phonics instruction gives children skills to decode words in print. Reutzel and Cooter (2013) recommend teaching consonant letters and sounds first, followed by the vowel letters and sounds.

There are many variations in consonant letter sounds, such as the rule for the letters *C* and *G*. For example, the letter *C* in certain words sounds like *K* or *S*, referred to as a hard *C* and soft *C*, respectively (Reutzel & Cooter, 2013). The letter *G* also represents two different sounds: a hard *G* sound and a soft *G* sound. In addition to these rules, there are also consonant blends and consonant digraphs. **Consonant blends** are two or more consonants blended together (Rasinski & Padak, 2008; Reutzel & Cooter, 2013)— for example, *cloud, clown, drown, small*.

On the other hand, **consonant digraphs** are consonant blends that make very distinctive sounds, such as *trunk, plunk, sunk; ship, shrank, sham, shrink;* or *tree, train, trip.* Together, they represent up to 96 sounds (Reutzel & Cooter, 2013), although there are only five to seven letter vowels.

Types of Phonics Instruction: Analytic, Synthetic, and Contemporary

All approaches to the teaching of phonics should lead down the path to a balanced classroom literacy program. Early reading programs use a mixture of analytical and synthetic phonics, as well as contemporary approaches. See Table 12.8 for an outline of the differences among these approaches and their applications (Fox, 2000).

Table 12.8 Characteristics of Analytic, Synthetic, and Contemporary Phonics

Analytic Phonics	Synthetic Phonics	Contemporary Phonics
Indirect instruction	Direct instruction	Spelling based, embedded in authentic stories, analogy based
Whole-to-part instruction	Part-to-whole instruction	Both whole-to-part and part-to-whole instruction
Teacher points out a word with a long vowel sound, and students identify examples in words read.	Teacher has students segment long-vowel words into sounds—beginning, middle, and end.	Children use known long-vowel word parts to identify known words (families), learn phonics through spelling words with long vowel sounds, or identify long-vowel words through reading (and also writing) authentic texts.
Assessment formats include sticky notations, whole-class chart paper activities, and checklists.	Assessment formats include Elkonin boxes, word ladders, and word chains.	Assessments include spelling activities, word family assessments, and locating examples from texts and then identifying them with sticky notes.

Source: Fox (2000).

When to Teach Foundational Phonics

The bulleted information that follows, from *K–5 Teachers: Laying Foundations for the Common Core* (Literacy Leadership State Team & Oregon Department of Education, n.d.), presents the Common Core Foundational Skills by grade level. When looking at the skills progression, notice the emphasis on print concepts and phonological awareness in kindergarten and first grade. Phonics and **word recognition** and fluency are addressed in kindergarten through fifth grade. Also, notice the skills students need at the end of each grade level.

- By the end of *kindergarten*, students are comfortable recognizing and writing letters of the alphabet and know the primary sound/symbol relationship for every letter. Students are able to read emergent-reader texts with purpose and understanding so they will be ready to read grade-level texts in first grade.

- *First grade* students leave first grade reading grade-level texts with purpose and understanding. Students will also use context to confirm or self-correct word recognition and understanding, rereading as necessary. When reading grade-level texts orally, students will be reading with accuracy, appropriate rate, and expression.
- Finally, by the time they complete *second grade*, students are decoding automatically and reading with fluency. Overall, by the end of second grade, it is essential that students be able to read independently with automaticity and flow to ensure that they have full attentional resources available for high level comprehension.
- By the end of *first grade*, students should have sufficient working knowledge of English spelling patterns and conventions to decode regular, one- and two-syllable words, including those with inflections. First grade students are also expected to apply their knowledge of English spelling patterns and conventions in writing, so they can produce regular one- and two-syllable words that are phonemically complete and decipherable, even if not formally correct.
- Learning about irregularly spelled words needs to be distributed across grades in accordance with the language demands of children's texts. The introduction of irregular words begins in kindergarten with very high-frequency grammatical words, including articles, prepositions, and common irregular verbs such as *is* and *do*. (pp. F-4–F-5)

Teachable Opportunities

Teachable moments are one of the best ways to engage children in real-life learning opportunities. These moments could be based on a child's experience on the way to school, the weather, a trip to the grocery store, a classroom problem, or even a service project.

Environmental print, consisting of any print in a child's environment, provides excellent incidental opportunities for word learning, alphabetic recognition, and literacy discussions. As children explore their neighborhood or new locations, they naturally encounter print and symbols that can be used to stimulate interest. Teachers or parents/guardians can call attention to signs and text, and gently pose questions to the learner:

1. Notice the sign on that house (for sale, beware of dog, or residents' names)? What can you guess is its purpose?

2. See the large bold letters on the billboard? Can you tell me the names of those letters (alphabetic recognition)? Are they capital or lowercase letters? How do you know?

3. Note the traffic sign at the end of the street. What do you think it means for us to do (yield, stop, or watch for oncoming traffic)?

4. Can you think of words that begin with the letter _____ that you see straight ahead? Tell me some other words that begin with the same letter.

5. See the shape of that (fence, stairway, or rooftop)? What letter does the shape remind you of and why?

Taking a field trip to stroll through the neighborhood (with extra supervision from parents) can be a wonderful way to give children a chance to authentically note environmental print, nature symbols, pictures, or images. Provide students with small clipboards and pencils to note environmental print and symbols they appreciate. While on the neighborhood stroll, have students write or draw environmental objects of significance that they can highlight once they are back in the classroom.

Labeling classroom features, writing sticky notes, and posting schedules, in addition to other types of print found within the classroom, promotes functional print and supports word learning and teachable moments. Theme books developed by young learners can be an engaging strategy to promote word work.

Making Connections

Theme books can be put together using environmental print found in magazines, junk mail, newspapers, and other print sources. For example, if the unit of study is on families (a popular kindergarten unit), students can cut out and paste into bound theme notebooks logos, pictures, and words that characterize families. It is a good idea to avoid commercialized logos or symbols as much as possible. When the books are complete, the teacher can cut out and add words, and students can guess their meaning and connection to the unit. Make sure students can provide justification for inserting certain word, symbols, and pictures.

As a teacher, challenge yourself to make a theme book based on your environment that you can use as a model for your students. As you present your theme book to students, make sure to explain why you included each particular element: word, symbol, picture, or photograph. As a test run, present your theme book to your learning partner.

Environmental print walls can assume various formats, such as "words we see" walls, sight word walls, theme walls, math walls, writing word walls, or story walls. The resulting wall can be used for practicing words, supporting spelling, providing starters for writing, exercising letter or word part recognition, and more.

Name walls are an effective strategy teachers can use to teach new words while also highlighting a "student of the week." The name wall might contain features such as characteristics of the student, likes and dislikes, family members, favorite foods, and pets. At the end of the week, students take their name wall home (Rasinski & Padak, 2000; see Figure 12.4 for an example).

K	A	S	E	Y
kindergarten	allergies	Sue—sister	elephants	yellow
Kathy—mother	apples	skiing	enthusiastic	yells
Kim—dog	Aunt Liz	skating	eggs—hates them	you

Figure 12.4
Sample of a Name Wall

Making Connections

Construct a name wall using your name or your partner's. This exemplar or sample will be valuable as a model for primary students. Remember to start with letters of your name in listing likes/dislikes, pets, family members, favorite foods or colors, and so on. Have fun!

Teachers should become proficient in offering specific prompts for children who struggle with word identification when encountering new words. Diller (2007) provides a chart that lists explicit teacher prompts to help students. In addition, several possible prompts based on semantic context are provided in Table 12.9.

Table 12.9 Semantic Context Prompts

When Students Struggles With . . .	Possible Teacher Prompts
Initial letter sounds	• Look at the first letter. What sound does it make? • Get your mouth ready to form the word. • Check the pictures and the first letter. • Try the word out. Does it fit in the sentence and with the picture?
Final letter sounds	• Focus on the word. Check the last letter. • Check it. What would you expect to see at the end of that word? Were you right? • Try the word out. Does it fit in the sentence and with the picture?
Short vowel sounds	• What sound does that letter make? • Use the vowel sound for help. • Think of a word that uses the vowel, like _____. • You know that sound. It's in this word, too.
Consonant-vowel-consonant patterns and blending sounds	• Say the sounds. Put them together fast. • Use your finger to blend the sounds. • Is that a real world? Does it fit in the sentence and with the picture?
Long vowel sounds	• Flip it. Try the other sound. • Use the vowel chart to help. Look at the long vowels. • Long _____ can be spelled many different ways. That is correct.
Vowel plus *r* patterns	• What sound could these letters make? • It's like in the word _____. • Use the vowel plus *r* or vowel combinations.
Long words	• Read a part at a time. • Look for a word or word parts in the longer word. • Use your finger to cover up the rest of the word, and read it a part at a time. Move your finger across the word and read the sounds in order.
Connections:	

Literacy charts can be codeveloped by teacher and students to use as a reference while students are figuring out tricky words or struggling with combination vowel sounds, for example. Charts are developed as the students and teacher discuss, provide examples, and make choices. They should be hung on classroom walls throughout the year, where all students can access the information. Many teachers use them for the school year and discard them to formulate a new literacy chart as needs arise during the next school year (daCruz Payne, 2005).

Literacy charts displayed on chart paper have become a popular strategy in classrooms to support student metacognition. When learning charts are displayed, students can refer to the information on their own as a reminder of a skill they have acquired. An example of a literacy chart about encountering long words is shown in Figure 12.5. The creators of the chart may decide to provide examples or more graphics; furthermore, frequent review of the strategy is helpful for retention and use.

Figure 12.5

Literacy Chart Example

How to Read LONG Words

1. Read a part at a time.

2. Look for a word or word parts in the longer word.

3. Use your finger to **cover up** the rest of the word and read it a part at a time. Move your finger across the word and read the sounds in order.

4. See if the word **makes sense** in the context of the sentence.

Making Connections

Devise a literacy chart based on the list of possible teacher prompts or other teacher resources. Cut and paste Google pictures or clip art to add graphics. Work with a partner to develop the chart. Last, role-play a class session, with students helping develop and design your specific literacy chart. Reflect on the "teacher talk" you used to dialogue with the class.

Phoneme Level (Segmenting and Blending)

Phoneme awareness is being able to recognize the smallest sounds in a word (segmenting) and then blend them back together to make the word. Blending strategies for sound awareness are critical for beginning and striving readers. Arm blending and finger blending are both considered tactile or kinesthetic approaches to sound awareness. Furthermore, they require no materials—just a body and a word with three or four phonemes or sounds, as represented by three graphemes or letters. Have fun!

1. *Arm blending:* Children imagine that they are placing sounds on their arms, and then they blend the sounds by saying them. To blend *c-a-t*, children put their right hand on their left shoulder and say *c*, then their hand in the crook of their arm and say *a*, and last their hand on their wrist and say *t*. This process can be done several times. Then children slide their right hand down from shoulder to wrist in one sweep, blending the sounds together. When they are finished, ask what word they pronounced.

2. *Finger blending:* This anchors sounds in the memory and takes somewhat more dexterity, so it may be more appropriate for older readers and four-letter words. For the word *l-a-z-y*, students use their thumb to touch each finger on the same hand in order while making the sound associated with each word. To have students blend, they place each finger on the thumb as they pronounce sounds and then say the word.

> ### Making Connections
>
> Make several practice runs using arm blending or finger blending with the letter words. When you feel comfortable with the approach, teach it to your partner. Discuss the usefulness of the approach, particularly for striving learners.

Picture or graphic approaches to sound awareness include engaging activities such as picture blending and sliding sounds together. Use familiar objects or pictures as visual cues to support scaffolding. See Figures 12.6 and 12.7 for examples of blending activities.

> ### Making Connections
>
> Cut images from magazines or find graphics that will work well for picture blending. Set up five picture blends with words that first graders would benefit from knowing. Place in a file folder with individual letters cut out for practice.

Phonics Checks and Reinforcement

Check the understanding of letter–sound associations on a daily basis for primary word learners. Reinforcement activities can be active and engaging for students. Use multimodal learning activities such as visual–tactile body manipulation. Action phonics

Picture Blending

Picture blending provides students with a concrete visual to reference, illustrating the idea of sound blending with a familiar picture.

TRAIN   TR AI N   TRAIN

Steps for picture blending:

1. Show students a picture, say its name, and then cut it into as many equal parts as there are sounds in the word.

2. Next, point to each piece and say the sound represented.

3. Explain that the pieces of the word can be "blended" back together just as the picture can.

4. Collect a selection of pictures that can be cut to illustrate the idea of blending

Figure 12.6
Picture Blending

Source: Fox (2000).

Sliding Sounds Together

The slide provides a visual aspect to word blending.

Steps for activity:

1. Draw a large slide on the board or chart paper.

2. Write a three-letter word, with a letter at the top, then the middle, and finally the bottom.

3. To show blending, teacher pronounces each letter and slides hand under each sound.

4. Ask students the word, and write it at end of slide.

5. Students can be the "slider" and follow this process, name the word, and even direct the whole class.

Figure 12.7
Sliding Sounds

Source: Fox (2000).

has students present their graphemes (letters) on a large piece of oak tag paper, along with phonemes (sounds) as represented in the word. As students read their phoneme section, they then move together to pronounce the word in unison. Action phonics is a powerful method to reinforce phoneme–grapheme correspondence.

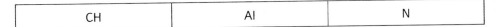

CH	AI	N

Word whoopers, which resemble fly swatters with a square opening in the middle, work well to highlight phonemes in words for instructional purposes. When a poem or excerpt from a book is placed on chart paper, the word whooper can be used to draw attention to graphemes or phonemes. The short sample exercise in Figure 12.8 asks students to read and locate the -*oy* rime.

Figure 12.8

Word Whoopers

The boy was looking for his toy. With joy, he found it. His friend Roy had taken it.

Word Sorting and Word Hunting

A student's maximum level of reading comprehension is determined by his or her knowledge of words. An effective strategy for helping emergent readers, English language learners (ELLs), and students with special needs develop a keen sense of word study is word sorting. Word sorting exercises and activities require readers to look at words analytically to identify any number of similarities or differences (Bear, Invernizzi, Templeton, & Johnston, 2011). Research also suggests that devoting time to word study is beneficial in building readers' vocabulary (Duke & Moses, 2003; Graves & Watts-Taffe, 2002; Nagy & Scott, 2000; Stahl & Fairbanks, 1986), which is key for vocabulary development for ELLs and students with special needs. Typical sorting patterns and features vary across the different volumes, but this series is found in thousands of classrooms across the country.

Word Sorts

Word sorts are an excellent way to teach students to find patterns that make decoding easier. Word sorts are used extensively to teach concepts from elementary word families to more sophisticated language concepts. Exercises such as those found on word sort websites enable students to recognize word families more easily, which helps in decoding new words with similar patterns (Literacy Connections, n.d.). The word sort series *Words Their Way* (Bear, Invernizzi, Johnston, & Templeton, 2009; Helman, Bear, Templeton,

Invernizzi, & Johnston, 2012) offers many workbooks for early letter/word learners. The authors describe the features of the first volume this way:

> *Words Their Way Letter and Picture Sorts for Emergent Spellers*, 2/E: This first volume introduces the idea of concept sorts for students in the emergent stage of spelling development (Pre-K through Grade 1). The word study lesson plan format of demonstrate, sort, check, and reflect is expanded in this stage to include reading aloud and writing activities. The early concept sorting activities are followed with picture sorts that develop phonemic awareness and include activities for rhyming, syllabication, and sound play. Alphabet knowledge and letter recognition are then covered, along with sorts that look at concept of word in print, as well as poems, jingles and short text selections that can be shared with children. Students are then ushered into sorts that introduce beginning consonants with pictures, laying the foundation for the letter-name stage. (Bear et al., 2009)

Other useful word sort volumes include *Words Their Way: Word Study for Phonics, Vocabulary, and Spelling Instruction* (Bear et al., 2008) and *Words Their Way: Emergent Sorts for Spanish-Speaking English Learners* (Helman, Bear, Invernizzi, Templeton, & Johnston, 2008).

A word sort template is shown in Figure 12.9. Many available websites showcase word sorting, and "make-your-own" sorts specifically targeting your classroom words are probably the most effective use of this strategy. Targeting high-frequency words for word sort review is important in early grades. Challenge students to use these words in sentences, silly poems, or hinky pinkies (riddles that have two or more rhyming words as their answer). Likewise, for older adults, irregularly spelled words should be targeted through word sorts.

Word Hunts

Word hunts are also effective strategies for helping all students become attentive to words. Students are instructed to look for specific patterns or features within a previously read text. Using a familiar text allows the students to read for meaning before returning

-en	-in	-an

Word Bank: win, hen, tan, ban, tin, ten, can, fan, man, den, men

Figure 12.9
Word Sort Templates

to the text to look for specific words. Constructing a word wall in the classroom is another way to actively engage students in word study. Word walls should be accessible to both the teacher and students and should be dynamic (always changing). Encourage all your students to refer to the wall if they need help spelling a word; an interactive word wall is a very effective instructional and learning tool. This strategy is also an effective Tier 2 or 3 intervention. The same patterns and features suggested for word sorts work well for word hunts.

Skills

Word sorts and word hunts teach students to pay attention to the following aspects of words during acquisition of reading skills:

- Spelling patterns
- Morphemes (smallest unit of)
- Affixes (prefixes, suffixes)
- Word structure
- Roots and base words
- Meaning of words (in a variety of contexts)
- Etymology (word history)
- Increasing vocabulary

Making Connections

In small groups, design a word-sort checklist for your group members for the following words: *affix, alphabetic, auditory discrimination, automaticity, base word, fluency, grapheme, letter, phoneme, phonemic awareness, prefix, root word, sound, syllable,* and *suffix*. Create a word wall card for each word. Sort the words as many ways as possible, and record each group member's sort on the chart.

Making and Breaking Words

Effective readers and writers understand the importance of knowing how to construct and deconstruct words (Johnston, Invernizzi, & Bear, 2004; Pinnell & Fountas, 1998). This can be accomplished in a variety of ways. One particular skill, called morphemic analysis, enables the reader and writer to look at units of meaning (morphemes) within words more efficiently. Morphemes are the smallest units of meaning in the language (Harris & Hodges, 2005), which means they cannot be divided into smaller units that contain meaning. Morphemes include base words, root words, and affixes (prefixes and suffixes). Helping your students understand and learn morphemic units will prepare them with an effective skill for word building, spelling, vocabulary, and word recognition.

There are several different instructional strategies for word building. Frequently, when you are teaching word building you are also teaching students to recognize other morphemic units. Research supports the notion that students learn and remember word study when it is taught in context, which is why these strategies are suggested for use during reading (Blachowicz & Fisher, 2010; McKeown & Curtis, 1987). Teaching students how to analyze words and identify the roots, base words, and etymologies is essential for teaching "making and breaking" words.

The next most important decision you will make is determining when to teach the strategies. The chart in Table 12.10 lists several instructional strategies, the academic language associated with each one, use in the content areas, and uses in pre-, during, and postreading/writing exercises.

Table 12.10 Instructional Strategies for Teaching the Skills of Making/Breaking Words (Word Construction/Deconstruction)

Instructional Strategy	Academic Language	Common Core English Language Arts Standards	Use in the Content Areas	Application in the Reading Processes	Application in the Writing Process
Root word	Root word Spelling pattern	Reading—Literature and Informational Text: Standard 4 Reading—Foundational Skills: Phonics and Word Recognition	*ELA:* Teach students Greek and Latin roots *Math:* Teach students math Greek and Latin roots (e.g., *graph, tract, meter, centi*) *Science:* Teach students science Greek and Latin roots (e.g., *bio, aero, geo, sphere*) *Social studies:* Teach students Greek and Latin roots (e.g., *trans, demo, cracy, theo*)	**Prereading:** • Supports vocabulary **During Reading:** • Supports word identification • Supports vocabulary **Postreading:** • Supports comprehension	**Prewriting:** • Supports vocabulary **During Writing:** • Supports vocabulary • Supports spelling • Supports text clarity **Postwriting:** • Supports text clarity
Base word	Base word Spelling pattern	Reading—Literature and Informational Text: Standard 4 Reading—Foundational Skills: Phonics and Word Recognition	*ELA:* Teach commonly used base words (e.g., *plot, climax, grammar, narrate*) *Math:* Teach commonly used base words (e.g., *add, sum, number, formula*)	**Prereading:** • Supports vocabulary **During Reading:** • Supports word identification • Supports vocabulary	**Prewriting:** • Supports vocabulary **During Writing:** • Supports vocabulary • Supports spelling • Supports text clarity

(Continued)

Table 12.10 (Continued)

Instructional Strategy	Academic Language	Common Core English Language Arts Standards	Use in the Content Areas	Application in the Reading Processes	Application in the Writing Process
			Science: Teach commonly used base words (e.g., *hypothesis, law, theory, experiment*)	**Postreading:** • Supports comprehension	**Postwriting:** • Supports text clarity
			Social studies: Teach commonly used base words (i.e., *continent, economy, civil, govern*)		
Prefixes	Prefix Spelling pattern Parts of speech	Reading—Literature and Informational Text: Standard 4 Reading—Foundational Skills: Phonics and Word Recognition	*ELA:* Teach commonly used prefixes (e.g., *un-, pre-, con-, re-*) *Math:* Teach commonly used prefixes (e.g., *centi-, milli-, quad-, equi-*) *Science:* Teach commonly used prefixes (e.g., *mili-, centi-, tri-, bi-*) *Social studies:* Teach commonly used prefixes (e.g., *anti-, micro-, macro-, pro-*)	**Prereading:** • Supports vocabulary **During Reading:** • Supports word identification • Supports vocabulary **Postreading:** • Supports comprehension	**Prewriting:** • Supports vocabulary **During Writing:** • Supports vocabulary • Supports spelling • Supports text clarity **Postwriting:** • Supports text clarity
Suffixes	Suffix Spelling pattern Parts of speech	Reading—Literature and Informational Text: Standard 4 Reading—Foundational Skills: Phonics and Word Recognition	*ELA:* Teach commonly used suffixes (e.g., *-tion, -able, -ment, -ful*) *Math:* Teach commonly used suffixes (e.g., *-ic, -tion, -metry*) *Science:* Teach commonly used suffixes (e.g., *-ology, -ist, -ic, -ar*)	**Prereading:** • Supports vocabulary **During Reading:** • Supports word identification • Supports vocabulary **Postreading:** • Supports comprehension	**Prewriting:** • Supports vocabulary **During Writing:** • Supports vocabulary • Supports spelling • Supports text clarity

Instructional Strategy	Academic Language	Common Core English Language Arts Standards	Use in the Content Areas	Application in the Reading Processes	Application in the Writing Process
			Social studies: Teach commonly used suffixes (e.g., *-tion, -al, -ist, -cian*)		**Postwriting:** • Supports text clarity
Inflectional endings	Inflectional ending Spelling patterns Tense Plural Singular	Reading—Literature and Informational Text: Standard 4 Reading—Foundational Skills: Phonics and Word Recognition	*All content areas:* Teach commonly used inflectional endings (e.g., *-s, -es, -ing, -ies*)	**Prereading:** • Supports vocabulary **During Reading:** • Supports word identification • Supports vocabulary **Postreading:** • Supports comprehension	**Prewriting:** • Supports vocabulary **During Writing:** • Supports vocabulary • Supports spelling • Supports text clarity **Postwriting:** • Supports text clarity
Derivational endings	Derivational ending Parts of speech Spelling patterns	Reading—Literature and Informational Text: Standard 4 Reading—Foundational Skills: Phonics and Word Recognition	*All content areas:* Teach commonly used derivational endings (e.g., *-tion, -ment, -able, -er*)	**Prereading:** • Supports vocabulary **During Reading:** • Supports word identification • Supports vocabulary **Postreading:** • Supports comprehension	**Prewriting:** • Supports vocabulary **During Writing:** • Supports vocabulary • Supports spelling • Supports text clarity **Postwriting:** • Supports text clarity
Syllables	Syllable Syllable patterns	Reading—Literature and Informational Text: Standard 4 Reading—Foundational Skills: Phonics and Word Recognition	*ELA:* Teach seven syllable patterns	**Prereading:** • Supports vocabulary **During Reading:** • Supports word identification • Supports vocabulary **Postreading:** • Supports comprehension	**Prewriting:** • Supports spelling **During Writing:** • Supports spelling **Postwriting:** • Supports spelling

Word-Solving Strategies and Teaching

Skilled readers learn how to effectively and efficiently recognize unfamiliar words very quickly (Stanovich, 1980). They are able to determine the most appropriate strategy for the word, which suggests that efficient emerging readers have learned a variety of word recognition strategies. Therefore, it is imperative that primary-grade readers be taught a variety of word-solving strategies. Using think-alouds, explain the implementation process and questions you ask yourself while reading. Think-alouds demonstrate the abstract, metacognitive component of word identification in a more concrete fashion. This is especially helpful for younger readers.

Helping emerging readers develop rapid word recognition skills is most effectively accomplished by teaching them a variety of strategies for each skill. Teaching strategies is similar to teaching vocabulary and spelling—the strategy should be taught in context, or at the same time the word is being taught. For instance, the best time to introduce the strategy of chunking is during the teaching of word families or phonograms. This simultaneous approach implicitly teaches readers how to analyze words as a natural component of reading. The strategies are also appropriate Tier 1 and Tier 2 interventions for students who are working toward becoming more efficient readers.

There are many word-solving strategies. Some of them were mentioned in the "Making and Breaking Words" section, and those will not be repeated here. Rather, this section will take a closer look at Ask It!, Bleep It!, Chunk It!, Look It Up!, Match It!, Phonic It!, Skip It!, Spot It!, and Wrap It! (adapted from Hendricks & Rinsky, 2006).

Ask It! When the reader has exhausted all the word-solving strategies or the strategies have been unsuccessful, he or she is encouraged to ask someone for help. The reader may ask an adult, a peer, or another child. The challenge in implementing this strategy is helping the reader determine when to use it. If the reader asks too soon in the reading or writing process, he or she will not develop the use of trial and error in the word identification process. On the other hand, if he or she waits too long, frustration will quickly derail and likely discourage the young reader. One guideline is an adaptation of the "five-finger rule": Tap a finger on the nonwriting hand for every word-solving strategy the reader tries; when all five fingers have been tapped, it is time to "Ask It!" This strategy is effective for complex text, informational text, and content text. The mnemonic chant for this strategy is, "If five fingers you have tapped, now it's time to 'Ask It' fast."

Bleep It! One way to keep early readers encouraged and engaged in the text is to keep them moving through it. Frequent or long pauses devoted to identifying unfamiliar words require the reader to put previously read information in working-term memory while trying to determine the unfamiliar word in short-term memory. The more time and effort the brain devotes to word identification, the less time and attention it can devote to understanding the text. One way to help emerging readers keep moving through the text is to have them "bleep" the unfamiliar word and continue reading. Instruct the reader to complete the sentence and then return to the "bleeped" word to reattempt it. Encourage the reader to look at the initial grapheme, structure of the word, context clues, or spelling pattern to determine the word. This strategy works well for informational, content, and complex texts. The mnemonic chant for this strategy is "Bleep the word and keep on reading, then go back and try rereading."

Chunk It! This strategy dovetails nicely with the teaching of word families, phonograms, and word chunks. Since many publishers incorporate the instruction of one or more of these "chunks," it is very easy to simultaneously teach the word analysis skill of identifying chunks of letters or spelling patterns. When the reader encounters an unfamiliar word, instruct him or her to scan it and look for chunks of consecutive letters that look familiar. If the reader recognizes only one or two consecutive letters, guide him or her to look for larger chunks. This strategy works well for most types of text. The mnemonic for this strategy is "Scan the letters in the word, and look for chunks that you have learned."

Look It Up! Instructing young readers to use the dictionary to identify a word should be the strategy of last resort. Too frequently, readers are sent to find a word in the dictionary to confirm its spelling. If we stop to think about this approach, we are assuming that the student has an understanding of three primary skills: alphabetical order, text features and purposes, and dictionary skills. This strategy is much more developmentally appropriate for older, more advanced readers, because readers should be instructed in dictionary skills before being asked to implement it. This strategy works well for informational, content, and complex texts. The mnemonic is "This new word I still don't know, so to the dictionary I will go."

Match It! Emerging readers need to be taught how to look metacognitively at an unfamiliar word and find a familiar matching word in their lexicon. This strategy employs the skill of analogy to solve the mystery of an unfamiliar word. For instance, if a young reader stumbled on the word dove in a story, he or she could think of a familiar word with the same spelling pattern to help him or her identify the new word. You might guide the reader using the word love. Help him or her analyze the word for similarities and differences. A think-aloud would help the reader use prior knowledge to read an unfamiliar word. This strategy works well for predictable texts, poetry, and rhyming texts. The mnemonic for this strategy is "Does this word look like one I know?"

Phonic It! "Sound it out" is probably one of the most frequently used word identification strategies. The process of determining a word by applying letter–sound relationships and rules is called decoding. This approach to identifying unknown words is a very effective method if the reader has an understanding of phonics. The drawback to this strategy is that it takes time to decode a word letter by letter. Word solving is much faster when the reader recognizes larger chunks of consecutive letters. This strategy works well for words in isolation, unfamiliar texts, and most proper nouns. The mnemonic for this strategy is "If this word is completely new, sound out the letters and blend them, too."

Skip It! This strategy gives readers permission to skip over an unfamiliar word and continue to read, which helps the reader maintain the flow of reading and the simultaneous construction of meaning. This strategy works well in three situations: (1) with more difficult or informational text (skipping an unknown word allows the reader to use context words), (2) with cold reads (first reading of a new text), and (3) with longer passages or paragraphs. The mnemonic for this strategy is "Skip over the word you don't know, but don't forget to go back and read it slow."

Spot It! Another way to study and analyze words is to look for words within a word. The observant reader can spot smaller words in larger words. This enables the reader to add the remaining letters or chunks as he or she constructs the unknown word. This strategy works well with unfamiliar, informational, and content text, and with unfamiliar proper nouns. The mnemonic for this strategy is "Look real close and you might see a smaller word, or two or three."

Wrap It! A word solver knows how to uncover the context clues wrapped around the unfamiliar word. The reader has the ability to look for or remember tidbits of information that may provide clues to help him or her identify the unknown word (Harris & Hodges, 2005). This strategy is most effectively introduced using a think-aloud to help the young reader study the word. During the think-aloud, be sure to point out the types of questions the reader must ask while trying to locate appropriate clues. This strategy is effective for informational, content, complex, and descriptive texts. The mnemonic for this strategy is "Use the clues around the word, and wrap them up to guess the word."

Additional strategies for ELLs and students with special needs include the following:

1. Identify vocabulary words that you think might be difficult.

2. Model think-alouds.

3. Demonstrate fix-up strategies.

4. Partner with stronger classmates followed by independent practice (Colorín Colorado, 2007c).

Instruction in Using Rimes

Introduction to using rimes can be fun and engaging for early learners, especially when the teacher gets creative with rhyming poetry, hinky pinkies, read-aloud pattern books, and other ideas. Figure 12.10 provides a list of the most common rimes (Fry, 1998; Wylie & Durrell, 1970), which can be used to make more than 650 one-syllable words. In addition, these beginning rimes can be used to decode longer multisyllabic words. If a primary teacher decides to instruct using the most common rimes twice a week, he or she should be able to cover the whole list easily in one school year (Rasinski & Padak, 2000). Rasinski and Padak (2000) and Rasinski, Rupley, and Nichols (2008) suggest the following instructional program on a weekly or biweekly basis:

1. Introduce a rime—for example, *am*. Print the rime on chart paper, and say the sound it represents multiple times. Ask students to repeat several times.

2. Brainstorm and list on the chart paper several one-syllable words that contain the rime. If students come up with multisyllabic words, that is fine. Place several of the trickier words on sentence strips and assign students to become "rime experts."

3. Read the words with students several times. Mix up the reading with groups, pairs, the whole class, echo reading, and so on. Rime experts are responsible for being

able to pronounce and spell their word using the word family approach. As you continue to collect rimes, circulate among students and establish a phonogram word wall.

4. Challenge students with a hinky pinky. They should connect with words that answer the riddle and that contain *am*. The sillier the better—for example, "What did the boy say to the woman when she asked what type of sandwich he wanted?" HAM, MA'AM.

5. Introduce two or three rhyming poems, either commercial or written by the teacher. Read each poem in a variety of ways—choral, solo oral or silent, whole group, listening to a recording, or partner reading. Have students notice and identify rimes and other unique words. If appropriate, students might develop a poem using the chosen rime. Student drawings or graphics might accompany the poetry.

Phonogram	Words Using the Phonogram
-ab	blab, cab, crab, dab, drab, gab, grab, jab, lab, scab, slab, stab, tab
-ack	back, black, clack, crack, flack, hack, lack, knack, pack, quack, rack, sack, slack, stack, tack, whack
-ag	bag, brag, drag, flag, gag, hag, lag, nag, rag, sag, shag, slag, stag, tag, wag, zag
-ail	bail, hail, jail, mail, nail, pail, rail, sail, snail, tail, trail, wail
-ain	chain, drain, gain, grain, main, pain, plain, rain, strain, train
-ake	bake, brake, cake, drake, fake, flake, lake, make, quake, rake, sake, shake, stake, take, wake
-am	clam, dam, gram, ham, jam, ram, slam, swam, tram
-an	ban, can, clan, fan, flan, man, pan, plan, ran, span, tan, van
-ank	bank, blank, drank, prank, rank, sank, spank, tank
-ap	cap, chap, clap, flap, gap, knap, lap, map, nap, sap, slap, strap, tap, trap, wrap
-at	bat, brat, cat, chat, fat, flat, gnat, hat, mat, pat, rat, sat, slat, spat, tat, that, vat
-ay	bray, clay, gay, hay, lay, may, pay, play, ray, say, slay, spray, stay, stray, tray, way
-eed	breed, creed, deed, greed, heed, reed, seed, speed, weed
-ell	bell, dell, fell, sell, shell, smell, spell, tell, yell
-est	best, chest, crest, guest, nest, pest, rest, vest, west
-ew	blew, brew, chew, drew, grew, knew, new, pew, spew, stew

Figure 12.10

37 Most Common Phonograms

Source: Fry (1998) and Wylie and Durrell (1970).

(Continued)

Figure 12.10
(Continued)

Phonogram	Words Using the Phonogram
-ick	brick, chick, knick, quick, pick, prick, sick, stick, thick, tick, trick, wick
-ight	blight, bright, fight, flight, knight, light, might, night, plight, right, sight
-ill	bill, chill, dill, drill, fill, frill, gill, grill, hill, kill, mill, pill, shrill, sill, skill, spill, still, thrill, till, will
-in	bin, chin, fin, gin, grin, pin, shin, skin, spin, thin, tin, twin, win
-ine	brine, dine, line, mine, nine, pine, shine, shrine, spine, spline, twine, vine, wine
-ing	bing, bring, cling, ding, king, ping, ring, sing, sting, string, wing
-ink	blink, brink, chink, clink, drink, kink, link, mink, pink, plink, rink, shrink, sink, slink, think, wink
-ip	chip, dip, drip, grip, hip, lip, nip, quip, rip, ship, sip, tip, trip, whip
-ob	bob, blob, cob, dob, fob, gob, glob, knob, lob, mob, rob, sob
-ock	block, clock, crock, dock, hock, knock, lock, mock, rock, shock, sock, stock, tock
-op	chop, cop, crop, flop, hop, mop, plop, pop, shop, sop, stop, top
-ore	bore, chore, core, fore, gore, lore, more, shore, sore, spore, store, tore, wore, yore
-ot	blot, clot, cot, dot, got, hot, knot, lot, plot, pot, rot, shot, spot, tot, trot
-out	clout, grout, pout, shout, spout, sprout, trout
-ow	bow, chow, cow, how, now, pow, sow, wow
-ow	bow, crow, glow, grow, know, low, mow, row, show, sow, tow
-uck	buck, chuck, cluck, duck, luck, puck, stuck, truck, tuck
-ug	bug, drug, dug, hug, lug, mug, plug, rug, shrug, thug, tug
-um	bum, chum, drum, glum, gum, hum, mum, plum, rum, sum, strum,
-unk	bunk, chunk, clunk, dunk, flunk, funk, gunk, hunk, punk, shrunk, spunk, sunk, trunk
-y	by, cry, dry, fly, fry, my, ply, pry, shy, spry, sty, try

Continue to repeat the rime patterns in diverse and challenging ways for students throughout the week. Each morning, the rime experts should begin the practice by reading and noting their specific word family words. Be sure to follow up with activities such as word sorting, where students categorize words based on the rime pattern or lack thereof. Other practice ideas are highlighted next.

Practice Ideas for Using Rimes or Onsets

1. *Make lists:* Students can be challenged to make lists of words that rhyme with food names, holidays, pets, community places, games, or toys. From there, they can develop and collect personalized rime lists.

2. *Egg words:* With colorful plastic eggs, use a permanent marker to write an onset on one half of the egg and a rime on the other. Challenge students to make words from the onsets and rimes combined.

3. *Word chains:* Using colorful strips of paper, have students develop a three- or four-link chain connecting several rimes with one onset. Have them present their rime chains at the front of the class and read the words out loud.

4. *Rime pick-up:* Write various rimes on pick-up sticks. Scatter the sticks and play the game pick-up sticks, with students providing a beginning sound to make a word (one letter or a combination).

5. *Rime tic-tac-toe:* Using laminated tic-tac-toe cards and erasable markers, challenge students to look for words that share the same rime or onset.

6. *Rime trains:* Using four to six large envelopes, draw a train engine and caboose on two of them. On the others, write rimes to which children will add onsets in the form of tickets (teacher can find and replicate train tickets). Ask students to read their words to ride the train.

7. *Fish for rimes:* Using a plastic bucket for a fish pond, the teacher provides a fishing pole with a magnet on the end to collect "fish" rimes with paper clips attached. Students go fishing to catch a rime that will make a word with their given onset (Fox, 2005).

Segmenting

Sound segmentation requires that students recognize and identify all the constituent sounds in a word, starting out with onsets and rimes in short, two-sound words (Rasinski & Padak, 2000). Elkonin boxes, described in Chapter 2, are a popular tool to help develop and practice sound segmentation. The website Online Activities 4 DIBELS (sites.google.com/site/onlineactivities4dibels/dibels-psf) offers great ideas for providing active segmentation challenges for young students. Additional activities are described in the sections that follow.

Jump Along With Phonics

Mark the floor or sidewalk with a series of 12 lines (the number of lines is changeable). Children begin by standing in a row along the first line. The teacher calls out a word, such as *top*. Then the teacher says, "Go." Children jump forward as many lines as there are phonemes in the word. If the children are correct (in this case, they have jumped forward three rows), they keep their place. If incorrect, they move back to the starting line. The game ends when all children have passed the 12th line, and everyone applauds their success.

Blocks

Teach children how to stretch words, saying a word slowly so they can hear the sounds that make it up. Demonstrate the process, and then invite children to say the word slowly as they listen for the individual phonemes. You may want to have them stretch a pretend rubber band as they say the word. Be sure they are actually saying the word. After children have learned how to say the word slowly, use small, colored blocks to mark the different phonemes. For example, say, "Go"—"G-o-o-o-o-o"—and use two different-colored blocks to represent the sounds. Later, ask children to tell how many blocks they will need to represent the sounds in other words.

It's in the Bag

This game can be played with a small group or pairs of children in a center or at home with a parent. Give each child a small brown-paper bag with several objects inside. Have the child peek inside and select one item, but tell him or her not to show the object to the other player(s). The child holding the bag then segments the name of the object, and the other player(s) guess what the object is by blending the sounds back together to make the word. Take the object out, show it, segment the object name again together, and set it aside. The children take turns segmenting the name of an object in their bag for the other player(s). (Some suggested items to get you started are a fork, pen, shell, sock, bottle, or brush.)

Mini Lessons for Direct Instruction: Teaching Consonant Diagraphs

Objective: Student will be able to recognize and identify the sound of *ch*.

Activities:

- Show the video for the song "Chicka Chicka Boom Boom" (available at www.youtube.com/watch?v=Yot9pWy_Txk).
  - Essential questions: What letters did you see? What did the letters do? What was your favorite part?

- Read the book *Chicka Chicka Boom Boom* by Bill Martin Jr.
  - Teach the sounds *ch*, *sk*, and *fl*.
  - Guide students in finding *ch*, *sk*, and *fl* in the book, in the classroom, and in the school.
  - Write the words on a word wall.
  - Have the students create their own word wall.
  - Guide the children in making words that rhyme with *ch*, *sk*, and *fl*.

- Writing extension activities
  - Have the students write or draw pictures using the consonant digraphs
  - Write a song using their new words

Strategies for English Language Learners

English language learners (ELLs) need multiple opportunities to hear and see learning in action. Through the use of children's videos, audiobooks, images, choral reading, and repeated reading opportunities, ELLs will be more engaged and achieve greater success in learning and developing phonemic awareness and phonics skills. Many of the strategies described in this chapter take into account ELLs. In fact, the *Report of the National Literacy Panel on Language-Minority Children and Youth* (August & Shanahan, 2006) found that ELLs benefit from instruction in phonemic awareness, oral reading development, writing, reading comprehension, and vocabulary. Further findings suggest that ELLs benefit from learning in their own language and that phonics instruction is crucial to their reading success. Some specific considerations for instructing ELLs apply to all early readers:

> In order for the speller to be successful at his or her task in both English and Spanish, he or she must possess adequately functioning phonological and visual modules, master the phoneme-to-grapheme and grapheme-to-phoneme conversion mechanisms, and be capable of reproducing the serial order of letters in words. (Canado, 2011, p. 524)

It should be noted, Spanish spelling contains three practically identical deviations that produce challenges similar to those found in English. Teachers should note these three deviations in Spanish when teaching early ELLs (Canado, 2011):

- One phoneme can be represented by diverse phonograms or letters. In Spanish, this type of polygraphy is sometimes regular (e.g., the phoneme /g/ is written as *g* before *a*, *o*, and *u* and as *gu* before *e* and *i*) and sometimes irregular (e.g., /k/ can be represented by *c*, *k*, or *qu*).
- One particular phonogram or letter can fulfill more than one phonemic assignment (e.g., the letter *c* is pronounced as /k/ prior to *a*, *o*, and *u* but as /z/ before *e* and *i*).
- Sometimes variations in spelling are not accompanied by a linguistically relevant change in pronunciation or meaning (e.g., uniform morphemes finished in /k/ or in /g/—/sak/ from *sacar* is sometimes written *sac* and sometimes *saqu*; /pag/ is sometimes written *pag* and sometimes *pagu*).

Strategies for Students With Special Needs

Phonics lessons for students with developmental considerations should be interactive, explicit, and reviewed continuously, and should employ multiple modalities, especially tactile. Well-organized and well-executed lessons in phonics or phonological awareness will benefit word acquisition. The use of strategy charts that are reviewed continuously will encourage growth and self-confidence.

Schnorr (2011) recommends using the following materials to support an explicit lesson in phonics: picture cards; letter cards, pocket chart, or alphabet chart; electronic formats for teacher-prepared lessons in making words; picture sorts; or word sorts (e.g., software, touchscreen, interactive whiteboard). In addition, encourage students to run their fingers below the line of poetry or text they are reading.

Wiki sticks are valuable as a concrete prop for struggling early learners. These flexible sticks with a waxy covering can be cut to varying lengths and used to highlight letters, words, or phrases. Placing wiki sticks to underline words and make them stand out with more permanence is beneficial while the teacher and student discuss characteristics of the word and note features or specific sounds associated with phonemes. For example, when working with poetry that emphasizes word families, the teacher might request that students place a wiki-stick circle around a word or several that contain the -*ack* rime. There are multiple ways wiki sticks can help struggling students "bookmark" words to be discussed.

Phonemic awareness and the degree of scaffolding necessary for struggling learners can vary from intense levels of support to minimal levels of support. When teachers are working with very early learners with special needs or ELLs on isolating first sounds in words—initial phonemes—as represented by letters, children who are unsure of the initial letter represented by a phoneme may react in various ways, such as casting their eyes down, looking to the teacher, not responding, or acting unsure of what is being asked of them. Students who react in these ways are often helped with intense support. In providing this level of support, the teacher isolates and exaggerates the phoneme on its own and in the word, points to her mouth or says "watch my lips," and tells children to watch and repeat the correct response. In providing moderate support, the teacher will follow the same procedure without offering the correct response. Minimal support would be simply to ask what the initial sound in the word is (McGee & Ukrainetz, 2009).

Key Terms

alphabetic principle	phonemic awareness
consonant blends	phonics
consonant digraphs	rime
environmental print	word families
explicit and systematic phonics	word recognition
onset	word work

Website Resources

- **Family Learning**

Phonics games will help your students practice sounding out words, which will help them read. Initially, children will learn basic letter sounds, such as *c-a-t* for *cat*. Later, they will move on to sounds such as *th*, *sh*, and *ch*, then *oo*, *oa*, and so on. Once they recognize a few basic letter sounds, they will be able to work out for themselves what a written word says, a skill they will be very proud to show off! For more information on the purchase of research-based phonics software or apps, visit **www.cnkdigital.com/about**, or see **freephonicslessons .com/about.html** for free sequential phonics lessons and activities.

- **PBS Learning Media**

PBS Kids is a website designed to promote phonics and reading in an interactive way. The site features all the same educational programs for kids as the PBS television station offers. Each program features different types of engaging games and activities to help kids learn several skills. Kids can have stories read to them while watching their favorite characters and seeing the words across the bottom of the screen. Kids can learn how to spell words with many games and songs specifically targeting spelling. For more, **visit pbskids.org.**

- **Word Sort Websites**

Word Study Activities From Words Their Way: **www.literacyconnections.com/WordsTheirWay .php**

Create Your Own Word Sort: **www.spunkyenglish.com/MagnetMaker/sortMaker.php**

Student Interactive Word Family Sort: **www.readwritethink.org/classroom-resources/ student-interactives/word-family-sort-30052.html**

Student Study Site: Visit the Student Study Site at **www.sagepub.com/grantlit** to access additional study tools including eFlashcards, web resources, and online-only appendices.

CHAPTER 13

Comprehension and Writing Strategies

Penny Soboleski
and Nance S. Wilson

Common Core State Standards

Text Types and Purposes	*W.3.1* Write opinion pieces on topics or texts, supporting a point of view with reasons.
Production and Distribution of Writing	*W.3.4* With guidance and support from adults, produce writing in which the development and organization are appropriate to task and purpose.
Research to Build and Present Knowledge	*W.3.8* Recall information from experiences or gather information from print and digital sources; take brief notes on sources and sort evidence into provided categories.
Range of Writing	*W.3.10* Write routinely over extended time frames (time for research, reflection, and revision) and shorter time frames (a single sitting or a day or two) for a range of discipline-specific tasks, purposes, and audiences.

FOCUS QUESTIONS

1. What makes reading and writing meaning-making processes?

2. What is the difference between a skill and a strategy?

3. How can teachers modify strategies to meet the individual needs of readers?

4. What is the Gradual Release of Responsibility Model? Where does assessment fit in this model?

5. What are graphic organizers?

6. How do bookmarks and strategy posters help students learn strategies?

7. What are some specific strategies that you could use when reading your textbooks?

8. What classroom structures support the teaching of strategies?

Words in Action

Mr. Readmore

Mr. Readmore's class is buzzing with activity during the reading block of language arts. One table is working on a magnetic word sort with the -*ank* and -*ant* word families before they begin their new decodable reader featuring the same word families. A second table is engaged in partner-reading the newest classroom picture book. The third table is practicing a reader's theatre on "The Three Little Pigs." The readers at a fourth table are working with Mr. Readmore as he models how to use a main idea/details graphic organizer during reading. These students have clipboards and are practicing completing a main idea/detail graphic organizer with partners. Mr. Readmore steps back and wonders if this workshop model is the best way to meet his students' needs. "How can I help them develop the skills they will need to become independent readers?" His first year of teaching has been challenging. First grade is such an important time for the development of foundational reading and writing skills. Nine of his twenty-four students have significant needs, and he quickly recognized that his first lesson plans were not effective for all his students. Some students have modality preferences (visual, aural, tactile, reading and writing, kinesthetic), all have natural tendencies that Gardner refers to as multiple intelligences, seven students are on Individualized Education Programs with specific modifications and accommodations, three students have difficulty maintaining focus and attention, and his newest student has been in the United States for only 3 months. He must provide instructional strategies for comprehension and writing to meet the needs of his diverse first-grade classroom. Keep Mr. Readmore's class in mind throughout this chapter.

Reading and writing are both constructive processes during which the reader and/or writer builds meaning through engagement. In reading comprehension, an understanding is forged through the transaction between the reader and the text, which occurs when there is a "blending of components" (Rosenblatt, 1985, p. 98). The transaction involves a give and take among the reader (what he or she knows and can do), the text (the difficulty and background knowledge necessary to understand it), and the context (the setting of and purpose for the reading). This transaction requires that the reader be engaged as words are decoded, prior knowledge is activated, and new knowledge is constructed (Adams, 1990; Anderson, Hiebert, Scott, & Wilkinson, 1985; Rosenblatt, 1985; Rumelhart, 1975).

The importance of constructing meaning is also present in the **writing process**. The writer creates meaning through composition. The writer must use knowledge of content, language structure, text types, and graphophonics to compose even simple sentences. As the writer works to communicate meaning, he or she has a purpose for writing—to access or build knowledge, develop meaningful sentences, and revise and monitor writing for clarity. The writer makes meaning of ideas and language as he or she composes (Fitzgerald & Shanahan, 2000; Graham & Hebert, 2010; Tierney & Shanahan, 1991).

Being an active reader and writer requires metacognition. Metacognition is the kind of thinking you do when you engage in learning. "Metacognitive thinking helps students [readers and writers] to identify tasks, monitor performance, choose appropriate strategies, and solve problems" (Wilson, 2011, p. 32). It is the enactment of strategies and the recognition of the need for a strategy; therefore, it is important that the teacher first understand the difference between skills and strategies.

Skill or Strategy?

Reading strategies are deliberate, goal-directed attempts to control and modify the reader's efforts to decode text, understand words, and construct meanings of text. Reading skills are automatic actions that result in decoding and comprehension with speed, efficiency, and fluency and usually occur without awareness of the components or control involved. (Afflerbach, Pearson, & Paris, 2008, p. 368)

Skills and strategies serve different purposes during the reading and writing process. **Skills** provide the automatic application of knowledge, such as decoding or encoding words, whereas strategies provide readers with intentional application of knowledge to solve a problem. A strategy will require that the reader use several skills. For instance, to predict what will happen in a text, the reader or writer will need to note the details of the text, sequence the text, and identify the main idea of the text (Honig, Diamond, & Gutlohn, 2012). Proficient readers and writers have a repertoire of strategies to use depending on the type and the difficulty of the text or piece of writing.

Knowing the difference between skills and strategies enables you to consider the skills and strategies your students will need to meet their course objectives. This can be illustrated using a Common Core English Language Arts Standard for Writing in Grade 5: "With guidance and support from peers and adults, develop and strengthen writing as needed by planning, revising, editing, rewriting, or trying a new approach" (Common Core State Standards Initiative, 2014c, W.5.5). For students to master this writing objective, they must have the skills of handwriting and/or keyboarding, must be able to encode or spell a large bank of words, and must be able to compose even simple sentences effectively. Additionally, they must have the strategies to effectively plan for the writing piece, revise it throughout the writing process, edit it, and rewrite it as needed.

Independent, effective readers and writers have acquired a variety of skills and strategies that enable them to engage with the text on a variety of levels, in a variety of ways, at a variety of times to make sense of the text. Your responsibility is to help readers and writers develop skills, strategies, experiences, and interests to become independent, effective readers and writers. And how do you accomplish this? By teaching them a range of strategies and providing them with opportunities to practice them.

Teaching Students to Become Strategic

When proficient readers and writers use strategies, more often than not, they are engaging in an invisible thinking process. Thus, teaching students to be strategic readers and writers requires modeling the mental processes that make readers and writers metacognitve. **Modeling** provides students with a window into the reasoning processes that occur when readers and writers need to identify and solve problems to construct meaning.

Below is an example of a teacher model that could be used to show students how to plan for an informational writing piece on desert animals:

Okay, so I need to write a piece about animals that live in the desert. I have read a number of books and have kept a reading journal with my notes from reading. The first step for my planning is to review my notes. As I review, I have to keep my purpose in mind and take notes that support writing about animals in the desert. I decide to use a bubble map graphic organizer. This will help me organize my thoughts visually and help me describe the qualities of desert animals. I put "desert animals" in the center. Then I make a spoke for each animal. For each spoke, I put additional spokes for animal family—for instance, I label the cactus wren a bird—survival techniques, and place in the food chain. I think these three spokes are important for teaching others about the different animals in the desert, because a person reading my essay will know the animals, how they survive, and where they fit in the food chain. The bubble map [see Figure 13.1] will be my tool for planning my writing project.

Notice how the teacher in the example shares both the procedural steps of making the bubble map and her thinking process. The thinking process helps students "see" metacognition in action. Demonstration of the thinking process behind reading and writing is key to the **Gradual Release of Responsibility Model** of teaching and learning (Fisher & Frey 2008; Pearson & Gallagher, 1983). This model (see Figure 13.2) requires that the responsibility for

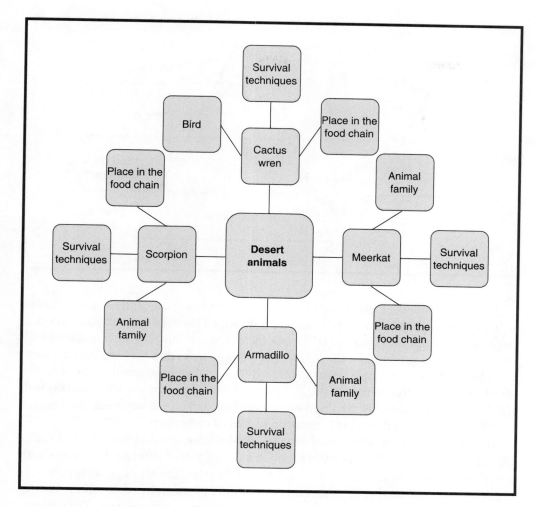

Figure 13.1
Graphic Organizer to Support the Mental Model for Helping Students Plan an Informational Writing Piece

being strategic shift from the teacher to the student through scaffolding. The model has four components: focus lesson, guided instruction, collaboration, and independent work.

The first component is the focus lesson (Fisher & Frey, 2008). At this point of instruction, the teacher is doing the bulk of the strategy work, taking the time to ensure that students know the metacognitive moves to be successful with the strategy. This is like the previous example, where the teacher is modeling the planning process for writing about desert animals. During this stage, the teacher does the bulk of the work.

The second component is guided instruction. During guided instruction, teachers and students are working together to develop proficiency in a strategy. The purpose of this component is for the teacher to provide supported opportunities for practice with the strategy. The practice is provided through verbal and written prompts that give students clues to the metacognitive moves that make strategy implementation successful. Throughout this stage in the process, the teacher is formatively assessing students' thinking and understanding of the strategy. Based on their understanding, the teacher may need to create additional models to support them. In guided instruction, the teacher and the students work together to accomplish the strategy.

Figure 13.2
Gradual Release
of Responsibility
Model

Source: Fisher and
Frey (2008).

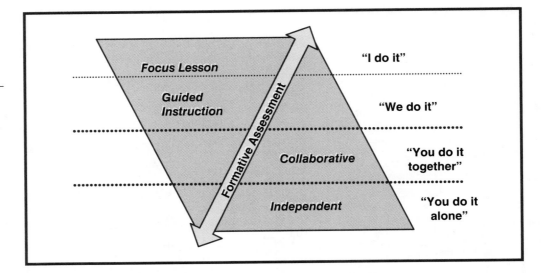

The third component, collaboration, allows students to work together as they continue to build their understanding of how to apply a strategy. This stage in the process is critical because it requires that students talk about their strategic thinking while working with their peers. During this stage, the teacher must design tasks that hold students accountable during the collaborative process and lead to formative assessment of the students' strategic thinking. Teachers will modify the process as they assess students' success with the strategy. Some students may need more modeling, and others may need more guided practice; still others will be able to move on to the last component.

The final component is independent work. By this time, the students have had multiple demonstrations of the strategy in action, have been guided through the strategy with a variety of prompts and activities, and have rehearsed the strategy with peers. As needed, the teacher has provided students with additional mental models and/or prompts based on formative assessment to help them become more independent. The students should now be ready to try the strategy on their own. They will practice independently using a range of texts and/or prompts, with the teacher continuously monitoring their strategic thinking and providing support as needed.

The four components of the Gradual Release of Responsibility Model should not be thought of as a linear process (Fisher & Fey, 2008). As students work through the components, they will need additional demonstrations, guidance, and/or collaboration throughout the process. The model will not be implemented over the course of a single day but, rather, as part of an ongoing program to help students become strategic.

When helping English language learners (ELLs) and students with special needs, the classroom teacher should add the following steps (Colorín Colorado, 2007b):

- Identify any vocabulary that may be difficult for students, and provide them with written definitions related to their existing knowledge.
- Partner students with other students who are more proficient in the strategy, asking the stronger students to demonstrate the strategy using a think-aloud.
- Provide students with a checklist to use when implementing the strategy to guide them as they work independently.

Determining the Strategies Students Need

Effective instruction that builds strategic readers and writers begins with assessment to determine what strategies your students need to achieve the required standards. Teachers use both formative and summative assessments to identify students' strengths and weaknesses. As teachers assess students, they need to document their strengths and weaknesses using techniques such as charts and anecdotal records. Teachers should use many of the assessment techniques described in Chapter 8, as well as the think-aloud to analyze students' strategic thinking.

Think-alouds are student demonstrations of their thinking while reading or writing (Oster, 2001). They are similar in nature to the teacher mental modeling presented earlier. Students will read or write, stopping occasionally to share questions, predictions, confusions over difficult information, and other strategic moves. As students verbalize their thinking, the teacher can assess their reading and writing strategic thinking.

Charting or graphing results and notes makes recognizing patterns and trends much easier. It also helps identify students' performance levels. Efficiency in recording the results is imperative in busy classrooms. Two quick recording tools are provided in Tables 13.1 and 13.2. Modify them to meet your needs.

Table 13.1 Checklist for Informal Data Collection

Name	8/21	8/22	8/23	8/24	8/25	8/28	8/29	8/30	8/31	9/1	9/4	9/5	9/6
Buford													
Cheyanne													

Table 13.2 Guided Reading Notes

Name: Buford	8/21	8/23	8/25
Reading level	1.4		
Oral reading fluency	NAEP Level 2, word by word		
Comprehension	Still struggling with details; introduce him to web graphic organizer		
Reading text and pages	"Pat Takes a Trip" (pp. 3–6)		

Once you have an understanding of the strengths and weaknesses of your students' comprehension and writing abilities, you can begin to plan instruction in strategies that build metacognitive readers and writers.

Strategies for Building Metacognitive Readers and Writers

The instruction can be organized by general tools that support students' strategic thinking and specific strategies that students can apply during the reading and writing process. The tools are key to the guided practice and collaboration components of the Gradual Release of Responsibility Model. Tools such as graphic organizers, bookmarks, and strategy posters can support the implementation of strategic thinking. Whereas specific strategies, such as the Frayer Model (see Figure 13.6 later in this chapter), will help students meet the Common Core State Standards (CCSS), in this section you will first learn about the general tools that support strategies and some specific strategies that can help your students achieve the standards.

Graphic Organizers

Graphic organizers are visual tools that display the relationships between ideas. They help readers and writers as they look for patterns. The human brain is designed to look constantly for patterns as the eyes scan the environment. This is especially true during the reading process and the process of comprehending the meaning of the text. Graphic organizers are one tool for helping the reader make sense of what he or she has read (Barron, 1979). This tool provides the reader with a structure for brainstorming, recording bits of information, making predictions, and/or arranging thoughts in a way that makes sense. "Graphic organizers are thought to activate a reader's prior knowledge and to encourage encoding strategies that will eventually result in increased retention" (Alverman, 1981, p. 44). Providing readers, especially ELLs and students with special needs, with charts and diagrams facilitates a tangible medium to record thoughts, details, and other information from the reading that helps them develop a deeper understanding.

For ELLs and students with special needs, graphic organizers help consolidate information into a meaningful whole and improve organization of writing. They enable students to use a combination of pictures, symbols, models, numbers, and written and spoken words. By associating these images with new words, ELLs and students with special needs reinforce critical thinking skills.

There are numerous types of graphic organizers that can be used in many ways to engage all learners (see Table 13.3).

Bookmarks

Bookmarks are another tool that can support students' strategic thinking. They provide students with a visual reminder of the strategies needed for active comprehension during the reading process. A bookmark is simply a slip of paper that a student can keep in a book during reading. On the paper are clues to support the student as he or she implements strategic thinking. These markers can be used as a tracking aid, a page marker, or a strategy reminder. The edge of the marker can be used to help readers keep their place while reading. It can also be used to mark their place or to identify pages that are particularly difficult to read. However, it also makes a good visual reminder of the strategies students are learning to use as they learn to read. Many templates for creating

Table 13.3 Graphic Organizers for the Reading Process				
Type of Graphic Organizer	Use	Before Reading	During Reading	After Reading
Alphaboxes	Brainstorming, details	X	X	X
Clock	Details		X	X
Cluster web	Details, characteristics, brainstorming		X	X
Continuum	Examining one main concept		X	X
Flow chart	Sequence		X	
Herring bone	Details		X	X
Hierarchy	Sequence		X	
Ice cream cone	Main idea and supporting details			X
Inverted triangle	Summarizing			X
KWL (student *knows*, *wants* to know, has *learned*) chart	Setting a purpose for reading	X	X	X
Ladder	Details, shades of meaning			X
Matrix	Comparison of more than one concept or item		X	X
Semantic feature analysis	Comparison of more than one concept or item		X	X
Story map	Sequence		X	
T-chart	Details, comparison/contrast		X	X
Tic-tac-toe	Major points/details			X
Timeline	Sequence		X	X
Two-, three-, or four-column chart	Details, comparison of more than one concept or item		X	X
Venn diagram	Compare/contrast more than one concept or item		X	X
Web	Brainstorming	X		

bookmarks are available online (e.g., see www.sanjuan.edu/webpages/gguthrie/resources
.cfm?subpage=122409 or it.pinellas.k12.fl.us/Teachers3/gurianb/bookmarks.html), so
very little preparation time is required. You can enter the phrase "bookmark templates
for reading" into a search engine to find preprinted and blank templates.

The most appropriate strategy bookmarks are those created and used by the students. Most of us learn best when we create our own products, and this rings true for bookmarks as well. Creating bookmarks can be an individual, small-group, or whole-class activity. The readers add new strategies (word recognition or comprehension) as they are introduced, practiced, and learned individually. Bookmarks that remain stuffed between pages are not nearly as effective as those that are used.

Making Connections

Visit one of the websites provided above and print a strategy bookmark to use while reading the remainder of this chapter. After reading, talk with your classmates about how the bookmark helped you keep the strategy at the forefront of your thinking during reading.

Strategy Posters

Strategy posters, like bookmarks, are visual instruction reminders that support student strategy learning. They come in a variety of forms, including posters, word walls, and timelines. Designing strategy posters that reflect the strategies the class has learned provides the students with an accessible reminder of previously learned strategies. Teacher-designed posters enable the teacher to create posters uniquely relevant to the class; the same list can be transcribed on the strategy bookmarks to provide students with portable support. When thinking about creating your strategy posters, keep it simple. Use good penmanship and dark letters on a light background, or vice versa, for visual clarity. List the strategy name (remember, this is just a reminder), and clearly title the poster to help students. If you choose to use graphics as a mnemonic device, keep them simple. The same graphic can be used on the strategy poster and to provide repetition from a variety of sources.

Making Connections

Graphic organizers, bookmarks, and strategy posters are general tools that can assist with a range of reading and writing strategies. Think about classrooms you have visited, and reflect on what tools you have seen. Share your reflection with your classmates.

Specific Strategies

In addition to the general tools described above, some specific strategies can build students' reading and writing strategic thinking. When implementing these strategies, it is important to use the Gradual Release of Responsibility Model to ensure that students become independent when working with grade-level texts. Following is a sampling of strategies that can support students to achieve the CCSS.

Reading Anchor Standards

The CCSS for reading are designed to build college- and career-ready students who can critically read and understand text.

The reading anchor standards are organized around four concepts:

- Key ideas and details
- Craft and structure
- Integration of knowledge and ideas
- Text complexity

Below are 11 strategies organized by the specific reading anchor standards they can support through instruction with the Gradual Release of Responsibility Model.

Key Ideas and Details. The standards under this concept ask that students learn to identify the key points in a text. Students need to read closely to analyze the texts' ideas and point to evidence supporting those ideas.

> *Anchor Standard 1 (CCSS.ELA-Literacy.CCRA.R.1).* Read closely to determine what the text says explicitly and to make logical inferences from it; cite specific textual evidence when writing or speaking to support conclusions drawn from the text.

Text Coding. Text coding helps students monitor comprehension during the reading process. As students read, they use a simple coding system to record what they are thinking. Sample codes include the following:

V = Visualize or make a picture in my head

Q = Question; something I don't understand

+ = This information is new for me

C = I can connect this information to another text, my life, or something else I read

W = I don't know what this word means

! = This information is new to me

Checklist. The checklist strategy is another one to use during reading. This strategy requires that students actively read a text to confirm true-or-false statements. It helps them constantly monitor a text for evidence. In this strategy, the teacher prepares a list of true-or-false statements on a reading. As the students read the passage, they mark the statements true or false. At the end of the reading, students go back to the false statements and correct them (Devries, 2004, p. 238).

Figure 13.3 shows a sample checklist completed while reading *Turtle Tide* (Swinburne, 2005).

> *Anchor Standard 2 (CCSS.ELA-Literacy.CCRA.R.2):* Determine central ideas or themes of a text and analyze their development; summarize the key supporting details and ideas.

Figure 13.3

Sample Checklist for *Turtle Tide*

F	1. The mother turtle lays her eggs on the sandy bottom of the ocean.
T	2. Sea turtles need to surface to breathe.
T	3. Sea turtles use their flippers to help them bury their eggs.
F	4. Sea turtle eggs are the size of baseballs.
Correction of False Statements	
1.	The mother turtle lays her eggs on the sandy beach by digging a hole.
4.	Sea turtle eggs are the size of Ping-Pong balls.

Two-Column Notes for Main Idea/Details. Students can use this chart to help them differentiate main ideas from supporting details as they read informational texts. Students divide their paper into two columns, as shown in Figure 13.4, placing main ideas in the left column and details in the right column. As students first work with this strategy, it is helpful for the teacher to provide the main ideas for students and then have them identify the supporting ideas. Another way you can use this form is to have students first write out the supporting details and then use those details to help them identify the main idea.

Figure 13.4

Two-Column Notes for Main Idea/Details Template

Main Idea	Supporting Details
1.	a. b. c.

Anchor Standard 3 (CCSS.ELA-Literacy.CCRA.R.3): Analyze how and why individuals, events, or ideas develop and interact over the course of a text.

Semantic Feature Analysis. Semantic feature analysis uses a chart to create a visual representation of how things are related to one another. To create a semantic feature analysis chart, the teacher creates a table and lists the terminology of the text students are studying down the left side and the characteristics of the terminology along the top. Students place a plus sign in the corresponding row and column to indicate if a characteristic applies to a term or a minus sign if it does not apply. Then the teacher leads the class in a discussion of the similarities and differences among the terminology being studied. See Figure 13.5 for an example.

Craft and Structure. For these standards, students analyze how language is used in a text to convey meaning. Students will need to analyze figurative language, vocabulary, sentences, and paragraphs to build an understanding of how craft and structure affect their comprehension of the text.

Anchor Standard 4 (CCSS.ELA-Literacy.CCRA.R.4): Interpret words and phrases as they are used in a text, including determining technical, connotative, and figurative meanings, and analyze how specific word choices shape meaning or tone.

	Carnivore	Herbivore	Omnivore
Frog			
Raccoon			
Lion			
Squirrel			
Elephant			

Figure 13.5

Sample Semantic Feature Analysis Chart on Animals

Frayer Model. The Frayer Model is a graphic organizer that helps students gain a deep understanding of a vocabulary concept. Students place the new term at the center of the model and then put the definition in one corner, facts about the term or concept in the next corner, and examples and nonexamples in the two remaining corners (see Figure 13.6).

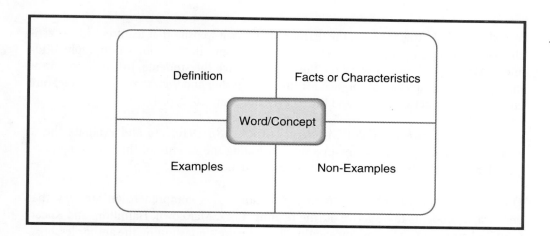

Figure 13.6

The Frayer Model

Anchor Standard 5 (CCSS.ELA-Literacy.CCRA.R.5): Analyze the structure of texts, including how specific sentences, paragraphs, and larger portions of the text (e.g., a section, chapter, scene, or stanza) relate to each other and the whole.

Detecting Patterns of Organization. Review the different text structures—description, sequence, problem and solution, and compare and contrast. As students read, have them try to answer the following questions to determine the structure of the text. Have students practice with different texts to become proficient in using the questions to determine text structure.

- *Cause and effect:* How did cause lead to effect? What are people's reactions?
- *Chronology:* What is the time span from first event to last? How does the author transition to each event? What do all the events explain?
- *Compare and contrast:* What is being compared? What are the similarities and differences? What are the most significant similarities and differences?
- *Problem and solution:* What has caused the problem? Is there more than one solution? Has the problem been solved, or will it continue into the future? (Dixon, Mainville, Farquer, & Gray, 2012).

Anchor Standard 6 (CCSS.ELA-Literacy.CCRA.R.6): Assess how point of view or purpose shapes the content and style of a text.

3-2-1 Strategy. The 3-2-1 strategy helps students discover the purpose of a text. Students identify three discoveries they made during reading, two interesting ideas, and one question they still have after reading (Zygouris-Coe, Wiggins, & Smith, 2004).

Integration of Knowledge and Ideas. These standards ask that students integrate and evaluate ideas within and across texts. Students will need to think about the big ideas presented in the texts and see how they relate to ideas within the same text or across multiple texts.

Anchor Standard 7 (CCSS.ELA-Literacy.CCRA.R.7): Integrate and evaluate content presented in diverse media and formats, including visually and quantitatively, as well as in words.

Website Walk. In this strategy, the teacher identifies a website that features videos, articles, charts, diagrams, and/or maps focused on one topic. Both National Geographic Kids and TIME for Kids would work for this activity. Have the students, in small groups or individually, find an example of each feature listed earlier and then share how that feature enables them to better understand the text (Dixon et al., 2012, p. 47).

Anchor Standard 8 (CCSS.ELA-Literacy.CCRA.R.8): Delineate and evaluate the argument and specific claims in a text, including the validity of the reasoning as well as the relevance and sufficiency of the evidence.

Questioning the Author. Questioning the author is a comprehension strategy that encourages students to be active during reading. Beck, McKeown, Hamilton, and Kucan (1997) identify specific steps you should follow during a questioning the author lesson:

1. Select a passage.
2. Decide appropriate stopping points that will support students in developing a deeper understanding of the passage.
3. Create questions to encourage critical thinking for each stopping point, such as the following:
   a. What is the author trying to say?
   b. Why do you think the author used the following phrase?
   c. Does this make sense to you?
   d. Why do you think the author chose to use this phrase or wording in this specific spot?
   e. How has the author let you know that something has changed?

Anchor Standard 9 (CCSS.ELA-Literacy.CCRA.R.9): Analyze how two or more texts address similar themes or topics in order to build knowledge or to compare the approaches the authors take.

Compare and Contrast Chart. Have students read two books on the same topic. After reading, students should identify two similarities and two differences between the texts (see Figure 13.7).

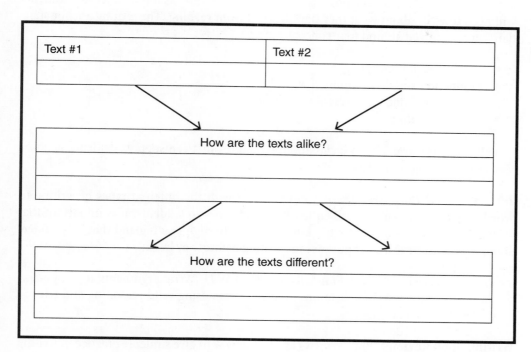

Figure 13.7
Compare/Contrast
Chart Template

Range of Reading and Level of Text Complexity. This standard addresses the need for students to work with texts that are of appropriate difficulty. Teachers should review the qualitative and quantitative difficulty of the text, as well as the difficulty of the task, in conjunction with the reader's ability prior to choosing texts (see Appendix A for more detail). We caution against using one-dimensional measures of text complexity, as you cannot match the text to the reader using this method. As in choosing any materials and techniques, you must use assessment data to inform your choices of appropriately complex text for students.

> *Anchor Standard 10 (CCSS.ELA-Literacy.CCRA.R.10):* Read and comprehend complex literary and informational texts independently and proficiently.

Reciprocal Teaching. Reciprocal teaching guides students in working together to improve comprehension. Teachers model the strategies of summarizing, questioning, clarifying, and predicting so that students can apply the strategies when working together in small groups. More information on how to use reciprocal teaching can be found at www.reading rockets.org/strategies/reciprocal_teaching.

The preceding strategies are not meant to be either an exclusive or exhaustive look at all the techniques teachers can use to build students who construct meaning throughout the reading process.

Writing Anchor Standards

The writing anchor standards provide a framework for understanding the types of writing in which students are required to engage. The implementation of these standards requires that teachers see the process of reading and writing as interconnected. Students will need to write about what they have learned from reading. The writing anchor standards are organized around four concepts:

- Text types and purposes
- Production and distribution of writing
- Research to build and present knowledge
- Range of writing

Following are strategies and classroom structures that can support students' acquisition of the writing standards.

Text Types and Purposes. These standards deal with the different types of writing in which students will engage. When teaching text types to students, it is important that they gain experience with different kinds of texts through reading and that they understand they must have a clear purpose for writing before they begin.

Anchor Standard 1 (CCSS.ELA-Literacy.CCRA.W.1): Write arguments to support claims in an analysis of substantive topics or texts using valid reasoning and relevant and sufficient evidence.

Writing Book Reviews. Book reviews are a great way to give students practice in writing supported opinion pieces. They require that students use the evidence from the text to support their claims regarding the quality of the book. A book review should include the follow parts:

- The book's title and author
- A brief summary of the book
- Comments on the book's strengths and weaknesses, using quotes directly from the book
- A personal response about the quality of the book, supported by at least three specific examples from the book to support the claim

Anchor Standard 2 (CCSS.ELA-Literacy.CCRA.W.2): Write informative/explanatory texts to examine and convey complex ideas and information clearly and accurately through the effective selection, organization, and analysis of content.

Writing a How-To. A how-to explains how to complete a task. Students can use a how-to organization chart to help them gather their thoughts for writing. Using the chart will help students break down complex ideas and guide them in organizing their content (see Figure 13.8).

Anchor Standard 3 (CCSS.ELA-Literacy.CCRA.W.3): Write narratives to develop real or imagined experiences or events using effective technique, well-chosen details, and well-structured event sequences.

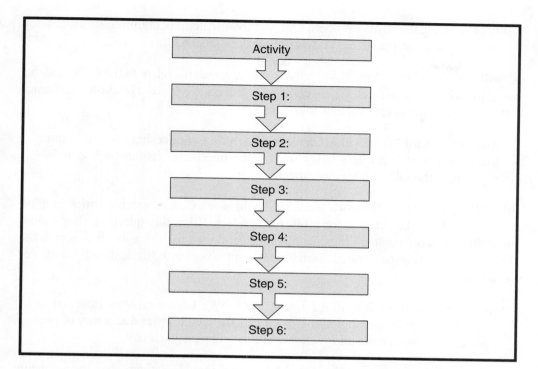

Figure 13.8
Student Guide for
Writing a How-To

Zooming In. This strategy helps students add details to their writing by using "binoculars" to zoom in on mental snapshots, visualizing the details that would make their writing deeper and more specific (Lane, 1992). This will enable students to write narratives with well-chosen details and events with specific sequences that will engage the reader.

Production and Distribution of Writing. The standards organized by this concept have to do with the writing process; therefore, they are presented together with a short description of the writing process to support teachers as they guide students to achieve these standards.

Anchor Standard 4 (CCSS.ELA-Literacy.CCRA.W.4): Produce clear and coherent writing in which the development, organization, and style are appropriate to task, purpose, and audience.

Anchor Standard 5 (CCSS.ELA-Literacy.CCRA.W.5): Develop and strengthen writing as needed by planning, revising, editing, rewriting, or trying a new approach.

Anchor Standard 6 (CCSS.ELA-Literacy.CCRA.W.6): Use technology, including the Internet, to produce and publish writing and to interact and collaborate with others.

The Writing Process. The writing process—prewriting, drafting, revising and editing, rewriting, and publishing—mirrors the way proficient writers work. Student engagement in the writing process provides them with a view into the thinking processes writers use when composing. Although writers may not always engage in these processes in a linear fashion, they do work through each part of the process distinctly. For more information on implementing the writing process, visit www.readwritethink.org/professional-develop ment/strategy-guides/implementing-writing-process-30386.html.

Research to Build and Present Knowledge. These standards relate to the skills students need to write using research. These standards address the process of asking questions, researching, and drawing evidence from text.

> *Anchor Standard 7 (CCSS.ELA-Literacy.CCRA.W.7):* Conduct short as well as more sustained research projects based on focused questions, demonstrating understanding of the subject under investigation.

Identifying Effective Keywords. Students should have a clear research question in mind before searching the Internet for a research project. Using this question, they should underline the words that tell them its main idea and then use these words to search the Internet. By keeping their search down to a few simple keywords, students will have fewer results to evaluate.

> *Anchor Standard 8 (CCSS.ELA-Literacy.CCRA.W.8):* Gather relevant information from multiple print and digital sources, assess the credibility and accuracy of each source, and integrate the information while avoiding plagiarism.

Determining the Credibility of a Website. Students should ask themselves the following questions when determining the reliability of a website:

- Who is the author of the webpage, and what are the author's credentials?
- What does the URL say about the author or the publisher?
- How current is the information?

Teachers should provide students with opportunities to practice asking these questions in relation to a variety of websites.

> *Anchor Standard 9 (CCSS.ELA-Literacy.CCRA.W.9):* Draw evidence from literary or informational texts to support analysis, reflection, and research.

Inquiry Chart. The inquiry chart helps students gather information about a topic from a variety of resources (see Figure 13.9). Students go through three steps in completing an inquiry chart: planning, interacting, and integrating/evaluating (Hoffman, 1992). In the planning stage, the teacher and/or students identify the topic and questions to be researched and collect the resources. During the interacting stage, students read the materials to answer their questions. As they engage in the integrating/evaluation stage, students will need to compare the responses to their questions to compose a summary response for each one.

Range of Writing. To accomplish the standards above, students need dedicated time to practice a range of writing pieces. They will need to learn how to work through longer pieces over an extended period as well as to produce on-demand writing pieces that must be completed in a short prescribed time (e.g., 50 minutes).

	Question 1	Question 2	Question 3	Other Interesting Facts
Source 1				
Source 2				
Summary				

Figure 13.9
Inquiry Chart
Template

Anchor Standard 10 (CCSS.ELA-Literacy.CCRA.W.10): Write routinely over extended time frames (time for research, reflection, and revision) and shorter time frames (a single sitting or a day or two) for a range of tasks, purposes, and audiences.

Writer's Workshop. For students to meet this standard, they need time to engage in extended writing time. Writer's workshop is a technique for structuring your classroom to support students' writing development. Writer's workshop is described in detail in the next section.

Making Connections

Choose one reading and writing strategy from above, and create a bookmark and/or strategy poster that you could use to guide students in the application of that strategy.

Classroom Structures for Strategy Instruction

The Gradual Release of Responsibility Model provides a structure for teaching strategies. Graphic organizers, bookmarks, and strategy posters provide the tools students need as they learn strategies. Writer's workshop and guided reading help you organize your classroom time to build strategic students.

Writer's Workshop

The concept of writer's workshop is a holistic instructional model that provides students with extended periods to do the work of writers (Calkins, 1994; Graves, 1983, 1994). The model has eight primary principles: (1) The process of learning is largely accomplished through authentic and natural tasks; (2) effective instruction is built on student-centered learning; (3) the role of the teacher in the workshop is that of a personalized coach and guide; (4) most instruction is provided in the conference, in mini-lessons, by modeling, and through spontaneous dialogue; (5) the purpose of the learning rests on the process of writing rather than the content and conventions; (6) significant chunks of time are devoted to writing during the academic day; (7) students are guided using a gradual release model to select their own topics and reading materials; and (8) sharing work with peers and others is strongly encouraged (Atwell, 1987; Graves, 1983, 1994).

Figure 13.10

Writer's Workshop in the Elementary Classroom

9:00 Writing workshop (center rotations every 20 minutes)

- *Center 1: Prewriting.* Students at this center are actively working on their next writing project. This station is stocked with a variety of graphic organizers for brainstorming and planning, samples of the genre students are to be creating, writing and highlighting utensils, scraps of paper for recording questions or ideas, and a writing process checklist.
- *Center 2: Beginning Writing.* This center is an active area. It is designed to facilitate thinking and exploration of the topic of the current writing piece. Students are sharing their ideas with one another, creating graphic organizers, pausing to read portions of their work to peers for feedback, looking through resources, and tracking their progress in their writing logs. The center is loaded with genre templates, writing tip bookmarks, writing strategies bookmarks, reference materials, writing paper, and room for partner writing.
- *Center 3: Editing.* Students who are in the midst of editing their work gather at this center for peer and teacher feedback. Strategy posters and bookmarks provide visuals to help the students as they evaluate and modify the cognitive arrangement of their piece. It, too, is stocked with colored writing utensils, sticky notes, and scraps of paper to annotate their editing process.
- *Center 4: Meet With Me.* The heart of the writing conference is students' visits to this center. Here they spend one-on-one time with the teacher to discuss their current project, possible obstacles, questions, and an accountability check of goals and progress. This center may also be used for guided writing.
- *Center 5: Mini-Lessons.* This center is devoted to housing mini-lessons. These 10-minute lessons are used to work with homogenous groups of students who need a bit more instruction in the same area. Guided writing support and instruction can easily be facilitated here.

10:00 Whole-class debrief (the class meets to share their discoveries and challenges during writer's workshop and to formulate plans for the next workshop; 20 minutes)

The writing conference is a key part of the writer's workshop. Writing conferences can be approached from two perspectives: teacher led or student led. They can be used to review goals, set goals, identify problems, perform formative assessment, and determine instructional changes. During the writing conference, the teacher must take anecdotal notes to use in assessment of students' writing skills and strategies. The writer's workshop supports individualized instruction to meet students' writing instructional needs.

Guided Reading and Writing

Guided reading is also designed to provide dynamic, individual instruction and support for the use and implementation of strategies to help children as they are learning how to read. Guided reading is reading instruction where the teacher works with small groups of students to support their acquisition of reading skills and strategies. Most groups share a similar structure: (1) Groups are small (three to six students), (2) sessions last 20 to 30 minutes, (3) students use leveled and/or common texts, (4) pre-, during, and postreading instruction are provided, (5) groups meet two to three times per week, and

(6) other students are involved in center or seatwork. While the teacher is working with a small group, the remainder of the class is working on applying reading and writing strategies individually, with a partner, or in a small group.

The small number of students per group facilitates individualized support and instruction, which is very valuable for students receiving intervention, as well as for ELLs and students with special needs. Groups can be determined by reader needs (gather students who need to work on the same skill or strategy), ability (gather students at the same reading level), mixed ability (gather students at various reading levels for partner or buddy reading), or text (gather students reading the same text or with the same interests). Because the guided groups are built around need, their composition is dynamic and changes as the students' needs change. The short sessions help prevent the students from becoming too fatigued as they wrestle with more difficult tasks. The design of each group meeting is simple: A prereading activity prepares the readers for the implementation of the strategy during reading. The session usually ends with a postreading review or reflection on the strategy of the day.

Setting up your classroom to implement guided reading and the writer's workshop versus traditional whole-class instruction allows you the flexibility to meet students' individual needs. This is of particular importance in supporting ELLs and students with special needs, because your instructional decisions are not made for a whole class but based on students' individual learning needs. Just as guided reading and writer's workshop provide students with opportunities to practice their reading and writing strategies in the classroom, activities that promote family reading and writing provide additional practice outside the classroom. Following are some engaging ways to involve families in writing.

Promoting Family Writing: Dialogue Journals, Special Events Books, and Parodies

Involving families in writing and writing projects is an effective way to create support and community in the classroom. Several ideas are presented for you to consider as you begin working with students and planning instruction. Writing with family members also facilitates intergenerational opportunities not often found in the elementary curriculum. The opportunities and project ideas are limited only by your imagination. Two helpful websites for the support of family writing and writing ideas are www.familywritingprojects.com and the National Writing Project website (www.nwp.org). When thinking about implementing a family writing project, consider the following:

1. Are the audience and project authentic? Authentic writing opportunities are far more meaningful and engaging for early and struggling writers, regardless of age. More important, writing for an authentic audience is more meaningful and engaging for all writers (Peterson, 2001).

2. Does the project require special resources? If so, consider modifying it so all families can participate.

3. Is the project reasonable for your students' families? Are your expectations appropriate? If the project is too time-consuming, it is likely you will not receive the participation you are hoping to get. Limit the time investment to 30 minutes or less for family members.

4. How will the project be published? Taking writing to publication sends a message of value and validation to the writers. Be sure to include a time and place for publication.

5. How will the project be assessed? Take a moment to consider how students without familial support will be scaffolded and evaluated. Make certain it is reasonable and equitable.

Three particular ideas for including families in writing are dialogue journals, special events books, and parodies. Dialogue journals are informal exchanges written between parents or family members and their children. Regular responses to entries between the students and family members resemble a conversation, where the responses are connected rather than corrected. Dialogue journals offer students and family members a nonthreatening opportunity to communicate with each other and to develop language, reading, and writing skills in an unrestrictive environment (McGrail, 1991; Peyton & Staton, 1993). Because the journals can easily be adapted for all learners throughout the elementary grades, they provide an effective means of cultivating an authentic literacy opportunity for young readers and writers and of managing a wide variety of abilities. It is as simple as preparing a number of stapled pages and establishing a purpose for the students to write. The purpose might be asking their grandparents what Christmas was like when they were children. The student would begin the journal and ask the question, then deliver the journal to the grandparent. The grandparent would respond to the question and then return the journal to the student. The student would read the response and write back, continuing the exchange. This could also be modified to use electronic text, such as e-mail, Facebook, Twitter, or text messaging.

Chronicling special events is another way to engage in family writing during the elementary years. Similar in many ways to a diary, families begin compiling descriptions and memories of meaningful shared events in one location, either by hand or electronically. One way to implement this in the classroom is to ask students to pick their favorite family activity, such as Friday evening popcorn and a movie. Have your students begin their book by introducing and describing the cherished event. After they are finished, they pass their books to a family member, who writes about his or her perception of the event and passes the book to another family member, and the cycle continues. When the event has been exhausted, start over with a new event, school project or occasion, trip, or tradition. Each family can decide the format for the book, such as how/where the author's name will appear, how the writing will be dated, and if/how illustrations and pictures will be added. Special events books make cherished gifts and records that can be enjoyed for generations.

Parodies are another engaging way to draw families into shared writing. A parody is simply making fun of an existing story. The process for writing the parody is quite easy: Select a familiar story, decide how you want to rewrite it to make it comical, rename the characters and places to match the new perspective, and try to extend the storyline. For instance, one family may want to rewrite *Brown Bear, Brown Bear, What Do You See?* because their family beagle runs into everything. They might title their new story "Blind Beagle, Blind Beagle, Why Can't You See?" Members of the family can collaboratively write about the exploits of their beloved family pet, or they can take turns writing paragraphs or short chapters.

As with the previously mentioned family writing projects, including students' families in the writing process provides much more than homework. It links the families and the school into a supportive partnership; provides opportunities for families to spend time together; increases students' exposure to reading, writing, and language; and creates memorable family writing pieces.

Reading and writing are meaning-making processes that require multiple opportunities for guidance and practice. As a teacher, you can provide the support students need by teaching them to be strategic using the Gradual Release of Responsibility Model, showing them a range of strategies to achieve the standards, and providing a classroom structure that promotes student practice of strategies in a variety of situations for a variety of purposes.

Key Terms

Gradual Release of Responsibility Model	skills
modeling	writing process

Website Resources

- **"Spelling and Vocabulary," Kids' Place**

This site offers educators, students, and parents a wide variety of word sorting, building, and hunting activities. It is recommended for students in Grades 1–6. There are a variety of units, each increasing in difficulty at each grade level. There is also an audio component that allows students to hear the words being sorted, hunted, and built. This is great for ELLs and students with special needs as well. For more information, go to **www.eduplace.com/kids/sv**.

- **"Graphic Organizers," Education Oasis**

This site offers 50+ graphic organizers to choose from to get the best from your students. The graphic organizers are arranged by category, including cause and effect, character and story, compare and contrast, sequence, cycle, timeline and chain of events, and vocabulary and concept development. For more information, go to **www.educationoasis .com/curriculum/graphic_organizers.htm**.

(Continued)

(Continued)

- **"What Is Balanced Literacy?" Instructional Strategies Online**

This site provides an outline of how guided reading and writing support student learning. It includes lessons to do with your students and suggestions for ways to assess that guide further instruction. For more information, go to **olc.spsd.sk.ca/DE/PD/instr/strats/balancedliteracy**.

- *Welcome to Writer's Workshop,* **Teaching That Makes Sense Inc.**

This document offers a complete guide to effective writing workshops and how to get the most from your students. It explains what writing workshops are, how they look, and how to manage them. It also includes examples of students' work, organizational tips, lesson plans, and pointers for managing sharing time. The information is broken into sections so that it is applicable for K–12 students. Find the full document at **www.ttms.org/PDFs/05%20 Writers%20Workshop%20v001%20(Full).pdf**.

Student Study Site: Visit the Student Study Site at **www.sagepub.com/grantlit** to access additional study tools including eFlashcards, web resources, and online-only appendices.

CHAPTER 14

Strategies for Fluency Through Reading

Sheila Morris and Kathy B. Grant

Common Core State Standards	
Text Types and Purposes	*W.5.2* Write informative/explanatory texts to examine a topic and convey ideas and information clearly.
Production and Distribution of Writing	*W.5.4* Produce clear and coherent writing in which the development and organization are appropriate to task, purpose, and audience.
Research to Build and Present Knowledge	*W.5.9* Draw evidence from literary or informational texts to support analysis, reflection, and research.
Range of Writing	*W.5.10* Write routinely over extended time frames (time for research, reflection, and revision) and shorter time frames (a single sitting or a day or two) for a range of discipline-specific tasks, purposes, and audiences.

FOCUS QUESTIONS

1. What is fluency, and what strategies do you use to promote reading fluency in your students?

2. How does fluency support increased understanding of selections?

3. What is the role of the student during literature circles?

4. How are reader-response questions different from text-dependent questions? What are the benefits of each type of question?

5. How does writing instruction support fluency?

6. What is the difference between writing in response to reading and the more formal writing required for students to complete an informational piece?

Words in Action

My Teacher Taught Me to Love Words!

The following passage was written by a young boy who worked closely with a novice teacher on his vocabulary and fluency. Prior to this encounter, this student didn't know what fluency meant. But his teacher's enthusiasm for words, word play, and word recognition made the learning process not only a memorable experience but something he chose to write about.

"This summer I went to summer school to help me catch up on my reading. I wasn't happy to spend my summer this way. I had visions of happy hunting, fancy fishing and flawless flaunting of football formations. Instead I was learning the difference between interpret and interrogate. I practiced rolling R's and saying 'hapless' out loud. I drew pictures of what I thought words sounded like. I even had to spend time rereading stories and writing about fishing instead of doing it.

"Fortunately for me, my teacher was a lot of fun. We did drawings, riddles, poems and word plays to learn new words and the differences in meanings for each. Mrs. D called them tier 2 words. She says these are the words that are not specific to a story, but which are used with the assumption that we know what they mean. Prior to this summer, I didn't know what an assumption was, even though I make them all the time. I think of an assumption as like a prediction. Sometimes I am right, but sometimes I am not.

"One of my teacher's favorite things to say was, 'ecoute, et repete!' This means 'listen and repeat' in French, which is what we do a lot with new words. Our teacher has us say them out loud. We practice seeing them in print and saying them out loud. We get pretty silly when we say them. We rhyme with them, time with them and smack the words around pretty well. We pull words from a Golden Hat and have to practice pronouncing them, and then using them in a sentence. Then we all say the word aloud together. I really enjoyed learning new words this summer. Knowing more tier 2 words has improved my fluency because I don't trip over these words anymore."

Understanding Fluency

A fluent reader accurately decodes words while simultaneously recognizing them and employing correct oral expression while reading (Rasinski, 2004). The goal of any successful reading instruction program is comprehension—understanding and being able to critique what one is reading. And the key to successful, *independent* comprehension is fluency. Fluency, by definition, means reading with speed, confidence, and expression (Reading Rockets, 2014). Fluency affects comprehension, because when reading too quickly or without expression, one has difficulty holding on to the meaning of the passage. Therefore, only when a reader becomes fluent will true comprehension and higher-level thinking take place.

A key factor in promoting students' fluency is a focus on phonics. When students can decode words automatically, then their fluency will be accurate and at the appropriate speed. However, when students struggle to identify words, their reading will become labored and it will be difficult to hold on to meaning during reading. Students who struggle with fluency are known as nonfluent readers—those who are slow and labor over reading, place attention on decoding words, and have an inability to comprehend the words they are finally able to recognize (Faver, 2008). Rasinski (2010) calls for a strong word study program in the classroom to ensure that students gain automaticity when reading.

Oral reading rate is the speed at which a student can accurately read a passage in 1 minute, which determines his or her words correct per minute (WCPM) score. A reader's WCPM score can be assessed by recording the number of words in the passage, the number of errors a reader makes when reading the passage, and the time in seconds it takes the reader to complete the passage. The formula for determining WCPM is as follows:

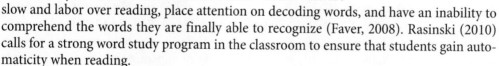

WCPM = (Number of words in passage ÷ Reading time [in seconds]) × 60

But fluency is more than just automaticity and reading rate. Reading rate is the number of words a reader can accurately read aloud in a minute. Reading rate is only one part of fluency. Fluency also involves reading with expression and with words in meaningful phrase groups, called prosody. A student can have a high reading rate but not read with expression and/or not place words in phrase groups, which detracts from the meaning of the text.

Making Connections

The emphasis on increasing reading rate as a form of assessment is suspect. Many commercial reading assessments claim that growth in reading rate as a single measure of fluency

(Continued)

(Continued)

should be used; however, this method alone is dubious. Students may be "word calling" to aim for a faster rate, but the true measure is comprehension of what is read.

One unintended and unfortunate consequence of using reading rate as a measure of fluency, however, has been that instructional approaches for fluency have assumed that the goal of fluency instruction is to increase reading rate. Thus, in many classrooms and in several published reading fluency programs, assisted and repeated readings of texts have been employed for the primary purpose of increasing reading rate. Students are encouraged to read a text repeatedly until they can read it at a certain rate, regardless of their level of understanding. Many students come to identify fast reading as proficient reading. This, we feel, is a disturbing and unwarranted approach to fluency instruction. We feel that this approach to fluency may lead to the development of a generation of readers who may read quickly but have little understanding of what they read and get little enjoyment or satisfaction from their reading. (Young & Rasinski, 2011, p. 5)

To help teachers understand the developmental levels of fluent and nonfluent readers, the U.S. Department of Education, Institute of Education Sciences, and National Center for Education Statistics (2002) developed a fluency scale called the National Assessment of Educational Progress (NAEP) Oral Reading Fluency Scale (see Table 14.1). This scale can be used as a guide for identifying students who may need intervention to improve their fluency.

When using the table to identify students who are nonfluent, some districts designate student fluency scores at Levels 1 and 2 as warranting academic remediation under Response to Intervention (RtI). What follows remedially may be word lists the student frequently reads aloud for speed to increase reading rate (they call it fluency, but it is not). When providing intervention for students who struggle with fluency, it is important to ensure that focus is also on reading with expression and phrasing words in meaningful groupings.

Although the scale divides readers into two groups—fluent and nonfluent—caution should be used with this instrument. Slow and precise readers may be misunderstood and labeled nonfluent when they are simply attending to meaning in their methodical manner. Likewise, speedy readers may be missing the meaning of the selection in their quest for quick reading, especially if they are aware that they will not be questioned about their understanding of the passage. Of course, English language learners and struggling readers may labor over a passage and score no more than Level 1 even when they are striving for comprehension. In the words of Weaver (2002), "fluency must not replace the focus on meaning as the goal of reading" (p. 215).

Fluency Strategies

Teaching strategies to build students' fluency must focus on improving the subskills of fluency: automaticity, prosody, rate, and expression during reading. The three strategies below provide opportunities for students to demonstrate and practice these subskills so

Table 14.1 NAEP Oral Reading Fluency Scale		
Fluent	Level 4	Reads primarily in larger, meaningful phrase groups. Although some regressions, repetitions, and deviations from text may be present, these do not appear to detract from the overall structure of the story. Preservation of the author's syntax is consistent. Some or most of the story is read with expressive interpretation.
	Level 3	Reads primarily in three- or four-word phrase groups. Some small groupings may be present. However, the majority of phrasing seems appropriate and preserves the syntax of the author. Little or no expressive interpretation is present.
Nonfluent	Level 2	Reads primarily in two-word phrases with some three- or four-word groupings. Some word-by-word reading may be present. Word groupings may seem awkward and unrelated to larger context of sentence or passage.
	Level 1	Reads primarily word-by-word. Occasional two-word or three-word phrases may occur— but these are infrequent and/or they do not preserve meaningful syntax.

Source: U.S. Department of Education, Institute of Education Sciences, and National Center for Education Statistics (2002).

teachers can recognize which one is causing the reader problems with fluency while also providing the student practice in the other fluency subskills.

Repeated Readings

The purpose of repeated readings is to allow students to read short passages until they achieve a satisfactory level of fluency with the passage. The goal of this strategy is to build automaticity, prosody, rate, and expression of oral reading. The texts need to be at the students' *independent* or *instructional* reading level, and formal feedback *needs* to be given to the students during the reading process. Repeated readings also help build a child's **reading stamina**—that is, a child's ability to focus and read independently for substantial periods of time (Reading Rockets, 2012).

Repeated readings could be as simple as partner reading, echo reading, or choral reading the stories from the reading series (Blau, 2014). They could be set up like coaching sessions, where a teacher facilitates the first reading, gives the student feedback, and then has the student try again, keeping in mind the miscues he or she made. Repeated readings can help students by teaching them what they should be doing independently; how to monitor and adjust their rate, speed, and intonation; and to set personal goals for themselves. This strategy can be used with students as soon as they are considered "readers." Kids love challenging their peers and themselves by setting goals; this is the same concept, only with texts. Students will begin to internalize these strategies when reading independently.

The text should be at or above the student's *instructional* reading level, with the proper vocabulary and background instruction to build their schema completed prior to reading. The Common Core State Standards (CCSS) concentrate on this goal to develop analytical students.

The purpose of repeated reading should be explained to students; the strategy should be explicitly taught, and the teacher should always act as a facilitator during a repeated reading session to give feedback until a common language and atmosphere are established in the classroom. Repeated reading does not have to be done the same way every time; as with any strategy, determine what is best for the particular cohort of students in the class, because this will change continually.

Research clearly demonstrates the efficacy of repeated readings:

1. Rasinski, Padak, Linek, and Sturtevant (1994) found that repeated readings helped improve the fluency of second-grade readers over a 6-month period.

2. Therrien and Kubina (2006) noted that repeated readings are beneficial for students between first- and third-grade levels.

3. Meyer and Felton (1999) suggested three types of repeated readings: read-alongs—an adult or teacher reads along with a student; assisted repeated readings—students are paired and read in unison; and unassisted repeated reading—students read alone independently.

For younger students, sight words, context vocabulary, songs, sentence strips, and short books can be used. Songs on CD paired with printed lyrics in a first-grade classroom literacy center offers an opportunity for early readers to practice fluent reading as they read along with the music. Teacher Terri Poffenberger (in Rasinski, Fawcett, Lems, & Ackland, 2010) describes the joy children express when using song to enhance fluency:

Terri reports that they "simply love it. . . . It's hilarious to hear a child so engaged that they are belting out a song during your reading group. You know the child is so into what he's doing, he doesn't realize there's a world around him." (pp. 27–28)

Making Connections

Poetry is an excellent tool to engage students in repeated reading. The Poetry Academy, specifically developed to support students struggling in fluency,

> used poetry for literacy with positive results. Teachers, students, volunteers, and parents mentioned the short format of poetry, combined with its usually humorous text, in conjunction with the improvement of the apprentices in their reading skills and attitudes towards reading. (Wilfong, 2008, p. 11)

With your partner, brainstorm some uses of poetry to promote fluency. What benefits from using poetry can you delineate? Are there any drawbacks for particular students? If so, discuss them.

Reader's Theatre

Reader's theatre is another strategy that can develop students' fluency subskills. It provides students opportunities to engage in repeated readings with a script, without the memorization or props required of traditional plays. This is a fun way to enable students to exhibit voice, intonation, rate, and speed. It is used to build confidence and comprehension while having fun—yes, fun! Additionally, research shows that the frequent use of reader's theatre in a classroom has been demonstrated to improve reading performance (Griffith & Rasinski, 2004). This strategy also fits in nicely with the Common Core expectations for creating and presenting a play and facilitating repeated readings.

There are many places to buy and obtain reader's theatre scripts, especially on the Internet, but one of the most authentic ways to help students comprehend complex material in social studies, math, or science is to have them write their own scripts. Strong readers could choose a chapter from the novel they are reading and create a script from that, or read a poem, such as Longfellow's "Paul Revere's Ride," each taking a part. Students could write scripts on how the Earth was formed or create one for the order of operations in math. Activities such as these are what make learning meaningful to students, which will help them comprehend what they are learning. With the emphasis on practice with expository text, students could transform any topic into a short script, highlighting disciplinary vocabulary. See Table 14.2 for a sample first-grade reader's theatre script that uses an expository text.

When first implementing reader's theatre, Rasinski, Fawcett, et al. (2010) suggest establishing a "routine" for instruction. Choosing stories that children are familiar with will help scaffold striving readers.

Monday: Teacher and students collaboratively pick a script based on a piece of literature or expository text recently read in class. Copies are made and distributed. The teacher reads the reader's theatre aloud, having students mark unknown vocabulary words. Vocabulary instruction occurs. The theme (narrative) or key facts (expository) may be discussed. The teacher introduces the fluency goal-setting activity, which is partner based.

Tuesday: Students read aloud through the script with a partner and then switch parts. Students read silently to themselves. The teacher checks on understanding of the script. The teacher introduces a self-assessment checklist (see Table 14.3) for their oral reading of the script (without yet knowing their parts). Students and the teacher cooperate on deciding parts, making sure all students get to read or narrate something.

Wednesday: Each student reads through the script again, assuming his or her assigned role. The focus is on the goals they set, reading with expression at a reasonable rate (as in conversation) and with intonation based on punctuation, word stress, and other textual factors. Repeated reading for practice is important. The teacher and the students codevelop criteria for the teacher's rubric to assess the group's performances.

Thursday: Scripts are read one more time for practice, with an emphasis on projection, or making sure the audience can hear the reader. The teacher and others should form the audience and monitor projection levels. The teacher may need to model voice projection several times since students are most likely unpracticed in this skill and may be hesitant. Note their hesitancy; it may be due to not decoding words correctly or fear of that happening.

Table 14.2 Reader's Theatre Script: Expository Text (Grade 1)

Who Lives in a Tree?

Narrator: Today we are going to talk about animals that live in trees. Trees provide food and shelter for many different kinds of animals. We'll begin by telling the following story.

Raccoon 1: Hi! I am a raccoon. I live here with my family. We use hollow logs as our homes to keep us safe and dry.

Raccoon 2: For fun we like to play with the bark on the trees. When we are hungry we eat the fruit from the tree.

Raccoon 1: We have lots of friendly neighbors. Let's learn more about them!

Raccoon 2: The fox family lives right next door. Let's go say hi!

Fox 1 (baby): Hi there. I am a baby fox. My mother and I live here together. She makes our home in the hollow tree trunk where we huddle together to keep warm. My mother must go out and gather food while I stay safe in the tree.

Raccoon 2: Now that we've met the fox family, let's find out who else lives in the tree.

Woodpecker: Hello! I am a woodpecker. I live higher up in the trees. I peck holes in the bark to find my food. I eat insects. My neighbors eat nuts. Let's meet them!

Chipmunk: I am a chipmunk, and I love to eat nuts. I also like to plan ahead and be ready for the winter months.

Woodpecker: How do you prepare for the winter?

Chipmunk: I gather nuts by stuffing them in my cheeks. Then I store them in the hollow tree trunks for safe keeping. I try to make as few trips as possible.

Woodpecker: I must say, that is very smart of you! Do you know any other animals that live in trees?

Chipmunk: Yes! My friend the hedgehog also likes hollow trees. When he is scared, he rolls up in a ball and shows his prickly spines, scaring any attacker away.

Woodpecker: Prickly spines? Do you know anyone else that uses prickly spines for protection?

Chipmunk: I do! My other friend the porcupine also has prickly quills to defend himself with. Trust me, you don't want to scare him! If an enemy gets close, he backs into them and releases his quills.

Woodpecker: So, who else lives in our neighborhood?

Chipmunk: There is another family that lives here, but we don't see them much. Mr. Owl uses twigs to make a nest for his young to keep them safe. He is nocturnal.

Woodpecker: What does nocturnal mean?

Chipmunk: It means that owls sleep during the day and stay awake at night to hunt for their food.

Woodpecker: Well, we have lots of neighbors don't we?! And we all have our special way of staying safe and warm.

Source: Canizares and Moreton (1997).

Friday: The group performs in the classroom or in front of a larger audience. They revisit their goals with their partners and complete a reader's theatre self-assessment checklist individually. Teacher scores the reader's theatre rubric as a group effort and discusses observational notes.

Note that the routine will change if students cowrite their own scripts based on a text they read; this is recommended once students do several "run-throughs" with ready-made scripts. We encourage teachers to take the next step by having the whole class or small groups of students write their original scripts based on informational texts or stories.

To evaluate student progress with fluency skills, it is important that teachers evaluate students' presentations of reader's theatre. Teachers can do this by establishing class goals and student self-assessment checklists.

Establishing Readers' Fluency Goals for Reader's Theatre

In class discussion, we talked about some goals of fluent reading. Now that you are comfortable with reading aloud, your confidence as a presenter will grow. With your partner, talk about specific goals you want to set for your presentation of your script. Be specific and list your "talking points" after the discussion.

- Making your voice mirror the line to be read, or *expression*
- Reading pace/flow, or *rate*
- Marking phrase boundaries with your voice, or *intonation*
- Clearness and volume of your voice, or *projection*

Reader's theatre is an active and engaging activity for all readers at various levels of ability, helping unmotivated readers turn into motivated and enthusiastic readers. Many great sources exist for ready-made reader's theatre scripts. Some of the best are listed below, along with their web addresses.

Best Sources for Reader's Theatre Scripts

- Aaron Shepard's RT Page, www.aaronshep.com/rt
- Teaching Heart: Reader's Theatre Scripts and Plays, www.teachingheart.net/readerstheater.htm
- Dr. Young's Reading Room, www.thebestclass.org/index.html
- Judy Helton's reader's theatre Pinterest board, pinterest.com/judyhelton/readers-theater
- Busy Teacher's Café: Reader's Theatre, www.busyteacherscafe.com/literacy/readers_theater.html

Making Connections

Check out the reader's theatre websites listed above. With the renewed focus on informational book engagement, locate a "teaching" script that might work for a grade level you are interested in teaching. Think about the number of reading roles, opportunities for expressive reading, and projection. Explore using the script as a content teaching tool through conceptual development and vocabulary instruction. As the teacher, what "talking" points would you note to prepare students prior to reading?

Table 14.3 Self-Assessment for Reader's Theatre Fluency Checklist

Directions: Place a + next to areas you feel you are able to do. Next, place a * next to areas you will focus on to improve. Write out a brief plan to show how you will evidence the improvement.

	Student	Comments
Expression Reading was natural and not phrase by phrase. Raised or lowered voice and showed emphasis where the script indicated, especially on exclamation or question marks.		
Pace or Rate Pace of reading was just fine, neither too fast nor too slow. Read without hesitation; knew all the words.		
Accuracy Able to read fluently and make words sound like they fit in the script.		
Projection Displayed clearness and volume in reading.		

Next time I will focus on _____

_____

I will do this by _____

_____

Source: Ideas taken in part from Zygouris-Coe (2010).

Fluency Checks

A fluency check is a quick assessment of a student's application of the fluency sub-skills. A teacher can check a student's fluency with an oral reading fluency check, and students can monitor their own fluency through the use of checklists. When doing a fluency check, the passage should be unfamiliar to the student and the focus should be on the student's automaticity, rate, prosody, and expression. Fluency checks result in a

WCPM score and a check of prosody using a rubric such as the NAEP Oral Reading Fluency Scale presented in Table 14.1.

Remember that automaticity refers to the capacity of capable readers to read the words in a text correctly with ease so they may use their mental resources to attend to meaning while reading. As we learned, prosody refers to readers' skill in reading a text with appropriate expression and phrasing to reflect the content of the passage. Readers should be taught to monitor and check their reading to support growth in fluency.

Teaching students how to check in with themselves while reading not only helps the teacher collect data on what kind of reader the student is but, with guidance and discussion from the teacher, can help the student become aware of what he or she is misreading and what to look out for. Students can be shown how to take an informal running record with a friend or by themselves. This is a perfect activity for centers while the teacher is meeting with reading groups. They will understand, firsthand, what they are being asked to do and how to get better at reading aloud.

The three most common questions readers can use to check for fluency independently or with peers are provided in Table 14.4. Fluency checks are simple to implement daily in the classroom. These strategies do not take a long time to complete, but they do require the proper amount of time to establish and model for the students what fluent reading is and is not, and how to give constructive feedback.

Table 14.4 Fluency Check Questions for Read-Aloud

Does that look right?	Graphophonic (visual)
Does that sound right?	Syntax
Does that make sense?	Semantic (meaning)

Making Connections

How would you explain to your school principal how fluency is much more than rate per minute or fluency drills to get students to read sight words as quickly as possible without concern for understanding. Tie your ideas about comprehension and fluency into your explanation.

From Fluency to Understanding

Reading fluency is the cornerstone in understanding what is read. Often, what sets "good" readers apart from striving readers is their ability to move from decoding to comprehension. Klauda and Guthrie (2008) found that students who could proficiently comprehend grade-appropriate material could also recognize words in isolation, engage in appropriate prosody, and read with expression during oral reading. As discussed in the previous chapter, comprehension is when the reader makes meaning from the text through the active process of monitoring comprehension and applying appropriate **comprehension strategies** before, during, and after reading.

Building Fluency Through Comprehension Strategies

Teaching strategies to build students' comprehension must focus on improving their thinking before, during, and after reading. The three strategies described below provide opportunities for students to demonstrate and practice these thinking processes in small groups and individually.

Literature Circles

They [students] need substantive opportunities to develop and pursue their own tastes, curiosities, and enthusiasms in the world of books. (Daniels, 2002b, p. 20)

Literature circles are not a new concept for helping students interact with texts independently. They are small temporary groups of students that come together to read and discuss a book they have chosen. Literature circles are about giving students choice and freedom to talk about the texts they want to read. The basic idea behind a literature circle is to get students to talk about literature in an in-depth and focused way, thereby supporting growth in fluency. The conversations are text based and are purposeful and meaningful. Students become the source of inquiry and choose the parts of the text they would like to discuss—where they made connections, what they thought was important, and what kind of language stood out to them—continually returning to the text for evidence/support.

Literature circles can be modified to meet any student's needs or personality (see Figure 14.1 for a list of key features). The adoption of the CCSS has strengthened the necessity for students to become independent "thinkers." The consistent use of literature circles in the English language arts classroom will compel students to think about the text's structure and theme, the author's purpose, and figurative language. It allows students to practice the isolated skills being taught in the required modules, curriculum, or reading series in a real-world setting through discussion, which is exactly what the CCSS is asking them to do.

Reading choices can be focused by selecting books based on themes and genres connected to what students are studying in the reading series, science, or social studies (again, exactly what the CCSS wants us to be doing). A good place to start is by selecting two or three different books of the same theme/genre and holding a whole-group book talk to spark students' interest. Then allow students time to check the books out and write on a slip of paper their name and book choice; a secret ballot helps ensure that students will choose based on interest rather than their friends' choices.

One way to help students focus on what they need to do during literature circles is to use role sheets. Role sheets provide each student with a job, such as discussion director, to focus his or her reading on a particular comprehension strategy. The role of discussion director helps students learn how to ask questions during reading to build comprehension. The role sheets have been adapted with descriptions and examples of the "jobs" (see Appendix E at **www.sagepub.com/grantlit**). Instead of asking students to complete all the jobs, try asking them to complete one job, which makes it less stressful for them. The reading and role sheets are to be completed as homework.

Literature circles provide teachers with the opportunity not only to assess students' comprehension skills through the use of role sheets but also to assess their speaking and

Figure 14.1
Key Ingredients to
Literature Circles

Source: Daniels
(2002b).

Students *choose* their own reading materials.

Small temporary groups are formed, based on book choice.

Different groups read different books.

Groups meet on a regular, predictable schedule to discuss their reading.

Kids use written or drawn notes to guide both their reading and discussion.

Discussion topics come from the students.

Group meeting aims to be open, natural conversations about books, so personal connections, digressions, and open-ended questions are welcome.

The teacher serves as a facilitator, not a group member or instructor.

Evaluation is by teacher observation and student self-evaluation.

A spirit of playfulness and fun pervades the room.

When books are finished, readers share with their classmates and the new groups form around new reading choices.

listening skills. When the students meet for literature circles, they are to share with and listen to their group members. To keep all students on task during group time and to evaluate their listening skills, provide them each with a note-taking sheet (see Appendix F at **www.sagepub.com/grantlit** for an example). Group members are required to jot down notes while listening and sharing. This sheet will be turned in at the end of each group and can be used as a formative assessment. The rubric in Table 14.5 can also be used to assess students' listening, speaking, and writing skills. Assessments drive instruction; by observing the students interacting with the text, you can identify skills needing reinforcement—for example, summarizing, context clues, author's point of view, and higher-level questioning.

Table 14.5 Rubric for Literature Circles				
	Wow 4	Strong 3	Developing 2	Emerging 1
Comprehension	Shows a high level of comprehension. All of the job relates to reading and went beyond the literal level.	Shows high comprehension. Most of the job relates to reading.	Shows a medium level of comprehension. Parts of the job relate to reading.	Shows a low level of comprehension. Job does not relate to reading.
Completion of Job	All aspects of the job are detailed, clear, and relate to reading. Follows directions completely.	Job is complete and includes adequate details. Follows directions.	Job is complete but has limited responses. Some may not relate to reading. Does not follow directions completely.	Work is incomplete. Does not follow directions.
Writing/ Speaking Performance: Organization	Superbly organized and focused.	Organization helps the ideas flow logically.	Organization is unclear and loosely focused.	Organization is very confusing.
Writing Performance: Conventions	Grammar usage contributes to clarity. Free from conventional errors.	One or two grammar and/ or punctuation errors.	Grammar and/ or punctuation errors are common.	Frequent serious disruption in grammar and/ or punctuation.

Making Connections

Literature circles are a powerful tool to support comprehension through group responsibility. Describe what challenges may arise for a student who does not enact his or her role in literature circles. What would be your response as a reading teacher?

Reader Response

Reader response is an incredible way to indulge students in comprehension and fluency through writing about what they are reading or listening to. In the reader response approach to comprehension instruction, the teacher acknowledges that the reading process is a collaboration among the author, the text, and the reader to elicit responses and build comprehension. This type of response to literature is most effective when baseline data are used to create specific questions based on students' needs, but it can also take the form of open-ended questions or journals.

The benefit of using this type of response to literature is that students will begin to analyze and interpret texts guided by questions that help scaffold their thinking. A "while-you-read" question is posed for students to note and to focus their attention while reading or listening to a text. A "takeaway" question, which students must answer in paragraph form, provides scaffolding.

Responding to reading with writing using the "right" guided questions or prompts allows learning to take place and encourages readers to build understandings of the text and their responses to it. Students who are able to answer prompts with paragraphs and/ or complete sentences are consistently working on their writing skills, spelling, grammar, and style. Thus, this strategy, like literature circles, goes beyond ensuring that students meet the reading standards and also ensures that they meet the writing standards.

Figure 14.2 demonstrates how a teacher can collect reader response data on students by providing questions/prompts that assess the students' purpose while reading and their take-away after the reading. The purpose of the "while-you-read" question is to focus students during reading on a particular strategy or literary element, whereas the "takeaway" question reviews students' overall comprehension of the section read. The needs of the group of students in the Figure 14.2 response journals were sequencing, inferencing, figurative language, opinion, and social issues and class systems. Students could share their purpose at the end of the reading and share their response with their partner/group before each new reading.

Close Reading

The idea of a close reading is a new one for many teachers. The CCSS states that students should have time to read texts deeply to build stamina and rigor in their reading abilities. Close reading is a strategy that will help teachers accomplish this requirement of the standards. A close reading is a "careful and purposeful *rereading* of a text" (Fisher, 2014). The text chosen for a close reading should be a **complex text** for students. Students are asked to reread with guided text-based questions and closely analyze the text. The CCSS asks students/teachers to shift away from making connections with the text, which takes students out of a text to analyze it with guided questions and look back into it to find the answers or evidence to support their claims.

The process of a close reading can be varied, and many people have different ideas about how to complete one. The common elements in a close reading are use of short texts, allowing students just to read before "teaching" with the text, text-based questioning, and rereading of the text (Fisher, 2014). At the heart of a close reading, students will read a text multiple times to examine it as if under a microscope. When engaging in a close reading, students use what they find explicitly in the text to answer questions and build understanding.

Close readings must be directly related to the text being read. Some teachers will argue that reading will become stale and boring if students are not allowed to make connections to their knowledge of the world and/or personal knowledge. Close reading requires that when students make connections, they take an extra step to say, "I felt this way when the text said . . ." This very small but vital push on the part of the teacher to have students support their thoughts/ideas with evidence from the text validates the connection as relating to the text.

Figure 14.2
Example Reader Response for *Blood on the River* by Elisa Carbone

Pages 1-18   RJ 1   Chapter 1-3

Today's purpose:

Setting:	Time:	Place:

Response Question:

Reread the last paragraph on page 18. How do you think "power" can be more damaging than fists?

Pages 35-51   RJ 3   Chapter 6 & 7

Today's purpose:

a <u>simile</u> is a figure of speech used to compare two things using the words "like" or "as"	as busy as a bee	
a metaphor is another figure of speech to compare two things; instead of using "like" or "as," it states that one thing "is" another	he is a big fish	

Response Question:

In the book, people are treated differently based on who their parents are: lower born or higher class.

**Should people be treated equally in the New World?

When guiding students to engage in a close reading, teachers have to create **text-dependent questions.** These questions can be answered only by referring explicitly back to the text being read. They do not rely on students' background knowledge or any information extraneous to the text. Text-dependent questions privilege the text itself and what students can extract from that text. This is different from the questions a teacher may use for reader response, in that reader-response questions expect students to use their background knowledge and any outside information they have on the topic of the text.

To assist teachers in developing text-dependent questions, we have included two resources. The first is a guide created by the writers of the CCSS to give teachers a starting point for formulating text-dependent questions (see Table 14.6). The second is a bookmark teachers can use when prereading a text prior to teaching, if they need help determining the text-dependent questions they will ask students (see Figure 14.3).

Table 14.6 Brief Guide to Creating Text-Dependent Questions

Step One: Identify the Core Understandings and Key Ideas of the Text

As in any good reverse engineering or "backwards design" process, teachers should start by reading and annotating the text, identifying the key insights they want students to understand from the text. Keeping one eye on the major points being made is crucial for fashioning an overarching set of successful questions and critical for creating an appropriate culminating assignment.

Step Two: Start Small to Build Confidence

The opening questions should be ones that help orient students to the text. They should also be specific enough so that students gain confidence to tackle more difficult questions later on.

Step Three: Target Vocabulary and Text Structure

Locate key text structures and the most powerful academic words in the text that are connected to the key ideas and understandings, and craft questions that draw students' attention to these specifics so they can become aware of these connections.

Step Four: Tackle Tough Sections Head-On

Find the sections of the text that will present the greatest difficulty and craft questions that support students in mastering these sections (these could be sections with difficult syntax, particularly dense information, and tricky transitions or places that offer a variety of possible inferences).

Step Five: Create Coherent Sequences of Text-Dependent Questions

Text-dependent questions should follow a coherent sequence to ensure that students stay focused on the text, so that they come to a gradual understanding of its meaning.

Step Six: Identify the Standards That Are Being Addressed

Take stock of what standards are being addressed in the series of questions and decide if any other standards are suited to being a focus for this text (forming additional questions that exercise those standards).

Step Seven: Create the Culminating Assessment

Develop a culminating activity around the key ideas or understandings identified earlier that (a) reflects mastery of one or more of the standards, (b) involves writing, and (c) is structured to be completed by students independently.

Source: Student Achievement Partners (n.d., pp. 2–3).

Enacting a close-reading activity promotes fluency at the highest level. Comprehension of the text is enhanced through building deep knowledge of the key information and important ideas located in the text.

Figure 14.3

Bookmark of Text-Based Questions (Close Reading of a Text)

Always ask, "What in the text made you say that?"

Nonfiction Text-Based Questions	Fiction Text-Based Questions
1. How does the information in this text fit with what you already know?	1. What does the author want us to know about _____? (Main idea)
2. What are some of the most important ideas related to this topic?	2. What does _____ mean? How do you know? (Context clues)
3. How has the author made it easy for you to find information?	3. How do the author's words help you paint a picture in your head? (Figurative language)
4. How do the text features (illustrations, graphs, captions, photos) help you understand the passage?	4. What is the author's message to the readers? (Theme)
5. How does the author present information on this topic?	5. How does the sequence of events help develop the story (e.g., first, next, last)? (Plot/story structure)

Building Fluency Through Writing Activities

Writing can be a vehicle for improving reading. (Graham & Hebert, 2010, p. 6)

Writing helps students understand the texts they are reading and helps them learn the skills and processes writers use to create a text. Also, through the act of rereading and writing in response to text, fluency is built. In this section, we present you with writing strategies that will build students' fluency as they engage with text.

Writing in Response to Reading

When students write in response to reading, they build their comprehension of the text. From the earliest stages of literacy learning, students should be encouraged to respond to reading selections. At first, responses will be oral, and then as a child learns to write, he or she can react to teacher read-alouds or instructional reading through the act of writing. Writing in response to reading can take many forms, from oral responses to teacher-directed questions, to reader response journals, to exit slips.

Exit slips, or questions students answer in writing at the end of a lesson, can effectively be used to stimulate deep thinking about events in a reading selection. They function as a check for understanding or formative assessment of the reading selection. Exit slips elicit quick student responses to a question posed by the teacher at the end of a literacy lesson. Likewise, admit slips are used as students enter the classroom; they can function as a check for the previous day's reading concepts or skills (see Figure 14.4).

Admit Slip	Exit Slip
Yesterday we started to read *Blood on the River* in class. Please respond to the following question: In one sentence, tell me what you remember about characters in the book being treated differently based on being a member of the lower class.	We continued to read *Blood on the River* today in class. Please respond to the following question: In one sentence, provide one piece of evidence from the text that details how one character was treated differently based on membership in the lower class.

Figure 14.4

Admit and Exit Slip Examples

Writing to Convey Ideas

One way to encourage students to write about nonfiction texts they are reading is with Gallagher's (n.d.) "Article of the Week" format. This technique is usually used for middle- to upper-level grades to have students analyze, interpret, and respond to a nonfiction text on a weekly basis. Table 14.7 shows a modified outline of this strategy used in a fifth-grade classroom with a *TIME for Kids* article, and Table 14.8 provides a modified rubric for the task.

Table 14.7 Outline for Composing Article of the Week (Fifth-Grade Classroom)

Article of the Week

Questions you need to answer in your response

(Paragraph for each)

Summary

Topic: What is the topic (main idea) of this article?

Use TDDDC to form a paragraph, using facts to prove your answers (yellow highlighted information).

Audience: Who is this article written for? Who is the intended audience?

Purpose: Why was this article written? To entertain, inform, instruct, or persuade?

Use TDDDC to form a paragraph, using facts to prove your answers (yellow highlighted information).

Response

Bias: What is the mood of the article? Do you think the author agrees or disagrees with the topic, or is he or she neutral? Use quotes from the text to support your opinion. (Example of word choice: *father, dad*)

What have you learned from the article this week? Use TDDDC to form a paragraph, using facts to prove your answers (yellow highlighted information).

(Continued)

Table 14.7 (Continued)

*Make sure to use facts, evidence, and relevant details from the article to support your summary and response.

Source: Gallagher (n.d.).

Note: TDDDC is an acronym to help students remember all the structural elements of a paragraph:

Topic sentence

Detail/evidence

Detail/evidence

Detail/evidence

Conclusion sentence

Table 14.8 Article of the Week Rubric (Fifth-Grade Classroom)

Category	4 Excellent	3 Good	2 Fair	1 Unsatisfactory
Topic/ Audience	There is one clear, well-focused topic. Main idea stands out and is supported by detailed information.	Main idea is clear, but the supporting information is general.	Main idea is somewhat clear, but there is a need for more supporting information.	The main idea is not clear. There is a seemingly random collection of information.
Bias and Author's Purpose	Clearly defined the mood of the article. Defines/supports the author's point of view with text evidence. Author's purpose is clearly understood and stated.	Defines the mood of the article. Defines/ supports the author's point of view with some text evidence. Author's purpose is stated.	Defines/supports the author's point of view with little text evidence. Author's purpose is not clearly stated.	Section is missing most or all of the elements of the assignment.
What Have You Learned From This Article? (Personal Reflection)	Paragraph of at least five well-written sentences that includes your personal thoughts in reaction to the ideas presented in the article. Observations are relevant, telling, detailed, and go beyond the obvious and predictable	Personal observation is at least five well-written sentences but may be missing one element of the assignment.	Personal observation may be missing some of the assignment.	Summary is missing many elements of the assignment.
Conventions	Writing contains no errors in spelling or grammar.	Writing contains some errors in spelling or grammar that do not distract the reader from the content.	Writing contains multiple errors in spelling or grammar that somewhat distract the reader from the content.	Errors in spelling and grammar distract the reader from the content of the writing.

Category	4 Excellent	3 Good	2 Fair	1 Unsatisfactory
Evidence of Close Reading (Coding the Text)	Text is well marked with thoughtful annotations throughout. Words are written noting ideas, notes, reminders, and connections. Evidence of a symbol system. Has evidence that you have asked yourself questions about the text (written questions).	Text is marked but missing an element of the required assignment.	Text is marked but missing more than one element.	Text is not marked.

Writing to Promote Fluency

With the advent of the CCSS for writing in Grades 3–5, focus moves from developing creative pieces to "writ[ing] informative/explanatory texts to examine a topic and convey ideas and information clearly" (CCSS.ELA-LITERACY.W.5.2). To generate this type of writing, students draw from prior knowledge, informational children's books, and online resources. With practice, intermediate students become better able to develop a controlling idea and a logical focus on a topic, and more expert at selecting and incorporating pertinent examples, facts, and details in their writing.

The spotlight on **informational/explanatory writing** has the following goal: to convey information accurately. This kind of writing serves one or more closely related purposes:

1. To increase readers' knowledge of a subject

2. To help readers better understand a procedure or process

3. To provide readers with an enhanced comprehension of a concept (New York State Education Department, 2011).

Informational/explanatory writing addresses matters such as

- types (*What are the different types of poetry?*) and components (*What are the parts of a motor?*);
- size, function, or behavior (*How big is the United States? What is an X-ray used for? How do penguins find food?*);
- how things work (*How does the legislative branch of government function?*);
- and why things happen (*Why do some authors blend genres?*) (New York State Education Department, 2011).

They are also able to use a variety of techniques to convey information, such as naming, defining, describing, or differentiating among types or parts; comparing or contrasting ideas or concepts; and citing an anecdote or a scenario to illustrate a point.

Informational/explanatory writing includes a wide array of genres, including

- academic genres such as literary analyses,
- scientific and historical reports,
- summaries, and
- forms of workplace and functional writing such as instructions, manuals, memos, reports, applications, and résumés (New York State Education Department, 2011).

Opportunities for writing in response to expository and narrative text selections are essential to complete the fluency loop. When students compose as a method to engage with text, they necessarily increase their comprehension and fluency overall. This facility is further enhanced when students grow in fluency through multiple interactions with text through reading, rereading, retelling, writing, performing, and discussing. The goal of having a classroom of fluent readers is a worthwhile one.

Students With Special Needs and English Language Learners

Supporting English language learners (ELLs) and students with special needs in developing strategies for fluency and comprehension through reading and writing requires that teachers understand the unique needs of these learners. Fluency can be particularly difficult for ELLs because they struggle with oral language development and may not have a clear understanding of the English language. In addition, students with special needs may have trouble with fluency due to difficulties with memory and/or coding language. Instruction for both of these groups requires that teachers look deeply at how they can extend and expand instruction to meet their students' needs.

> It seemed that our problem-solving meetings were becoming more centered on RTI tiers that identified rate-deficient readers. These students were then placed in intervention groups designed to increase rate and accuracy. Although these interventions did render progress in reading speed, we noticed that many of our students were beginning to ignore punctuation and lack intonation. Worst of all, some could not provide an accurate retelling. (Marcell & Ferraro, 2013, p. 608)

The above quote from teachers Marcell and Ferraro (2013) underscores their objective in developing the Superhero Intervention Plan for Improving Fluency. Although not originally targeted as an intervention plan for struggling ELLs, the strategy would prove valuable for modeling the components of fluent reading in English.

The Superhero Intervention Plan presents an engaging means for turning disfluent readers into prosody superstars. Each week, students ally with Poetry Power Man and his superhero friends to battle the evil Robot Reader and his sidekicks. The Fluency Foursome help students adhere to the multidimensional aspects of fluency, where expression and comprehension are addressed along with rate and accuracy. By the end of the week, students are flying through phrases, leaving Robot Reader in the dust!

Teachers used the fluency development lesson (FDL) as a basis for the battle against disfluency. Weekly elements included (a) the introduction of a short passage or poem, (b) a read-aloud, (c) a content-based discussion, (d) choral reading, (e) paired reading, (f) word study, (g) home practice, (h) performance, and (i) a final rereading, preceding the introduction of the next FDL passage (Rasinski, 2010). Teachers aligned each rereading with a fluency feature or superhero specialty.

Practice #1 introduced Super Scooper and his phrasing technique, Practice #2 brought in Expression Man and his call for voice inflection, and Practice #3 featured Captain Comprehension advocating for summarizing and connecting to deepen understanding. As with the FDL, the final day entailed performances. (Marcell & Ferraro, 2013, p. 609)

As you read this chapter, you recognized that practice building fluency takes many forms. Be reminded of the ultimate fluency goal for readers: mastering the printed text so they may comprehend its deeper meaning (Rasinski, Fawcett, et al., 2010).

Beware! Educators need to be critical consumers of commercial fluency materials such as kits, worksheets, and packages. Schools are lured into buying materials with promises of quick and easy fluency assessments. They abound online and can be limited to measuring reading rate in a push to gain reading speed without comprehension. We do not discount reading rate, as it is an important overall indicator of reading progression; however, recognize that fluency is ultimately "gaining meaning and comprehending the text" (Rasinski, Fawcett, et al., 2010, p. 5).

Key Terms

complex text	oral reading rate
comprehension strategies	reading stamina
informational/explanatory writing	text-dependent questions

Website Resources

- "Reader's Theatre Tips," Reading A–Z

This website contains a wealth of information about reader's theatre, including how it promotes students' oral reading fluency and other literary skills. The site also offers guidelines on using and rehearsing scripts and preparing to perform. There is also a link to 70+ free scripts covering a wide range of abilities. For more information, go to **www.readinga-z.com/ guided/theater.html.**

(Continued)

(Continued)

- **"Literature Circles Build Excitement for Books!" EducationWorld: The Educator's Best Friend**

This article explains what literature circles are, how to use them, and the benefits to students. It includes a clear breakdown of student roles and checklists for student use. It also details how literature circles can be effective for ELLs, poor readers, and reluctant readers. For more information, go to **www.educationworld.com/a_curr/curr259 .shtml.**

- **"Close Reading and the CCSS," Common Core State Standards Toolbox: English Language Arts and Literacy**

This page provides details on what close reading is, its purpose, and how this activity benefits students. It also explains how close reading aligns with the CCSS and includes a YouTube video of Dr. Douglas Fisher discussing close reading and the CCSS. For more information, go to **www.mhecommoncoretoolbox.com/close-reading-and-the-ccss-part-1.html.**

- **"Reader's Theatre," Reading Rockets**

This website contains information on why reader's theatre is effective. It also provides a video showing reader's theatre in action. The site offers guidelines for using and rehearsing scripts and preparing to perform. There are also links to other websites for reader's theatre scripts across content areas. For more information, go to **www.readingrockets .org/strategies/readers_theater.**

- **"Reader's Theatre: A Reason to Read Aloud," EducationWorld: The Educator's Best Friend**

This website contains information on how to implement reader's theatre and how it improves students' oral reading fluency. It provides characteristics of reader's theatre and describes what makes a good script. The site also offers guidelines on using and rehearsing scripts and preparing to perform. There are also links to other websites for accessing scripts and additional information on reader's theatre. For more information, go to **www.education world.com/a_curr/profdev/profdev082.shtml.**

- **"Fluency Passages," Reading A–Z**

This website contains information on fluency and how to conduct an oral reading fluency assessment. The site also gives advice regarding the materials needed to conduct such an assessment, along with a link to 70+ free oral reading fluency passages. For more information, go to **www.readinga-z.com/guided/fluency.html.**

- "Close Reading Packs," Reading A–Z

This website provides texts and text-dependent questions for use in close reading. The resources are leveled so that teachers can easily find complex texts appropriate for any student. For more information, go to **www.readinga-z.com/comprehension/close-reading-packs**.

- "Text-Dependent Question Resources," Achieve the Core

This website contains links to guides for developing text-dependent questions. It also provides techniques for evaluating the questions. For more information, go to **www.achieve thecore.org/page/710/text-dependent-question-resources**.

Student Study Site: Visit the Student Study Site at **www.sagepub.com/grantlit** to access additional study tools including eFlashcards, web resources, and online-only appendices.

SECTION IV

Connecting Readers to Texts

How Can Teachers Decide When Students Are "Connected" to a Text That Meets Their Reading Needs?

Throughout this text, we have highlighted that assessment and instruction are not separate parts of teaching but part of an integrated teaching and learning process. This final section continues this holistic view of literacy assessment and teaching. Chapter 15 discusses matching texts to readers. It highlights how teachers can use what they know about their students to find books and implement classroom procedures that build students who are readers and writers. Chapter 16 takes reading and writing into the realm of new literacies. This chapter focuses on what students need to be successful readers and writers using Internet communication technologies. It highlights the skills and strategies students need to be successful readers and writers in this new modality, in addition to assessment and classroom techniques that can develop student competencies.

CHAPTER 15

Connecting Kids to Texts

Colleen Carroll, Melanie O'Leary, and Nance S. Wilson

Common Core State Standards	
Key Ideas and Details	*RL.3.1* Ask and answer questions to demonstrate understanding of a text, referring explicitly to the text as the basis for the answers.
Craft and Structure	*RL.3.6* Distinguish their own point of view from that of the narrator or those of the characters.
Integration of Knowledge and Ideas	*RL.3.7* Explain how specific aspects of a text's illustrations contribute to what is conveyed by the words in a story (e.g., create mood, emphasize aspects of a character or setting).
Range of Reading and Level of Text Complexity	*RL.3.10* By the end of the year, read and comprehend literature, including stories, dramas, and poetry, at the high end of the grades 2–3 text complexity band independently and proficiently.

Source: © Copyright 2010. National Governors Association Center for Best Practices and Council of Chief State School Officers. All rights reserved.

FOCUS QUESTIONS

1. What is text complexity?

2. How can you match text to students?

3. Think about your classroom library—how diverse is it? Are there plenty of choices for all your students?

4. Have you used graphic novels as part of your instruction? How could they be used to reach reluctant readers or English language learners?

5. Do you make time to conference with students about their reading? What can you learn about your readers?

Words in Action

Finding the Right Book

"Mr. Readmore, Mr. Readmore, look at the book I found in the library. It's all about my favorite baseball player, Derek Jeter!" exclaimed Hank as he ran into the classroom with *The Life You Imagine: Life Lessons for Achieving Your Dreams* (Jeter, 2001).

Mr. Readmore glanced at the book and began to wonder, "How do I know if this book is right for Hank? I know he is interested in baseball, but the audience for this book is typically adults. How can I weigh the text difficulty, Hank's interest, and the requirements of our upcoming independent reading project to ensure that reading this book will be a pleasurable experience for Hank that he can also learn from? How can I make sure that this book is the right match for Hank?"

Students' reading choices do not always match what they should be reading. We want students to have a say, make choices, and be engaged; however, some students will pick the too-easy route, while others will choose an excessively challenging book. We want students to be using books at an appropriate level of difficulty for them, providing a balance between support and challenge; this means matching readers to texts. According to Clay (1991), the text should be easy enough to develop confidence and facilitate comprehension, yet difficult enough to require the reader to do some "reading work."

Students also need opportunities to select from a wide range of texts and to talk about the texts they are reading, independently and with the teacher. In this chapter, we talk about how to match a text to a reader, how to find books for students, and how to help ensure that readers are connecting with the books you have chosen.

> **Making Connections**
>
> Make a list of reasons why you select your reading material. Have you ever asked your students to do this? Compare your answers. How could you use this information to help them and inform your teaching?

Matching Readers to Texts

Just-right text is used for instructional purposes. With this sort of text, the reader can read about 9 out of 10 words and comprehend the meaning of the passage with little difficulty (Clay, 1991). When a child can read 90% to 95% of the words easily, the text is considered to be at that child's instructional reading level—the degree of difficulty at which instruction will be most effective. Easier text is considered to be at the student's independent reading level, while more difficult text is at the frustration level and will require additional teacher support.

Text Complexity

Text complexity is a term brought to the forefront by the Common Core State Standards (CCSS) to highlight that different texts present different reading challenges—challenges students need to experience to ensure that they engage in "reading work," which will continue to develop their skills and strategies. Text complexity is determined by quantitative readability formulas, qualitative features, and an evaluation of the reader and the demands of the task the reader will be asked to perform with the text.

Quantitative Readability Formulas

Quantitative analysis of text leveling has been described by numerous researchers and publishers to guide teachers in determining the text levels for reading instruction. This analysis occurs in the form of **readability formulas**, primarily used to assess the difficulties of a reading passage in the English language. They are also used to assess the grade level of a reader. These formulas evaluate the difficulty of a text based on the length of sentences and words, how often words are repeated, and other issues involving syntactic and semantic features of text. These formulas assume that the longer the sentences and the more complex the words, the more difficult the text. A readability formula is an analytic evaluation of a text that is most often determined by a computer.

The oldest, most trusted readability formula is known as the Flesch method, named after Rudolph Flesch in the 1940s. The Flesch method has become the standard formula used by the U.S. Department of Defense, as well as many other government agencies ("The Flesch

Reading Ease Readability Formula," n.d.). In this formula, the average sentence length and average number of syllables per word determine the reading ease of a text between 0 and 100. The higher the score, the easier the text is to understand (see Table 15.1).

Table 15.1 The Flesch Reading Ease Readability Formula

The specific mathematical formula is

$$RE = 206.835 - (1.015 \times ASL) - (84.6 \times ASW)$$

ASL = Average sentence length (i.e., the number of words divided by the number of sentences)

ASW = Average number of syllables per word (i.e., the number of syllables divided by the number of words)

RE = Readability ease

The output (i.e., RE) is a number ranging from 0 to 100. The higher the number, the easier the text is to read.

- Scores between 90.0 and 100.0 are considered easily understandable by an average fifth grader.
- Scores between 60.0 and 70.0 are considered easily understood by eighth and ninth graders.
- Scores between 0.0 and 30.0 are considered easily understood by college graduates.

Source: "The Flesch Reading Ease Readability Formula" (n.d.).

Another method is the Flesch–Kincaid Grade Level Readability Formula (see Table 15.2), which takes the readability formula a step further and produces a grade-level score. A grade-level score is particularly helpful to parents and teachers because it provides a readability level that can correlate with a student's grade level. Flesch collaborated with Jon Kincaid on this method, and it has been traditionally used in the U.S. Navy, although it is particularly useful in education ("The Flesch Grade Level Readability Formula," n.d.).

Several additional options are available, including the Gunning-Fog Score, the Coleman–Liau Index, the SMOG Index, the Dale–Chall Formula, and the Linsear Write Index. Readability formula calculators can be found online. One such tool, which uses seven different readability formulas to give you a variety of feedback, is the Text Readability Consensus Calculator (available at www.readabilityformulas.com/free-readability-formula-tests.php).

A Lexile score helps determine readability as well and is readily available through school libraries and bookstores. A Lexile can be used to determine either the level of difficulty for a particular text or a reader's ability level. Lexiles are shown as a number ranging from 200 to 1500, usually followed by an L (e.g., 860L). While beginning

Table 15.2 The Flesch–Kincaid Grade Level Readability Formula

Step 1: Calculate the average number of words used per sentence.

Step 2: Calculate the average number of syllables per word.

Step 3: Multiply the average number of words by 0.39, and add it to the average number of syllables per word multiplied by 11.8.

Step 4: Subtract 15.59 from the result.

The specific mathematical formula is

$$FKRA = (0.39 \times ASL) + (11.8 \times ASW) - 15.59$$

ASL = Average sentence length (i.e., the number of words divided by the number of sentences)

ASW = Average number of syllables per word (i.e., the number of syllables divided by the number of words)

FKRA = Flesch-Kincaid reading age

Analyzing the results is a simple exercise. For instance, a score of 5.0 indicates a grade-school level; that is, a score of 9.3 means that a ninth grader would be able to read the document. This score makes it easier for teachers, parents, librarians, and others to judge the readability level of various books and texts for the students.

Theoretically, the lowest grade-level score could be −3.4, but since there are no real passages that have every sentence consisting of a one-syllable word, it is a highly improbable result in practice.

Source: "The Flesch Grade Level Readability Formula" (n.d.).

readers are at Lexiles below 200L, the range can reach up to more than 1600L for the most advanced readers. MetaMetrics (2014) determines the Lexile level of text. The score given is based on two measures, or predictors, of how difficult the text is to comprehend: word frequency and sentence length. Lexile scores are rounded to the nearest 10L.

Lexiles are a good way to begin the book selection process for readers. Once a book's Lexile is known, you can match it to the child's reading level. If measurements to determine a reader's Lexile score are in place, matching children to texts becomes much easier. One such measurement is the *Scholastic Reading Inventory*, a computer-based assessment providing teachers immediate data on student growth to inform instruction. The inventory will provide a teacher with a Lexile score that can help determine if a text is appropriate for students (Scholastic, 2014).

The above quantitative measures of text complexity are only part of the puzzle in matching the reader to a text. This is important to remember, because readability formulas are imperfect. Informational text difficulty can be overestimated and narrative text underestimated (Hiebert, 2012). Thus, it is imperative that prior to matching a text to a reader, the teacher considers the qualitative nature of the text.

Qualitative Analysis

The second factor to enter into the text complexity equation is a **qualitative analysis** of the text. A qualitative analysis reviews the meaning, structure, language, and knowledge demands of a text. The levels of meaning or purpose of the text asks that the teacher evaluate if the text purpose is implicit or explicit and if there are multiple levels of meaning throughout the text. In reviewing the structure, teachers are asked to consider the text organization, use of graphics, and genre in analyzing the text. A text that uses a lot of figurative language, dialects, or academic words should also be considered as more difficult when analyzed by teachers for complexity. Finally, in reviewing the qualitative complexity of a text, the teacher needs to consider the student's background knowledge, as developed by school, life, and cultural experiences.

These reviews are completed by teachers and reading specialists, and are established through comparison with benchmark texts. **Benchmark texts** are those that a range of educators believe can be used as a comparison or guide for analyzing the qualitative nature of texts. When using benchmark texts, it is very important to make sure they have been validated by multiple educators (Hiebert, 2012). Two text-leveling tools that include both qualitative and quantitative analysis of books for readers are guided reading level and Reading Recovery level:

- *Guided reading level (Fountas and Pinnell text-level gradient).* Books are analyzed based on the text characteristics of fiction and nonfiction to determine a level on the gradient of difficulty from A to Z. Fountas and Pinnell (2005) have aligned their letter grades to grade-level equivalencies.
- *Reading Recovery level.* Reading Recovery is a brand-name program that districts can purchase as an intervention for early struggling readers. This system rates books from 1 to 20 on a range of difficulty (Reading Recovery Council of North America, 2014).

Both of these text-leveling systems look at semantic and syntactic difficulty along with genre, content, theme, language, literacy features, and print/book features to determine the appropriate text level:

Evaluation of Reader and Task

The third variable in the text complexity triangle is the reader and the task. When choosing just the right text for students, the teacher must consider the reader's ability as well as the tasks of the reading activity. Reading ability includes a reader's facility with decoding, fluency, and comprehension, along with the reader's background knowledge. Two commercial assessments that can assist teachers in determining a reader's level are the *Developmental Reading Assessment* and Leveled Literacy Intervention:

- The *Developmental Reading Assessment* is used to assess a child's reading level, specifically with accuracy, fluency, and comprehension, to determine his or her independent (instructional) reading level (Pearson Education, 2005). Reading levels range from A, then 1 through 80.
- Leveled Literacy Intervention is a scientifically based system designed to prevent literacy difficulties (Pinnell & Fountas, 2008). The system is a supplemental,

small-group intervention for students who find reading and writing difficult. The goal is to bring students to grade level using leveled texts that place increased demands on the reader, with a gradual challenge. The intensively supportive, yet engaging lessons provide English language learners (ELLs) with the opportunity to expand their abilities (Pinnell & Fountas, 2008).

These levels can be used in conjunction with classroom formative assessment and other measures previously discussed in this text. After teachers determine students' reading levels, they must gauge students' motivation and prior knowledge to determine the appropriateness of a text.

Now the teacher needs to determine if the tasks he or she requires of students will provide them with an appropriate amount of "reading work" to learn reading skills and strategies and to learn from the text during reading. The teacher can do this by asking two general questions:

- *What is the purpose of the reading?* If students are reading a text independently (e.g., for a book report), they may need a text that is less complex than one they are reading as part of the instructional program.
- *What types of questions will be asked of the readers?* Teachers will need to determine if students will be asked to engage in literal, inferential, or analytical thinking as they read the text. They need to evaluate how students will gather evidence to support their responses to questions and what difficulties they may encounter when engaging in these activities.

Once a teacher is armed with this information, he or she can use it along with the quantitative and qualitative evaluation of the text to determine if it is complex enough to be "just right" for the student.

Classroom Libraries

By knowing the levels of available texts, teachers can build a differentiated classroom library that supports the variety of reading abilities in the classroom. Well-developed libraries are established over time, as it takes effort and financial resources to fill the library and keep it stocked, orderly, and up-to-date. A classroom library that meets the needs of all the readers in the classroom will have books of varying genres and subjects to entice readers with all different interests. It will also span the range of readability levels of the students in the classroom so there is an appropriate independent book choice for everyone.

A classroom should emit a welcoming aura that gives students a sense of comfort and belonging. A well-stocked, organized classroom library can be the heart of the classroom and one of the main areas that help students feel connected and comfortable. Involving students in the organization process and even setup of the library is one way to create a sense of belonging (Fountas & Pinnell, 2001). When students have ownership in the process, they are more likely to take advantage of the resources, account for their whereabouts, and keep the materials organized. Surveying students on their interests as well as favorite authors and genres can give a teacher a solid baseline of information for what to include on the shelves, as well as help him or her learn about the students as readers. Table 15.3 is a sample of a survey to give your students at the beginning of the school year.

Table 15.3 Student Reading Interest Survey

Name: _____

1. Why do you read?

_____

_____

_____

_____

2. What do you like to read?

_____

_____

_____

_____

3. How often do you read at school and home?

_____

_____

_____

_____

4. What is the best thing you ever read and why?

_____

_____

_____

_____

5. What have you learned from reading?

_____

_____

_____

_____

6. How would you help someone who is learning to improve his or her reading?

_____

_____

_____

_____

7. As a reader, is there some way you would like to improve your reading?

_____

_____

_____

_____

8. How could I help you improve?

_____

_____

_____

_____

9. Is there anything else you would like to share about reading?

_____

_____

_____

_____

Making Connections

During a long-term substitute teaching position for a Grade 4 class, I was fortunate to be in a classroom with a wide range of rich reading material for students. To make sure we were taking advantage of this resource, each student was responsible for a weekly bag of books. The rules were to exchange books on their assigned day and choose at least four to five new books: two to three that were "just right," one that was easy, and one "just because." "Just because" meant that the book was a favorite or funny or a challenge or looked like it might be interesting. These student-chosen books were then used during individual conferences, which guided group and whole-class workshop instruction. The student survey in Table 15.3 was used during conferences and aided in workshop organization.

A classroom library may be the most accessible resource for reading materials that a student has all year. Therefore, a varied, interesting, and accessible collection is critical

(Fountas & Pinnell, 2001). There are many ways to set up a thriving classroom library; however, a diverse collection should include the following:

- Leveled books for guided reading
- Independent reading books in various levels and genres
- Reference books to use as resources for reading or writing (e.g., dictionaries, thesauruses, atlases)
- Short-story collections
- New, award-winning books (e.g., Caldecott, Newbery, Coretta Scott King)
- Books in a series (e.g., *Harry Potter*, *Junie B. Jones*, *Diary of a Wimpy Kid*)
- Poetry anthologies
- Age-appropriate, high-interest short texts (e.g., magazines, newspapers, journals)
- Environmental print (e.g., maps, charts, graphs, infographics, labels and boxes on a ring)
- Picture and illustrated books, particularly related to the current theme in science or social studies
- Teacher read-aloud collection
- Student-published books/writing
- Books about the arts (e.g., fine art, dance, theatre, music)
- High-interest nonfiction texts (e.g., space, animals, oceans)

The organization of the library is important. Be thoughtful about the arrangement, showcasing new and interesting reads and pulling out books that relate to the current themes either in the news or curriculum. Display books on stands, on top of bookcases, and in open plastic bins organized by level or category for easy student access. The books that get seen the most get chosen the most, so rotate the top books often. If space allows, comfortable seating areas with lamps, plants, and other welcoming features create a relaxing and inviting space that beckons readers.

Students need to experience that reading is related to the real world. By consistently giving book talks, reading aloud to the class, and making connections among different texts (e.g., the picture book, the nonfiction text, and the magazine article on space exploration), students will have a much easier time finding the resources they need or want to study. Students should keep track of their independent reading as well. This helps them (and you) visually account for the amount of reading each student is getting done. The most fluent students typically read more words per year than their peers. A student reading log, such as the one in Table 15.4, can be helpful in tracking this information.

A teacher's knowledge of his or her collection, as well as his or her enthusiasm, is very important in "selling" a good read. However, don't forget that students can often be the best "salespeople." Ask students to give a quick book talk by summarizing a piece of the story, making sure to leave out the ending. Getting students excited about the contents of the library and then giving them time to browse and choose from its contents are the keys to independent reading interest.

Interactive Book Reports

Connecting kids to texts is a fascinating exercise in coercion, and who better to do that than the kids themselves. This harks back to the need for book reports—not the traditional

Table 15.4 Student Reading Log

Name: _____

Directions: As you read, it is necessary to keep track of your reading. Please fill in the table, beginning with the title and author. Once you have finished the book, fill in the date, the genre, and whether it was easy (E), just right (JR), or too hard (H).

Title	Author's Name	Date	Genre	E, JR, or H

book report we may remember and dread but the sales-pitch book report, with a voting component that will appeal to the creativity of our young students while also fulfilling the CCSS literacy need of public speaking.

Much like a "show and tell" where students share an experience with their classmates, the sales-pitch book report is a little telling about the book followed by reasons why someone else might like it. There could/should be a marketing component and a "thumbs-up" rating by the students as to whether they think anyone else should read the book.

Leading questions might include the following:

- Why did you choose the book? What made you want to read it?
- Did it live up to your expectations? Was it about what you thought it would be about?
- What was your favorite part of the book? Favorite chapter? Favorite character? Why?
- What didn't you like about the book, if anything?
- Who would like this book? Kids who like what kinds of stories?
- Do you think it would appeal more to girls or boys?
- How would you rate this book? On a scale of 1 to 5 thumbs-up, how many thumbs-up would you give this book?

Supporting media for the book report may be a poster or picture; a sculpture or model of a scene, character, or incident; a little video; or even a role play. It could be anything the student thinks will help others decide whether or not to read the book.

After the book report, have the other students indicate, on a scale of 1 to 5, what their inclination is to read this book, based on the student's report. Track the students' progress on their ability to speak publicly, form an effective persuasive argument, and garner votes. The payoff for you is a list of books that kids will enjoy to add to your classroom library!

Multicultural Children's Literature

A fully stocked classroom library should include a selection of multicultural books and stories to reflect the world we live in and that children today are growing up in. Consider representing not only different racial groups but also various religions, ages, and genders. Wonderful books at appropriate levels exist today, and with a little effort, your classroom library can be an excellent resource for introducing children to the wide world of culture. Children need to see themselves reflected in the stories they read to help them make connections. Conversely, many children are not exposed to the differences among people if not through their classroom environment, mainly through books and stories.

Some of your children's favorite stories will include exciting tales of others' lives, traditions, rituals, and ceremonies. Be sure to read the selections first with a critical lens to ensure that the choices do not include any overt or covert stereotyping, bigoted language or racism, sexism, or ageism. The Council for Interracial Books for Children provides excellent guidelines to assess what you include in your library. The wide variety of multicultural literature available today leaves no excuses for having an ethnocentric collection (Fountas & Pinnell, 1996).

Multicultural children's literature may also provide the hook to reading that many ELLs need. They may more easily construct meaning from a text that contains familiar elements because their background knowledge helps them make predictions and inferences about a story (Freeman & Freeman, 2004). Culturally relevant books support ELLs' understanding of their reading, resulting in increased engagement and motivation.

Making Connections

My first teaching assignment was a Grade 5 class in North Carolina. All my students were African Americans and ELLs from Mexico with varying English-language abilities. I am a white Canadian—how could I relate to and teach these students? The answer was multicultural literature. We read *The Watsons Go to Birmingham* (by Christopher Paul Curtis), *Esperanza Rising* (by Pam Munoz Ryan) and *Anne of Green Gables* (by Lucy Maud Montgomery), and searched for the common theme—people moving in search of a better life. All the while, we shared our own stories and learned about one another—building connections among the stories, our connections to the stories, and connections among ourselves.

Children's Choice Book Lists

Children's feedback on their favorite books is invaluable to you as a teacher. In a perfect world, you would be able to read every book you'd like to recommend to children. Since that is not possible, feedback from children allows you to put into your students' hands books they may like, based on classmates' referrals. While you can encourage book referrals among peers in your own classroom, the annual Children's Choices Reading List, published by the International Reading Association with the Children's Book Council, accepts submissions from children with the help of an adult. For more information about the International Reading Association and the Children's Choices Reading List, see the "Website Resources" section at the end of this chapter.

Self-Selected Text

Students need adult support and guidance in choosing texts that are appropriate for them. Factors such as level and interest come into play, as well as more subtle areas of teacher concern such as ensuring that students are reading a wide variety of genres. Therefore, it is necessary to teach students how to select appropriate texts for their own independent reading. Enticing them to choose books beyond what their friends are reading (and are capable of reading, as this may be very different) should be in every teacher's bag of tricks.

Books selected at the appropriate reading level for the student are often known as "good-fit" books (Boushey & Moser, 2009). These books are in an appropriate Lexile range so that a student can comprehend what he or she is reading with little difficulty. Too often, students, especially in the upper elementary grades, equate being a "good reader" with word calling. They believe that reading means fluency and expression; however, comprehension is sometimes missing. In many cases, the child does not even realize it. A teacher needs to explicitly instruct students to choose books that are appropriate for them.

Gail Boushey and Joan Moser (2009), authors of *The Café Book*, liken the process of choosing a "good-fit" book to that of choosing a pair of shoes to wear. They bring in a bag of all kinds of footwear to help students connect purpose with choice. One would not wear rain boots to play soccer or cleats to a birthday party. Likewise, book choice is based on purpose as well, such as when pursuing a favorite author, reading the third book in a series, or conducting research on a nonfiction topic of interest. They continue the analogy with the subject of interest as well. We choose shoes to match our interests, such as the shoes we wear for certain sports. Likewise, we pursue books that match our interests. Helping students recognize that interest plays an important role in choosing the right book will make them more apt to read independently, which in turn will make them better readers. Once the shoe analogy is presented to students, it can be used as a fun reference all year long.

Graphic Novels

There was a time when graphic novels had only a small, almost cult-like fan base of enthusiasts, much like the comic-book crowd. More recently, however, graphic novels—complete with interesting characters and plots, and captivating illustrations—have risen in their appeal to a wider audience of children, and they are now being considered as a positive alternative to more traditional forms of literature. While graphic novels are unusual in style, resembling a comic book more than they do "real text," their usefulness as a means of motivating reluctant readers cannot be denied.

The word *graphic* in this sense refers to the sequential series of illustrations that tell a story when viewed in order (Graphix, n.d.). A **graphic novel** tells a story in comic format but is longer in length and development of the narrative. This combination is a winner with many children, who are highly attracted to this style. Teachers and librarians are catching on, too, and are filling their libraries and classrooms with books by authors such as Jeff Smith, who writes the *Bone* series, and Dav Pilkey, author of the well-known *Captain Underpants* and *Super Diaper Baby* series. Acceptance for these types of books is growing, as the quality of those being published increases. The American Library Association has recognized graphic novels as a form of storytelling much like traditional novels, or movies or picture books, and established an annual list of Great Graphic Novels for Teens (Graphix, n.d.). With literary awards also going to graphic novelists in recent years, this book style has established a firm foothold in modern-day reading.

The myth about graphic novels is that they are easy reading and do not challenge students enough. This theory is inaccurate for contemporary work. In fact, graphic novels can be leveled the same way as other books and can be given a Lexile measure, a grade-level equivalent score, and an appropriate age range based on maturity. Even as they attract lower-achieving and reluctant readers, these books are often known to include more difficult vocabulary than other books at the same age or interest level. The reader is required to stay actively engaged with the text and illustrations to get through and understand the story, which demands critical thinking skills and simultaneously drawing on numerous reading strategies, such as decoding and monitoring comprehension. Add this to the high interest level for so many readers, and one can understand why graphic novels are creating a big buzz in literature today.

An additional feature of graphic novels is their benefit to struggling readers, students with special needs, and ELLs. The illustrations in graphic novels provide contextual clues to support the written narrative. For autistic readers, the illustrations provide clues to emotional content, and for ELLs, they motivate students to acquire new vocabulary and increase English proficiency (Graphix, n.d.).

Book Introductions

A book introduction may provide one of the student's first impressions of a story. It is not only the teacher's opportunity to "sell" the book to students but also a way to prepare students for a guided reading lesson or unit. The way a book is introduced may be different each time, depending on the needs of the students or the book itself.

The amount of support given in an introduction is reflected in the needs of the group. Some books may have unusual concepts or vocabulary that need explaining. Beginning readers often need more detailed introductions than do experienced readers. It is also important that students know the parts of a book and that they check the title and pictures on the cover. Ann Staman (n.d.) suggests trying to give equal emphasis to meaning, language, and print cues in introductions, because the cues you stress in your introduction can influence how your students read that text.

Summarizing the book should also include a talk about the illustrations. Make sure to take the time to clarify misconceptions if you think students will become confused during reading.

Checking Connections

Student Think-Alouds

Using think-alouds during reading is an excellent way to assess what students are thinking about or attending to while they are reading. Think-alouds give teachers insight into how much sense the student is able to make of the text. According to Serafini (2010), they are a window for generating immediate reactions to texts. They are a great way to assess how students are connecting to the text. Some possible think-aloud questions to ask during reading include the following:

- What has happened so far?
- What has caught your eye in the illustrations?
- What is most important in the story so far?
- What are you noticing?
- What are you thinking about?
- What connections are you making to the text and illustrations?

Connections help us understand text. Not being able to relate a text to anything we have experienced can significantly diminish our comprehension of that text (Serafini, 2010).

Peer Connections

Working with their peers provides students with an authentic audience and increases motivation, especially for reluctant readers. Students become excited about sharing opportunities, forming book clubs and discussion groups, and having read-aloud sessions. They value the social interactions with peers to help them choose their own books. Peer connections also allow students to receive different views and learn to read critically, because collaborative peer-led groups promote achievement, higher-level thinking skills, and the intrinsic desire to read, as well as helping develop social insights, creativity, and literacy skills (Gambrell, Mazzoni, & Almasi, 2000).

Building reading connections through peer work is especially important for ELLs and students with special needs. According to Hollenbeck (2010), for this to be successful, it is essential to root comprehension strategies in the foundation of active engagement with constructing meaning while reading. Students of all ability levels must be taught that successful readers employ comprehension strategies for a variety of purposes before, during, and after reading, and this must be transparent for all readers during discussions about books. Orfano (2012) notes that when working with peers, students with special needs

- strengthen their communication skills through conversing and socially interacting with classmates,
- strengthen their critical thinking skills, and
- model the problem-solving and behavioral techniques exhibited by peers in the group.

Conferencing With Readers

Independent reading block is an excellent opportunity for teachers to take a few minutes to chat with each child about the book he or she is reading. Where we once engaged in DEAR time, when students and teachers would "drop everything and read," we now recognize that although the modeling of independent reading is important, teachers' time is more valuably spent conversing with students about their reading and taking notes on what they learn (Fountas & Pinnell, 1996). During this quiet independent reading time, the teacher will work with one student at a time, listening to him or her read, having a quick discussion, and taking notes on what occurred.

Conferences should be focused conversations with students that provide detailed information about their reading in a short amount of time; to be effective, conferences must be specifically tailored to the needs of each student. Teachers should ask questions and take notes, recording student answers and their own observations to track growth over time (see Table 15.5 for a sample template for recording these observations). The most productive conferences occur when teachers act as "reading coaches," creating goals for students to work toward and guiding them in using the reading strategies taught in class while they read independently. Conferences should occur daily if possible, especially with struggling readers. Conferences with ELLs and students with special needs provide the teacher with insights about reading development and allow students to showcase their reading progress over time; ideally, these should happen several times per week. Conferences with proficient or advanced readers should happen once or twice a week.

Conferencing about what skills the student is working on during independent reading time helps the child think about the strategies used while reading and builds ownership of and

Table 15.5 Student–Teacher Conference Observations

Student Name: _____

Date and Book Title	Focus Question	Observation–Student Response

independence in his or her reading. This is an important practice, as noted throughout the CCSS. It also gives you information about the students' abilities today, whereby you can set practical, relevant next steps to help students continue to achieve incremental growth in their reading ability. Students, too, become comfortable with the language that helps them understand themselves as readers. Conferences, as with direct instruction, are an opportunity for discussions around the words that describe the reading process, such as *fluency, comprehension,* and *vocabulary* (Boushey & Moser, 2009). As students learn to use these words appropriately to describe themselves as readers, they will gain independence in their own learning.

Reader Self-Assessment

Good readers think critically and monitor their understanding while they are reading. They think about what they are reading and make connections to the text from their own lives and the world around them. They realize when the text is hard to read and when their comprehension breaks down. Good readers automatically employ several strategies while reading to help them understand complex text, while struggling readers do not. It is critically important that readers self-assess while reading and, when the text is no longer making sense, that they use strategies to help. Several examples of self-assessment while reading include the following:

- *Summarizing information:* Readers should be able to stop and summarize what they have read. If they cannot, then good readers know that their understanding has broken down.

- *Asking questions:* By asking questions and trying to find the answers in the text, readers can tell if they are comprehending or not. If they cannot find the answers to their questions or if the text is so difficult that even the questions are hard to ask, then this technique should highlight the problem.
- *Visualization:* Texts that use vivid language should allow the reader to visualize the information. A reader who is unable to create a picture in his or her mind may be having difficulty understanding the text.
- *Making a prediction:* Readers can assess their understanding by determining if they can make a prediction of what will happen farther along in the text. If they have enough information that they can attempt to predict the outcome, their understanding of the material is most likely higher than if they cannot.

By using these and other techniques to determine if they understand the text, readers can self-assess the appropriateness of the text level as well as their interest in it. If the text is too hard, they can move to an easier Lexile level and begin these techniques again to see if the text is a better fit. If the text is very easy for the reader, the above should happen quickly and without struggle, in which case the reader may want to choose a more challenging book. It is essential that teachers explicitly instruct students in these methods to ensure that they are monitoring their reading and assessing their comprehension.

Matching texts to readers requires that teachers evaluate text complexity, have an in-depth understanding of their students' reading abilities and interests, have access to a wide range of texts, and keep tabs on their readers during the reading process. The teacher needs to continually develop his or her knowledge of available books while building the classroom library to ensure that students have access to a range of options. Furthermore, the teacher needs to ensure that the classroom environment supports not just formative assessment of reading but also the discussion of books and reading.

Key Terms

benchmark texts

graphic novel

just-right text

multicultural children's literature

qualitative analysis

quantitative analysis

readability formulas

text complexity

Website Resources

- "50 Multicultural Books Every Child Should Know," Cooperative Children's Book Center (CCBC)

The CCBC is a library in the School of Education at the University of Wisconsin–Madison; its book collection includes current, historical, and retrospective books for children and adolescents. The CCBC is committed to identifying excellent literature for children and adolescents and to bringing this literature to adults who have an academic or professional interest in connecting young readers with books. They believe that children and adolescents "deserve excellent literature which reflects their own experience and encourages them to imagine experiences beyond their own," satisfying their curiosity and giving them an invitation to dream. To see their recommended list of multicultural books for children and adolescents, go to **ccbc.education.wisc.edu/books/detailListBooks.asp?idBookLists=42.**

- **"Reading Partnerships," Scholastic**

This site outlines a strategy for engaging all students in meaningful reading partnerships through instruction for inventing open-ended questions and regular meetings to discuss a familiar text. For the lesson plans and required reproducibles, go to **www.scholastic.com/teachers/lesson-plan/reading-partnerships.**

- **"Children's Choices Reading List," International Reading Association (IRA)**

The IRA is a nonprofit, global network of individuals and institutions devoted to worldwide literacy. It supports literacy professionals through a wide range of resources, including professional development, research and advocacy, lesson plans, awards, and grants. One of the website's features is the Children's Choices Reading List, developed using recommendations submitted online by teachers, librarians, parents, and children. For more information, go to **www.reading.org/Resources/Booklists/ChildrensChoices.aspx.**

- **National Council of Teachers of English (NCTE)**

NCTE is a professional organization that supports research and teaching in the language arts at all levels of education, from kindergarten to university. Its website provides a wealth of resources for both members and nonmembers, including professional development opportunities, advocacy, public education, grants, newsletters, and lesson plans. NCTE is committed to supporting all classroom learners. For more information, go to **www.ncte.org.**

- **"Reading Tips for Children With Special Needs," First 5: Contra Costa Children and Families Commission**

This article provides parents and teachers with nine easy-to-follow tips and suggestions to keep children with special needs engaged in their reading and to make reading a positive experience. To view the tips and for more information, go to **www.firstfivecc.org/blog/index.php/2011/09/reading-tips-for-children-with-special-needs.**

Student Study Site: Visit the Student Study Site at **www.sagepub.com/grantlit** to access additional study tools including eFlashcards, web resources, and online-only appendices.

CHAPTER 16

Assessing New Literacies and Media Literacies

Justin Gray and Laura Baker

Standards	
Creativity and Innovation	*ISTE Standard 1* Students demonstrate creative thinking, construct knowledge, and develop innovative products and processes using technology.... Create original works as a means of personal or group expression.
Communication and Collaboration	*ISTE Standard 2* Students use digital media and environments to communicate and work collaboratively, including at a distance, to support individual learning and contribute to the learning of others.... Communicate information and ideas effectively to multiple audiences using a variety of media and formats.
Integration of Knowledge and Ideas	*CCRA.R.7* Integrate and evaluate content presented in diverse media and formats, including visually and quantitatively, as well as in words. (Please see the writing standards on "research to build and present knowledge" and speaking and listening standards on "comprehension and collaboration" for additional standards relevant to gathering, assessing, and applying information from print and digital sources.)
Production and Distribution of Writing	*CCRA.W.6* Use technology, including the Internet, to produce and publish writing and to interact and collaborate with others.

Source: © Copyright 2007. International Society for Technology in Education. © Copyright 2010. National Governors Association Center for Best Practices and Council of Chief State School Officers. All rights reserved.

FOCUS QUESTIONS

1. What kinds of technology do you use in your classroom? Explain why you make the technology choices you do.

2. Have you read an e-book? Would you be willing to allow your students to use them? Why or why not?

3. How can your English language learners or students with special needs benefit from using technology in the classroom?

4. After reading about podcasting, what benefits for classroom literacy do you envision?

5. Would you consider using digital storytelling and WebQuests as ways to assess your students? Why or why not?

6. What classroom applications do you see for blogging? How could blogging support writing practice?

Words in Action

Charlie

Charlie is in Mrs. O's Grade 4 class. He is well liked and is involved in a lot of extracurricular activities, but Mrs. O is worried about him. As part of the regular class routine, on Mondays students write to her about their weekend. Charlie labors the whole writing time and generally ends up with just three sentences: "It was a good weekend," "I had fun," and a final sentence stating one thing he did. There are usually several spelling mistakes and never any details. But talking to Charlie about his weekend is a completely different story; he would talk for more than half an hour if given the opportunity.

After attempts at partner writing, scribing, and time on the computer and on the computer with a cowriter, Mrs. O gave Charlie an iPad with Dragon Dictation (a free voice-to-text app). The results were astounding. Charlie "wrote" two pages about his weekend, including organization, extensive details, and a humorous incident.

Now Charlie can hardly wait for writing time, and using the iPad to assist is part of his daily routine.

Introduction and Rationale for Assessment

As we equip kindergarten classrooms with iPads . . . , middle school students with Kindles . . . , and high school libraries with Nooks . . . , it is realistic to imagine a time when the traditional conceptualization of a book no longer exists. (Karchmer-Klein & Shinas, 2012, p. 288)

Literacy no longer exists solely on the page; rather, the digital revolution has brought with it new forms and ideas of what it means to become literate. As technological literacy becomes a larger part of everyday life, and a requirement for many careers, it becomes necessary for teachers to integrate these new literacies into instruction. With this in mind, it is then the teacher's responsibility to employ appropriate means of assessing student understanding of the unique skills that come with this relatively new territory. Additionally, with the advent of the Common Core State Standards and initiatives such as the Partnership for 21st Century Skills (www.p21.org), expectations are set for students to use and become literate in these new technologies.

iStock.com/Feverpitched

Many of the technologies that fall under the umbrella of new media are referred to as **information communication technologies** (ICTs) and come in many different forms, such as the Internet, Facebook, e-books, iPads, and so on (Henry, 2006). Essentially, any method that delivers information electronically, or digitally, can be considered an ICT. Just like the rapid evolution of technology, ICTs are always changing, making it the responsibility of the literacy teacher to be up-to-date on the latest technology (International Reading Association, 2009).

⌐ Making Connections

Turn to your partner and discuss some of the ICTs you are familiar with. What was available to you when you were a student? How have things changed over the years? What might be some challenges in using this form of ICT in the classroom?

The students of today's classrooms are already exposed to the digital world and technology culture that surrounds them—and they have been since birth. Many of these students have grown up with computers in the home, have surfed the Internet, and have, in some capacity, used a smartphone or tablet computer. These wired individuals born after 1980 are referred to as **digital natives**. Those who were not born into this digital world are known as **digital immigrants** (Prensky, 2001).

- *Digital natives:* Those born into technology. Those who are well versed in computers, video games, and the Internet. Technology comes naturally to them.
- *Digital immigrant:* Those born before the digital age who have adopted many aspects of technology but still have difficulty fully understanding it and integrating it into their lives. They can often struggle with learning new technology.

The challenge for many teachers, whether digital natives or digital immigrants, is to understand that this technology is the new language of today's students—and of the professional world. Students are more connected now than ever. An effective literacy teacher can use these trends to aid in the instruction of his or her students, connecting them to students around the world, helping them grasp a more effective understanding of the English language, and providing additional scaffolding to students with special needs. However, the literacy teacher must understand that these new technologies and literacies demand new understandings and, therefore, new means of assessment. While the ICTs may continuously change as technology evolves—and, typically, students are at the forefront of nascent technology trends—developing a framework for new literacy assessment has become a hot educational topic.

> Today's students have mastered a large variety of tools that we will never master with the same level of skill. From computers to calculators to MP3 players to camera phones, these tools are like extensions of their brains. Educating or evaluating students without these tools makes no more sense to them than educating or evaluating a plumber without his or her wrench. (Prensky, 2005, p. 12)

As can be seen in Table 16.1 and the quote above, a heavy emphasis has been placed on giving students the technological tools they are familiar with and will need in their future careers.

Table 16.1 International Reading Association's Student Rights Regarding ICTs

Students have a right to...	
Peers who use ICTs responsibly and actively share effective strategies applied to a range of literacy purposes and settings.	Teachers who use ICTs skillfully for teaching and learning effectively.
A literacy curriculum that offers opportunities to collaboratively read, share, and create content with peers from around the world.	Literacy instruction that embeds critical and culturally sensitive thinking into print and digital literacy practices.
State reading and writing standards that include new literacies.	State reading and writing assessments that include new literacies.
School leaders and policymakers committed to advocating the use of ICTs for teaching and learning.	Equal access to ICTs for all classrooms and all students.

Source: International Reading Association (2009, p. 1).

With this in mind, we turn to both the integration of these forms of ICT in the classroom and best practices in assessing student use of this technology. If students are going to be expected to use these new literacies in both the classroom and the workplace, then it is important to develop a framework for the assessment of these new skills and understandings. As you will see, assessing student reading comprehension based on a webpage requires a different array of skills and understandings than if that student were reading a passage on a written page. Table 16.2 highlights some key principles that will make understanding the goals of assessing these new literacies a bit clearer.

Table 16.2 Four Principles for Supporting New Literacies in the Classroom	
1. Keep Your Eye on the Moving Target Literacy is always changing as technology advances. An effective teacher should try to keep up-to-date on new technologies as much as possible.	**2. Recognize the Complexity of New Literacies** Technological literacy demands a new set of skills that differ from the traditional reading comprehension activities.
3. Digital Natives Still Have a Lot to Learn A teacher cannot assume that a student knows everything about technology simply because he or she is a digital native. A teacher should never go into instruction with the assumption that the students are skilled with a particular form of ICT.	**4. Reconsider Assessment Methods** A teacher attempting to teach new literacies in the classroom must also find new ways of assessing these literacies. Each form of ICT used in the classroom should be assessed based on the student's use of the technology features in addition to the traditional features of literacy.

Source: Adapted from Karchmer-Klein and Shinas (2012).

To support these goals, in this chapter we discuss a variety of ICTs that are critical to new literacies and can be assessed and integrated into classroom instruction. This chapter also addresses other forms of technology enactment that can be used in lesson plans and other classroom activities to heighten student engagement and help digital natives use the technology that is present in their everyday lives.

Online Reading Comprehension

We can no longer assume that a standardized assessment of a student's offline reading comprehension ability will adequately measure important skills that influence online reading performance. (Coiro, 2009, p. 60)

As previously alluded to in this chapter, successfully reading an offline document requires different skills than reading a document online. Just as it is important for students to understand the various features included in a physical text, so, too, is it imperative for students to become familiar with the features that are unique to reading online. In the world of Google, Facebook, and Twitter, students must become familiar with new ways of searching for and comprehending information (Coiro, 2009). Our digital native students, even though they may be familiar with the technology they are using, still need to be provided with and assessed on the skills that will allow them to use the powerful technology they have access to.

Unlike traditional books and texts, the information provided online is presented through different multimedia features. Learning to navigate, synthesize, and understand interactive graphs, tables, photo albums, timelines, and navigation bars is integral to online reading comprehension. Additionally, the manner and methods in which online reading takes place in the classroom differ greatly from the reading of traditional books.

As noted in Table 16.3, the skills necessary for online reading comprehension include being able not only to repeat information and understand text features but also to evaluate the validity of the information presented and to navigate and search through a nonlinear web of information. Due to the differences between offline and online reading, it has been noted that many high-achieving offline readers struggle with online reading because of the new skills required (Coiro, 2009).

Table 16.3 Traditional Reading Versus Online Reading	
Traditional Reading	**Online Reading**
Reading can take place mostly with the whole class or in small groups. Readers can be grouped together by level.	Reading is often a more individualized experience. Each student is typically at his or her own computer.
Writers/sources are generally thought of as authoritative by virtue of being published.	The validity of information often takes evaluation, since anyone can publish material on the Internet.
Information typically consists of text, with some pictures and graphs.	Multimedia such as hyperlinks, audio, video, and pictures are often part of the reading experience.
Information usually flows sequentially, starting at the beginning of the book and finishing at the end.	Information can be nonlinear, with hyperlinks leading to other pieces of writing. The reading experience is not sequential.
Reading is focused on the page. The reader does not have much of a choice in what he or she is reading.	Reading can be full of choice. Hyperlinks can take students to pages of interest as well as provide opportunities for responding and giving feedback.

Source: Adapted from Hodgson (n.d.).

This is not to say that the skills required for the comprehension of a traditional text no longer apply. As with reading a traditional text, students must become familiar with all the different textual and visual features. For example, a webpage could include pictures, diagrams, and sidebars, just like a traditional book, but all the other options, such as hyperlinks, can confuse students (Malloy & Gambrell, 2006). Therefore, understanding exactly what the new literacies of online reading entail is important to properly assess a student's abilities in this area (see Table 16.4).

The four new literacies of online reading comprehension can be applied to any sort of task students might be asked to complete. Additionally, these literacies spiral throughout the K–12 curriculum, with the expectation of increased complexity. Typically, these literacies would be assessed on a research task for which students have to search the Internet using a search engine (Google, Bing, Yahoo, etc.) or search the content of a selected website (see Table 16.5 for an example). By applying these

Table 16.4 The New Literacies of Online Reading Comprehension

Reading to Locate Information	A student must be able to use the features of the webpage or online document to locate relevant information based on the task given.
Reading to Critically Evaluate Online Information	A student must be able to determine the validity and credibility of the website in question. Is the website created by a legitimate entity? Is it a community webpage on which anyone can post?
Reading to Synthesize Online Information	Unlike offline reading, students are continuously creating a singular and cohesive text in their heads as defined by the choices they make in online reading, such as skipping certain pages and following relevant hyperlinks.
Reading to Communicate Online Information	Once students have synthesized the text, they should communicate what they have learned through e-mail, text message, or instant message. Students should reread messages before they send them to make sure they are clear. The communication of information in real time is critical to problem solving and collaboration with colleagues and peers.

Source: Adapted from Neag School of Education, University of Connecticut (2011).

literacies as the criteria in a checklist or rubric, the teacher is able to guide students through the necessary steps. These criteria were adapted from the ORCA (Online Reading Comprehension Assessment) Project out of the University of Connecticut (orca.uconn.edu), which is an upcoming standardized assessment of these skills that will be discussed later in this section.

In the task described in Table 16.5, the four literacies of online reading comprehension are integrated into a research task asking students to find information about an early explorer of the Americas. In this particular example, the students are given a website to visit and are asked to navigate the site to find information about their explorer. This particular website features an alphabetical navigation bar at the top of the page, numerous pictures, and a variety of hyperlinks to follow. As students complete the task, they are to fill out their process, showing that they are thinking parallel to the online reading comprehension literacies, which concludes with posting to a class message board and responding to a classmate's post.

Once students have completed the activity, it is simple for the teacher to go back and determine each student's level of online reading comprehension. Using a checklist (see Table 16.6), the teacher is able to go through the various aspects of the activity and easily pinpoint student weaknesses and opportunities for reteaching.

Students are generally excited about using technology. Therefore, employing this approach to have students do research and share what they have learned will go a long way toward enhancing student engagement and scaffolding key skills and understandings that will prove to be so important going forward.

Table 16.5 Example Online Reading Comprehension Activity

Directions: This rubric shows how the four new literacies of online reading comprehension can be assessed through an authentic research task. This rubric can be modified as necessary but is best suited to Grades 2–5.

This is an example of a Grade 4 task:

Task (what you need to do): You have been studying the people who have explored America! Now you are going to find out some more information on the Internet about an explorer that you have been assigned!

My Explorer: _____

Step 1: Locating Information • Go to the website http://www.enchantedlearning.com/explorers/namerica.shtml. • You will see a list of explorers. You need to use the different parts of the website to find your explorer!	• How did you find the information about your explorer? • What parts of the website did you click on? • Did you follow any links to get more information?
Step 2: Evaluating Information • Take a look at the website. Does this look like a website you can trust?	• Do you think you can trust this website? Why or why not? • What is one clue that you can trust this website?
Step 3: Synthesizing (Understanding) Information • Make sure you read the information about your explorer. Look at the different links, and be sure to pay attention to any pictures or videos!	• Summarize what you have learned about your explorer. • What parts of the website did you use to find out about your explorer? Pictures, words, videos?
Step 4: Communicating Information • Now that you are an expert on your explorer, please go to the class webpage and post a comment on our class message board, telling the class about why your explorer was important. • Be sure to read and reread your message before posting it!	• After you have posted your message, read some of the other messages left by your classmates and write a response about one of their explorers! Be sure to be nice and to read and reread your message!

Table 16.6 Explorers Online Reading Comprehension Checklist

Name: _____

Explorer: _____

Criteria	GOT IT!	NOT YET
Step 1: Locating Information Student shows evidence of an understanding of searching for relevant information about his or her explorer. The student is aware of how he or she arrived at the information.	☐	☐
Step 2: Evaluating Information The student provides appropriate insights about why he or she believes that the website is reliable.	☐	☐
Step 3: Synthesizing (Understanding) Information The student is able to construct a cohesive story from the information presented and explain how he or she learned the information.	☐	☐
Step 4: Communicating Information The student appropriately posts relevant information on the message board and replies to another post, providing evidence of understanding.	☐	☐

Online Reading Comprehension for Students With Special Needs and English Language Learners

Assessments and performance tasks such as the one presented earlier can easily be adopted for both students with special needs and English language learners (ELLs). With help from the many translation services available on the Internet (see Table 16.7), ELLs will be able to translate words in real time as they run into difficulties. These real-time translation services do have drawbacks, however, since the translation provided is often too literal. Likewise, many educational websites offer alternate language versions, enabling students to switch back and forth between English and their native language.

Internet capabilities also aid students with special needs, in that many websites feature videos and pictures along with the written text. Additionally, many computers feature screen-reading technology, which will read the text on the screen aloud to aid with the student's reading comprehension.

Table 16.7 Instant Online Text Translation Services

For many current translation services, the user simply needs to copy and paste a website address or a difficult word and then choose the desired language.

Google Translate: translate.google.com

Bing Translator: bing.com/translator

Free Translation: www.freetranslation.com

Technology-Based Reading Assessments

As much of what students are expected to learn moves into the digital age, so, too, have many of the assessments that gauge various student proficiencies. In the field of literacy, there are several computer-based assessments that can be given to students. These assessments can quickly aggregate scores for the teacher, giving him or her a comprehensive look at how each student is faring.

STAR Reading

The STAR Reading assessment is a computer-adaptive test developed by Renaissance Learning (2014). The assessment is aligned to the Common Core State Standards and can be used to assess early literacy. Students are exposed to questions on literacy topics such as vocabulary, author's craft, comprehension, and literary elements, among others. As students take the test, it adapts to how the student is doing. Once students answer questions correctly, the test chooses more difficult questions. Likewise, if a student is answering questions incorrectly, the test chooses simpler questions. The test is designed to be brief so that all the students in a class can be assessed without taking up too much class time.

ORCA

The ORCA (Online Reading Comprehension Assessments) Project is a series of assessments developed by the University of Connecticut to gauge student online reading comprehension. Unlike STAR Reading, the ORCA attempts to assess new literacies using text formats that students will likely see online, such as on Facebook and in e-mail. As of the time of this writing, the ORCA assessments are still being developed (Neag School of Education, University of Connecticut, 2011).

Rating E-Books

A first step toward integrating new literacies into existing reading programs often involves redefining the notion of what constitutes text, as teachers seek alternative text sources including digital texts and electronic books. (Larson, 2010, p. 15)

Interchangeable terms:

E-book	eBook
electronic book	digital book

While e-books and e-picture books are stepping into the limelight, they are certainly not brand new. Reading books in a digital format dates back at least to 1997, when the electronic version of *Stellaluna* made its debut after being published by Living Books (Guernsey, 2011). However, e-books are certainly beginning to make more of a splash as parents, educators, and school librarians turn to them to bridge reading gaps, increase reading motivation, and integrate new literacies and technology into the lives of students. Although this book format has been around for more than a decade, it is a fresh and relatively unexplored topic in literacy research.

The term *e-book* itself is a murky one. It is a broad term that covers what is, in reality, a variety of digital content formats that can be used on multiple platforms or physical devices (see Table 16.8). The types of digital content include apps, CD-ROMs, online content, and downloaded files. Downloaded files can also come in a variety of formats: JPEG, MP3, Flash, HTML, or even PowerPoint. While the digital content is the meat of the e-book, it cannot be accessed without some type of platform, whether it be a computer, smartphone, tablet, or dedicated e-reader, such as a Nook or a Kindle.

Table 16.8 E-Book Platforms

- Netbooks
- Laptops
- Desktop computers
- Dedicated e-book readers·
- Mobile phones
- Portable media players

Source: Buczynski (2010).

There is even some debate as to what digital content actually qualifies as an e-book. E-books can now include animated scenes, multimedia (such as embedded videos), interactive elements, quizzes, and games. These elements can help students learn new literacies, since "some forms of electronic books, with their potential for multimodal texts and multidimensional representations of a message, challenge the linear, right-to-left and top-down processing that is the norm for most written texts" (Larson, 2010, p. 16). While many believe that these elements are valuable, some are concerned about how much is too much. When does a multimedia e-book cross the line into being a movie with text? While some publishers have come up with their own e-book definitions, there has been no official definition to guide manufacturers (Guernsey, 2011). As a result, e-books are highly varied, ranging from scanned book pages to highly complex creations that integrate text, sound effects, multimedia, interactive elements, and narration.

The complexity and lack of standardization in e-books makes selecting them for our young readers a challenging task. Having a working knowledge of Lexiles or of Fountas and Pinnell's leveling systems only scratches the surface of what educators need to know to evaluate e-books. E-books are not yet deeply rooted in most elementary schools, in part due to the challenges mentioned in this section; however, it is necessary for educators to become familiar with the elements of e-books that should be assessed as they continue to be integrated into school systems (see Table 16.9 for criteria for rating e-books, which are discussed in more detail in the following).

Table 16.9 Criteria for Rating E-Books

1. Accessible
2. Reader controlled
3. User friendly
4. Interactive
5. Meaningful
6. Durable

The lack of standardization makes selecting appropriate e-books a challenge, even when considering just the type of digital content and the hardware available with which to read it. Due to the fact that different devices require different types of digital content, an app purchased for a tablet will not necessarily be accessible through a smartphone. Likewise, digital content that is readable on a computer may not be accessible on a tablet or e-reader. Additionally, many e-book manufacturers have their own proprietary format that is not compatible with other e-book readers (Buczynski, 2010). For example, an e-book bought through Amazon will certainly be readable on Amazon's Kindle e-reader; however, it will not be compatible with Barnes and Noble's Nook e-reader. While many parties are campaigning for increased standardization as a way to boost the accessibility of e-books, we must learn to negotiate this complex and shifting digital landscape.

As a result, educators must first evaluate how they plan to use e-books. E-books that are being used in the classroom must be compatible with the e-book platforms available at schools. Before deciding to make e-books available for student use at home, it is necessary to evaluate your student body and the way the digital divide impacts them. The term **digital divide** refers to the gap between students who have access to technology, such as computers and the Internet, and those who do not (Judge, Puckett, & Cabuk, 2004). When creating opportunities for learning, it is important that the information be accessible across socioeconomic and ethnic lines. Once the method of e-book access is decided, one can move on to evaluating the software, or the actual meat of the e-book.

E-books, like physical books, should be reader controlled. Unlike a movie, where the audience passively watches, readers should have control as they navigate from page to page through the story they are constructing. The digital format of e-books allows for a variety of features that children can control. In many books, they can turn narration and music on or off as they read though sections on their own or look for the support of a narrator during difficult passages (Bircher, 2012). E-books can offer word-by-word assistance that is activated only when children click the words they need to have defined or read to them. The navigation system should allow children to skip pages or return to other sections of the story that they may need to reread (Bircher, 2012). An auto-play option can offer support to emergent readers before they try to tackle new words on their own. The packaging of the e-book should allow children to visit, revisit, and review the story with different levels of support in accordance with their needs.

While physical books have a predictable format, there is no standard way of navigating through e-books. This makes it especially important for e-books to be user friendly (Bircher, 2012). A variety of cues can be used to help children navigate through e-books. Verbal cues can give readers instructions, or even reminders of what to do next after a significant pause in reader activity. Textual cues can tell students where to click next or how to activate different features. Visual elements, such as arrows or flashing buttons, can also aid students as they progress through the story.

E-books should also take advantage of their medium by making stories interactive. However, it is important that the added elements do not overwhelm or distract readers from the focus of the story (Bircher, 2012). Interactive opportunities should be brief and scattered throughout, so as not to cause significant delays and diversion from the plot (Bircher, 2012). Ideally, interactive activities should be accessible to readers after they are finished with the story so they can revisit them after the story as well.

E-books should be durable. Just as a truly good book stands up to multiple revisits, so should a good e-book. As in a physical book, story and characters should be engaging, and the subject matter should be relatable and ring true to the reader. Where e-books really have the potential to shine is through increasing the novelty of a story by rotating animations and interactive elements (Bircher, 2012). With the addition of rotating elements, stories can remain new and fresh even after multiple retellings.

Above all, the sum total of the e-book—text, images, narration, music, sound effects, embedded videos, extensions to websites—should be cohesive and meaningful. While interactive elements should be integrated into the text, they should also have a level of meaning that adds to and extends the experience, rather than simply mirroring the text or providing superfluous add-ons (Bircher, 2012). Just as pictures extend the information and experience of a successful picture book beyond the text, so should the multimedia elements extend the information and experience in a successful e-book. Table 16.10 details how e-books can be especially helpful for ELLs, students who are visually impaired, and struggling readers. Table 16.11 provides a handout that can help parents choose quality e-books for their children outside of class.

The International Children's Digital Library

The mission of the International Children's Digital Library Foundation (ICDL Foundation) is to support the world's children in becoming effective members of the global community—who exhibit tolerance and respect for diverse cultures, languages and ideas—by making the best in children's literature available online free of charge. (ICDL Foundation, n.d.)

Table 16.10 E-Books for ELLs, Students Who Are Visually Impaired, and Struggling Readers

The customizable format of e-books allows for a greater degree of differentiation. On computers, e-readers, and other platforms, text can be enlarged to support the visually impaired. ELLs and struggling readers can use the visual cues from images, animations, and integrated video to support their reading of the text. They can use additional support through text tools that provide definitions and pronounce words that are giving readers trouble (Larson, 2010).

Table 16.11 Helping Parents Understand How to Evaluate E-Books

Choosing E-Books

Here in the classroom, we use e-books to help teach reading and technology skills. We think very hard about which e-books to include in our reading collection. Below is a checklist of things we consider when we make our selections. If you buy or borrow e-books for your children, these are some things you can think about to help you with your selection.

Is this e-book

- accessible?
  - Will it work on the computer, e-reader, or tablet you have?
  - Is it at a reading level that will allow your child to participate in reading?

- child controlled?
  - Can your child turn music or narration on and off?
  - Can you easily skip parts of the story or return to a section you already read?
  - Does the e-book give definitions or pronunciations of words when you click on them?

- interactive?
  - Is this story something that the student can interact with (click to make animations appear, play games, hover mouse over images to produce sounds, etc.)?
  - Does the book have a feature that makes the e-book format a better choice than a paper book?

- user-friendly?
  - Is it easy for your child to move through the book?
  - Is it easy to figure out how to use interactive elements?

- meaningful?
  - Is the story one that your child can relate to?
  - Do the interactive parts of the story add meaning to the story?

- durable?
  - Is this something that your child could read again and again and not get bored?
  - Do any of the animations or features change with each retelling, keeping it fresh and new?

While e-books are available to buy or borrow in a variety of places, there are also collections of e-books that can be accessed at any time free of charge via the Internet. One of the most notable is the ICDL, which is the "most popular and accessible collection of digital children's literature" (Houston, 2011). The ICDL is a digital library for the whole world, offering 4,643 e-books appropriate for 3- to 13-year-old children in more than 60 languages (ICDL Foundation, n.d.). Even the user-friendly interface, which was designed in collaboration with children from around the world, can be translated into 18 of the world's major languages. While the e-books available there may not be familiar titles, they were purposefully chosen to help children learn about other cultures, lifestyles, and societies around the world.

Many books are available in more than one language, which makes the ICDL a great option for ELLs and multilingual classrooms. Students have the opportunity to visit the same story in two texts—one in English and one in their native language. The cultural concepts in the e-books also empower students, who can read stories that reflect their own cultures and share their backgrounds with the rest of the class (Hutchinson, Rose, Bederson, & Weeks, 2005). These multilingual and multicultural stories also give parents who do not have a firm grasp of English an opportunity to share in reading with their children, in their home language and about their native culture.

Although the e-books in the ICDL are simply scanned pages, readers can zoom in on page features to see details more clearly. The pages are not interactive, nor are they accented by funky music or animations; however, that does not mean this type of e-book is not valuable. The value of the e-book format in the case of this collection is that it feeds directly into the mission of the ICDL Foundation—it is limitless in its geographic scope and is accessible to anyone with access to technology. The ICDL is a success in its own right, with a mission that supports 21st century skills and the creation of global citizens. See Table 16.12 for a list of other open-access e-book collections.

Table 16.12 Other Open-Access E-Book Collections

Visit these other sites to see the variety of free e-book collections available for children to use in school and at home.

- Children's Books Online: The Rosetta Project (www.childrensbooksonline.org)
  - Traditional and historic children's literature
  - Adult supervision recommended due to biases in older literature

- Children's Storybooks Online (www.magickeys.com/books)
  - Illustrated, modern stories
  - Some available as iPhone app

- Story Place (www.storyplace.org)
  - Truly multimedia
  - Personalization of character's names and other story elements

Evaluating Author Websites

Author websites are a wonderful way to explore literary text beyond the books themselves. Offering biographical information about the author, examples of other books he or she has written, and the motivation behind his or her writing career, author websites can be a great way for the whole class or individual students to dive into an author study. Students can draw information from the website's text and images and relate it to the literature studied in class.

Just as there are vast varieties of books within the K–5 reading spectrum, the types of author websites also vary (see Table 16.13 for some examples). Before assigning a student an author to study independently, make sure to read through the website to evaluate whether it would be understandable and navigable for one of your students. Keep in mind that children's authors may not always address their young readers on their websites; some instead write to the audience of teachers and parents.

Table 16.13 Examples of Author Websites	
Monica Brown www.monicabrown.net	The Common Core encourages teachers to highlight nonfiction for younger students and infuse multiculturalism into the curriculum. Brown's website demonstrates her love of biographies and shows how her Peruvian-American heritage has influenced her writing.
Christopher Paul Curtis www.nobodybutcurtis.com	This website hosts videos, news articles, interviews, and author's notes for Curtis's most notable books. Accessible for fourth and fifth graders, this website lies at the more complex and information-heavy end of the spectrum.
Patricia Polacco www.patriciapolacco.com	Polacco's website, in addition to having all the elements evaluated by the Table 16.14 checklist, demonstrates the writing process. From showing images of unpublished early works to displaying images and explanations of her working in her studio, she gives budding writers a glimpse into the author's world.
Cynthia Rylant www.cynthiarylant.com	While Rylant's website is not flashy and full of information, it is a good place for young readers to start evaluating and learning from author websites. A simple layout with simple language can help students focus on content.
Jon Scieszka www.jsworldwide.com	As funny and unpredictable as his books, Scieszka's website fuses humor and information. Most notable is the way that he incorporates hyperlinks into his biography to direct readers to pictures of his family, the website for his college, or his hometown's location on Google Maps. Making the most of the web, he encourages students to look beyond his website in their search for knowledge.

Older students can evaluate author websites on their own. For younger students, it may be better to evaluate websites as a class or with one-on-one guidance. Students who are researching their author from home can use a checklist to help guide them through the research process (see Table 16.14).

Table 16.14 What Can I Learn From My Author's Website?	
Can I learn about my author's life?	☺ ☺ ☹
Can I learn what my author likes?	☺ ☺ ☹
Can I learn how my author got interested in writing?	☺ ☺ ☹
Can I learn what other books my author wrote?	☺ ☺ ☹
Can I learn what books my author is working on now?	☺ ☺ ☹
Can I e-mail or write my author?	☺ ☺ ☹

Podcasting and Rubrics

> In our quest to use and integrate current technology to enhance literacy instruction, we seek to match well-researched literacy strategies with technological tools that enhance the strategy and make it stronger. (Vasinda & McLeod, 2011, p. 486)

While this chapter has discussed many of the ways technology can aid literacy instruction, there is one specific technological application that can provide a unique avenue for students to create, write, speak, listen, and learn: the podcast.

Podcasting is a term for creating, recording, and then sharing an audio (and sometimes video) presentation meant to be broadcast over the Internet (Vasinda & McLeod, 2011). The term is a joining together of the words *iPod*, which was the original destination for podcasts, and *broadcast* (Lee, McLoughlin, & Chan, 2008). Therefore, a podcast is any audio or video recording that is meant to be shared with others digitally. Due to many schools' privacy policies, however, podcasts can also be shared among students over a local school intranet or simply through exclusive broadcast in the classroom.

While previously created podcasts about a wide variety of subjects and topics can be found easily on the Internet, this section focuses on learner-created podcasts and how this technology can enhance existing literacy strategies.

> Young people want hands-on experience, action, interaction, identity in cyberculture, and connectivity with the world. (Panday, 2009, p. 251)

Using podcasting as a support for literacy strategies is an excellent way to engage students with hands-on creation and connectivity. Podcasting has been used to support literacy in many ways, from enhancing a reader's theatre activity (Vasinda & McLeod, 2011) to providing a platform for students to respond to literature (Saine & Kara-Soteriou,

2010). The format is so successful in the classroom because it has students actively engaged in and excited to read, write, speak, and share their creations. Furthermore, the podcasting format is adaptable to nearly any literacy task.

Panday (2009) talks about student interaction in the world of computers but also speaks about how podcasting can be used to help students work together and communicate with one another (p. 259). Additionally, podcasting can be used as an effective literacy technique because it allows one to "'listen to oneself,' [which] provides an opportunity to learn from mistakes" (p. 260). Therefore, students have the ability to record, listen to, make modifications, and rerecord their podcasts until they achieve their desired results.

Due to the traits Panday described, podcasting is also an effective strategy to use with ELLs or students with special needs. ELLs are given the opportunity to listen to and emulate the language of their peers, while the ability to record, listen to, and rerecord their own contributions allows these students to develop their own unique voice in a dynamic way. Likewise, students with special needs are able to work at their own pace and create multiple "takes" if necessary. Figure 16.1 offers some key steps to introducing podcasting in the classroom.

Figure 16.1

What You Need to Get Started Podcasting in the Classroom

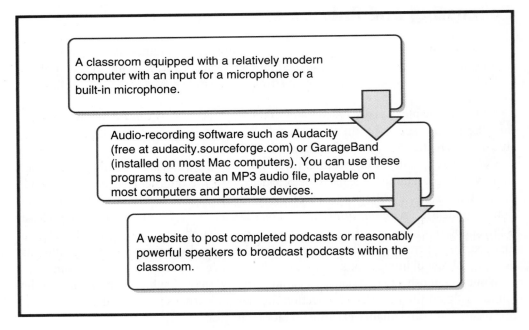

No matter the task, podcasts are an excellent way to assess student understandings and for students to share with their classmates what they have learned. If they are posted to a class webpage, podcasts are also a great way to communicate with parents what their children have learned. In many cases, gaining the consent of parents to post student work to the Internet will allow for an authentic opportunity to involve parents in what their children are working on in the classroom.

The following is a sample letter to a parent explaining a podcasting activity based on an online reading comprehension research task.

Sample Letter to Parent

Dear Parent,

In class we have been learning all about the explorers of the early Americas. Your child has spent a lot of time and effort on locating information on the Internet about his or her assigned explorer.

To share what we have discovered with everyone in the class, we will be creating podcasts about our explorers. A podcast is an audio file that is recorded and posted on the Internet. Your child will be working in a group with some other students to write a script, choose roles, and perform and record a podcast. With your permission, we would like to post these podcasts on our class webpage so that other students from all across the nation and the world will be able to learn about these explorers. This will also give you, the parent, the opportunity to hear what your student has worked on.

I look forward to having you listen to your child's podcast, and I hope that you learn a little something from it as well!

For most podcasts, the teacher will want his or her students to work together in a small group. Once the students have been assigned a task, they will then be asked to create a short script. As the students work together to develop a script, they need to pay attention to who will be the speaker for certain sections or roles, as well as how their podcast should be organized. In the case of reader's theatre, students can be assigned (or select) a section of the reading to be acted out and debate who will portray which roles in the selection. Naturally, depending on the task, the assessment vehicle used will vary slightly.

In the example rubric in Table 16.15, students are assessed based on their adherence to the task, the creation of a script (for planning), the use of their voices, and their ability to work together. If the students are performing a reader's theatre task, the script criteria can simply be removed or replaced with sound effects or even music.

In all, podcasting is a great way to incorporate technology (which will help increase student engagement) with traditional literacy strategies (Vasinda & McLeod, 2011). From reader's theatre to online reading comprehension, having students contribute in the form of a podcasting project that they are able to listen to over and over again, and also share with their classmates and parents, will go a long way toward building both traditional skills and new competencies.

Digital Storytelling

Creating digital stories invites students to employ old and new literacies, and through the process of creating a movie they erect, explore, and exhibit other literacies. (Sylvester & Greenidge, 2009, p. 284)

Digital storytelling, like podcasting, gives students a new way of expressing themselves in a digital format. Generally, a digital story is a combination of narrated soundtrack

Table 16.15 General Rubric for Podcasting With a Student-Created Script			
Podcasting Elements	☺	☺	☹
Task	Students followed all instructions for the podcast activity.	Students mostly followed instructions for the podcast activity.	Students did not follow instructions for the podcast activity.
Script	A clear script was written. Everyone has a part to play.	Some of the script might be written out. Most everyone has a part to play.	There is no script for this podcast. Only one or two people have a part to play.
Voice	Voices are clear and easy to understand.	Voices are a little quiet but can mostly be understood.	Voices are impossible to understand.
Working Together	Students worked together with no problems to create this podcast.	Students worked together with few problems to create this podcast.	Students had difficulty working together to create this podcast.

and still images that work together to tell a story. It can also feature occasional short video clips and a soundtrack. See Table 16.16 for some of the traditional story elements and technologies that can be woven together to create a digital story. Since the format of presentation engages all the senses, "digital storytelling represents a particularly powerful method of expression that can amplify a writer's voice" (Kajder, Bull, & Albaugh, 2005). It is a product that allows students to express creativity while developing new and traditional literacies.

Table 16.16 Making Your Own Digital Story	
Video Editors	Microsoft Photo Story 3, iMovie, Windows Movie Maker
Story Elements to Include	Setting, character, plot, climax, and resolution
Hosting	Youtube.com, teachertube.com, your school website, or a live showing

Students find digital storytelling appealing on a variety of levels. Since digital stories have visual, auditory, and written components, creating them appeals to multiple learning styles. Like podcasts, they are meant to be viewed by an audience beyond the teacher. As a result, students are motivated to present their story and message to an authentic audience. High levels of motivation can bolster students through the academically rigorous process of writing a script, planning their images and text, learning a new technology, and communicating their story.

Struggling writers are seldom strategic writers; however, the components of creating digital storytelling may help them compose more strategically. (Sylvester & Greenidge, 2009, p. 291)

Struggling writers can particularly benefit from digital storytelling. The seven-step process of creating the digital story requires deliberate planning and reflection (see Table 16.17). Students must take the time to plan and reflect on the structure of their story as they set up their storyboard. A storyboard is a page that allows students to outline and sequence their stories using drawings and text, much like one would find in a comic strip. Struggling writers can also scaffold their traditional literacy skills by building off of their visual and new literacy skills in the creation of their digital story (Sylvester & Greenidge, 2009). Students can fill gaps in their narrative with photographs that more explicitly demonstrate their meaning. When combined with the motivational factors mentioned above, digital storytelling gives struggling writers the opportunity to be successful and increase their confidence.

Table 16.17 Seven Steps to Creating a Digital Story

1. Write script
2. Plan storyboard
3. Reflect and revise
4. Sequence images in video editor
5. Add narrative track
6. Add special effects
7. Add soundtrack

Source: Kajder et al. (2005).

As students follow Kajder et al.'s seven-step process to create a digital story, a rubric can help guide them to their final product. Through each major step of the process, the rubric should remind them what is expected, such as attendance to task, the guiding structures of the script and storyboard, the importance of strong communication through voice, and the smart (rather than flashy) use of music and images. If time is running short on the project, the seven steps are designed to be easily paired down to five steps by ending with the addition of the narrative track. The rubric in Table 16.18 can be used as a basic assessment for digital stories.

WebQuests

Another way teachers are able to assess new technological literacies is through the use of WebQuests. A **WebQuest** is a "web-based inquiry learning activity" (Ikpeze & Boyd, 2007, p. 645) that allows students to problem-solve in an authentic manner using the

Table 16.18 Digital Storytelling Rubric			
Digital Storytelling Elements	☺	☺	☹
Task	Students followed all instructions for the digital storytelling activity.	Students mostly followed instructions for the digital storytelling activity.	Students did not follow instructions for the digital storytelling activity.
Script	A clear script was written.	Some of the script might be written out.	There is no script for this digital story.
Storyboard	The storyboard shows all the images and how they match the script.	The storyboard shows all the images but not how they match the script.	There is no storyboard for this digital story.
Voice	Voice is clear and easy to understand.	Voice is a little quiet but can mostly be understood.	Voice is impossible to understand.
Pictures and Music	Pictures and music add meaning and emotion to the story.	Pictures and music sometimes add meaning and emotion to the story.	Pictures and music have nothing to do with the story.

Internet. Much as the name indicates, WebQuests include a variety of tasks, or "quests," that students must complete to achieve an understanding of a particular topic or idea. No matter the content, WebQuests have students watching videos, navigating websites, completing web searches, and following hyperlinks. These activities help students learn about content, in addition to providing many of the skills necessary for effective online reading comprehension, developing 21st century skills, and problem solving. Often, WebQuests are completed as companions to a book students have just read or as part of research they are in the process of conducting. In many instances, WebQuests can be completed in groups, creating an authentic opportunity for collaboration and discussion among peers.

Making Connections

What About ELLs and Students With Special Needs?

Many of the ELL and special needs strategies used for online reading comprehension apply to WebQuests. ELLs may translate webpages as needed, and both kinds of students will be able to work with groups to accomplish necessary tasks. For classrooms rich with ELLs and students with special needs, it is important to select a WebQuest that has a wide variety of resources presented in multiple formats.

While many different WebQuests are available on the Internet, the majority of them follow the same basic format. A standard WebQuest includes these key parts:

- *Introduction:* This explains the concept and goal of the WebQuest to students. This should be used to draw students into the activity as well as to give them an idea of where they will be going.
- *Task:* As the name implies, this section gives students an explanation of what they will be doing and what the final goal/product of the WebQuest is.
- *List of resources:* These are the links to relevant websites, videos, pictures, and more that students should visit as part of the aforementioned task. It is best to give students a variety of resources so they are able to discover information in a way that appeals to their own learning style. Having a variety of resources also helps develop a student's ability to sift through and organize nonsequential information. Sometimes this information will be listed under "Process."
- *Process:* This is a description of how students will go about completing the task at hand and a step-by-step explanation of what students will need to do to succeed. The process can encompass everything from doing research to posting a blog entry about one's findings.
- *Evaluation:* A rubric or checklist is typically used to evaluate a student's completion of the task. This usually follows the process of a particular WebQuest.
- *Conclusion:* This wraps up the WebQuest and provides a sense of closure.

Even though many WebQuests follow this format, some are more in-depth than others. While some WebQuests may take a class or two, others may take a week or longer. Due to this variation, the assessment vehicle to be used differs greatly depending on the task and process. The flexibility of the WebQuest is one of the reasons it is such an effective literacy technique.

Many websites, specifically WebQuest.org and Zunal.com, have collected wonderful WebQuests and made them available online for teachers and students to use. These WebQuests are easily searchable by topic and grade level. Additionally, WebQuest.org and Zunal.com enable teachers to create their own WebQuests using the standard format. Table 16.19 lists some WebQuests to get you started. More can be found at WebQuest.org and Zunal.com.

Web-Enhanced Lessons

Since our digital native students have new needs and new literacy expectations (Coiro, 2009), it is important to be sure that lessons and instructions consistently require students to use the Internet (Prensky, 2001). Fortunately, the array of tools and programs available on the Internet is vast, allowing a teacher to work new literacies and the web into almost any type of lesson. Furthermore, integrating the web and other technologies into lessons can help reach ELL students and provide extra scaffolding for those with special needs. In many instances, students can be assessed on their online reading comprehension (with a modified version of the rubric provided in Table 16.5) in addition to

Table 16.19 Some Useful WebQuests	
Safari WebQuest: Grades 3–5 zunal.com/webquest.php?w=175258	This WebQuest is a companion activity for *The Great Kapok Tree* by Lynne Cherry. It has students pretending they are an animal from the story and writing a narrative Facebook page about a day in the life of their animal, based on research they have done.
Around the World With Our Pen Pals: Grades 2–3 questgarden.com/150/59/9/121106152700/	This WebQuest splits students up into groups, having them each search the web for information about an assigned country to prepare a poster with pictures and other facts to share with their classmates.
Poetry WebQuest: Grades 3–5 zunal.com/webquest.php?w=152750	This WebQuest has students discovering and researching various forms of poetry, culminating in writing their very own poem.

traditional literacies. The following are just some examples of the wide variety of methods that can be used to enhance a lesson.

Smartphones or iPads

This generally works for older students who have cell phones, although iPads or other tablets can be substituted. In many instances, smartphones can provide a means for students to find real-time information that relates to a book they are reading or a concept they are learning about.

Smartphones can be used to look up complicated vocabulary as students encounter the words in a book; they can also be used to look up relevant facts or questions students form as they read. Bromley (2012) presents an excellent list for how students can use smartphones as they read an informational text (see Figure 16.2).

Blogging/Message Boards

As mentioned earlier in this chapter, one of the major tenets of the new online reading comprehension literacies is learning to read and communicate using the electronic medium. Using a blogging or message-board service is a wonderful way to keep students sharing information with one another, as well as an effective way to use a new medium for responses to literature (O'Dell, 2010). A blog is a website on which a user is able to post information in journal or diary form for others to read. A message board is a website that features topics, or "threads," where users can communicate and participate in a linear discussion. (See Table 16.20 for a list of some free blogging and message-board services.) Unlike podcasting, which can be used in many of the same ways, blogging or posting to message boards requires far less preparation and could conceivably be sustained throughout the entire year.

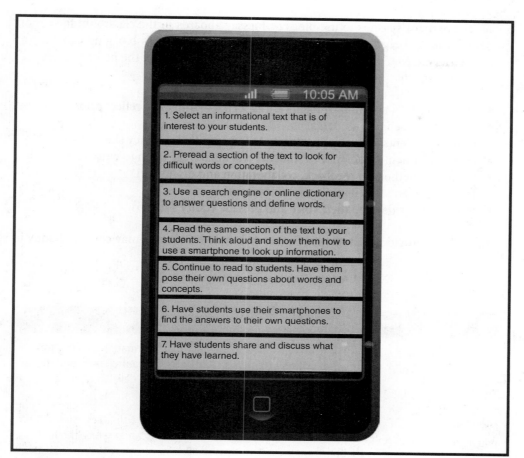

Figure 16.2

Using a Smartphone as a Supplement to an Informational Text

Source: Adapted from Bromley (2012, p. 343).

Table 16.20 Some Free Blog and Message-Board Services

Blogger www.blogger.com	This is a basic blogging website through which a teacher can set up a blog for the class and then have students sign up for accounts to post on it. This site features lots of customization, but beware that some of the other blogs hosted by this website might not be appropriate for school.
ClassChatter www.classchatter.com	This website, created by a teacher for teachers, features a free centralized hub for a message board and individual student blogs. A teacher can register his or her class to the website and give each student a login. The site features no ads and is safe for the classroom. However, uploading of pictures and sounds is not permitted.
Edublogs www.edublogs.com	This website is much like ClassChatter but with many more features. Some of the premium features do come with a price, however.

There are many reasons to use blogs or message boards in the classroom to support student learning. Berger and Trexler (2010) provide seven ways blogging can support student learning. Note that many of these represent the criteria of the new literacies.

Blogging can

- Support critical thinking. Students are expected to think and reflect prior to writing.
- Motivate and engage students.
- Provide students with an opportunity to improve their literacy skills.
- Offer an authentic audience to students and encourage them to write responsibly.
- Provide a method for feedback, collaboration and discussion.
- Involve students in a community of learners.
- Help students develop their voice and provide equity. (p. 105)

Table 16.21 provides a short list of other web-based tools that may come in handy in the classroom.

Table 16.21 Other Web-Based Tools to Enhance Lessons	
Wikis www.wikispaces.com www.pbworks.com	A wiki (a collaborative compendium of information about a topic or topics) can be created by a class while reading an informational text or even a piece of fiction. Students can develop pages about characters, topics, or even research they do.
Glogster EDU edu.glogster.com	This is a website students can use to create a digital poster. Within the poster, students can add text, pictures, animations, thought bubbles, and clipart.
Audio/Visual www.animoto.com www.voicethread.com	Using these websites, students can create short animations with text or their own voices. Students could create a video to complement a poem or even a short story using visuals.
Visualizing Ideas www.wordle.org www.bubbl.us	These tools can be used to visualize concepts, including key words. Wordle will create a "word cloud" of frequently used words in a story. Bubbl.us can be used to create a web of character or topic relationships.

Key Terms

digital divide

digital immigrants

digital natives

digital storytelling

information communication technologies

podcasting

WebQuest

Website Resources

- **Online Practice Reading Tests, Pearson Education**

This site provides information and samples on online reading comprehension tests and how to use and score them. There are two-page practice tests for students in Grades 1–8 that include multiple-choice, short-answer, and long-answer questions. This is a great way for ELLs to experience and practice how to take reading comprehension assessments. For more information, go to **www.pearsonlongman.com/ae/marketing/sfesl/practicereading.html**.

- **Oxford Owl Reading**

This site provides children ages 3 to 12 with 250 free e-books. This site is a great resource for educators and parents, offering tips on phonics, grammar, punctuation, spelling, and struggling readers, encouraging reading for all. Online games also accompany the resources. For more information, go to **www.oxfordowl.co.uk/Reading**.

- **"Podcasts: The Nuts and Bolts of Creating Podcasts," ReadWriteThink**

ReadWriteThink is associated with the International Reading Association and National Council of Teachers of English. This webpage provides a useful two-page printout with steps, tools, links to tutorials, and extras for all your podcasting needs. There are also ideas on how to use podcasting in the classroom and additional lesson plan resources for using them in middle and high school. For more information, go to **www.readwritethink.org/classroom-resources/printouts/podcasts-nuts-bolts-creating-30311.html**.

- **Digital Storytelling With the iPad**

Created by teachers, this site provides detailed information on how to use digital storytelling in the classroom. It also offers tutorials and detailed app recommendations for the iPad, including prices and options, and links to additional resources. For more information, go to **sites.google.com/site/digitalstorytellingwiththeipad/home**.

- **TeachersFirst: Blog Basics for the Classroom**

This is a comprehensive site that gives step-by-step setup instructions, explains how blogs may be linked to the curriculum, provides various grade-level samples of blogs already in progress, and offers details on how to keep a blog cybersafe. For more information, go to **www.teachersfirst.com/content/blog/blogbasics.cfm**.

Student Study Site: Visit the Student Study Site at **www.sagepub.com/grantlit** to access additional study tools including eFlashcards, web resources, and online-only appendices.

Appendix A

International Reading Association Standards for Reading Professionals

Standards 2010: Standard 3

Assessment and Evaluation

Candidates use a variety of assessment tools and practices to plan and evaluate effective reading and writing instruction.

The Assessment and Evaluation Standard recognizes the need to prepare teachers for using a variety of assessment tools and practices to plan and evaluate effective reading and writing instruction. The elements featured in this standard relate to the systematic monitoring of student performance at individual, classroom, school, and systemwide levels. Teacher educators who specialize in literacy play a critical role in preparing teachers for multifaceted assessment responsibilities.

The following are the major assumptions of the Standards 2010 Committee for developing this standard and its elements:

- The most fundamental goal of assessment and evaluation is to optimize student learning.
- Effective assessment practices inform instruction.
- Competent reading professionals appreciate the importance of assessment.
- Effective reading professionals demonstrate a skilled use of assessment processes and results.
- Competent reading professionals are knowledgeable of standardized tests and their uses and limitations in the assessment process.
- Effective reading professionals are able to analyze data and communicate findings and implications to appropriate audiences.

Source: International Reading Association (2010b). Standards 2010: Standard 3: Assessment and Evaluation. Retrieved from www.reading.org/General/CurrentResearch/Standards/ProfessionalStandards2010/ProfessionalStandards2010_Standard3.aspx. Reprinted with permission.

Appendix B

Common Core State Standards, State Assessments

Arizona: www.azed.gov/azcommoncore/m

Arkansas: ideas.aetn.org/commoncore/institutes

California: www.cde.ca.gov/re/cc/

Colorado: www.colorincolorado.org/educators/common_core

Connecticut: www.sde.ct.gov/sde/cwp/view.asp?a=2618&q=322592

Delaware: www.doe.k12.de.us/commoncore/math/teachertoolkit/assessement.shtml

Florida: www.fldoe.org/BII/curriculum/SSS/

Georgia: www.georgiastandards.org/common-core/Pages/default.aspx

Idaho: www.sde.idaho.gov/site/common

Illinois: www.isbe.net/common_core/default.htm

Indiana: learningconnection.doe.in.gov/Standards/About.aspx?art=11

Kansas: www.ksde.org/Default.aspx?tabid=1678

Kentucky: education.ky.gov/curriculum/docs/pages/kentucky-core-academic-standards—new.aspx

Louisiana: www.louisianabelieves.com/assessment/common-core-assessments

Maine: www.maine.gov/education/lres/commoncore/index.html

Maryland: www.hcpss.org/academics/math/md_common_core.shtml

Massachusetts: www.doe.mass.edu/candi/commoncore

Michigan: www.michigan.gov/mde/0,4615,7-140-28753_64839_64848—,00.html

Minnesota: education.state.mn.us/MDE/EdExc/StanCurri/K-12AcademicStandards/

Mississippi: www.mde.k12.ms.us/curriculum-and-instruction/curriculum-and-instruction-other-links/common-core-state-standards

Missouri: www.missourilearningstandards.com/common-core-state-standards/english-language-artsmath/

Montana: opi.mt.gov/groups/mtl/wiki/c245e/Montana_Common_Core_State_Standards_and_Assessment.html

Nebraska: www.edutopia.org/blog/common-core-state-standards-3-virginia-goatley

Nevada: www.doe.nv.gov/APAC_Nevada_Academic_Standards_Implementing_Common_Core/

New Hampshire: www.education.nh.gov/spotlight/ccss/index.htm

New Jersey: www.state.nj.us/education/sca/ccss

New Mexico: newmexicocommoncore.org

New York: engageny.org/resource/test-guides-for-english-language-arts-and-mathematics

North Carolina: www.ncpublicschools.org/acre/standards/common-core-tools

North Dakota: www.dpi.state.nd.us/standard/common_core.shtm

Ohio: www.ode.state.oh.us/GD/Templates/Pages/ODE/ODEPrimary.aspx?page=2&TopicRelationID=1699

Oklahoma: ok.gov/sde/oklahoma-c3-implementation-timeline

Oregon: www.ode.state.or.us/search/page/?id=3298

Pennsylvania: www.portal.state.pa.us/portal/server.pt/community/state_academic_standards/19721

Rhode Island: www.ride.ri.gov/InstructionAssessment/Literacy/CommonCoreStateStandardsforELALiteracy.aspx

South Carolina: ed.sc.gov/agency/programs-services/190

South Dakota: www.doe.sd.gov/octe/commoncorestandards.aspx

Tennessee: www.tncore.org

Utah: www.uen.org/commoncore

Vermont: sites.google.com/site/commoncoreinvermont

Virginia: www.doe.virginia.gov/testing/common_core/index.shtml

Washington: www.k12.wa.us/corestandards

West Virginia: wvde.state.wv.us/commoncore

Wisconsin: standards.dpi.wi.gov/stn_ccss

Wyoming: edu.wyoming.gov/in-the-classroom/content/common-core/

Glossary

academic resiliency   Developing the ability to persevere in tackling challenging academic work with confidence and resilience

accountability   Schools and teachers are accountable for adequate progress in student learning.

affective   The emotional end of reading; negative or positive emotions that support or prevent students from engaging in purposeful reading

alliterate   Label used to describe a student who can read well enough but chooses not to read

alphabetic awareness   Refers to the ability to recognize the shapes, names, and sounds each letter represents

alphabetic principle   Understanding that spoken words are broken into phonemes and that the letters in written words represent the phonemes in spoken words when spoken words are represented in text

analytic rubric   A template for assessing student work that provides criteria for scoring based on categories of academic achievement, such as exemplary, proficient, or weak

anchor chart   A chart hung on the wall to remind students of literacy information they need to know for their daily reading work

anecdotal record keeping   A written record of a student's progress, using notations and abbreviations developed by the teacher

assessment accommodation   Can be a change in format, response, scheduling, setting, or timing that does not alter in any significant way what the test measures or the comparability of scores (Phillips, 1993)

assessment calendar   A calendar of the common interim assessments administered two to three times a year

assessment modification   A change in administration that alters the constructs or skills assessed or the comparability of scores (Phillips, 1993)

authentic data collection   Ongoing systematic collection, analysis, and interpretation of student-selected artifacts

authentic measures   Instruments that inform us what learners have learned and are capable of doing

automaticity   The ability to read and decode words without thinking about the process

background information   Individualized student information that helps teachers effectively prepare and plan to meet each student's needs

bell curve   A visual representation of scores on a standardized assessment, where the scores are distributed symmetrically with more scores toward the middle and fewer at the extremes

benchmark texts   Texts that a range of educators believe can be used as a comparison or guide for analyzing the qualitative nature of texts

buddy reading   An older student reads aloud to a younger student, thereby increasing literacy confidence, motivation, and fluency.

characterizations Describing the character traits of a specific character to present a fully formed identity

cognitive development The process of developing information processing, conceptual resources, perceptual skills, and language learning as children acquire intelligence and increasingly advanced thought and problem solving into adulthood

Common Core State Standards National learning standards that have been disseminated and adopted by the states

complex text Text that has complex syntax, semantics, concepts, and/or requires a significant amount of knowledge from the reader to comprehend. The Common Core State Standards provide teachers with tools to determine text complexity using quantitative, qualitative, and reader and task considerations.

comprehension (reading) The ability to read, process, and understand the meaning of text as a result of a transaction between the reader, the text, and the context

comprehension strategies Metacognitive strategies that help students improve their understanding of text before, during, and after reading

consonant blends Two or more consonants blended together that retain their minimal sounds—for example, *bl* in *block* and *str* in *string*

consonant digraphs Consonant blends that make very distinctive sounds, such as *trunk*, *plunk*, *ship*, *shrank*, *sham*, *shrink*, *tree*, *train*, and *trip*

construction of knowledge The learner's ability to analyze and interpret new information or situations by applying basic and prior knowledge at higher levels of thinking

content area literacy Literacy skills that focus on helping students understand the content in their grade-level textbooks on subjects such as social studies, science, math, or health

criterion-referenced tests Test takers are compared with a fixed standard or criterion.

cueing systems Graphophonic, semantic, syntactic, and pragmatic development are the four major systems a child relies on during the act of reading. These systems are interdependent and critical during reading performance.

cultural discontinuity Disconnection within a student's cultural milieu—for example, Latino students' exclusively hearing read-alouds focusing on white children as characters

data-driven instruction Using collected and analyzed student data to determine instruction

decode The ability to apply knowledge of letter–sound relationships to solve for unknown words

diagnostic tests Tools that are used to identify students' strengths and weaknesses in a particular skill area. Initial screening and progress monitoring data inform decisions about the level and type of interventions needed to help individual students make progress (University of the State of New York, 2010).

digital divide This refers to the gap between students who have access to technology, such as computers and the Internet, and those who do not.

digital immigrants Those born before the digital age who have adopted many aspects of technology but still have difficulty fully understanding it and integrating it into their lives. They can often struggle with learning new technology.

digital natives Those born into technology. Those who are well versed in computers, video games, and the Internet. Technology comes naturally to them.

digital storytelling Similar to podcasting, allows students a new way of expressing themselves in a digital format.

disciplinary literacy The literacy demands of a discipline

driven by data Based on quantifiable data gathered to guide the teacher in determining students' next steps

eco-resiliency The ability to exert control over the reading task when called for

Elkonin or sound boxes   A strategy that supports student graphophonic word pronunciation

emergent reading   Early reading characteristics of readers who strive to decode words and seek meaning

emotive language   Highly charged or emotional language found in reading selections

engagement   Sustained enjoyment of the reading selection

English orthography   This consists of three layers: the alphabetic, pattern, and meaning layers.

environmental print   Examples of print sources in a child's everyday environment that help with early attention to literacy

evaluation   Analyzing the results of assessment

explicit and systematic phonics   An extensive, prespecified set of letter–sound correspondences or phonograms that are directly taught or explicit

extrinsic rewards   Rewards given for engaging in the act of reading

family conference   A genuine discussion of student growth and progress as evidenced by student-selected artifacts

fix-up strategies   Quick literacy strategies that help students monitor their understanding of texts

fluency   The ability to read with accuracy, speed, and correct expression so as to understand what is being read

formative assessment   Assessment for learning; contrasted with summative assessment, which is an assessment of what was learned

grade- and age-equivalent scores   Compare the student being tested to others in his or her same age or grade

Gradual Release of Responsibility Model   A model for teaching that includes a focus lesson, guided instruction, collaboration, and independent work

graphemes   A letter or group of letters representing one sound

graphic novel   Tells a story in comic format but is longer in length and development of the narrative

graphic organizers   Visual tools that support connections among ideas, vocabulary, and content to aid in student learning

graphophonics   The cueing system that focuses on grapheme–phoneme correspondence or letter–sound relationships

high-frequency words   The most common words in English; make up most of written material

high-stakes testing   National, state, and local testing that carries consequences for students, schools, and districts as far as retention, funding, or closure

holistic rubric   Sometimes called a simple rubric, judges student mastery levels without specific criteria

informal reading inventories   Individually administered reading passages designed to help educators determine a student's reading instructional needs

information communication technologies   Any hardware or software that allows a person to access, store, transmit, and/or modify digital information

informational or expository texts   A nonfiction genre of literature focusing on topical information

informational/explanatory writing   A form of writing focused on conveying information; provides students with enhanced comprehension of a topic

instructional level   The level at which a student can read with support from the teacher

just-right text   A text in which the reader can read about 9 out of 10 words and comprehend the meaning of the passage with little difficulty

kidwatching   An observational technique where the teacher intensely watches a child for a short time frame and jots down academic, social, or affective student reactions

language experience approach   A strategy in which students orally dictate their invented story to the recorder, who then writes it on chart paper for the student to read back aloud

learning styles   Individual characteristics of cognitive, affective, and physiological traits that serve as a measurement of how a learner perceives, interacts with, and responds to his or her learning environment

Lexile   A rough calculation of a student's reading level based on the student's achievement on the test given

mastery   Level of understanding of a learning standard or skill

Matthew effect   A reading theory that posits "the weak (readers) get weaker and the strong (readers) get stronger" through practice and increasing competence

maturity   Reading maturity is developed when students experience challenges and success with textual encounters and develop practice strategies that support understanding.

maze   To create a maze task, the teacher uses a narrative passage at the appropriate reading level for the student and replaces key words in the passage with a choice of three words.

metacognition   Thinking about the best way to learn something; includes the ability to self-assess one's strengths and weaknesses in literacy

modeling   When a teacher shares his or her thinking and reasoning processes to construct meaning with students

morphology   Morphology deals with how words are formed or put together from smaller, meaning-based affixes (roots, prefixes, and suffixes) and units of meaning (morphemes).

multicultural children's literature   Literature that accurately portrays a distinct cultural group

norm group   A sample of the intended test takers that is used as a benchmark to compare scores on a norm-referenced test

normal curve equivalent   Shows where a student falls along the normal bell curve of achievement

norm-referenced tests   The test takers' scores are compared with the norm group having taken the test.

onset   The initial consonant or consonants in a syllable

oral reading fluency   The ability to read, speak, or write easily, smoothly, and expressively

oral reading miscues   Any departure from the text when reading orally; strategies that students use to make sense of their understanding of the text

oral reading rate   The speed at which students can accurately read a grade-level passage in 1 minute

organizational aids   Help with textual organization of a book; include sidebars, glossary, table of contents, and so on

orthographic awareness   The knowledge of the symbols in a writing system

orthographic development   Spelling development as an essential component of growth in reading

orthographic features   Letters, their correct usage, and spelling

percentile rank   Shows the student's position relative to the norm group

performance level   An assigned level of performance that correlates with a range of scaled score

phonemes   The smallest unit of sound in our language system and the basic unit of speech; combines with other phonemes to make words

phonemic awareness   The ability to conceptualize that the sound of letters creates the spoken word and that one needs to recognize and segment the smallest part of a word and then blend the sounds of the letters to make the spoken word

phonics   The relationships between the sounds of a language and the letters used to represent those sounds; a way of teaching reading and spelling that stresses symbol–sound relationships

phonological awareness   Understanding of the sound structure of spoken words; an important and reliable predictor of reading ability

picture book   A genre of book that employs pictures to support the text content; great for read-aloud activities in the classroom

podcasting A term for creating, recording, and then sharing an audio (and sometimes video) presentation meant to be broadcast over the Internet

pragmatics One of the essential systems students rely on when reading, based on their background experiences, race, ethnicity, state or country of origin, or other factors that impact comprehension

primary prevention or Tier 1 Targeted needs-based learning that includes systematic processes of research-based interventions and frequent monitoring of student progress

print awareness Refers to print concepts and print language

print concepts An awareness that print carries and message

proctor A supervisor during an examination

progress monitoring Progress monitoring can occur every 2 weeks or every week through curriculum-based measurement that calculates targeted skills. Periodic checks (fidelity checks) are conducted to ensure that the delivery of instruction was provided in the way it was intended (University of the State of New York, 2010).

prosody Reading with expression and with words in meaningful phrase groups

purposeful reading Establishing a purpose, such as reading for a specific question, as determined by the teacher or student

qualitative analysis Evaluation of the features of a text

quantitative analysis A numerical evaluation of text difficulty

raw score Tallied by total number of questions the student has answered correctly on an assessment

readability formulas Analytic evaluations of a text that are most often determined by a computer

reading choice Students' ability to self-select texts to read

reading comprehension The act of understanding what is being read

reading motivation Student enthusiasm to approach the literacy task with self-assurance and confidence

reading rate The speed at which one reads; influenced by reading fluency

reading resiliency A reader's ability to read for sustained periods, seeking meaning as he or she goes. The reader may struggle with the selection but can persevere to gain fluency.

reading stamina The ability to focus and read independently for extended periods of time

rebuses Picture clips substituted for words for early readers

reliable When an assessment yields the same results when given to the student again under the same circumstances

reluctant readers Readers who demonstrate various avoidance traits in lieu of reading

repeated reading Multiple readings of the same reading selection for the purpose of fluency, comprehension, and increasing rate

Response to Intervention (RtI) Academic intervention used to provide early, systematic assistance to students who are having difficulty learning

retelling The student lists the main point or events in a narrative or expository selection. Retelling promotes knowledge of sequence, key ideas, and details.

rime The vowel or any consonant that follows the onset in a syllable

scaled score Converts a student's raw score to a common scale to adjust for differences in test items and/or form

schemas The background knowledge held by individuals at a certain time and under certain circumstances

screening Assessments conducted to identify students who may be at risk for poor learning outcomes

secondary prevention or Tier 2 Targeted student intervention that includes individualized assessments, interventions, and referral for specially designed interventions as needed

self-monitoring strategies   Enable students to select and use strategies to improve comprehension. Students are able to know when their reading makes sense and when it does not, and can then repair it.

self-regulated learning   Students self-monitor, employ fix-up strategies, and reflect on their ability to learn.

semantics   The cueing system that focuses on meaning cues from sentences, paragraphs, and the whole selection as a student reads the text

silent reading proficiency   Occurs when individuals access the ever-increasing stores of knowledge within texts

skills   Automatic applications of knowledge, such as decoding or encoding words

skills view of reading   Otherwise known as the bottom-up model; places emphasis on graphophonics or word recognition at the expense of comprehension

stamina   The growing ability to read for a significant length of time with comprehension and fluency

standard score   Represents how well a student performed on an assessment compared with the mean, or average

stanine   Group percentile ranks into relative areas of achievement on a scale of 1 to 9

strategies   Intentional applications of knowledge to solve a problem. Reading strategies include inferencing, making connections, visualizing, determining importance, synthesizing, questioning, and using effective text structures.

striving reader   Students who read below grade level

struggling reader   Students who find reading difficult due to disability, lack of literacy experience, or inadequate instruction. Literacy researchers suggest that the term *striving reader* may present a more positive connotation for these students.

syntactics   The cueing system that focuses on how students learn and practice the grammatical forms and structures of sentences

tertiary prevention or Tier 3   Increased intensity of specially designed learning that allows for accommodations or adaptations

text complexity   Determined by quantitative readability formulas, qualitative features, and an evaluation of the reader and demands of the task the reader will be asked to perform with the text

text-dependent questions   Questions that can be answered only by referring explicitly back to the text being read

text features   How the text is written, including the elements found in the text; might include pictures, graphics, bolded words, and so forth

think-aloud process   The teacher makes his or her thinking clear while processing a literacy challenge; after that, students mimic the teacher's thinking to share their mental processes.

tiering   Differentiating or making different levels for instruction or assessment to support student acquisition of learning skills

tracking   The ability to control the fine eye movements required to follow a line of print

transformational literacy   Reading has the ability to transform our knowledge of ourselves and the world.

tunnel vision   Limited or restricted sight in which objects cannot be properly seen if not close to the center of the field of view; no or reduced peripheral vision

valid   When an assessment has demonstrated that it assesses what it claims to assess

vocabulary   The collection of words and their meanings used in a particular language or by a particular person

wait time   Pausing for 3 to 5 seconds to allow students time to process a question, frame an answer, and then respond

WebQuest   A "web-based inquiry learning activity" (Ikpeze & Boyd, 2007, p. 645)

word consciousness   Developing in students a curiosity about words, with the goal of adding new vocabulary words to their schemas

word families   A group of words that share a rime

word recognition   The process of determining the pronunciation and meaning of a word

word work   The investigation of words throughout the curriculum

writing process   The creation of meaning through writing; involves planning, drafting, revising, proofreading, and publishing

zone of proximal development   Concept developed by Lev Vygotsky; the distance between the actual developmental level as determined by independent problem solving and the level of potential development as determined through problem solving under adult guidance or in collaboration with more capable peers (i.e., what the child can learn alone vs. what the child can learn in cooperation with others)

References

Abedi, J., Kao, J., Leon, S., Sullivan, L., Herman, J., Pope, R., Nambiar, V., & Mastergeorge, A. (2009). *Exploring factors that affect the accessibility of reading comprehension assessments for students with disabilities: A study of segmented text.* Minneapolis: University of Minnesota, Partnership for Accessible Reading Assessment.

Ackland, R. T. (1994). *Let's look at reading: Interactive professional development using informal reading inventories.* Unpublished doctoral dissertation, University of Illinois at Chicago.

Adams, M. J. (1990). *Beginning to read: Thinking and learning about print.* Cambridge: MIT Press.

Addy, S., & Wight, V. R. (2012, February). *Basic facts about low-income children, 2010: Children under age 18.* New York: National Center for Children in Poverty. Retrieved from http://www.nccp.org/publications/pub_1049.html

Afflerbach, P. (2005). National Reading Conference policy brief: High stakes testing and reading assessment. *Journal of Literacy Research, 37*(2), 151–162.

Afflerbach, P. (2007). *Understanding and using reading assessment, K–12.* Newark, DE: International Reading Association.

Afflerbach, P., Pearson, P. D., & Paris, S. G. (2008). Clarifying differences between reading skills and reading strategies. *The Reading Teacher, 61*(5), 364–373.

Alber-Morgan, S. (2010). *Using RTI to teach literacy to diverse learners, K–8: Strategies for the inclusive classroom.* Thousand Oaks, CA: Corwin.

Allington, R. L. (1983). Fluency: The neglected goal. *The Reading Teacher, 36,* 556–561.

Allington, R. L. (2006). Research and the three tier model. *Reading Today, 23*(5), 20.

Allington, R. L. (2007). Intervention all day long: New hope for struggling readers. *Voices From the Middle, 14*(4), 7–13.

Allington, R. L. (2012). *What really matters for struggling readers: Designing research-based programs.* Boston, MA: Pearson Education.

Allington, R. L., & Gabriel, R. E. (2012). Every child, every day. *Educational Leadership, 69*(6), 10–15.

Alverman, D. E. (1981). The compensatory effect of graphic organizers on descriptive text. *Journal of Educational Research, 75,* 44–48.

American Speech-Language-Hearing Association. (2009). *Summary of ED's 2% rule for students with disabilities: Alternate assessments based on modified academic achievement standards.* Retrieved from http://www.asha.org/uploadedFiles/advocacy/federal/nclb/NCLB2PercentRule.pdf#search=%22alternate%22

Anderson, R. C., & Freebody, P. (1981). Vocabulary knowledge. In J. Guthrie (Ed.), *Comprehension and teaching: Research reviews* (pp. 77–117). Newark, DE: International Reading Association.

Anderson, R. C., Hiebert, E. H., Scott, J. A., & Wilkinson, I. A. G. (1985). *Becoming a nation of readers: The report of the Commission on Reading.* Champaign: University of Illinois, National Academy of Education.

Annenberg Foundation. (2014). *Literature: Exploring point of view.* Retrieved from http://www.learner.org/interactives/literature/read/pov1.html

Anxiety Disorders Association of Canada. (2007). *Childhood anxiety.* Retrieved from http://www.anxietycanada.ca/english/childhood.php

Apple Classrooms of Tomorrow–Today. (n.d.). *Social and emotional connections with students.* Retrieved from http://education.apple.com/acot2/connections/#more

Applegate, A. J., Applegate, M. D., & Turner, J. D. (2010). Learning disabilities or teaching disabilities: Rethinking literacy failure. *The Reading Teacher, 64*(3), 211–213.

Armbruster, B. B. (2010). *Put reading first: The research building blocks for teaching children to read: Kindergarten through Grade 3.* Washington, DC: National Institute for Literacy..

Atwell, N. (1987). *In the middle: Writing, reading, and learning with adolescents.* Portsmouth, NH: Boynton/Cook.

Au, K. (2002). Multicultural factors and the effective instruction of students of diverse backgrounds. In A. E. Farstrup & S. Samuels (Eds.), *What research has to say about reading instruction* (pp. 392–413). Newark, DE: International Reading Association.

August, D., & Shanahan, T. (Eds.). (2006). *Developing literacy in second-language learners: Report of the National Literacy Panel on Language-Minority Children and Youth.* Mahwah, NJ: Erlbaum. Retrieved from http://www.cal.org/projects/archive/nlpreports/Executive_Summary.pdf

Australian Disability Clearinghouse on Education and Training. (n.d.-a). *Fact sheet: Assessment: Strategies for students with physical impairments or chronic health conditions.* Retrieved from http://www.adcet.edu.au/View.aspx?id=4272

Australian Disability Clearinghouse on Education and Training. (n.d.-b). *Fact sheet: Teaching and assessment strategies for deaf and hearing impaired students.* Retrieved from http://www.adcet.edu.au/view.aspx?id=3956

Bailey, A. L., & Heritage, M. (2008). *Formative assessment for literacy, Grades K–6: Building reading and academic language skills across the curriculum.* Thousand Oaks, CA: Corwin.

Bambrick-Santoyo, P. (2010). *Driven by data: A practical guide for improving instruction.* San Francisco, CA: Jossey-Bass.

Bandura, A. (1977). Self-efficacy: Toward a unifying theory of behavioral change. *Psychological Review, 84*(2), 191–215.

Barnhouse, D., & Vinton, V. (2012). *What readers really do: Teaching the process of meaning making.* Portsmouth, NH: Heinemann.

Barron, R. F. (1979). The use of vocabulary as an advance organizer. In H. L. Herber & P. L. Sanders (Eds.), *Research on reading in the content areas: The fourth report* (pp. 171–176). Syracuse: NY: Syracuse University Press.

Bean, R., & Lillenstein, J. (2012). Response to Intervention and the changing roles of school personnel. *The Reading Teacher, 65*(7), 491–501.

Bear, D. R., Invernizzi, M. A., Johnston, F. R., & Templeton, S. R. (2009). *Words their way: Letter and picture sorts for emergent spellers* (2nd ed.). Boston, MA. Pearson.

Bear, D., Invernizzi, M., Templeton, S., & Johnston, F. (2008). *Words their way: Word study for phonics, vocabulary, and spelling instruction* (4th ed.). Boston, MA: Pearson.

Bear, D. R., Invernizzi, M. A., Templeton, S. R., & Johnston, F. R. (2011). *Words their way: Word study for phonics, vocabulary and spelling instruction* (5th ed.). Boston, MA. Pearson.

Beck, I. L., McKeown, M. G., Hamilton, R. L., & Kucan, L. (1997). *Questioning the author: An approach for enhancing student engagement with text.* Newark, DE: International Reading Association.

Bennett-Armistead, S. V., Duke, N. K., & Moses, A. M. (2005). *Literacy and the youngest learner: Best practices for educators of children from birth to 5.* New York: Scholastic.

Berger, P., & Trexler, S. (2010). *Choosing Web 2.0 tools for learning and teaching in a digital world.* Santa Barbara, CA: Libraries Unlimited.

Betts, E. A. (1946). *Foundations of reading instruction: With emphasis on differentiated guidance.* New York: American Book Company.

Biemiller, A. (2003). Oral comprehension sets the ceiling on reading comprehension. *American Educator, 27*, 1–13.

Billman, J., & Sherman, J. (2003). *Observation and participation in early childhood settings: A practicum guide.* Boston, MA: Allyn & Bacon.

Bircher, K. (2012). What makes a good picture book app? *Horn Book Magazine, 88*(2), 72–78.

Blachowicz, C. L. Z., & Fisher, P. J. L. (2010). *Teaching vocabulary in all classrooms* (4th ed.). Columbus, OH: Merrill/Prentice Hall.

Blachowicz, C. L. Z., & Obrochta, C. (2005). Vocabulary visits: Virtual field trips for content vocabulary development. *The Reading Teacher, 59*(3), 262–268.

Blair, T. R., Rupley, W. H., & Nichols, W. D. (2007). The effective teacher of reading: Considering the "what" and "how" of instruction. *The Reading Teacher, 60*(5), 432–438.

Blau, L. (2014). Five surefire strategies for developing reading fluency. Retrieved from http://www.scholastic.com/teachers/article/5-surefire-strategies-developing-reading-fluency

Block, J. H., & Block, J. (1980). The role of ego-control and ego-resiliency in the organization of behavior. In W. A. Collins (Ed.), *Development of cognition, affect, and social relations: The Minnesota symposia on child psychology* (Vol. 13, pp. 39–101). Hillsdale, NJ: Erlbaum.

Bluestein, N. A. (2010). Unlocking text features for determining importance in expository text: A strategy for struggling readers. *The Reading Teacher, 63*(7), 597–600.

Börsch-Haubold, A. (2006, December 20). Sleep and learning. *Science in School, (3).* Retrieved from http://www.scienceinschool.org/2006/issue3/sleep

Boushey, G., & Moser, J. (2006). *The Daily Five: Fostering literacy independence in the elementary grades.* Portland, ME: Stenhouse.

Boushey, G., & Moser, J. (2009). *The café book: Engaging all students in daily literacy assessment and instruction.* Portland, ME: Stenhouse.

Boyd-Batstone, P. (2004). Focused anecdotal records assessment: A tool for standards-based authentic assessment. *The Reading Teacher, 58*(31), 230–239.

Bradley, B. A., & Jones, J. (2007). Sharing alphabet books in early childhood classrooms. *The Reading Teacher, 60*(5), 452–463.

Bridges, L. B. (1995). *Creating your classroom community.* York, ME: Stenhouse.

Bromley, K. (2002). *Stretching students' vocabulary: Best practices for building the rich vocabulary students need to achieve in reading, writing, and the content areas.* Jefferson City, MO: Scholastic.

Bromley, K. (2012). Using smartphones to supplement classroom reading. *The Reading Teacher, 66*(4), 340–344.

Brown, H., & Cambourne, B. (1990). *Read and retell.* Portsmouth, NH: Heinemann.

Brozo, W. G., & Flynt, E. S. (2007). Content literacy: Fundamental tool kit. *The Reading Teacher, 61*(2), 192–194.

Brozo, W. G., Moorman, G., Meyer, C., & Stewart, T. (2013). Content area reading and disciplinary literacy: A case for the radical center. *Journal of Adolescent and Adult Literacy, 56*(5), 353–357.

Brozo, W. G., & Simpson, M. L. (2007). *Content literacy for today's adolescents: Honoring diversity and building competence.* Upper Saddle River, NJ: Merrill/Prentice Hall.

Buczynski, J. A. (2010). Library eBooks: Some can't find them, others find them and don't know what they are. *Internet Reference Services Quarterly, 15*(1), 11–19.

Buehl, D. (1995). *Classroom strategies for interactive learning.* Schofield: Wisconsin State Reading Association.

Burke, J. (2000). *Reading reminders: Tools, tips, and techniques.* Portsmouth, NH: Boyton/Cook.

Calkins, L. M. (1994). *The art of teaching writing.* Portsmouth, NH: Heinemann.

Cambourne, B. (2001). Conditions for literacy learning: Turning learning theory into classroom instruction: A minicase study. *The Reading Teacher, 54*(4), 414–417.

Canado, M. L. P. (2011). English and Spanish spelling: Are they really different? *The Reading Teacher, 56*(6), 522–531.

Canizares, S., & Moreton, D. (1997). *Who lives in a tree?* New York: Scholastic.

Carnine, D. W., Silbert, J., Kame'enui, E. J., & Tarver, S. G. (2004). *Direct reading instruction* (4th ed.). Upper Saddle River, NJ: Merrill Prentice Hall.

Center for the Improvement of Early Reading Achievement. (2010). *Putting reading first, kindergarten through Grade 3: The research building blocks for teaching children to read* (3rd ed.). Washington, DC: National Institute for Literacy.

Centers for Disease Control and Prevention. (2014). *Child maltreatment prevention.* Retrieved from http://www.cdc.gov/ViolencePrevention/childmaltreatment

Cerullo, M. M. (1996). *Coral reef: A city that never sleeps.* Dutton, NY: Cobblehill Books.

Chall, J. S. (1983). *Stages of reading development.* New York: McGraw-Hill.

Chall, J. S. (1996). *Stages of reading development* (2nd ed.). Fort Worth, TX: Harcourt Brace.

Chall, J. S., & Jacobs, V. A. (2003). Poor children's fourth-grade slump. *American Educator, 27,* 14–15.

Cheyney, W. (n.d.). *Early language and literacy: The home–school connection.* San Antonio, TX: Pearson Education. Retrieved from http://assets.pearson-school.com/asset_mgr/legacy/200747/ReaAutMon0505594Lit2Cheyney_4007_1.pdf

Children's Defense Fund. (2012a, September 20). *Families struggle: Child poverty remains high* [Press release]. Retrieved from http://www.childrensdefense.org/newsroom/cdf-in-the-news/press-releases/2012/child-poverty-remains-high.html

Children's Defense Fund. (2012b). *Policy priorities: Child nutrition and obesity.* Retrieved from http://www.childrensdefense.org/policy-priorities/childrens-health/child-nutrition/

Children's Vision Information Network. (n.d.). *Vision and reading: Important information about why your child may be struggling.* Retrieved from http://www.childrensvision.com/reading.htm

CLAN. (2012). *Chronic conditions.* Retrieved from http://www.clanchildhealth.org/Chronic-Conditions

Clark, D. (2000, May 29). *Learning styles and preferences.* Retrieved from http://www.nwlink.com/~donclark/hrd/styles.html

Clay, M. M. (1979). *The early detection of reading difficulties* (2nd ed.). Portsmouth, NH: Heinemann.

Clay, M. M. (1985). *The early detection of reading difficulties* (3rd ed.). Portsmouth, NH: Heinemann.

Clay, M. M. (1991). *Becoming literate: The construction of inner control.* Auckland, New Zealand: Heinemann.

Clay, M. M. (1993). *An observation survey of early literacy achievement.* Portsmouth, NH: Heinemann.

Clay, M. M. (1998). *By different paths to common outcomes.* York, ME: Stenhouse.

Clay, M. M. (2000). *Concepts About Print: What have children learned about the way we print language?* Portsmouth, NH: Heinemann.

Clay, M. M. (2001). *Change over time in children's literacy development.* Portsmouth, NH: Heinemann.

Clay, M. M. (2002). *Observation survey of early literacy achievement.* Portsmouth, NH: Heinemann.

Clay, M. M. (2005a). *Literacy lessons: Designed for individuals.* Portsmouth, NH: Heinemann.

Clay, M. M. (2005b). *An observation survey of early literacy achievement.* Portsmouth, ME: Heinemann.

Clay, M. M. (n.d.). Clay's Observation Survey: Planned observations can capture evidence of early progress. Retrieved from http://readingrecovery.org/reading-recovery/teaching-children/observation-survey

Clymer, T. (1963). The utility of phonic generalizations in the primary grades. *The Reading Teacher, 16,* 252–258.

Coffey, H. (2012). *Benchmark assessments.* Retrieved from The University of North Carolina at Chapel Hill, Learn NC website: http://www.learnnc.org/lp/pages/5317

Cohen, H. (2012). *Children and depression.* Retrieved from http://psychcentral.com/lib/2007/children-and-depression

Cohen, L. (2009). *Exploring cultural heritage in a kindergarten classroom.* Retrieved from http://www.naeyc.org/files/yc/file/200905/BTJCohen.pdf

Coiro, J. (2009). Rethinking online reading assessment. *Educational Leadership, 66*(6), 59–63.

Collard, S. N., III. (2000). *The forest in the clouds.* Boston, MA: Charlesbridge.

Colorín Colorado. (2007a). Informal assessments for English language learners. Retrieved from http://www.colorincolorado.org/educators/assessment/informal

Colorín Colorado. (2007b). Reading comprehension strategies for English language learners: Additional steps for ELLs. Retrieved from http://www.colorincolorado.org/article/14342/

Colorín Colorado. (2007c). Vocabulary development. Retrieved from http://www.colorincolorado.org/educators/teaching/vocabulary/

Comber, B., & Kamler, B. (Eds.). (2005). *Turn-around pedagogies: Literacy interventions for at-risk students.* Newton, NSW, Australia: Primary English Teaching Association.

Common Core State Standards Initiative. (2014a). *College and career readiness anchor standards for reading.* Retrieved from http://www.corestandards.org/ELA-Literacy/CCRA/R/

Common Core State Standards Initiative. (2014b). *Reading: Foundational skills—Kindergarten.* Retrieved from http://www.corestandards.org/ELA-Literacy/RF/K/

Common Core State Standards Initiative. (2014c). Writing: Grade 5. Retrieved from http://www.corestandards.org/ELA-Literacy/W/5

Connecticut Administrators of Programs for English Language Learners. (2011). *English language learners and special education: A resource handbook.* Retrieved from http://www.sde.ct.gov/sde/lib/sde/pdf/curriculum/bilingual/CAPELL_SPED_resource_guide.pdf

Cramer, E. H. (1980). Informal reading inventories go commercial. *Curriculum Review, 19,* 424–429.

Cunningham, P., & Allington, R. (2011). *Classrooms that work: They can all read and write* (5th ed.). Boston, MA: Allyn & Bacon.

Cziko, C., Greenleaf, C., Hurwitz, L., & Schoenbach, R. (2000). What is reading? An excerpt from reading for understanding. *The Quarterly, 22*(3), 38–39.

daCruz Payne, C. (2005). *Shared reading for today's classroom.* New York: Scholastic.

Daniels, H. (2002a). Expository text in literature circles. *Voices From the Middle, 9*(4), 7–14.

Daniels, H. (2002b). *Literature circles: Voice and choice in book clubs and reading groups.* Portland, ME: Stenhouse.

Daniels, H. (Ed.). (2011). *Comprehension going forward.* Portsmouth, NH: Heinemann.

Daniels, H., & Steineke, N. (2011). *Texts and lessons for content-area reading.* Portsmouth, NH: Heinemann.

Danili, E., & Reid, N. (2006). Cognitive factors that can potentially affect pupils' test performance. *Chemistry Education Research and Practice, 7*(2), 64–83.

Darling, S. (2005). Strategies for engaging parents in home support of reading acquisition. *The Reading Teacher, 58*(5), 476–479.

Darling-Hammond, L. (2006). No Child Left Behind and high school reform. *Harvard Educational Review, 76*(4), 642–667.

Dechant, E. V. (1993). *Whole-language reading: A comprehensive teaching guide.* Lancaster, PA: Technomic.

Deshler, D. D., Palincsar, A. S., Biancarosa, G., & Nair, M. (2007). *Informed choices for struggling adolescent readers: A research-based guide to instructional programs and practices.* Newark, DE: International Reading Association.

Devries, B. (2004). *Reading assessment and intervention for the classroom teacher.* Scottsdale, AZ: Holcomb Hathaway.

Diamond, L., & Thornes, B. J. (Eds.). (2008). *Assessing reading: Multiple measures for kindergarten through twelfth grade* (2nd ed.). Novato, CA: Arena Press.

Diederich, P. (1974). *Measuring growth in English.* Urbana, IL: National Council of Teachers of English.

Diller, D. (2007). *Making the most of small groups: Differentiation for all.* Portland, ME: Stenhouse.

Dixon, B., Mainville, S., Farquer, T., & Gray, T. (2012). *Common Core teaching and learning strategies: English and language arts, reading informational text, Grades K–5.* Springfield: Illinois State Board of Education. Retrieved from http://www.isbe.net/common_core/pdf/ela-teach-strat-read-text-k-5.pdf

Dozier, C., Garnett, S., & Tabatabai, S. (2011, October). Responsive teaching through conversation. *The Spot: The ESA's Magazine,* 10–11. Retrieved from http://issuu.com/esa_magazine/docs/thespot.oct.11

Duke, N., & Moses, A. (2003). *10 research-tested ways to build children's vocabulary.* New York: Scholastic. Retrieved from http://teacher.scholastic.com/products/readingline/pdfs/ProfessionalPaper.pdf

Duke, N. K., & Pearson, P. D. (2002). Effective practices for developing reading comprehension. In A. E. Farstrup & S. J. Samuels (Eds.), *What research has to say about reading instruction* (3rd ed., pp. 205–242). Newark, DE: International Reading Association.

EDGE₄ (Education Data Gathering Engine). (n.d.). What is EDGE₄? Retrieved from https://www.edge4.ca/whatis.aspx

Edmunds, K. M., & Bauserman, K. L. (2006). What teachers can learn about reading motivation through conversations with children. *The Reading Teacher, 59*(5), 414–424.

Education Department of South Australia. (1990). *Children's writing development.* Crystal Lake, IL: Rigby.

Educational Testing Service. (2009). *Guidelines for the assessment of English language learners.* Retrieved from http://www.ets.org/s/about/pdf/ell_guidelines.pdf

EducationFever.com. (n.d.). *Print awareness: Concepts of print.* Retrieved August 11, 2013, from http://www.educationfever.com/?page_id=12

Ehri, L. C. (1991). Development of the ability to read words. In R. Barr, M. L. Kamil, P. Mosenthal, & P. D. Pearson (Eds.), *Handbook of reading research* (Vol. II, pp. 383–417). White Plains, NY: Longman.

Ehri, L. C., & McCormick, S. (2004). Phases of word learning: Implications for instruction with delayed and disabled readers. In R. B. Ruddell & N. J. Unrau (Eds.), *Theoretical models and processes of reading* (5th ed., pp. 365–389). Newark, DE: International Reading Association.

EngageNY. (2011). *What to do when there's a "2": Recommended action steps to increase proficiency on the DDI rubric (draft).* Retrieved from http://www.engageny.org/sites/default/files/resource/attachments/9b-implementation_rubric_ddi-what_to_do_with_2s_7-11.pdf

EngageNY. (2013, August 5). New York State Common Core sample questions. Retrieved from http://engageny.org/resource/new-york-state-common-core-sample-questions

Enriquez, G., Jones, S., & Clarke, L. W. (2010). Turning around our perceptions and practices, then our readers. *The Reading Teacher, 64*(1), 73–76.

Ereading Worksheets. (2011). Point of view. Retrieved from http://www.ereadingworksheets.com/point-of-view/

Fang, Z., & Coatoam, S. (2013). Disciplinary literacy: What you want to know about it. *Journal of Adolescent and Adult Literacy, 56*(8), 627–632.

Fauth, R. C., Brady-Smith, C., & Brooks-Gunn, J. (2012). *Poverty and education: Overview, children and adolescents.* Retrieved from http://education.stateuniversity.com/pages/2330/Poverty-Education.html

Faver, S. (2008). Repeated reading of poetry can enhance reading fluency. *The Reading Teacher, 62*(4), 350–352.

Feeding America. (2014). *Hunger in America: Child hunger facts.* Retrieved from http://feedingamerica.org/hunger-in-america/hunger-facts/child-hunger-facts.aspx

Feezell, G. (2012). Robust vocabulary instruction in a readers' workshop. *The Reading Teacher, 56*(3), 233–237.

Fink, R. (2006). *Why Jane and John couldn't read—and how they learned.* Newark, DE: International Reading Association.

Finn, J. D. (1993). *School engagement and students at risk.* Washington, DC: National Center for Educational Statistics.

Fisher, D. (2014). Close reading and the CCSS: Part 1. Retrieved from http://www.mhecommoncoretoolbox.com/close-reading-and-the-ccss-part-1.html

Fisher, D., & Frey, N. (2008). *Better learning through structured teaching: A framework for the gradual release of responsibility.* Alexandria, VA: Association for Supervision and Curriculum Development.

Fisher, D., & Frey, N. (2012). Motivating boys to read: Inquiry, modeling, and choice matter. *Journal of Adolescent and Adult Literacy, 55*(7), 587–596.

Fitzgerald, J., & Shanahan, T. (2000). Reading and writing relations and their development. *Educational Psychologist, 35*(1), 39–50.

Flanigan, K., Hayes, L., Templeton, S., Bear, D. R., Invernizzi, M., & Johnston, F. (2011). *Words Their Way with struggling readers: Word study for reading, vocabulary and spelling instruction, Grades 4–12.* Boston, MA: Pearson.

The Flesch Grade Level Readability Formula. (n.d.). *Readability Formulas.* Retrieved from http://www.readabilityformulas.com/flesch-grade-level-readability-formula.php

The Flesch Reading Ease Readability Formula. (n.d.). *Readability Formulas.* Retrieved from http://www.readabilityformulas.com/flesch-reading-ease-readability-formula.php

Ford, H. (2009, December 23). Norm-referenced testing. Retrieved from http://www.education.com/reference/article/norm-referenced-testing

Fountas, I. C., & Pinnell, G. S. (1996). *Guided reading: Good first teaching for all children.* Portsmouth, NH: Heinemann.

Fountas, I. C., & Pinnell, G. S. (1998). *Word matters: Teaching phonics and spelling in the reading/writing classroom.* Portsmouth, NH: Heinemann.

Fountas, I. C., & Pinnell, G. S. (2001). *Guiding readers and writers: Teaching comprehension, genre, and content literacy.* Portsmouth, NH: Heinemann.

Fountas, I., & Pinnell, G. S. (2005). *Leveled books K–8: Matching text to readers for effective teaching.* Portsmouth, NH: Heinemann.

Fountas, I. C., & Pinnell, G. S. (2008). *Benchmark assessment system* (2nd ed.). Portsmouth, NH: Heinemann. Retrieved from http://www.heinemann.com/fountasandpinnell/BAS2_Overview.aspx

Fountas, I., & Pinnell, G. S. (2009). *Fountas and Pinnell benchmark online data management system.* Portsmouth, NH: Heinemann. Retrieved from http://www.heinemann.com/products/DMS0010.aspx

Fountas, I. C., & Pinnell, G. S. (2010). *The continuum of literacy learning: Grades pre-K through 6.* Portsmouth, NH: Heinemann.

Fountas, I. C., & Pinnell, G. S. (2012). Guided reading: The romance and reality. *The Reading Teacher, 66*(4), 268–284.

Fox, B. J. (2000). *Word identification strategies: Phonics from a new perspective* (2nd ed.). Upper Saddle River, NJ: Prentice Hall.

Fox, B. J. (2005). *Phonics for the teacher of reading* (9th ed.). Boston, MA. Pearson.

Francis, D. J., Fletcher, J. M., Stuebing, K. K., Lyon, G. R., Shaywitz, B. A., & Shaywitz, S. E. (2005). Psychometric approaches to the identification of LD: IQ and achievement scores are not sufficient. *Journal of Learning Disabilities, 38*(2), 98–108.

Fredricks, J. A., Blumenfeld, P. C., & Paris, A. H. (2004). School engagement: Potential of the concept, state of the evidence. *Review of Educational Research, 74*(1), 59–109.

Freeman, Y., & Freeman, D. (2004). Connecting students to culturally relevant texts. *Talking Points, 15*(2), 7–11. Retrieved from http://www.ncte.org/library/NCTEFiles/Resources/Journals/TP/0152-aprilmay04/TP0152Connecting.pdf

Friedland, E. S., & Truesdell, K. S. (2004). Kids reading together: Ensuring the success of a buddy reading program. *The Reading Teacher, 58*(1), 76–83.

Fry, E. (1998). The most common phonograms. *Reading Teacher, 51*, 620–622.

Fuchs, D., & Fuchs, L. S. (2009). Responsiveness to intervention: Multilevel assessment and instruction as early identification and disability identification. *The Reading Teacher, 63*(3), 250–252.

Fusaro, M. (2008). Measure for measures: What do standardized tests really tell us about students and schools? *Harvard Graduate School of Education: Usable Knowledge.* Retrieved from http://www.uknow.gse.harvard.edu/decisions/DD315-608.html

Gadamer, H.-G. (1989). *Truth and method* (2nd ed., J. Weinsheimer & D. G. Marshall, Trans.). New York: Crossroad. (Original work published 1960)

Gallagher, K. (n.d.). Article of the week. Retrieved from http://kellygallagher.org/resources/articles.html

Gallaudet University. (n.d.). *Emotional/behavioral disorders.* Retrieved from http://www.gallaudet.edu/clerc_center/information_and_resources/info_to_go/educate_children_(3_to_21)/students_with_disabilities/emotionalbehavioral_disorders.html

Gambrell, L. B. (1996). Creating classrooms that foster reading motivation. *The Reading Teacher, 50*(1), 14–25.

Gambrell, L. B. (2011). Seven rules of engagement: What's most important to know about motivation to read. *The Reading Teacher, 65*(3), 172–178.

Gambrell, L. B., Mazzoni, S. A., & Almasi, J. F. (2000). Promoting collaboration, social interaction, and engagement with text. In L. Baker, M. J. Dreher, & J. T. Guthrie (Eds.), *Engaging young readers: Promoting achievement and motivation* (pp. 119–139). New York: Guilford Press.

Ganske, K. (2014). *Word journeys: Assessment-guided phonics, spelling, and vocabulary instruction* (2nd ed.). New York: Guilford Press.

Gardner, H. (1991). *The unschooled mind: How children think and how schools should teach.* New York: Basic Books.

Gay, G. (2010). Teaching literacy in cultural context. In K. Dunsmore & D. Fisher (Eds.), *Bringing literacy home* (pp. 161–183). Newark, DE: International Reading Association.

Gaylord, V., Quinn, M., McComas, J., & Lehr, C. (Eds.). (2005). *Impact: Feature issue on fostering success in school and beyond for students with emotional/behavioral disorders 18*(2). Minneapolis: University of Minnesota, Institute on Community Integration.

Gill, S. (2006). Teaching rimes with shared reading. *The Reading Teacher, 60*(2), 191–193.

Glover, D. (1997). *Simple machine: Wheels and cranks.* Portsmouth, NH: Heinemann.

Gonzalez, N., Moll, L. C., Floyd-Tenery, M., Rivera, A., Rendón, P., Gonzalez, R., & Amanti, C. (1993). *Teacher research on funds of knowledge: Learning from households* (Educational Practice Report 6). Santa Cruz: National Center for Research on Cultural Diversity and Second Language Learning, University of California.

Goodman, K. S. (1969). Analysis of reading miscues: Applied psycholinguistics. *Reading Research Quarterly, 5*(1), 9–30.

Goodman, K. S. (1973). Miscues: Windows on the reading process. In K. S. Goodman (Ed.), *Miscue analysis: Applications to reading instruction* (pp. 3–14). Urbana, IL: ERIC Clearinghouse on Reading and Communication Skills.

Goodman, Y. M. (1985). Kidwatching: Observing children in the classroom. In A. Jaggar & M. T. Smith-Burke (Eds.), *Observing the language learner* (pp. 9–18). Newark, DE: International Reading Association.

Goodman, Y. M., & Marek, A. M. (1996). *Retrospective miscue analysis: Revaluing readers and reading.* Katonah, NY: Richard C. Owen.

Graham, S., & Hebert, M. (2010). *Writing to read: Evidence for how writing can improve reading.* New York: Alliance for Excellent Education.

Graphix. (n.d.). *Using graphic novels with children and teens: A guide for teachers and librarians.* Retrieved from http://www.scholastic.com/graphix/Scholastic_BoneDiscussion.pdf

Graves, D. H. (1983). *Writing: Teachers and children at work.* Portsmouth, NH: Heinemann.

Graves, D. H. (1994). *A fresh look at writing.* Portsmouth, NH: Heinemann.

Graves, M. F. (2000). A vocabulary program to complement and bolster a middle-grade comprehension program. In B. M. Taylor, M. F. Graves, & P. van den Broek (Eds.), *Reading for meaning: Fostering comprehension in the middle grades* (pp. 116–135). New York: Teachers College Press; Newark, DE: International Reading Association.

Graves, M. F., & Watts-Taffe, S. M. (2002). The place of word consciousness in a research-based vocabulary program. In A. E. Farstrup & S. J. Samuels (Eds.), *What research has to say about reading instruction* (3rd ed., pp. 140–165). Newark, DE: International Reading Association.

Graves, M. F., & Watts-Taffe, S. (2008). For the love of words: Fostering word consciousness in young readers. *The Reading Teacher, 62*(3), 185–193.

GreatSchools Staff. (2014). *Accommodations, modifications, and alternative assessments: How they affect instruction and assessment.* Retrieved from http://

www.greatschools.org/special-education/legal-rights/713-accommodations-IEP.gs

Green, C. R., & Halsall, S. W. (2004). Head Start families sharing literature. *Early Childhood Research and Practice, 6*(2). Retrieved from http://ecrp.uiuc.edu/v6n2/green.html

Greenwood, S. C. (2007). Simple to sophisticated, abhorring to adoring: Students define reading. *Journal of Reading Education, 32*(3), 37–39.

Gregg, M., & Sekeres, D. C. (2006). Supporting children's reading of expository text in the geography classroom. *The Reading Teacher, 60*(2), 102–110.

Griffith, L. W., & Rasinski, T. V. (2004). A focus on fluency: How one teacher incorporated fluency with her reading curriculum. *The Reading Teacher, 58*(2), 126–137.

Guernsey, L. (2011). Are ebooks any good? *School Library Journal, 57*(6), 28–32.

Gunning, T. G. (2010). *Assessing and correcting reading and writing difficulties.* Boston, MA: Allyn & Bacon.

Gunning, T. G. (2013). *Creating literacy instruction for all students* (8th ed.). Boston, MA: Pearson.

Guskey, T. R. (2003). How classroom assessments improve learning. *Educational Leadership, 60*(5), 6–11.

Guthrie, J. T., Seifert, M., Burnham, N., & Caplan, R. (1974). The maze technique to assess, monitor reading comprehension. *The Reading Teacher, 28*, 161–168.

Guthrie, J. T., & Wigfield, A. (2000). Engagement and motivation to read. In M. L. Kamil, P. B. Mosenthal, P. D. Pearson, & R. Barr (Eds.), *Handbook of reading research* (Vol. 3, pp. 403–422). Mahwah, NJ: Erlbaum.

Halladay, J. L. (2012). Revisiting key assumptions of the reading level framework. *The Reading Teacher, 66*(1), 53–62.

Hammill, D. (2004). What we know about correlates of reading. *Exceptional Children, 70*(4), 453–468.

Harris, A. J., & Sipay, E. R. (1990). *How to increase reading ability: A guide to developmental and remedial methods* (9th ed.). New York: Longman.

Harris, T. L., & Hodges, R. E. (Eds.). (2005). *The literacy dictionary.* Newark, DE: International Reading Association.

Harste, J. C. (2009). Reading as identity. *Journal of Reading Education, 34*(3), 5–7.

Hart, B., & Risley, T. (1995). *Meaningful differences in the everyday experiences of young American children.* Baltimore, MD: Brookes.

Hart, D. (1994). *Authentic assessment: A handbook for educators.* Menlo Park, CA: Addison-Wesley.

Hedin, L. R., & Conderman, G. (2010). Teaching students to comprehend informational text through rereading. *The Reading Teacher, 63*(7), 556–563.

Heisey, N., & Kucan, L. (2010). Introducing science concepts to primary students through read-alouds: Interactions and multiple texts make the difference. *The Reading Teacher, 63*(8), 666–676.

Helman, L., Bear, D. R., Invernizzi, M. A., Templeton, S. R., & Johnston, F. R. (2008). *Words their way: Emergent sorts for Spanish-speaking English learners.* Boston, MA: Pearson.

Helman, L., Bear, D. R., Templeton, S. R., Invernizzi, M. A., & Johnston, F. R. (2012). *Words their way with English learners: Word study for phonics, vocabulary, and spelling* (2nd ed.). Boston, MA: Pearson.

Hempenstall, K. (2011). *Phonemic awareness: What does it mean?* Retrieved from http://www.educationoasis.com/resources/Articles/phonemic_awareness.htm

Hendricks, C., & Rinsky, L. A. (2006). *Teaching word recognition skills* (7th ed.). Boston, MA: Pearson Education.

Henk, W. A., & Melnick, S. A. (1995). The reader self-perception scale (RSPS): A new tool for measuring how children feel about themselves as readers. *The Reading Teacher, 48*(6), 470–482.

Henry, L. A. (2006). Searching for an answer: The critical role of new literacies while reading on the Internet. *The Reading Teacher, 59*(7), 614–627.

Hiebert, E. H. (2012). The Common Core State Standards and text complexity. In M. Hougen & S. Smartt (Eds.), *Fundamentals of literacy instruction and assessment, Pre-K–6* (pp. 111–120). Baltimore, MD: Brookes.

Hilden, K., & Jones, J. (2011). Rewards for student reading: A good idea or not? *Reading Today, 29*(2), 6–7.

Hodgson, K. (n.d.). Strategies for online reading comprehension. Retrieved from http://www.learnnc.org/lp/pages/6958

Hoffman, J. (1992). Critical reading/thinking across the curriculum: Using I-charts to support learning. *Language Arts, 69*(2), 121–27.

Hollenbeck, A. F. (2010). Instructional makeover: Supporting the reading comprehension of students with learning disabilities in a discussion-based format. *Intervention in School and Clinic, 46*(4), 211–220.

Hollingsworth, L. (2007). Five ways to prepare for standardized tests without sacrificing best practice. *The Reading Teacher, 61*(4), 339–342.

Honig, B., Diamond, L., & Gutlohn, L. (2012). *Teaching reading sourcebook* (updated 2nd ed.). Novato, CA: Academic Therapy.

Houston, C. (2011). Digital books for digital natives: A tour of open access children's digital literature collections. *Children and Libraries, 9*(3), 39–45.

How Many Syllables (2014). Retrieved from http://howmanysyllables.com

Huck, S. W. (2012). Stanine scores. Retrieved from http://www.readingstats.com/fifth/email2d.htm

Hurst, B., Scales, K. B., Frecks, E., & Lewis, K. (2011). Signing up for reading: Students read aloud to the class. *The Reading Teacher, 64*(6), 439–443.

Hutchinson, H. B., Rose, A., Bederson, B. B., & Weeks, A. C. (2005). The International Children's Digital Library: A case study in designing for a multilingual, multicultural, multigenerational audience. *Information Technology and Libraries, 24*(1), 4–12.

Ikpeze, C. H., & Boyd, F. B. (2007). Web-based inquiry learning: Facilitating thoughtful literacy with WebQuests. *The Reading Teacher, 60*(7), 644–654.

Institute of Education Sciences. (2007). *National Assessment of Education Progress.* Retrieved from http://nces.ed.gov/nationsreportcard

Institute of Education Sciences. (2008). *National Assessment of Education Progress.* Retrieved from http://nces.ed.gov/nationsreportcard

Institute of Reading Development. (2014). *The stages of reading development.* Retrieved from http://reading-programs.org/our-approach/stages-of-reading-development

International Children's Digital Library Foundation. (n.d.). Mission. Retrieved from http://en.childrenslibrary.org/about/mission.shtml

International Reading Association. (2000a). *Excellent reading teachers: A position statement of the International Reading Association.* Newark, DE: Author. Retrieved from http://www.reading.org/General/AboutIRA/PositionStatements/ExcellentTeachersPosition.aspx

International Reading Association. (2000b). *Making it right means making it different: Honoring children's rights to excellent reading instruction.* Newark, DE: Author. Retrieved from http://www.reading.org/General/AboutIRA/PositionStatements/ChildrensRightsPostion.aspx

International Reading Association. (2003). *Investment in teacher preparation in the United States: A policy statement.* Retrieved from http://www.reading.org/Libraries/position-statements-and-resolutions/ps1060_TeacherPreparation_web.pdf

International Reading Association. (2009, May). *New literacies and 21st-century technologies.* Retrieved from http://www.reading.org/Libraries/position-statements-and-resolutions/ps1067_NewLiteracies21stCentury.pdf

International Reading Association. (2010a). *Response to Intervention: Guiding principles for educators from the International Reading Association.* Retrieved from http://www.reading.org/Libraries/Resources/RTI_brochure_web.pdf

International Reading Association. (2010b). Standards 2010: Standard 3—Assessment and evaluation. In *Standards for reading professionals* (Rev. ed.). Retrieved from http://reading.org/General/CurrentResearch/Standards/ProfessionalStandards2010/ProfessionalStandards2010_Standard3.aspx

International Reading Association and National Council of Teachers Joint Task Force on Assessment. (1994). *Standards for the assessment of reading and writing.* Newark, DE: International Reading Association. Retrieved from http://www.reading.org/General/CurrentResearch/Standards/AssessmentStandards.aspx

International Reading Association and National Council of Teachers of English Joint Task Force on Assessment. (2010). *Standards for the assessment of reading and writing* (Rev. ed.). Newark, DE: International Reading Association. Retrieved from http://www.reading.org/General/CurrentResearch/Standards/AssessmentStandards.aspx

International Society for Technology in Education. (2007). ISTE standards: Students. Retrieved from http://www.iste.org/docs/pdfs/20-14_ISTE_Standards-S_PDF.pdf

Invernizzi, M., Meier, J., & Juel, C. (2010). *1–3 technical reference: Phonological Awareness Literacy Screening.* Charlottesville: University of Virginia Curry School of Education. Retrieved from http://www.palswisconsin.info/documents/1-3technical_ref.pdf

Invernizzi, M. A., Landrum, T. J., Howell, J. L., & Warley, H. P. (2005). Toward the peaceful coexistence of test developers, policymakers, and teachers in an era of accountability. *The Reading Teacher, 58*(7), 610–618.

Irujo, S. (2007, January–February). What does research tell us about teaching reading to English language learners? *ELL Outlook.* Retrieved from http://www.readingrockets.org/article/19757

Ivey, G., & Broaddus, K. (2001). "Just plain reading": A survey of what makes students want to read in middle school classrooms. *Reading Research Quarterly, 36*(4), 350–377.

Jeter, D. (2001). *The life you imagine: Life lessons for achieving your dreams.* New York: Broadway Books.

Johns, J. L., & Lenski, S. D. (2001). *Improving reading: Strategies and resources.* Dubuque, IA: Kendall/Hunt.

Johns, J. L. (1991). Emmett A. Betts on informal reading inventories. *Journal of Reading, 34*(6), 492–493.

Johns, J. L., & Lunn, M. K. (1994). History and development of the informal reading inventory. In J. L. Johns, *Basic reading inventory* (6th ed., pp. 82–90). Dubuque, IA: Kendall/Hunt.

Johns, J. L., & Magliari, A. M. (1989). Informal reading inventories: Are the Betts criteria the best criteria? *Reading Improvement, 26*(2), 124–132.

Johnson, H., Watson, P. A., Delahunty, T., McSwiggen, P., & Smith, T. (2011). What it is they do: Differentiating knowledge and literacy practices across content disciplines. *Journal of Adolescent and Adult Literacy, 55*(2), 100–109.

Johnson, J. C. (2005). What makes a "good" reader? Asking students to define "good" readers. *The Reading Teacher, 58*(8), 766–770.

Johnson, M. S., Kress, R. A., & Pikulski, J. J. (1987). *Informal reading inventories* (2nd ed.). Newark, DE: International Reading Association.

Johnston, F., Invernizzi, M., & Bear, D. R. (2004). *Words their way: Words for syllable and affixes spellers.* New York: Prentice Hall.

Johnston, P. (2005). Literacy assessment and the future. *The Reading Teacher, 58*(7), 684–686.

Johnston, P. H. (2004). *Choice words: How our language affects children's learning.* Portland, ME: Stenhouse.

Johnston, P. H. (2011). Response to Intervention in literacy: Problems and possibilities. *Elementary School Journal, 111*(4), 511–534.

Johnston, P. H., & Allington, R. L. (1983). How sharp is a unicorn's horn? *Reading Research Quarterly, 18*(4), 498–500.

Johnston, P., & Costello, P. (2005). Principles for literacy assessment. *Reading Research Quarterly, 40*(2), 256–267.

Joseph, L. M. (1998). Word boxes help children with learning disabilities identify and spell words. *The Reading Teacher, 52*(4), 348–356.

Judge, S., Puckett, K., & Cabuk, B. (2004). Digital equity: New findings from the early childhood longitudinal study. *Journal of Research on Technology in Education, 36*(4), 383–396.

Justice, L. M., Invernizzi, M. A., & Meier, J. D. (2002). Designing and implementing an early literacy screening protocol: Suggestions for the speech-language

pathologist. *Language, Speech, and Hearing Services in Schools, 33,* 84–101.

Kajder, S., Bull, G., & Albaugh, S. (2005). Constructing digital stories. *Learning & Leading With Technology, 32*(5), 40–42.

Kamil, M., & Hiebert, E. (2005). Teaching and learning vocabulary: Perspectives and persistent issues. In E. H. Hiebert & M. L. Kamil (Eds.), *Teaching and learning vocabulary: Bringing research to practice* (pp. 1–23). Mahwah, NJ: Lawrence Erlbaum.

Karchmer-Klein, R., & Shinas, V. (2012). Guiding principles for supporting new literacies in your classroom. *The Reading Teacher, 65*(5), 288–293.

Keefe, J. W. (1979). Learning style: An overview. In National Association of Secondary School Principals, *Student learning styles: Diagnosing and proscribing programs* (pp. 1–17). Reston, VA: Author.

Keene, E. O. (2008). *To understand: New horizons in reading comprehension.* Portsmouth, NH: Heinemann.

Kelley, J. G., Lesaux, N. K., Kieffer, M. J., & Faller, S. E. (2010). Effective academic vocabulary instruction in the urban middle school. *The Reading Teacher, 64*(1), 5–14.

Kendall, J., & Khuon, O. (2006). *Writing sense: Integrated reading and writing lessons for English language learners K–8.* Portland, ME: Stenhouse.

Killgallon, P. A. (1983). A study of relationships among certain pupil adjustments in reading situations. In L. M. Gentile, M. L. Kamil, & J. S. Blanchard (Eds.), *Reading research revisited* (pp. 563–575). Columbus, OH: Charles E. Merril. (Originally an unpublished doctoral dissertation, Pennsylvania State College, 1942)

King, E. N. (n.d.). *Emotional disability (also referred to as emotional disturbance in some school systems).* Retrieved from http://www.schoolpsychologistfiles.com/emdisability

Klauda, S. L., & Guthrie, J. T. (2008). Relationships of three components of reading fluency to reading comprehension. *Journal of Educational Psychology, 100*(2), 310–321.

Klein, A. (n.d.). Phoneme awareness assessment tools: Recognizing rhyme assessment. Retrieved from http://teams.lacoe.edu/documentation/classrooms/patti/k-1/teacher/assessment/tools/rhyme.html

Kosin, E. (2011, January 15). Interesting characters in children's biographies. *Salisbury Post.* Retrieved from http://www.salisburypost.com/Entertainment/011611-book-lib-notes-qcd

Kovalik, S. J., & Olsen, K. D. (2010). *Kid's eye view of science: A conceptual, integrated approach to teaching science, K–6.* Thousand Oaks, CA: Corwin.

Kurkjian, C., Livingston, N., & Cobb, V. (2006). Inquiring minds want to know: The info on nonfiction and informational series books. *The Reading Teacher, 60*(1), 86–94.

Lacour, M., & Tissington, L. D. (2011). The effects of poverty on low academic achievement. *Educational Research and Reviews, 6*(7), 522–527. Retrieved http://www.academicjournals.org/article/article1379765941_Lacour%20and%20Tissington.pdf

Lane, B. (1992). *After the end: Teaching and learning creative revision.* Portsmouth, NH: Heinemann.

Lane, H. B., & Allen, S. A. (2010). The vocabulary-rich classroom: Modeling sophisticated word use to promote word consciousness and vocabulary growth. *The Reading Teacher, 63*(5), 363–370.

Langer, J. A. (1982). Facilitating text processing: The elaboration of prior knowledge. In J. A. Langer & M. T. Smith-Burke (Eds.), *Reader meets author: Bridging the gap* (pp. 149–162). Newark, DE: International Reading Association.

Larson, L. C. (2010). Digital reader: The next chapter in e-book reading and response. *The Reading Teacher, 64*(1), 15–22.

Leach, J. M., Scarborough, H. S., & Rescorla, L. (2003). Late-emerging reading disabilities. *Journal of Educational Psychology, 95*, 211–224.

LearningRx. (2012). Cognitive learning styles. Retrieved from http://www.learningrx.com/cognitive-learning-styles.htm

Lee, M. J., McLoughlin, C., & Chan, A. (2008). Talk the talk: Learner-generated podcasts as catalysts for knowledge creation. *British Journal of Educational Technology, 39*(3), 501–521.

Lee & Low Books. (2014). *Children's Book Press.* Retrieved from http://www.leeandlow.com/p/overview_cbp.mhtml

Lehr, C. A., & McComas, J. (2005). Students with emotional/behavioral disorders: Promoting positive outcomes. *Impact, 18*(2). Retrieved from http://ici.umn.edu/products/impact/182/over1.html

Leipzig, D. H. (2001). What is reading? *Reading Rockets.* Retrieved from http://www.readingrockets.org/article/352

Leslie, L., & Caldwell, J. S. (2011). *Qualitative reading inventory* (5th ed.). New York: Pearson.

Lilly, E., & Green, C. (2004). Literacy development: Cambourne's conditions. Excerpted from *Developing partnerships with families through children's literature* (p. 5). Upper Saddle River, NJ: Merrill Prentice Hall. Retrieved from http://www.education.com/reference/article/Cambournes-literacy-development/

Lipson M. Y., Chomsky-Higgins, P., & Kanfer, J. (2011). Diagnosis: The missing ingredient in RTI assessment. *The Reading Teacher, 65*(3), 204–208.

Literacy Connections. (n.d.). Word study activities from Words Their Way. Retrieved from http://www.literacyconnections.com/WordsTheirWay.php

Literacy Leadership State Team & Oregon Department of Education. (n.d.). *K–5 teachers: Laying foundations for the Common Core.* Retrieved from http://www.ode.state.or.us/teachlearn/subjects/elarts/reading/literacy/foundations.pdf

Lose, M. K. (2007). A child's response to intervention requires a responsive teacher of reading. *The Reading Teacher, 61*(3), 276–279.

Lucariello, J. (2012). *How do I get my students over their alternative concepts (misconceptions) for learning? Removing barriers to aid in the development of the student.* Retrieved from http://www.apa.org/education/k12/misconceptions.aspx

Luke, S. D., & Schwartz, A. (2007). Assessment and accommodations. *Evidence for Education, 2*(1). Retrieved from http://nichcy.org/wp-content/uploads/docs/eeaccommodations.pdf

Lyons C. (2003). *Teaching struggling readers: How to use brain-based research to maximize learning.* Portsmouth, NH: Heinemann.

Macaulay, D. (2003). *Mosque.* Boston, MA: Houghton Mifflin.

Malloy, J. A., & Gambrell, L. B. (2006). Approaching the unavoidable: Literacy instruction and the Internet. *The Reading Teacher, 59*(5), 482–484.

Marentette, L. V. (2009, May 22). *Alternative assessment tools for students with complex disabilities.* Retrieved from http://www.slideshare.net/lynnmarentette/assessment-of-students-with-multiple-special-needs

Manyak, P. (2007). Character trait vocabulary: A schoolwide approach. *The Reading Teacher, 60*(6), 574–577.

Marcell, B., & Ferraro, C. (2013). So long, Robot Reader! A superhero intervention plan for improving fluency. *The Reading Teacher, 66*(8), 607–614.

Martin, N. A. (2006). *Test of visual-perceptual skills (non-motor)* (3rd ed.). Ann Arbor, MI: Academic Therapy.

McCarthy, P. A. (2008). Using sound boxes systematically to develop phonemic awareness. *The Reading Teacher, 62*(4), 346–349.

McGee, L. M., & Ukrainetz, T. A. (2009). Using scaffolding to teach phonemic awareness in preschool and kindergarten. *The Reading Teacher, 62*(7), 599–603.

McGrail, L. (1991). Full cycle: From journal writing to "codes" to writing. In J. K. Peyton & J. Staton (Eds.), *Writing our lives: Reflections on dialogue journal writing with adults learning English* (pp. 53–62). Englewood Cliffs, NJ: Regents Prentice Hall and Center for Applied Linguistics.

McGrath, A. (2005, February 28). A new read on teen literacy. *U. S. News & World Report, 138*(7), 68–70.

McKenna, M. C., & Dougherty-Stahl, K. A. (2011). *Assessment for reading instruction* (2nd ed.). New York: Guilford Press.

McKenna, M. C., & Picard, M. C. (2006). Revisiting the role of miscue analysis in effective teaching. *The Reading Teacher, 60*(4), 378–380.

McKeown, M. G., & Curtis, M. E. (Eds.). (1987). *The nature of vocabulary acquisition.* Hillsdale, NJ: Erlbaum.

McLeod, S. A. (2007). Lev Vygotsky. *Simply Psychology.* Retrieved from http://www.simplypsychology.org/vygotsky.html

McLeod, S. A. (2009). Jean Piaget. *Simply Psychology.* Retrieved from http://www.simplypsychology.org/piaget.html

McLeod, S. A. (2011). Bandura: Social learning theory. *Simply Psychology.* Retrieved from http://www.simplypsychology.org/bandura.html

McKenna, M. C., & Walpole, S. (2005). How well does assessment inform our reading instruction? *The Reading Teacher, 59*(1), 84–85.

McLaughlin, M., & Overturf, B. J. (2012). *The Hunger Games* and the Common Core: Determining the complexity of contemporary texts. *Reading Today, 30*(3), 8–9.

McTigue, E. M., Washburn, E. K., & Liew, J. (2011). Academic resilience and reading: Building successful readers. *The Reading Teacher, 62*(5), 422–432.

Mesmer, E. M., & Mesmer, H. A. E. (2008). Response to Intervention (RTI): What teachers of reading need to know. *The Reading Teacher, 62*(4), 280–290.

MetaMetrics. (2012). *The Lexile Framework for reading: Matching readers with targeted text.* Retrieved from https://d1jt5u2s0h3gkt.cloudfront.net/m/cms_page_media/123/The_Lexile_Framework_for_Reading_1.pdf

MetaMetrics. (2014). What is a Lexile measure? Retrieved from http://www.lexile.com/about-lexile/lexile-overview

Meyer, M. S., & Felton, R. H. (1999). Repeated reading to enhance fluency: Old approaches and new directions. *Annals of Dyslexia, 49*(1), 283–306. doi:10.1007/s11881-999-0027-8

Minnesota Association for Children's Mental Health. (n.d.). *Children's mental health disorder fact sheet for the classroom: Anxiety disorders.* Retrieved from http://www.schoolmentalhealth.org/Resources/Educ/MACMH/Anxiety.pdf

Mokhtari, K., Thoma, J., & Edwards, P. (2009). How one elementary school uses data to help raise students' reading achievement. *The Reading Teacher, 63*(4), 334–337.

Moll, L. C., Amanti, C., Neff, D., & Gonzalez, N. (1992). Funds of knowledge for teaching: Using a qualitative approach to connect homes and classrooms. *Theory Into Practice, 31*(2), 132–141.

Moll, L. C., & Cammarota, J. (2010). Cultivating new funds of knowledge through research and practice. In K. Dunsmore & D. Fisher (Eds.), *Bringing literacy home* (pp. 289–305). Newark, DE: International Reading Association.

Moore, J., & Whitfield, V. (2009). Building schoolwide capacity for preventing reading failure. *The Reading Teacher, 62*(7), 622–624.

Moore, R. A., & Gilles, C. (2005). *Reading conversations: Retrospective miscue analysis with struggling readers, Grades 4–12.* Portsmouth, NH: Heinemann.

Moss, B. (2004). Teaching expository text structures through information trade book retellings. *The Reading Teacher, 57*(8), 710–718.

Moustafa, M. (1997). *Beyond traditional phonics.* Portsmouth, NH: Heinemann.

Mueller, J. (2014). *Authentic assessment toolbox: What is authentic assessment?* Retrieved from http://jfmueller.faculty.noctrl.edu/toolbox/whatisit.htm

Murray, D. M. (1982). *Learning by teaching.* Portsmouth, NH: Boynton/Cook.

Nagy, W. E., & Scott, J. A. (2000). Vocabulary processes. In M. L. Kamil, P. B. Mosenthal, P. D. Pearson, & R. Barr (Eds.), *Handbook of reading research* (Vol. 3, pp. 269–284). Mahwah, NJ: Erlbaum.

National Association for the Education of Young Children and National Association of Early Childhood Specialists in State Departments of Education. (2003). *Early childhood curriculum, assessment, and program evaluation: Building an effective, accountable system in programs for children birth through age 8.* Retrieved from http://www.naeyc.org/files/naeyc/file/positions/pscape.pdf

National Center for Educational Statistics. (2013). English language learners. Retrieved from https://nces.ed.gov/programs/coe/indicator_cgf.asp

National Center on Response to Intervention. (2010, April). *Essential components of RTI: A closer look at Response to Intervention.* Washington, DC: U.S. Department of Education, Office of Special Education Programs, National Center on Response to Intervention.

National Clearinghouse for English Language Acquisition. (2011, February). *The growing numbers of English learners students: 1998/99–2008/09.* Washington, DC: U.S. Department of Education. Retrieved from http://www.ncela.us/files/uploads/9/growing-LEP_0809.pdf

National Reading Panel. (2000). *Teaching children to read: An evidence-based assessment of the scientific research literature on reading and its implications for reading instruction* (NIH Publication No. 00-4769). Washington, DC: U.S. Government Publishing Office.

National Research Council. (2000). *Eager to learn: Educating our preschoolers.* Washington, DC: National Academy Press.

Neag School of Education, University of Connecticut. (2011). *Developing and evaluating three formats for assessing online reading comprehension: The ORCA Project.* Retrieved from http://www.orca.uconn.edu/orca/assets/File/Conference%20Presentations/2011-AERA-Leu.pdf

Neuman, S. B., & Dickinson, D. K. (Eds.). (2002). *Handbook of early literacy research.* New York: Guilford.

New South Wales Department of Education and Training. (n.d.). *Best start kindergarten assessment: Literacy.* Retrieved from http://www.schools.nsw.edu.au/media/downloads/languagesupport/best_start/literacy/english.pdf

New York State Education Department. (2011). *New York State P–12 Common Core Learning Standards for English language arts and literacy.* Retrieved from http://www.p12.nysed.gov/ciai/common_core_standards/pdfdocs/p12_common_core_learning_standards_ela.pdf

Newlands, M. (1993). *Spelling sense: A guide for the classroom.* Hamilton, ON, Canada: Primary Junior Department, Hamilton Board of Education.

Newlands, M. (2011). Intentional spelling: Ten steps to eliminate guessing. *The Reading Teacher, 64*(7), 531–534.

Newmann, F. M., King, M. B., & Carmichael, D. L. (2007). *Authentic instruction and assessment: Common standards for rigor and relevance in teaching academic subjects.* Des Moines: State of Iowa Department of Education.

Nilsson, N. L. (2008). A critical analysis of eight informal reading inventories. *The Reading Teacher, 61*(7), 526–536.

Nitko, A. J. (2004). *Educational assessments of students.* Englewood Cliffs, NJ: Prentice Hall.

Norman, K. A., & Calfee, R. C. (2004). Tile Test: A hands-on approach for assessing phonics in the early grades. *The Reading Teacher, 58*(1), 42–52.

Oczkus, L. D. (2012). *Best ever literacy survival tips: 72 lessons you can't teach without.* Newark, DE: International Reading Association.

O'Dell, R. (2010). How blogging saved sustained silent reading. *Virginia English Bulletin, 60*(1), 40–43.

Office on Child Abuse and Neglect, Children's Bureau, ICF International. (2009). How parental substance use disorders affect children. In *Protecting children in families affected by substance use disorders* (Chap. 3). Retrieved from http://www.childwelfare.gov/pubs/usermanuals/substanceuse/chapterthree.cfm

Ogle, D., & Correa-Kovtun, A. (2010). Supporting English-language learners and struggling readers in content literacy with the "partner reading and content, too" routine. *The Reading Teacher, 63*(7), 532–542.

Ohio Department of Education. (n.d.). *Establishing a point of view in narratives—Grade four.* Retrieved from http://ims.ode.state.oh.us/ODE/IMS/Lessons/Content/CER_LP_S05_BD_L04_I04_01.pdf

O'Keefe, T. (1997). The habit of kidwatching. *School Talk, 3*(2), 4–6. Retrieved from http://fcit.usf.edu/assessment/classroom/ST0032November97.pdf

O'Malley, K., Francis, D. J., Foorman, B. R., Fletcher, J. M., & Swank, P. R. (2002). Growth in precursor and reading-related skills: Do low-achieving and IQ-discrepant readers develop differently? *Learning Disabilities Research & Practice, 17*(1), 19–34.

Ontario Ministry of Education. (2003). *Early reading strategy: The report of the expert panel on early reading in Ontario.* Toronto: Queen's Printer for Ontario. Retrieved from http://www.edu.gov.on.ca/eng/document/reports/reading/reading.pdf

Ontario Ministry of Education. (2007). *Supporting English language learners in kindergarten: A practical guide for Ontario educators.* Toronto: Queen's Printer for Ontario. Retrieved from http://www.edu.gov.on.ca/eng/document/kindergarten/kindergartenell.pdf

Orange County Public Schools. (1992). Checklist of reading development. Orange County Public Schools. Orlando, Florida.

Orfano, F. (2012). Benefits of collaborative learning for students with special needs. Retrieved from http://www.brighthubeducation.com/special-ed-inclusion-strategies/67912-advantages-of-special-needs-students-working-with-mainstreamed-peers

Oster, L. (2001). Using the think-aloud for reading instruction. *The Reading Teacher, 55,* 64–69.

Panday, P. P. (2009). Simplifying podcasting. *International Journal of Teaching and Learning in Higher Education, 20*(2), 251–261.

Paris, S. G., & Carpenter, R. D. (2003). FAQs about IRIs. *The Reading Teacher, 56*(6), 578–580.

Partnership for Assessment of Readiness for College and Careers. (2013, July). *Glossary of frequently used PARCC assessment system terms and definitions: Version 1.* Retrieved from https://www.parcconline.org/sites/parcc/files/PARCCGlossary07-01-13.pdf

Pattenaude, D. (2012, January 12). Are students losing the love of reading. *Petrolia Topic.* Retrieved from http://www.petroliatopic.com/2012/01/12/are-students-losing-the-love-of-reading

Pearson, P. D., & Gallagher, M. C. (1983). The instruction of reading comprehension. *Contemporary Educational Psychology, 8,* 317–344.

Pearson Education. (2005). *Developmental reading assessment* (2nd ed. PLUS). Retrieved from http://www.pearsonschool.com/index.cfm?locator=PSZw5u&PMDbSiteId=2781&PMDbSolutionId=6724&PMDbSubSolutionId=&PMDbCategoryId=3289&PMDbSubCategoryId=28139&PMDbSubjectAreaId=&PMDbProgramId=23661

Peebles, J. L. (2007). Incorporating movement with fluency instruction: Motivation for struggling readers. *The Reading Teacher, 60*(6), 578–582.

Peterson, A. (2001). NAEP/NWP study shows link between assignments, better student writing. *The Voice, 6*(2). Retrieved from http://www.nwp.org/cs/public/print/resource/112

Peyton, J. K., & Staton, J. (1993). *Dialogue journals in the multilingual classroom: Building language fluency and writing skills through written interaction.* Norwood, NJ: Ablex.

Phillips, D. A., Voran, M., Kisker, E., Howes, C., & Whitebook, M. (1994). Child care for children in poverty: Opportunity or inequity? *Child Development, 65*(2), 472–492.

Phillips, S. E. (1993). *Legal implications of high-stakes assessments: What states should know.* Oak Brook, IL: North Central Regional Laboratory.

Piaget, J. (1954). *The construction of reality in the child.* New York: Basic Books.

Piaget, J. (1973). *Main trends in psychology.* London: Allen & Unwin.

Piasta, S. B., Purpura, D. J., & Wagner, R. K. (2010). Fostering alphabet knowledge development: A comparison of two instructional approaches. *Reading and Writing, 23,* 607–626.

Pikulski, J. J. (1990). Informal reading inventories. *The Reading Teacher, 43*(7), 514–516.

Pikulski, J. J., & Shanahan, T. (1982). Informal reading inventories: A critical analysis. In J. J. Pikulski & T. Shanahan (Eds.), *Approaches to the informal evaluation of reading* (pp. 94–116). Newark, DE: International Reading Association.

Pinellas County Schools. (1998). Primary writing continuum. *Pinellas Writing Project.* Pinellas County Schools.

Pinnell, G. S., & Fountas, I. C. (1998). *Word matters: Teaching phonics and spelling in the reading/writing classroom.* Portsmouth, NH: Heinemann.

Pinnell, G. S., & Fountas, I. C. (2008). *When readers struggle: Teaching that works.* Portsmouth, NH: Heinemann.

Pinnell, G. S., & Fountas, I. C. (2011). *Literacy beginnings: A prekindergarten handbook.* Portsmouth, NH: Heinemann.

Pinnell, G. S., Fountas, I. C., & Giacobbe, M. E. (1998). *Word matters: Teaching phonics and spelling in the reading/writing classroom.* Chicago, IL: Heinemann.

Polacco, P. (2006). *Rotten Richie and the ultimate dare.* New York: Philomel.

Polacco, P. (2009). *January's sparrow.* New York: Philomel.

Popham, W. J. (2005a). *Classroom assessment* (4th ed.). Boston, MA: Pearson Education.

Popham, W. J. (2005b, March 23). Standardized testing fails the exam. *Edutopia.* Retrieved from www.edutopia.org/standardized-testing-evaluation-reform

Powell, W. R., & Dunkeld, C. G. (1971). Validity of the IRI reading levels. *Elementary English, 48*(6), 637–642.

Prensky, M. (2001). Digital immigrants, digital natives. *On the Horizon, 9*(5), 1–6.

Prensky, M. (2005). Listen to the natives. *Educational Leadership, 63*(4), 8–13.

Protacio, M. S. (2012). Reading motivation: A focus on English learners. *The Reading Teacher, 66*(1), 69–77.

Provost, M. C., Lambert, M. A., & Babkie, A. M. (2010). Informal reading inventories: Creating teacher-designed literature-based assessments. *Intervention in School and Clinic, 45*(4), 211–220.

Purves, A. C. (1992, February). Reflections on research and assessment in written composition. *Research in the Teaching of English, 26,* 108–122.

Raphael, T. E., & Au, K. H. (2005). QAR: Enhancing comprehension and test taking across grades and content areas. *The Reading Teacher, 59,* 206–221.

Rapp, D. N., van den Broek, P., McMaster, K. L., Kendeou, P., & Espin, C. A. (2007). Higher order comprehension processes in struggling readers: A perspective for research and intervention. *Scientific Studies of Reading, 11*(4), 289–312.

Rasinski, T. (2003). *The fluent reader: Oral reading strategies for building word recognition, fluency, and comprehension.* New York: Scholastic.

Rasinski, T. V. (2004). Creating fluent readers. *Educational Leadership, 61*(6), 46–51.

Rasinski, T. V. (2010). *The fluent reader: Oral and silent reading strategies for building word recognition, fluency and comprehension* (2nd ed.). New York: Scholastic.

Rasinski, T. V., Ackland, R., Fawcett, G., & Lems, K. (2011). *The fluent reader in action: A close-up look into 15 diverse classrooms—Grades 5 and up.* New York: Scholastic.

Rasinski, T. V., Fawcett, G., Lems, K., & Ackland, R. (2010). *The fluent reader in action: A close-up look into 15 diverse classrooms.* New York: Scholastic.

Rasinski, T., & Padak, N. (2000). *Effective reading strategies: Teaching children who find reading difficult* (2nd ed.). Columbus, OH: Merrill/Prentice Hall.

Rasinski, T., & Padak, N. (2008). *From phonics to fluency: Effective teaching of decoding and reading fluency in the elementary school.* Boston, MA: Pearson.

Rasinski, T., Padak, N., & Fawcett, G. (2010). *Teaching children who find reading difficult.* Boston, MA: Allyn & Bacon.

Rasinski, T. V., Padak, N. D., Linek, W. L., & Sturtevant, E. (1994). Effects of fluency development on urban second-grade readers. *Journal of Educational Research, 87*(3), 158–165.

Rasinski, T., Rupley, W. H., & Nichols, W. D. (2008). Two essential ingredients: Phonics and fluency getting to know each other. *The Reading Teacher, 62*(3), 257–260.

Reading Recovery Council of North America. (2014). *Online Reading Recovery book list.* Retrieved from http://readingrecovery.org/index.php?option=com_user&view=login&bl=yes&return=aHR0cDovL3JlYWRpbmdyZWNvdmVyeS5vcmcvYm9vay1saXN0

Reading Rockets. (2012). Building reading stamina. Retrieved from http://www.readingrockets.org/article/51787

Reading Rockets. (2014). Fluency. Retrieved from http://www.readingrockets.org/helping/target/fluency

Really Good Stuff. (2008). *Really Good Stuff activity guide: Character traits in literacy poster.* Retrieved from http://page.reallygoodstuff.com/pdfs/156499.pdf

Reilly, C., & Qi, S. (2011, October). *Snapshot of deaf and hard of hearing people, postsecondary attendance and unemployment.* Washington, DC: Gallaudet Research Institute. Retrieved from http://research.gallaudet.edu/Demographics/deaf-employment-2011.pdf

Reilly, M. A. (2007). Choice of action: Using data to make instructional decisions in kindergarten. *The Reading Teacher, 60*(8), 770–776.

Renaissance Learning. (2014). STAR Reading. Retrieved from http://www.renaissance.com/products/star-assessments/star-reading

Reutzel, D. R., & Clark, S. (2011). Organizing literacy classrooms for effective instruction. *The Reading Teacher, 65*(2), 96–109.

Reutzel, D. R., & Cooter, R. B. (2013). *The essentials of teaching children to read: The teacher makes the difference* (3rd ed.). Boston, MA: Pearson.

Reutzel, D. R., & Mitchell, J. (Eds.). (2005). High stakes accountability themed issue: How did we get here from there? *The Reading Teacher, 58*(7), 606–608.

Reutzel, D. R., Oda, L. K., & Moore, B. H. (1989). Developing print awareness: The effect of three instructional approaches on kindergarteners' print awareness, reading readiness, and word reading. *Journal of Reading Behavior, 21*(3), 197–217.

Reutzel, R., Read, S., & Fawson, P. C. (2009). Using information trade books as models for teaching expository text structure to improve children's reading comprehension: An action research project. *Journal of Reading Education, 35*(1), 31–38.

Rice, D. C. (2002). Using trade books in teaching elementary science: Facts and fallacies. *The Reading Teacher, 55*(6), 552–565.

Richardson, J. (2012). *The next step in guided reading.* New York: Scholastic.

Richek, M. A., List, L. K., & Lerner, J. W. (1989). *Reading problems: Assessment and teaching strategies* (2nd ed.). Englewood Cliffs, NJ: Prentice Hall.

Rieben, L., & Perfetti, C. A. (Eds.). (1991). *Learning to read: Basic research and its implications.* Hillsdale, NJ: Lawrence Erlbaum.

Risko, V. J., & Walker-Dalhouse, D. (2010). Making the most of assessments to inform instruction. *The Reading Teacher, 63*(5), 420–422.

Robb, L. (2009). *Literacy assessments for differentiating instruction.* New York: Scholastic.

Rosenberg, M. (2006). *Sound and letter time: Building phonemic awareness and alphabetic recognition through purposeful play.* New York: Scholastic. Retrieved from http://research.scholastic.com/sites/default/files/publications/SoundandLetterTime_ResearchFoundation_2006.pdf

Rosenblatt, L. M. (1985). Viewpoints: Transaction versus interaction—A terminological rescue operation. *Research in the Teaching of English, 19,* 96–107.

Roskos, K., & Christie, J. (2011). The play-literacy nexus and the importance of evidence-based techniques in the classroom. *American Journal of Play, 4*(2), 204–224.

Roskos, K., & Neuman, S. (2012). Formative assessment: Simply, no additives. *The Reading Teacher, 65*(8), 534–538.

Rubin, J. (2011). Organizing and evaluating results from multiple reading assessments. *The Reading Teacher, 64*(8), 606–611.

Ruddell, R., & Unrau, N. (Eds.). (2004). *Theoretical models and processes of reading* (Vol. 5). Newark, DE: International Reading Association.

Rumelhart, D. E. (1975). Notes on Schema for Stories. In D. C. Hobrow & A. Collins (Eds.), *Representation and understanding* (pp. 211–236). New York: Academic Press.

Sableski, M. (2009). Scaffolding as an impetus for change when working with struggling readers. *Journal of Reading Education, 34*(3), 30–37.

Sadler, D. R. (1989). Formative assessment and the design of instructional systems. *Instructional Science, 18*(2), 119–144.

Saine, P., & Kara-Soteriou, J. (2010). Using podcasts to enrich responses to global children's literature. *New England Reading Association Journal, 20*(2), 251–261.

Samuels, S. J. (1997). The method of repeated reading. *The Reading Teacher, 50*(5), 376–381.

Samuels, S. J. (2007). The DIBELS tests: Is speed of barking at print what we mean by reading fluency? *Reading Research Quarterly, 42,* 563–566.

Sanders, W. L., & Rivers, J. C. (1996). *Research progress report: Cumulative and residual effects of teachers on future student academic achievement.* Knoxville: University of Tennessee Value-Added Research and Assessment Center. Retrieved from http://www.cgp.upenn.edu/pdf/Sanders_Rivers-TVASS_teacher%20effects.pdf

Scanlon, D. M., Anderson, K. L., & Sweeney, J. M. (2010). *Early intervention for reading difficulties: The interactive strategies approach.* New York: Guilford Press.

Scharlach, T. D. (2008). START comprehending: Students and teachers actively reading text. *The Reading Teacher, 62*(1), 20–31.

Schnorr, R. F. (2011). Intensive reading instruction for students with developmental disabilities. *The Reading Teacher, 65*(1), 35–45.

Scholastic. (2014). Reading assessment program overview. Retrieved from http://teacher.scholastic.com/products/sri_reading_assessment/programoverview.htm

Schön, D. A. (1983). *The reflective practitioner: How professionals think in action.* Aldershot, UK: Ashgate.

Schoology. (2014). Schoology as a K–12 LMS. Retrieved from https://www.schoology.com/k-12-lms.php

Schumm, J. S., & Mangrum, C. T. (1991). FLIP: A framework for content area reading. *Journal of Reading, 35*(2), 120–124.

Scott, J. E. (1996). Self-efficacy: A key to literacy learning. *Reading Horizons, 36*(3), 195–213.

Scott-Little, C., & Niemeyer, J. (2001). *Assessing kindergarten children: What school systems need to know.* Greensboro, NC: SERVE Center. Retrieved from http://earlysuccess.org/sites/default/files/website_files/files/2012-10-Inter-State-Dicsussion-Time-Doc-2.M.Boyajian.pdf

Sears, L. A. (n.d.). *A short history of United States' reading research and instruction: 1900 to 2006.* Retrieved from http://www.historyliteracy.org/download/Sears3.pdf

Serafini, F. (2010). *Classroom reading assessments: More efficient ways to view and evaluate your readers.* Portsmouth, NH: Heinemann.

Shanahan, T., & Shanahan, C. (2008). Teaching disciplinary literacy to adolescents: Rethinking content-area literacy. Harvard Educational Review, *78*(1), 40–59.

Shaywitz, S. E. (1996). Dyslexia. *Scientific American, 275*(5), 98–104.

Shepard, L., Kagan, S. L., & Wurtz, E. (Eds.). (1998). *Principles and recommendations for early childhood assessments.* Washington, DC: National Education Goals Panel. Retrieved from http://govinfo.library.unt.edu/negp/reports/prinrec.pdf

Slapin, B., Seale, D., & Gonzales, R. (1996). *How to tell the difference: A guide for evaluating children's books for anti-Indian bias.* Berkeley, CA: Oyate.

Smarter Balanced Assessment Consortium. (2012). Computer adaptive testing. Retrieved from http://www.smarterbalanced.org/smarter-balanced-assessments/computer-adaptive-testing

Smith, F. (1985). *Reading without nonsense*. New York: Teachers College Press.

Smith, F. (1992). Learning to read: The never-ending debate. *Phi Delta Kappan, 73*(6), 432–441.

Smith, F. (1998). *The book of learning and forgetting*. New York: Teachers College Press.

Smith, F. (2006). *Reading without nonsense* (4th ed.). New York: Teachers College Press.

Smith, M. K. (2002, 2008). Howard Gardner and multiple intelligences. *Encyclopedia of informal education*. Retrieved from http://www.infed.org/thinkers/gardner.htm

Snow, C. E., Burns, M. S., & Griffin, P. (Eds.). (1998). *Preventing reading difficulties in young children*. Washington, DC: National Academy Press.

Solórzano, R. W. (2008). High stakes testing: Issues, implications, and remedies for English language learners. *Review of Educational Research, 78*(2), 260–329. doi:10.3102/0034654608317845

Sousa, D. A. (2007). *How the special needs brain learns* (2nd ed.). Thousand Oaks, CA: Corwin.

Spandel, V. (2009). *Creating writers through 6-trait writing: Assessment and instruction* (5th ed.). Boston, MA: Pearson.

SpanglishBaby. (2011). Retrieved from http://spanglishbaby.com

Sparrow, S. S., & Davis, S. M. (2000). Recent advances in the assessment of intelligence and cognition. *Journal of Child Psychology and Psychiatry, 41*(1), 117–131. Retrieved from http://www.psy.vanderbilt.edu/courses/hon182/overview_of_intelligence_testing.pdf

Spiegelman, A. (1986). *Maus I: A survivor's tale; My father bleeds history*. New York: Random House.

Stahl, K. (2010, June 29). *Diagnostic assessment in a tiered system: Who, what, and when?* Retrieved from http://www.nysrti.org/docs/Stahl_diagnostic_assessment_small_copy.pdf

Stahl, K. A. D. (2012). Complex text or frustration-level text: Using shared reading to bridge the difference. *The Reading Teacher, 66*(1), 47–51.

Stahl, S. A. (2006). Understanding shifts in reading and its instruction. In K. A. Dougherty Stahl & M. C. McKenna (Eds.), *Reading research at work: Foundations of effective practice* (pp. 45–75). New York: Guilford Press.

Stahl, S. A., & Fairbanks, M. M. (1986). The effects of vocabulary instruction: A model-based meta-analysis. *Review of Educational Research, 56*, 72–110.

Staman, A. (n.d.). *Guided reading strategies from Handprints*. Cambridge, MA: Educators Publishing Service. Retrieved from http://eps.schoolspecialty.com/downloads/articles/guided_reading_strategies.pdf

Stanford Achievement Test series (10th ed.). (2009). San Antonio, TX: Pearson Education. Retrieved from http://www.pearsonassessments.com/learningassessments/products/100000415/stanford-achievement-test-series-tenth-edition.html

Stanovich, K. E. (1980). Toward an interactive compensatory model of individual differences in the development of reading fluency. *Reading Research Quarterly, 16*, 32–71.

Stanovich, K. E. (2000). *Progress in understanding reading: Scientific foundations and new frontiers*. New York: Guilford Press.

Stanovich, K. E. (2005). The future of a mistake: Will discrepancy measurement continue to make the learning disabilities field a pseudoscience? *Learning Disability Quarterly, 28*(2), 103–106.

Stickgold, R. (2007). *Sleep, learning, and memory*. Retrieved from http://healthysleep.med.harvard.edu/healthy/matters/benefits-of-sleep/learning-memory

Strickland, D. S., Ganske, K., & Monroe, J. K. (2002). *Supporting struggling readers and writers: Strategies for classroom intervention 3–6*. Portland, ME: Stenhouse.

Strickland, K. (2005). *What's after assessment? Follow-up instruction for phonics, fluency, and comprehension*. Portsmouth, NH: Heinemann.

Student Achievement Partners. (n.d.). Guide to creating text-dependent questions. Retrieved from http://achievethecore.org/page/710/text-dependent-question-resources

Sugai, G., & Horner, R. H. (2002). Introduction to the special series on positive behavior support in schools. *Journal of Emotional and Behavioral Disorders, 10*(3), 130–135.

Swinburne, S. R. (2005). *Turtle tide: The ways of sea turtles*. Honesdale, PA: Boyds Mills Press.

Sylvester, R., & Greenidge, W.-L. (2009). Digital storytelling: Extending the potential for struggling writers. *The Reading Teacher, 63*(4), 284–295.

Taylor, B., Harris, L., Pearson, P. D., & Garcia, G. (1995). *Reading difficulties: Instruction and assessment*. New York: McGraw-Hill.

Taylor, S. (2011, November 11). *Strategies for teaching vocabulary in kindergarten.* Retrieved from http://www.scholastic.com/teachers/classroom-solutions/2011/11/strategies-teaching-vocabulary-kindergarten

Teale, W. H. (2008). What counts? Literacy assessment in urban schools. *The Reading Teacher, 62*(4), 358–361.

Temple, C., Ogle, D., Crawford, A., & Freppon, P. (2011). *All children read: Teaching for today's diverse classrooms* (3rd ed.). New York: Pearson.

Therrien, W. J., & Kubina, R. M., Jr. (2006). Developing reading fluency with repeated reading. *Intervention in School and Clinic, 41*(3), 156–160.

Tierney, R., & Shanahan, T. (1991). Research on the reading-writing relationship: Interactions, transactions, and outcomes. In R. Barr, M. Kamil, P. Mosenthal, & D. Pearson (Eds.), *The handbook of reading research* (Vol. 2, pp. 246–280). New York: Longman.

UN Educational Scientific and Cultural Organization. (2001). *Health education: Introduction.* Retrieved from http://www.unesco.org/education/tlsf/mods/theme_b/mod08.html

University of Michigan Health System. (2012). *Children with chronic conditions.* Retrieved from http://www.med.umich.edu/yourchild/topics/chronic.htm

University of Michigan Health System. (2013). Dyslexia and reading problems. *Your Child: Developmental and Behavioral Resources.* Retrieved from http://www.med.umich.edu/yourchild/topics/dyslexia.htm

University of Oregon Center on Teaching and Learning. (2014). *DIBELS letter naming fluency.* Retrieved from https://dibels.uoregon.edu/market/assessment/measures/lnf.php#admin

University of the State of New York, State Education Department. (2010, October). *Response to Intervention: Guidance for New York State school districts.* Retrieved from http://www.p12.nysed.gov/specialed/RTI/guidance-oct10.pdf

U.S. Department of Agriculture Food and Nutrition Service. (2013, September). *National School Lunch Program.* Retrieved from http://www.fns.usda.gov/sites/default/files/NSLPFactSheet.pdf

U.S. Department of Education. (2002). *Twenty-fourth annual report to Congress on the implementation of the Individuals with Disabilities Education Act (IDEA).* Washington, DC: Author.

U.S. Department of Education. (2006). *Individuals with Disabilities Education Act (IDEA) database.* Washington, DC: Author.

U.S. Department of Education. (2010). *Electronic book reader dear colleague letter: Questions and answers about the law, the technology, and the population affected.* Retrieved from http://www2.ed.gov/about/offices/list/ocr/docs/504-qa-20100629.pdf

U.S. Department of Education, Institute of Education Sciences, & National Center for Education Statistics. (2002). *National Assessment of Educational Progress oral reading study.* Retrieved from http://nces.ed.gov/nationsreportcard/studies/ors/

Vacca, R. T., Vacca, J. L., & Mraz, M. E. (2010). Content area reading: Literacy and learning across the curriculum (10th ed.). Boston: Pearson.

Valencia, S. W., & Buly, M. R. (2004). Behind test scores: What struggling readers *really* need. *The Reading Teacher, 57*(6), 520–530.

Vandergrift, K. E. (2014). Biography. *Vandergrift's Children's Literature Page.* Retrieved from http://comminfo.rutgers.edu/professional-development/childlit/ChildrenLit/index.html

Vasinda, S., & McLeod, J. (2011). Extending reader's theatre: A powerful and purposeful match with podcasting. *The Reading Teacher, 64*(7), 486–497.

Vellutino, F. R., & Fletcher, J. M. (2005). Developmental dyslexia. In M. J. Snowling & C. Hulme (Eds.), *The science of reading: A handbook* (pp. 362–378). Oxford, UK: Blackwell.

Vellutino, F. R., Scanlon, D. M., & Lyon, G. R. (2000). Differentiating between difficult-to-remediate and readily remediated poor readers: More evidence against the IQ-discrepancy definition of reading disability. *Journal of Learning Disabilities, 33*(3), 223–238.

Vlach, S., & Burcie, J. (2010). Narratives of the struggling reader. *The Reading Teacher, 63*(6), 522–525.

Vygotsky, L. S. (1978). *Mind in society: The development of higher psychological processes* (M. Cole, V. John-Steiner, S. Scribner, & E. Souberman, Eds. & Trans.). Cambridge, MA: Harvard University Press. (Original work published 1930–1935)

Vygotsky, L. S. (1986). *Thought and language* (A. Kozulin, Trans.). Cambridge: MIT Press. (Original work published 1934)

Wahlberg, H. J., & Tsai, S. (1983). Matthew effects in education. *American Educational Research Journal, 20*(3), 359–373.

Walcutt, C. C. (1967). Reading: A professional definition. *Elementary School Journal, 67*(7), 363–365.

Walmsley, S., & Allington, R. (2007). *No quick fix, the RTI edition: Rethinking literacy programs in America's elementary schools.* Newark, DE: International Reading Association.

Walsh, M. E., & Murphy, J. A. (2003). *Children, health, and learning: A guide to the issues.* Westport, CT: Praeger.

Watson, D. (1988). Knowing where we are coming from. In C. Gilles, M. Bixby, P. Crowldey, S. Crenshaw, M. Henrichs, F. Reynolds, & D. Pyle (Eds.), *Whole language strategies for secondary students* (pp. 3–10). New York: Richard C. Owen.

Weaver, C. (2000). *Reading process and practice.* Portsmouth, NH: Heinemann.

Weaver, C. (2002). *Reading process and practice* (3rd ed.). Portsmouth, NH: Heinemann.

Wertz, J. V. (1985). *Vygotsky and the social formation of mind.* Cambridge, MA: Harvard University Press.

White, S. (n.d.). *Building vocabulary for second grade students.* Retrieved from http://www.sfps.info/document center/view/6985

Whitney, A., Blau, S., Bright, A., Cabe, R., Dewar, T., Levin, J., Macias, R., & Rogers, P. (2008). Beyond strategies: Teacher practice, writing process, and the influence of inquiry. *English Education, 40*(3), 201–230.

Wiehardt, G. (n.d.). First person point of view. Retrieved from http://fictionwriting.about.com/od/glossary/g/firstperson.htm

Wiesner, D. (1991). *Tuesday.* New York: Houghton Mifflin.

Wilfong, L. G. (2008). Building fluency, word recognition ability, and confidence in struggling readers: The Poetry Academy. *The Reading Teacher, 62*(1), 4–13.

Wilson, N. S. (2011). The heart of comprehension instruction: Metacognition. *California Reader, 44*(3), 32.

Wixson, K. (2011). A systematic view of RTI research: An introduction to the special issue. *Elementary School Journal, 111*(4), 503–510.

Wolf, M. (2007). *Proust and the squid: The story and science of the reading brain.* New York: Harper Perennial.

Wolf, M., & Bowers, P. (1999). The double-deficit hypothesis for the developmental dyslexias. *Journal of Educational Psychology, 91*(3), 415–438.

Wood, K. D., & Harmon, J. M. (2001). *Strategies for integrating reading and writing in middle and high school classrooms.* Westerville, OH: National Middle School Association.

Wright, P. W. D., & Wright, P. D. (2005). *What you need to know about IDEA 2004 Section 142: State eligibility (the catch-all statute).* Retrieved from http:/www.wrightslaw.com/idea/art/sec.1412.overview.htm

Wylie, R. E., & Durrell, D. D. (1970). Teaching vowels through phonograms. *Elementary English, 47,* 787–791.

Yezerski, T. F. (2011). *Meadowlands: A wetland survival story.* New York: Farrar Straus Giroux.

Yopp, H. K. (1988). The validity and reliability of phonemic awareness tests. *Reading Research Quarterly, 23,* 159–177.

Young, C., & Rasinski, T. (2011). Implementing readers theatre as an approach to classroom fluency instruction. *The Reading Teacher, 63*(1), 3–13.

Zambo, D. (2006). Using thought-bubble pictures to assess students' feelings about reading. *The Reading Teacher, 59*(8), 798–802.

Zucker, S. (2004, April). *Assessment report: Administrative report for standardized testing.* San Antonio, TX: Pearson Education. Retrieved from http://images.pearsonassessments.com/images/tmrs/tmrs_rg/AdministrationPractices.pdf?WT.mc_id=TMRS_Administration_Practices_for_Standardized_Assessments

Zygouris-Coe, V. (2010). Reader's theatre student self-assessment. Retrieved from http://www.readwritethink.org/files/resources/30621_selfrubric.pdf

Zygouris-Coe, V., Wiggins, M. B., & Smith, L. H. (2004). Engaging students with text: The 3-2-1 strategy. *The Reading Teacher, 58*(4), 381–384.

Index

About the Authors

Kathy B. Grant is an associate professor of curriculum and instruction at State University of New York at Plattsburgh's School of Education. Her degrees include a master's in reading and a doctorate in literacy education. She has worked as a reading specialist (K–2), taught middle-grades reading, and worked as an elementary teacher. Her higher education teaching experiences, both graduate and undergraduate, include instruction in literacy foundations, reading diagnosis and correction, research methods in literacy, multicultural competencies, literacy instruction, and content area literacy. Her research interests include using role play in reading teacher education, multicultural literacy investigation, and guided reading strategies. As a literacy consultant in North Carolina, Grant worked with schools in collaborative development of guided reading programs, authentic classroom content literacy strategies, and vocabulary activities. Her lifelong love of reading has taken her down this path.

Sandra E. Golden has been in higher education since 1988 and her involvement in community development and engagement spans 20 years. Prior to joining the Sisters of Charity Foundation of Cleveland as associate director of Cleveland Central Promise Neighborhood, she taught for 7 years at Defiance College. She also provided administrative leadership as the associate provost of graduate studies and professional development. While at Defiance College, Dr. Golden earned tenure and was promoted to full professor of education. Prior to joining the faculty of Defiance College, she also taught for 7 years at Notre Dame College of Ohio in the teacher education program and provided administrative leadership for the graduate programs. Dr. Golden has 15 years of experience as a teacher educator and literacy educator. Her research interest includes culturally relevant pedagogy, reading and literacy development, and teacher education. She has written several book chapters and articles and is the co-editor of *Connecting the Literacy Puzzle: Linking the Professional, Personal, and Social Literacies* (Hampton Press, 2012). Currently, she is the managing editor of the *American Reading Forum Annual Yearbook*. She is also the co-founder and director of T-RUTH Academy for Young Adolescent Girls, a reading and writing program to support young girls in developing and enhancing reading and writing skills, promoting self-awareness and self-esteem, and engaging in service learning and project development.

Nance S. Wilson is an associate professor of literacy education at State University of New York at Cortland. Her research focuses on professional development, new literacies, comprehension, and adolescent literacy. Dr. Wilson's work has been published in the *Middle School Journal,* the *Journal of Adolescent and Adult Literacy, Reading Horizons, Literacy, Metacognition and Learning,* the *California Reader,* the *Florida Educational Leadership Journal,* and the *Florida Association of Teacher Educators,* among others. She serves in several editorial roles, including *Reading and Writing Quarterly: Overcoming Reading Difficulties and Reading in the Middle.* She has served in leadership positions in the American Reading Forum and the Middle School Reading Special Interest Group of the International Reading Association.

About the Contributors

Robert T. Ackland, PhD, is a teacher educator and literacy education professor at the State University of New York at Plattsburgh. He co-authored *The Fluent Reader in Action: A Close-Up Look Into 15 Diverse Classrooms—Grades 5 and Up* and a companion text focusing on Pre-K–4 (Scholastic, 2011). As an invited speaker at the TESOL Arabia Conference in 2012, he gave an address titled "Dynamic Idiolect: Moving Beyond a Stereoscopic VIEW with Multiple Languages." Bob was a reading specialist in elementary schools for 6 years in the Chicago area.

Dr. Stephanie Affinito holds a master's degree, a Certificate of Advanced Study, and a PhD in the field of reading education. In addition to her advanced educational degrees, Stephanie has experience in early childhood care and education, and elementary education through grade 6. She holds permanent New York certification as a Pre-K–6 elementary teacher and a K–12 reading specialist. Stephanie currently teaches as a full-time staff associate in the Reading Department at the State University at Albany and works as a literacy consultant for multiple schools and districts.

Laura Baker is a library media specialist in New York State. Her particular interests are in blending traditional research and literacy with new multiliteracies and online research to teach students the skills they need to excel in both physical and digital worlds. She has used various Web 2.0 tools and e-books to facilitate learning in the classroom.

Dr. Colleen Carroll is the assistant superintendent for curriculum, instruction, and personnel at the Union Free School District of the Tarrytowns in New York. She has also been a director of literacy, elementary principal, and sixth-grade teacher, with a focus on reading and writing instruction throughout her career. Her passion is working with secondary content area teachers in supporting all levels of readers achieve mastery in literacy for success in college and career beyond high school.

Kimberly Davidson received her bachelor's degree in animal science from Cornell University and her master's in adolescent education from State University of New York at Plattsburgh. She is a scientist, an engineer, a teacher, a farmer, and an advocate of all forms of literacy. Kimberly brings a hands-on, engaging, student-centered approach to the classroom. She resides in upstate New York on her farm with a herd of alpacas, a flock of chickens, several dogs, and a llama named Antonio.

Michael P. French is professor and director of graduate education at Lourdes University in Sylvania, Ohio. A former K–12 reading specialist and 7–12 English Teacher, Michael received his PhD from the University of Wisconsin–Madison in Reading; his MA is from the University of St. Thomas in St. Paul, Minnesota; and his AB in Linguistics from the University of Notre Dame. His research interests and specializations include neurodiagnosis of learning problems as associated interventions, as well as program assessment practices.

Justin Gray is a certified English teacher. He has worked to integrate podcasting, WebQuests, and other web technologies into his lessons with middle and high school students. In addition, he has researched student-created podcasting as a means of increasing student achievement in the classroom.

Jolene Malavasic, PhD, is on the faculty in the department of reading at the University at Albany. She is a former secondary reading specialist and her research explores how the relationships created between teachers and adolescent students working in collaborative spaces inform students' understanding, use, and creation of multimodal literacy practices both in and out of school.

Sheila Morris is a Nationally Board Certified Teacher (2012) currently teaching fifth grade. She studied education at State University of New York at Plattsburgh, earning her BS in childhood education in 2006 and her MS in literacy B–12 at the University of Albany in 2008. She lives in South Glens Falls, New York, with her husband, Nathan, and son, Alexander.

Melanie O'Leary is an elementary school teacher who has taught in both the United States and Canada. She recently completed her master's in education, inclusive studies. Melanie's interests include teaching math and science, and she is a passionate promoter of reading and assistive technology.

Gwyn W. Senokossoff is an assistant professor in literacy education at Florida International University. She has 28 years of experience in education as an elementary education teacher and professor in higher education. Her experiences include multiage teaching and Accelerated Literacy Learning, an early intervention program similar to Reading Recovery. Her research interests include early intervention in reading, reading comprehension instruction with delayed readers, including children with autism spectrum disorders and English language learners, and children's literature.

Penny Soboleski devotes most of her time to working with struggling readers of all ages. After earning her EdD in educational leadership studies through Bowling Green State University, Ohio, she spent 8 years teaching reading assessment and intervention courses, preparing teachers of reading, and researching effective multi-sensory reading interventions. Currently, she is a member of the School of Educational Leadership at Indiana Wesleyan University.

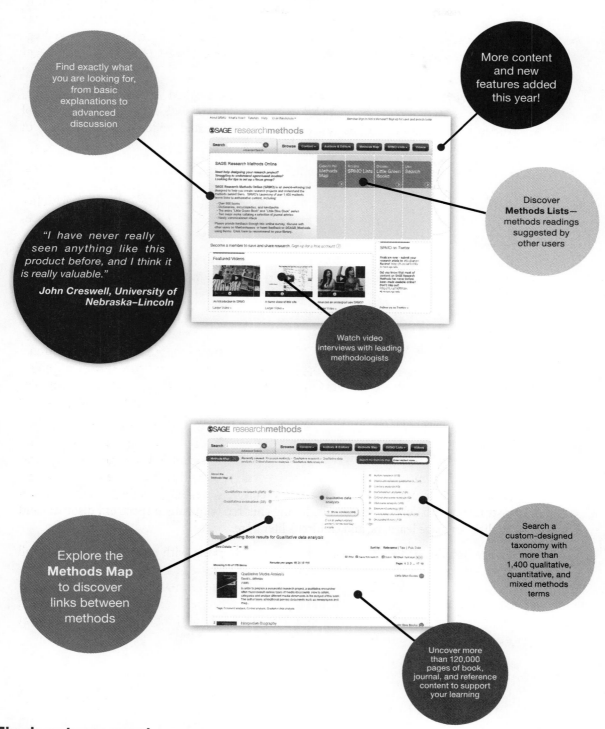

$SAGE researchmethods

The essential online tool for researchers from the world's leading methods publisher

Find exactly what you are looking for, from basic explanations to advanced discussion

More content and new features added this year!

"I have never really seen anything like this product before, and I think it is really valuable."

John Creswell, University of Nebraska–Lincoln

Discover **Methods Lists**— methods readings suggested by other users

Watch video interviews with leading methodologists

Explore the **Methods Map** to discover links between methods

Search a custom-designed taxonomy with more than 1,400 qualitative, quantitative, and mixed methods terms

Uncover more than 120,000 pages of book, journal, and reference content to support your learning

Find out more at
www.sageresearchmethods.com